Web Design Index by Content.02

THE PEPIN PRESS | AGILE RABBIT EDITIONS

COMPILED BY GÜNTER BEER

Compilation & layout by Günter Beer & Sigurd Buchberger
CD Master by Sigurd Buchberger

Cover and book design by Pepin van Roojen

Cover image by Karoly Kiralyfalvi (www.extraverage.net)

The cover image is an adaptation of an illustration used for www.drezign.hu (see page 232).

Introduction by Pepin van Roojen
Translations by Justyna Wrzodak (Polish), Vladimir Nazarov (Russian), Michie Yamakawa (Japanese), LocTeam (German, Spanish, Italian, French and Portuguese).

With special thanks to Magda Garcia Masana.

ISBN 978 90 5768 103 5
The Pepin Press | Agile Rabbit Editions
Amstedam & Singapore

The Pepin Press BV
P.O. Box 10349
1001 EH Amsterdam
The Netherlands

Tel +31 20 4202021
Fax +31 20 4201152
mail@pepinpress.com
www.pepinpress.com

10 9 8 7 6 5 4 3 2 1
2010 2009 2008 2007 2006

Manufactured in Singapore

Web Design Index By Content.02 contains a selection of 500 websites arranged by subject. Two pages from each site are included: one opening page and one page that is representative of the site. Enclosed is a CD-ROM containing a browser and a one-click facility to view and access the selected sites without having to be online. Together the book and CD offer a comprehensive overview of web design standards in many different fields.

With each site in the book, the URL is indicated. The names of those involved in the design and programming of the sites are stated as follows:

D design
C coding
P production
A agency
M designer's email address

Submissions & recommendations
Each year, brand new editions of all The Pepin Press' web design books are published. Should you wish to submit or recommend designs for consideration, please access the submissions form at www.webdesignindex.org.

The Pepin Press / Agile Rabbit Editions
For more information about The Pepin Press' many publications on design, fashion, popular culture, visual reference and ready-to-use images, please visit www.pepinpress.com.

Web Design Index By Content.02 (Modèles de sites Web par contenu.02) comprend une sélection de 500 sites Web classés par sujet. Deux pages sont consacrées à chaque site : une page d'ouverture et une page représentative du site. Un CD-ROM est inclus : il contient un navigateur et offre la possibilité de voir et d'accéder aux sites sélectionnés par simple clic, sans même avoir besoin d'être connecté à Internet. Livre et CD donnent un aperçu global des designs web standard dans chacun des domaines spécifiques.

L'URL de chaque site est indiquée. Les noms des personnes ayant participé à sa conception et à sa programmation sont indiqués comme suit :

D conception
C codage
P production
A agence
M adresse e-mail du concepteur

Suggestions et recommandations
Chaque année, de nouvelles éditions des ouvrages de design Web de The Pepin Press sont éditées. Si vous avez des designs à nous suggérer ou à nous recommander, vous pouvez accéder au formulaire de suggestions qui se trouve à l'adresse www.webdesignindex.org.

The Pepin Press / Agile Rabbit Editions
Pour en savoir plus sur les nombreuses publications de The Pepin Press consacrées au design, à la mode, à la culture pop, aux références visuelles et aux images prêtes à l'emploi, veuillez visiter le site Web www.pepinpress.com.

Web Design By Content.02收集了按主题分类的500个网址。对每个网址提供两页内容：一个是打开页面，另一个是体现该网址特色的代表性内容。此书还附有CD-ROM，包含一个浏览器和可单击观看并进入所选网址的工具。此套装可帮助你全面了解任何一个领域的网站设计标准。

书中的每个网址都标出其URL。 与网站设计和编程相关的名称如下:

D 设计
C 编码
P 制作
A 代理
M 设计师电子信箱

提交和推荐
每年Pepin出版社都都会推出全新的网站设计丛书。如果您想提交或推荐网站设计供我们参考，请登录www.webdesignindex.org填写提交表。

Pepin出版社/Agile Rabbit Editions
如果您想了解更多有关Pepin出版社的设计、时尚、流行文化、视觉参考和现成可用图片出版物方面的信息，请登录www.pepinpress.com。

Web Design Index By Content.02 (Disegno Web per contenuto.02) è una selezione di 500 siti ripartiti per argomento. Per ogni sito sono presentate una home page e una pagina interna per dare un'idea della sua natura. L'accluso CD-ROM contiene il browser e un sistema che consente di visualizzare e accedere alle pagine web desiderate senza la necessità di una connessione a Internet. Il libro e il CD insieme offrono una panoramica dello standard del web design in alcuni settori specifici.

Per ogni sito è indicato l'URL corrispondente. I nomi delle persone che hanno collaborato al design e alla programmazione di ogni sito sono riportati secondo i seguenti criteri:

D design
C codificazione
P produzione
A agenzia
M indirizzo e-mail del designer

Segnalazioni
Ogni anno The Pepin Press pubblica un'edizione aggiornata di tutte le opere che hanno come oggetto il web design. Se desiderate portare alla nostra attenzione un progetto di design, potete scaricare l'apposito modulo sul sito www.webdesignindex.org.

The Pepin Press / Agile Rabbit Editions
Per ulteriori informazioni sulle numerose opere inserite nel nostro catalogo che hanno come oggetto design, moda, cultura popolare, banca immagini e consultazione grafica potete visitare il sito www.pepinpress.com.

Web Design Index By Content.02 には、選りすぐりのウェブサイト500が、カテゴリー別に収録されています。全サイトについて、オープニング・ページと、そのサイトの特徴をよく表しているページを載せています。また、附録のCD-ROMには、ブラウザーがつき、各サイトにワンクリックで簡単にアクセスできます。本とCDを参照すれば、各分野で、現在どんなウェブサイトが人気があるのか、手軽に知ることができます。

本書には、各サイトのURLだけでなく、デザイナーとプログラマーの名前も載せています。表記方法は以下のとおりです。

- **D**　デザイン
- **C**　コーディング
- **P**　プロダクション
- **A**　エージェンシー
- **M**　デザイナーのEメール・アドレス

ウェブサイトの自薦・他薦

Pepin Press は、ウェブデザイン・ブックの改訂版を毎年出版しています。自分のウェブサイトを掲載ご希望の場合、また推薦したいサイトがある場合には、www.webdesignindex.orgにアクセスしてお申し込みください。

The Pepin Press / Agile Rabbit Editions

Pepin Press は、デザインやファッション、ポップ・カルチャーなどについて多様な出版物を出しています。すぐに使える画像などもありますので、当社の出版物や画像について、詳しい情報をお知りになりたい方は、www.pepinpress.comにアクセスしてください。

Web Design Index By Content.02 (Diseño de páginas web por contenidos.02) presenta una selección de 500 sitios web organizados por temas. De cada sitio web se incluyen dos páginas: una página inicial y una página representativa del sitio. Además, se adjunta un CD-ROM con un explorador que permite acceder a las páginas con total funcionalidad sin necesidad de estar conectado a Internet. Juntos, el libro y el CD ofrecen un panorama exhaustivo de los patrones utilizados en el campo del diseño web en numerosos ámbitos.

Se indica la URL de cada sitio que aparece en el libro. Asimismo, el nombre de las personas que han participado en el diseño y la programación de dichos sitios se recoge del modo siguiente:

D diseño
C codificación
P producción
A agencia
M dirección de correo electrónico del diseñador

Propuestas y recomendaciones
Cada año, se publican nuevas ediciones de todos los libros de diseño de páginas web de The Pepin Press. Si desea proponer o recomendar un diseño para que se tenga en cuenta para próximas ediciones, rellene el formulario que figura en www.webdesignindex.org.

The Pepin Press / Agile Rabbit Editions
Para obtener más información acerca de las numerosas publicaciones de The Pepin Press sobre diseño, moda, cultura popular, referencia visual e imágenes listas para utilizar, visite www.pepinpress.com.

Web Design By Content.02(내용별 웹 디자인.02)에는 주제별로 정렬된 500여개의 웹 사이트 디자인이 들어 있습니다. 각 사이트는 첫 페이지와 사이트의 특징을 잘 나타내는 기본 페이지 등 두 페이지로 구성되어 있습니다. 함께 제공된 CD-ROM에는 브라우저와 선택한 사이트를 보고 액세스할 수 있는 원 클릭 기능이 들어 있습니다. 또한 책과 CD에는 특정 분야의 표준 웹 디자인에 대해 알기 쉽게 설명되어 있습니다.

책에는 각 사이트의 URL이 표시되어 있습니다. 각 사이트의 디자인 및 프로그래밍 관련 이름은 다음과 같이 표기되어 있습니다.

D 디자인
C 코딩
P 제작
A 대행사
M 디자이너의 전자 메일 주소

제안 및 추천
일년마다 Pepin Press의 모든 웹 디자인 책이 새로운 버전으로 출판됩니다. 생각하고 있는 디자인을 제안하거나 추천하시려면 www.webdesignindex.org의 제출 양식에 액세스하시기 바랍니다.

Pepin Press / Agile Rabbit Editions
디자인, 패션, 대중문화, 영상 자료 및 기성 이미지와 관련된 수많은 Pepin Press의 출판물에 대한 자세한 내용은 www.pepinpress.com을 방문하시기 바랍니다.

Книга «Веб-дизайн по содержанию.02» содержит выборку из 500 веб-сайтов, сгруппированных по темам. Каждый сайт представлен двумя страницами: заглавной и содержательной. К книге прилагается компакт-диск с браузером и утилитой, позволяющей загрузить и просмотреть выбранный сайт одним щелчком мыши. Книга и компакт-диск вместе содержат полный обзор стандартов веб-дизайна во всех приведенных областях.

Для каждого сайта, приведенного в книге, указывается его адрес (URL). Фамилии людей, принимавших участие в проектировании и создании сайтов, отмечены следующим образом:

D дизайн
C программирование
P производство
A агентство
M адрес электронной почты дизайнера

Подача на рассмотрение заявок и рекомендации
Новые издания книг по веб-дизайну издательства The Pepin Press публикуются каждый год. Если вы желаете подать на рассмотрение заявку или порекомендовать какой-либо дизайн, заполните, пожалуйста, бланк заявки на сайте www.webdesignindex.org.

Издательство The Pepin Press / Agile Rabbit Editions
За дополнительной информацией об основных публикациях издательства The Pepin Press по дизайну, моде, современной культуре, визуальным справочникам и библиотекам высококачественных изображений, готовых к непосредственному использованию, обращайтесь на сайт www.pepinpress.com.

Web Design Index By Content.02 (Webdesign nach Thema.02) enthält eine thematisch gegliederte Auswahl von 500 Websites. Jede dieser Sites ist mit je zwei für die Gestaltung repräsentativen Abbildungen vertreten. Auf der beiliegenden CD-ROM können mit einem Internetbrowser die meisten der ausgewählten Websites offline in voller Funktionalität betrachtet werden. So bieten Buch und CD einen umfassenden Überblick über den aktuellen Stand des Webdesigns der unterschiedlichsten Bereiche.

Für jede im Buch genannte Website ist die URL angegeben. Die Namen der an Design und Programmierung der Websites beteiligten Personen sind wie folgt gekennzeichnet:

- **D** Design
- **C** Codierung
- **P** Produktion
- **A** Agentur
- **M** E-Mail-Adresse des Designers

Einsendungen & Empfehlungen

Jedes Jahr werden brandaktuelle Neuausgaben aller Websdesign-Bücher von The Pepin Press herausgebracht. Sollten Sie Designs einreichen oder empfehlen wollen, füllen Sie bitte das entsprechende Einsendeformular unter www.webdesignindex.org aus.

The Pepin Press / Agile Rabbit Editions

Weitere Informationen über die zahlreichen Publikationen von The Pepin Press zu den Themen Design, Mode, Kultur, visuelle Referenz und Bilder zur direkten Verwendung finden Sie auf unserer Website unter www.pepinpress.com.

Web Design Index By Content.02 (Web Design por Conteúdo.02) contém uma selecção de 500 sítios na Web, organizados por assunto. Foram incluídas duas páginas de cada sítio na Web: uma de abertura e uma representativa do mesmo. O CD-ROM anexo contém um programa de navegação e está estruturado de modo a permitir a visualização e o acesso offline aos sítios na Web seleccionados com um clique. Em conjunto, o livro e o CD proporcionam uma perspectiva abrangente do nível de Web design em diversas áreas.

É indicado o URL de cada sítio na Web presente no livro. Os nomes das pessoas envolvidas na concepção e programação dos sítios na Web são indicados da seguinte forma:

D design
C codificação
P produção
A agência
M endereço de correio electrónico do designer

Propostas e recomendações
Todos os anos, The Pepin Press publica edições novas de todos os seus livros sobre Web design. Para propor ou recomendar designs à nossa avaliação, aceda ao formulário de propostas em www.webdesignindex.org.

The Pepin Press/Agile Rabbit Editions
Para obter mais informações sobre as diversas publicações de The Pepin Press sobre design, moda, cultura popular, referências visuais e imagens prontas a usar, visite www.pepinpress.com.

Web Design Index By Content.02 zawiera wybór 500 ułożonych tematycznie stron internetowych. Każda z tych stron reprezentowana jest stroną startową oraz inną dla niej charakterystyczną stroną. Do książki dołączony jest CD-ROM zawierający przeglądarkę i funkcję pokazywania i wywołania wybranych stron internetowych poprzez jedno kliknięcie. Razem, książka i CD-ROM, oferują wyczerpujące zestawienie standardów projektowania stron internetowych w obrębie wielu dziedzin.

Na każdej stronie książki podawany jest URL danej strony internetowej. Nazwiska osób zaangażowanych w projektowanie i programowanie stron internetowych podawane są następująco:

D projektowanie
C kodowanie
P wykonanie
A agencja
M adres email projektanta

Propozycje i rekomendacje
Każdego roku wydawnictwo The Pepin Press publikuje nowe edycje książek Web Design. Jeśli mają Państwo życzenie przedłożyć lub polecić nam projekt, proszę wypełnić odpowiedni formularz na stronie internetowej www.webdesignindex.org.

Wydawnictwo The Pepin Press / Agile Rabbit Editions
Więcej informacji o licznych publikacjach wydawnictwa The Pepin Press na temat projektowania, mody, kultury, referencji wizualnych oraz gotowych do bezpośredniego użycia obrazów znajdą Państwo na stronie internetowej www.pepinpress.com.

fluidum contemporary interiors zürich

fluidum

news
the company
sofas and armchairs
beds
chairs
tables
low tables
services
references
where to buy
contact
sale

contact

address

fluidum GmbH
contemporary interiors
Bändlistrasse 29
CH-8064 Zürich

phone +41 1 440 42 85
fax +41 1 440 42 86

contact@fluidum.ch

e-news

join our mailing list

first name :

name :

E-Mail :

>>

fluidum contemporary interiors zürich

fluidum

news
the company
sofas and armchairs
beds
chairs
tables
low tables
services
references
where to buy
contact
sale

big spender
bird
club
deep
lizard
lizard de luxe
round

more information

Big Spender | Friedemann Ramacher 2000

< >

'big spender' is an exceptionally comfortable range of cushioned seating whose loose elements can be combined to the user's personal taste. Apart from linear sofas with or without armrests, 'big spender' elements can also compile into day beds, round-the-corner combinations and generously sized and varied 'seatscapes'. Its cushionless, somewhat pronounced voluminous design lends to 'big spender' a lucid and inviting keynote.

www.fluidum.ch

D: friedemann ramacher **C:** pierre morgadès **P:** pierre morgadès

A: wattstyle **M:** www.wattstyle.ch

A10

A10 is a new architecture magazine with a European focus. Six times a year, it presents the latest architecture on the ancient continent.

new European architecture

CLICK HERE FOR THE CONTENTS OF **A10 #8**

Sub-scribe here

about
inside
contact
get

Contents A10 #8

about
inside A10
contact
get

#1 | #2 | #3 | #4 | #5 | #6 | #7 | #8

#8 (Mar/Apr 2006)

On the spot

News and observations

www.a10magazine.com

D: arjan groot **C:** kim dijkstra

M: mail@a10magazine.com

Gregotti Associati International Site

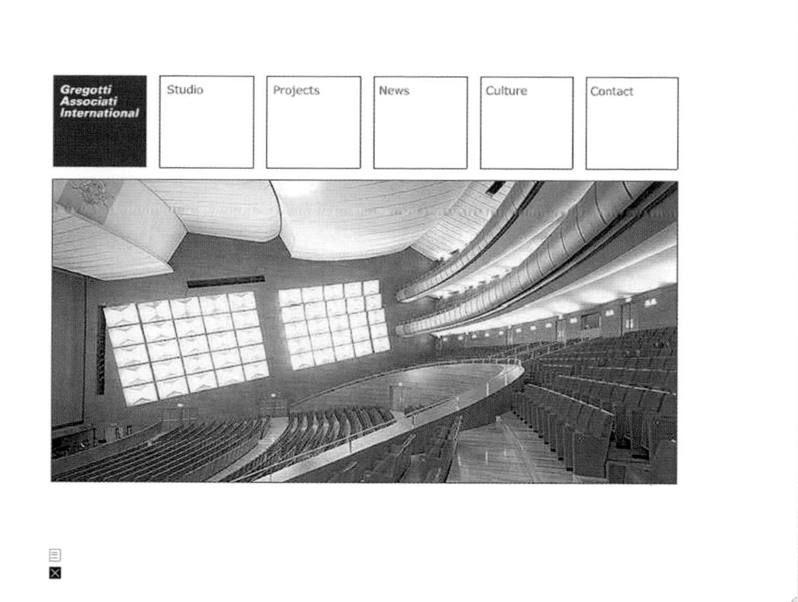

Gregotti Associati Site

STUDIO > **PRACTICE**

Gregotti Associati International was founded in 1974 by Vittorio Gregotti. Currently there are three partners, Vittorio Gregotti, Augusto Cagnardi and Michele Reginaldi, supported by twelve associates, a large group of young architects and an efficient and organizational structure.
Gregotti Associati International is an architectural design firm that collaborates regularly with engineering firms for the development of projects, and with experts and scholars when forming analysis groups for particularly demanding or complex issues.
Since the 1970s there has been a continuous increase in activities. In the course of these years there have been hundreds of projects developed in over 20 countries in Europe, the US, Africa, the Middle East, and Asia.
Numerous projects have been realised, such as master plans for big cities, redevelopment plans for urban areas, theaters, stadia, museums, public buildings, curches, university and research centers, banks, companies headquarters, housing districts, commercial and open spaces.
Gregotti Associati International has its main offices in

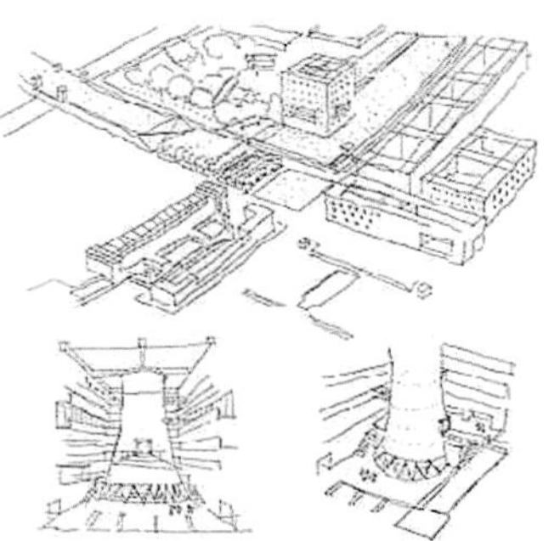

Print

www.gregottiassociati.com

D: dario zannier, fabio zannier **C:** caroline hue

M: gai.milano@gregottiassociati-link.it

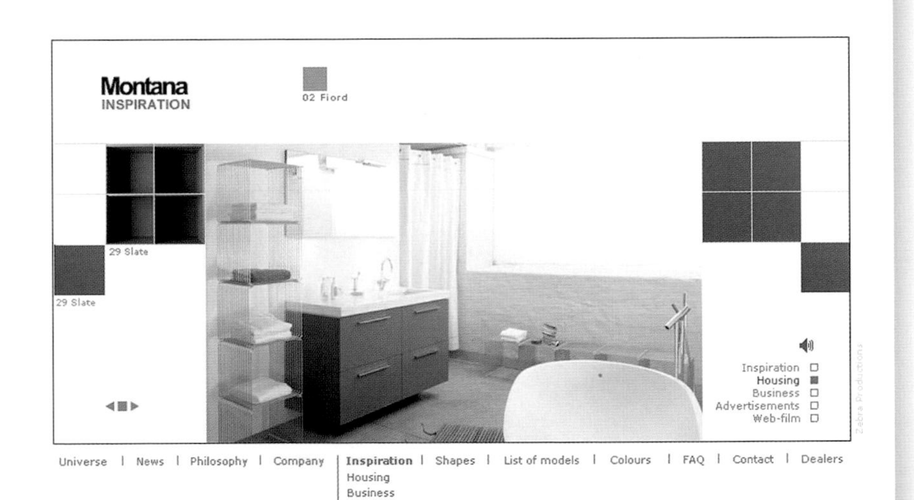

www.montana.dk

D: lars norman, birgit kristiansen **C:** gitte brinck, boris hansen **P:** birgit kristiansen

A: zebra productions **M:** zebra@zebra-pro.dk

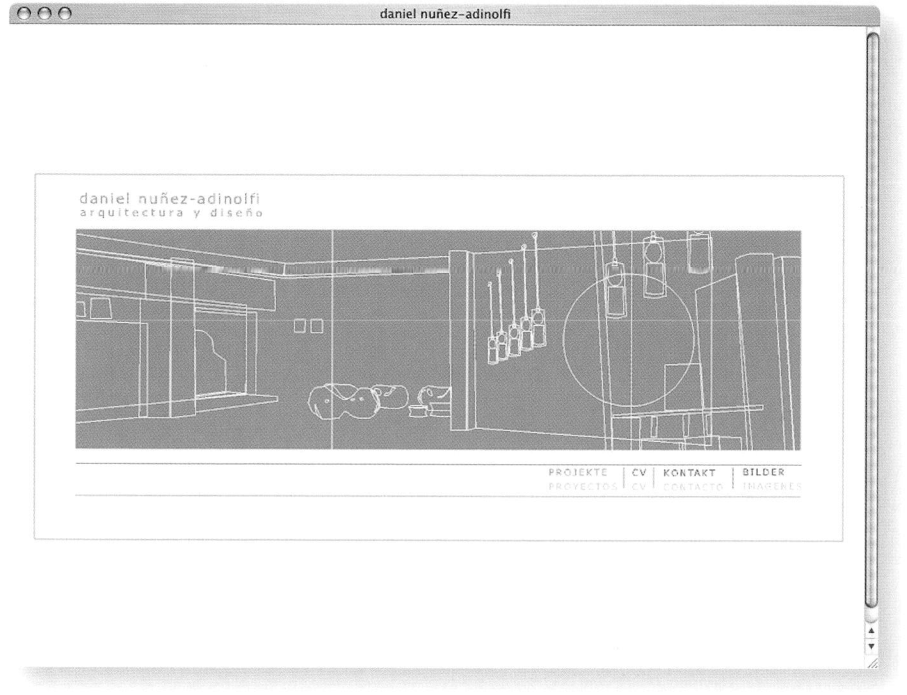

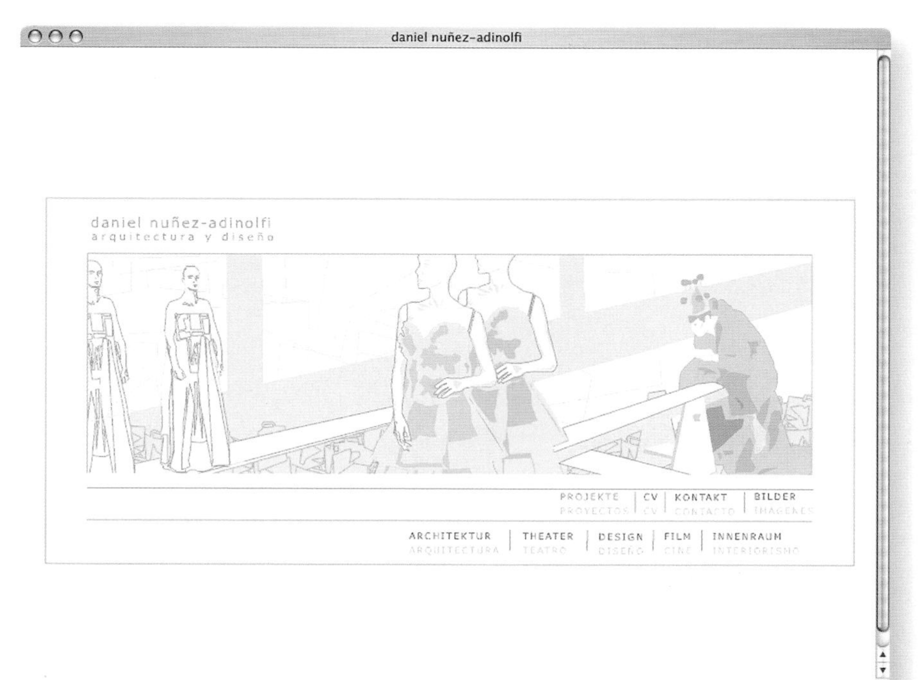

www.danuadi.de

D: diego gardón

M: chiclegalaxia@yahoo.com

www.gmp-architekten.de

D: pia danner **C:** wolfgang becker **P:** gmp architekten

A: macina **M:** pd@macina.com

yes architectes

Yes architectes

yes architectes

Yes architectes

Espace pro
Coordonnées
Newsletter

16 10 03 25 07 Recherche thématique
01 Équipe
Actualités 32 04 18 12
08 29 06 27
11 02 28 15 24 05 34 09

www.yesarchi.com

D: trafik **P:** yes architectes

A: trafik **M:** www.lavitrinedetrafik.com

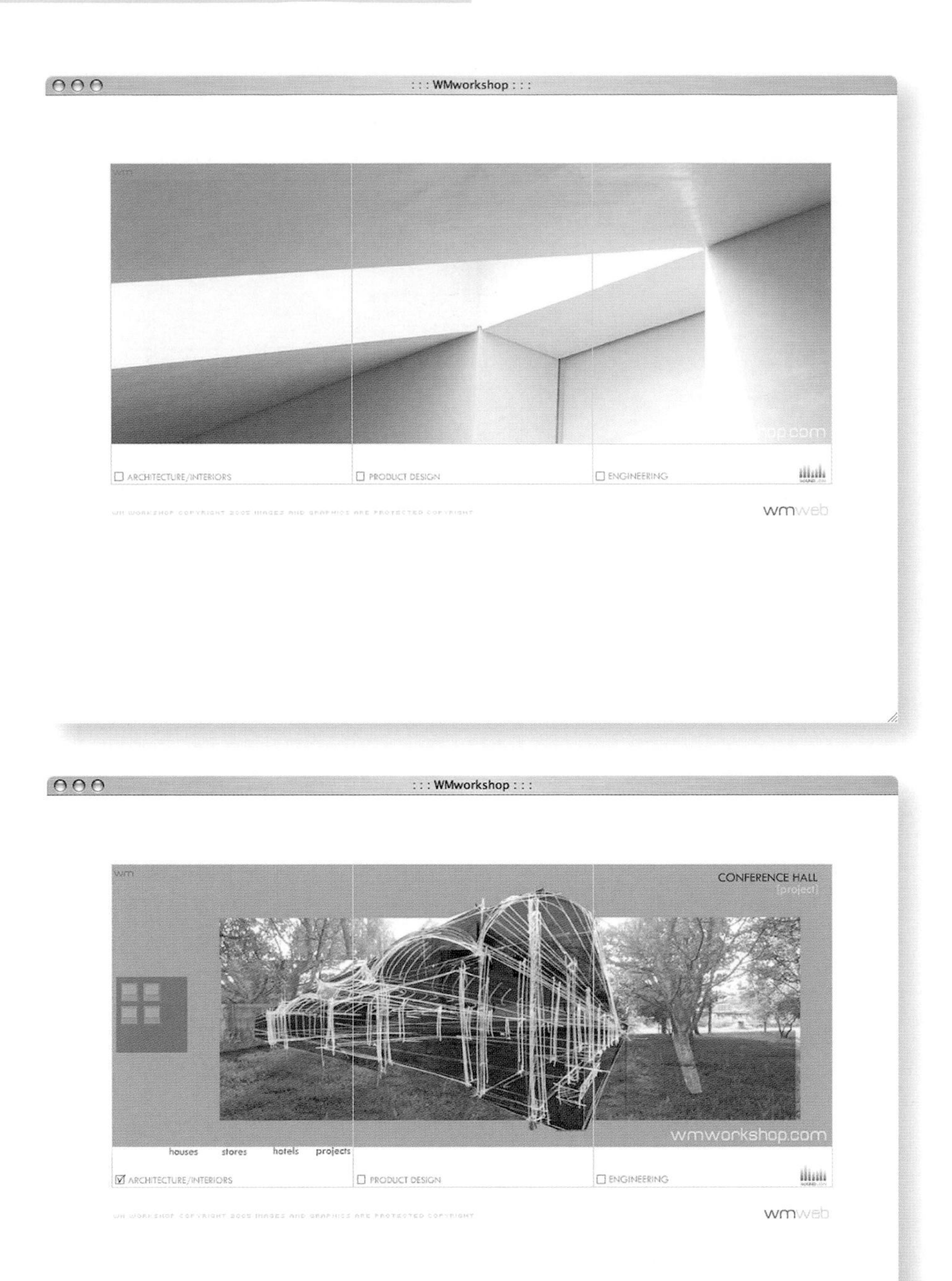

www.wmworkshop.com

D: donato dogali **P:** wmworkshop

A: wmweb **M:** info@wmweb.it

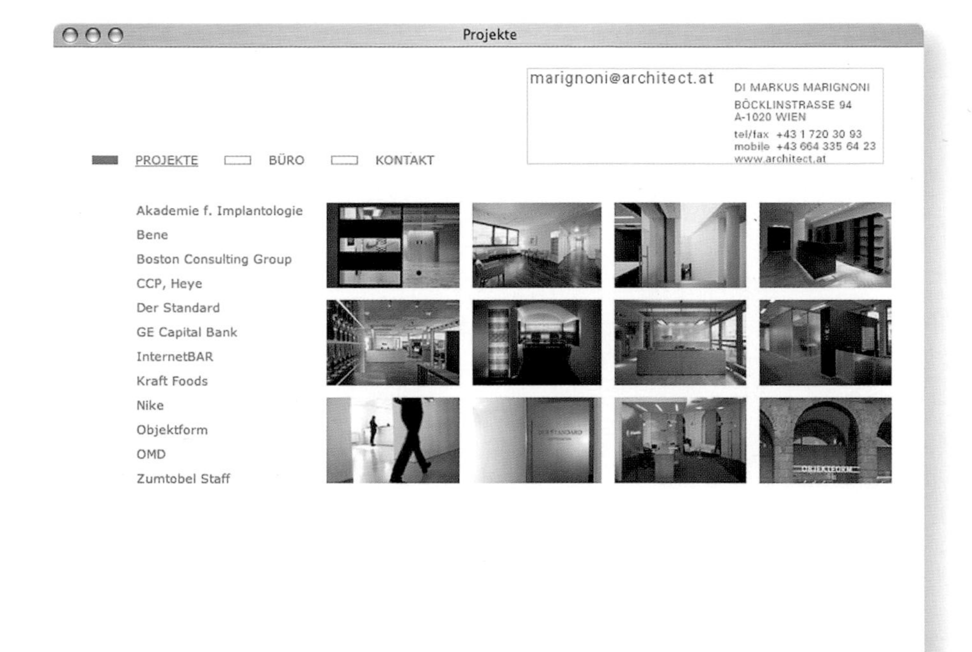

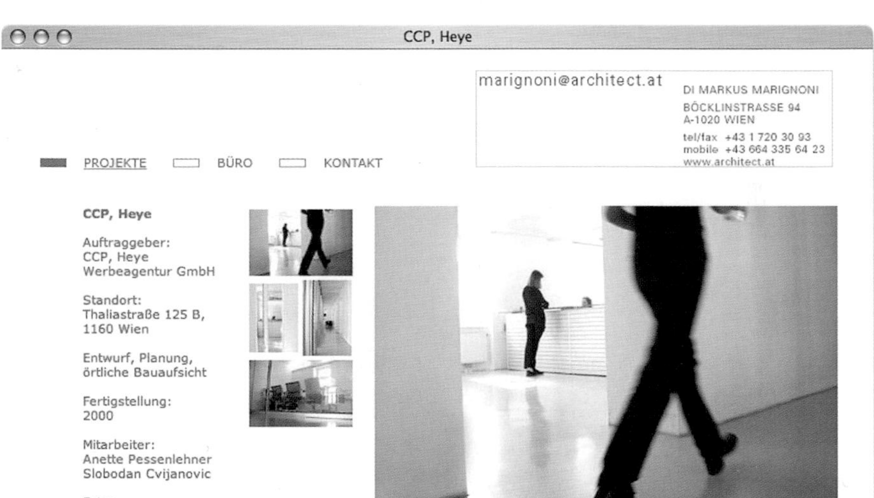

www.architect.at

D: christina kandlhofer

A: kashi_design **M:** www.kashi.at

www.dgaarquitectura.com

D: alex soteres, jordi cortada

A: artrivity disseny **M:** info@artrivity.com

www.camillindenny.com

D: thom bennett

A: thom bennett graphic design **M:** info@tbgd.co.uk

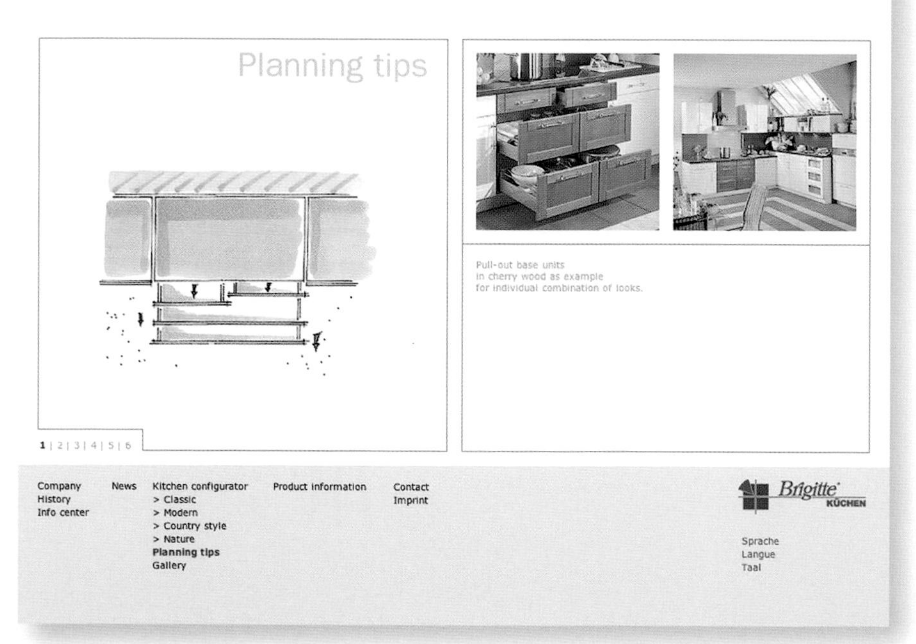

www.brigitte-kuechen.com

D: antje weber, hanno denker

A: quer-denker.com **M:** mail@quer-denker.com

www.homekeep.pt

D: sofia vitor **C:** wolfgang borgsmüller **P:** sofia vitor

A: aftamina **M:** www.aftamina.pt

www.ctpinvest.com

D: nydrle studio

A: nydrle studio **M:** helpdesk@nydrle.net

www.sartori-deco.be/xy

D: fx. marciat, j. veronesi **P:** sartori deco

A: xy area **M:** xy@xyarea.com

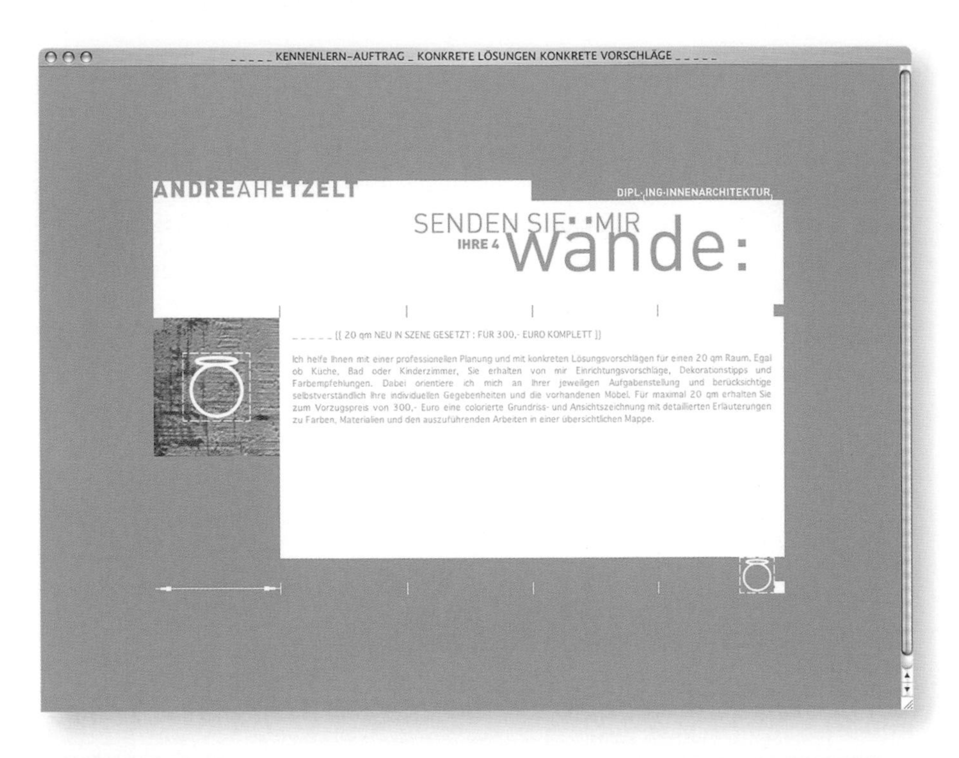

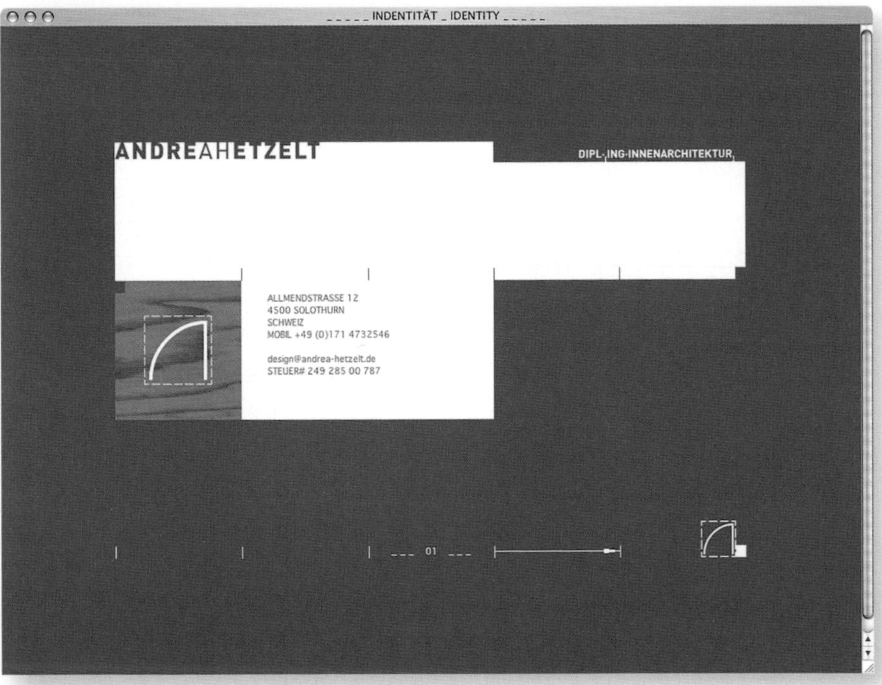

www.andrea-hetzelt.de

D: patricia prem **C:** patricia prem **P:** claus roland heinrich

A: heinrichplusprem kommunikationsdesign **M:** hallo@heinrichplusprem.com

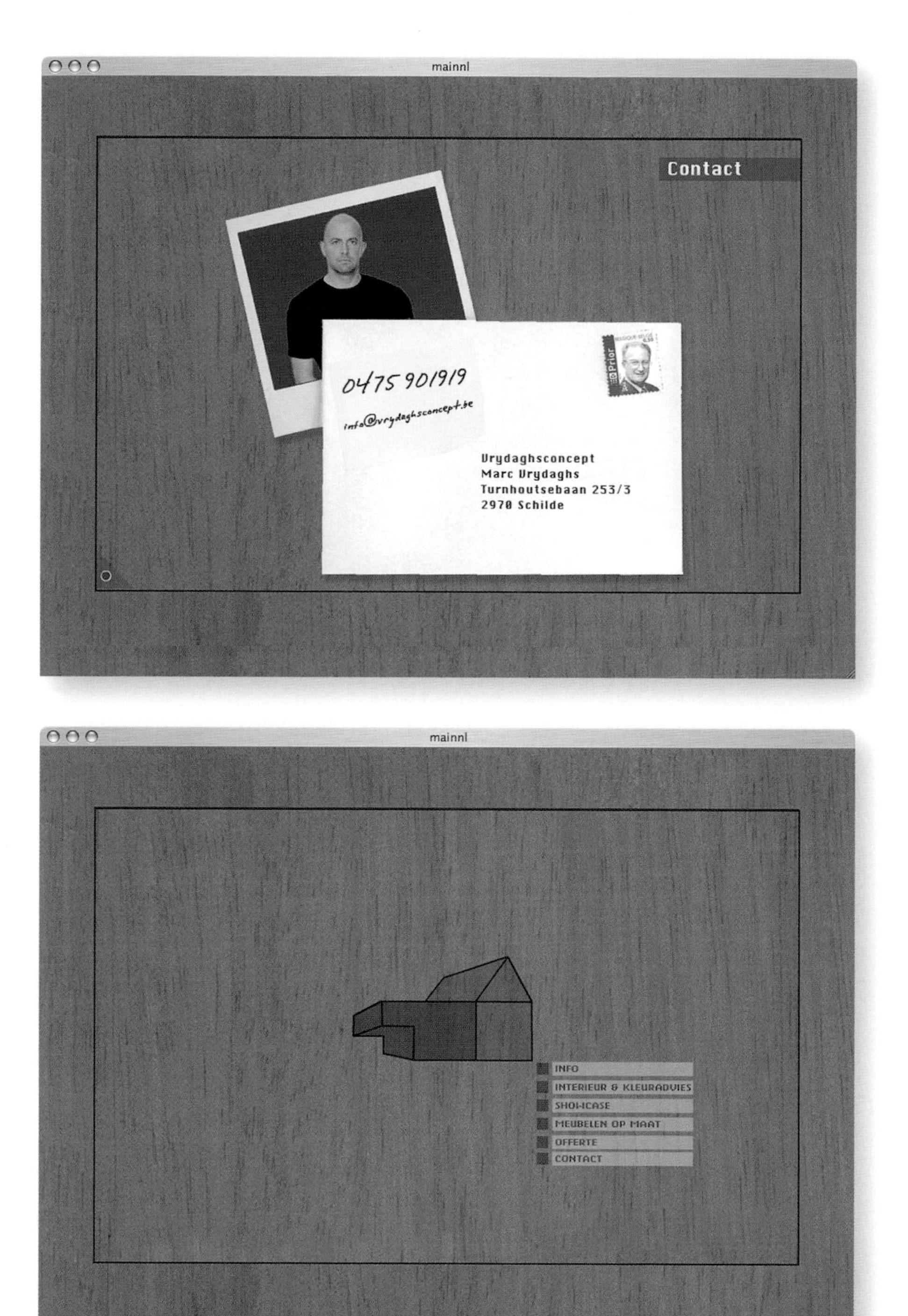

www.vrydaghsconcept.be

D: inés van belle

A: pinker **M:** ines@pinker.be

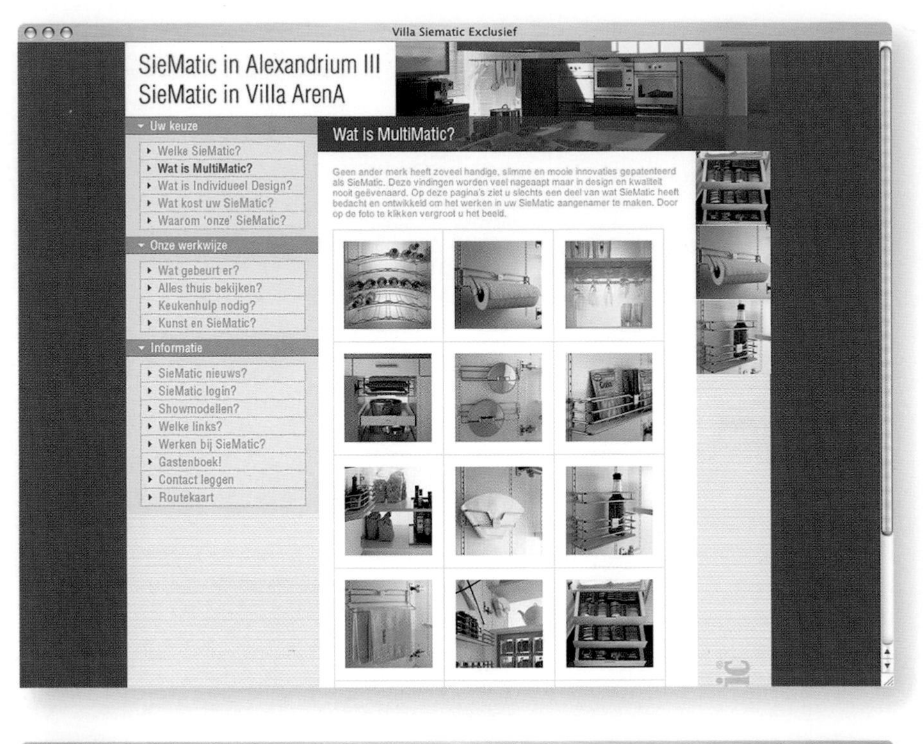

www.siematicindewoonmall.nl

D: mattijs janssen **C:** janssen, robert nouwens **P:** mattijs janssen, marcel geerts

A: janssen.nl reclamebureau **M:** info@janssen.nl

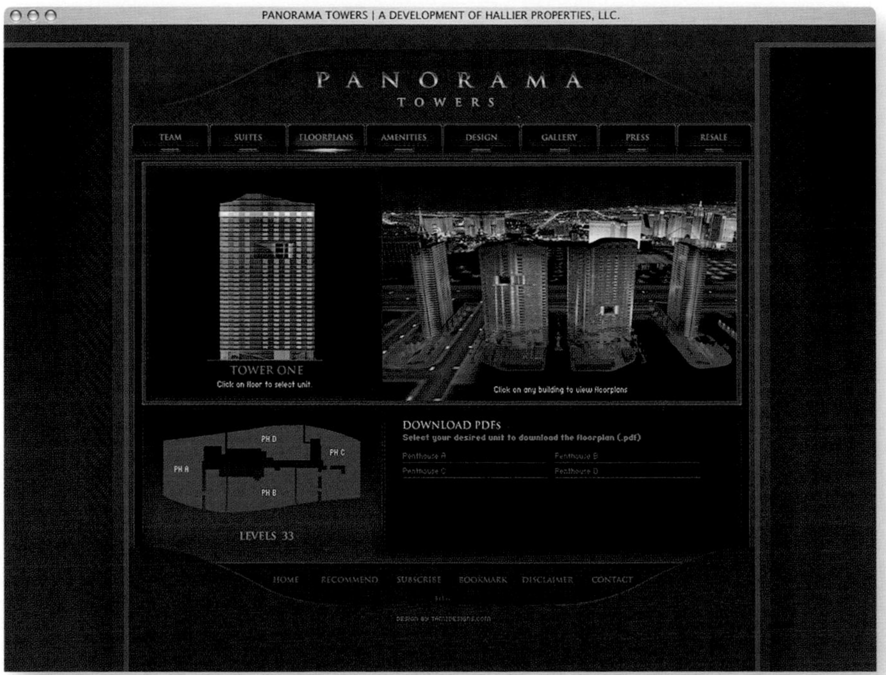

panoramatowers.com
D: tamzdesigns
A: tamzil inc. **M:** mtamzil@tamzdesigns.com

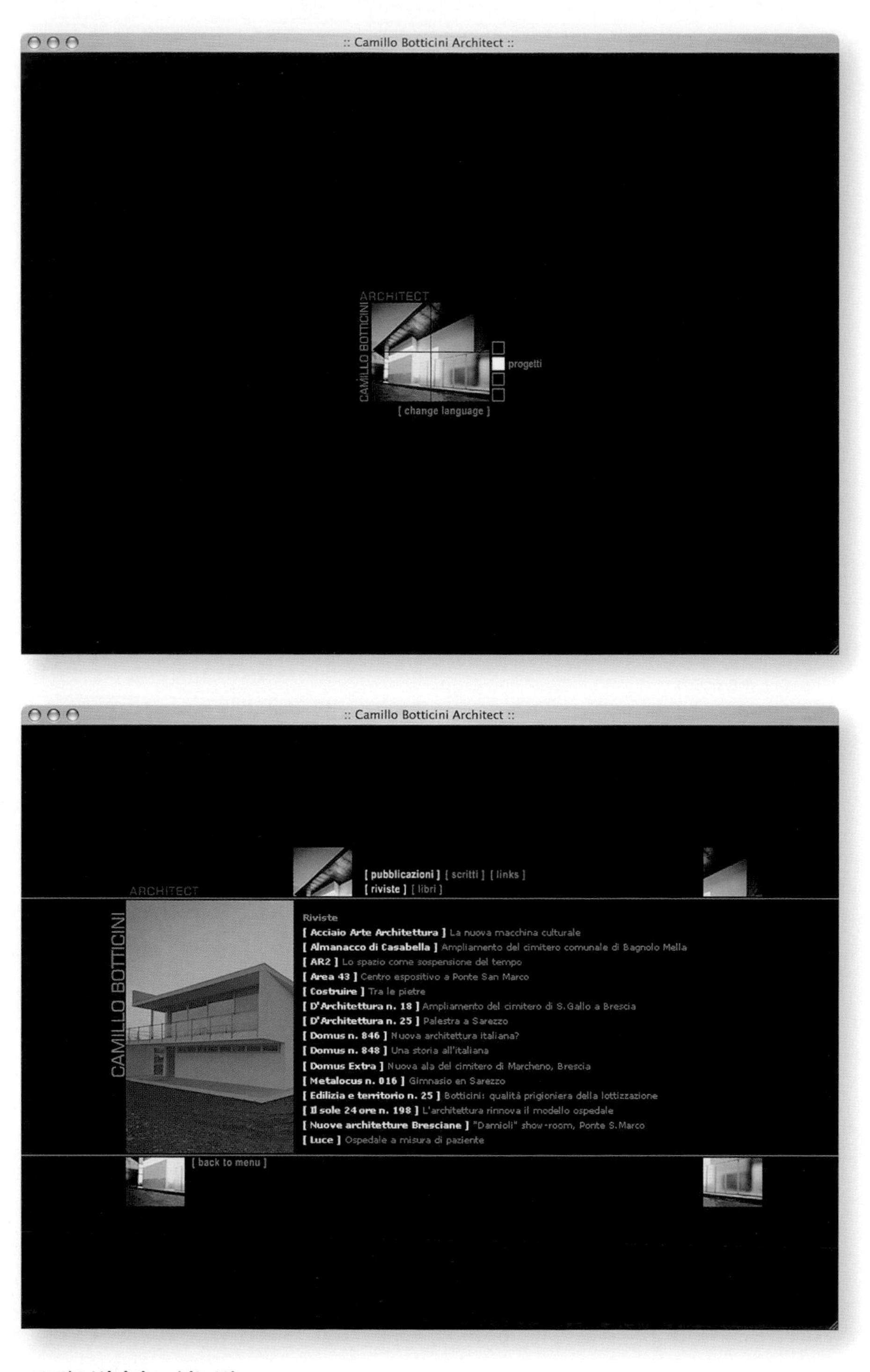

www.botticiniarchitetti.com

D: alessandro raimondo **P:** riccardo borsoni

M: info@design-r.com

[plug.in]

[plug.in]

2006

About
Calendar
Events
Exhibitions
2000
2001
2002
2003
2004
2005
2006
2007
Network
Projects
Resources
Links
Fotobot
Search

Jan
Feb
Mar
Apr
May
Jun
Jul
Aug
Sep
Oct
Nov
Dec

Thursday
21.9.2006, 14:00-18:00
Public Living Room

2006

14.09.06 Home Made
22.06.06 Einmal Kiew hin und zurück
01.06.06 Jan Torpus - TelcomGallery
27.05.06 Cyber seductions for virtual virgins
04.05.06 Rolf Pfeifer
28.04.06 electric rendez-vous
27.04.06 etoy - Mission Eternity
20.04.06 Bitnik
13.04.06 Rainer Fischbach - Mythos Netz
06.04.06 transmediale 06 - review and video-selection
30.03.06 Zone Interdite
29.03.06 Zone Interdite
25.03.06 Cyber seductions for virtual virgins
16.03.06 VIPER-Festival
25.02.06 Cyber seductions for virtual virgins
23.02.06 Artist talk with SONOgames
27.01.06 Night of the Museums
27.01.06 SONOgames - Leisureland II

Deutsch
To Bookmark
Sound

[plug.in]

[plug.in]

About
Calendar
Network
Projects
Resources
Links
Fotobot
Search

Fotobot

The [plug.in] fotobot's duty is to record what goes on in [plug.in]'s public living room: the new issues of our magazines, a new DVD in our collection, the current exhibition or our visitors. The photos of all these real life people, objects and events are beamed directly into the [plug.in] online picture archive,where the images can be commented on, downloaded, printed or sent out as digital postcards.

Partners
Belleville

Supporter
Credit Suisse

Links
belleville.ch
Credit Suisse

Deutsch
To Bookmark
Sound

www.iplugin.org

D: brian hoffer, franziska burkhardt **C:** urs beyeler, brian hoffer
A: brianhoffer.com, buka grafik **M:** hoffer@brianhoffer.com

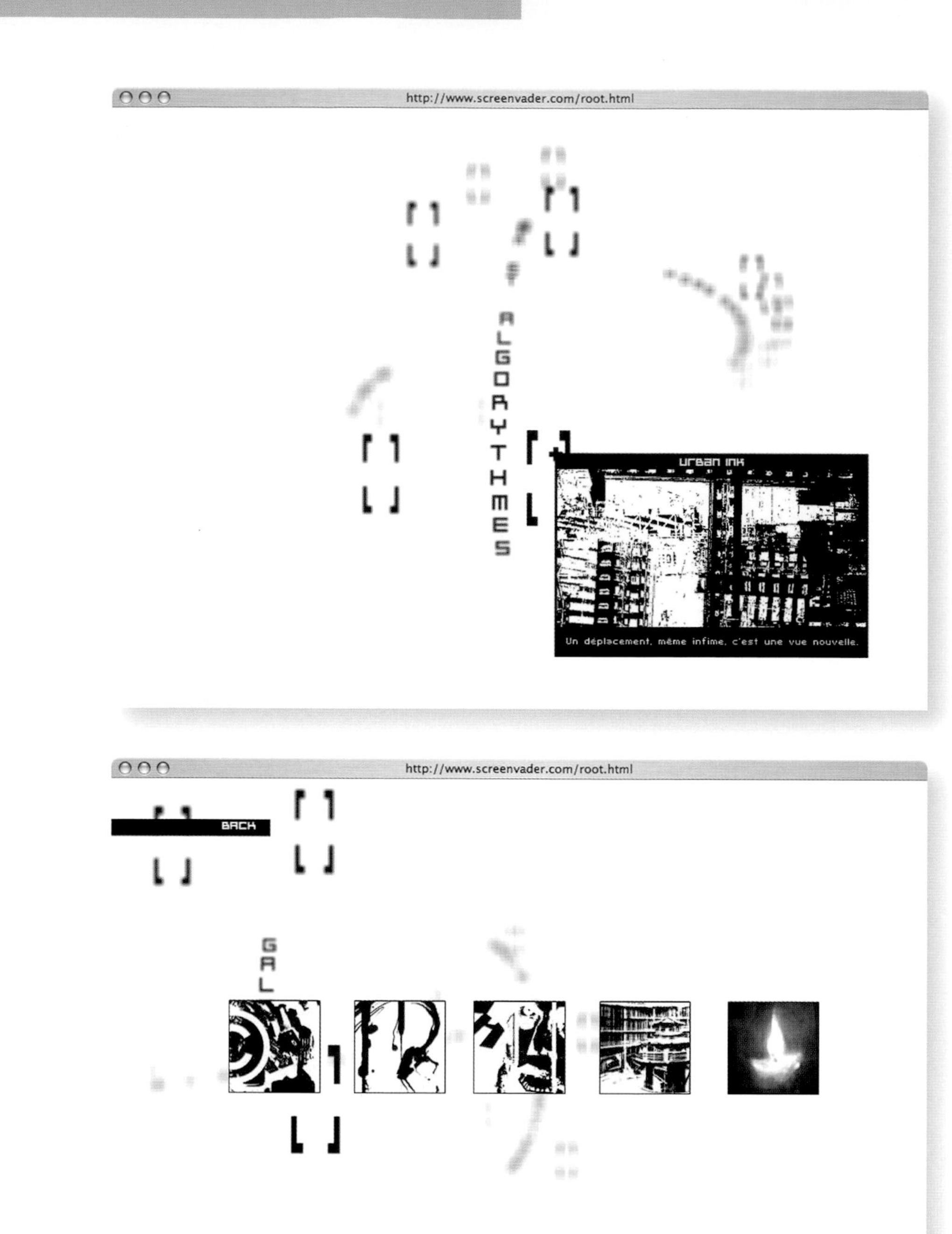

www.screenvader.com

D: stéphane bourez

M: stephane@screenvader.com

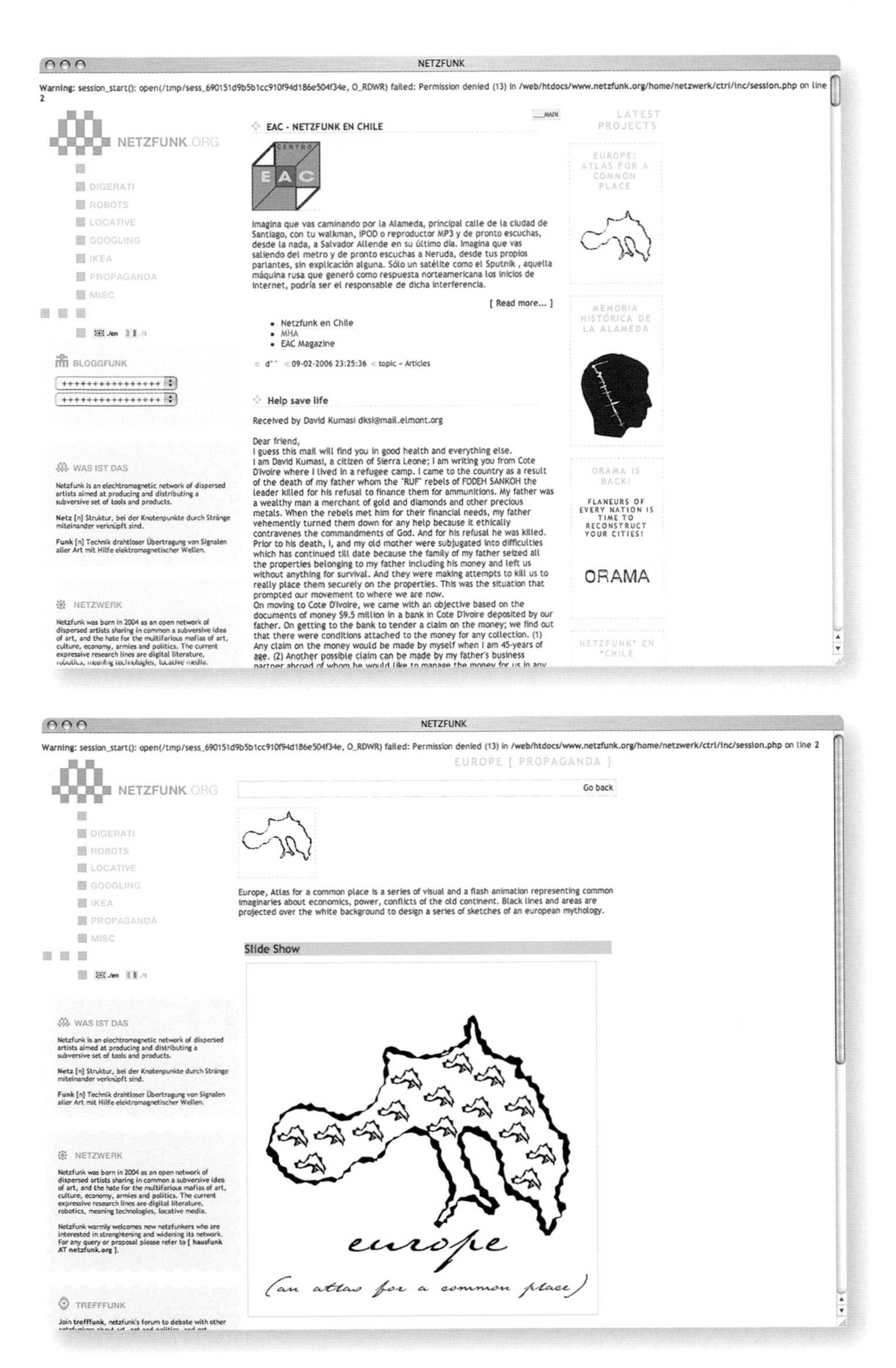

www.netzfunk.org

D: david boardman **C:** d-@netzfunk.org

M: d-@netzfunk.org

www.feedtank.com

D: jonah warren, steven sanborn

A: feedtank M: info@feedtank.com

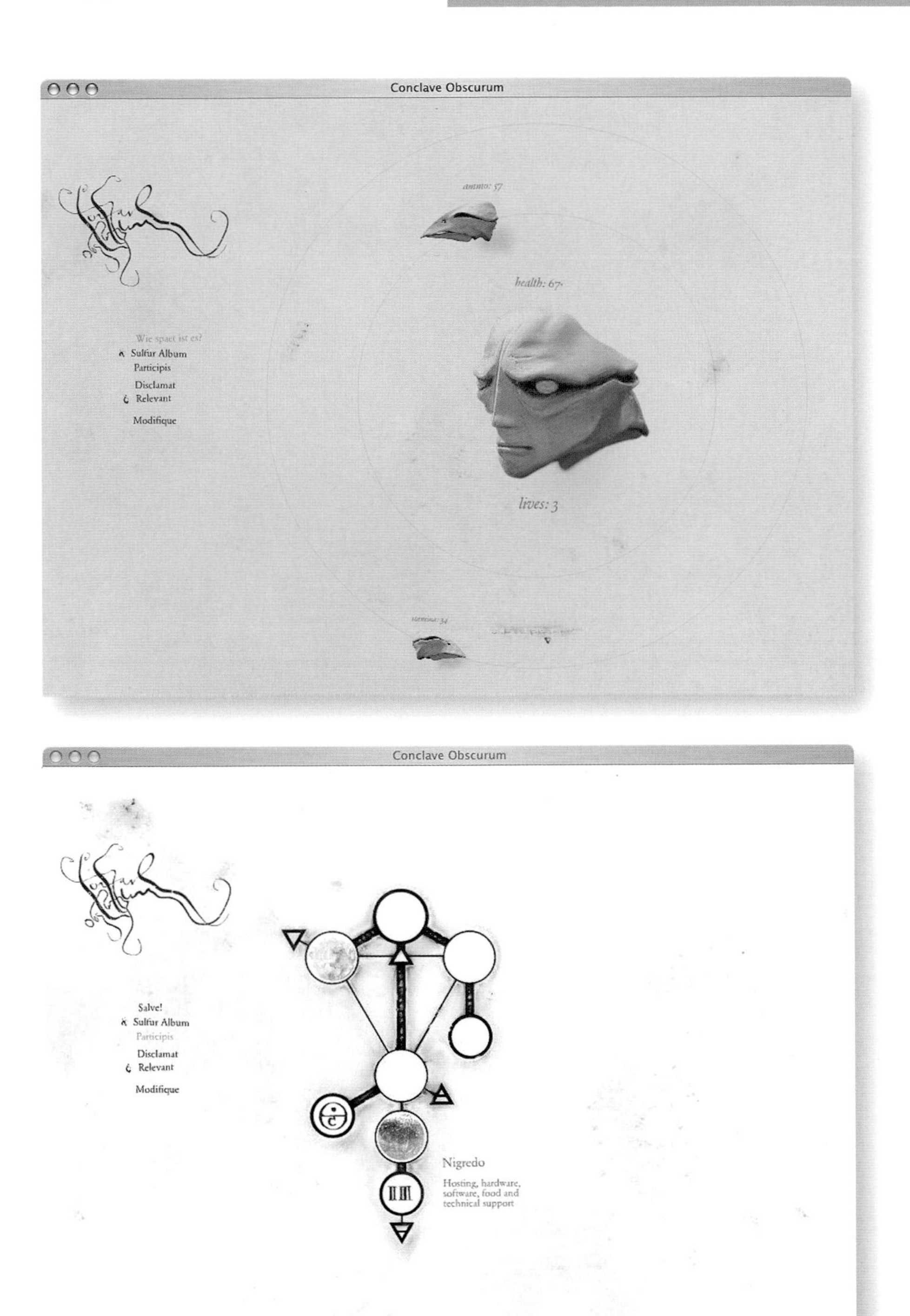

conclave.ru

D: oleg paschenko **C:** iv dembicki **P:** oleg paschenko

A: art. lebedev studio **M:** cmart@design.ru

c_cil _visiBle diFFerence_

c_cil

©2003, 2004 c_cil - c_lacomb@club-internet.fr

c_cil _visiBle diFFerence_

SEX

deCULottée

LOVE

©2003, 2004 c_cil - c_lacomb@club-internet.fr

www.c-cil.com

D: c_cil

M: c_lacomb@club.fr

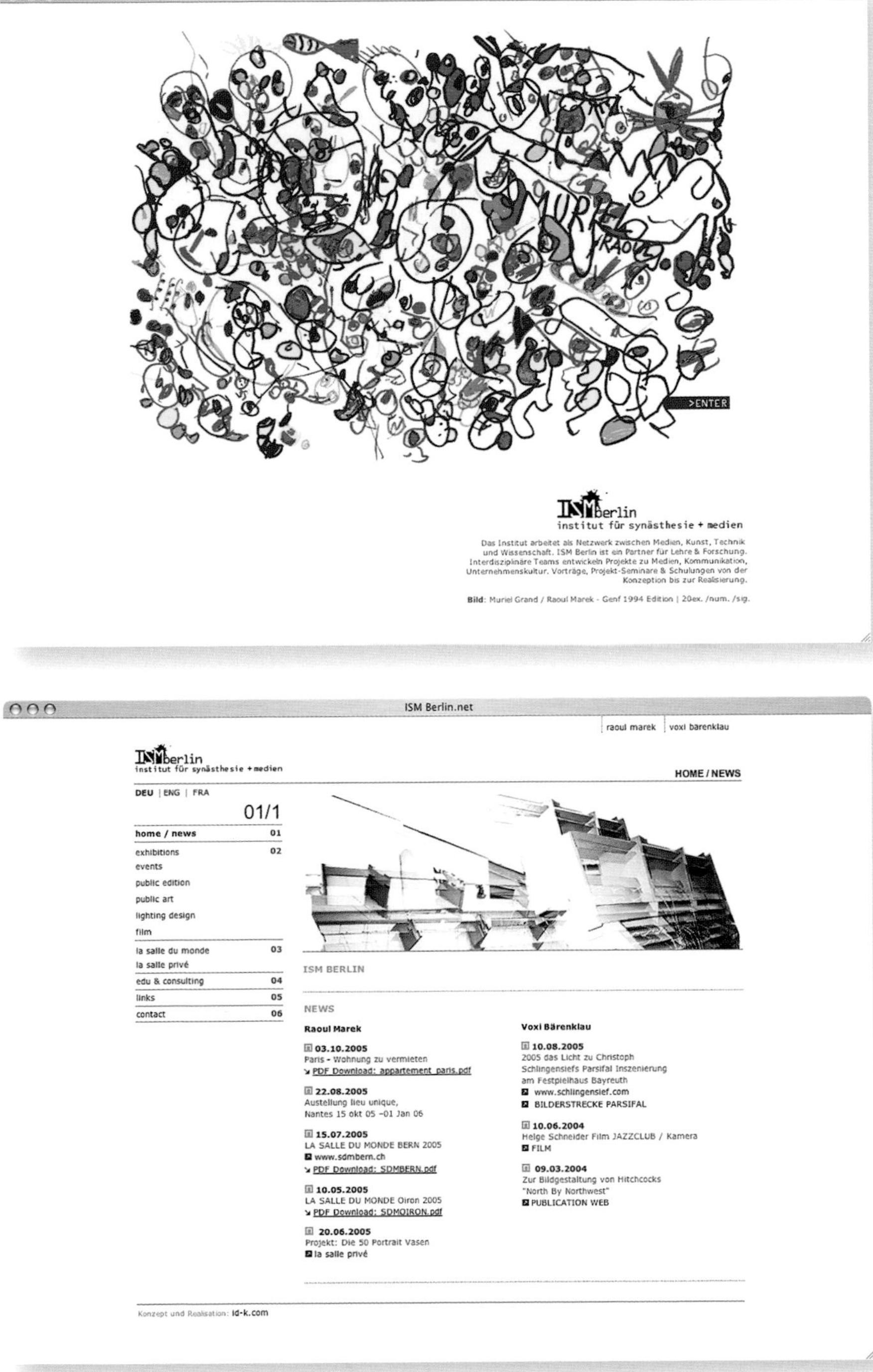

www.ism-berlin.net

D: gregory gasser **C:** gregory gasser **P:** id-k.com

A: id-k kommunikationsdesign **M:** g.gasser@id-k.com

Ágnes Elöd – Portfolio 2005

elöd ÁGNES

PORTFOLIO CV CONTACT

2005 '04 '03 '02 '01 '00 '99 '98 '97 '96 '95

2005

- harry potter
- star wars
- matrix
- i was young, and had to make a living from something
- my heart now belongs to someone else
- burda-style flaming heart
- burda-style chinese heavy metal heart
- erich von däniken sculptures I.
- erich von däniken sculptures II.
- erich von däniken sculptures III.

hu

HARRY POTTER, 2005
70x100 cm
print

In this picture I replaced the faces of the three main characters from "Harry Potter" with my own face, and the faces of my long-term studio partners. Ron Weasley's face is replaced by the face of Ádám Szabó, Harry Potter's is replaced by György Szász's face, and the face of Hermione Granger is replaced by my own.

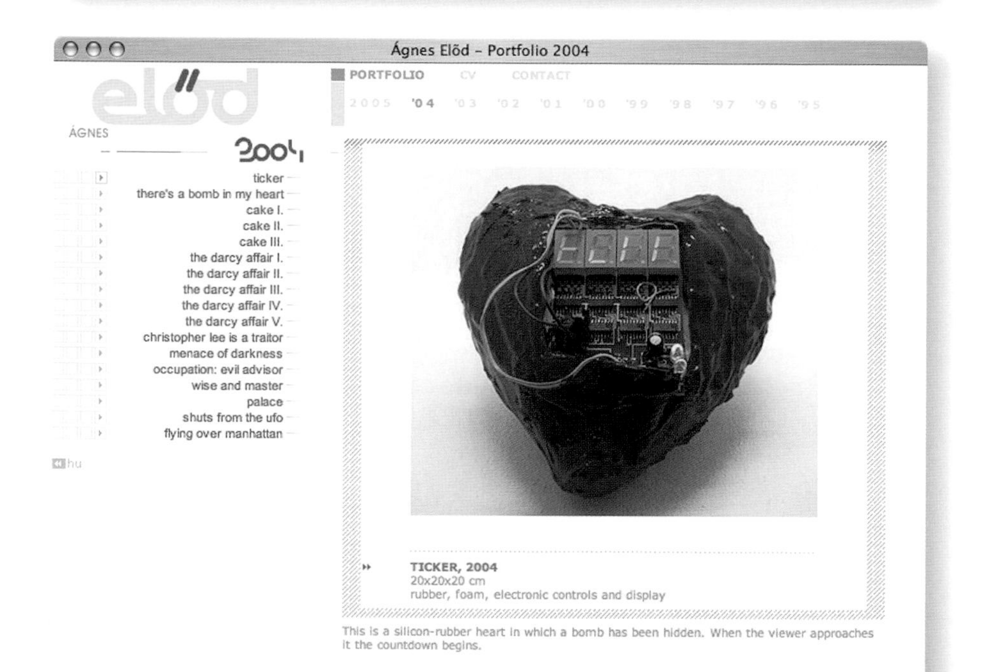

www.agneselod.hu

D: géza nyíry

A: nyk design **M:** info@nyk.hu

www.tokyoplastic.com

D: sam lanyon jones, andrew cope

A: tokyoplastic **M:** talk@tokyoplastic.com

menu

portafolio

curriculum

textos

contacto y presentación

Maider López

menu

<<<<< 1 2 3 4 5

Desde la playa 1

Intervención en la playa de Itzurun. 28 Agosto 2005. Zumaia.
Itzurun hondartzan egindako eskuhartze. 2005ko Abuztuaren 28a. Zumaia.
Intervention made in Itzurun beech. 2005/08/28. Zumaia
46 x 26,5 cm. Fotografía

Desde la playa 3

46 x 26,5 cm.
Photograph

Desde la playa 2

46 x 26,5 cm.
Argazkia

www.maiderlopez.com

D: josé maría martínez burgos, hafo **C:** josé maría martínez burgos **P:** maider lopez
A: animatu **M:** hafo@animatu.com

HUSTLE.. YEAR ROUND, SPRING, SUMMER, FALL, WINTER

ANTIGIRL; INTERIM (2006)

MEMOIRS · ARCHIVE · **HANDMADE**

mission: turbulence
> march 07, 2005
part of the passion & fury collection.

HUSTLE.. YEAR ROUND, SPRING, SUMMER, FALL, WINTER

ANTIGIRL; INTERIM (2006)

MEMOIRS · ARCHIVE · HANDMADE

we made two of these. one for the client and another to keep. this book contains a sample picture of every design that was created for the client lauren hart; this book was then given to her at the opening of the salon. a whole can of orange krylon paint was used to make the 2 books. and you can't tell from the pictures but it is shiny as hell. arik cut out the circle with precision, and derrick west illustrated the root drawing. 8x8x.25 inches.

> chip board, 80# semigloss, paint, wire.

www.antigirl.com

D: tiphanie brooke **C:** mike buzzard **P:** arik 1

A: antigirl **M:** t.tart@antigirl.com

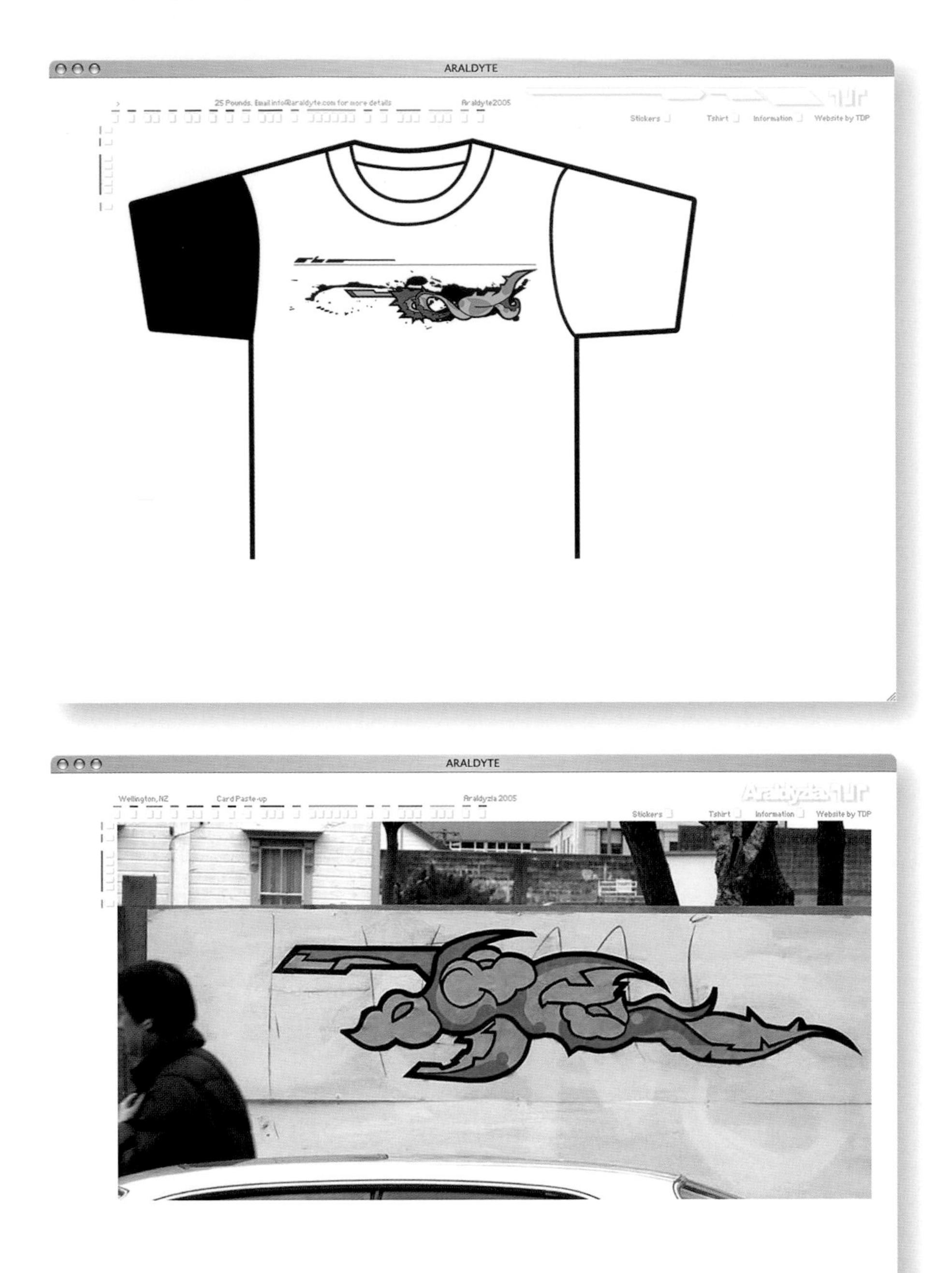

www.araldyte.com

D: tom painter

A: tdpstudio **M:** info@tdpdesign.com

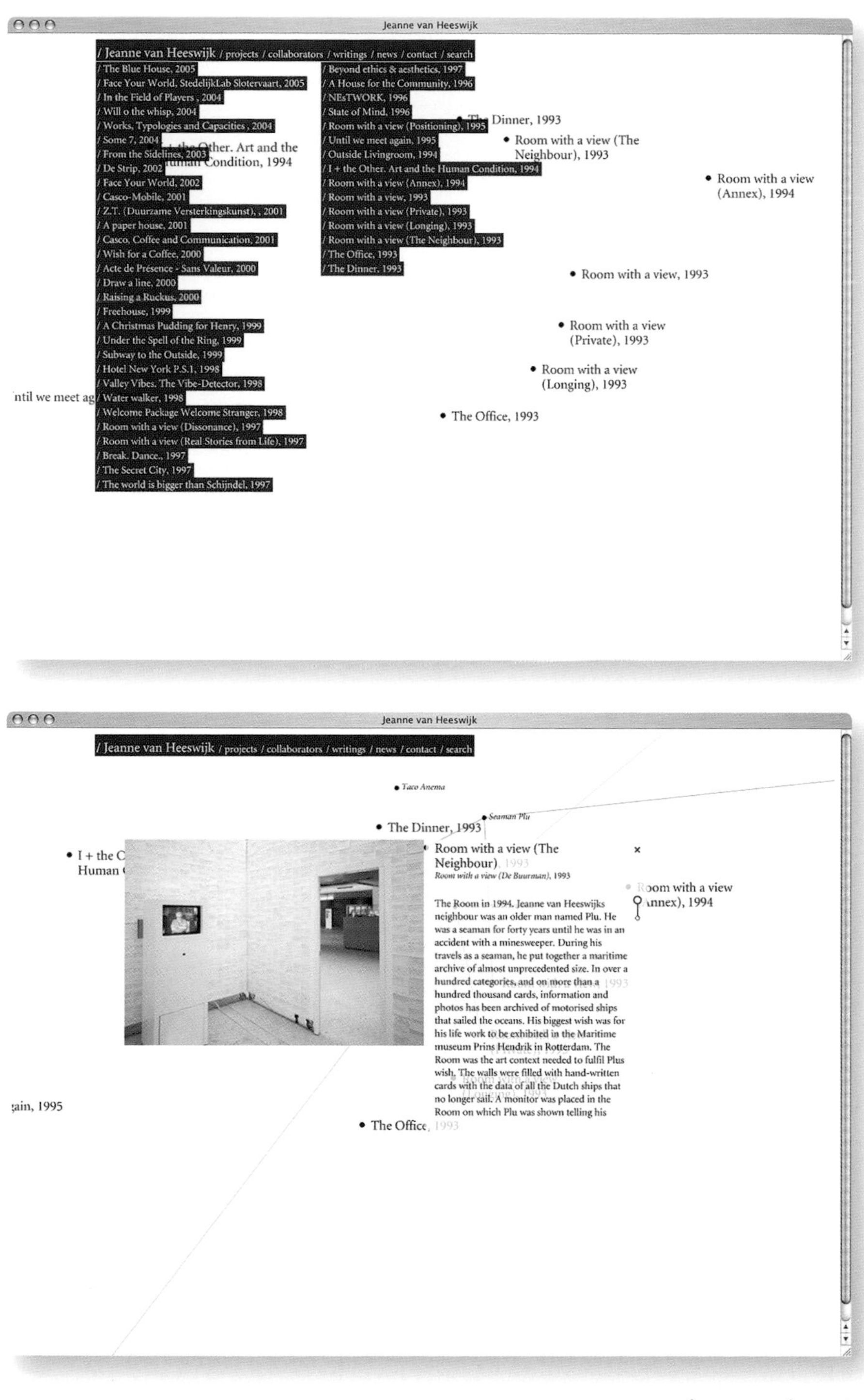

www.jeanneworks.net
D: maurits de bruijn
M: info@mauritsdebruijn.nl

010101.sfmoma.org

D: keiko hayashi, stephen jaycox **P:** stephen jaycox, perimetre-flux

A: perimetre-flux design **M:** webmaster@sfmoma.org

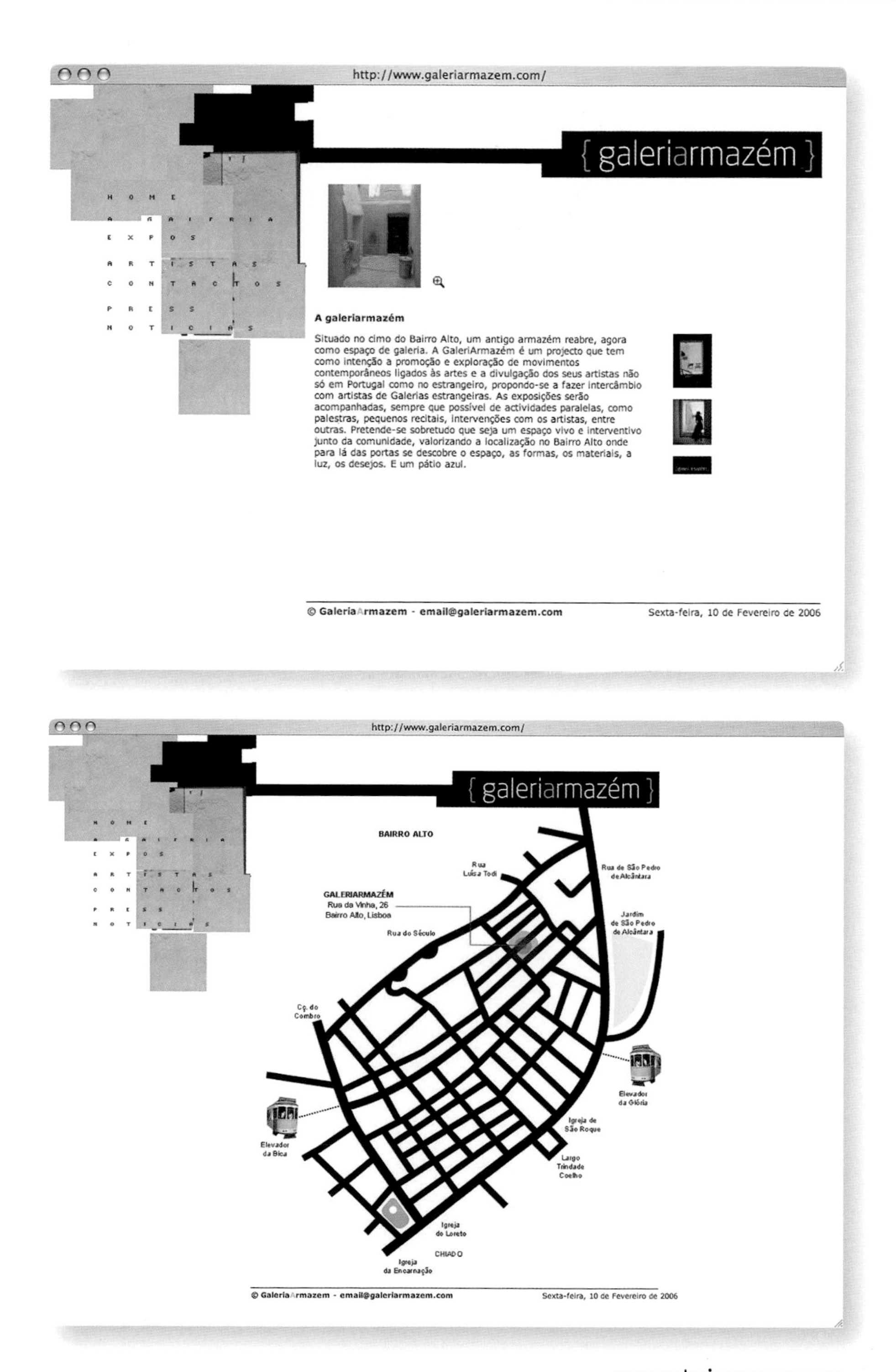

www.galeriarmazem.com

D: mário cameira **C:** hugo castanho

M: mariocameira@gmail.com

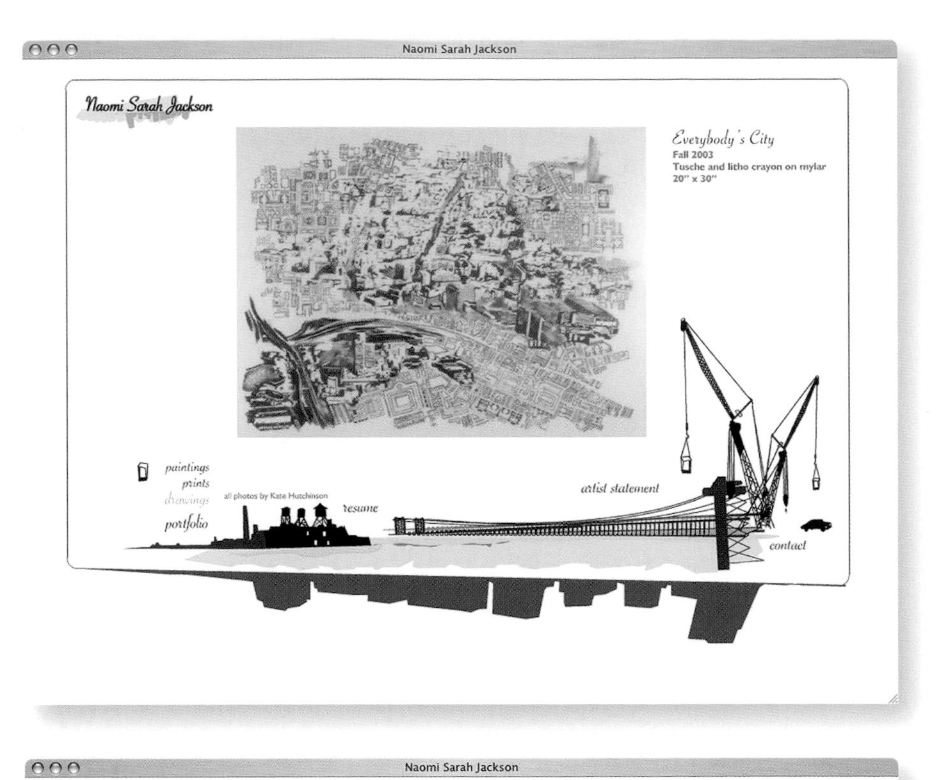

www.nsj.ca

D: chris tucker **C:** tyler hicks **P:** chris tucker

A: pretty girl designs **M:** tucker_chrisa@hotmail.com

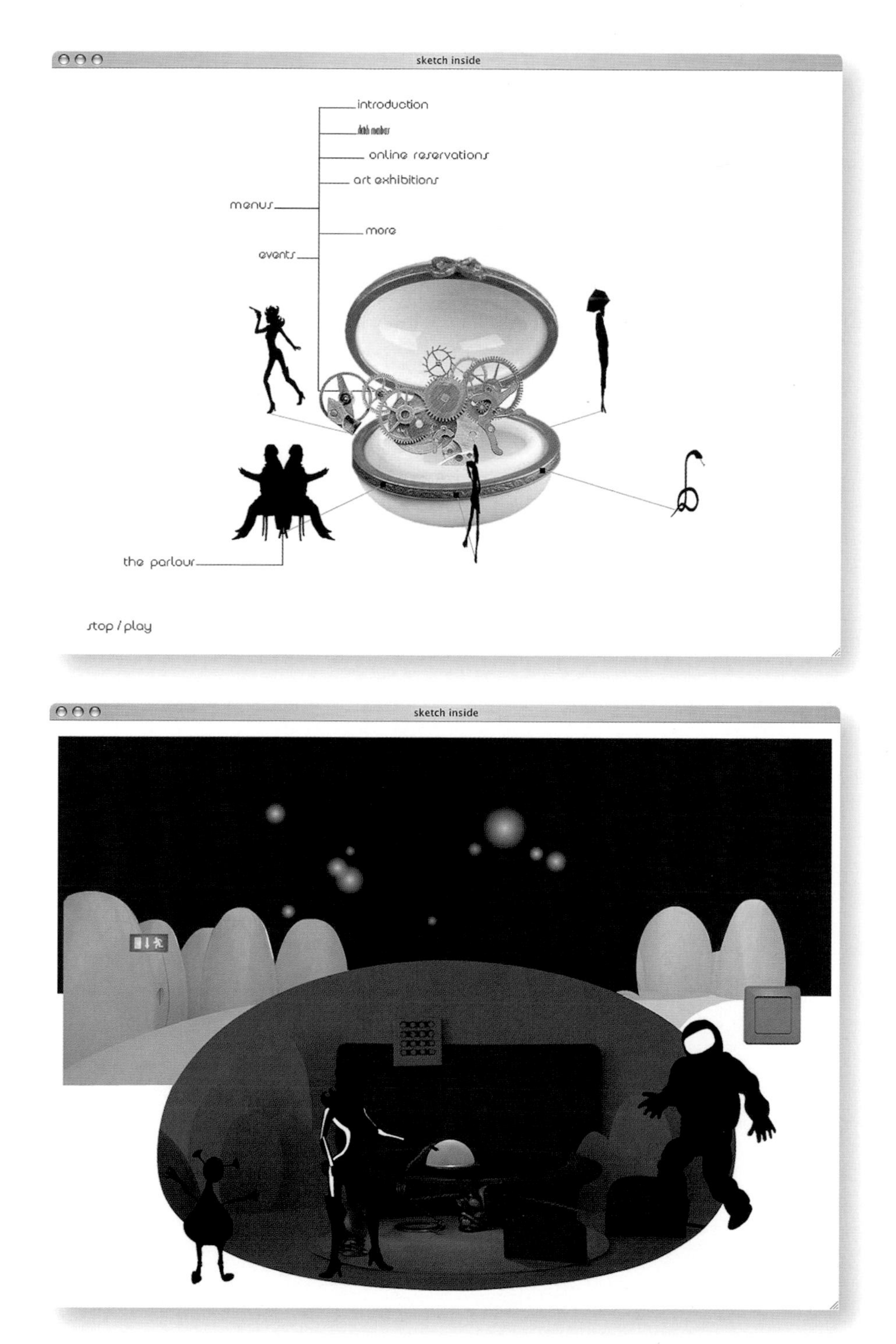

www.sketch.uk.com

D: katya bonnenfant
M: mail@katya-bonnenfant.com

Joël Guenoun

JOËL GUENOUN (NÉ À PARIS EN 1959) EST GRAPHISTE. IL A PUBLIÉ SIX LIVRES AUX ÉDITIONS AUTREMENT : **LES MOTS ONT DES VISAGES** , TOME 1 EN 1995 ET TOME 2 EN 1997 (UNE ÉDITION INTÉGRALE DES DEUX OUVRAGES EST PARUE EN 1998), **CLÉ** ET **ELLE** EN 1999 (ADAPTATIONS POUR ENFANTS DES "MOTS ONT DES VISAGES"), **OUI** EN 2000, **JOLI MONDE** EN 2005.

IL A ÉCRIT ET RÉALISÉ POUR CANAL + LES SÉRIES : **LE PROVERBE DU JOUR** (1994) ET **LES MOTS ONT DES VISAGES** (1997).

IL A RÉALISÉ DE NOMBREUSES **AFFICHES** (FESTIVALS SCÈNES NATIONALES, OPÉRA, THÉÂTRES...) ET QUELQUES LOGOS (**LE TOUR DE FRANCE**, OPÉRA COMIQUE...).

www.joelguenoun.com

D: arno roddier **C:** www.kodeagency.com **P:** joel guenoun

A: www.aruno.net **M:** contact@joelguenoun.com

www.justinfox.com.au

D: justin fox

M: justin@australianinfront.com.au

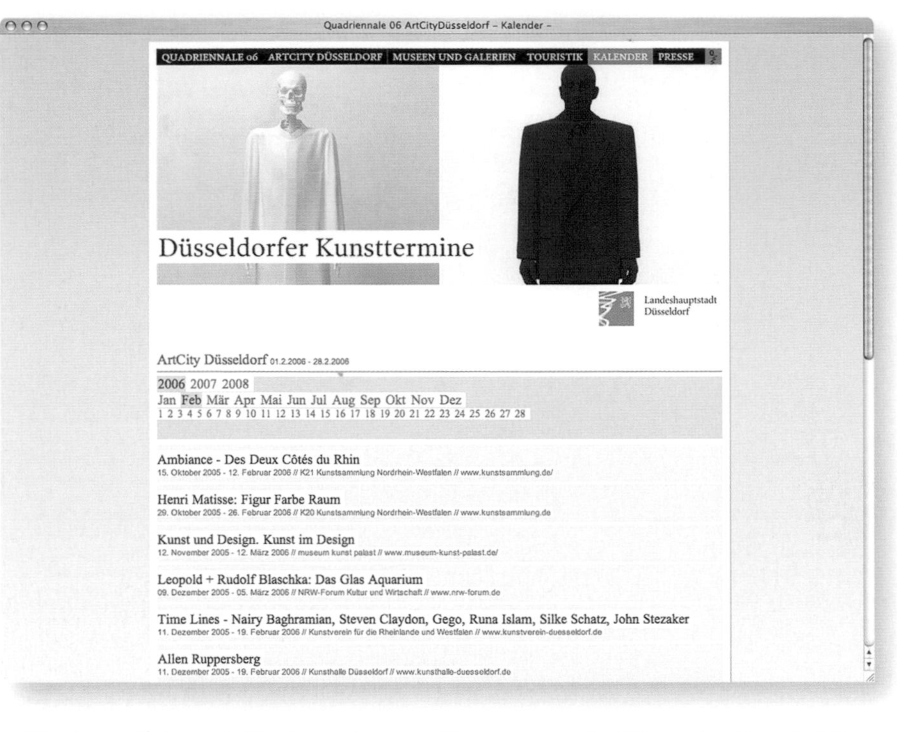

www.quadriennale.de

D: karsten blachke **C:** lars wöhning, marcel dickhage

A: v2a.net **M:** md@v2a.net

www.silviasimoes.com

D: nuno martins

A: nuno martins **M:** www.nunomartins.com

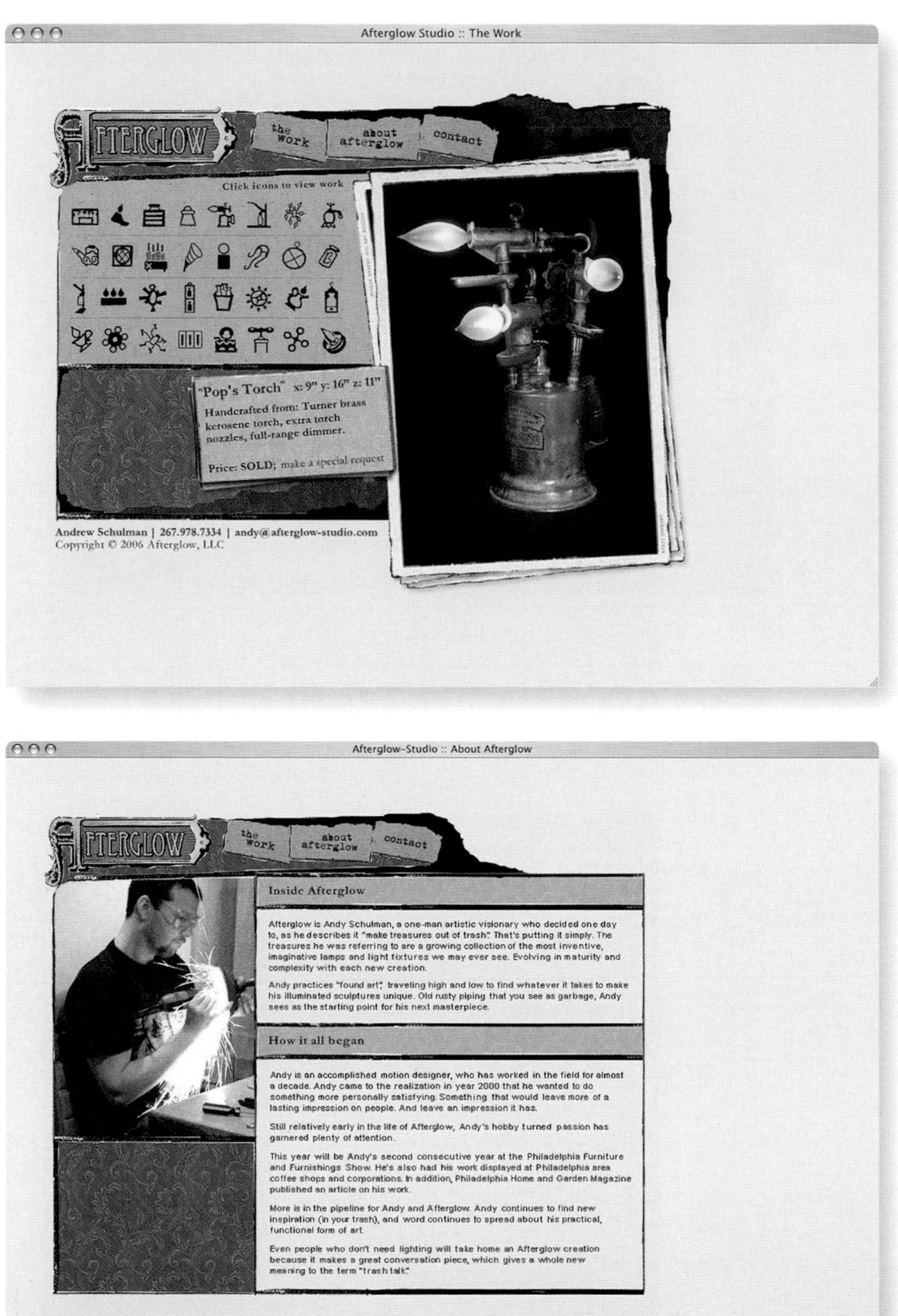

www.afterglow-studio.com

D: april donovan **C:** andrew schulman

A: april donovan **M:** www.grapeape.ws

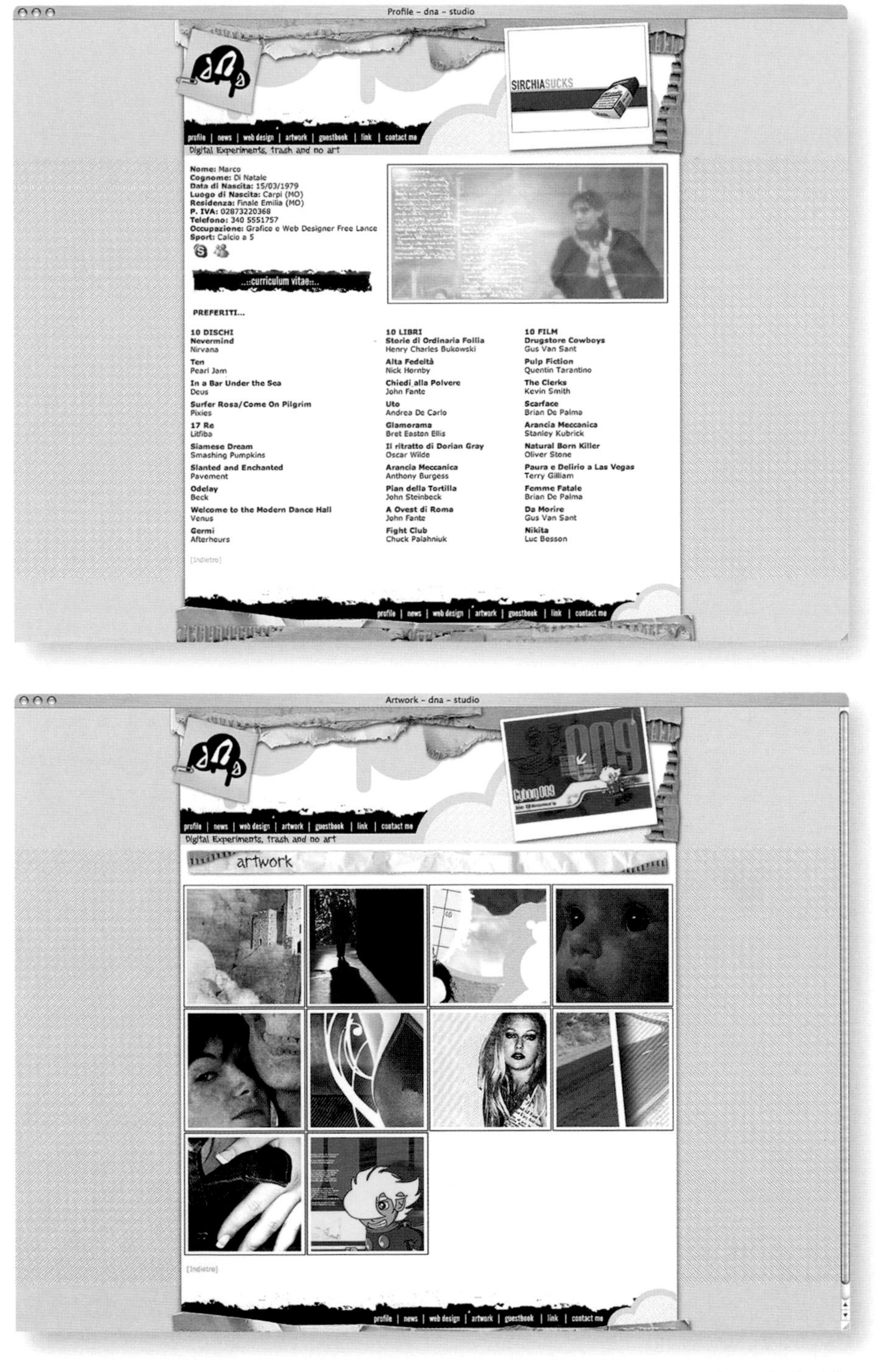

www.dna-studio.biz
D: marco di natale
M: marco@dna-studio.biz

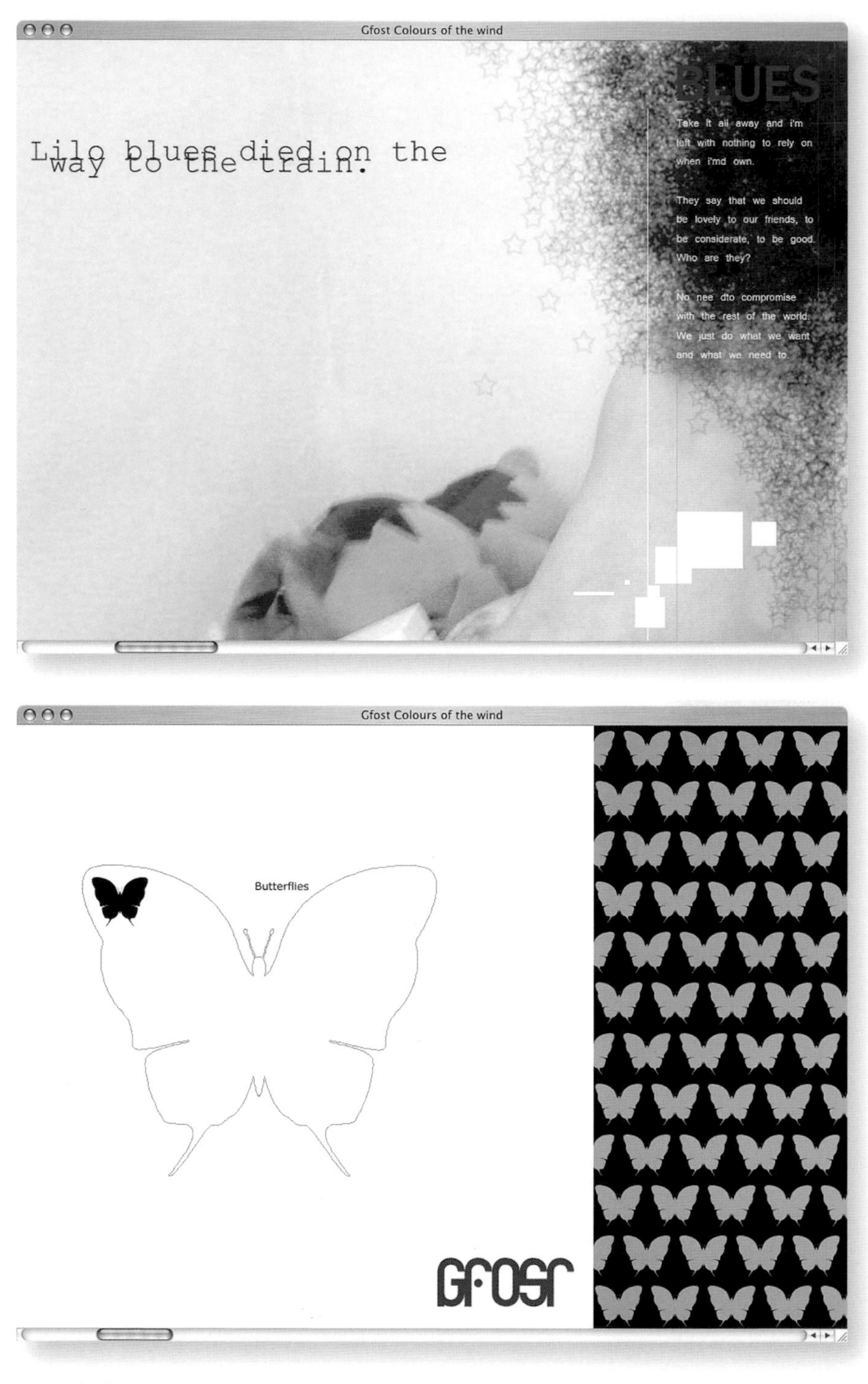

www.gfost.com

D: audi **C:** john7 **P:** captain crap

A: gfost **M:** johnmerques@hotmail.com

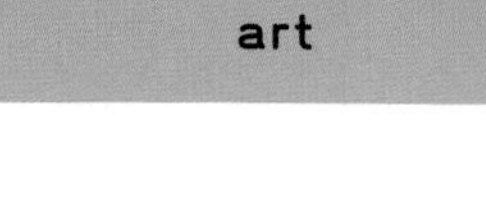

www.oculart.com
D: geoff lillemon
M: geoff@oculart.com

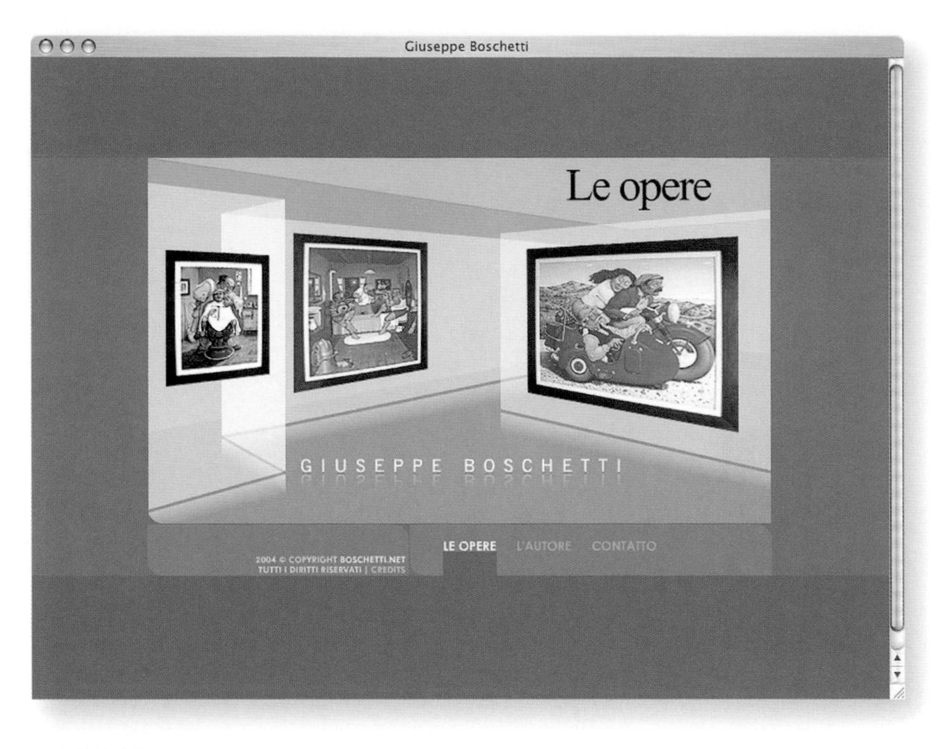

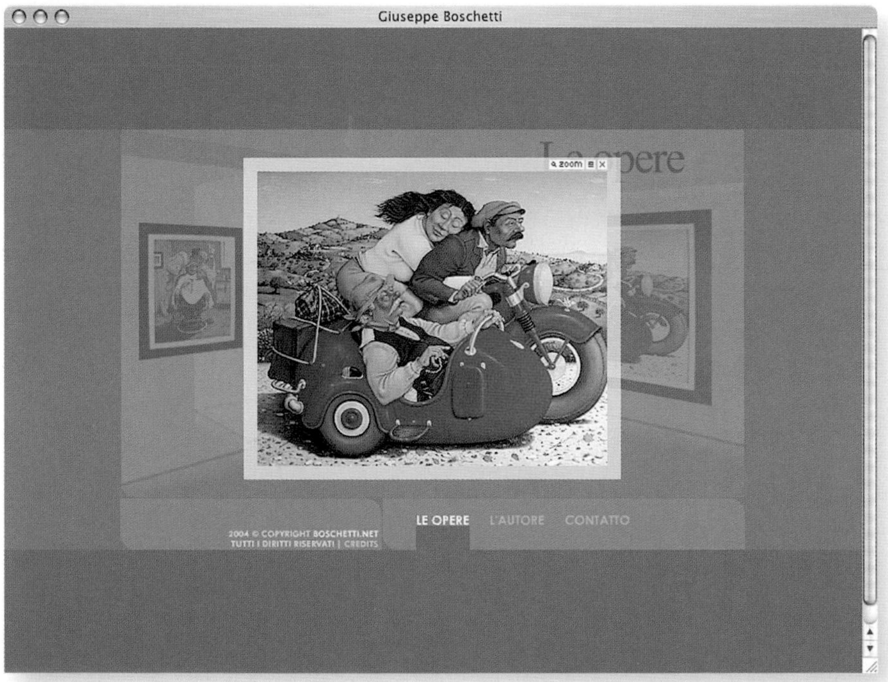

www.boschetti.net

D: marcello boschetti **C:** marcello boschetti **P:** giuseppe boschetti

A: bosqnet **M:** contact@boschetti.net

www.niciezalavilla.com

D: pablo reguera **C:** pablo reguera **P:** p_rc new media

A: p_rc new media **M:** www.pabloreguera.com

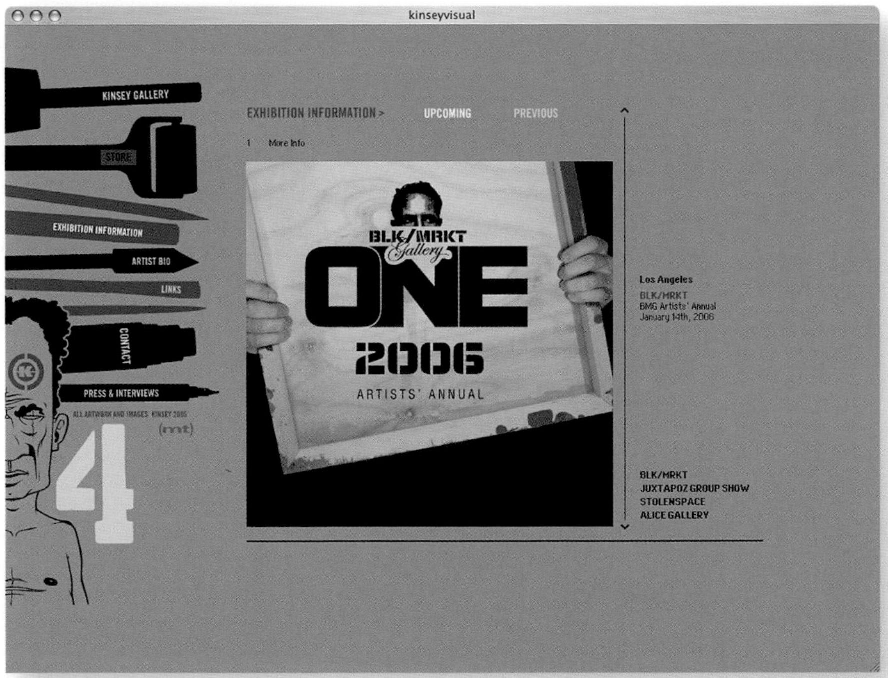

www.kinseyvisual.com

D: dave kinsey, jana desforges **C:** greg huntoon **P:** jana desforges

A: blk/mrkt **M:** contact@kinseyvisual.com

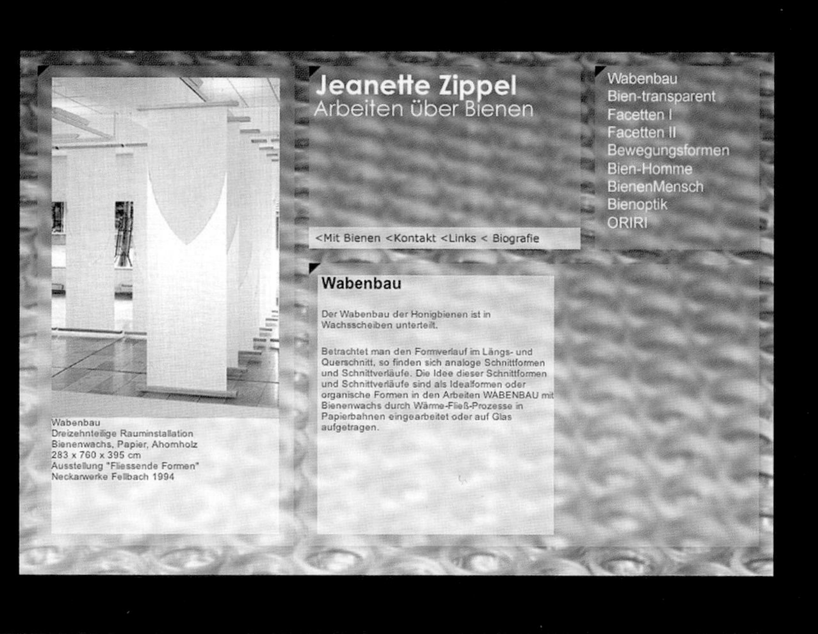

www.jeanettezippel.de

D: tobias wortmann
M: tob99@gmx.de

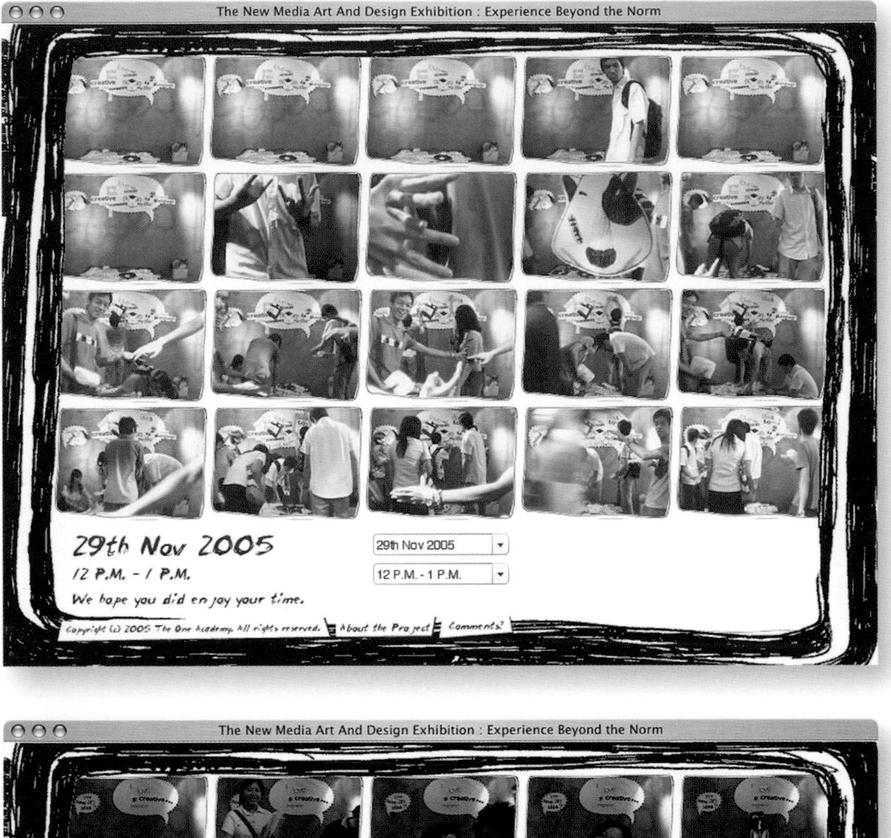

www.toa.edu.my/unplug

D: chui tuck loong **C:** ng man meng **P:** chienni chang

A: the one interactive **M:** info@theoneinteractive.com

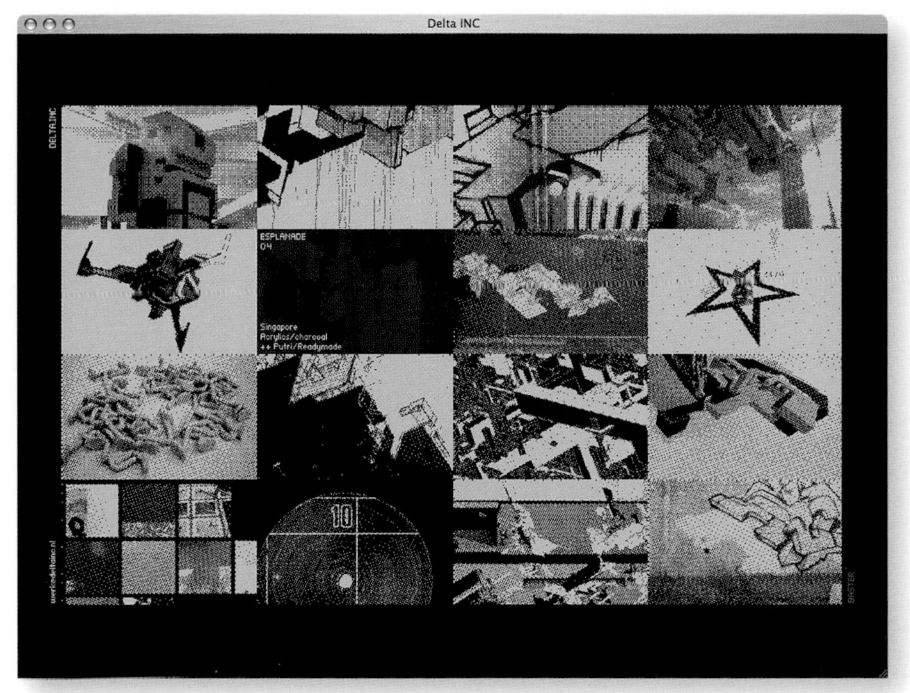

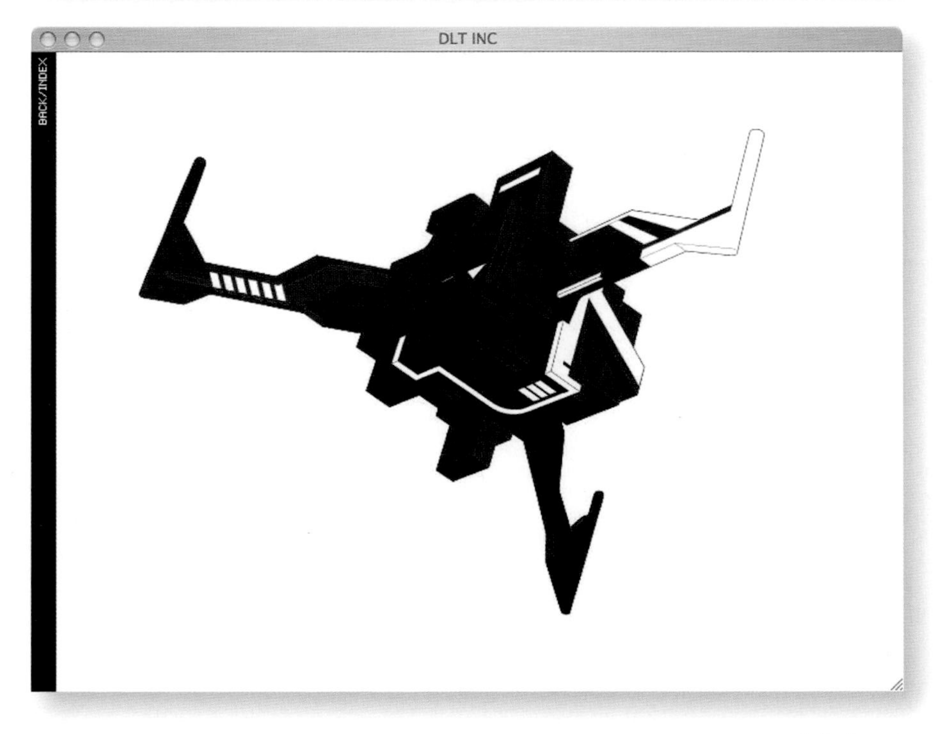

www.deltainc.nl

D: boris tellegen, bas koopmans

M: x@deltainc.nl

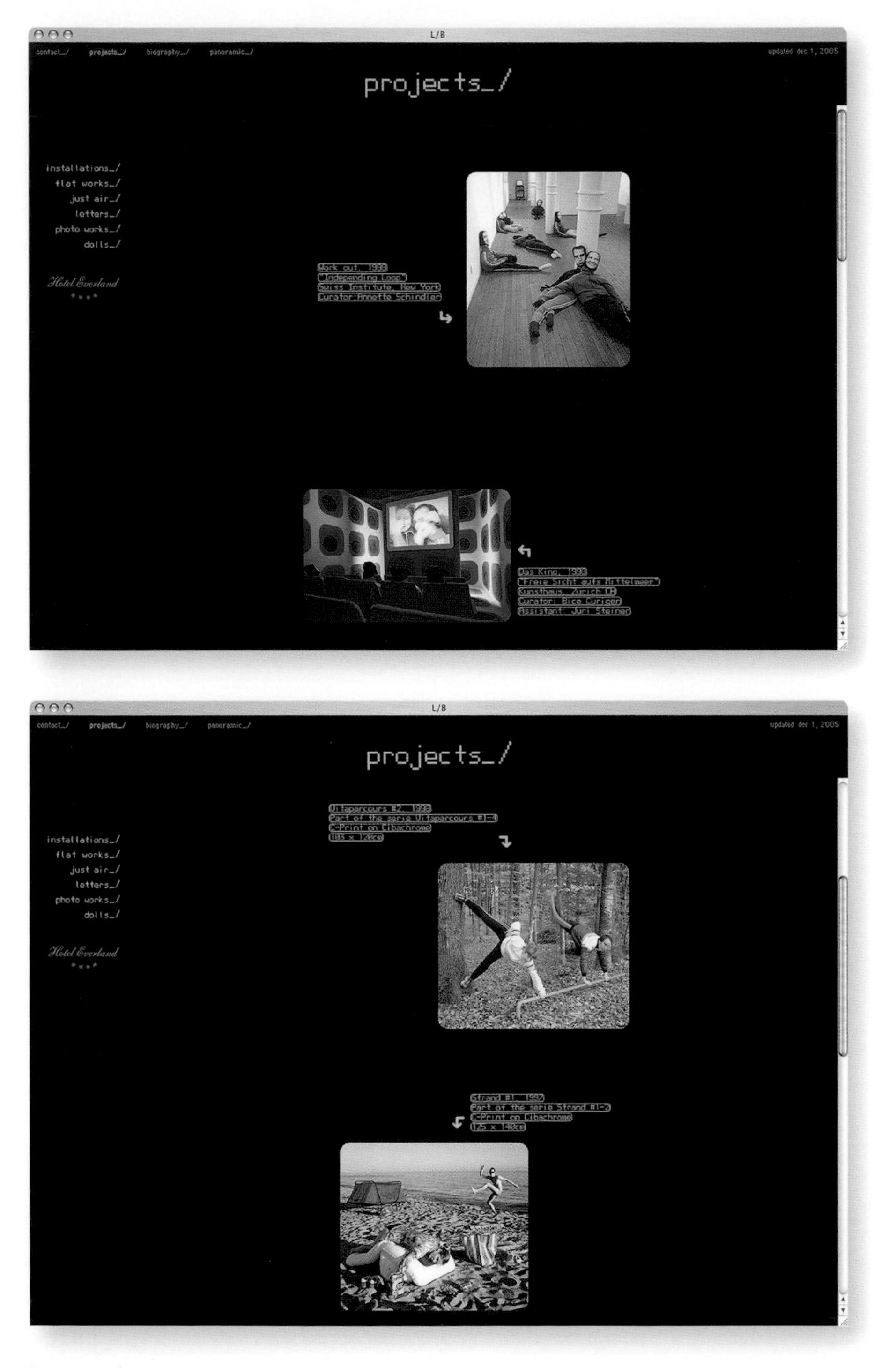

www.langbaumann.com

D: lang/baumann

M: lb@langbaumann.com

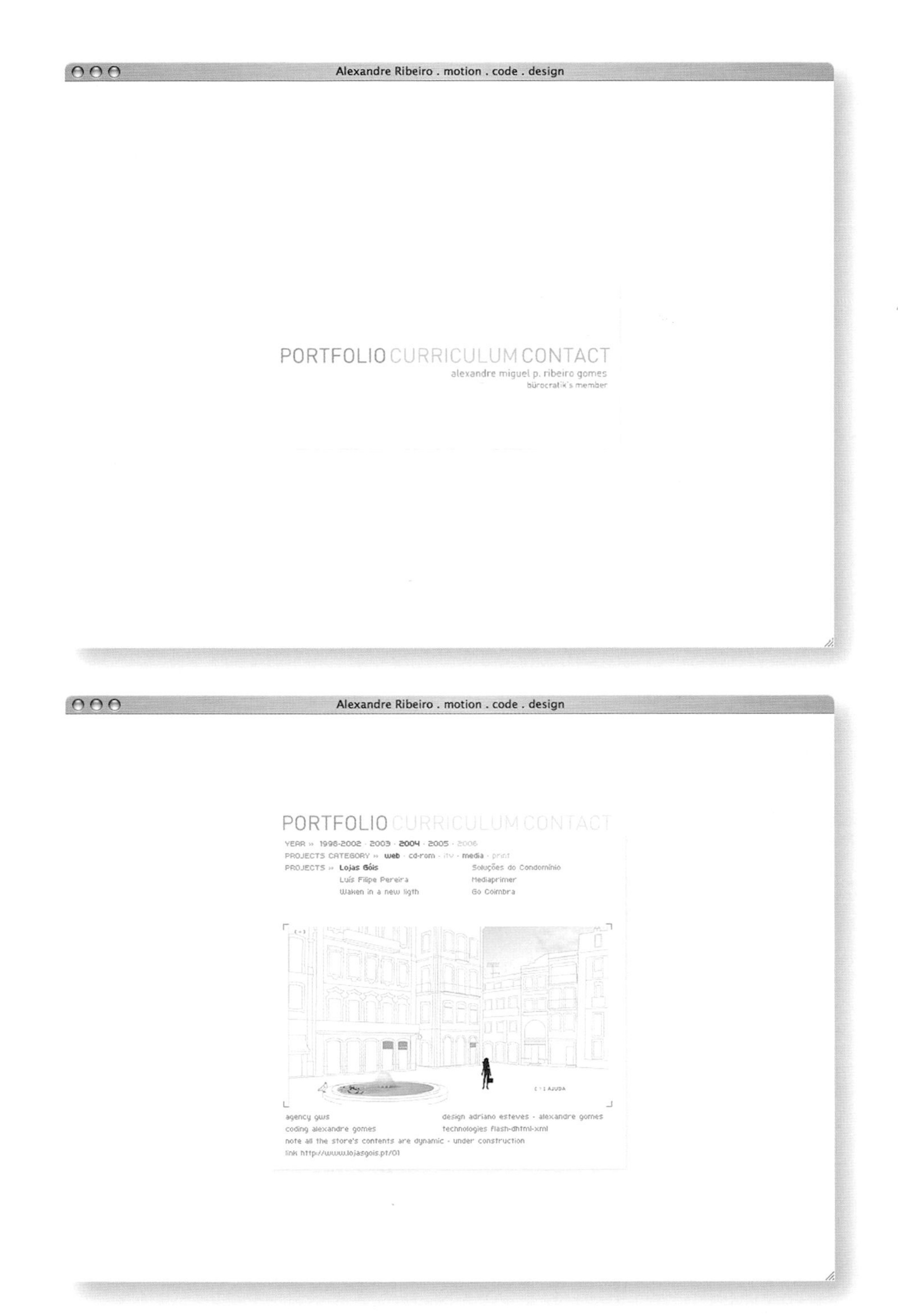

alex.gws.pt

D: alexandre ribeiro gomes

A: bürocratik **M:** alex@burocratik.com

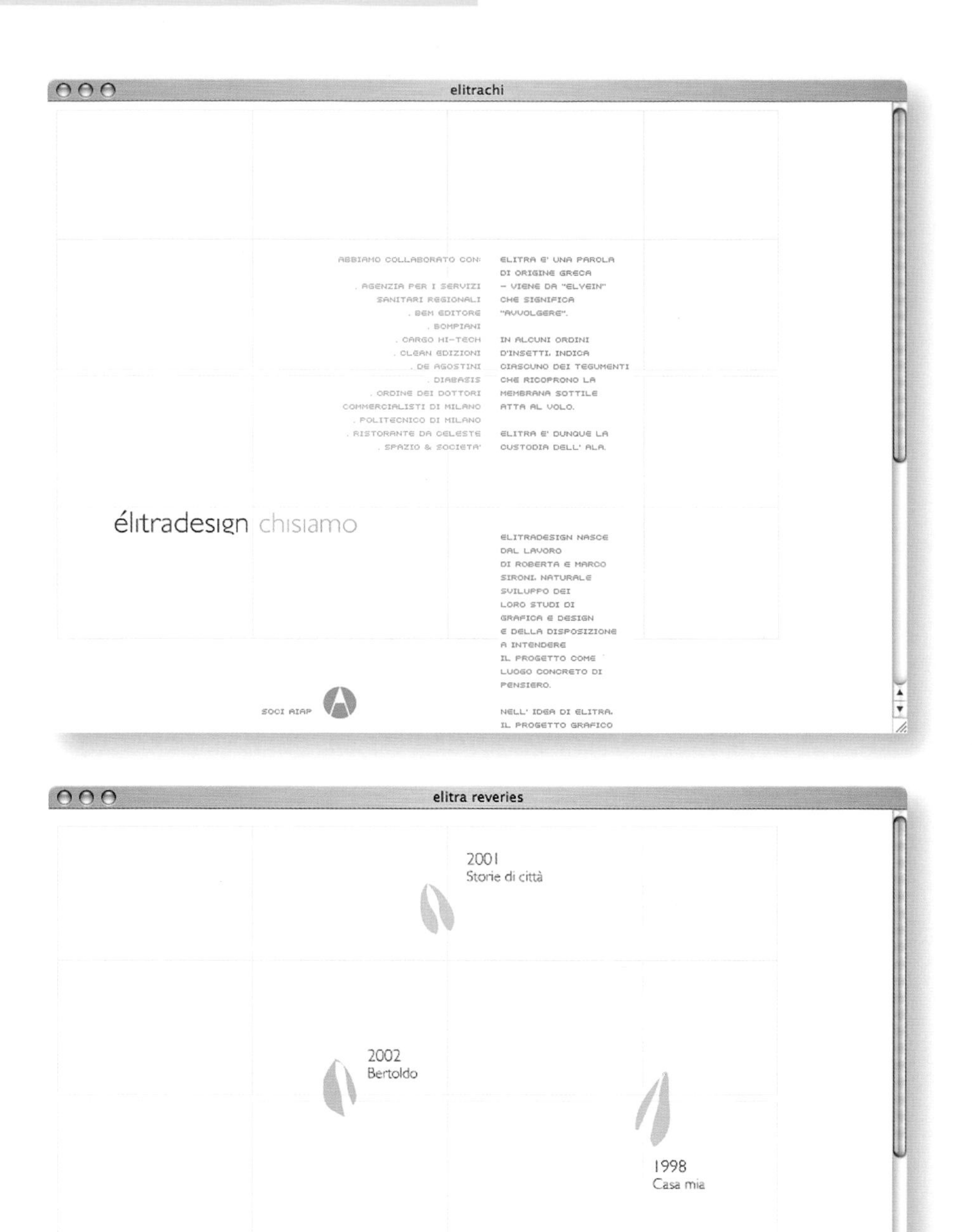

www.elitradesign.it

D: marco sironi, roberta sironi

A: elitradesign **M:** elitra@elitradesign.it

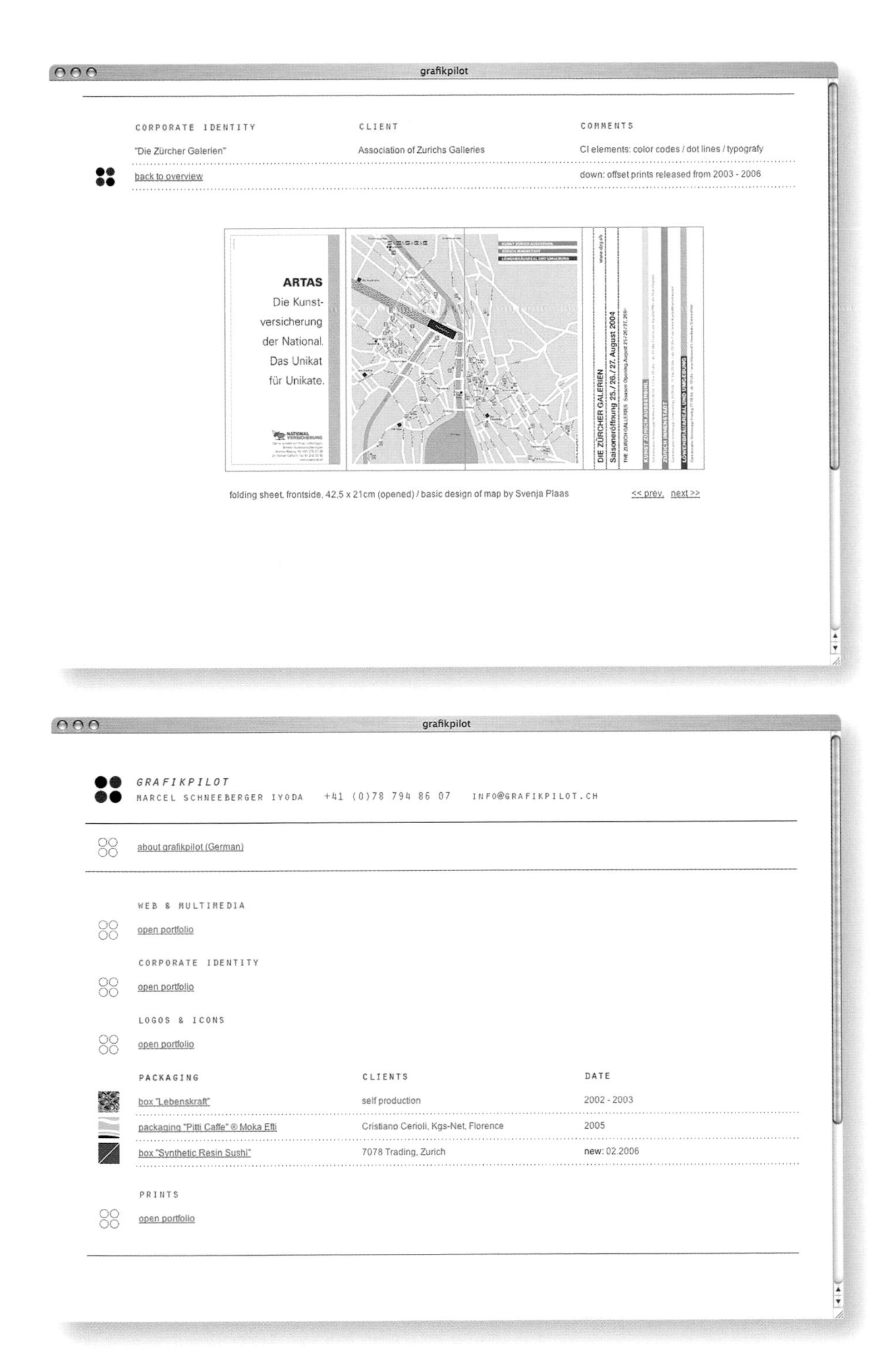

www.grafikpilot.ch
D: marcel schneeberger
A: grafikpilot **M:** kerosin@grafikpilot.ch

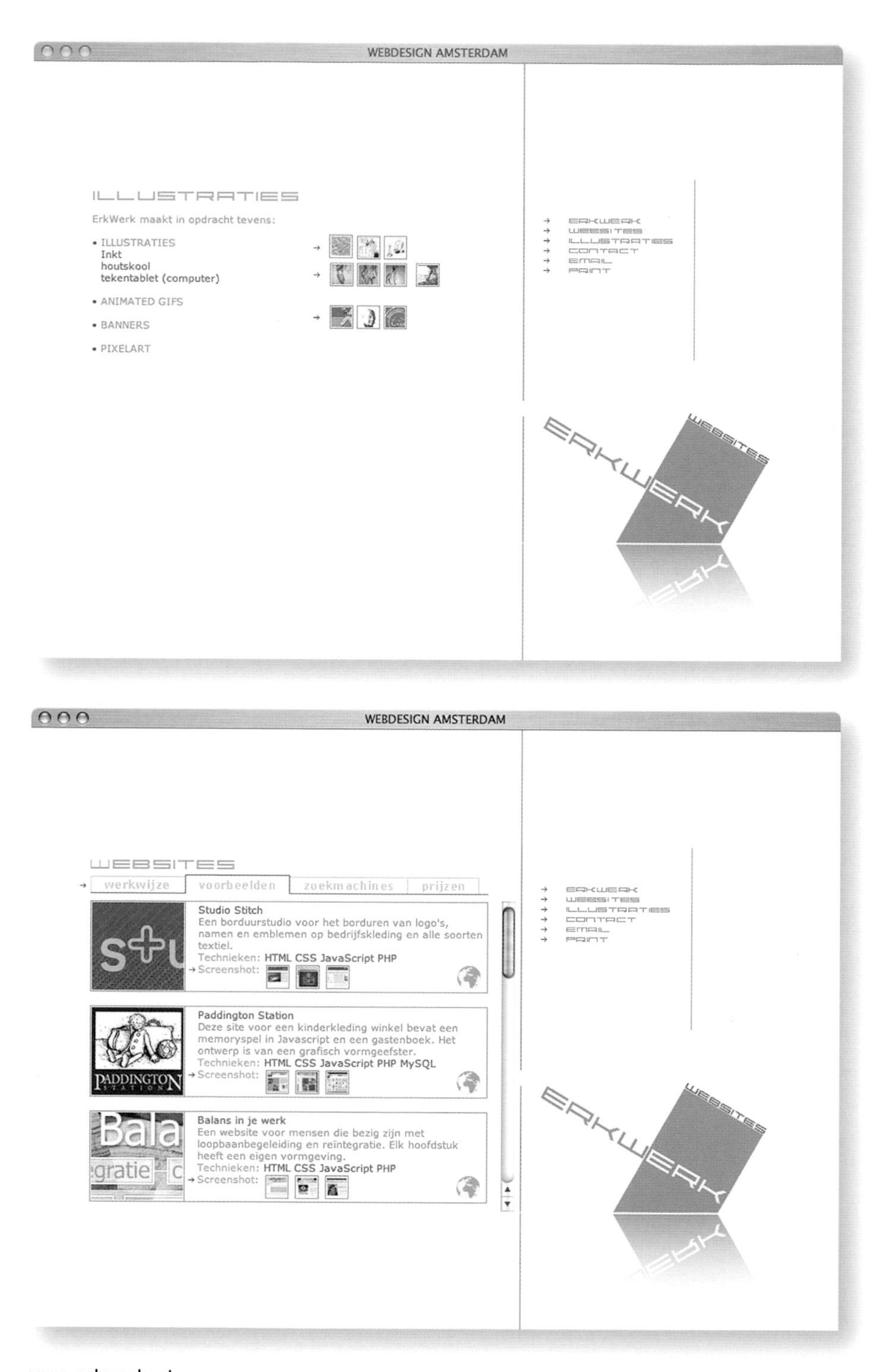

www.erkwerk.nl

D: erik visscher

A: erkwerk **M:** info@erkwerk.nl

::::: bulent bas :::::::

<!DOCTYPE html PUBLIC "-//W3C//DTD HTML 4.01 Transitional//EN">
<html>

<head>
<meta http-equiv="content-type" content="text/html;charset=ISO-8859-1">
<meta name="generator" content="bulent bas">
<title>::::::.. RESUME ...:::::::</title>

EDUCATION
1999 - 2001
CITY UNIVERSITY OF NEW YORK
MFA Media Arts Productions.

1992-1996
MARMARA UNIVERSITY
Bachelor's Degree in Fine Arts.

Fluent in Turkish and English. U.S. resident.
Portfolio and references available upon request.

<~~works~~ / ~~resume~~ / ~~contact /~~ main page >

</head>
</body>
</html>

::::: bulent bas :::::::

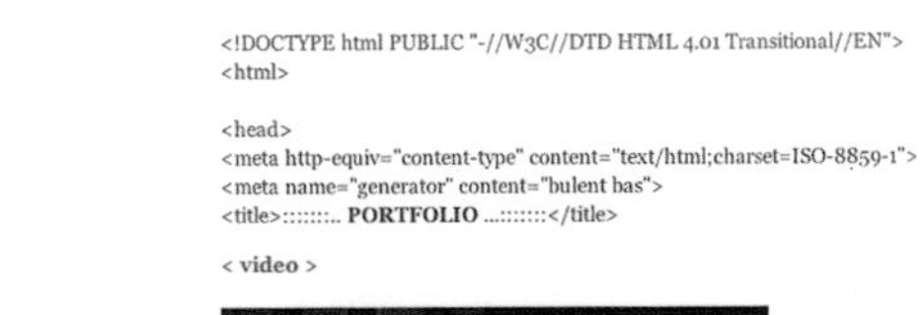
<!DOCTYPE html PUBLIC "-//W3C//DTD HTML 4.01 Transitional//EN">
<html>

<head>
<meta http-equiv="content-type" content="text/html;charset=ISO-8859-1">
<meta name="generator" content="bulent bas">
<title>::::::.. **PORTFOLIO** ...:::::::</title>

< video >

ZEKI DEMIRKUBUZ
Concept / Editorial / Animation
1 / 2 / 3 / 4 / 5 / ~~6~~ / ~~7~~ / 8 / 9

< print >

< web >

< ~~flash~~ >

<~~works~~ / ~~resume~~ / ~~contact /~~ main page >

</head>
</body>
</html>

www.bulentbas.com
D: bulent bas
A: bulent bas M: bulent@bulentbas.com

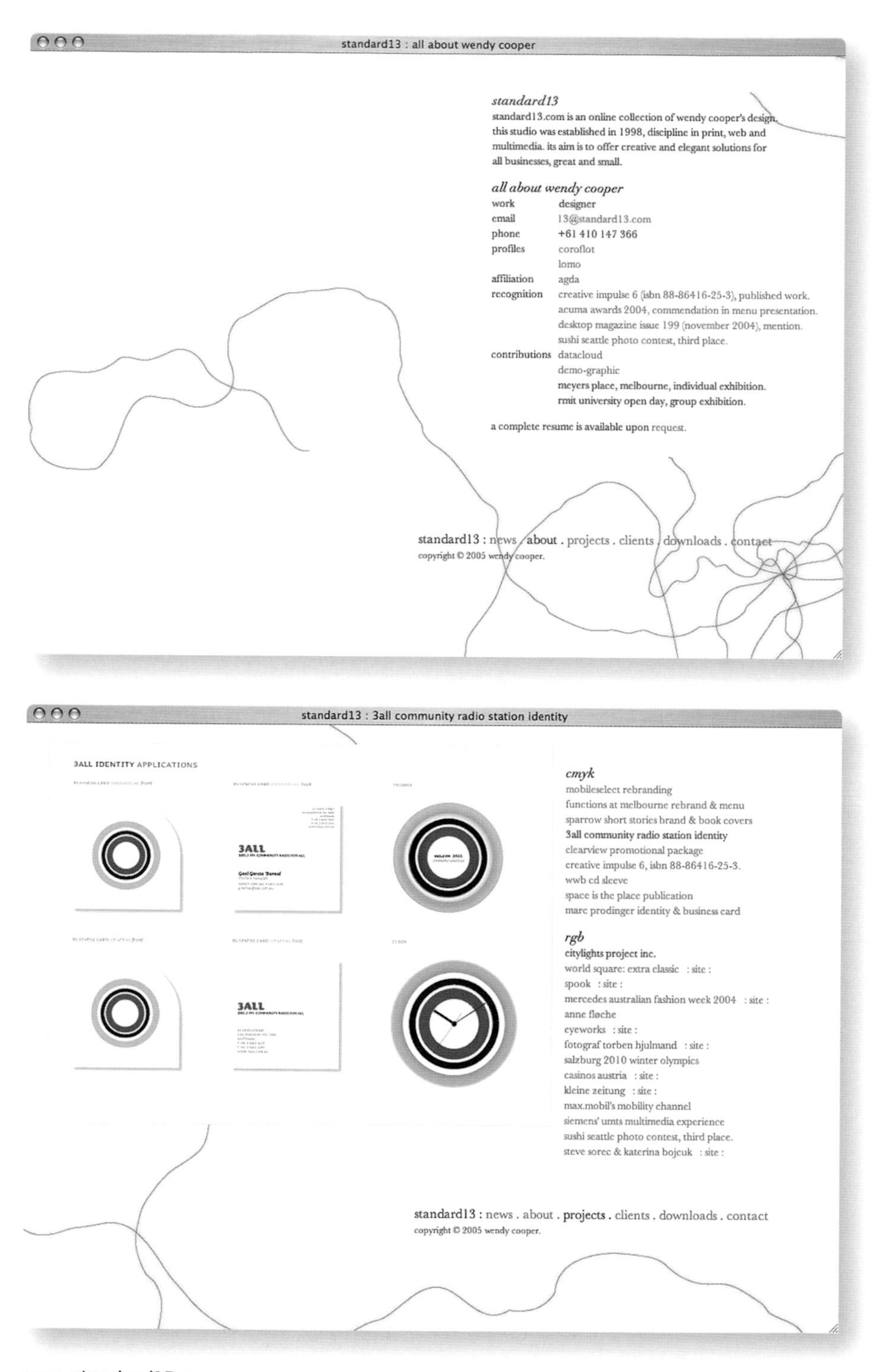

www.standard13.com

D: wendy cooper

A: standard13.com **M:** 13@standard13.com

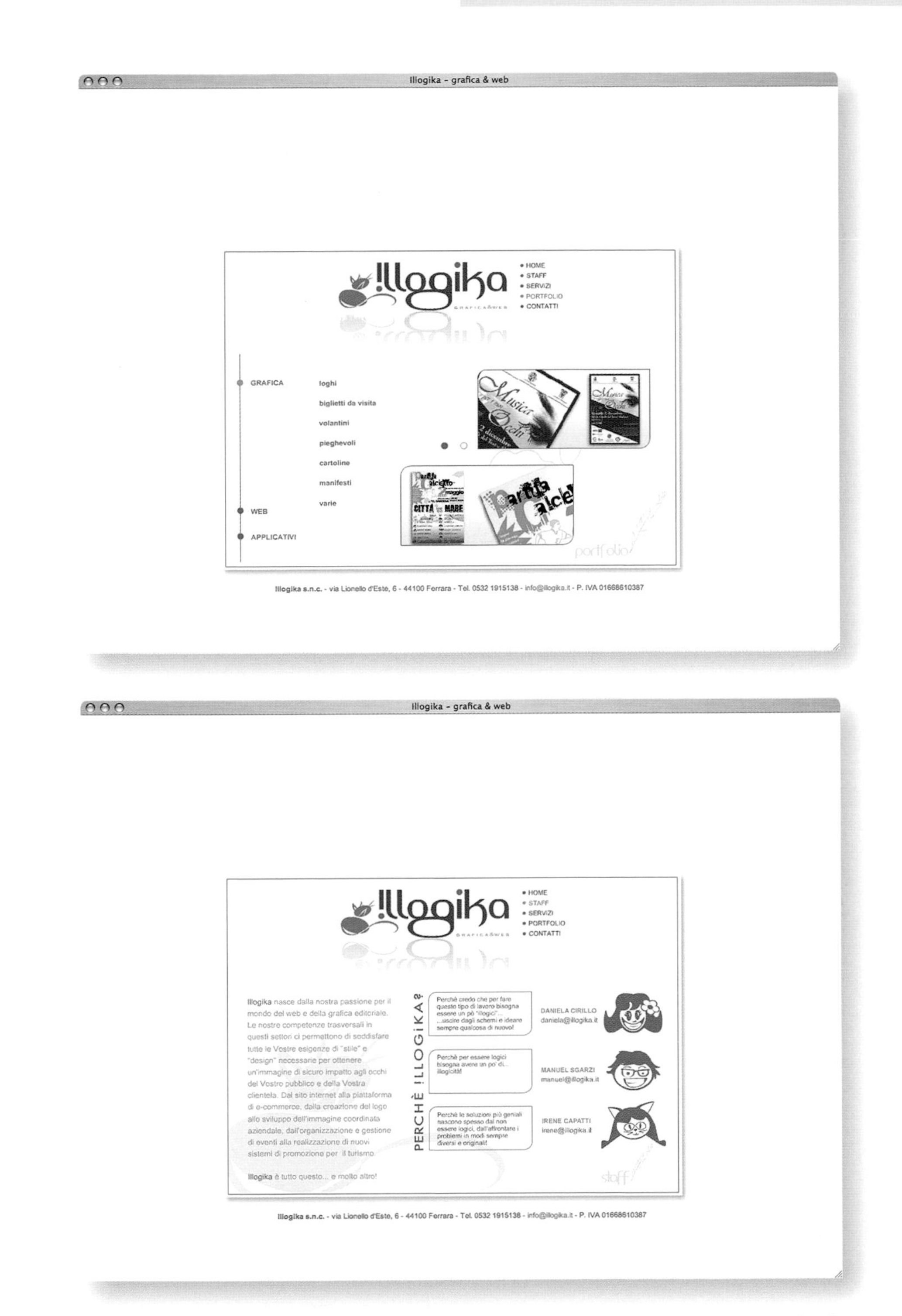

www.illogika.it

D: daniela cirillo, irene capatti, manuel sgarzi **P:** illogika s.n.c.

A: illogika s.n.c. **M:** info@illogika.it

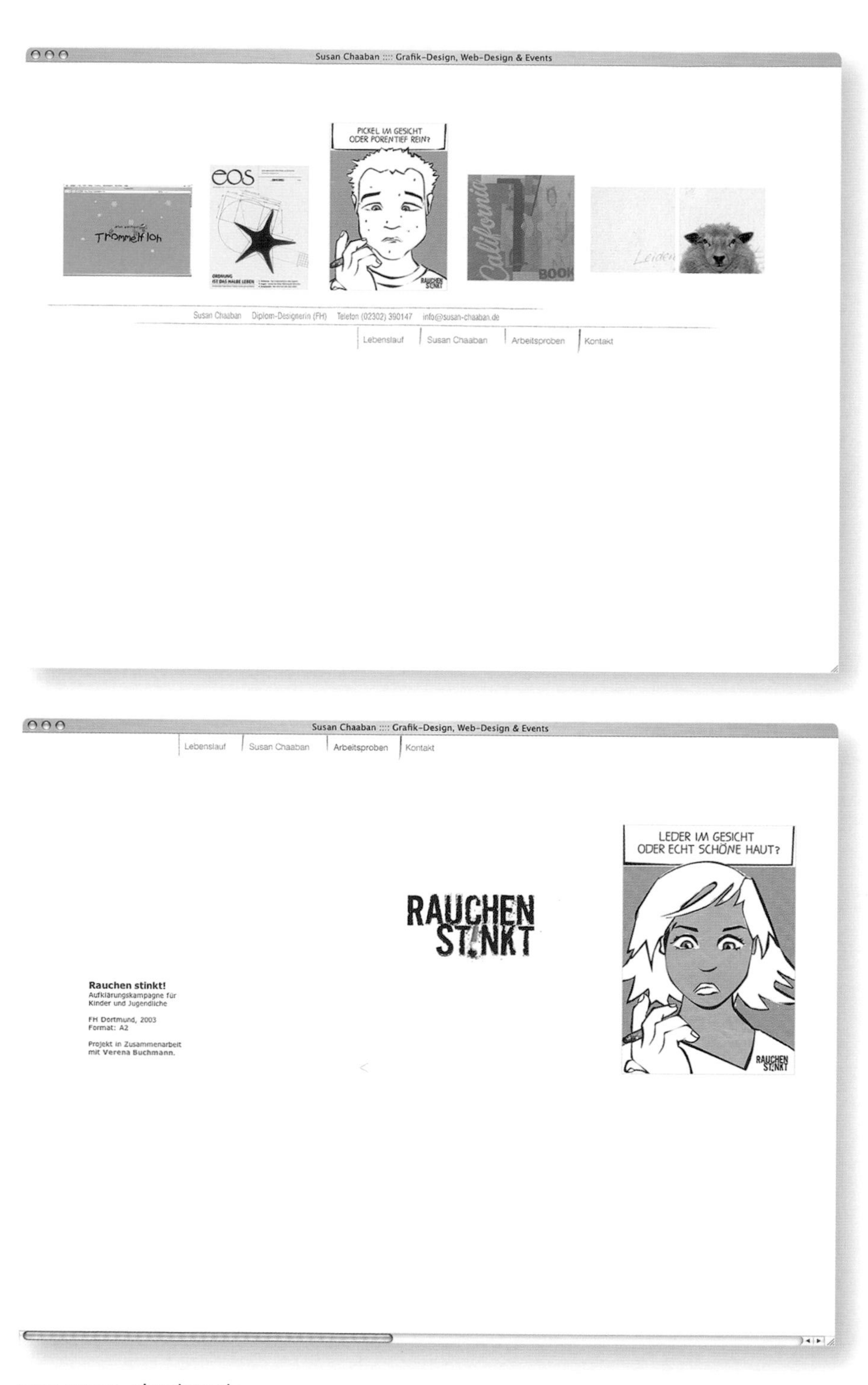

www.susan-chaaban.de

D: susan chaaban

A: susan chaaban **M:** info@susan-chaaban.de

www.marklucasdesign.co.uk

D: mark lucas

A: mark lucas design **M:** mail@marklucasdesign.co.uk

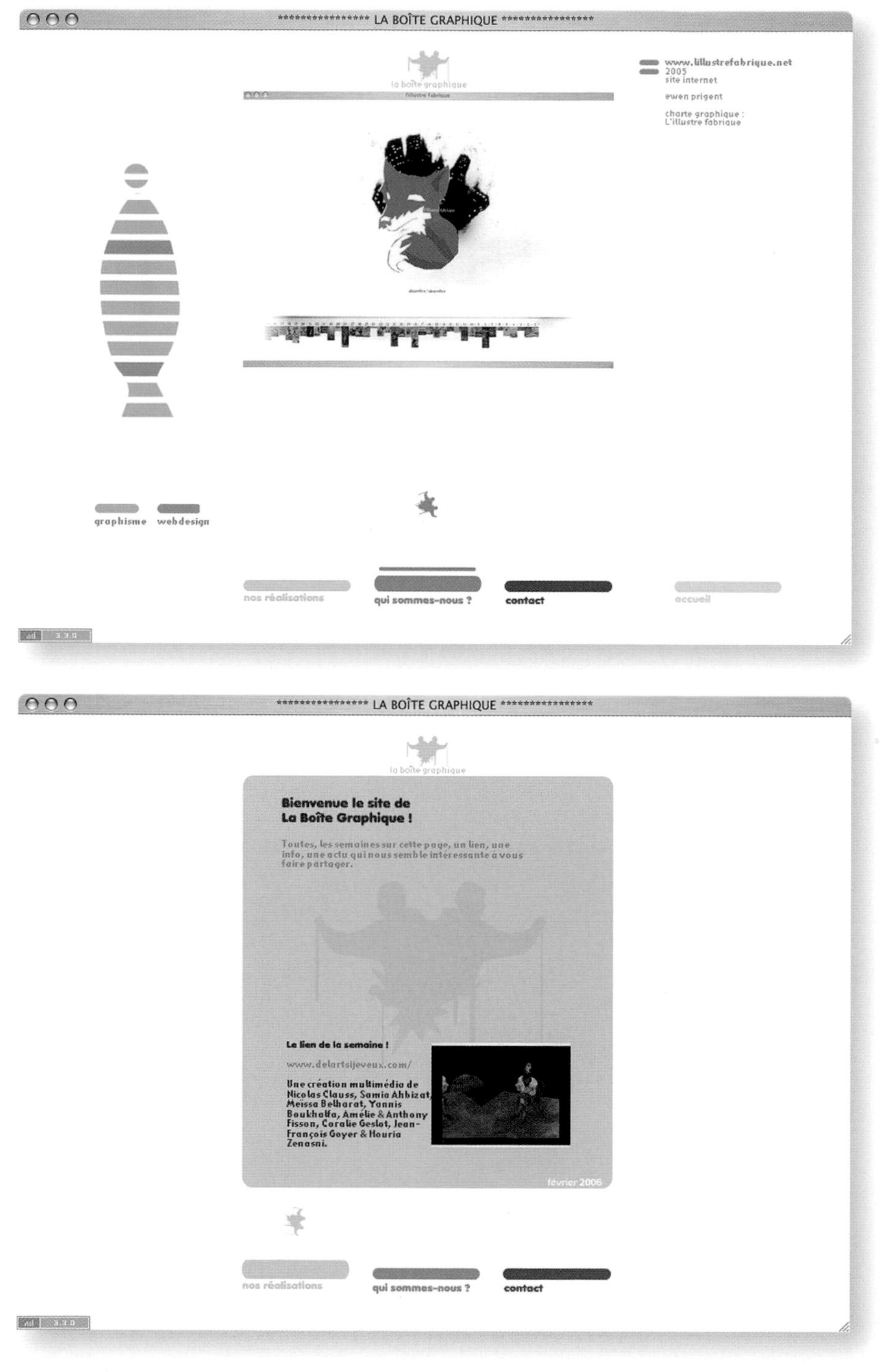

www.laboitegraphique.new.fr

D: prigent ewen

A: la boite graphique **M:** laboitegraphique@free.fr

blkmrkt.com

D: ana desforges, dave kinsey **C:** greg huntoon **P:** jana desforges

A: blk/mrkt **M:** contact@blkmrkt.com

RAUL HERNANDEZ -[PORTFOLIO MULTIMEDIA]

[i] PONG DISEÑADO POR RAÚL HERNÁNDEZ

PORTFOLIO MULTIMEDIA RAUL HERNANDEZ

ÉSTA ES UNA SELECCIÓN DE MIS TRABAJOS MÁS RECIENTES EN EL ÁMBITO BIDIMENSIONAL Y TRIDIMENSIONAL.MI ESTILO SE CENTRA EN UNA PERCEPCIÓN CLARA Y CONCISA DE FORMAS Y COLORES QUE OTORGAN UN VALOR Y UN SIGNIFICADO MUY ASIMILABLE.MIS CONOCIMIENTOS ABARCAN LENGUAJES DE PROGRAMACIÓN TALES COMO LINGO, ACTIONSCRIPT, HTML, JAVASCRIPT Y PROGRAMAS COMO CORELDRAW, PHOTOSHOP, MM FLASH, MM DIRECTOR, FINALCUTPRO, MM DREAMWEAVER , DVD STUDIO PRO Y MAYA 3D .

X

PONG • Juego interactivo • SOFTWARE UTILIZADO→ CorelDraw 12, MM Flash MX, MM dreamweaver MX • HISTORIA→ Remake del juego arcade de los 70, básicamente es un ejercicio de programación y aplicación de inteligencia al propio interactivo para una mayor jugabilidad [usuario-ordenador]. [2005]

RAUL HERNANDEZ -[PORTFOLIO MULTIMEDIA]

WWW.MERCADONEGRO.ORG • WebSite diseñado para la asociación Galeria • SOFTWARE UTILIZADO → MM Dreamweaver MX, MM Flash MX, CorelDraw12, Photoshop CS • HISTORIA→ Site informativo y promocional de eventos culturales trimenstrales dirigido a creativos, diseñadores y artistas en general para promoción y venta de sus obras.[2005]

www.raulhernandez.es

D: raul hernandez gracia

A: raul hernandez **M:** info@raulhernandez.es

www.19m2.ch/dominik

D: dominik buser
A: 19m2 atelierkollektiv M: dominik@19m2.ch

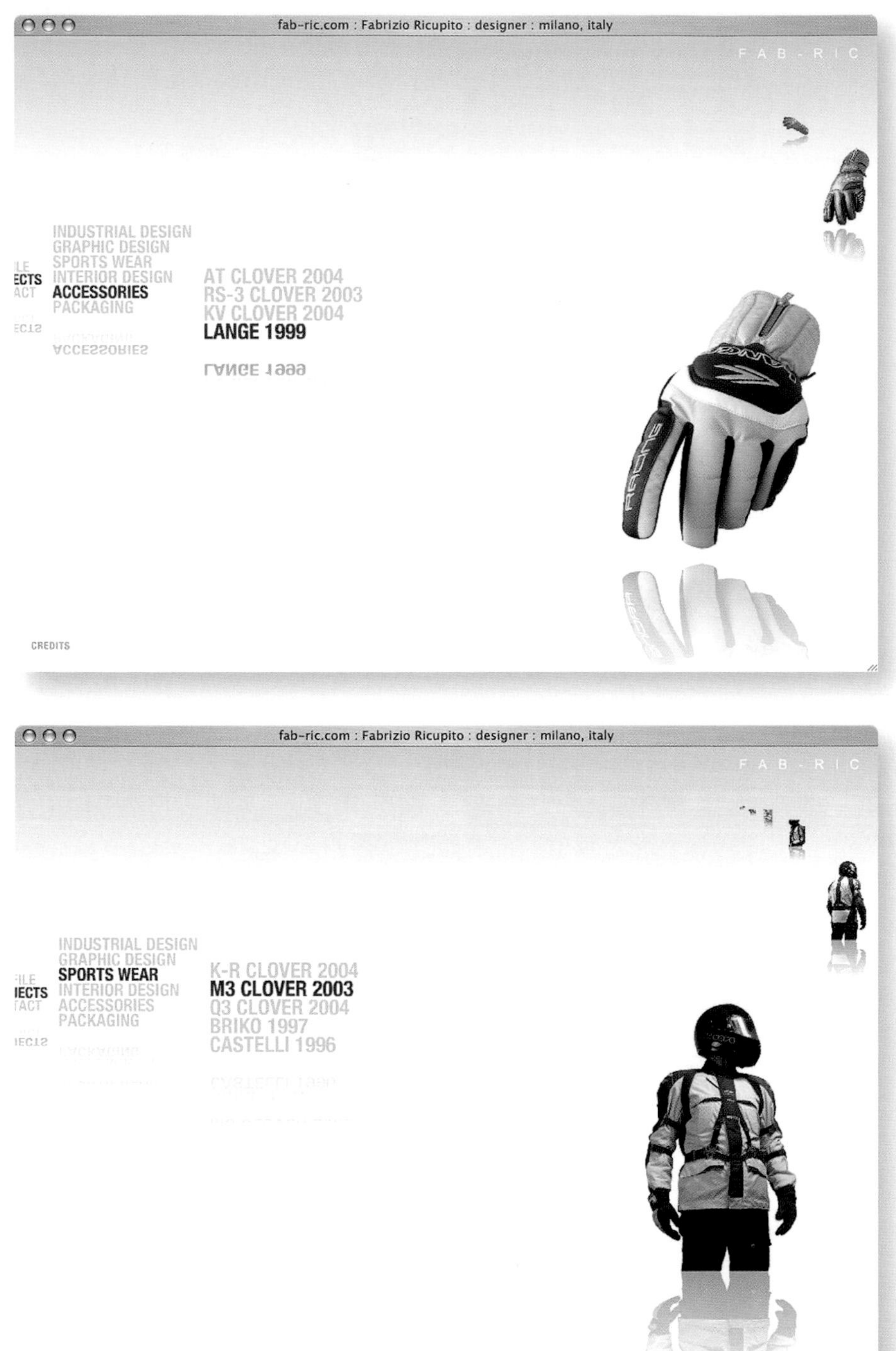

www.ricupitodesign.it

D: andrea luxich **C:** francesco m. munafò

A: pangoo design **M:** www.pangoo.it

www.piperboy.com

D: edvin lee

A: common brand M: hello@piperboy.com

www.kristinamatovic.com

D: kristina matovic

M: kris@kristinamatovic.com

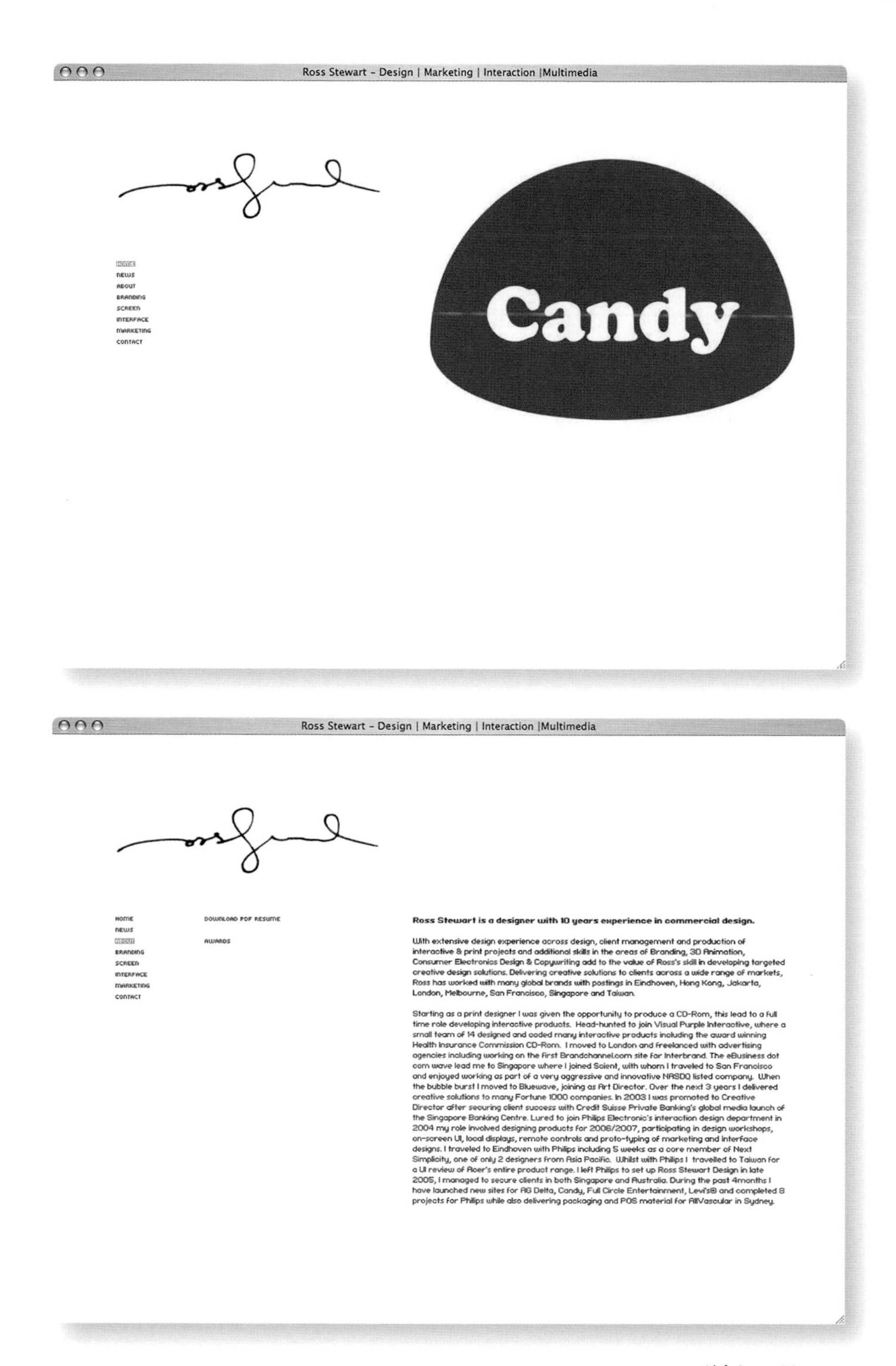

www.thirteen28.com
D: ross stewart
A: ross stewart design M: marketing@thirteen28.com

www.artiva.it

D: daniele de batté, davide sossi **C:** daniele de batté, davide sossi **P:** artiva

A: artiva design **M:** info@artiva.it

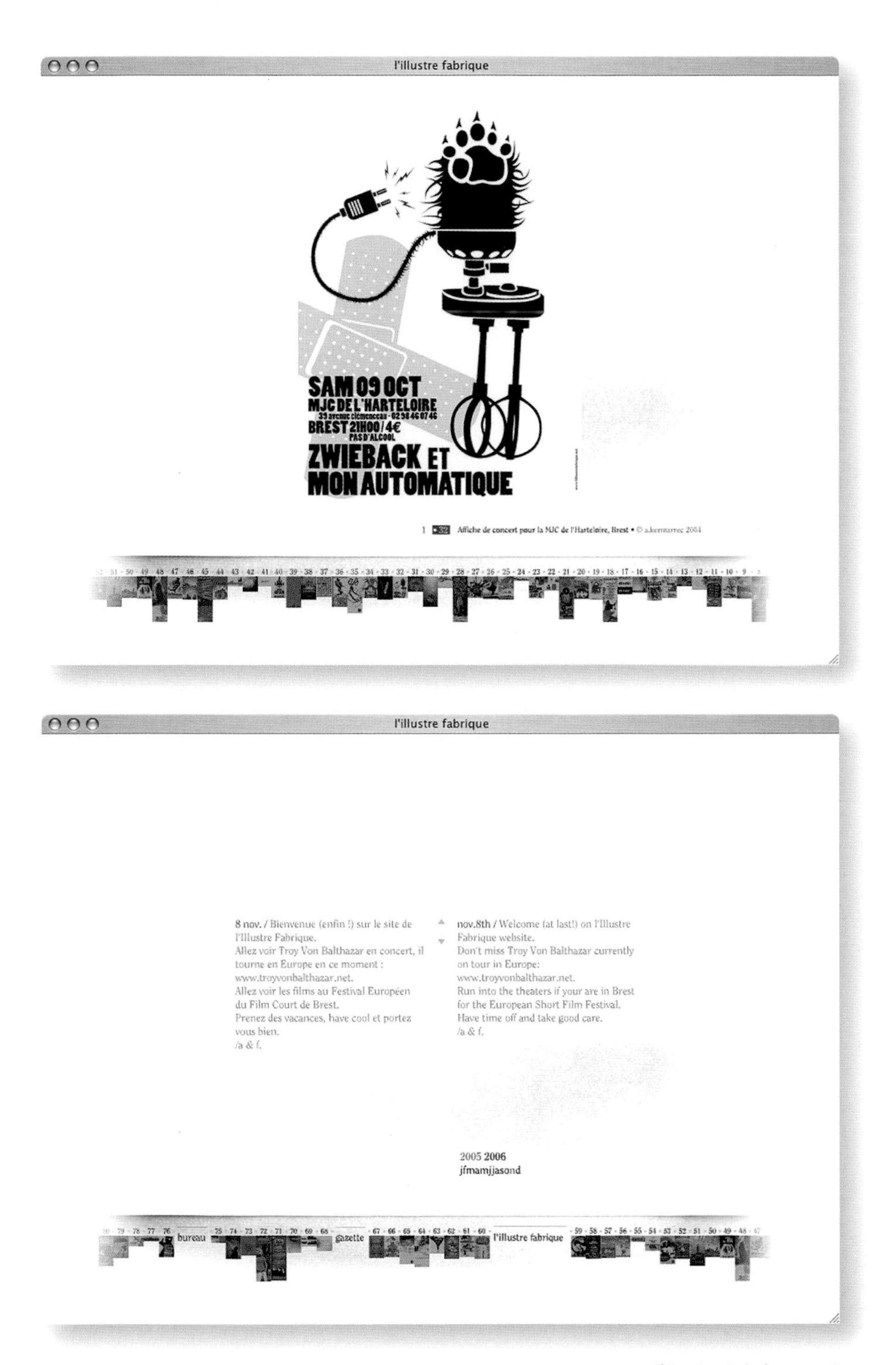

www.lillustrefabrique.net

D: prigent ewen

A: la boite graphique **M:** laboitegraphique.new.fr

The Consult – Creative Design Agency

TheConsult
Design & Art Direction

Profile
Selected work
Ascendis
Original Copywriting
Brighter Marketing
Leeds College of Art & Design
Diamond Days
Ready Planted
Jacqueline Callaghan
Designmash
Leeds Met University
The Consult
Terior
Get in touch

Prev. Next. 1 of 3

Following a three way pitch, Leeds College of Art & Design invited The Consult to design this year's prospectus.

we enco
rule bre

info@theconsult.com

The Consult – Creative Design Agency

TheConsult
Design & Art Direction

Profile
Selected work
Ascendis
Original Copywriting
Brighter Marketing
Leeds College of Art & Design
Diamond Days
Ready Planted
Jacqueline Callaghan
Designmash
Leeds Met University
The Consult
Terior
Get in touch

Prev. Next. 1 of 2

The Leeds School of Contemporary Art & Graphic Design at Leeds Met University commissioned us to design their new website. We focused on the processes and experiences of being a part of the School rather than past students work.

info@theconsult.com

www.theconsult.com

D: john-paul warner **P:** alex atkinson, rebecca keast

M: www.theconsult.com

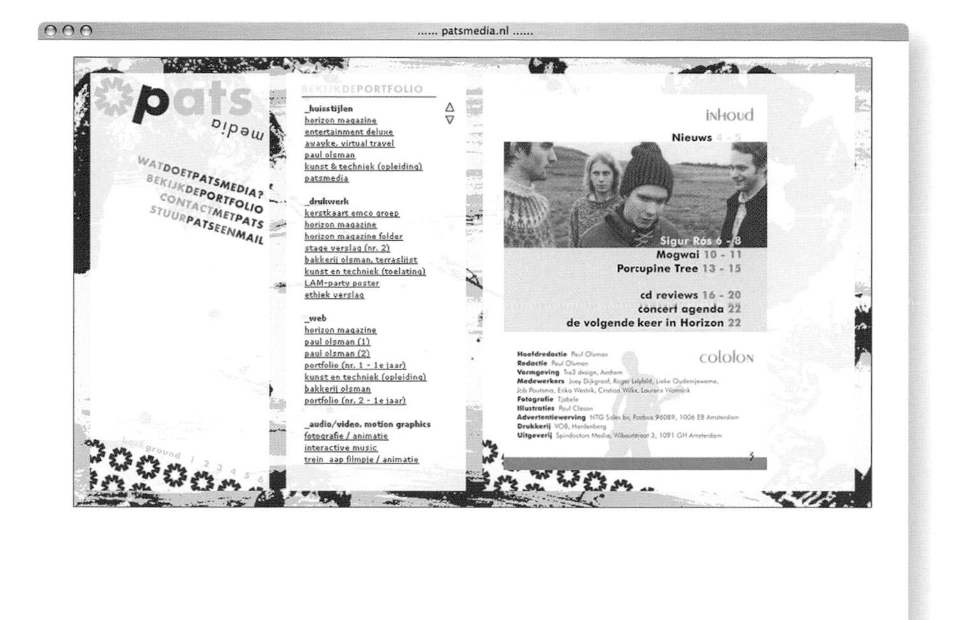

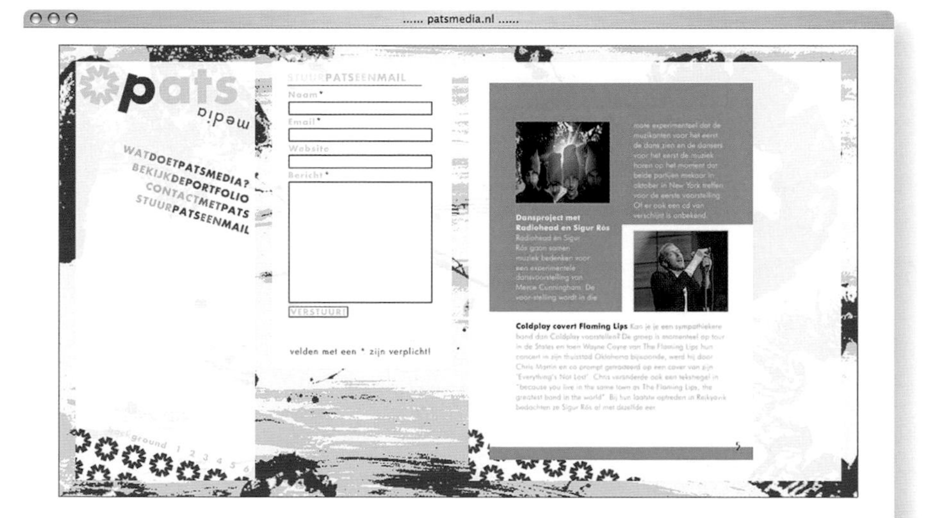

www.patsmedia.nl

D: paul olsman

A: patsmedia **M:** info@patsmedia.nl

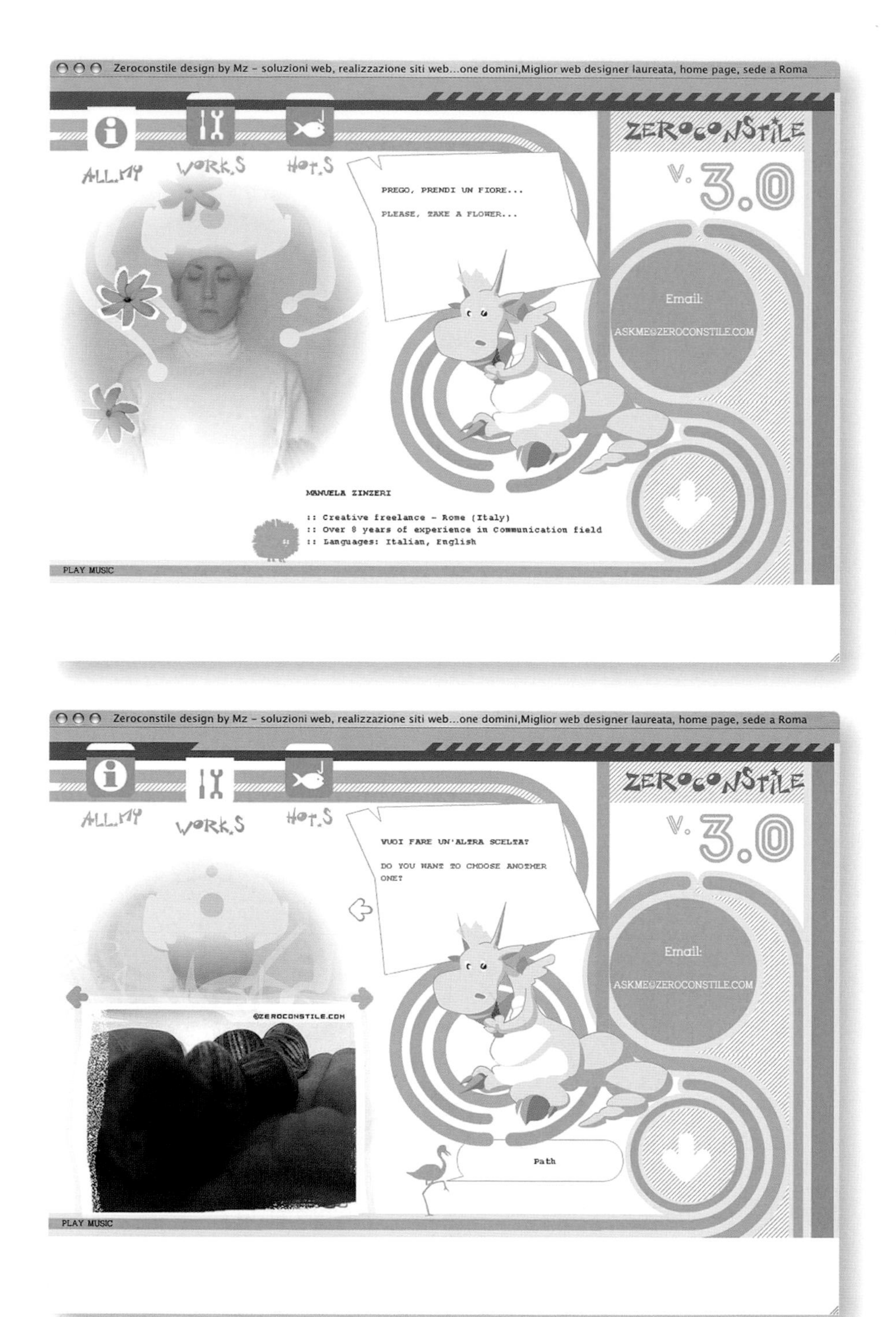

www.zeroconstile.com

D: manuela zinzeri

A: manuela zinzeri (freelance) **M:** askme@zeroconstile.com

www.limbus.fr

D: stefanos athanassopoulos **P:** emmanuelle ibara

A: limbus studio **M:** contact@limbus.fr

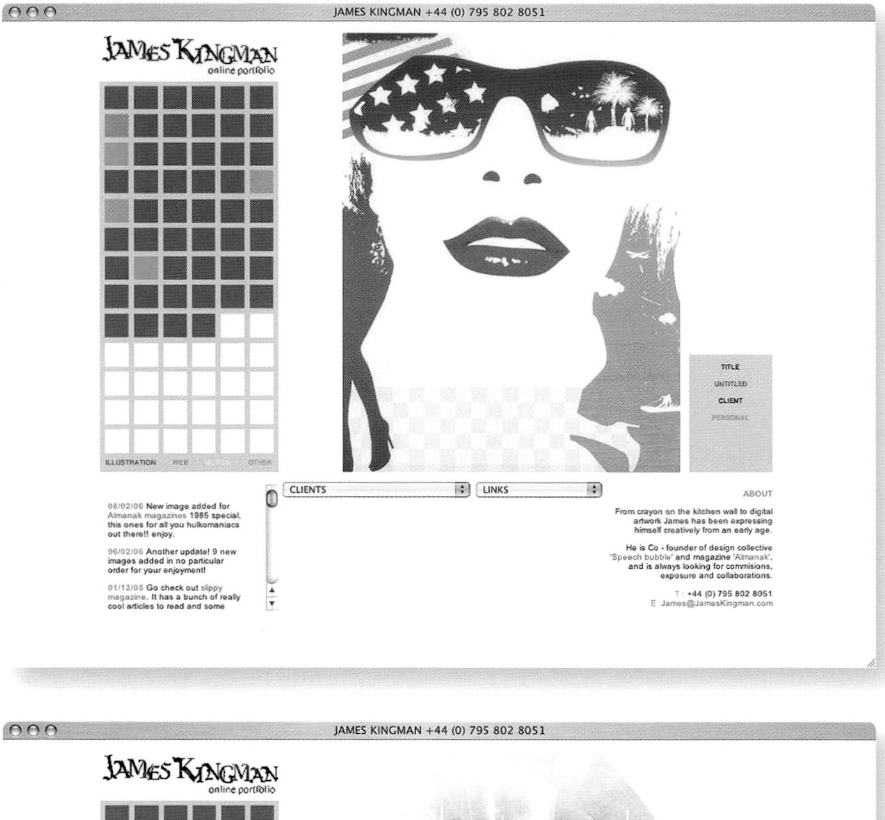

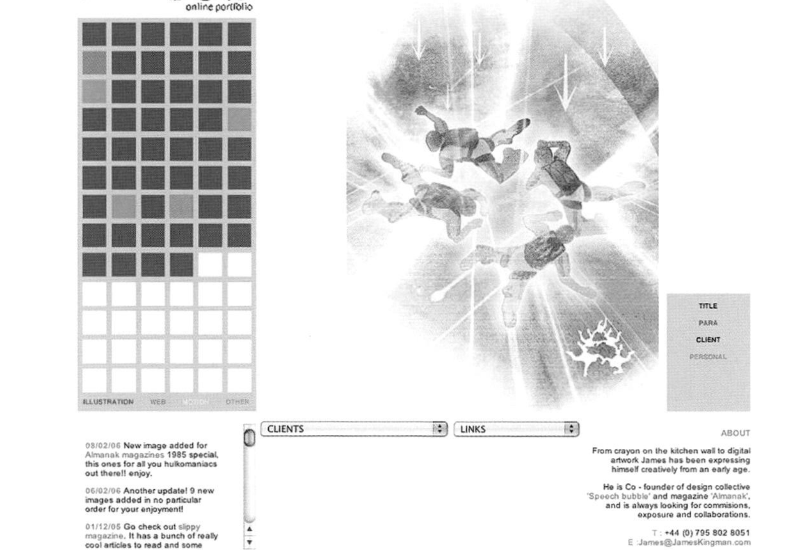

www.jameskingman.com

D: james kingman

M: james@jameskingman.com

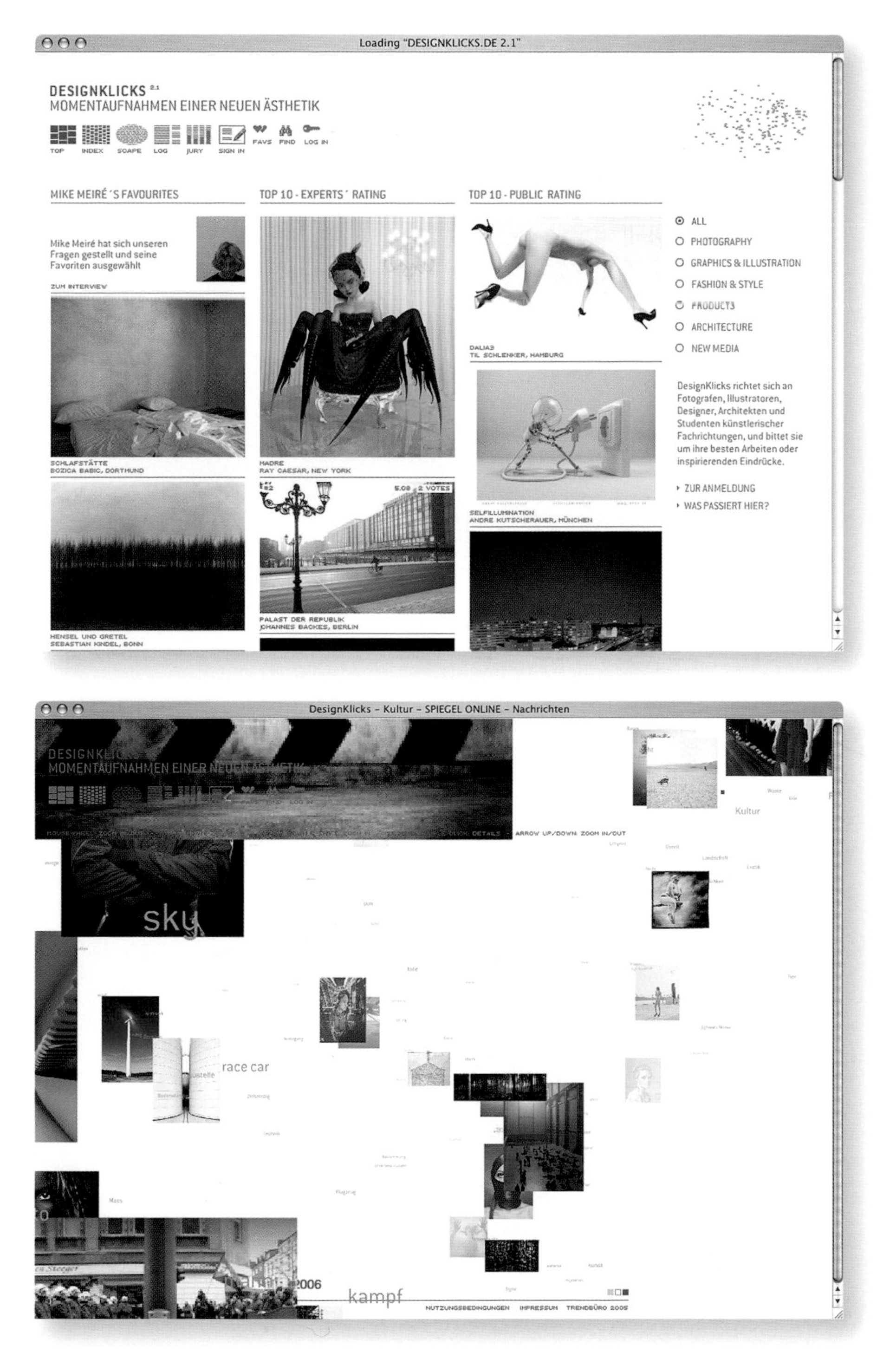

www.designklicks.de

D: stefan landrock **C:** deutschlandrock **P:** trendbüro hamburg

A: www.deutschlandrock.de **M:** designklicks@trendbuero.de

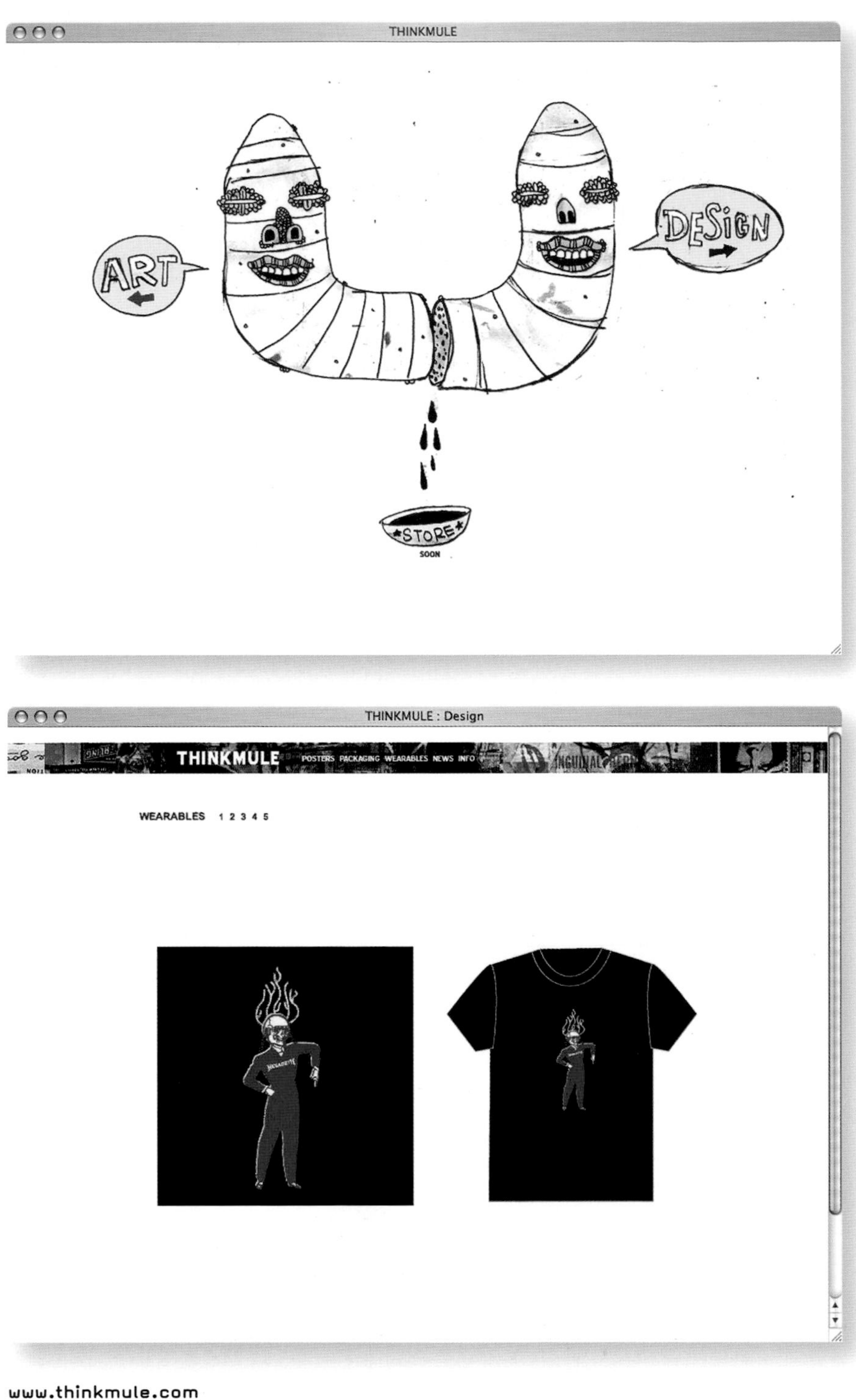

www.thinkmule.com

D: thinkmule **C:** aaron tanner

A: thinkmule **M:** www.thinkmule.com

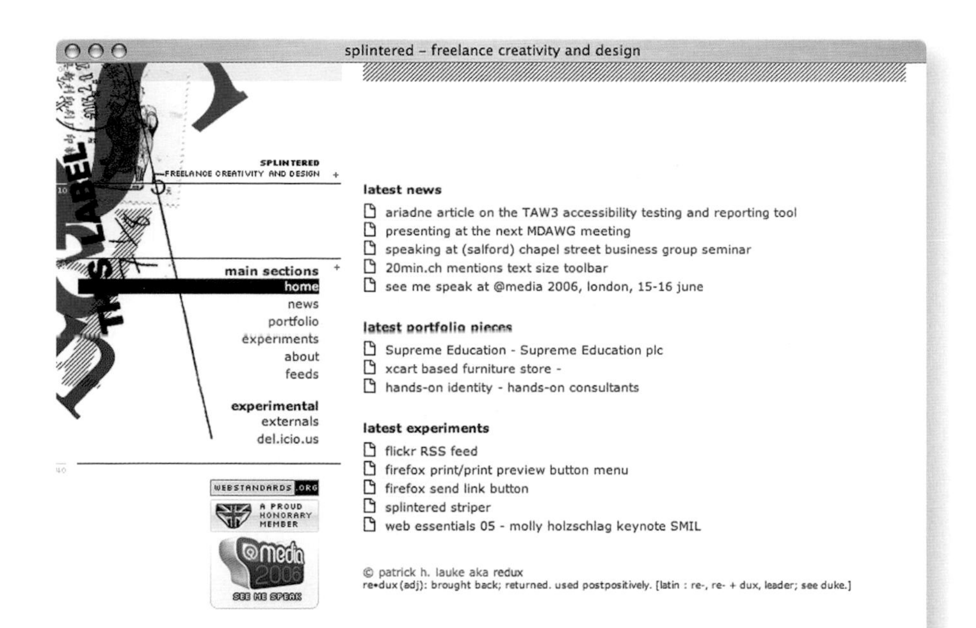

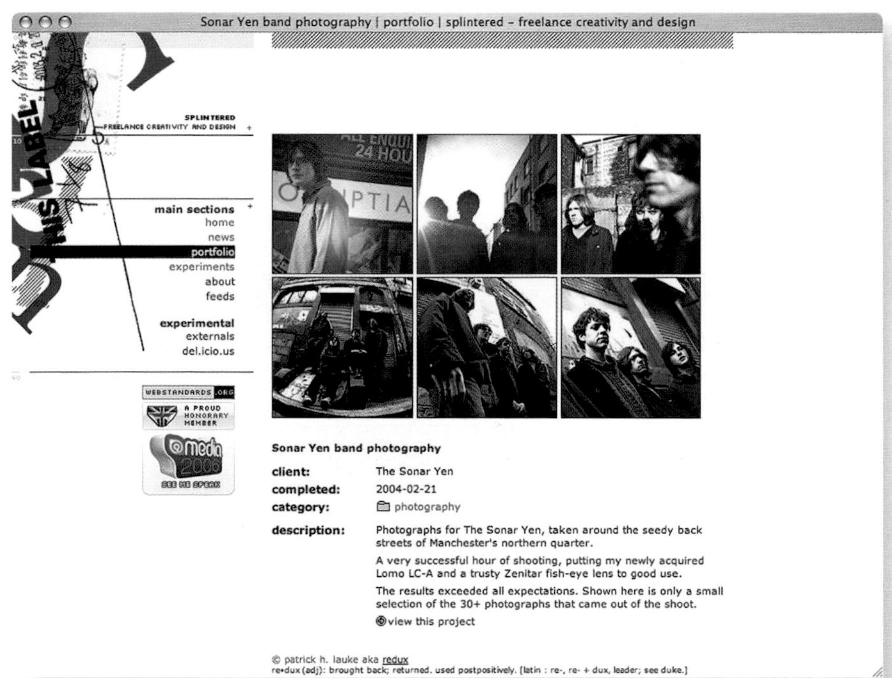

www.splintered.co.uk
D: patrick h. lauke
M: redux@splintered.co.uk

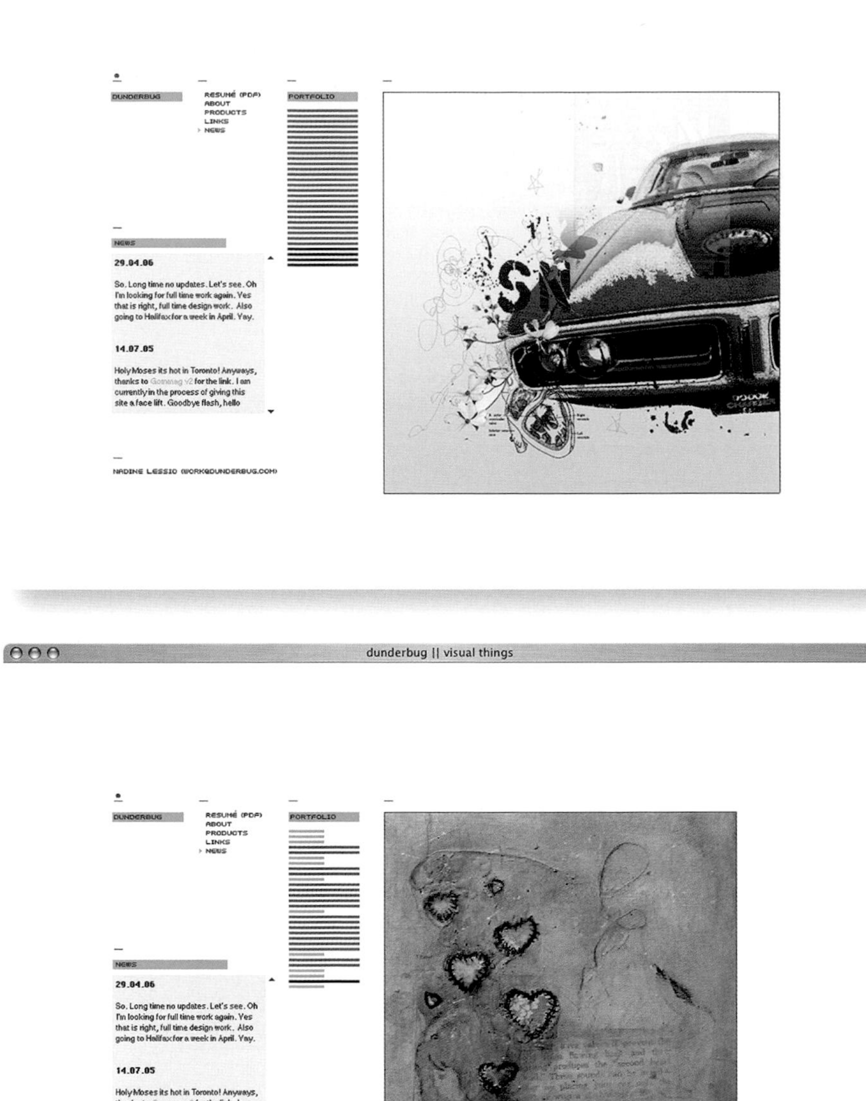

dunderbug.com

D: nadine lessio

M: work@dunderbug.com

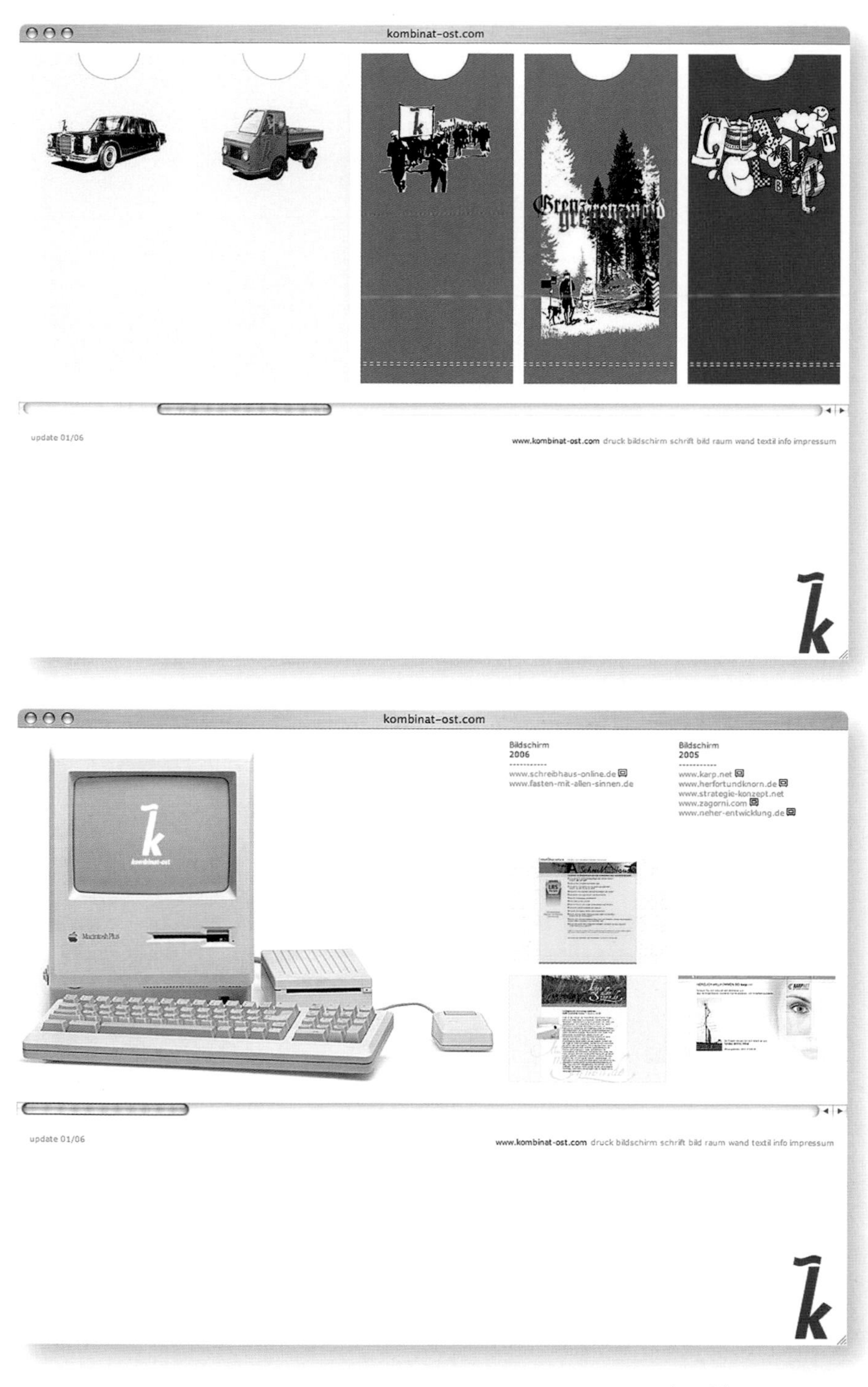

www.kombinat-ost.com

D: daniel knorn

A: kombinat-ost **M:** knorn@kombinat-ost.com

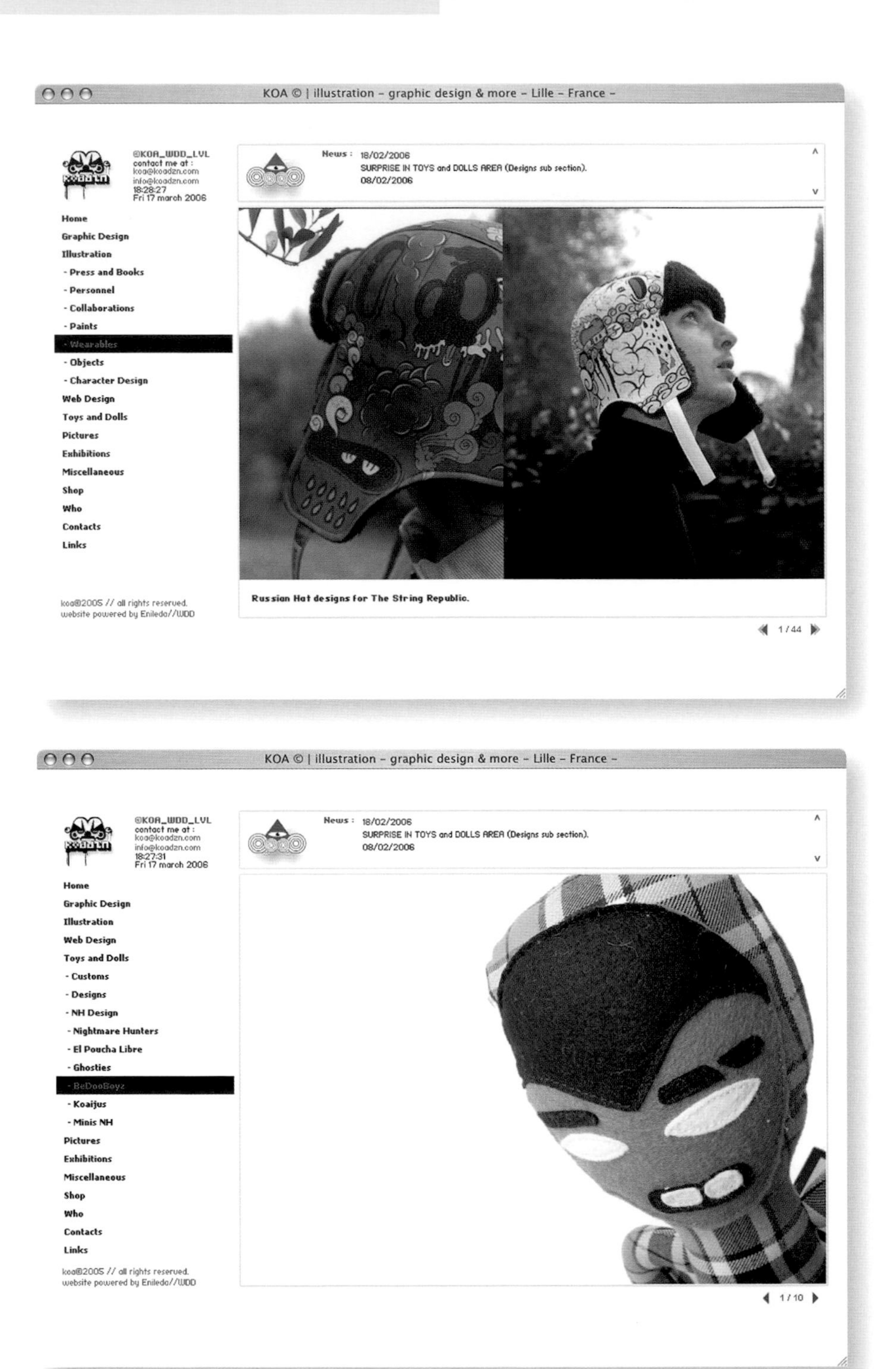

www.koadzn.com

D: koa C: enileda

M: koa@koadzn.com

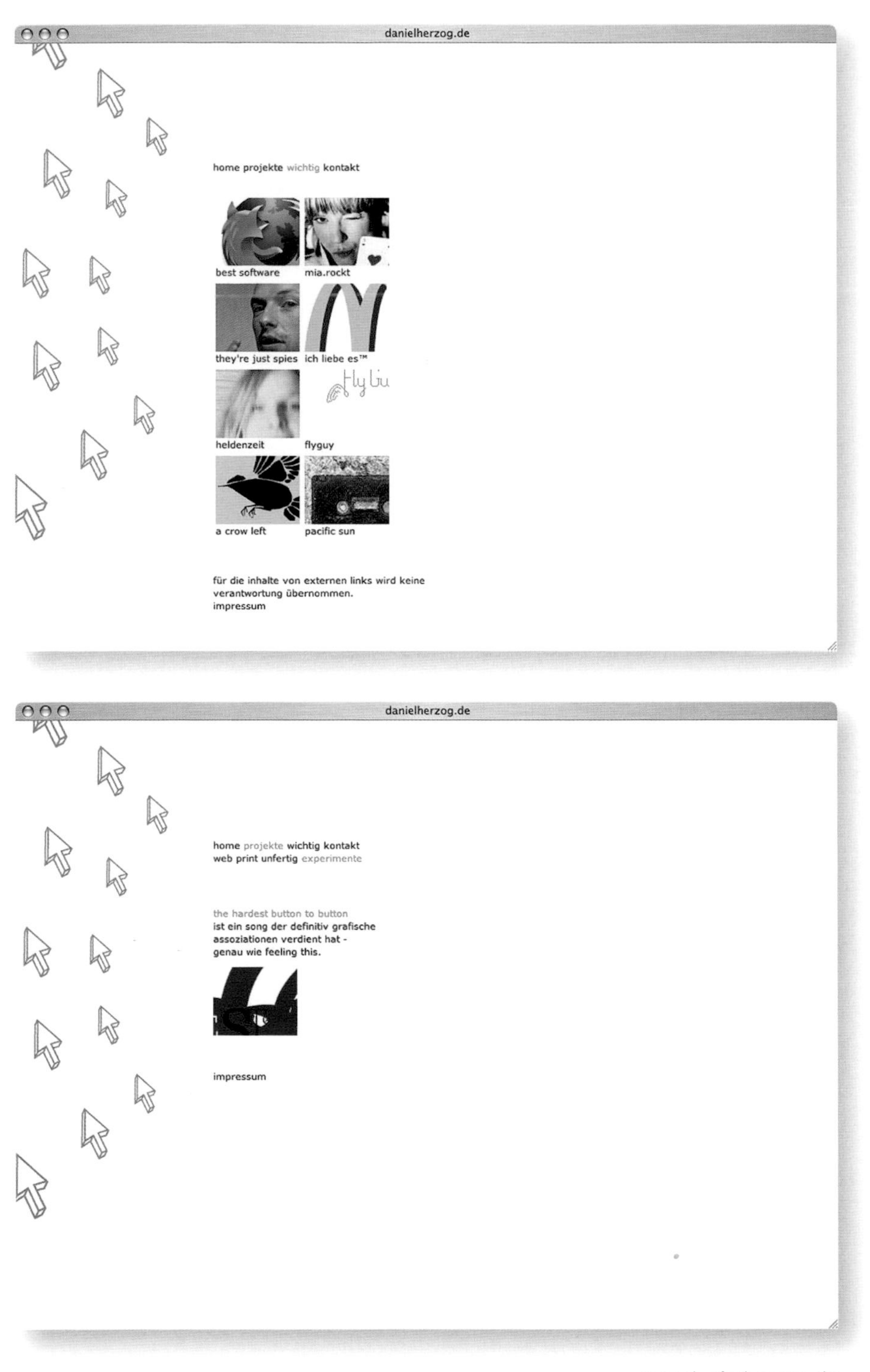

www.danielherzog.de
D: daniel herzog
M: daniel.herzog@gmail.com

www.thomasthiele.com

D: thomas thiele **C:** dirk thomas, sebastian petters

A: 4wd media **M:** kontakt@4wdmedia.de

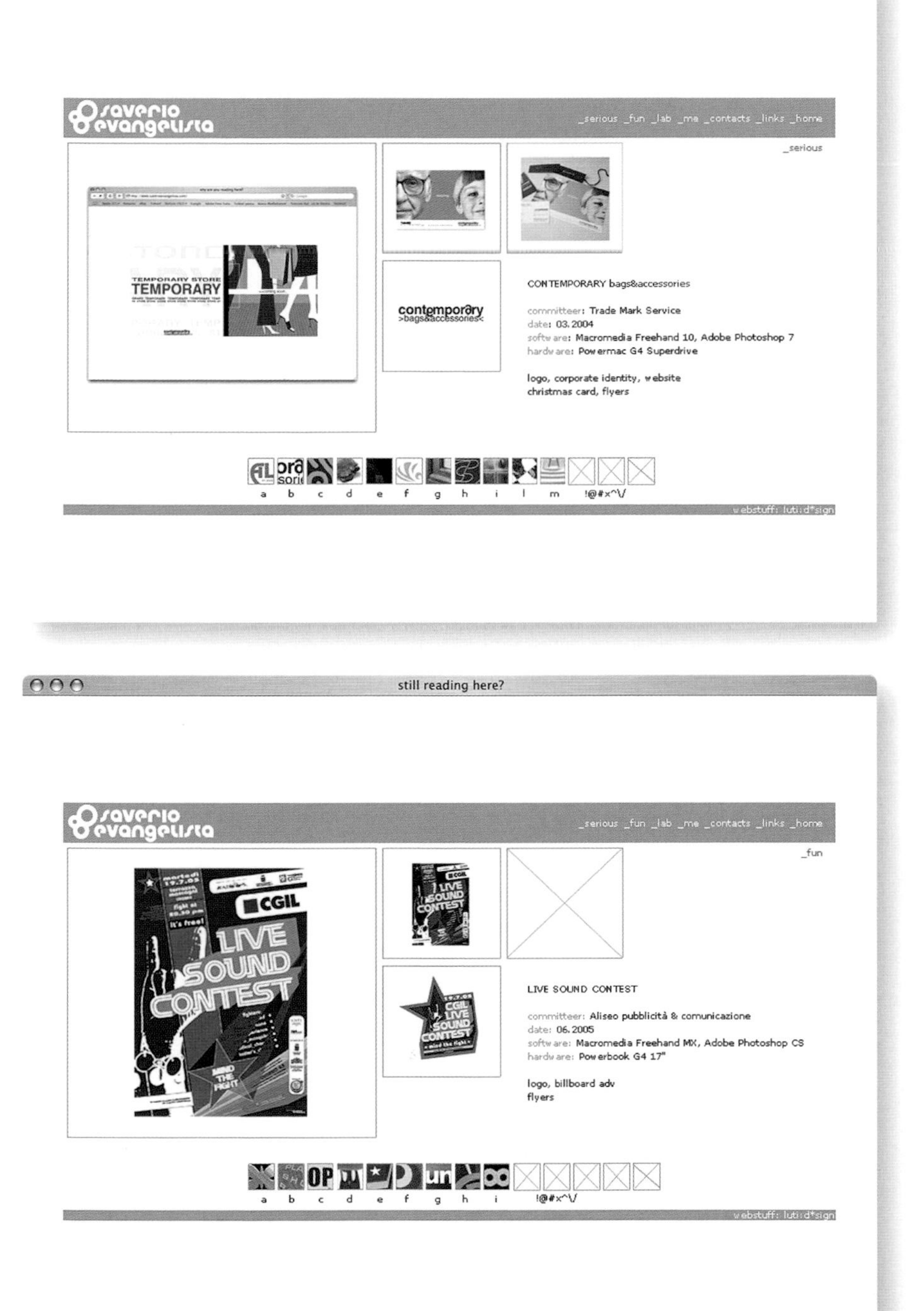

www.saverioevangelista.com

D: saverio evangelista **C:** saverio evangelista **P:** saverio evangelista, simone luti

A: luti*design **M:** www.luti.net

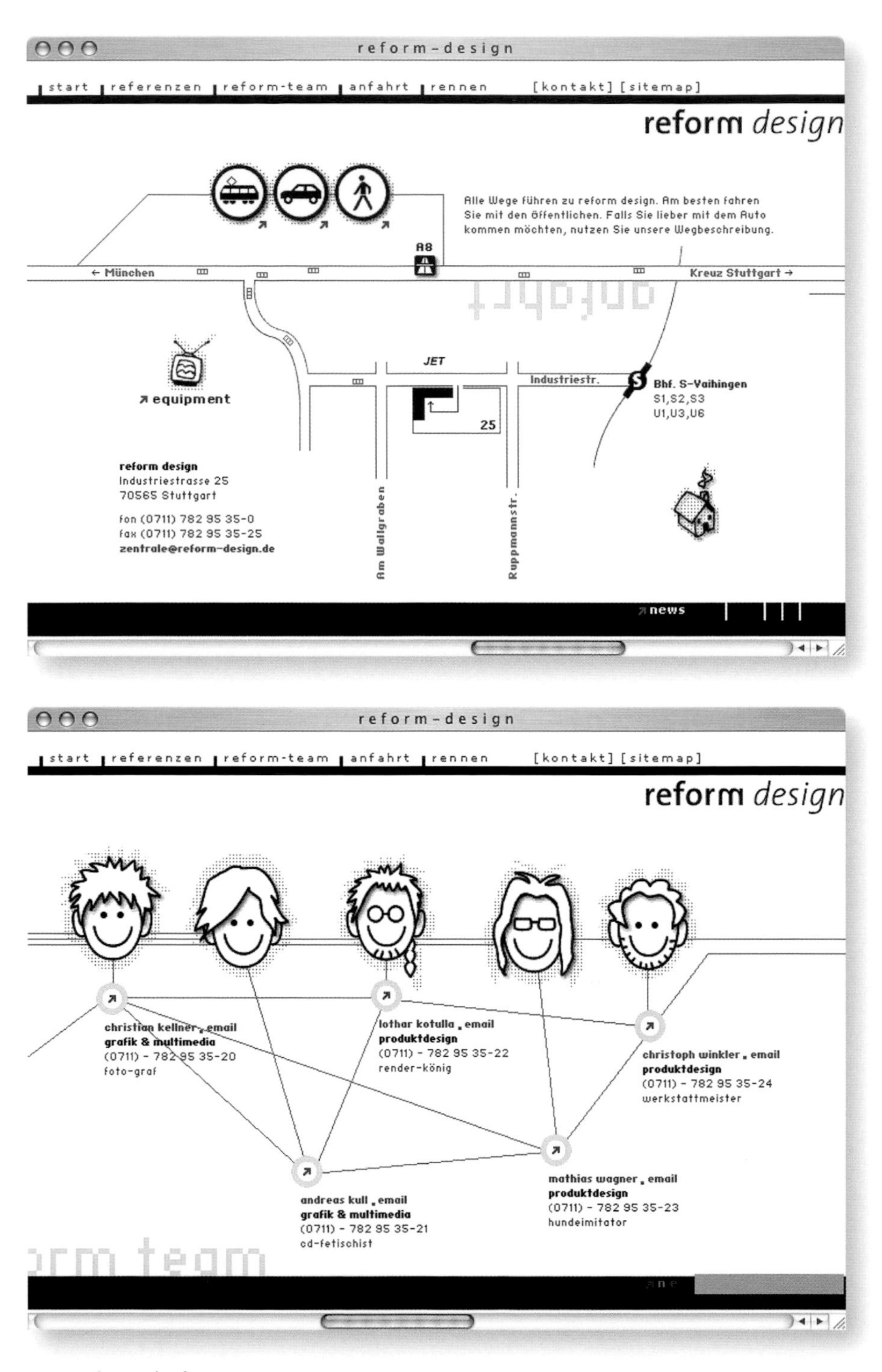

www.reform-design.com

D: christian kellner, andreas kull, christiane schulz C: christiane schulz

A: reform design M: andreas.kull@reform-design.de

www.pokelondon.com

D: nicky gibson **C:** simon kallgard **P:** peter beech

A: poke **M:** info@pokelondon.com

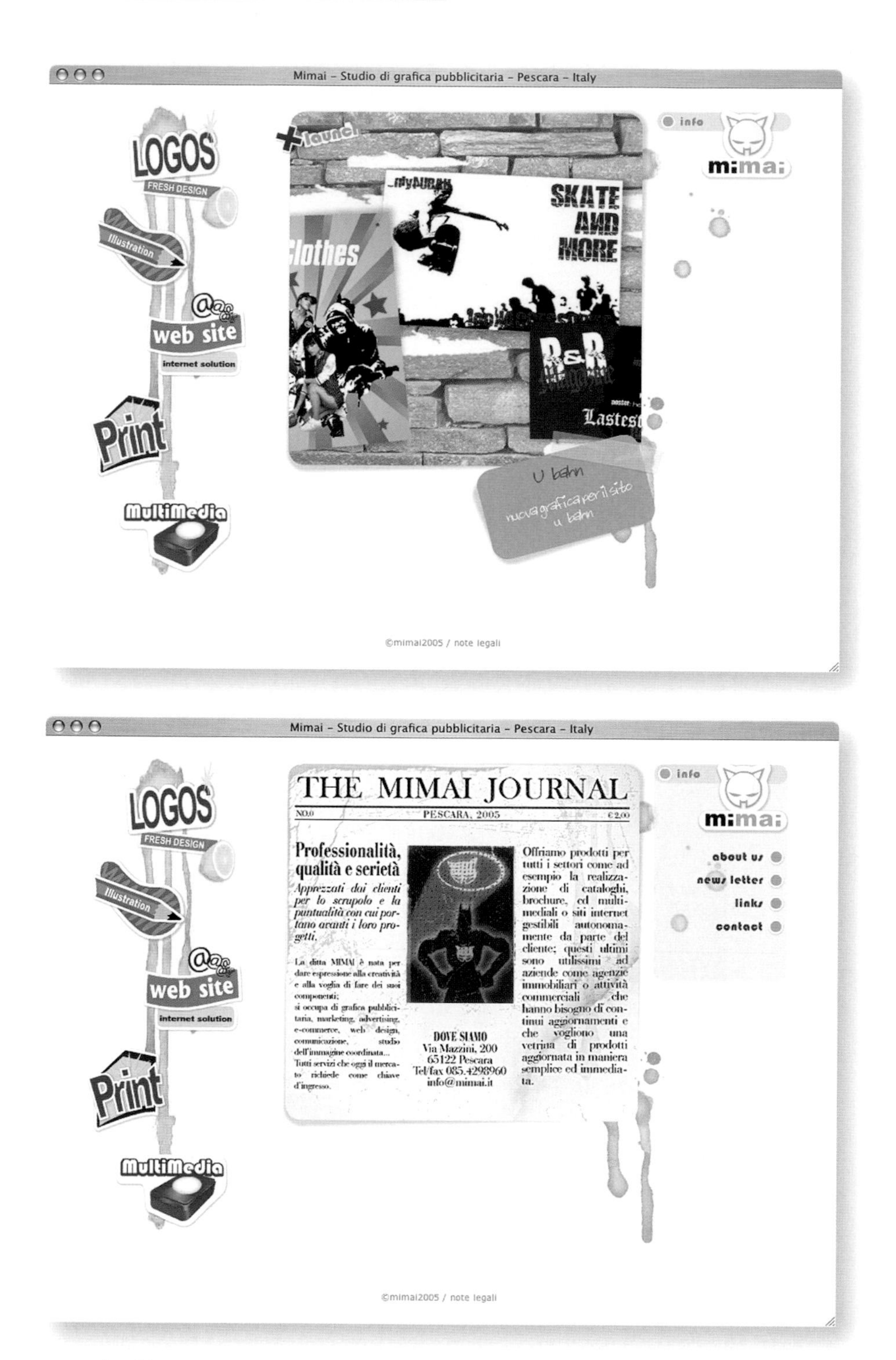

www.mimai.it

D: mimai group

A: mimai di mirko maiorano **M:** www.mimai.it

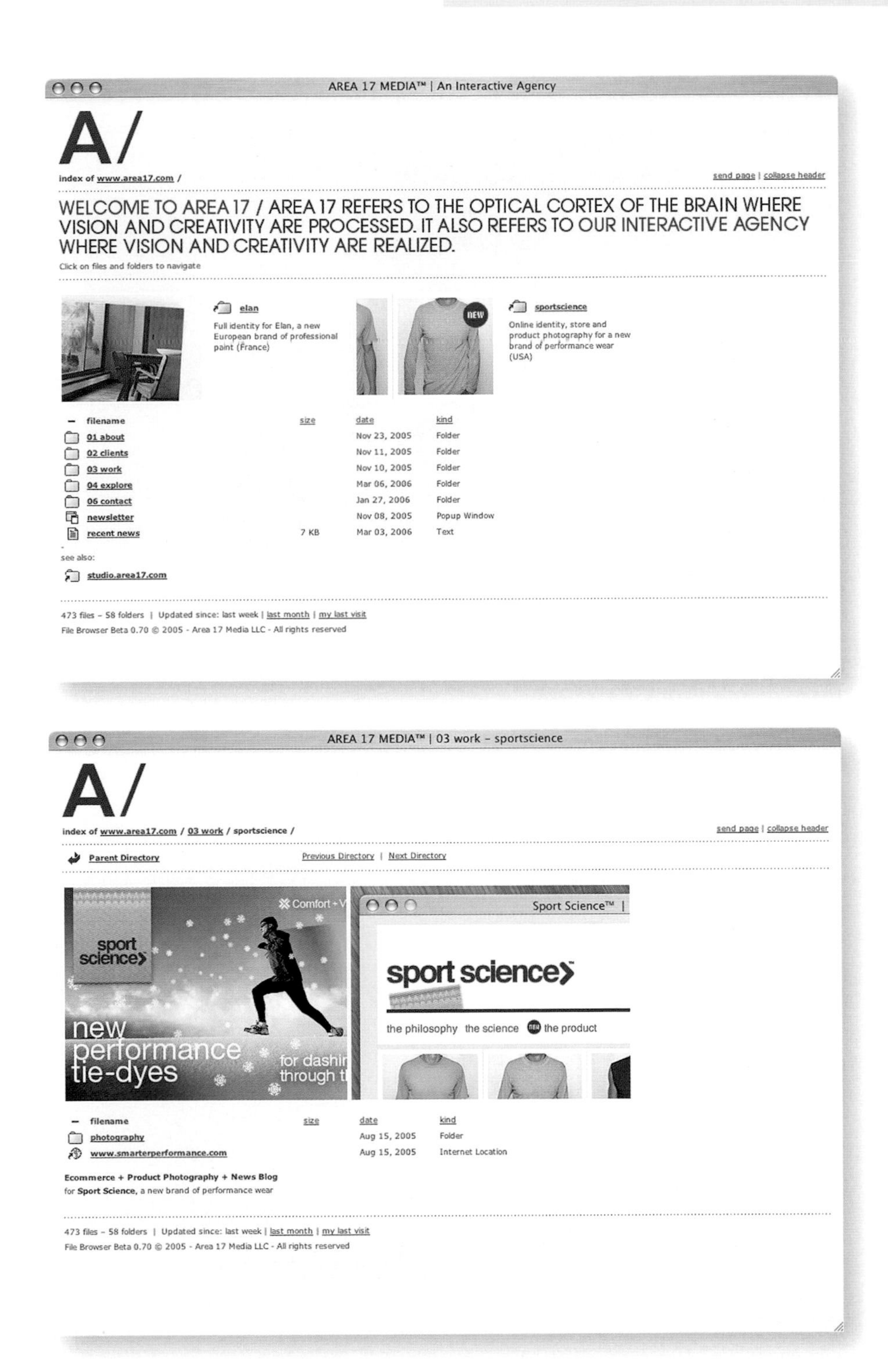

www.area17.com

D: arnaud mercier **C:** mubashar iqbal **P:** george eid

A: area 17 **M:** contact@area17.com

herfort+knorn I Design Werbung Medien

REFERENZEN Print Web Schrift KONTAKT IMPRESSUM herfort+knorn

Referenzen
Schrift

Diverse Illustrationen
Schriftentwicklung I CAF-Font
DDR-Modellautos.info I Berlin
Gerway Deutschland I Berlin
Heide Centrum I Senzig
kombinat-ost I Berlin

market I one I Leipzig
OSTBLOKK - Plattenbau I Berlin
Polo Dragracing Accociation I Berlin
Rochenkinder Schwimmschule I Berlin
Sikorski Sachverständigenbüro I Rangsdorf
STEELWORK GmbH I Berlin
Trabbi-Rallye.de I Berlin
umgestaltung.de I Berlin
WELT-IGLU I Xenos-Projekt I Pätz
X-Projekt I Xenos-Projekt I Pätz

Wie wird ein Logo entwickelt?
Ein Beispiel

Klicken Sie bitte hier!

herfort+knorn
Kontakt

Torsten Herfort
Konzeption + Organisation
Chausseestraße 207
15754 Senzig

Mobil: +49(0)172 - 383 88 71
Fax: +49(0)30 - 67 54 98 40

Daniel Knorn
Grafik, Layout + Web
H.-Heine Allee 43
15732 Eichwalde

Mobil: +49(0)163 - 787 19 77
Fax: +49(0)30 - 67 54 98 40

Kontaktformular
Name
Telefonnummer
email-Adresse
Rückruf
Ihr Anliegen
Abschicken

herfort+knorn
Impressum / Angaben gemäß §6 TDG

Verantwortlich für alle Inhalte: Torsten Herfort

Chausseestraße 207
15754 senzig

Mobil: +49(0)172 - 383 88 71
email: th(ä)herfortundknorn.de

Steuer-Nr.: 049/230/05574

Gesetzlicher Hinweis

Die auf diesen Seiten veröffentlichten Bilder und Texte sind urheberrechtlich geschützt. Eine Vervielfältigung für private oder kommerzielle Zwecke ist nur mit schriftlicher Genehmigung durch herfort+knorn zulässig.

Für die Inhalte externer Links sind die jeweiligen Anbieter verantwortlich.

herfort+knorn
Design Werbung Medien

www.herfortundknorn.de

D: daniel knorn

A: herfort+knorn **M:** dk@herfortundknorn.de

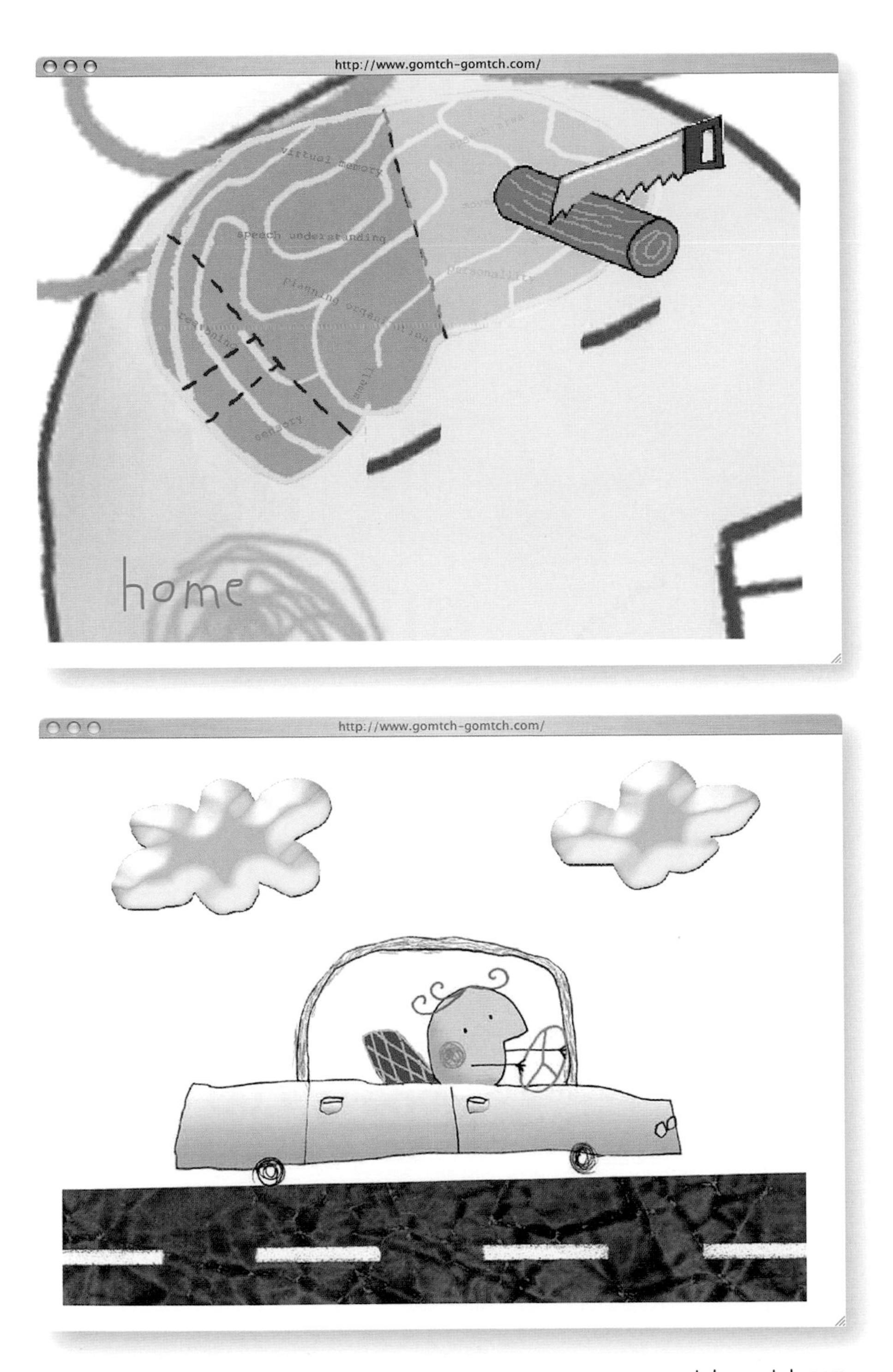

www.gomtch-gomtch.com

D: joana toste **C:** joana toste **P:** gomtch-gomtch

A: gomtch-gomtch **M:** mail@gomtch-gomtch.com

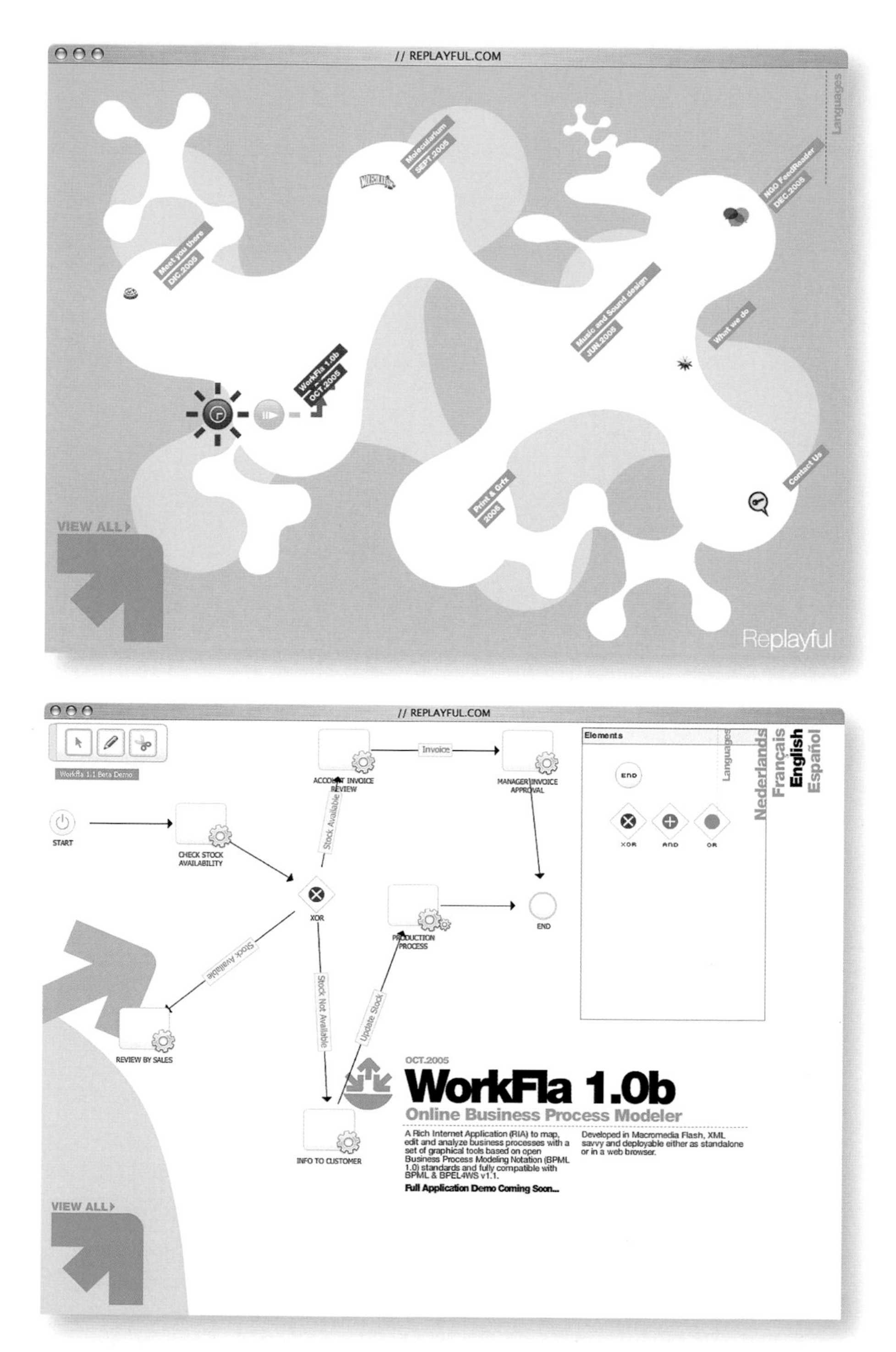

www.replayful.com
D: replayful
A: replayful M: info@replayful.com

www.ilustris.pl

D: andrzej tylkowski, marek charytonowicz C: marek charytonowicz

A: mediadream M: studio@mediadream.pl

www.ths.nu

D: thomas schostok

A: {ths} thomas schostok design **M:** www.ths.nu

www.thedesignersrepublic.com

D: the designers republic

A: the designers republic **M:** disinfo@thedesignersrepublic.com

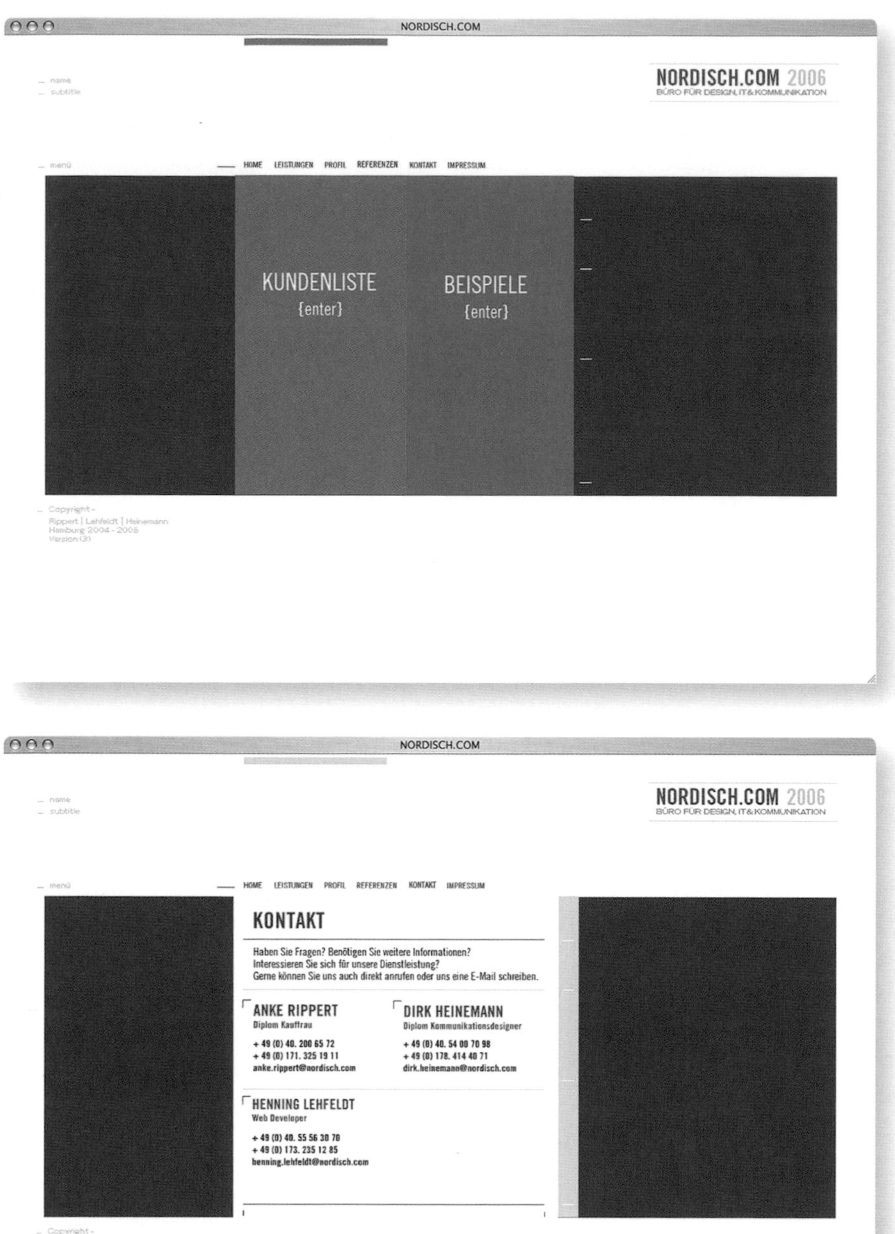

www.nordisch.com

D: dirk heinemann **C:** henning lehfeldt **P:** dirk heinemann

A: nordisch.com **M:** heinemann@nordisch.com

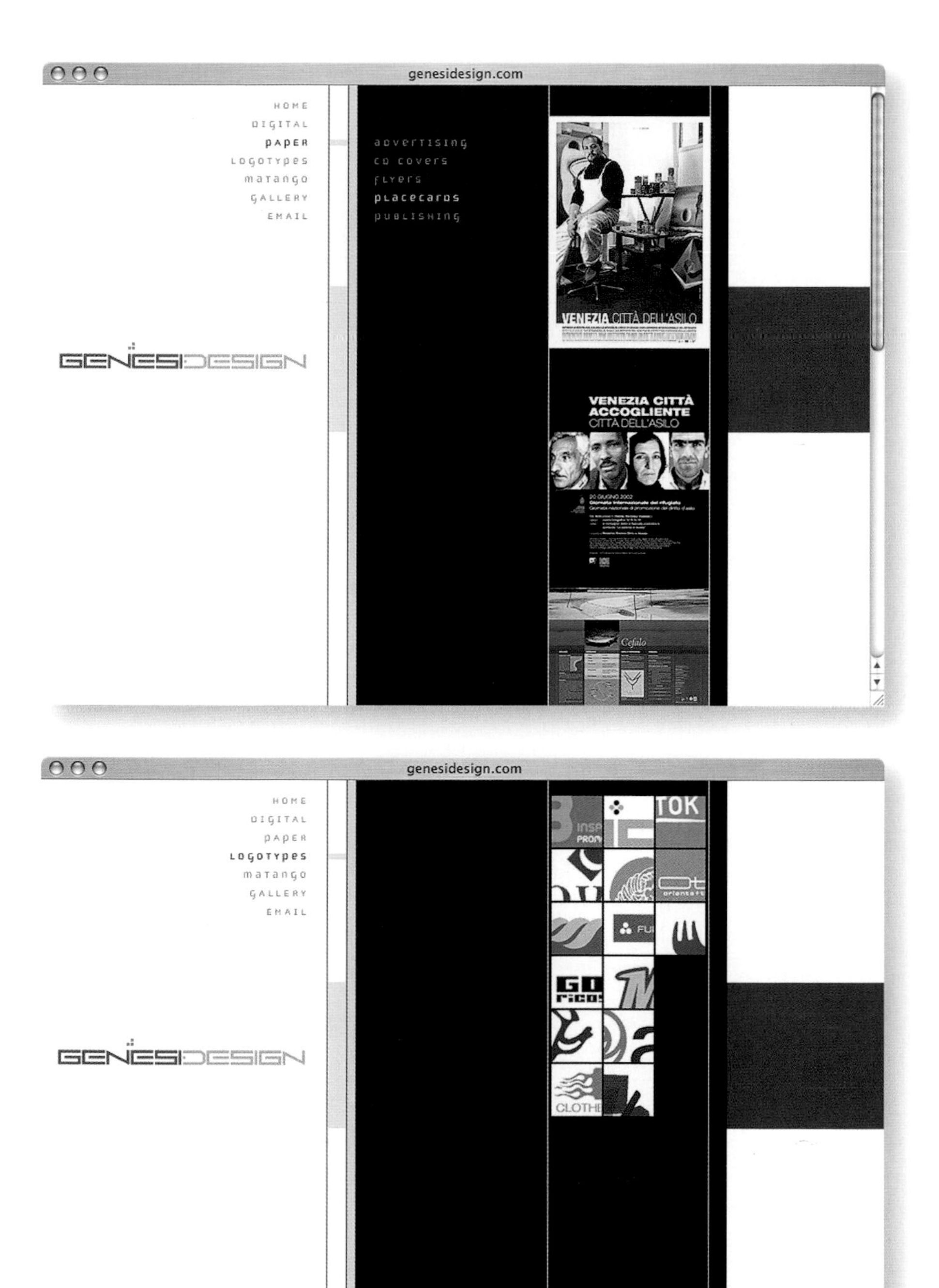

www.genesidesign.com
D: cristina mulinacci, maurizio ercole
A: genesidesign **M:** design@genesi.net

TWINPIX web.print.music

TWINPIX web.print.music

TWINPIX ist eine Agentur für Webdesign, Print (Anzeigen, Visitenkarten, Briefpapier, etc), Logo, Corporate Identity, Text und Sound-Design in Welzheim bei Stuttgart. Hinter TWINPIX stehen der Dipl. Designer (FH) und Master of Arts Joe Landen, sowie die Designstudentin Claudia Hahn.

TWINPIX mypage

Die kostengünstige und modulare Homepage mit 6 Kapiteln schon ab 450,- EUR (netto). Mehr Infos: mypage.twinpix.de

News

TWINPIX designt für die Cocolococlub-Veranstaltungen in Schorndorf und Stuttgart Plakate, Flyer, Anzeigen und Web-Banner.

TWINPIX gestaltet für Ludwig Bauer und sein Restaurant Ruccola ein Plakat und Visitenkarten.

TWINPIX entwirft für die Innen-Deko des Cocolococlubs diverse Werbeplanen und Transparente.

TWINPIX designt für den Cocolococlub Plakate, Flyer, Anzeigen und Web-Banner.

TWINPIX realisiert die Website von ak-projectmanagement. www.ak-projectmanagement.com

TWINPIX gestaltet die Website von M1-Bookings um, wegen der Namensänderung zu FAKE Artist Management. www.fakeartists.com

TWINPIX designt eine Zeitungsanzeige und ein Mailing für Auto Weimar.

TWINPIX entwirft zwei Anzeigen für den neuen Kunden Topper Electronics.

NEWS | AGENTUR | REFERENZEN | AUSZEICHNUNGEN | KONTAKT | ONLINE SHOP

TWINPIX web.print.music

Referenzen

| **Websites**
| Web-Banner
| Print
| Logo & CI
| Music
| Freelance

Website Projekte

FAKE Artists (Stuttgart)
M1-The Club (Stuttgart)
Großecker & Pyttel (Obersulm)
Tennisrado (Filderstadt)
mdproductions (Aichtal)
Tannhof (Alfdorf)
ak-projectmanagement (Stgt)
Armand van Helden (USA)
Netmen IHS (Hochwang)
DJ Thomsen (Berlin)
Bennett & Bennett (Herrenberg)
die Leute (Freiburg)
Felix da Housecat (USA)
Sunradio Creativo (Spanien)
van der Velden (Aachen)
Light Up! (Stuttgart)
Kirchheim teckt ... (Kirchheim)
Cafe Niethammer (Jettingen)
in the pink (Welzheim)

NEWS | AGENTUR | REFERENZEN | AUSZEICHNUNGEN | KONTAKT | ONLINE SHOP

www.twinpix.de

D: joe landen, claudia hahn **C:** joe landen **P:** joe landen

A: twinpix web.print.music **M:** info@twinpix.de

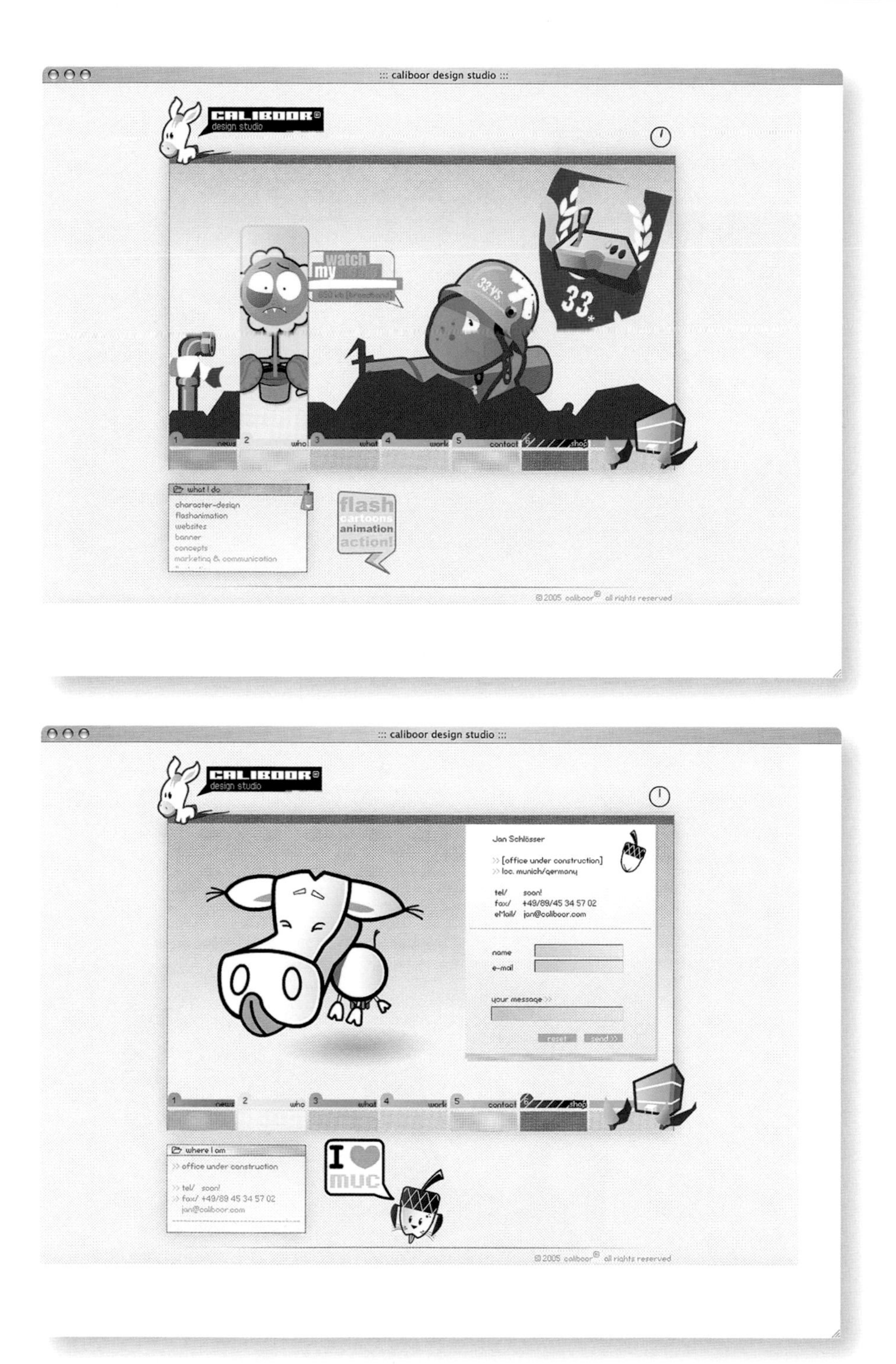

www.caliboor.com

D: jan schlösser

A: caliboor design studio **M:** jan@caliboor.com

stevescott.com.au

D: steve scott

M: steve@stevescott.com.au

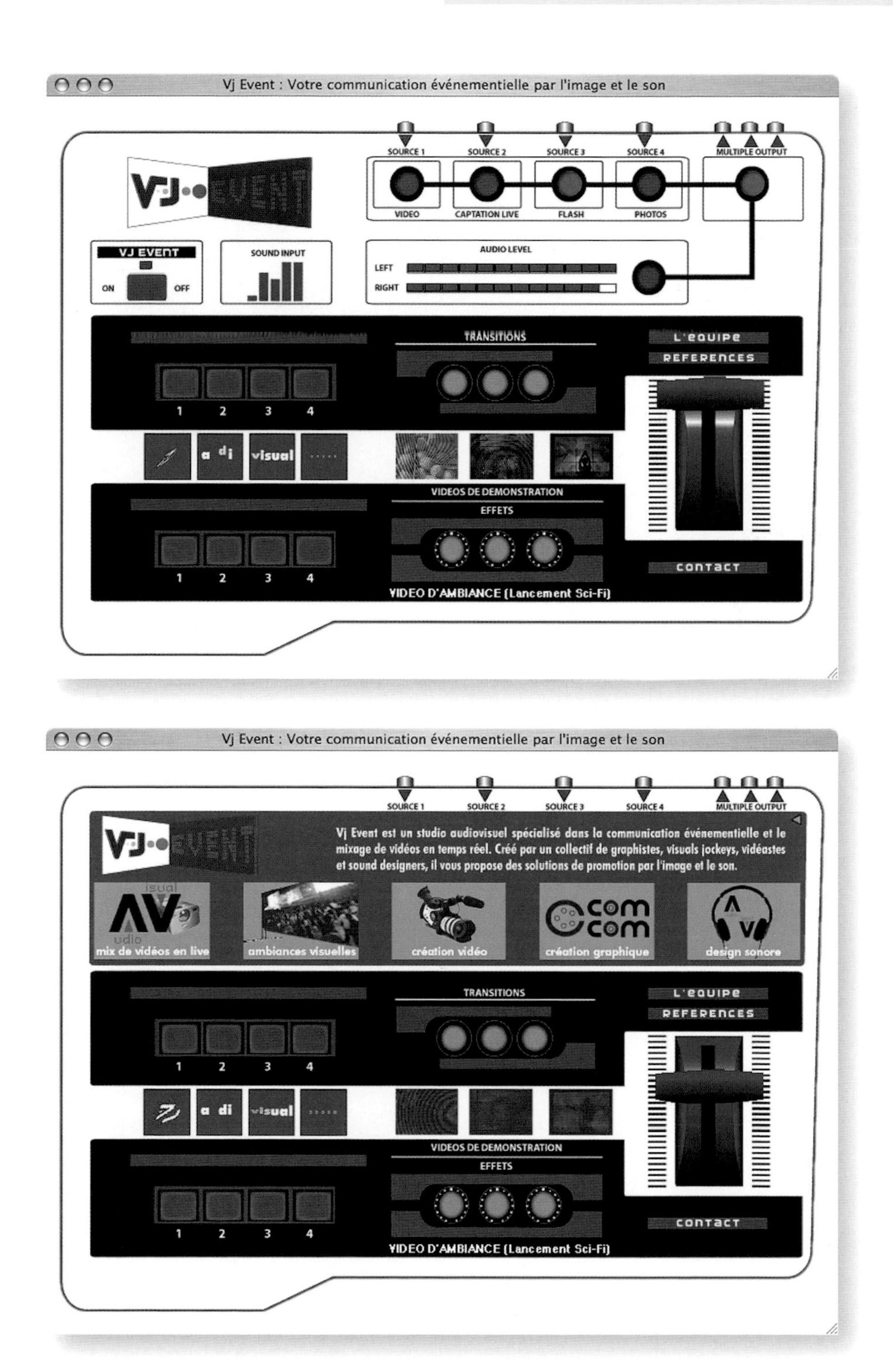

www.vievent.fr
D: florian raffene
M: infos@vievent.fr

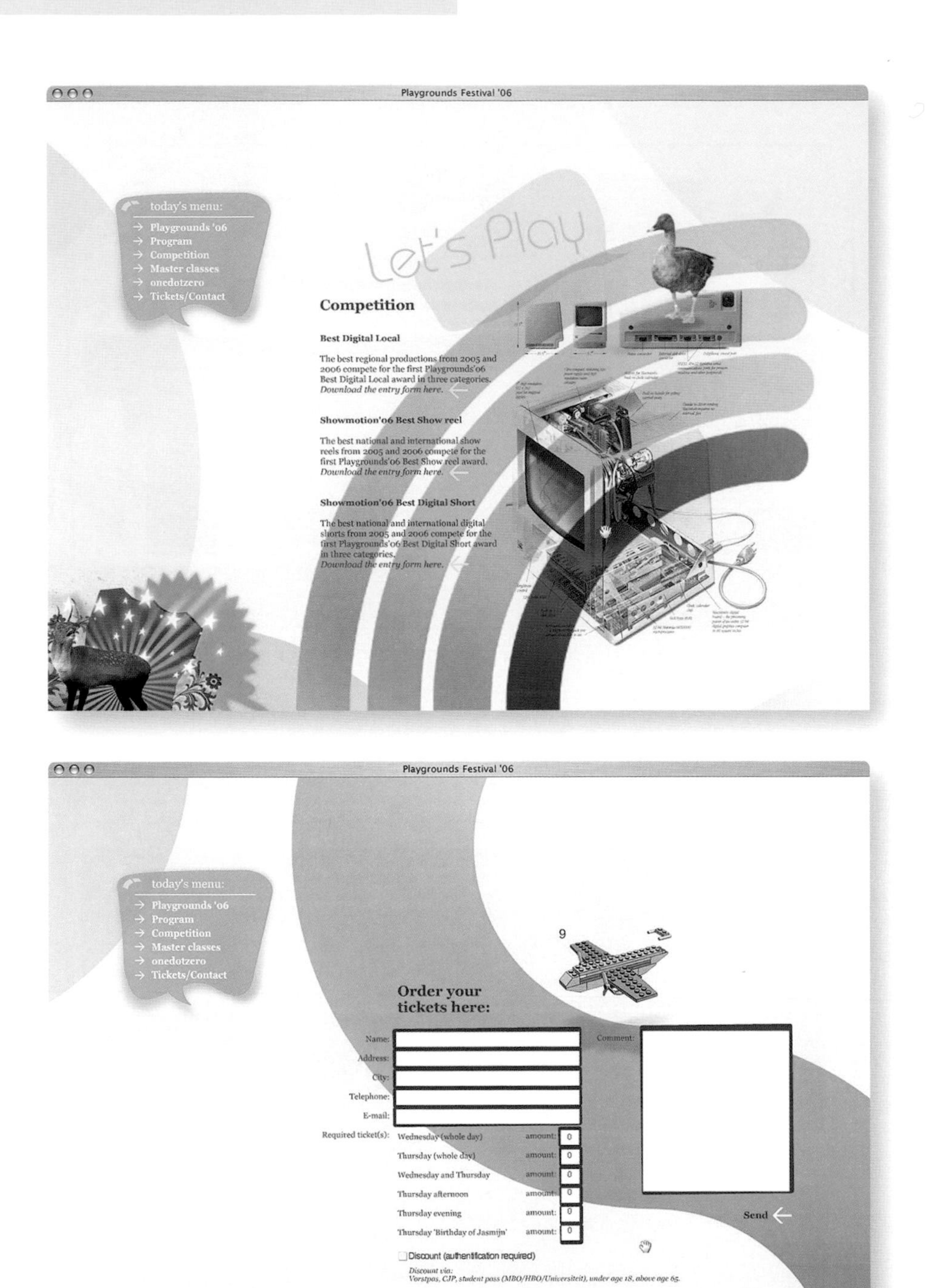

www.playgroundsfestival.nl

D: jorg van keulen, emiel van wanrooij **C:** c. raaijmakers, bas van hout **P:** loek jurres

A: the cre8ion.lab - schijndel **M:** www.cre8ion.com

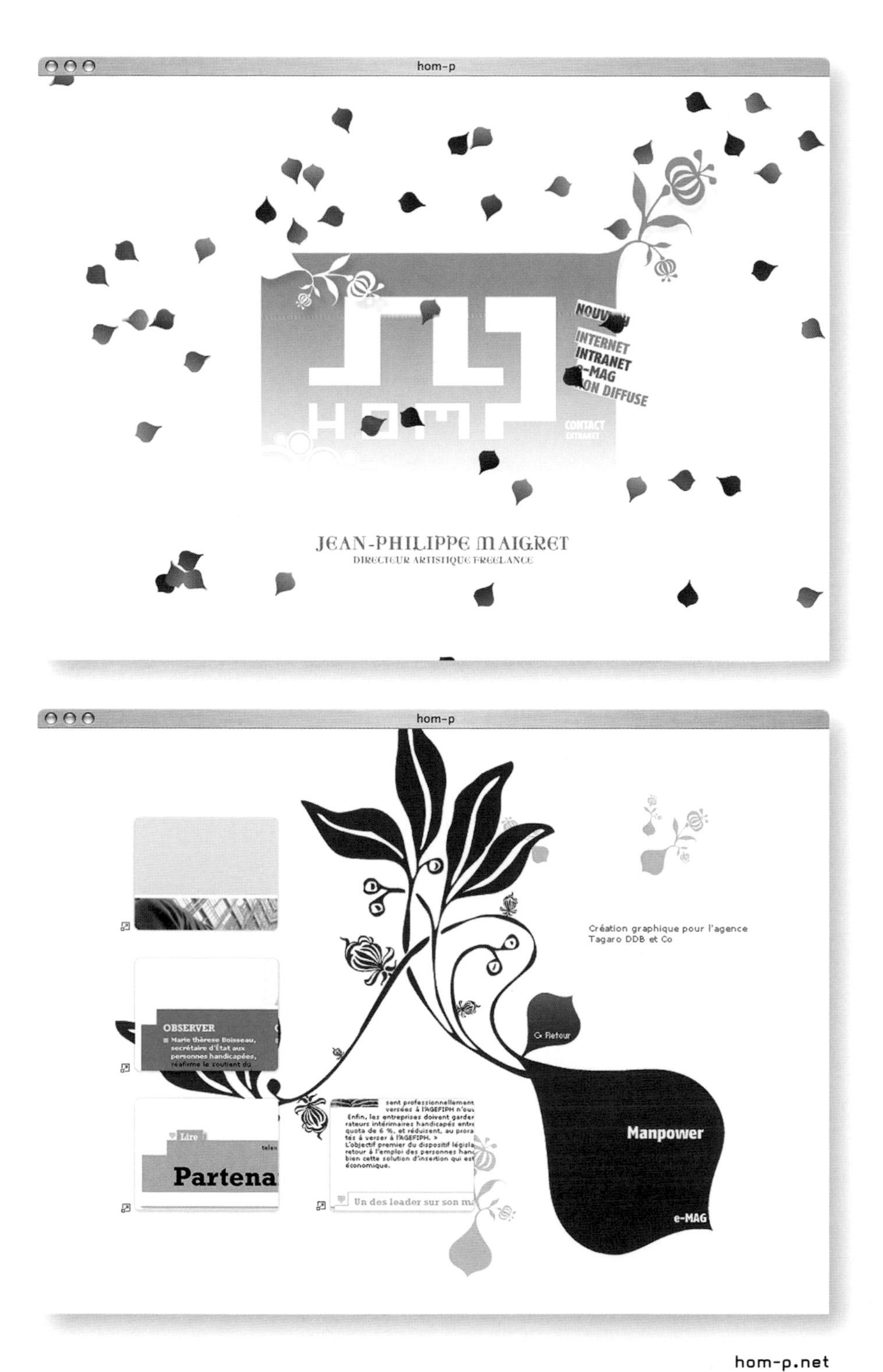

hom-p.net

D: jean-philippe maigret **C:** alexandre koch **P:** hom-p

A: hom-p **M:** contact@hom-p.net

www.z-design.it

D: marco zingoni

A: z-design **M:** zingoni@z-design.it

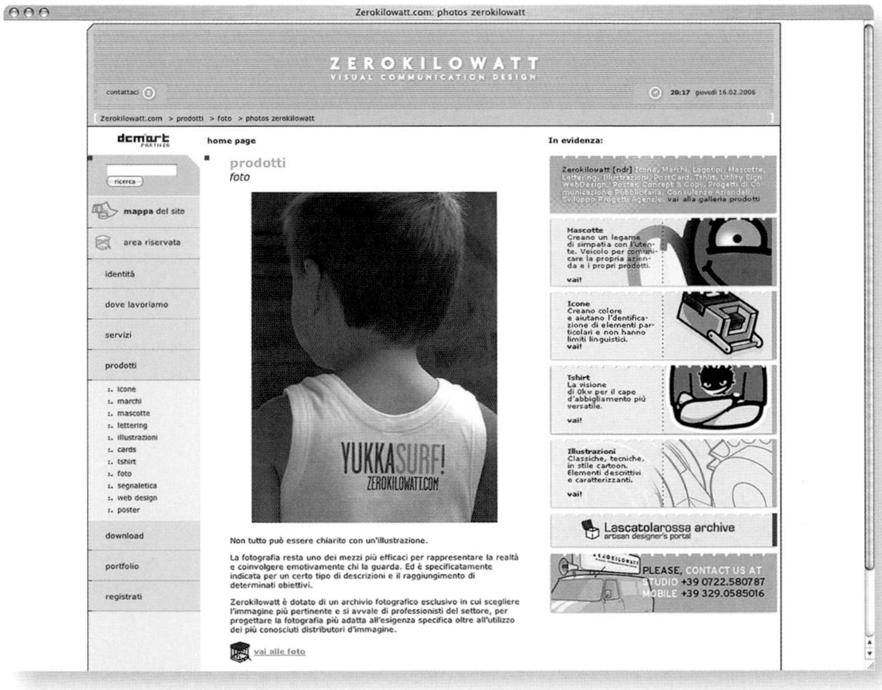

www.zerokilowatt.com

D: cristiano andreani C: maura battistoni P: dagomedia

A: zerokilowatt visual communication design M: cristiano@zerokilowatt.com

ホームページ Flash制作 グラフィックデザイン 映像制作 キャラクターデザイン ミヤシタカズヨ 和代★工房

Top

Web・映像・印刷物などのCGデザインを手がけている
『ミヤシタカズヨ』のWebサイトです。

★Flashなどを使用したPC＋モバイルWebサイトの構築とデザイン
>> 公式サイト、企業サイト、個人サイト、モバイルサイトなど

★AfterEffectsやMayaなどを使用した映像デザイン
>> 映画・TV・販売促進用映像など

★各種印刷物のデザイン・キャラクターデザイン
>> CDのジャケット・DVDのジャケット・メニュー画面など

KAZUYO ★ STUDIO

What's New
05/10/01
映画「ギミー・ヘブン」公式サイトデザイン
>>> let's go website!!

(c) 2004-2006 KAZYO★STUDIO All Rights Reserved.

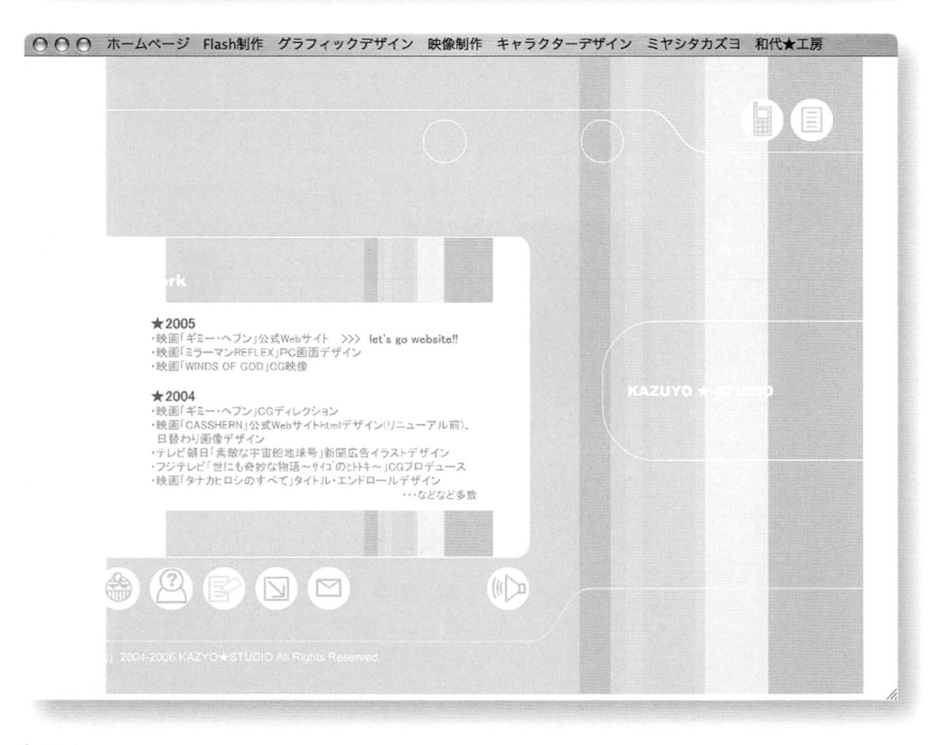

kazst.com

D: kazuyo miyashita

A: kazuyo*studio **M:** k_info@kazst.com

MARTIN HYDE | DESIGN – PRINT | WEB | MULTIMEDIA

MARTIN HYDE | DESIGN

MEDIA LINKS PDF WEB VIDEO SOUND MISC

NEWS ABOUT CONTACT LINKS

SOLAR HEATING IT WON'T COST THE EARTH

PLANET IN PERIL

conduction

SOLAR HEATING THE FUTURE LOOKS GREENER

conduction

[1]

NEWS

COPS N HOODIES BELT FOR UNCHASTE
06/02/06

ADDED THE COPS N HOODIES ART WORK FOR A BELT I HAVE DESIGNED FOR UNCHASTE.

ENVIROMENTAL ART WORK 2
04/02/06

ADDED THE SECOND PIECES OF ARTWORK FOR CONDUCTION.

ENVIROMENTAL ART WORK
21/01/06

ADDED THE FIRST IN A SERIES OF TWO PIECES OF ARTWORK FOR THE SOLAR HEATING COMPANY - CONDUCTION. THE APOCALYPTIC ARTWORK PROMOTES A STRONG MESSAGE FOR WHY WE SHOULD USE RENEWABLE ENERGY SOURCES.

INFO CONDUCTION POST CARDS DESIGN – ART | DESIGN

INFO PANNEL

LOGOS

TEL: +44 (0)1332 664438 | EMAIL: MARTIN@MARTINHYDE.CO.UK

© 2003 – 2006 MARTIN HYDE | DESIGN ALL RIGHTS RESERVED

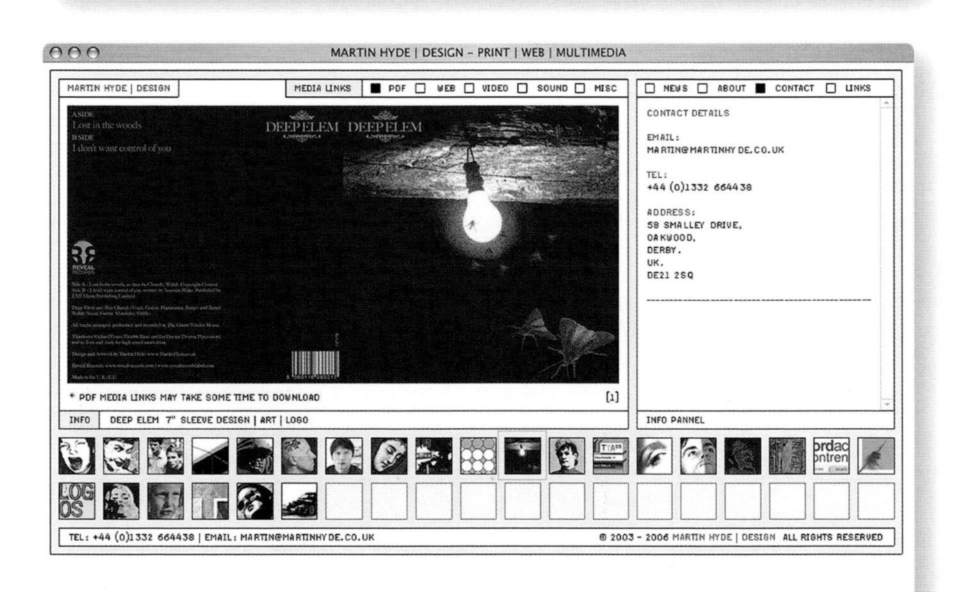

www.martinhyde.co.uk

D: martin hyde

A: martin hyde | design **M:** www.martinhyde.co.uk

www.freedominteractivedesign.com

D: shea gonyo, sabina hahn, mark ferdman **C:** josh ott, shea gonyo **P:** mark ferdman

A: freedom interactive design **M:** info@freedominteractivedesign.com

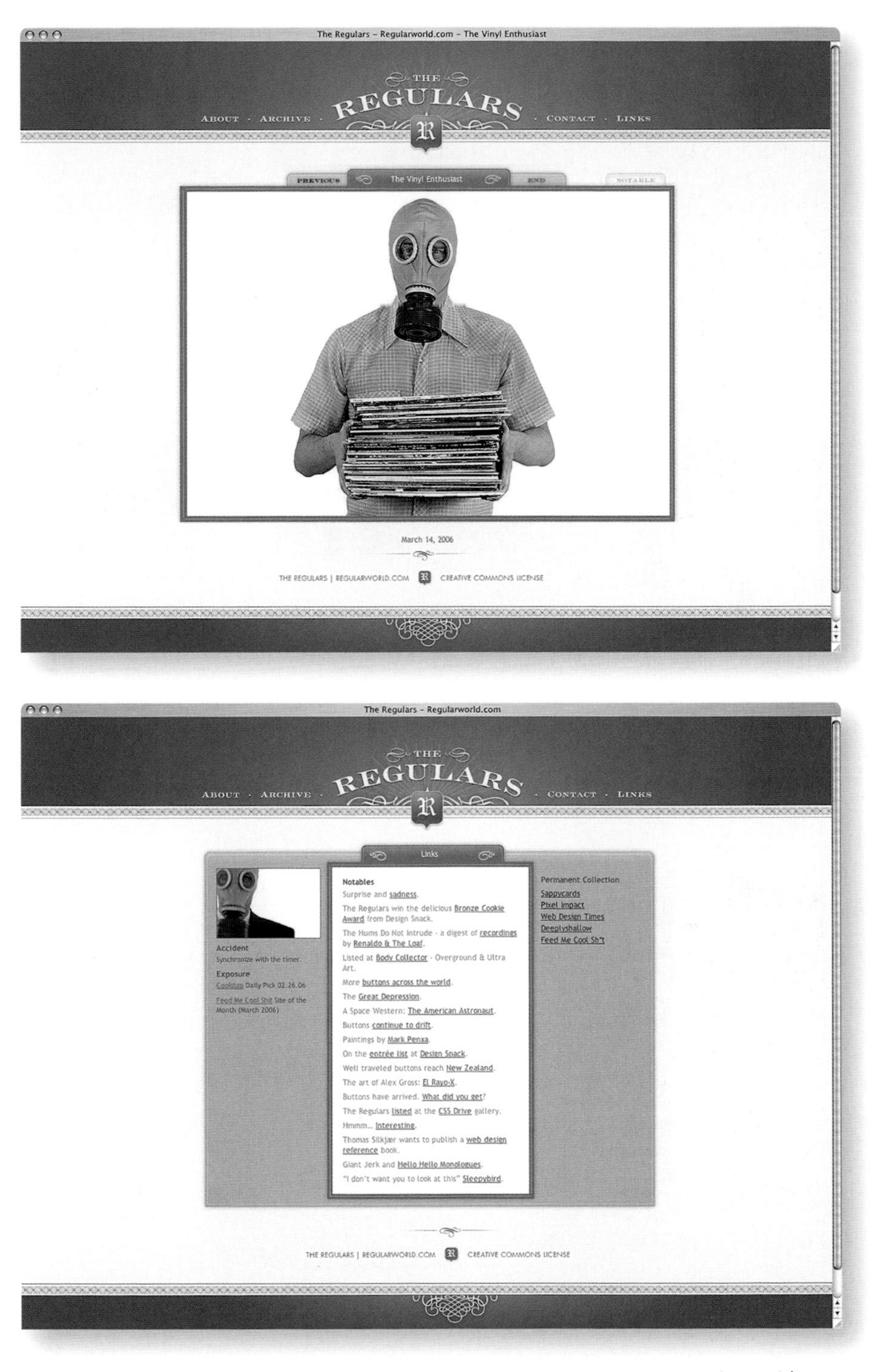

regularworld.com

D: gaston masque

A: the regulars **M:** regularworld.com

www.lettmotif.com

D: jean francois jeunet

A: lettmotif **M:** contact@lettmotif.com

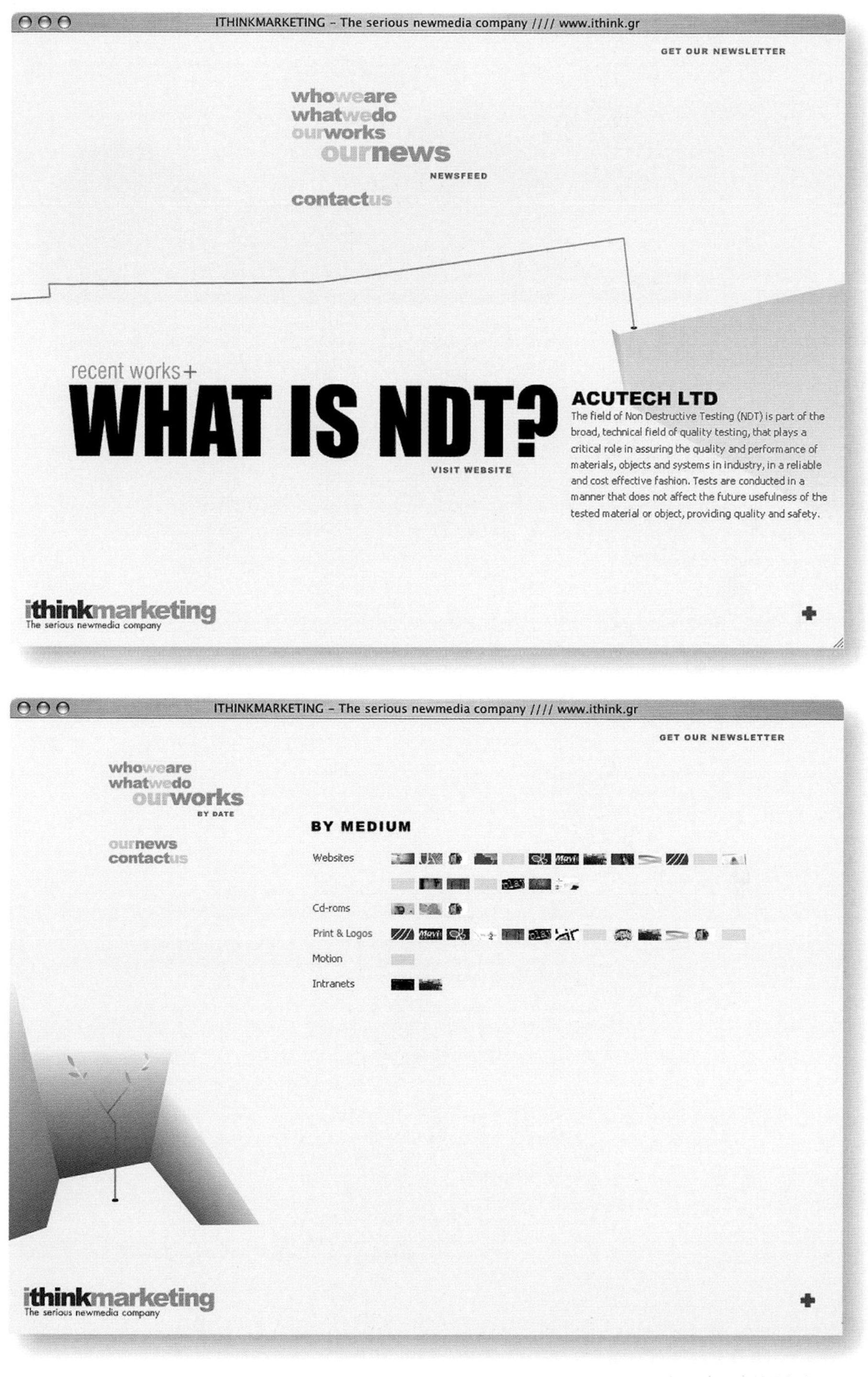

www.ithink.gr
D: ithinkmarketing **P:** stavros tsalikoglou
A: ithinkmarketing **M:** info@ithink.gr

www.cocoloco.com.au
D: mauricio perez
A: coco loco **M:** www.cocoloco.com.au

www.teil.ch
D: teil.ch
A: teil.ch **M:** info@teil.ch

www.darkybuthappy.free.fr

D: élisa bottin

M: elisa.bottin@free.fr

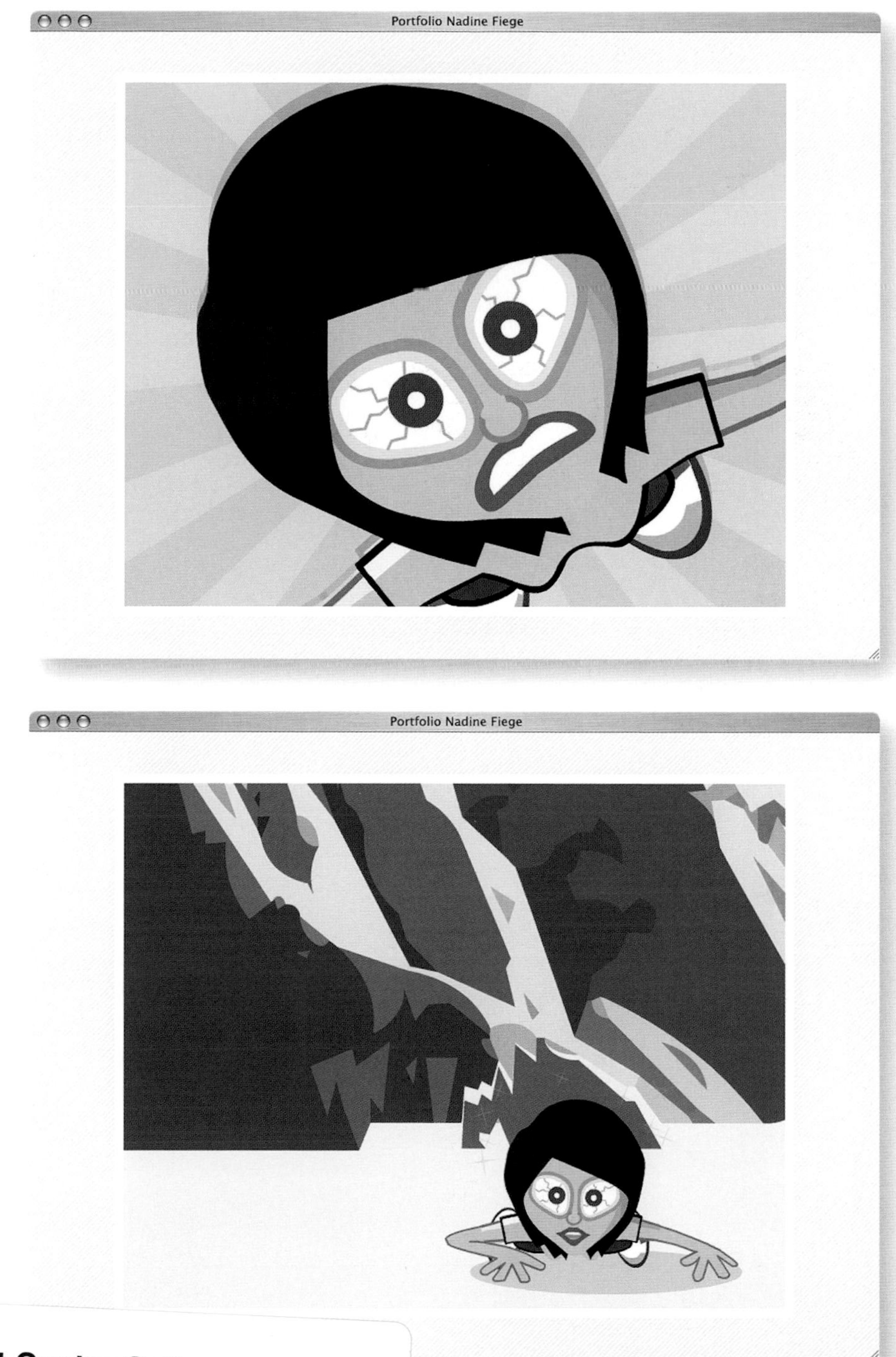

www.nadinefiege.de
D: nadine fiege
M: kontakt@nadinefiege.de

dixonbaxi welcomes you

dixonbaxi

UNIT 4D
PRINTING HOUSE YARD
HACKNEY ROAD
LONDON E2 7PR
T 0207 6131700

EMAIL US

ABOUT US

dixonbaxi welcomes you

IT'S GONNA BE BIG

www.dixonbaxi.com

D: dixonbaxi

A: dixonbaxi **M:** info@dixonbaxi.com

www.sonice.be

D: fred vandenbreede **C:** olivier leemans **P:** laurent duffaut

A: so nice **M:** info@sonice.be

www.insanelab.net

D: bibi gloaguen, juan díaz-faes **C:** alberto alvarez **P:** alberto alvarez

A: insane **M:** crash@insanelab.net

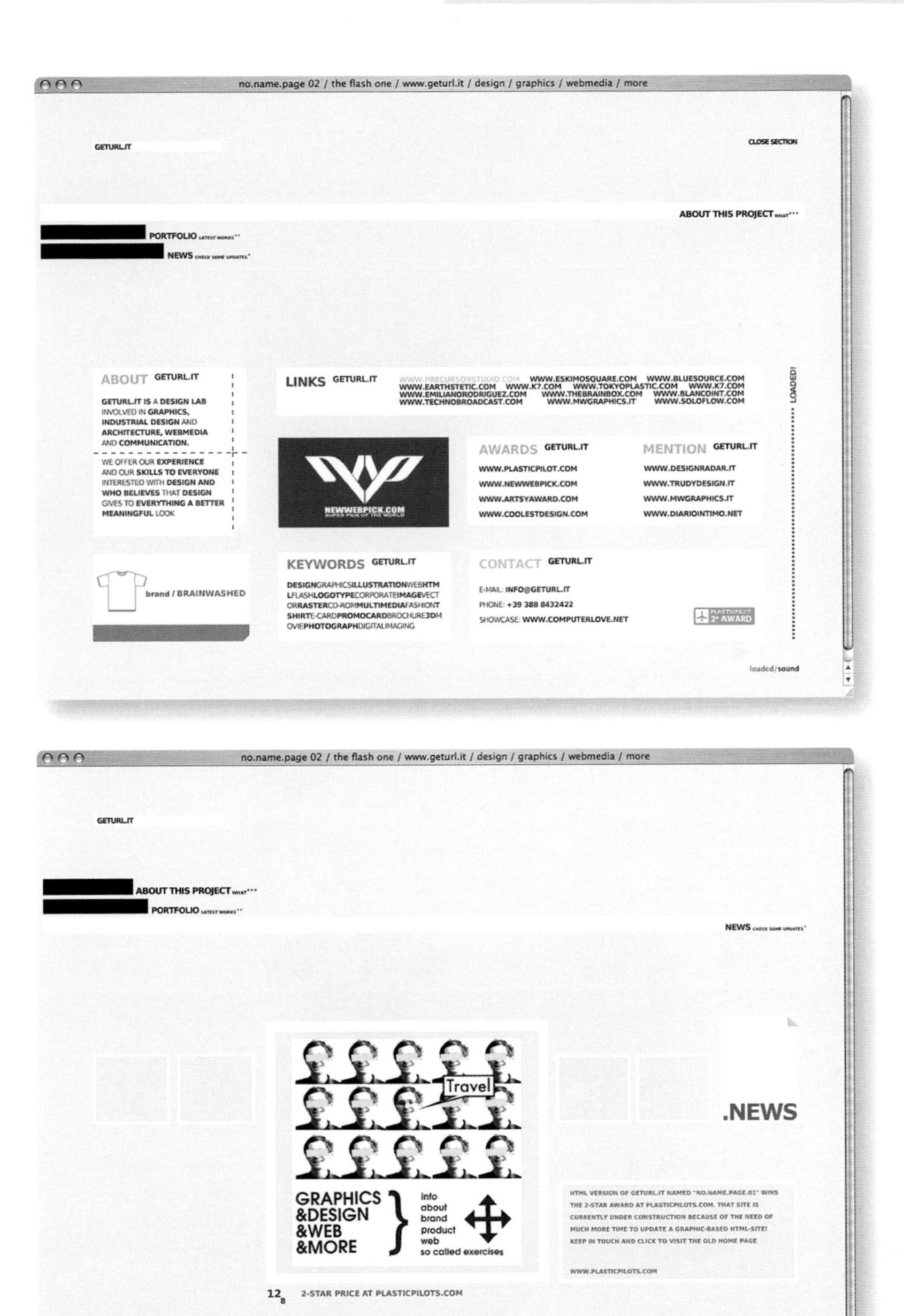

www.geturl.it
D: ivan pedri
A: ivan pedri M: info@geturl.it

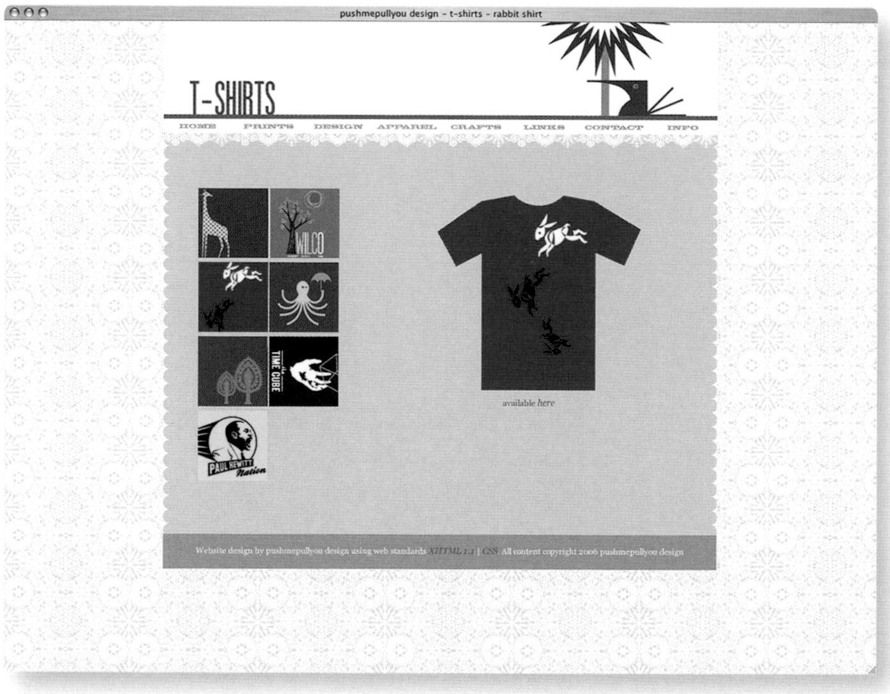

www.pushmepullyoudesign.com

D: eleanor grosch

A: pushmepullyou design **M:** pushmepullyoudesign@gmail.com

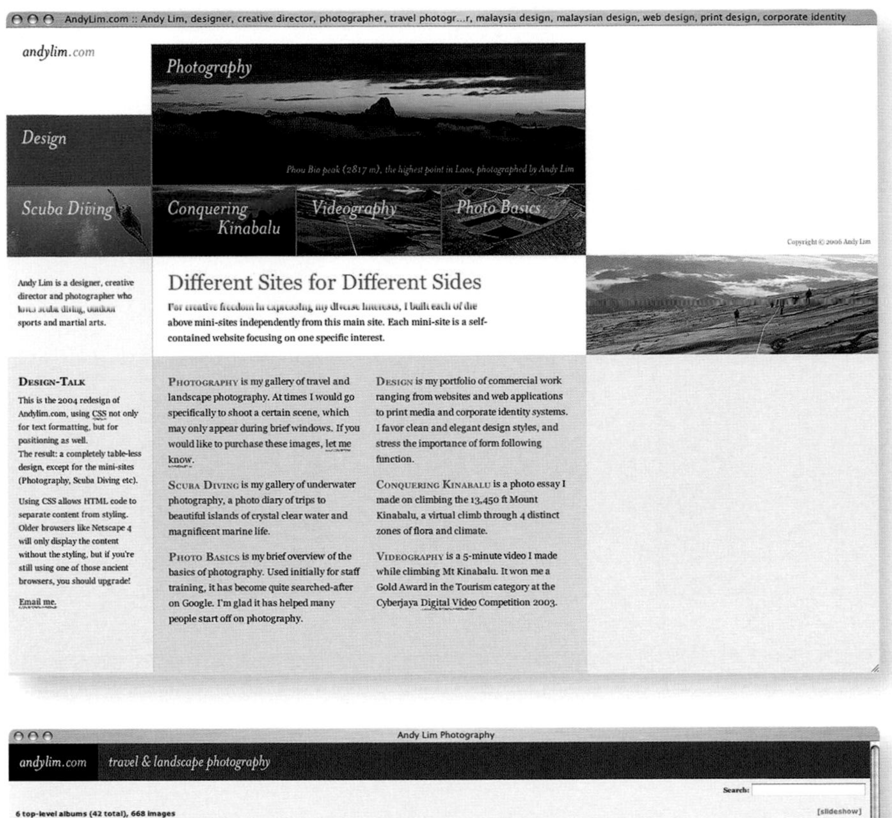

Andy Lim Photography

andylim.com travel & landscape photography

Search:

6 top-level albums (42 total), 668 images

[slideshow]

Welcome to a selection of my outdoor landscape and travel photography. All these and more are available from my portfolio at Alamy Images and my stock photography assignments at Inmagine Stock Photography. I'm also available for assignments and event photography.

Image Library:
All images in this gallery are protected by copyright and may not be copied, reproduced or republished in any form without my permission. If you would like to use any of these images, they are available for sale via Alamy Images, or you can contact me directly for a quote.

Technical Quality:
I pay painstaking attention to technical quality, both during the picture-taking moment as well as during post-production. All my images print to sizes of 30x45cm (11x17") at 300dpi with excellent sharpness. My panoramic images can be used at even bigger sizes, optimized for large high-quality printing. If you intend to buy an image but would like to inspect the image quality at 100% magnification, I can email partial crops of the original files for inspection.

Camera Gear:
Nikon D70 digital SLR, 10-20mm, 18-70mm, 70-300mm, 50mm, Manfrotto 055 Pro, Gitzo 1027, Nikon SB-600. For underwater photography I use a Canon S50. In the past, I shot 35mm slide film with Nikon and Pentax SLR cameras, and dabbled with black-and-white darkroom printing.

Selling Your Photos:
If you have some photos that are just sitting in your computer, you might as well let them make some money for you. Microstock agencies let almost anyone earn money from their photos:
Shutterstock (my current returns: USD130/mth)
iStockphoto (my current returns: USD70/mth)

- Andy Lim

Laos

8 albums of scenes from Luang Prabang, Vientiane, Xieng Khouang, Mekong River, Annam Highlands, Vang Vieng and rural Hmong village life.

Updated on 01/18/06.
8 items, 860 visits since 01/03/06.

Thailand

3 albums from Phi Phi Island, Pileh Bay, Maya Bay, Lo Sama Bay, Poda Island, Krabi and Bangkok.

Updated on 12/15/05.
3 items, 5258 visits since 11/05/03.

Malaysia

13 albums containing scenes from Mount Kinabalu, Bukit Tabur, Perhentian Island, Redang Island, Paya Indah, Langkawi, Pantai Kerachut, Batu Feringghi, Penang, Sabah, Selangor.

Updated on 10/05/05.
13 items, 10544 visits since 11/05/03.

www.andylim.com
D: andy lim
A: andy lim **M:** www.andylim.com

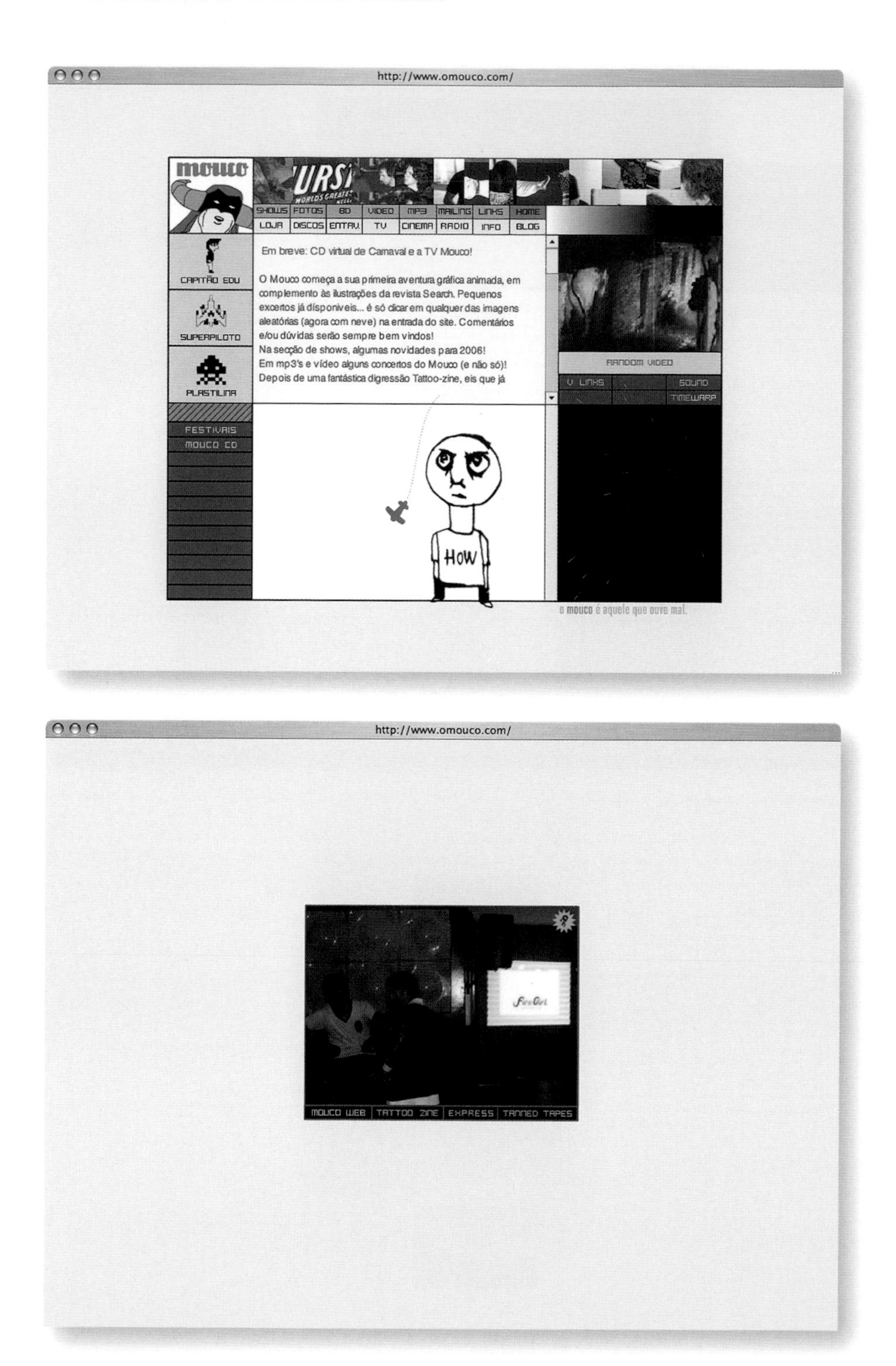

www.omouco.com

D: augusto lima

A: plastilina design **M:** plasti75@hotmail.com

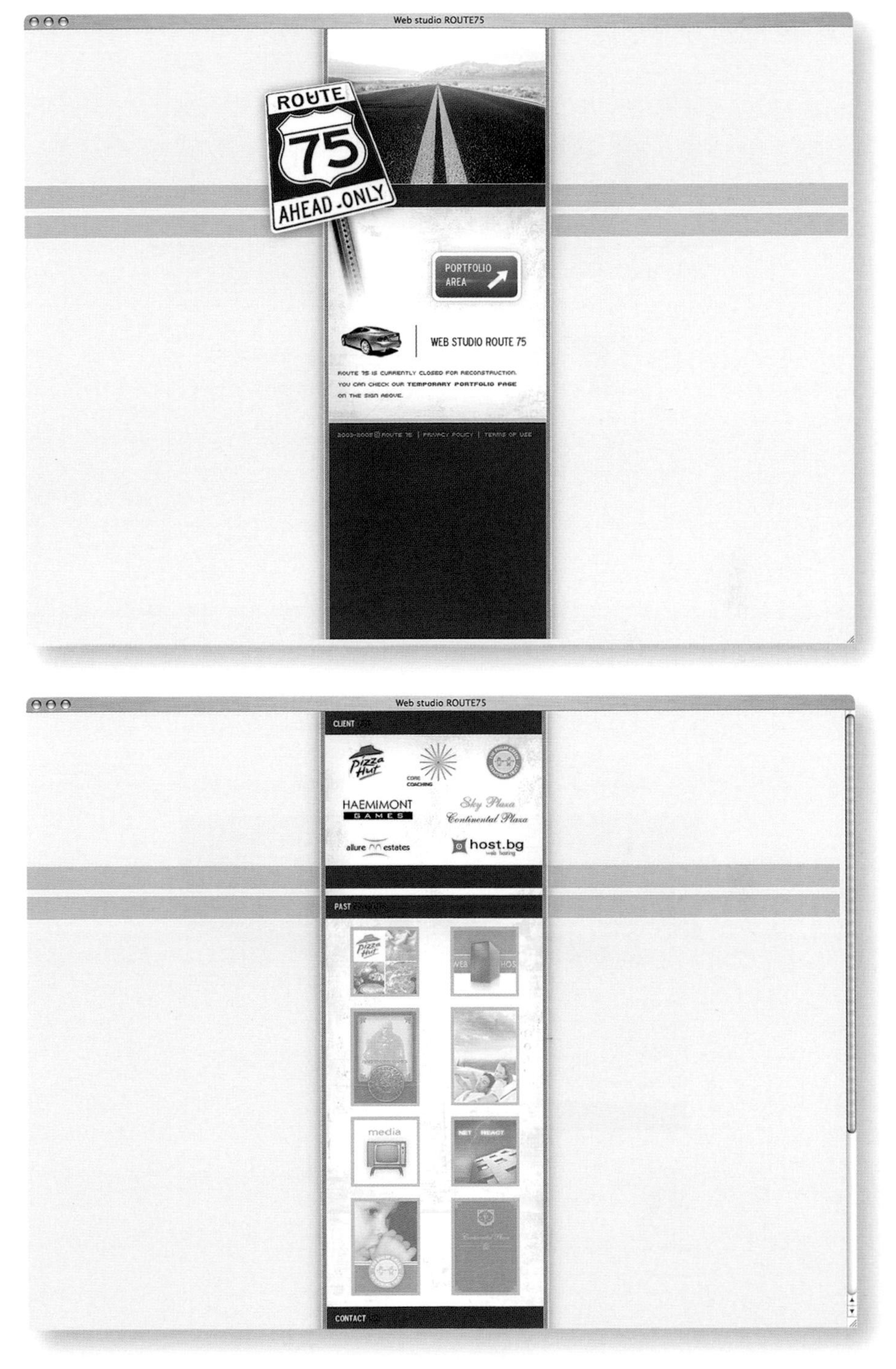

www.route75.com

D: hristo spasunin

A: route 75 M: info@route75.com

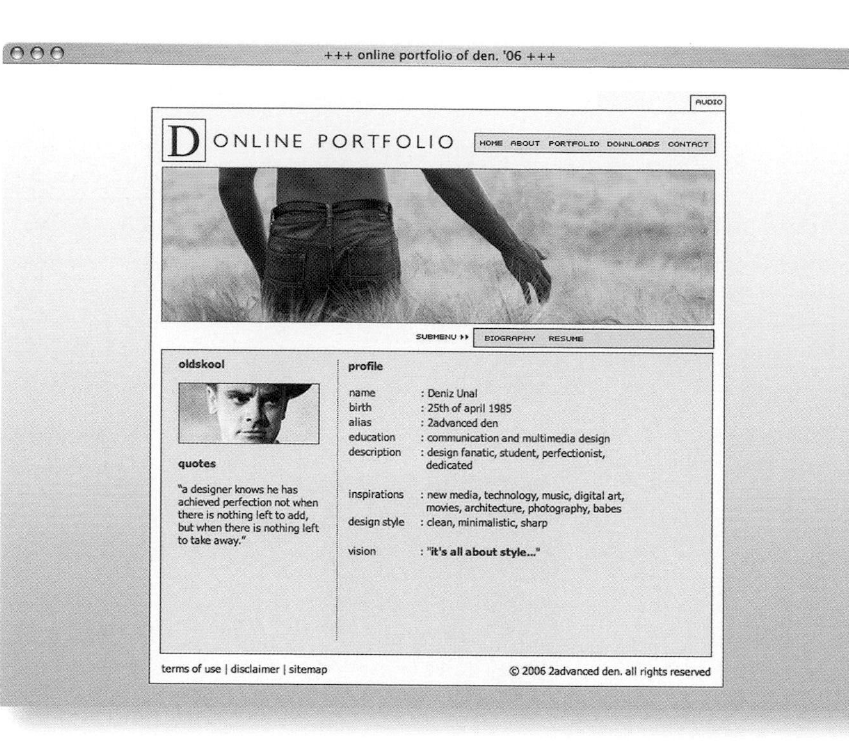

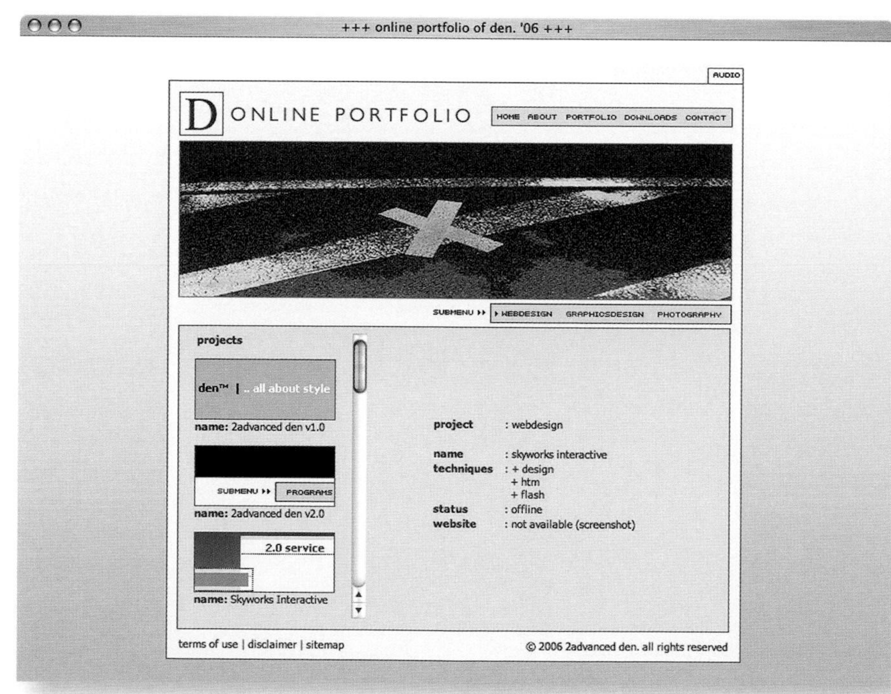

www.den-online.nl/home.htm

D: d. unal

M: mail@den-online.nl

www.vierhoog.nl

D: chris van seggelen

A: vier hoog grafisch ontwerp M: www.vierhoog.nl

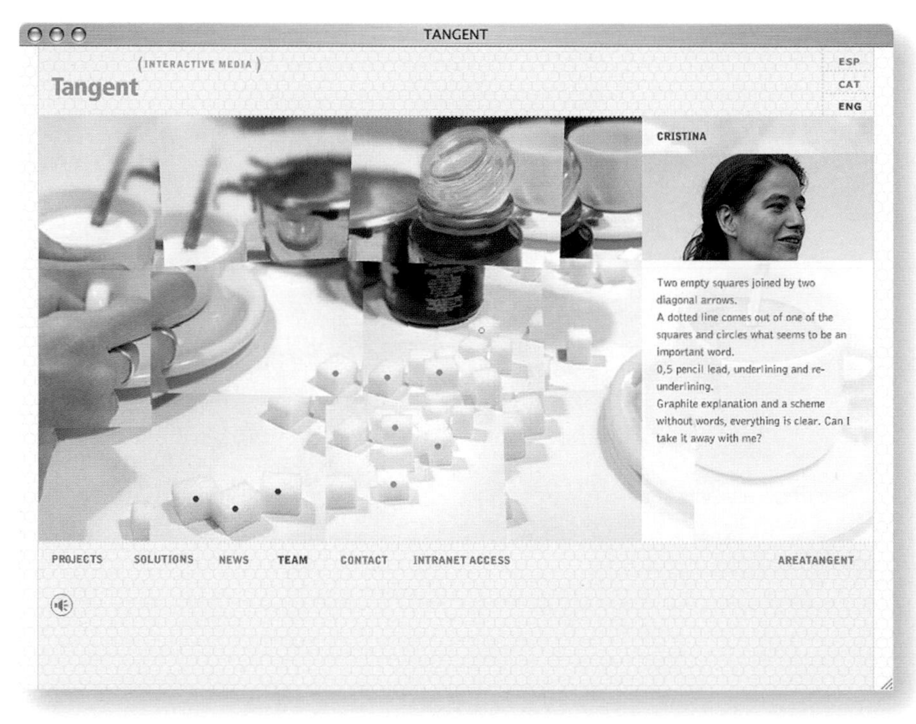

www.tangent.es

D: jorge ferrera **C:** raúl fernandez **P:** cristian cisa, josep mª marimon

A: tangent audiovisual **M:** info@tangent.es

:: CONSUMAestudio Proyectos con vida! :: Diseño Grafico :: Id... :: Diseño Web Corporativo :: Oviedo 984 084 987 Asturias ::

consumaestudio®

HOME EDITORIAL IDENTIDAD BRAND WEBSITES ILUSTRACION

:: DESARROLLO EDITORIAL

MAGISTRAL Hoteles
Residencial CAYON
AGENDA Escolar
PGMWin Producto
Jornadas ON ASTUR
Jornadas ON ITALIA
Jornadas ON ARROZ
ASACUNA Desplegable
Libro JGPA. Jean D.
Libro JGPA. Viviane R.

... editorial

AREAS

METODO

EL ESTUDIO

NEWS

AVISO LEGAL

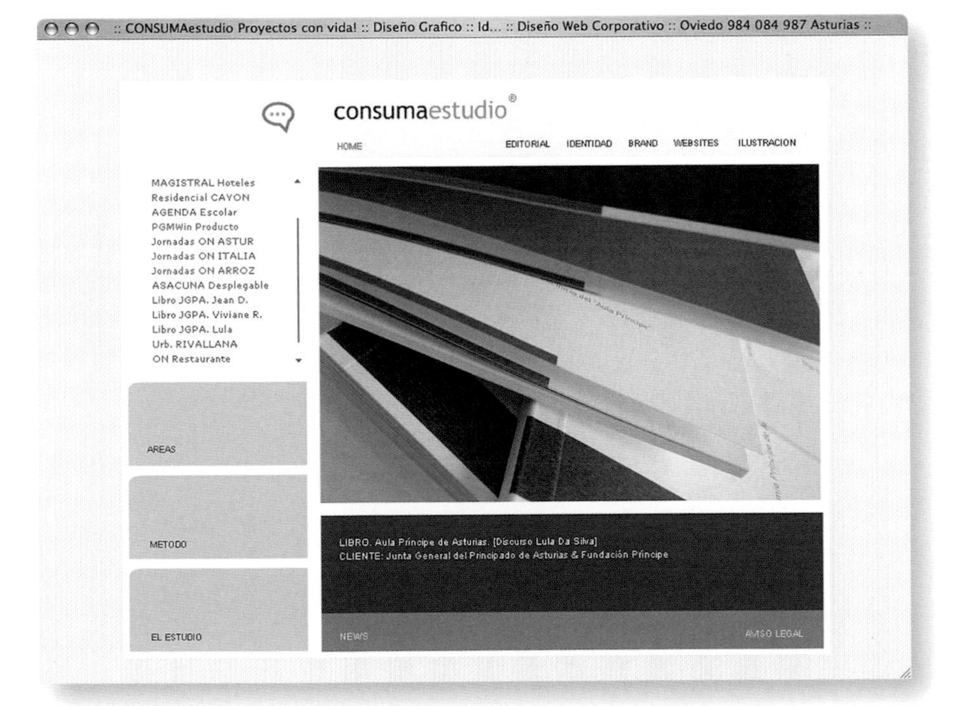

www.consumaestudio.com

D: frank pérez **C:** pablo rodríguez, angel garcía

A: consumaestudio® **M:** hola@consumaestudio.com

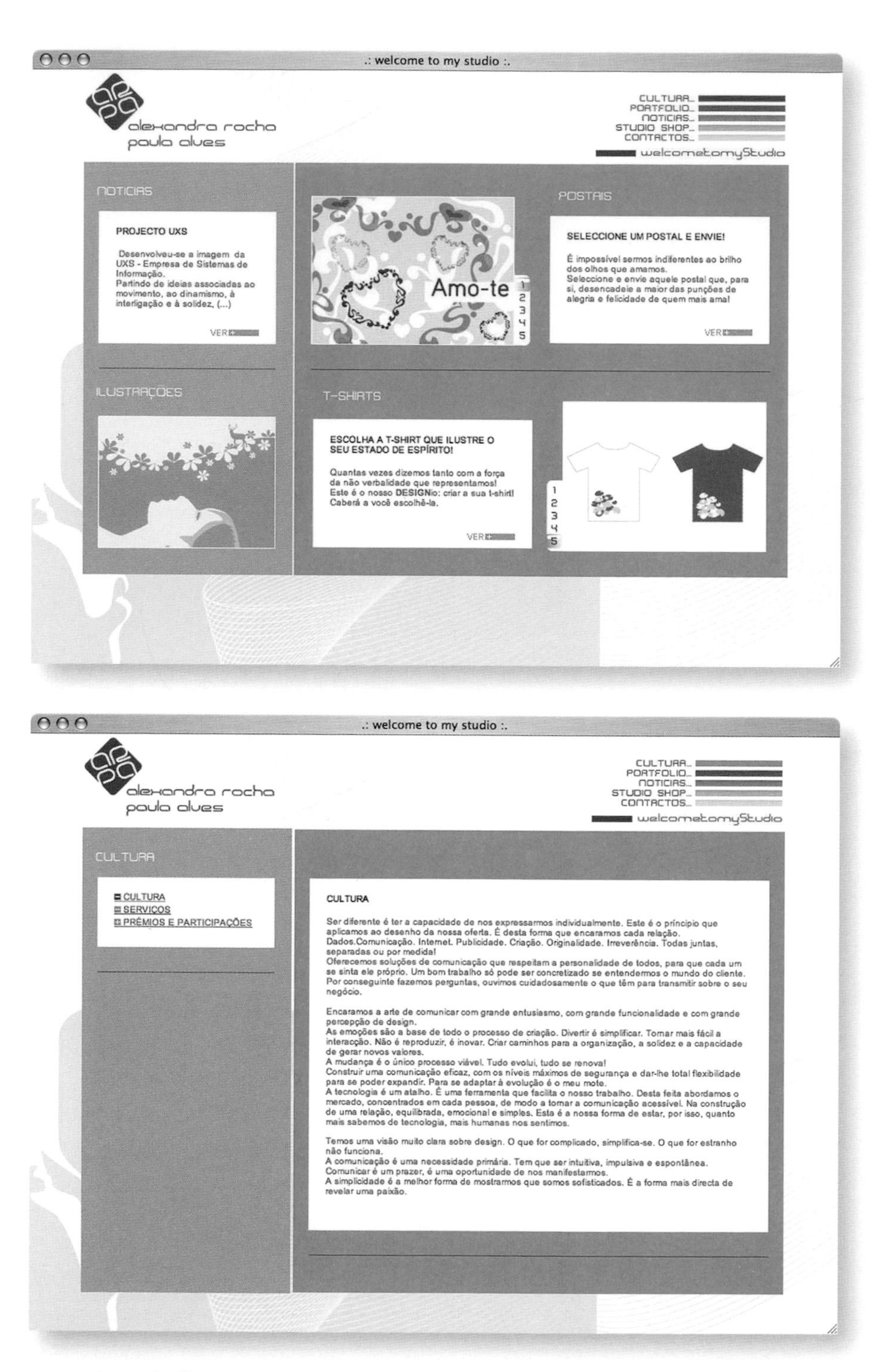

www.gotomystudio.com

D: alexandra rocha, paula alves **C:** alexandra rocha, susana teixeira, hélder ribeiro

M: geral@gotomystudio.com

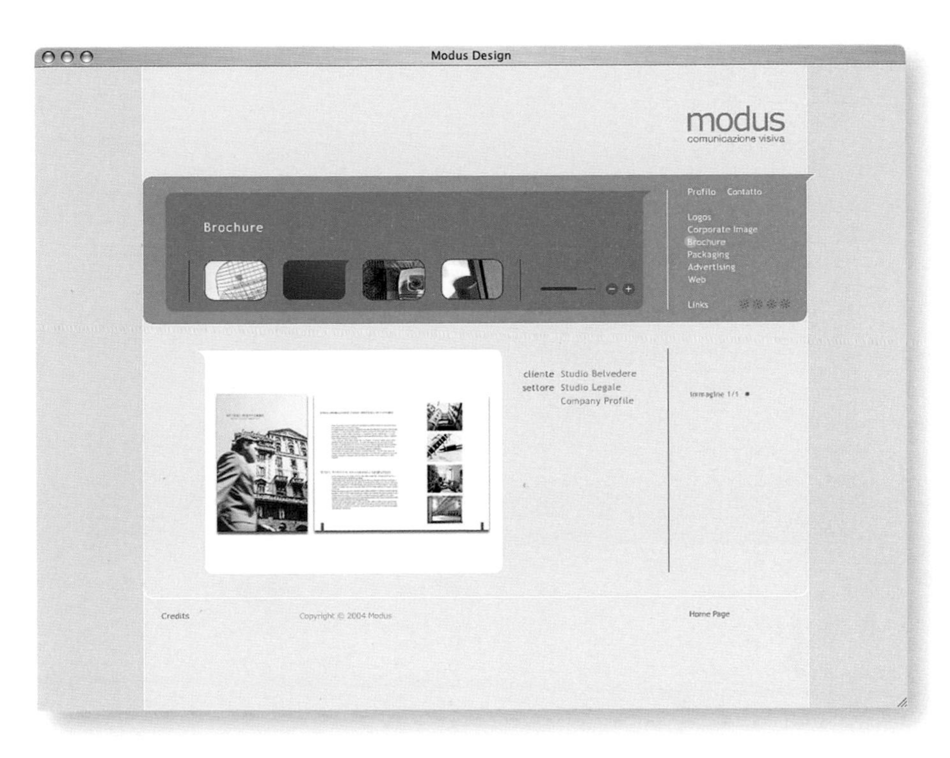

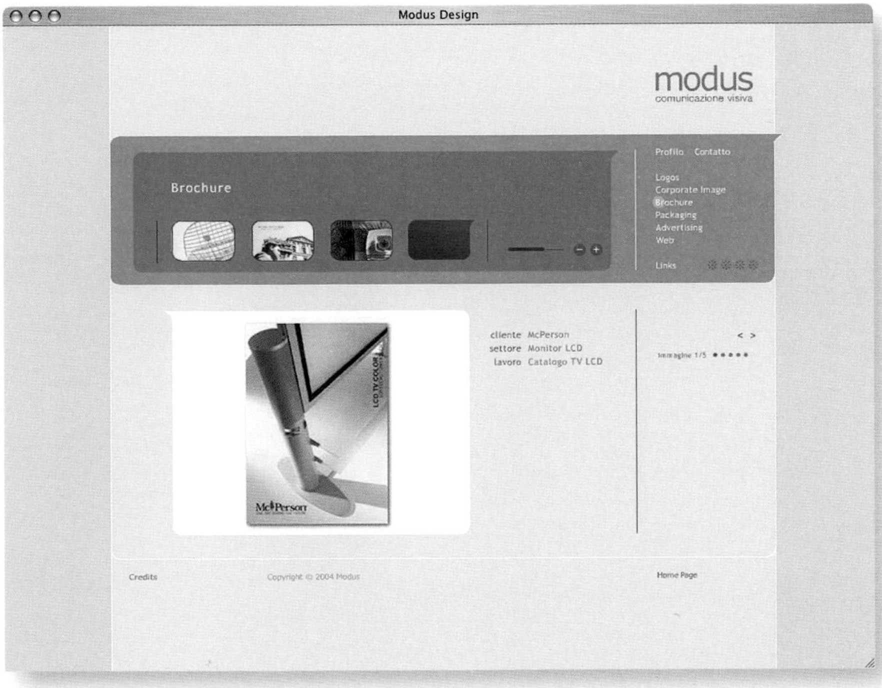

www.modus.it

D: cristina silva, luca basili **C:** alessandra tagliabue

A: modus comunicazione visiva, luca basili **M:** cristina@modus.it

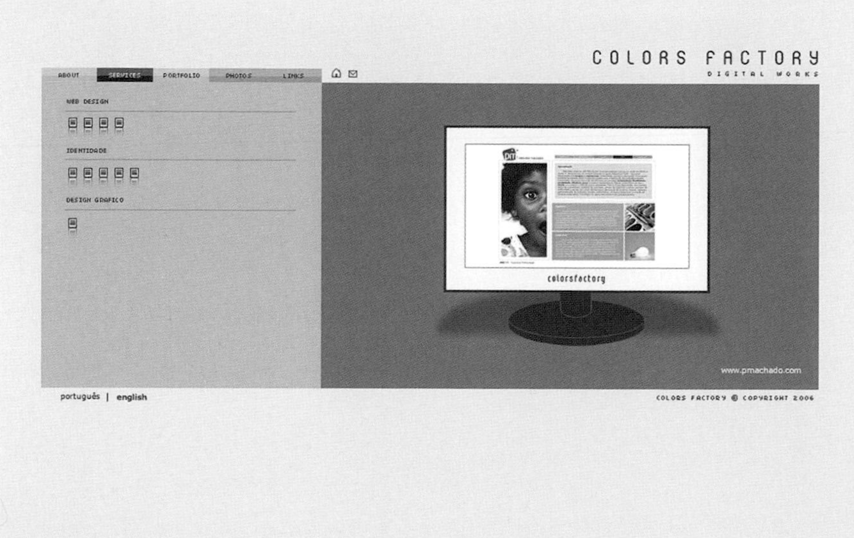

www.colorsfactory.com

D: ricardo ferreira

A: colors factory **M:** info@colorsfactory.com

www.liquiddesignsindia.com

D: kushal grover

A: liquid designs india **M:** kushalgrover@gmail.com

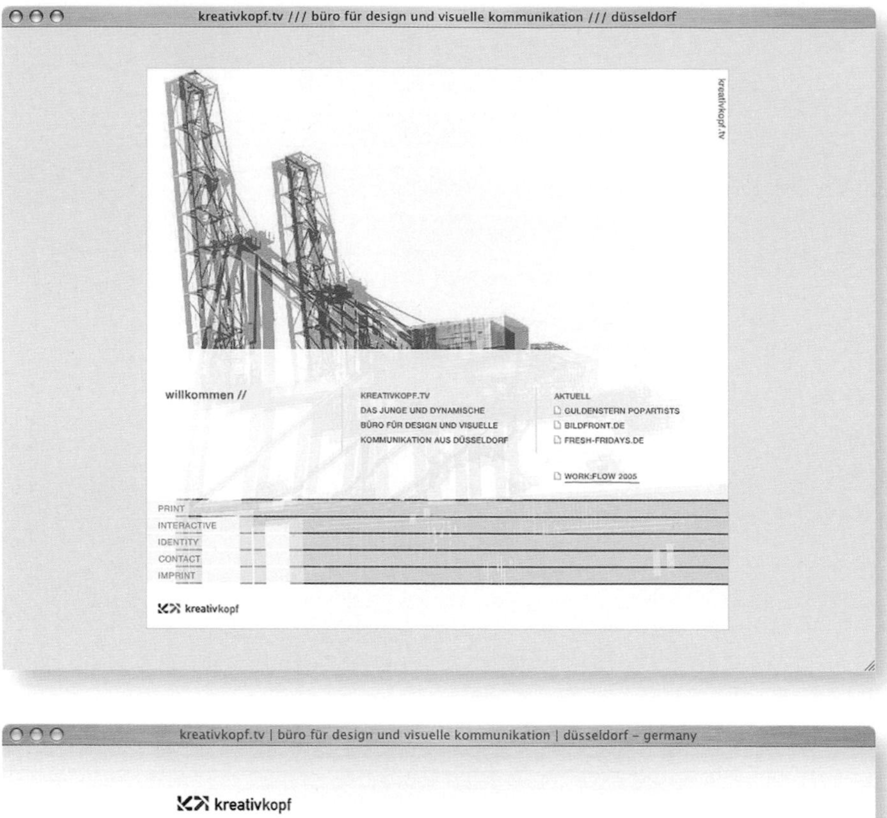

www.kreativkopf.tv

D: jan weiss

A: www.kreativkopf.tv **M:** j.weiss@kreativkopf.tv

www.julia-alic-design.de

D: julia alic C: mark siepen P: julia alic

M: info@julia-alic-design.de

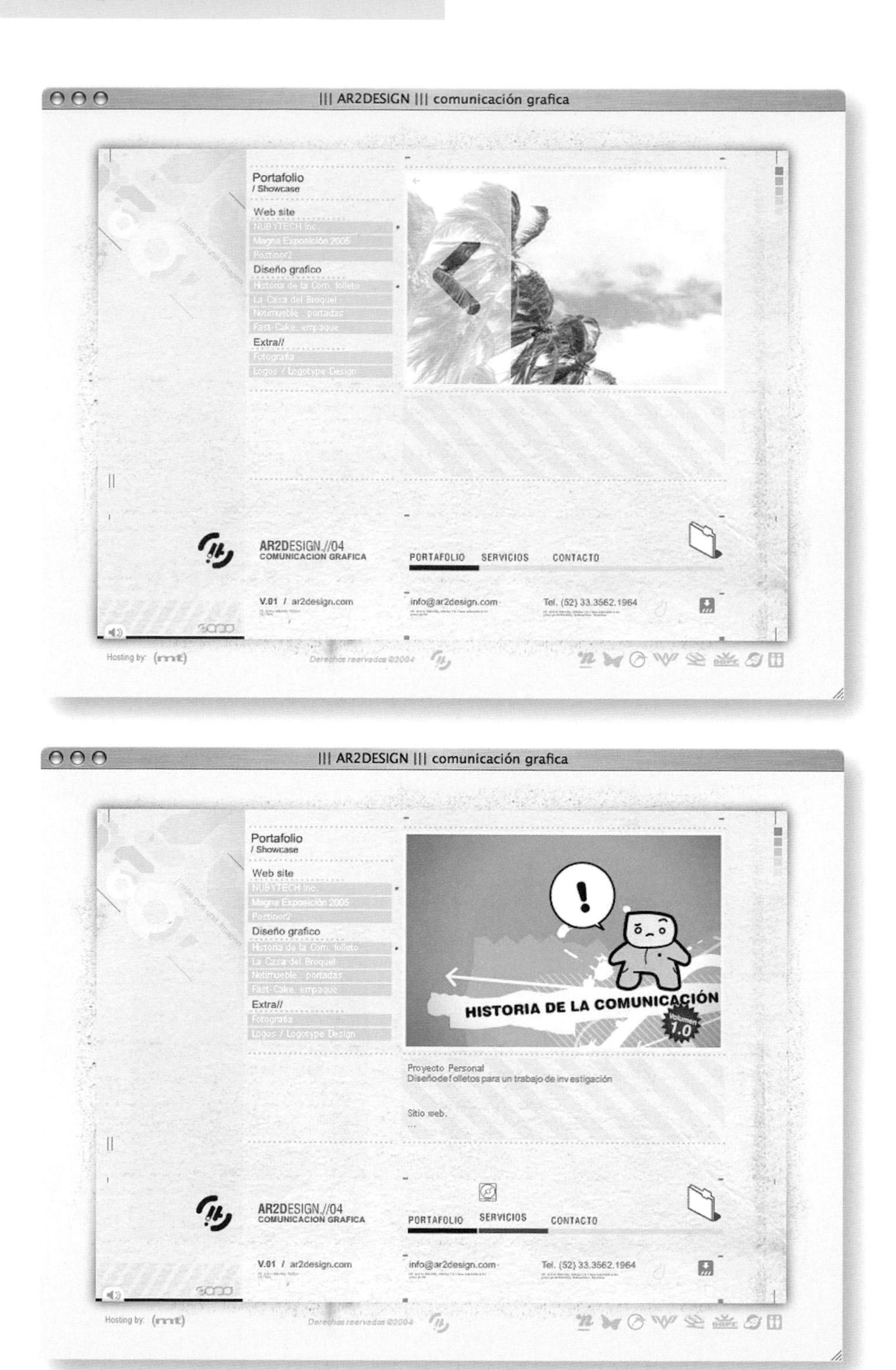

www.ar2design.com

D: arturo esparza

A: ar2design **M:** ar2@ar2design.com

www.djbfacilitair.nl

D: koos dekker

A: djbfacilitair **M:** koos@djbfacilitair.nl

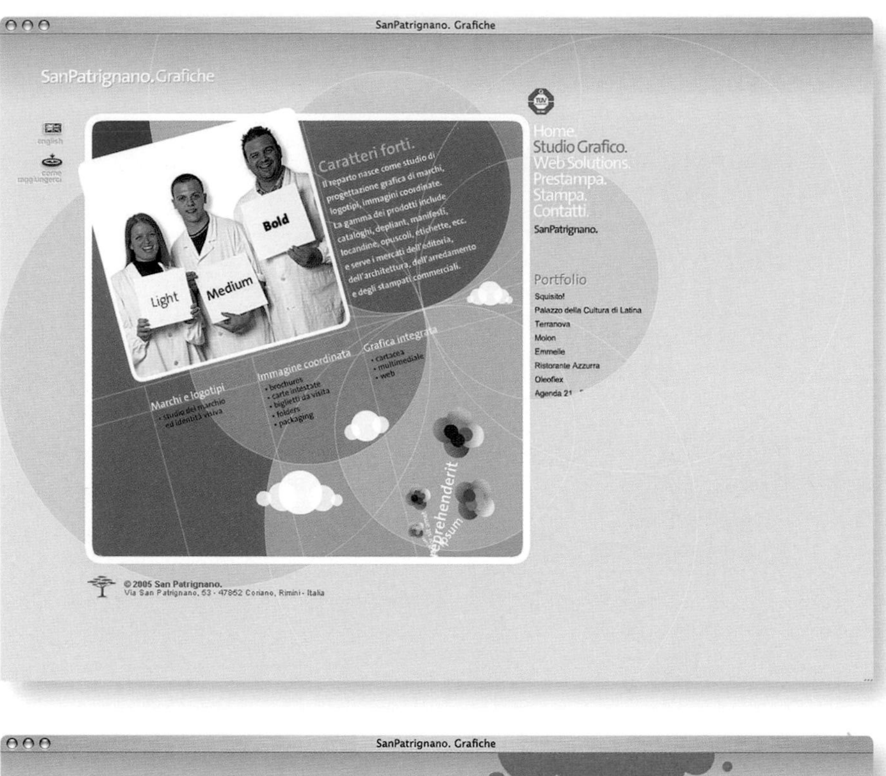

grafiche.sanpatrignano.org

D: andrea bianchi **P:** sanpatrignano. grafiche
A: sanpatrignano. grafiche **M:** andbia@gmail.com

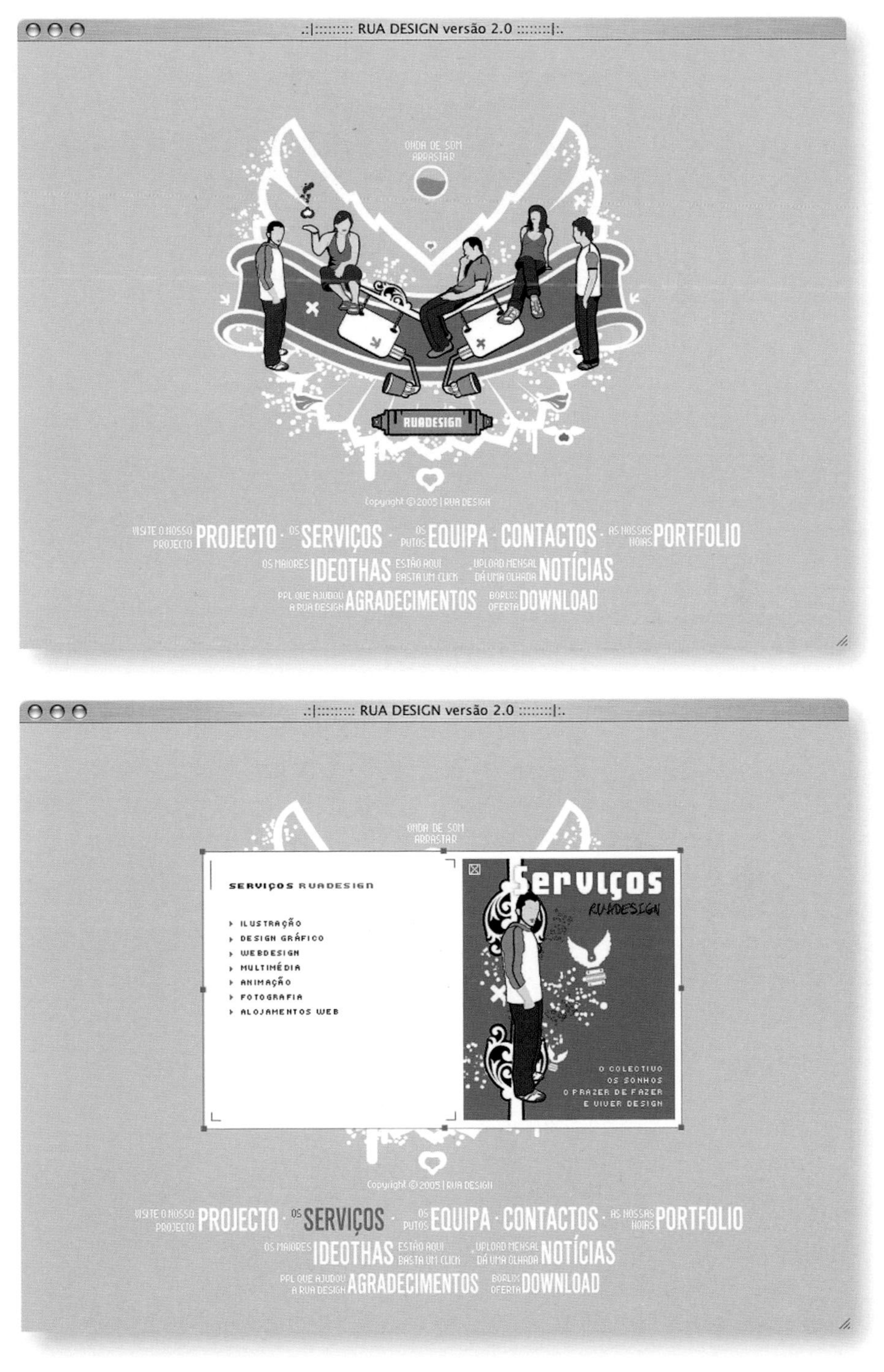

www.ruadesign.net

D: ruadesign

A: ruadesign **M:** geral@ruadesign.net

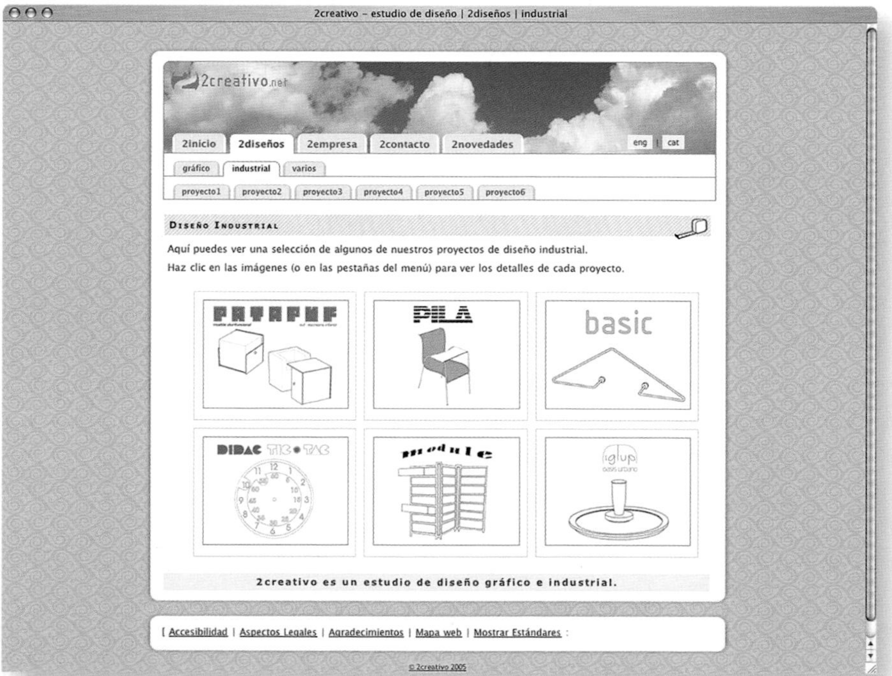

www.2creativo.net

D: 2creativo

A: 2creativo M: 2creativo@2creativo.net

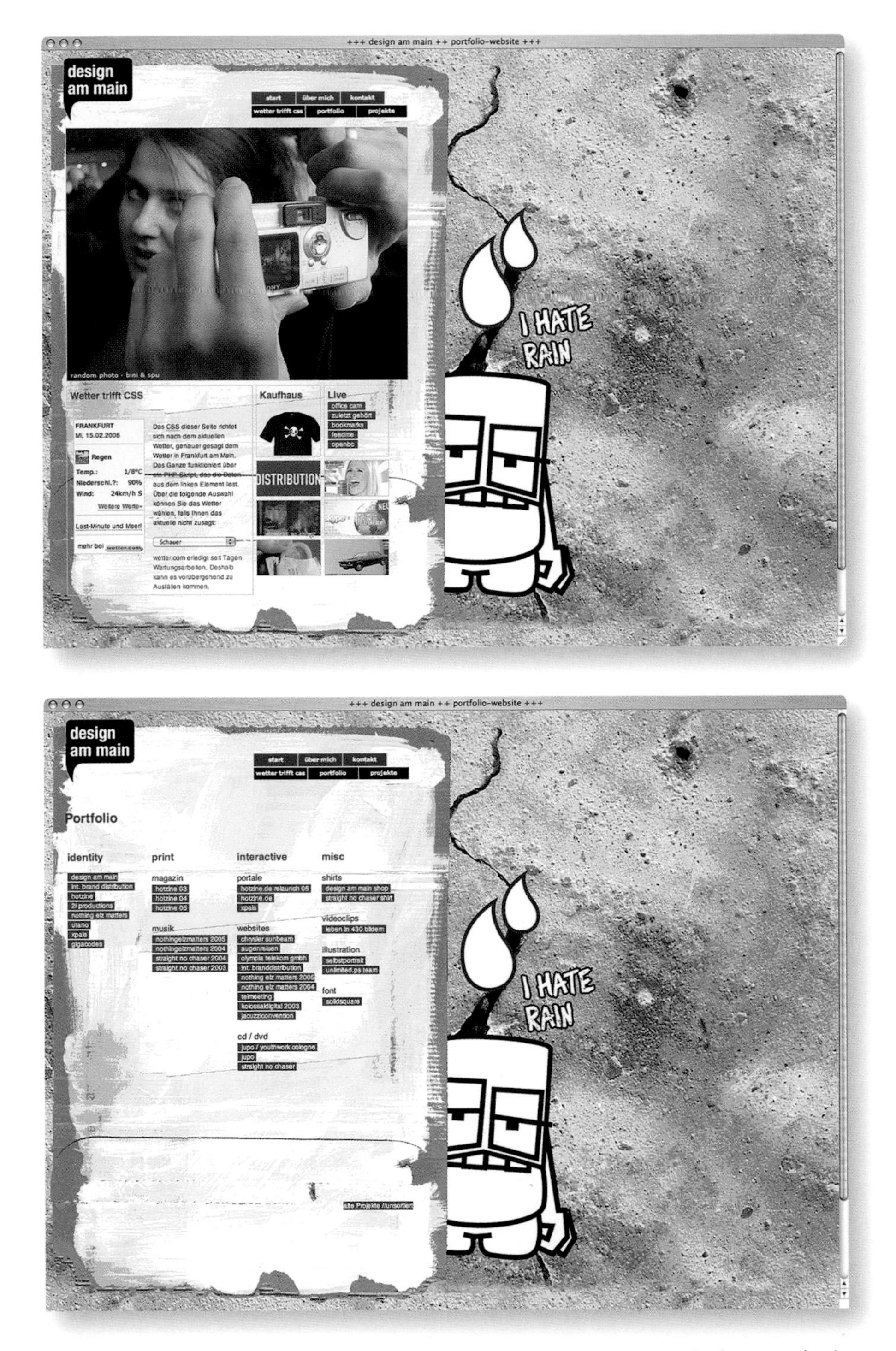

www.designammain.de
D: christian kunz
A: kolossaldigital.de **M:** ck@kolossaldigital.de

THIS WAY DESIGN

this way design

Cover photo: Kim Ramberhaug

This website features a selection of my work.

Some of the clients I've had the pleasure of working with include Telenor, Telia, Siemens, Tine, Nexans, St.Olavs Hospital, De Norske Bokklubbene, Egmont Serieforlaget, Filmtilsynet, Arthaus and Natt&Dag.

This Way Design
c/o Håvard Gjelseth
Stensgata 40b
0451 Oslo
Org: 981 885 236
Phone: +47 41 45 46 42

Thanx to: Almir Busevac for help with flash programming, Chris Pelsor for proofreading, and Ken Olling for inspiration.

Respect to my mentor
Tore Uluik

Portfolio Contents

03

RECENT WORK
SUPERMERCADO
ILLUSTRATION ETC.
PAGE 82

Supermercado started as an online project for artists from South Europe in April 2004. From 28th October to 6th November an exhibition was held in Oslo, Norway, and I did the promotion of the event, involving profile, poster, invitation and catalogue. Supermercado, meaning supermarket, I chose the shopping bag as the metaphor and object for the design. Also, I designed a logo for each of the artists, becoming a store within this supermarket.

CLICK, OR CLICK-DRAG CORNERS TO GO TO NEXT OR PREVIOUS PAGE
(you can also use your arrow keys)

THIS WAY DESIGN

this way design

One of Norway's best known schools of art and music, and the birthplace for bands such as Motorpsycho and production facility Stargate Studios. I did the profile and illustrations for both website and various print materials: a logo with a classic typeface and an energetic twist meets the photocopy-dada-style-illustrations in a happy marriage.

TRØNDERTUN
FOLKEHØGSKOLE

www.thiswaydesign.com

D: håvard gjelseth **C:** almir busevac **P:** håvard gjelseth

A: this way design **M:** hgjelseth@thiswaydesign.com

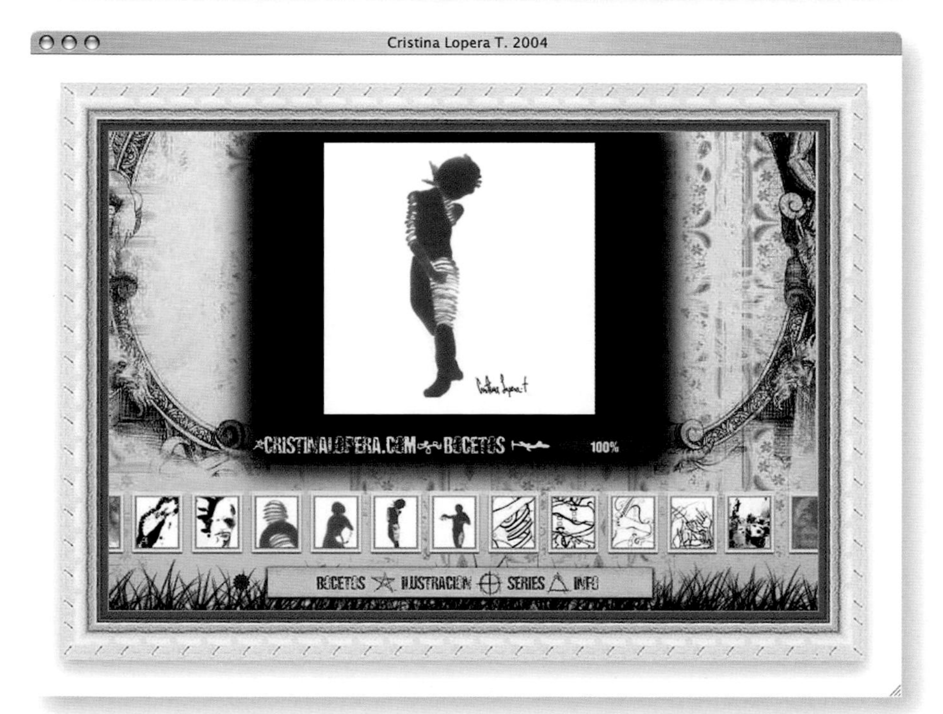

www.cristinalopera.com

D: ragde **C:** ragde **P:** cristina lopera

A: ragde.com **M:** info@ragde.com

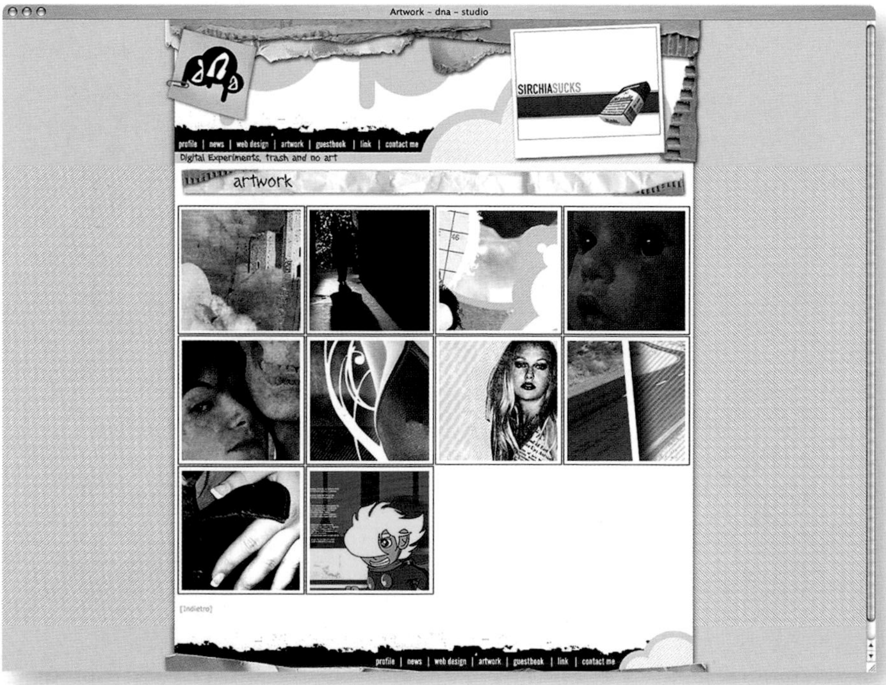

www.dna-studio.biz

D: marco di natale

A: dna studio **M:** marco@dna-studio.biz

www.sirang.com

D: mo. arian

A: sirang rasaneh **M:** arian@sirang.net

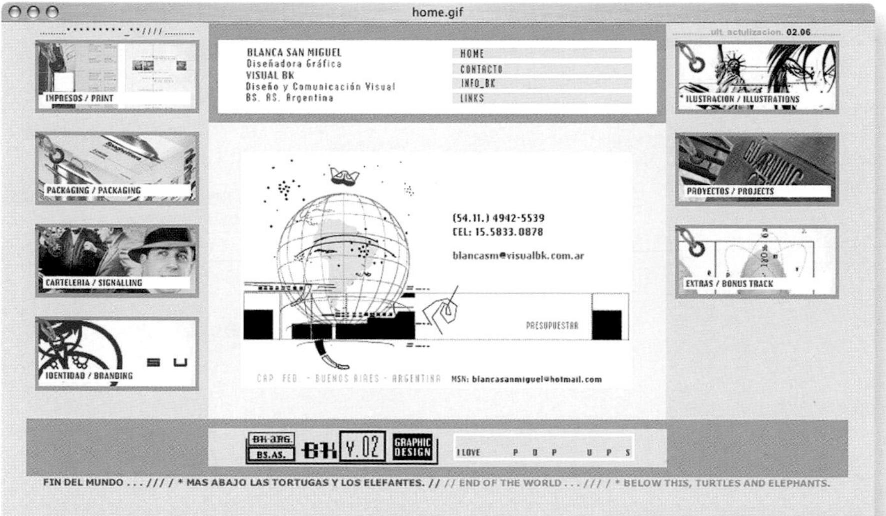

www.visualbk.com.ar

D: blanca san miguel

A: visual_bk **M:** blancasm@visualbk.com.ar

www.wtf7.com

D: nemanja nenadic

A: graphicstyle **M:** www.graphicstyle.net

+Lucky BeiJing:Graphic,Illustrator,Photos,Design+

THE-AOAO-VISION V1.0 ++

NEWS | ABOUT | VISUAL | GUESTBOOK | CONTACT

AOAOVISION.COM是结集了aoao和他朋友们独立创作作品的线上展示和交流平台，中文名叫“九喜”，取无穷无尽的中国传统意味。aoao是一位年轻的平面设计师。于2002年毕业于中国北京中央民族大学艺术设计专业，之后曾先后就职于北京经纬设计公司（ORBDESIGN）和一家位于北京老城边的颇具个性的名为“子午(ZERO)”的设计公司。目前，他效力于北京电通(DENTSU)广告公司任职平面设计师。

自从1998年开始，aoao开始了他的平面设计之旅，虽然这个行业现在有了各种花样不同的名称和性质，但他一直执着于他从儿时开始的兴趣并延伸至今－－－对于８０年代日本漫画的痴迷，并把喜爱的插图临摹下来。在2003年，他意识到中国大陆正在面临一个面对世界而重新建立自信的时代，在这样的洪流下，中国对外文化形象的输出成为这一代本土设计师不可逃避的责任之一。而视觉符号正是文化形象的载体之一，于是，他选择中国文化中心“北京”文化作为创作概念的出发点，开始尝试并付诸行动，希望基于一系列独立设计开而发出能够与世界沟通的具有北京文化特征的视觉符号，并在这种试验过程中体验独立创作的乐趣。

站点中的visual板块里包括了他近半年中的矢量图形和静态影像作品，第一期的主题是“Lucky BeiJing”。未来，他会从上述概念出发定期围绕不同的主题方向进行平面视觉表现并刊登；他还会在这里展示来自他朋友的声音和多媒体作品。有兴趣的话你可以通过留言板或者EMAIL、MSN的方式跟他在线交流。他说：“我感谢我的父母，爱人和朋友，同样感谢那些带给我创作灵感的在世界各地的前辈。从前活的太自我，现在到了该做些有意思的事的时候了...”

English

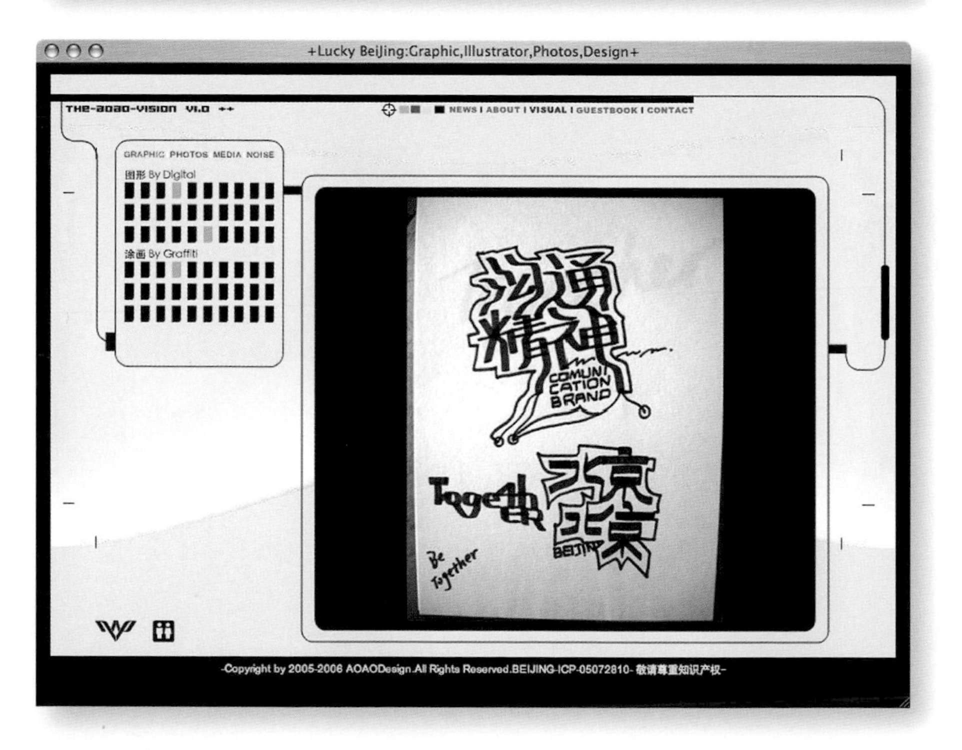

www.aoaovision.com

D: lin ao **C:** feng chen, lin ao **P:** nine-up studio

M: aoao@aoaovision.com

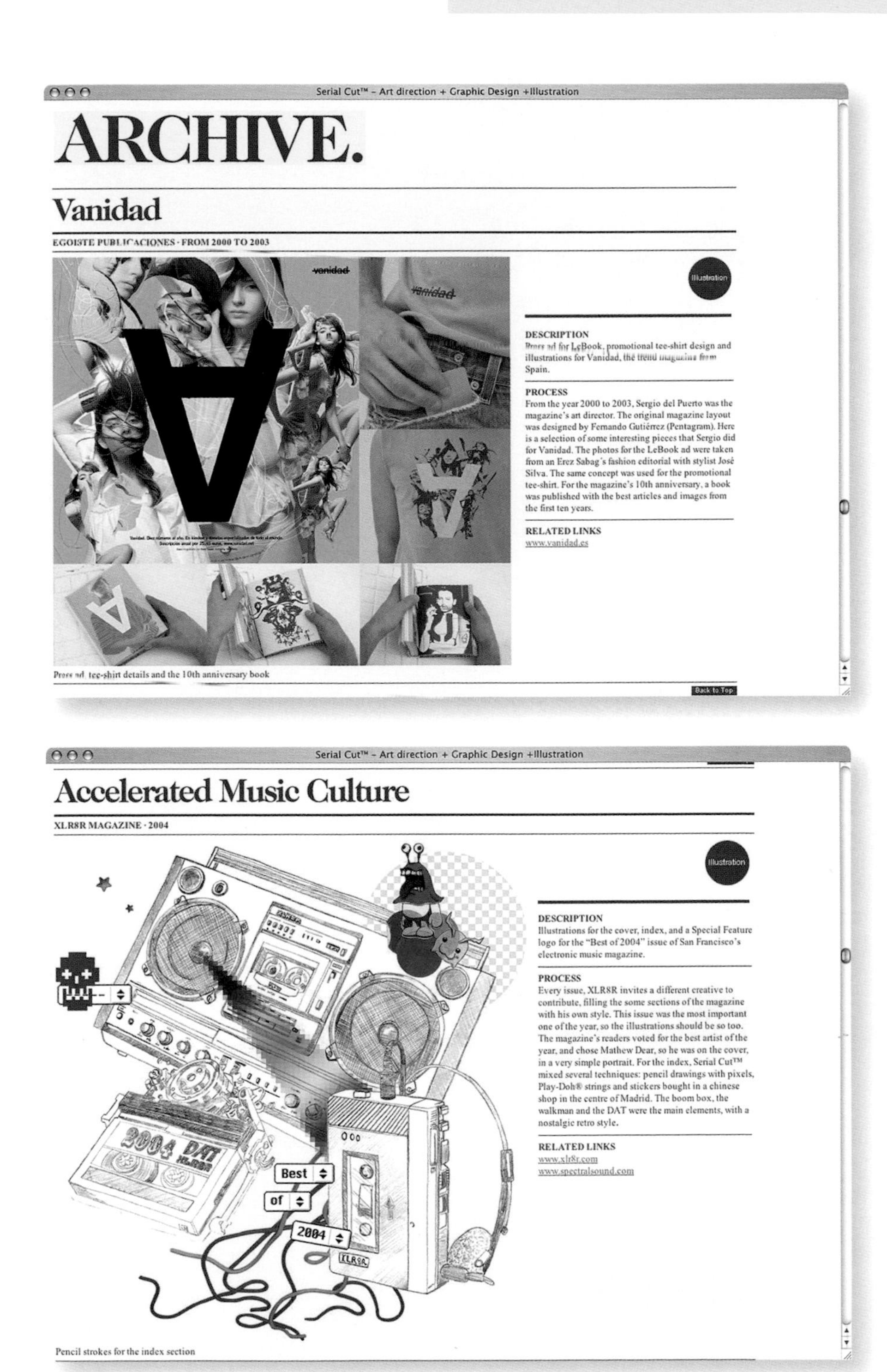

Serial Cut™ - Art direction + Graphic Design +Illustration

ARCHIVE.

Vanidad

EGOISTE PUBLICACIONES · FROM 2000 TO 2003

Illustration

DESCRIPTION
Press ad for LeBook, promotional tee-shirt design and illustrations for Vanidad, the trend magazine from Spain.

PROCESS
From the year 2000 to 2003, Sergio del Puerto was the magazine's art director. The original magazine layout was designed by Fernando Gutiérrez (Pentagram). Here is a selection of some interesting pieces that Sergio did for Vanidad. The photos for the LeBook ad were taken from an Erez Sabag´s fashion editorial with stylist José Silva. The same concept was used for the promotional tee-shirt. For the magazine's 10th anniversary, a book was published with the best articles and images from the first ten years.

RELATED LINKS
www.vanidad.es

Press ad, tee-shirt details and the 10th anniversary book

Back to Top

Serial Cut™ - Art direction + Graphic Design +Illustration

Accelerated Music Culture

XLR8R MAGAZINE · 2004

Illustration

DESCRIPTION
Illustrations for the cover, index, and a Special Feature logo for the "Best of 2004" issue of San Francisco's electronic music magazine.

PROCESS
Every issue, XLR8R invites a different creative to contribute, filling the some sections of the magazine with his own style. This issue was the most important one of the year, so the illustrations should be so too. The magazine's readers voted for the best artist of the year, and chose Mathew Dear, so he was on the cover, in a very simple portrait. For the index, Serial Cut™ mixed several techniques: pencil drawings with pixels, Play-Doh® strings and stickers bought in a chinese shop in the centre of Madrid. The boom box, the walkman and the DAT were the main elements, with a nostalgic retro style.

RELATED LINKS
www.xlr8r.com
www.spectralsound.com

Pencil strokes for the index section

www.serialcut.com
D: sergio del puerto
A: serial cut™ M: info@serialcut.com

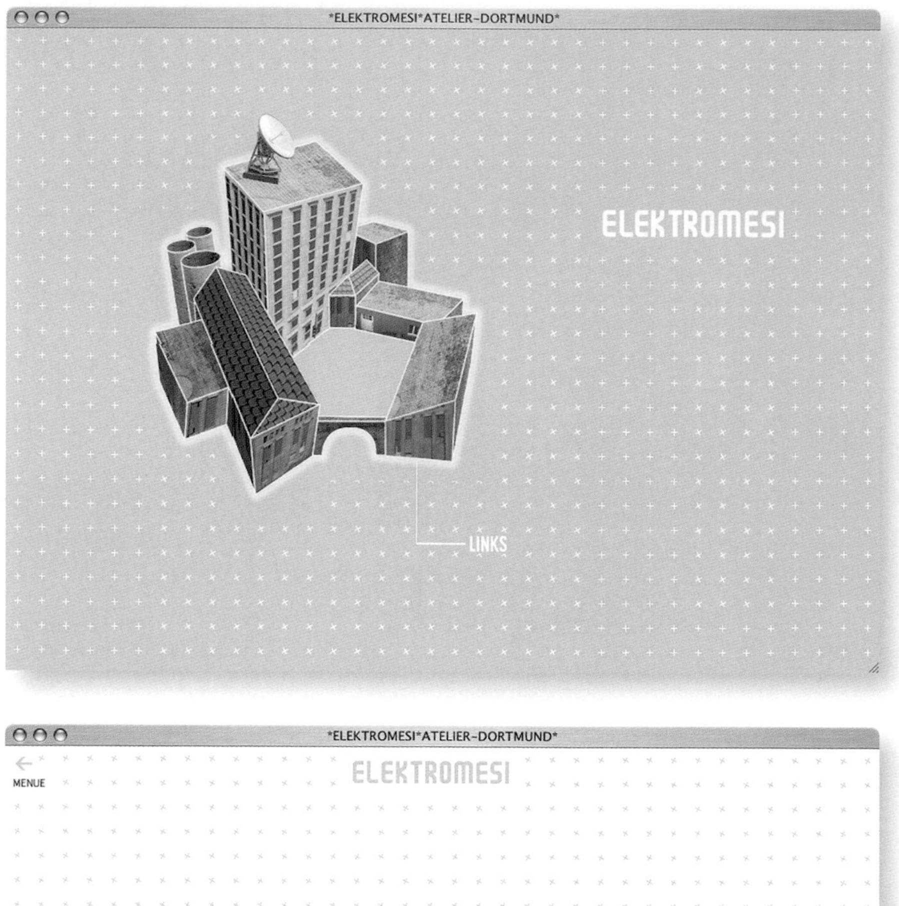

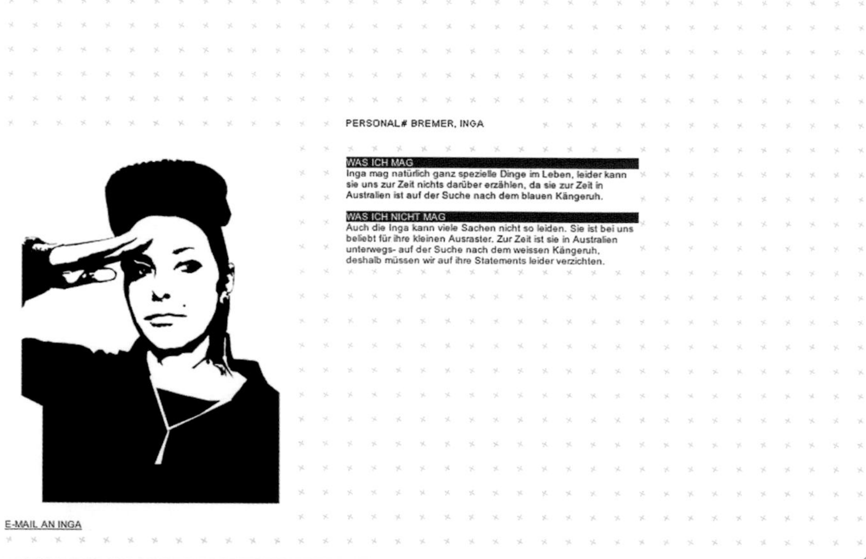

www.elektromesi.com

D: bruno bauch

M: post@elektromesi.com

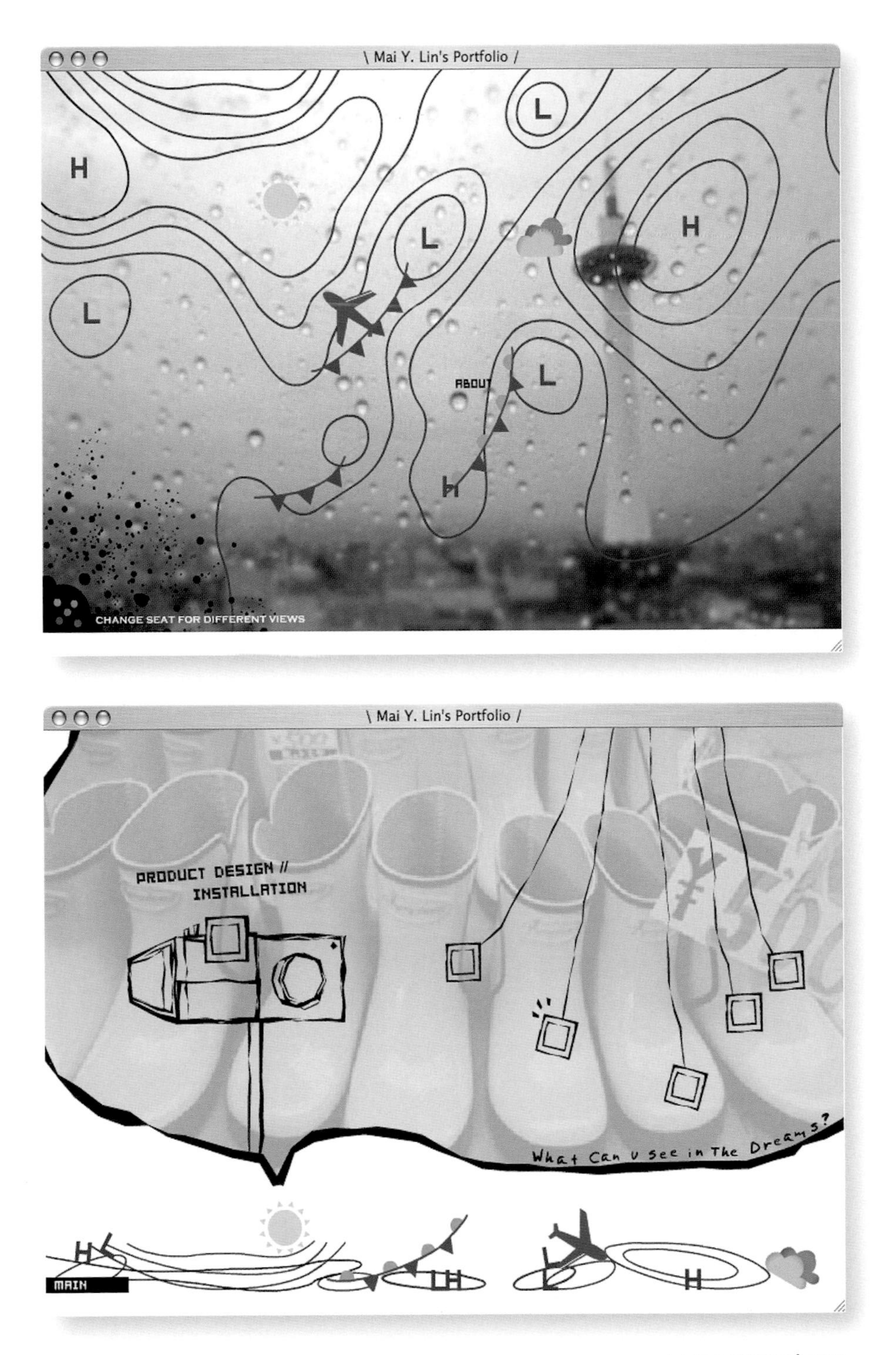

www.nevermai.com
D: mai yi-chun lin
M: maiylin@gmail.com

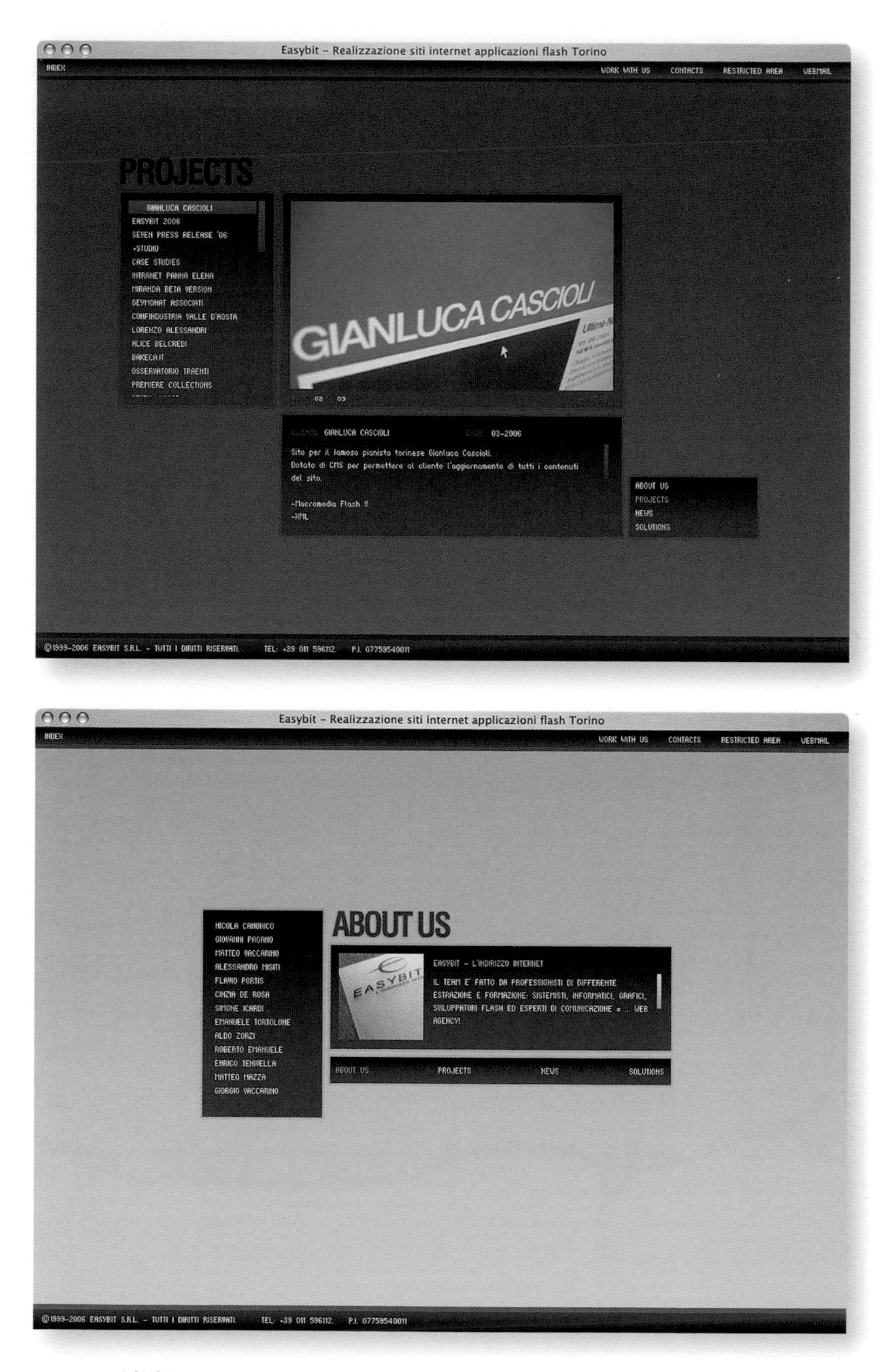

www.easybit.it

D: emanuele tortolone **C:** matteo vaccarino, aldo zorzi **P:** nicola canonico

A: easybit s.r.l **M:** marketing@easybit.it

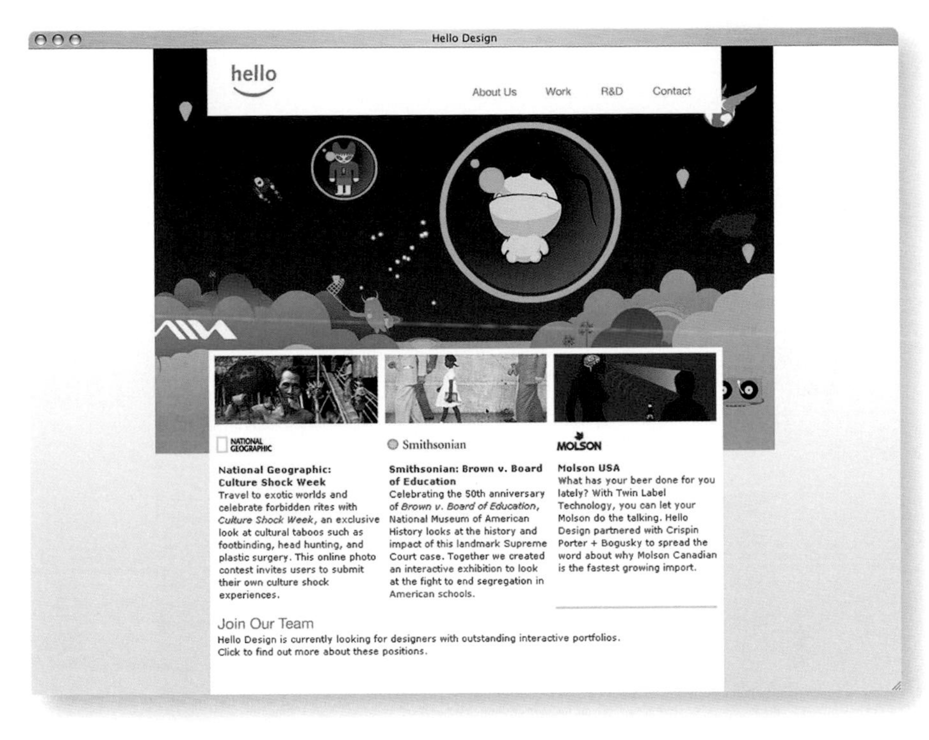

www.hellodesign.com

D: david lai, hiro niwa **C:** dan phiffer **P:** szu ann chen

A: hello design **M:** hello@hellodesign.com

www.funkbuilders.com

D: alan

A: funkbuilders **M:** www.funkbuilders.com

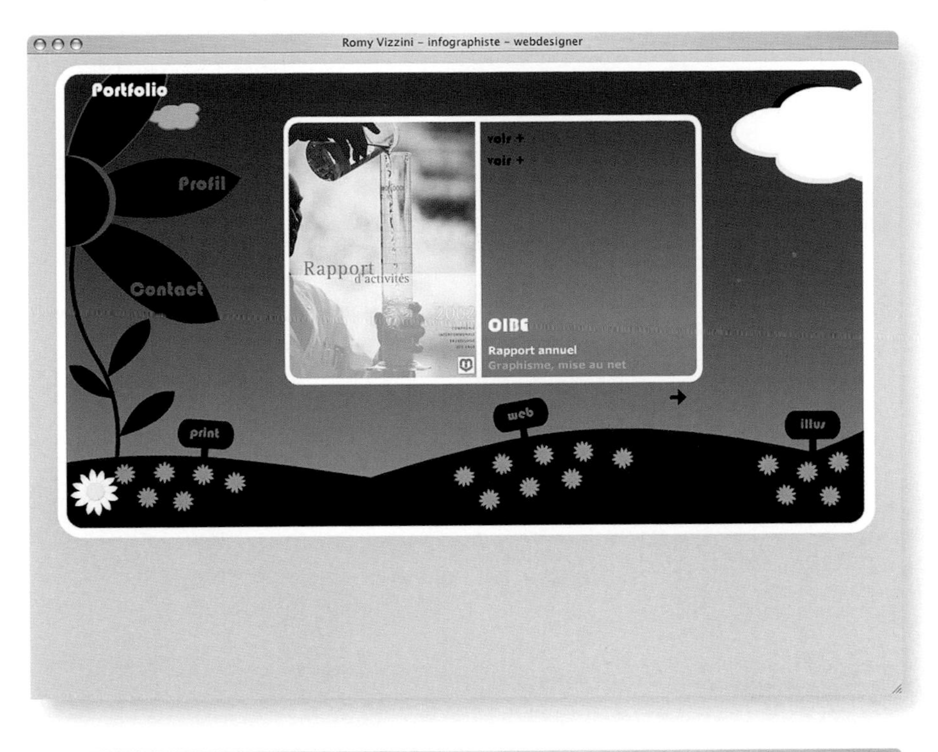

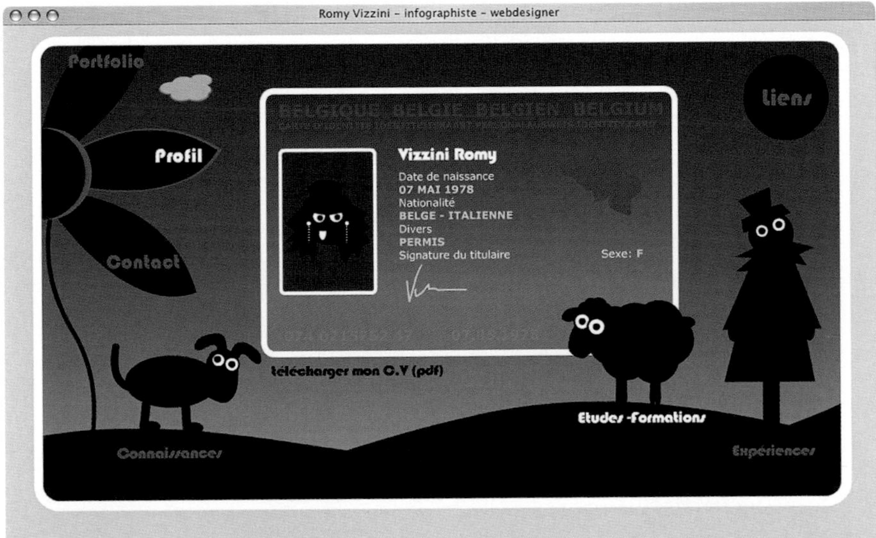

www.romy-vizzini.be
D: romy vizzini
M: info@romy-vizzini.be

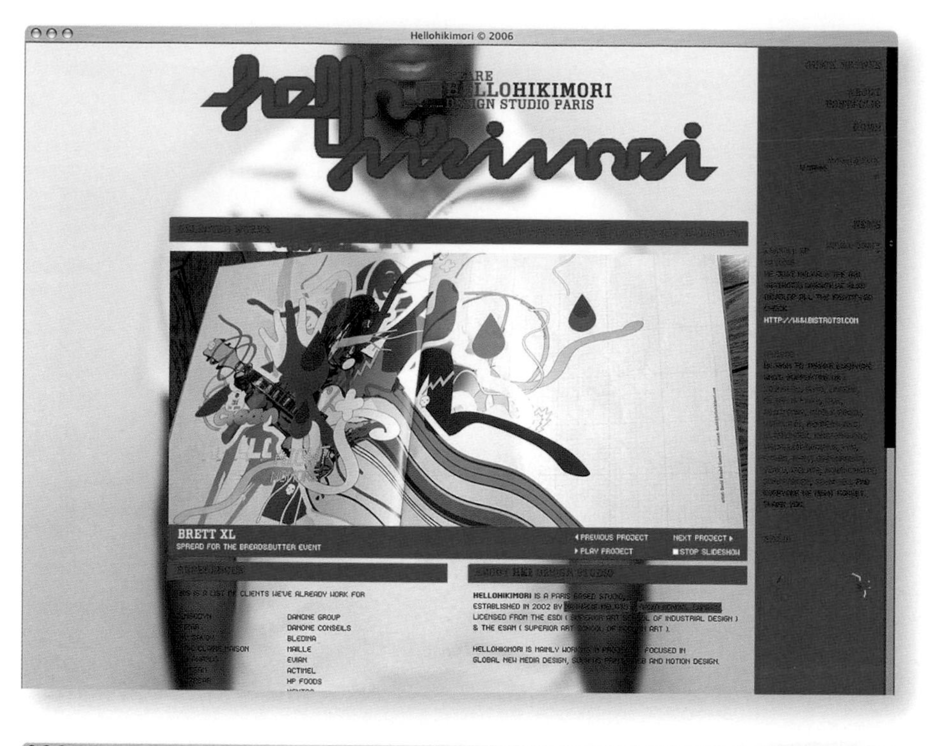

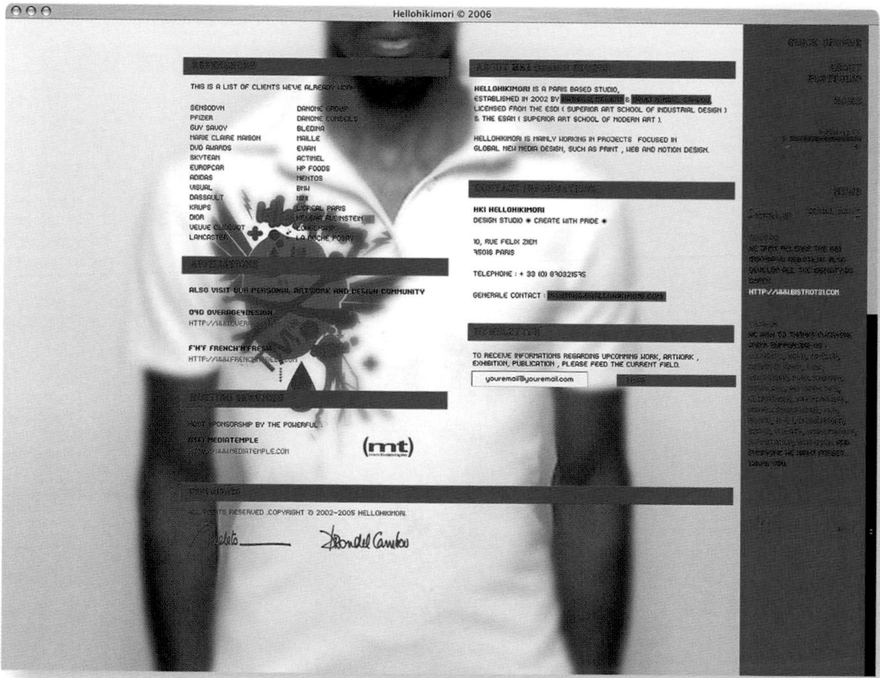

www.hellohikimori.com

D: nathalie melato, david rondel cambou **C:** vincent legrand **P:** hki

A: hellohikimori **M:** incoming@hellohikimori.com

www.lessrain.com

D: less rain

A: less rain **M:** reception@lessrain.com

www.lalozambrano.com

D: lalo zambrano

M: www.lalozambrano.com

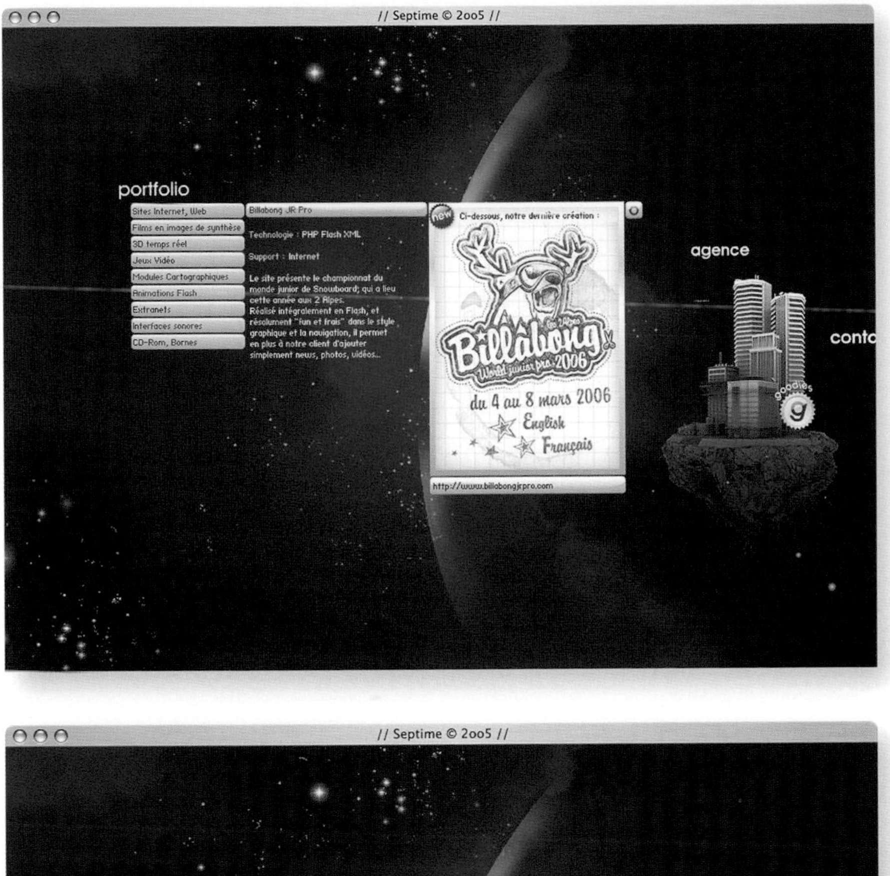

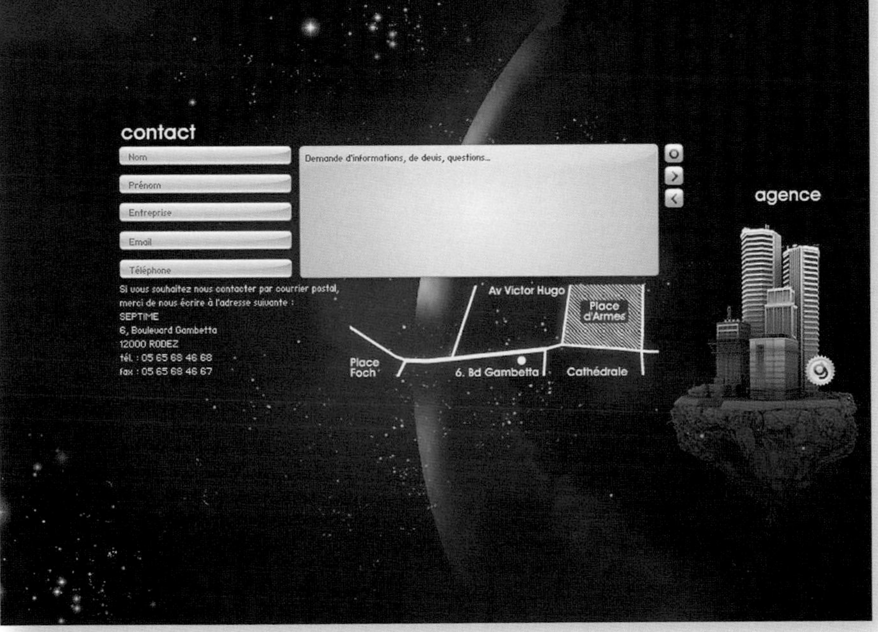

www.septime.net
D: nicolas combes, david polonia **C:** romain moussac **P:** ulysse lacombe
A: septime creation **M:** info@septime.net

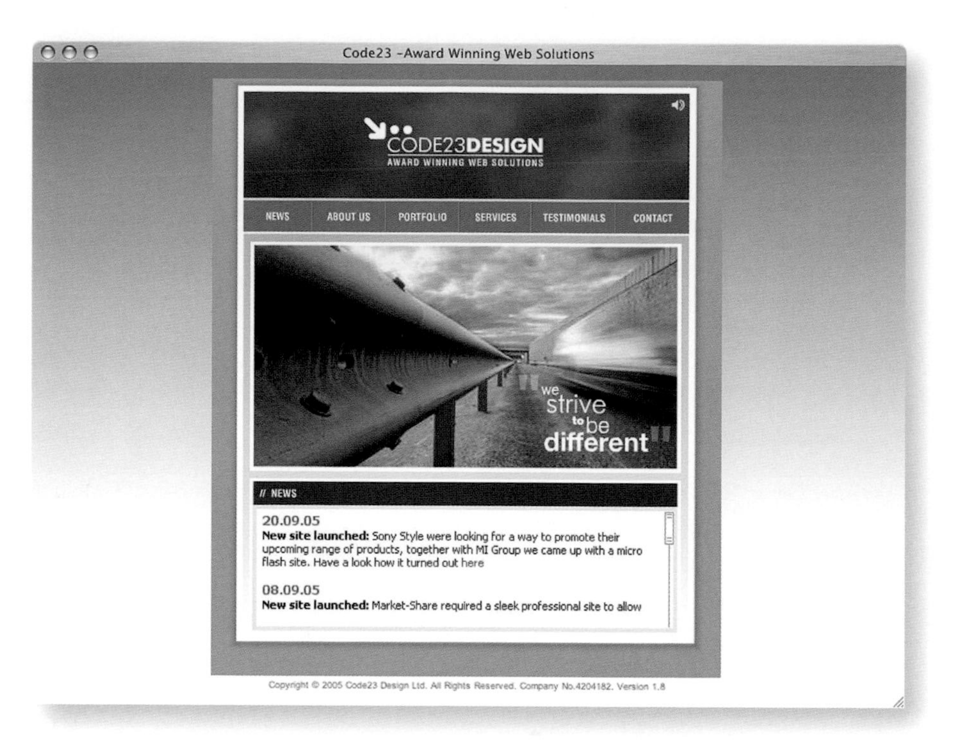

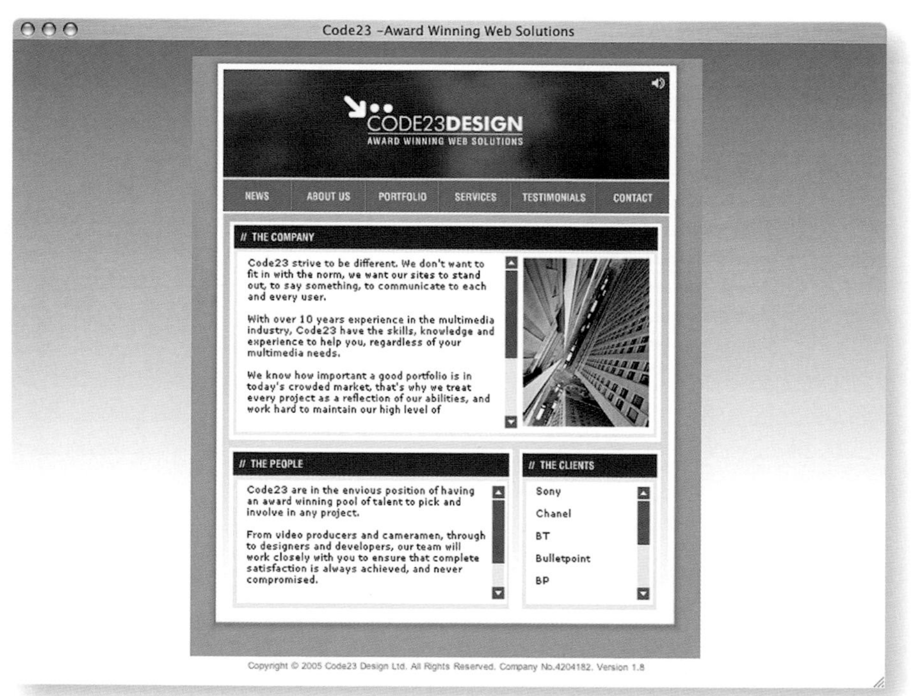

www.code23.com

D: james ansell

M: info@code23.com

www.tangerine-uk.co.uk

D: andy vinnicombe **C:** andy vinnicombe **P:** tangerine uk ltd

A: tangerine uk ltd **M:** andy@tangerine-uk.co.uk

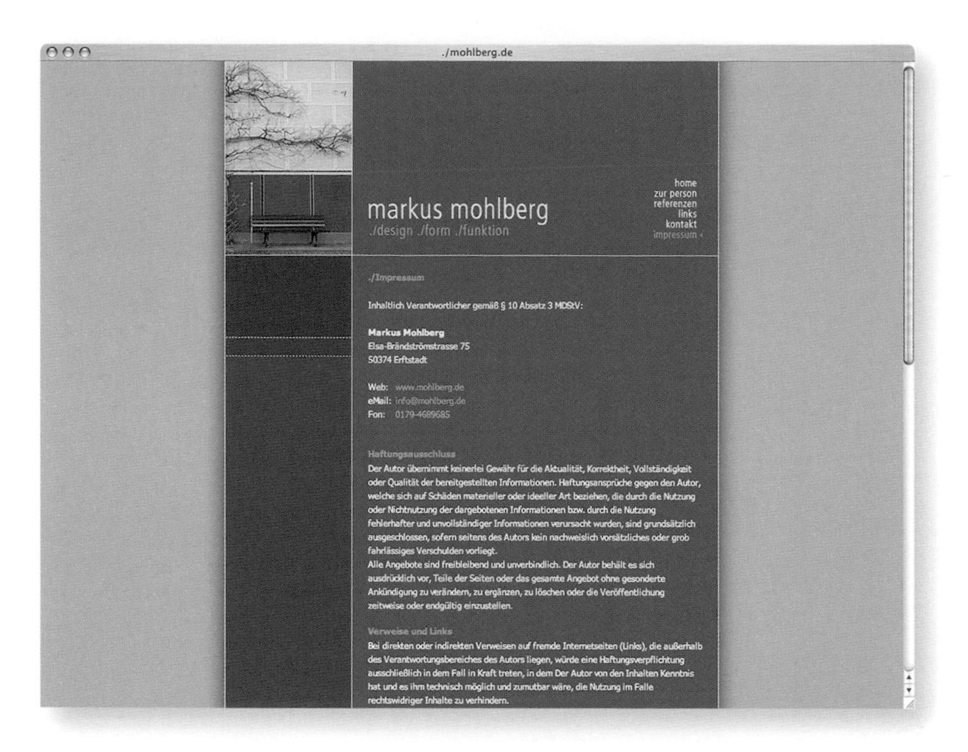

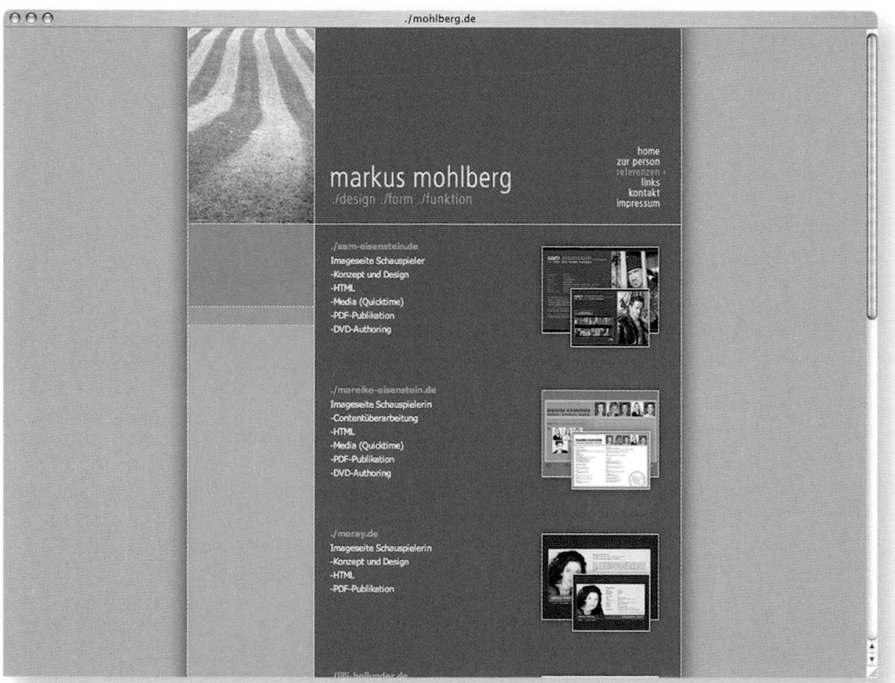

www.mohlberg.de

D: markus mohlberg

A: mohlberg.de **M:** markus@mohlberg.de

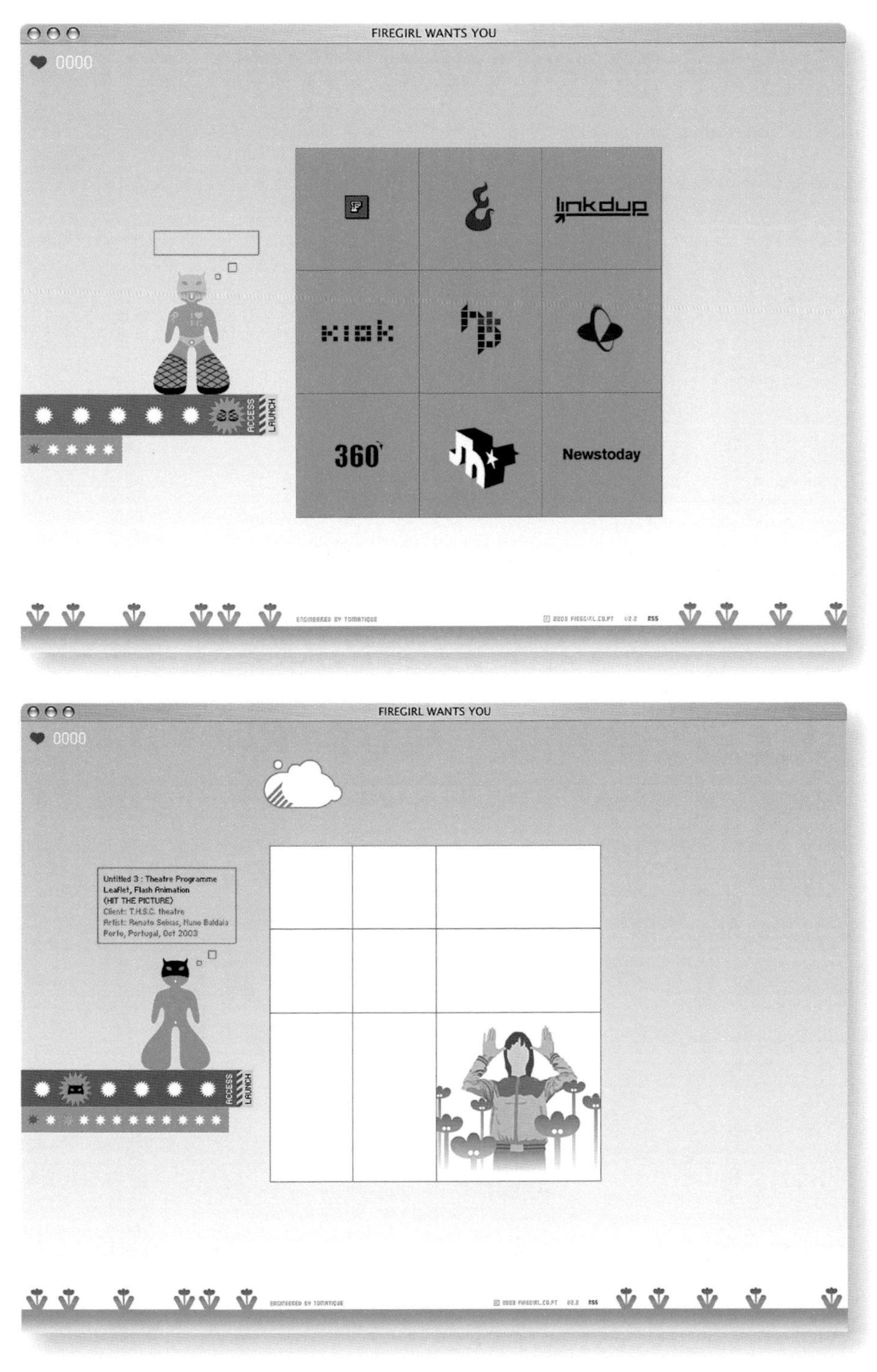

www.firegirl.co.pt

D: renato seixas **C:** nuno baldaia

A: firegirl **M:** info@firegirl.co.pt

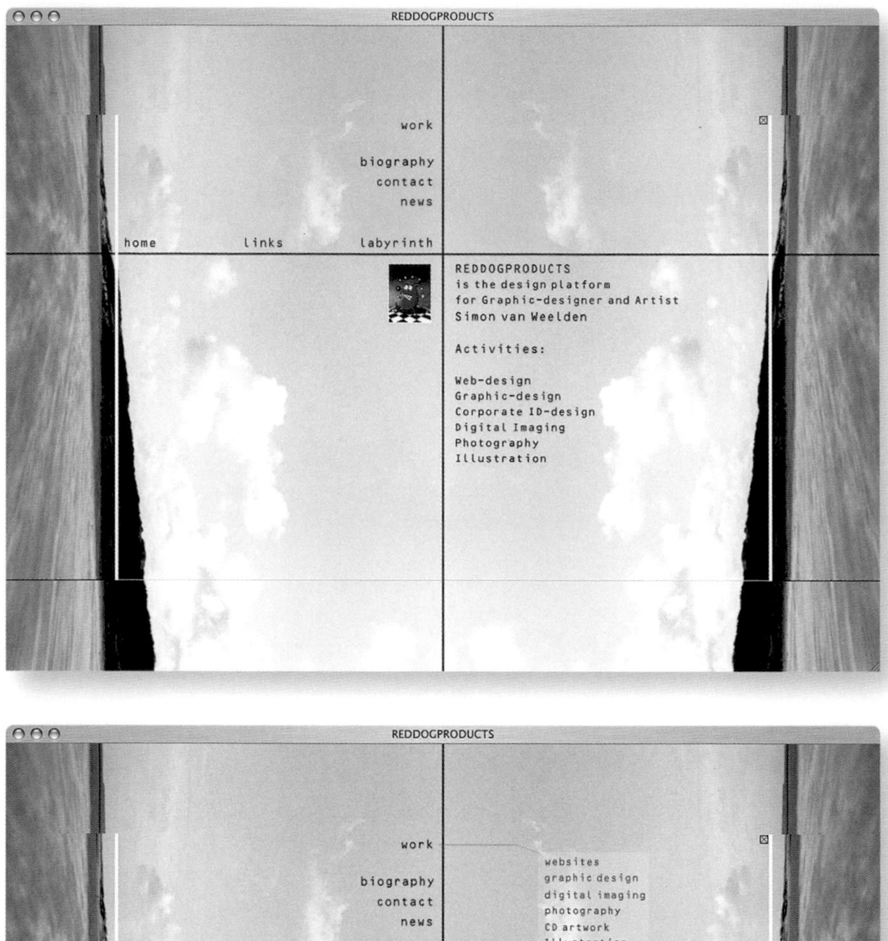

www.reddogproducts.com

D: simon van weelden

A: simon van weelden **M:** simon@projekt67.com

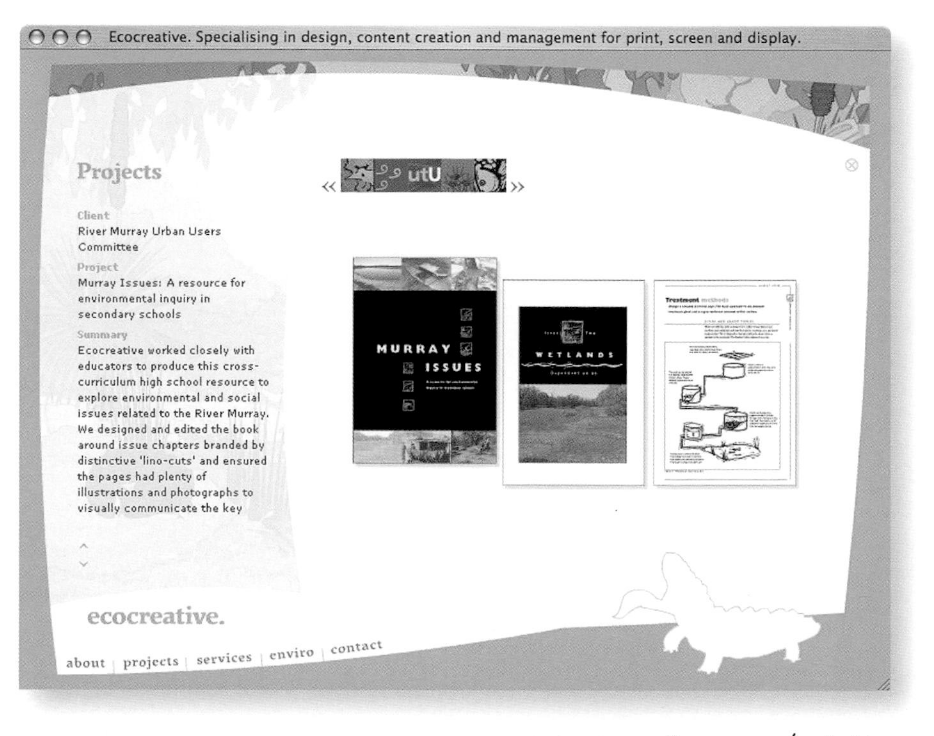

www.ecocreative.com.au/main.htm

D: robin green **P:** matthew wright-simon

A: ecocreative **M:** info@ecocreative.com.au

www.hemjeans.com

D: gary a. dorsey **P:** gary dorsey, kaysie dorsey

A: pixel peach studio **M:** info@pixelpeach.com

www.jongehazen.nl

D: de jongehazen **C:** quibuzz **P:** behappy

A: de jongehazen **M:** info@jongehazen.nl

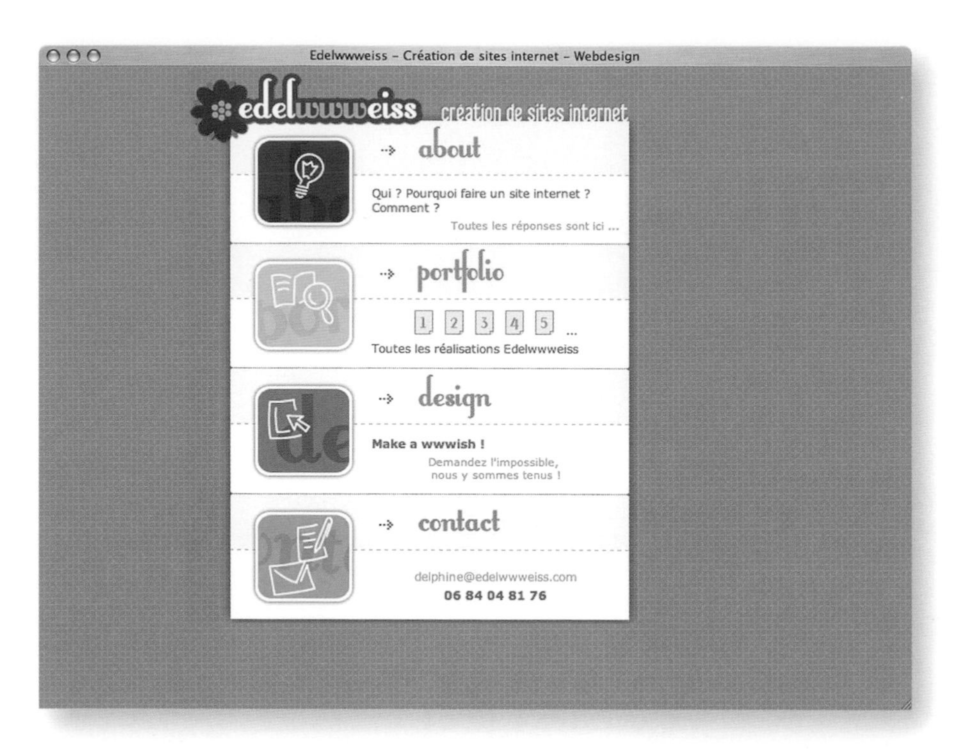

www.edelwwweiss.com

D: delphine pagès

A: edelwwweiss M: delphine@edelwwweiss.com

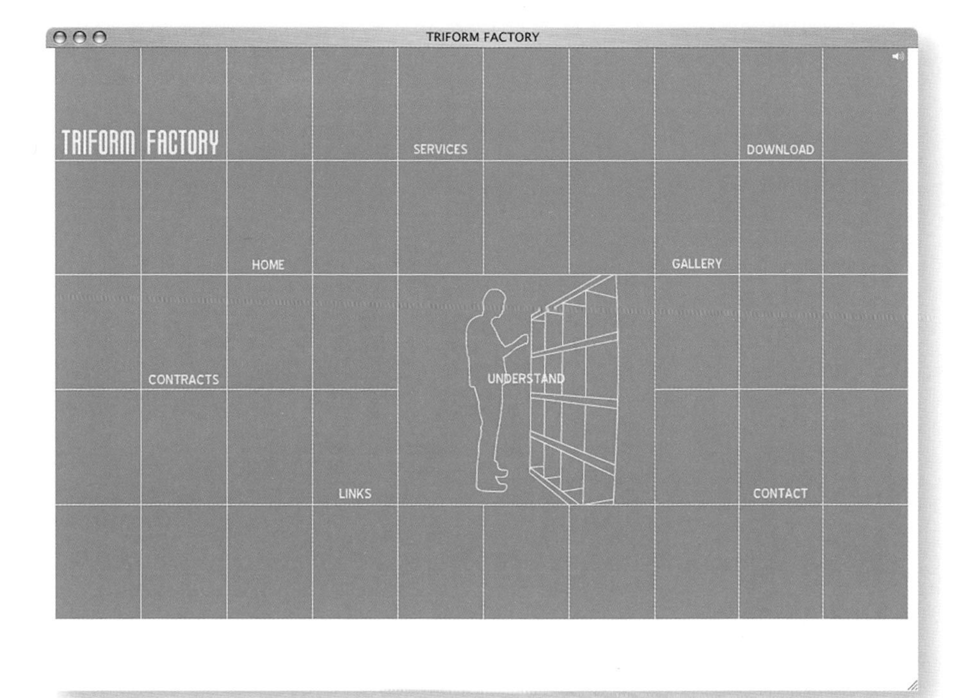

TRIFORM FACTORY

TRIFORM FACTORY HOME CONTRACTS SERVICES UNDERSTAND GALLERY LINKS DOWNLOAD CONTACT

TO UNDERSTAND DESIGN

The thing we understand is DESIGN.

We can recognise it: sometimes we'll know it by heart.

We can look it up for you, or seek it out.

We'll show you how to enjoy it, and make it suit you.

We'll re-make it, colour it, or shrink it if you want.

We can passionately debate it, fight for it, but also laugh at it.

ROZUMIEŤ DIZAJNU

SITE MAP

www.triform.sk

D: brano pepel **C:** brano pepel, rasto janko

A: kamikadze **M:** www.kamikadze.sk

www.twoto.com

D: patrick decaix

A: www.twoto.com **M:** patrick@twoto.com

www.mutanz.com

D: cesar jacobi

M: jacobi@mutanz.com

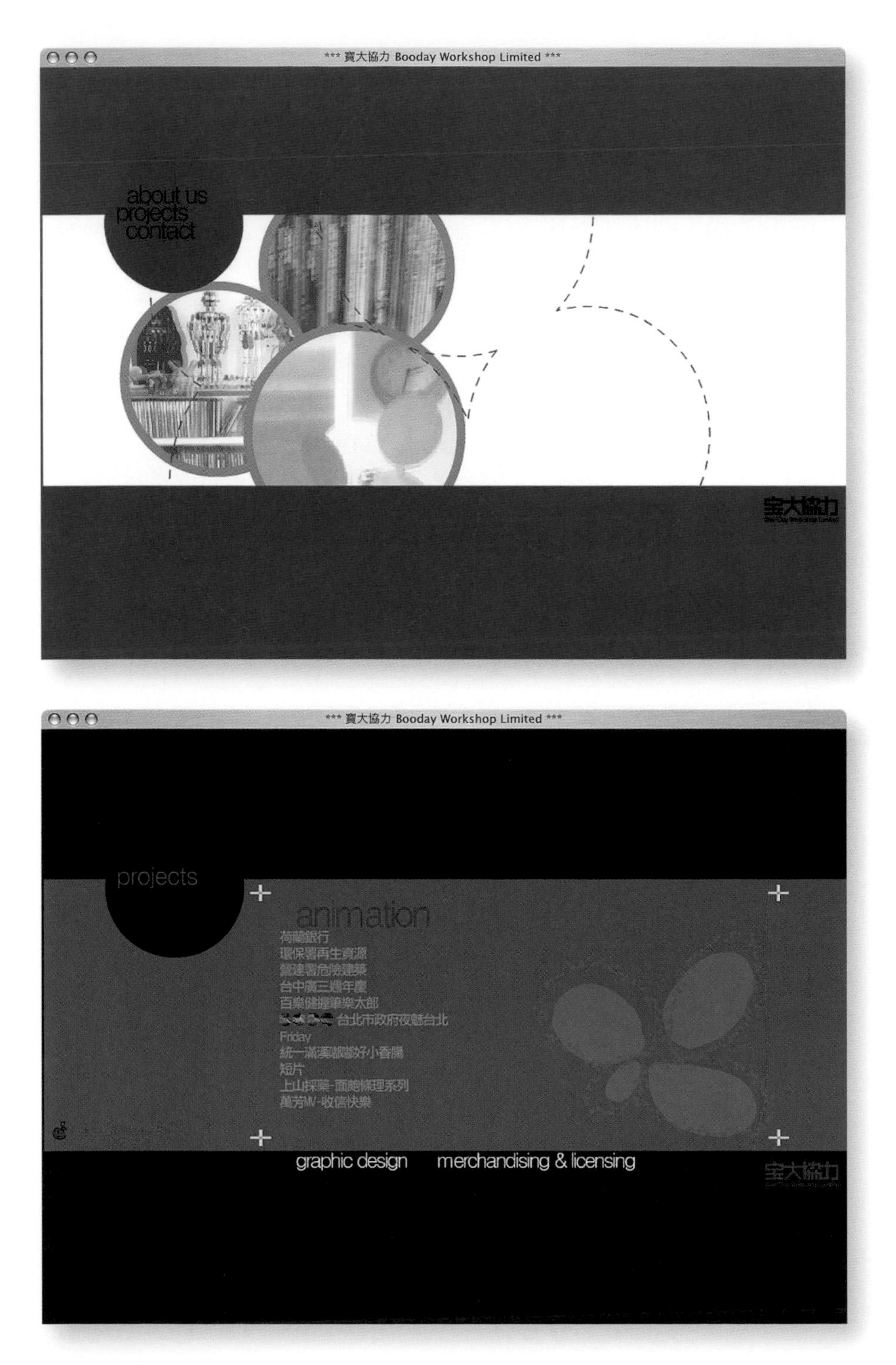

www.booday.com

D: mei-yu lee **P:** johnny chang

A: booday workshop limited **M:** johnny@mogu.com.tw

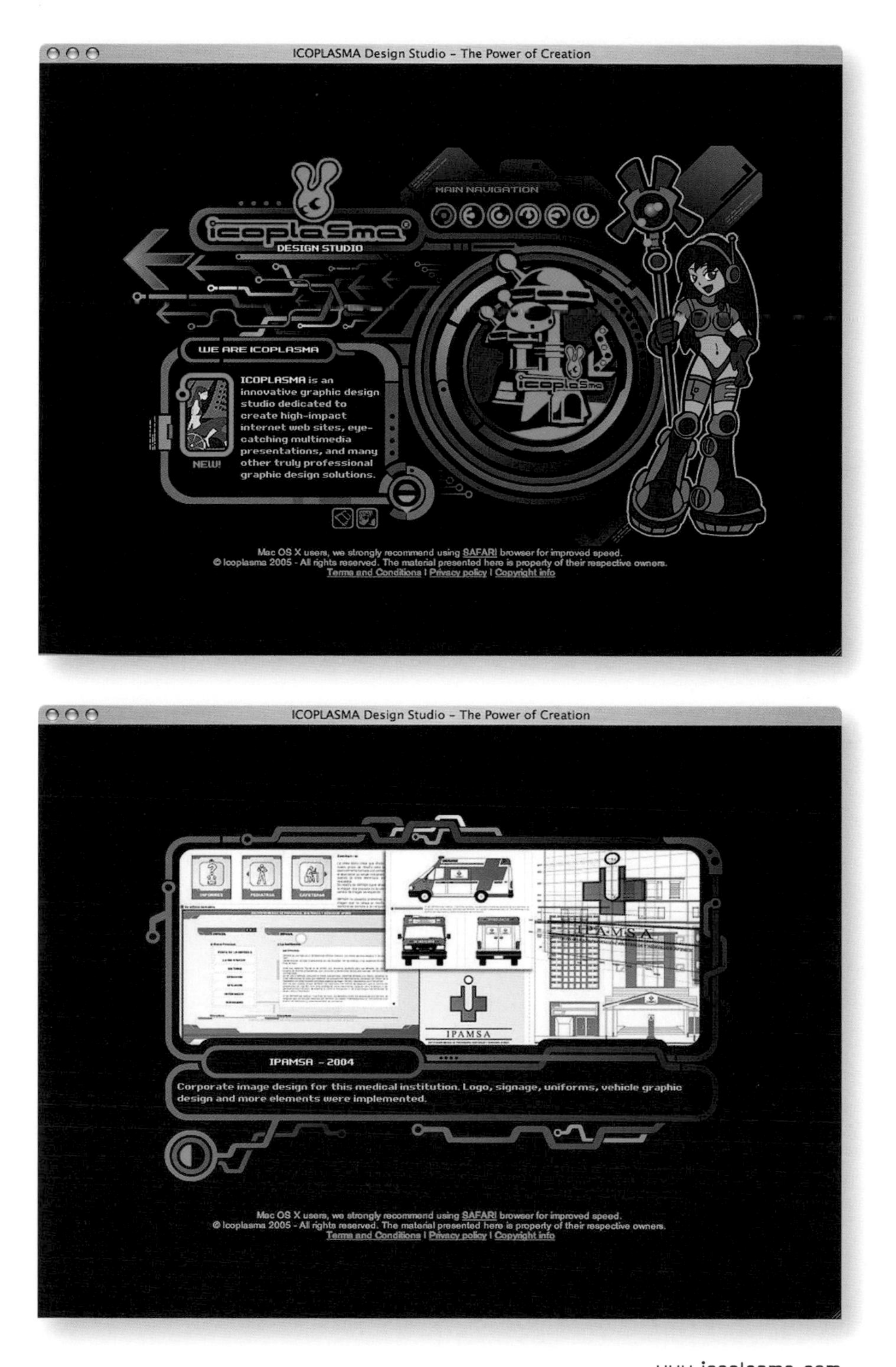

www.icoplasma.com
D: gerardo tato, jill lópez, alejandro tato C: gerardo tato P: gerardo tato
A: icoplasma design studio M: info@icoplasma.com

www.davidpareja.net

D: david pareja ruiz **C:** david pareja ruiz, miguel benitez, raul ledo

A: david pareja ruiz **M:** info@davidpareja.net

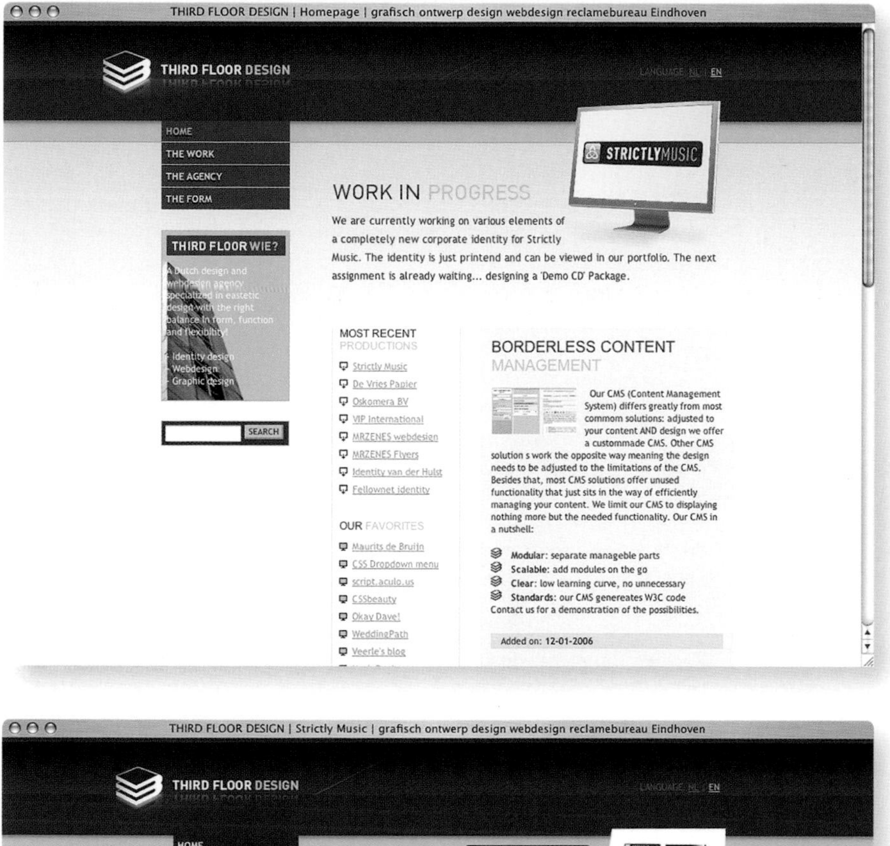

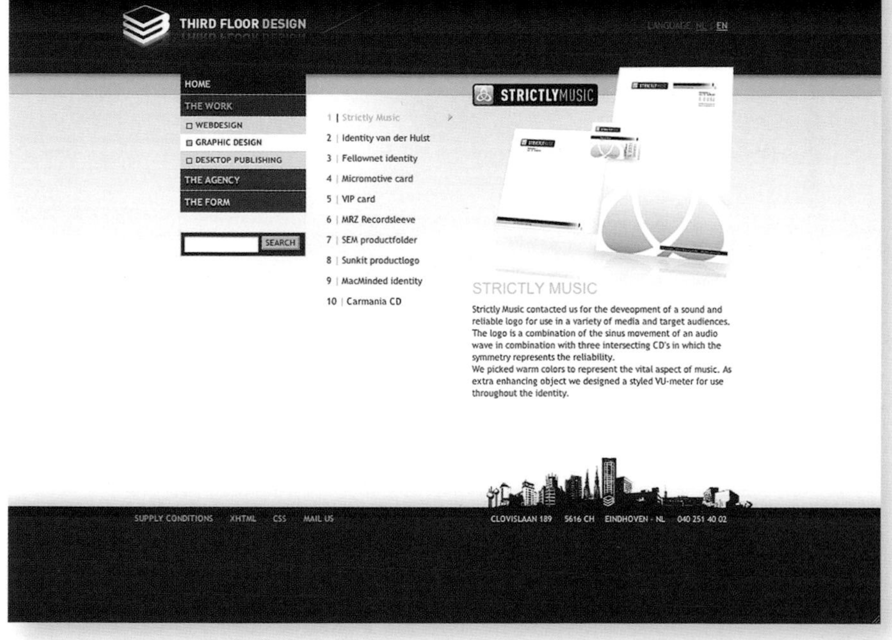

www.thirdfloordesign.nl
D: mark copal **C:** bob kersten
A: third floor design **M:** info@thirdfloordesign.nl

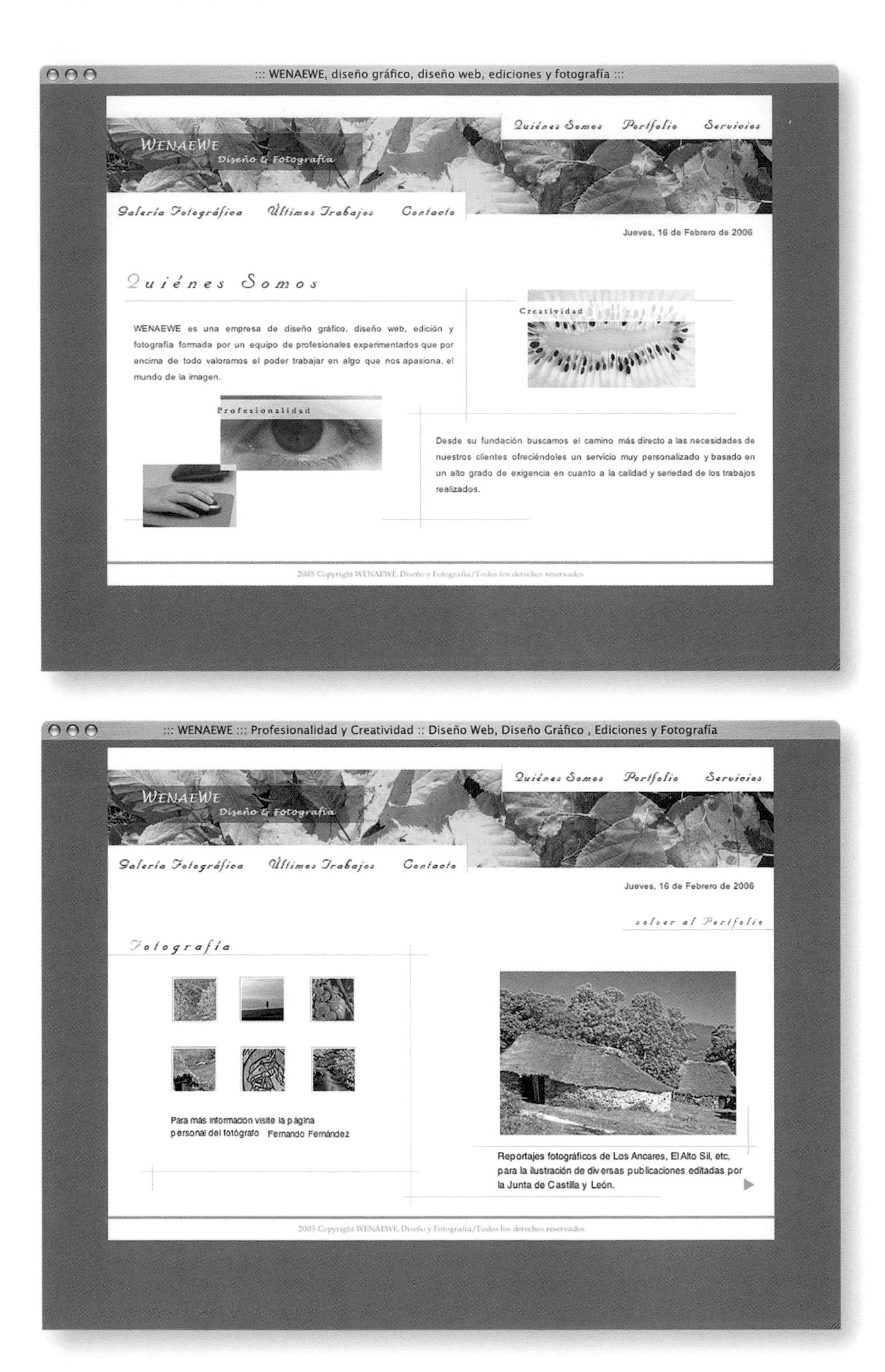

www.wenaewe.com

D: ef **C:** ef **P:** equipo wenaewe

A: wenaewe, diseño y fotografía **M:** dioxina2004@yahoo.es

www.fromscratch.us

D: cristian strittmatter C: gabriel toledano P: sandra strittmatter

A: from scratch design studio M: contact@fromscratch.us

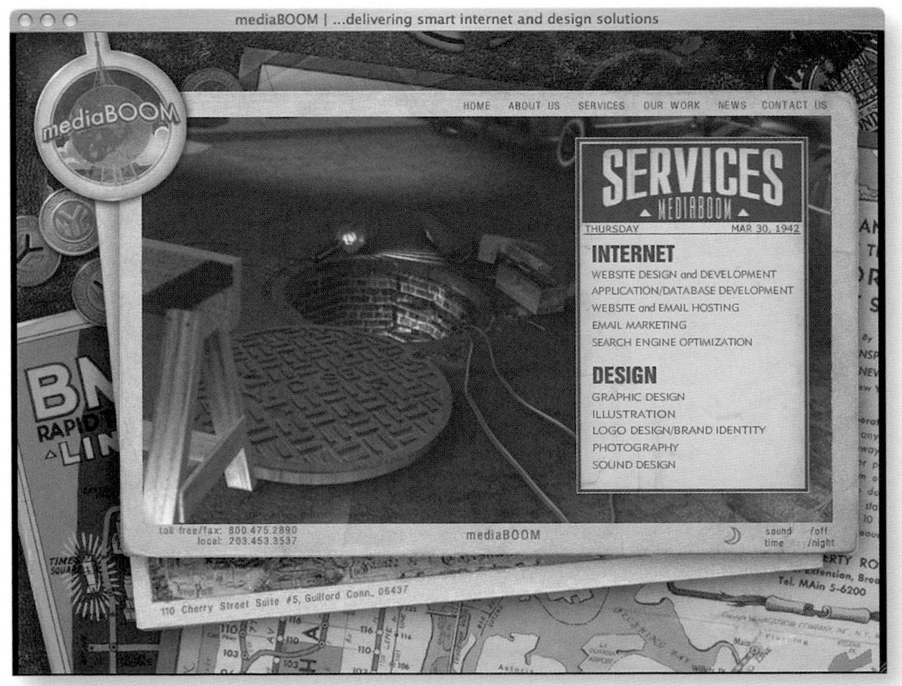

www.mediaboom.com

D: sean cooke **C:** sean cooke, frank depino **P:** frank depino

A: mediaboom **M:** www.mediaboom.com

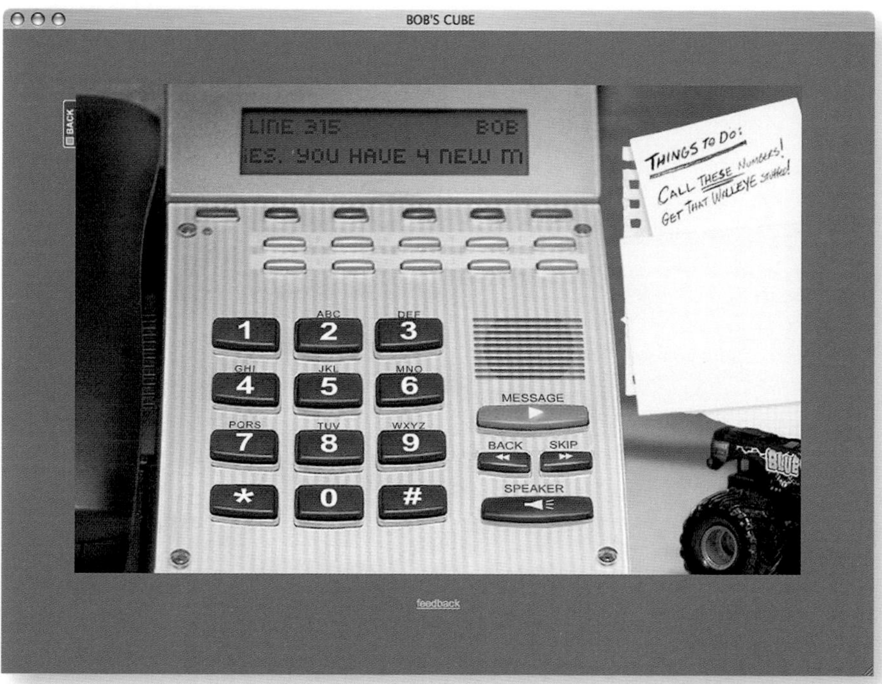

www.bobscube.com

D: 15 letters

A: 15 letters **M:** www.15letters.com

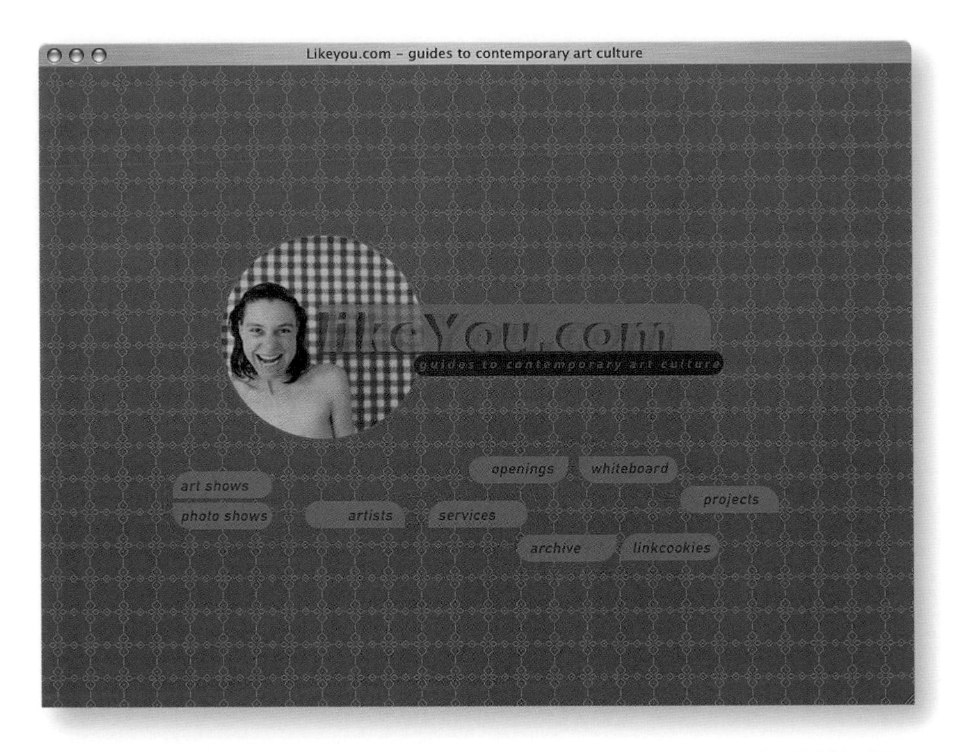

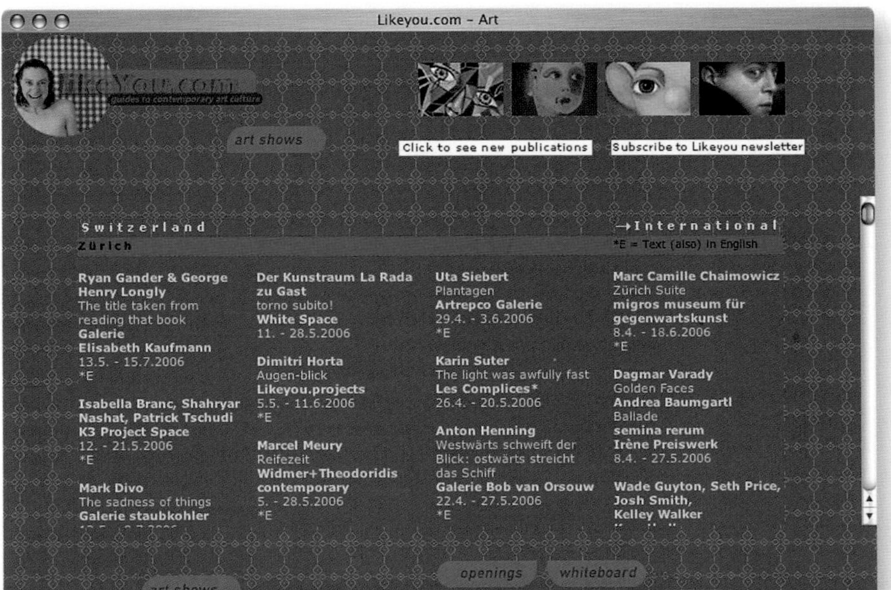

www.likeyou.com

D: centrik isler **C:** centrik isler, luc gross, hanna züllig **P:** centrik isler

A: the webfactory, cbc zurich **M:** www.likeyou.com

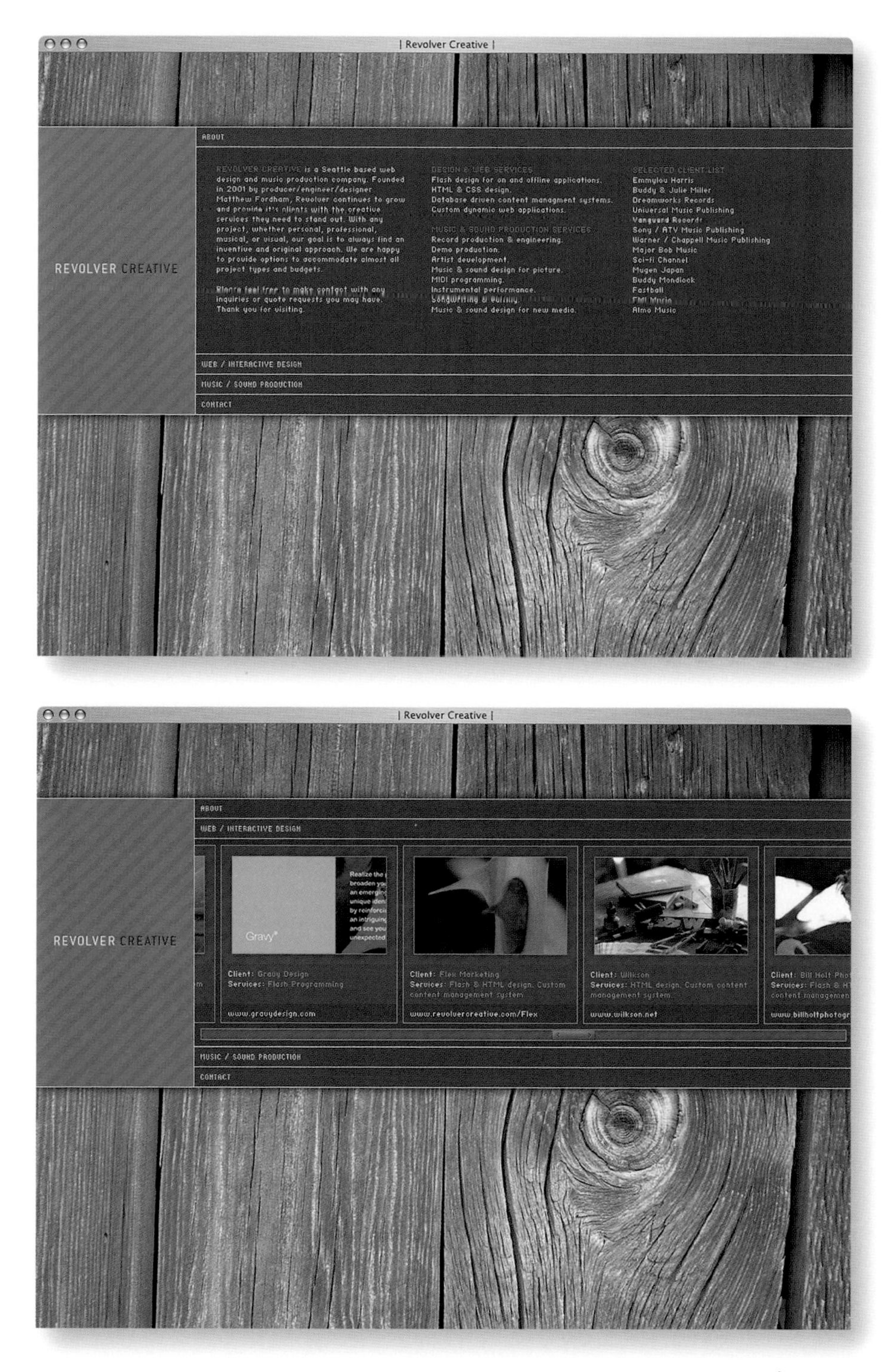

www.revolvercreative.com

D: matthew fordham

A: revolver creative **M:** www.revolvercreative.com

www.goweb.pt

D: peter steven **C:** helder vasconcelos **P:** josé fonseca, pedro ferreira

A: go web **M:** info@goweb.pt

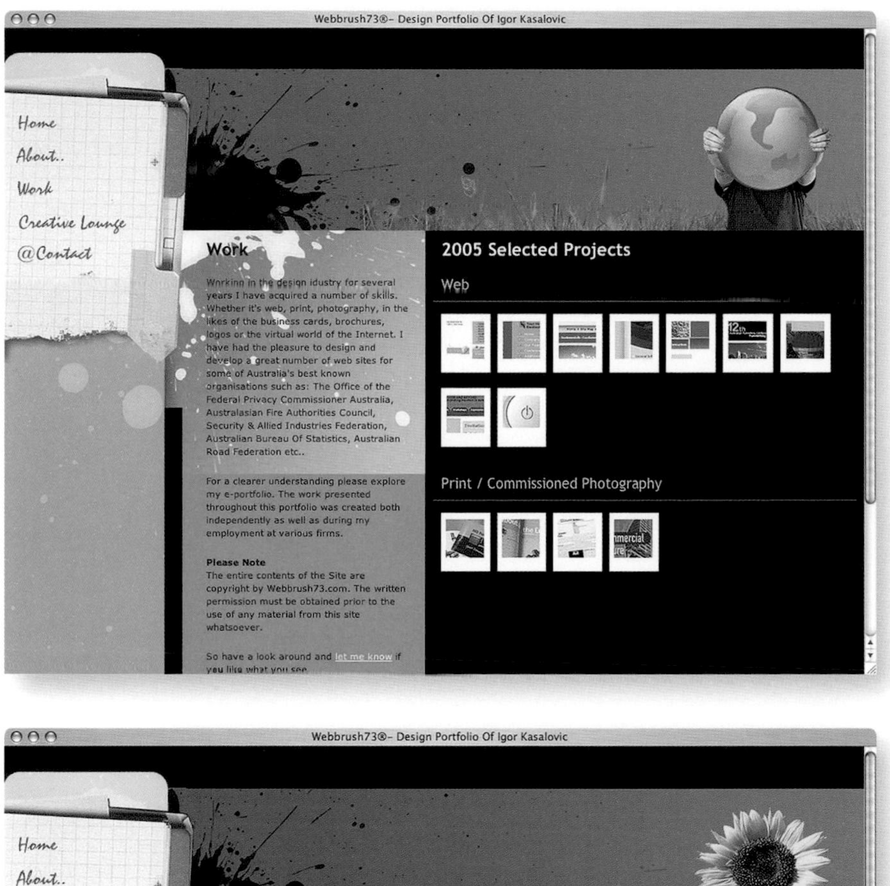

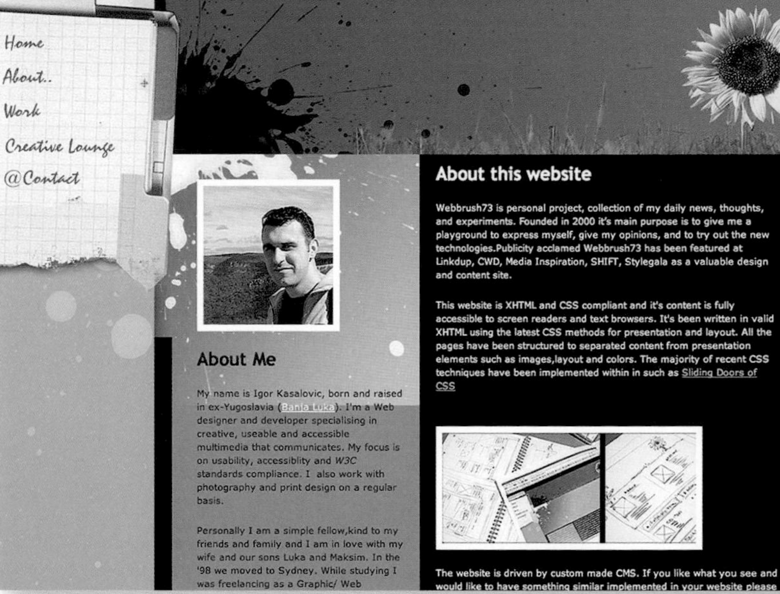

www.webbrush73.com
D: igor kasalovic
M: info@webbrush73.com

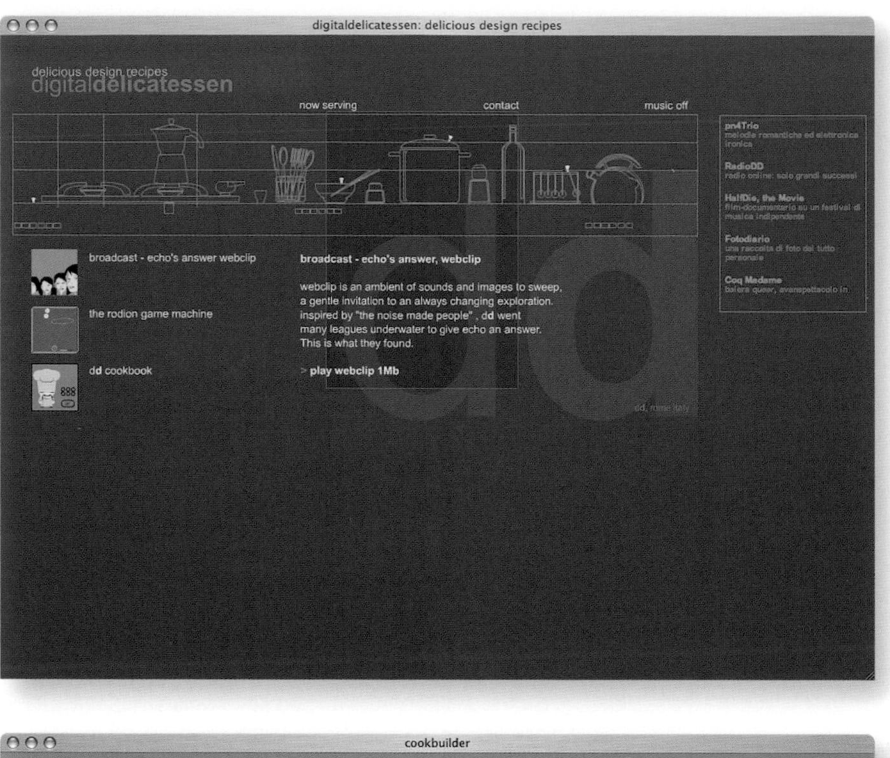

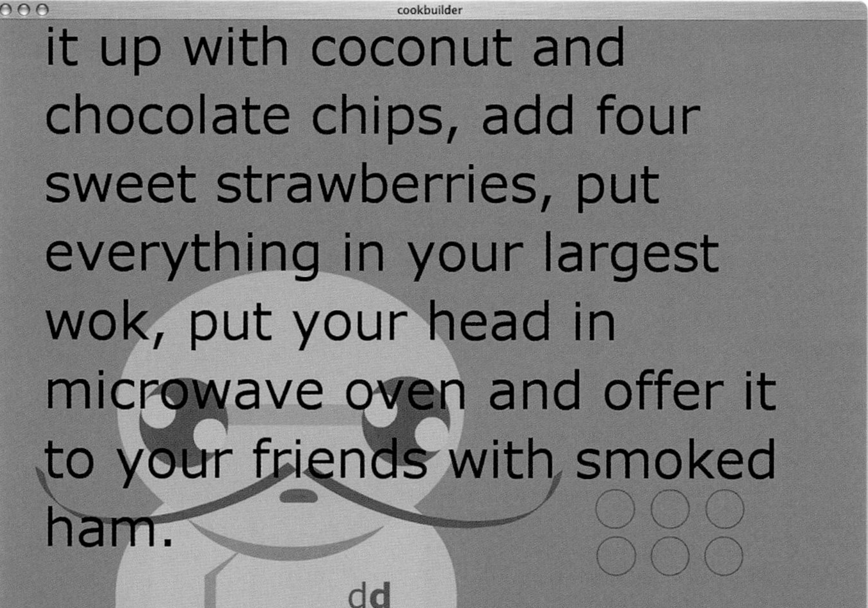

www.digitaldelicatessen.com

D: digitaldelicatessen

M: contact@digitaldelicatessen.com

www.strafefox.nl

D: jeroen bekker

A: strafefox M: jeroen@strafefox.nl

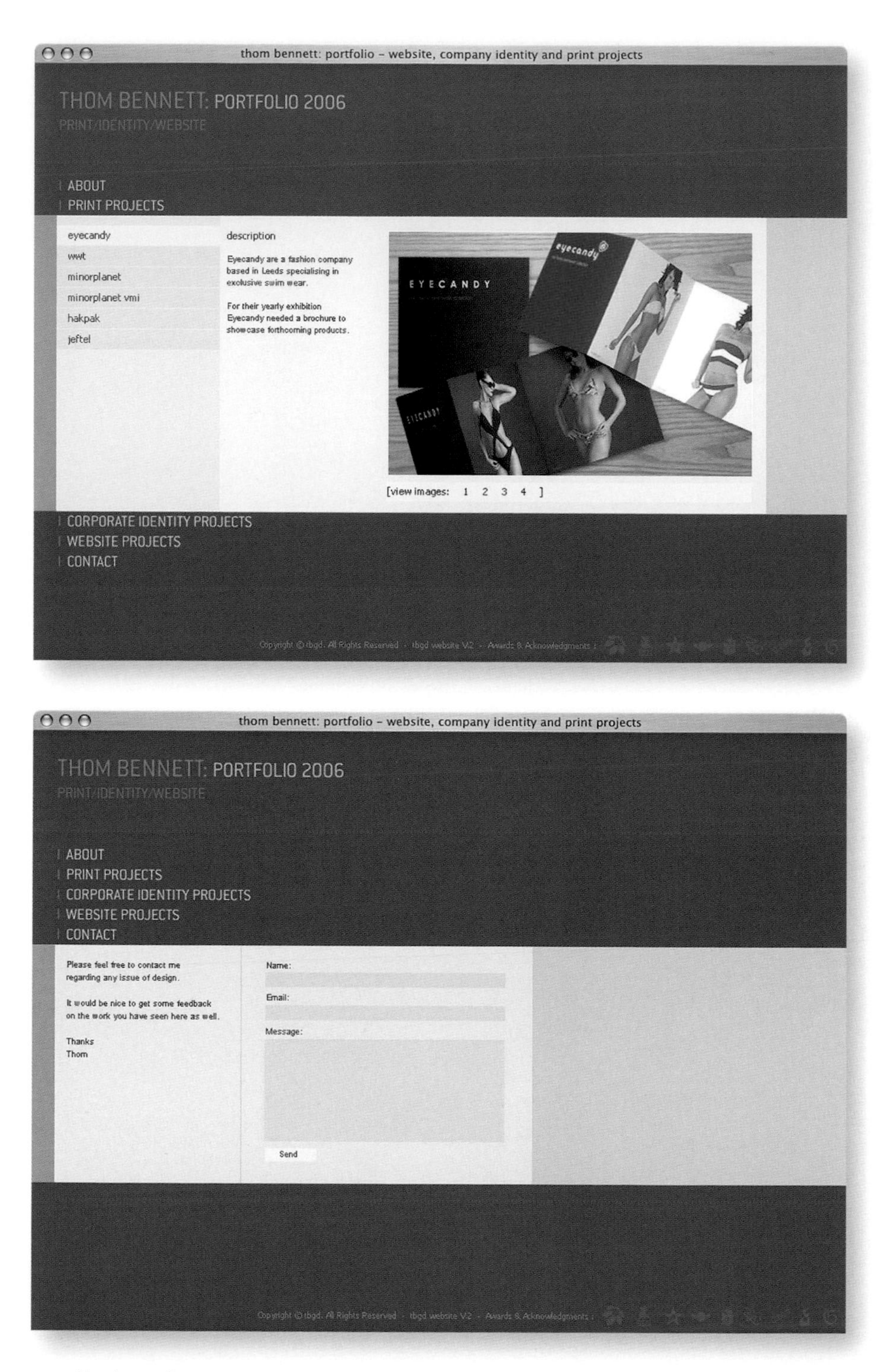

www.tbgd.co.uk

D: thom bennett

A: thom bennett graphic design **M:** info@tbgd.co.uk

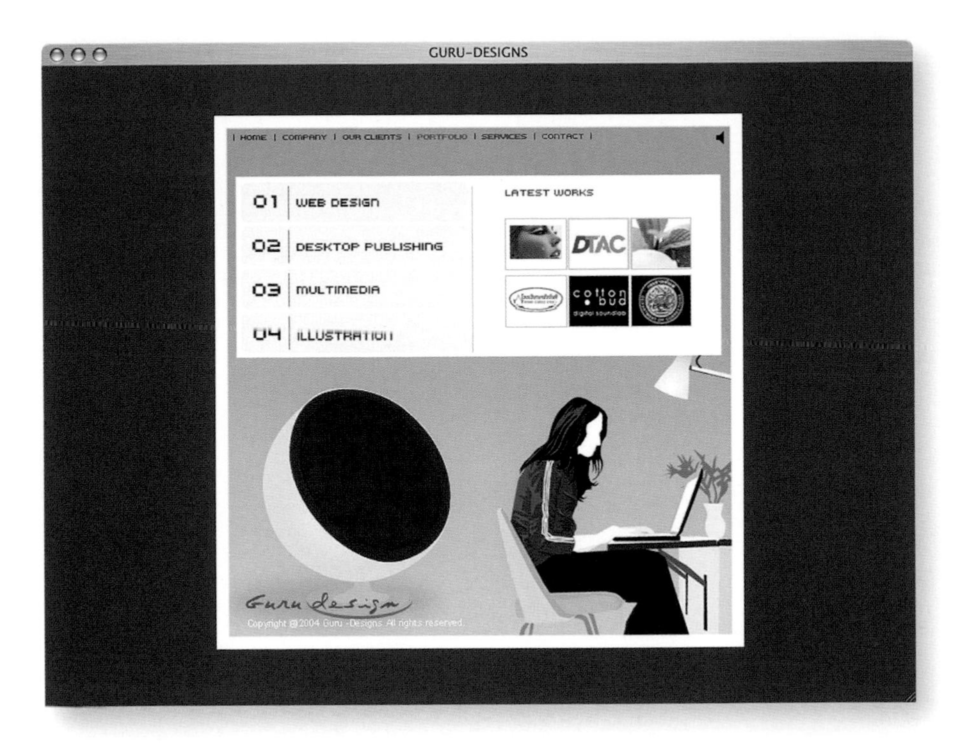

www.guru-designs.com

D: guru design

A: guru design **M:** info@guru-designs.com

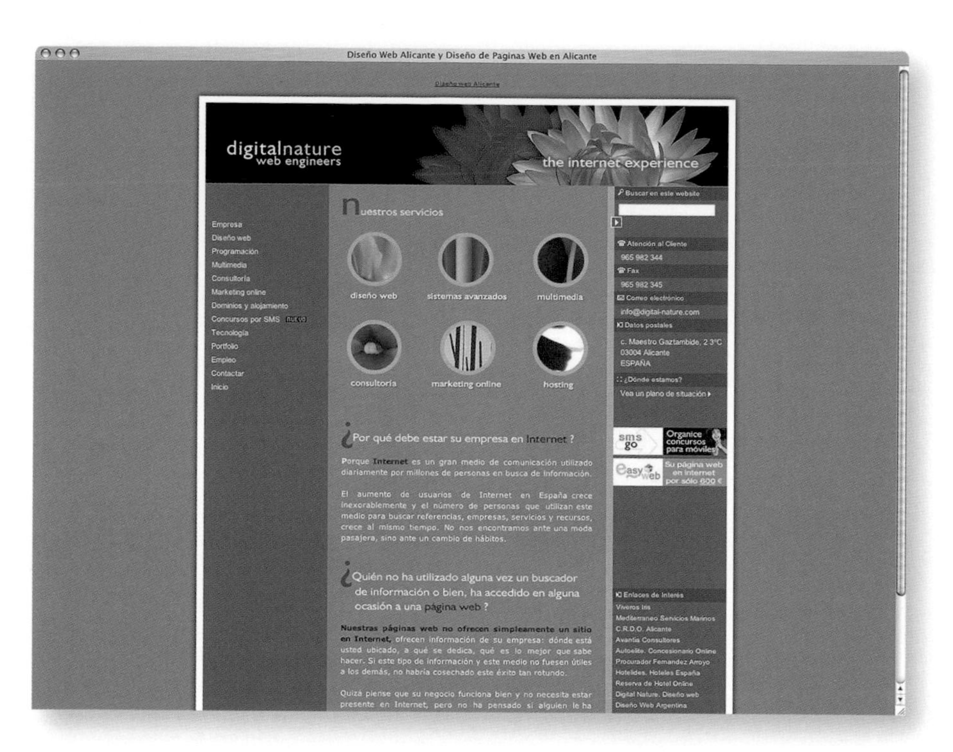

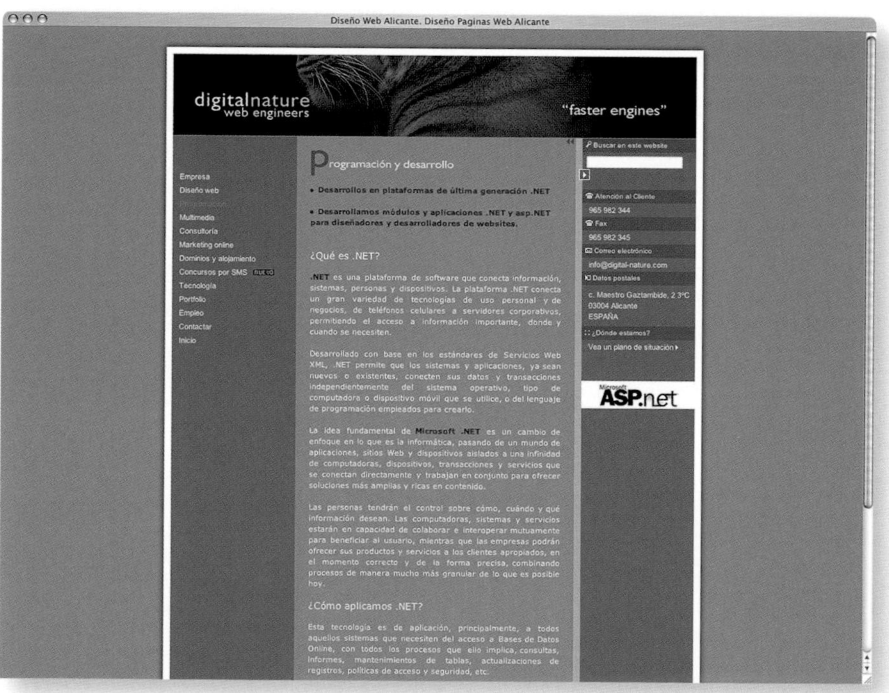

www.digital-nature.com

D: juan francisco berbejal rovira **C:** carlos berbejal rovira **P:** data click sl

A: digital nature **M:** info@digital-nature.com

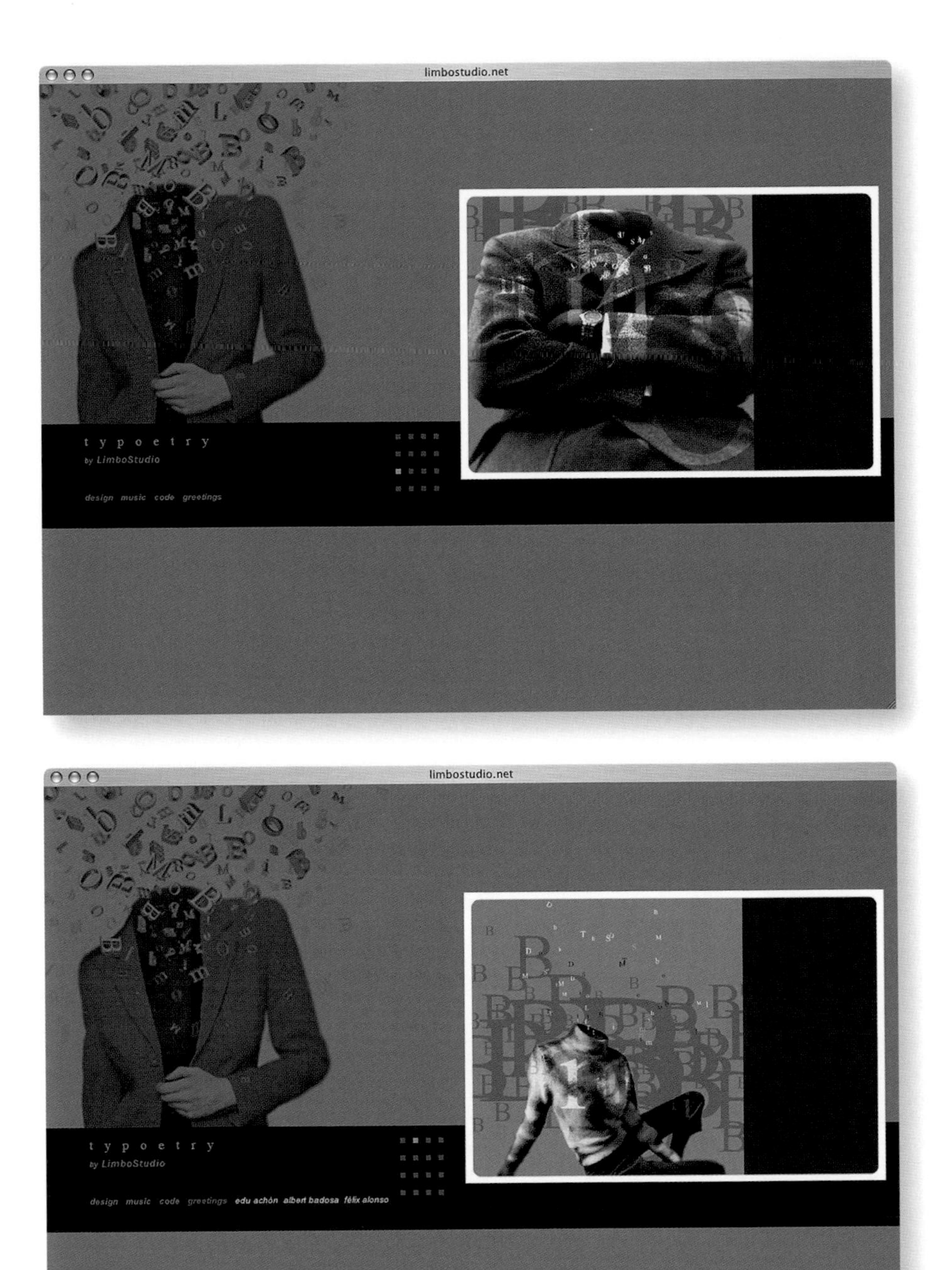

www.limbostudio.net

D: jordi carlos C: tecnoprog.com P: jordi carlos

A: limbostudio M: limbostudio@gmail.com

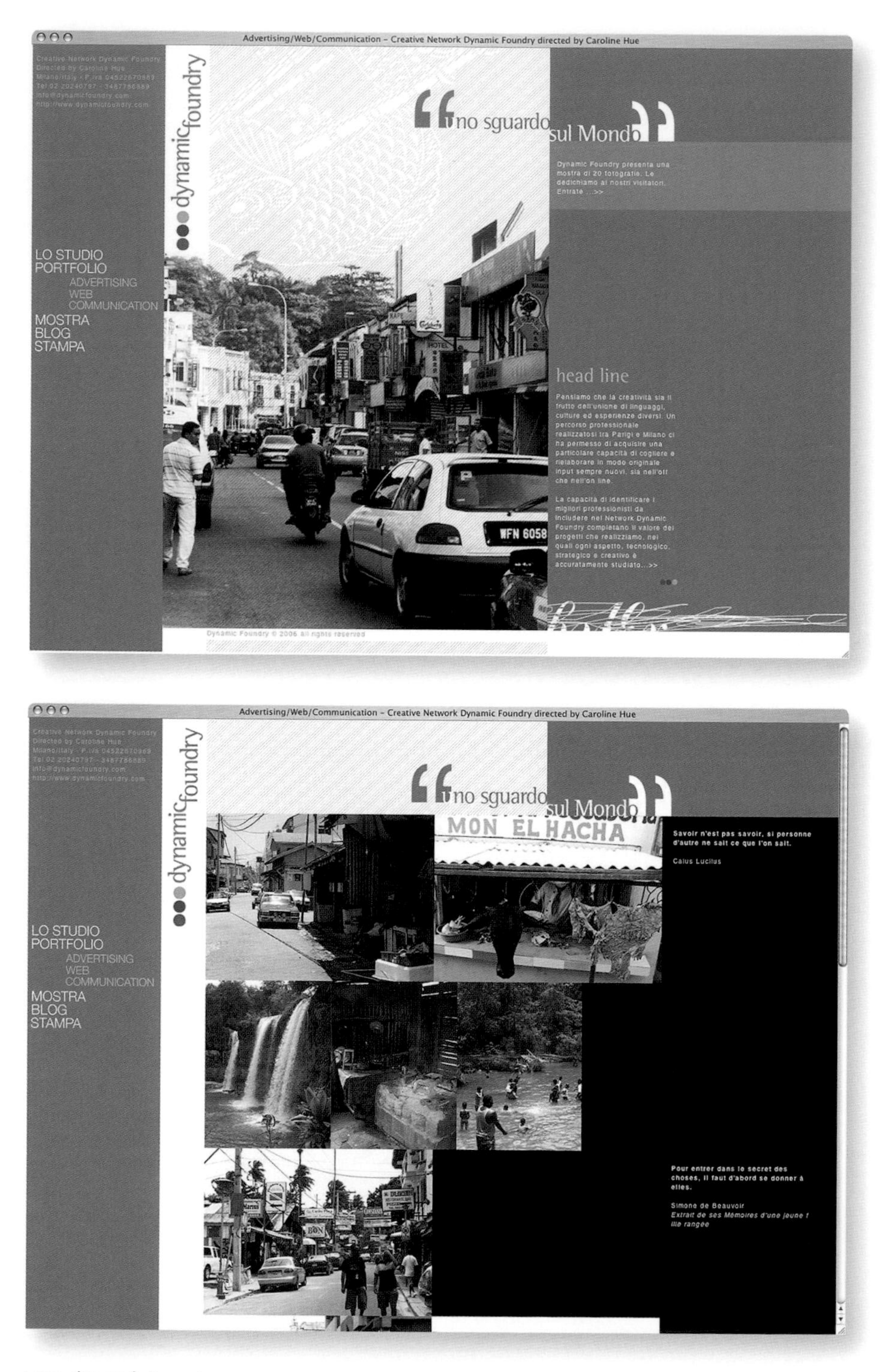

www.dynamicfoundry.com

D: caroline hue **C:** dynamic foundry staff **P:** dynamic foundry staff

A: dynamic foundry **M:** info@dynamicfoundry.com

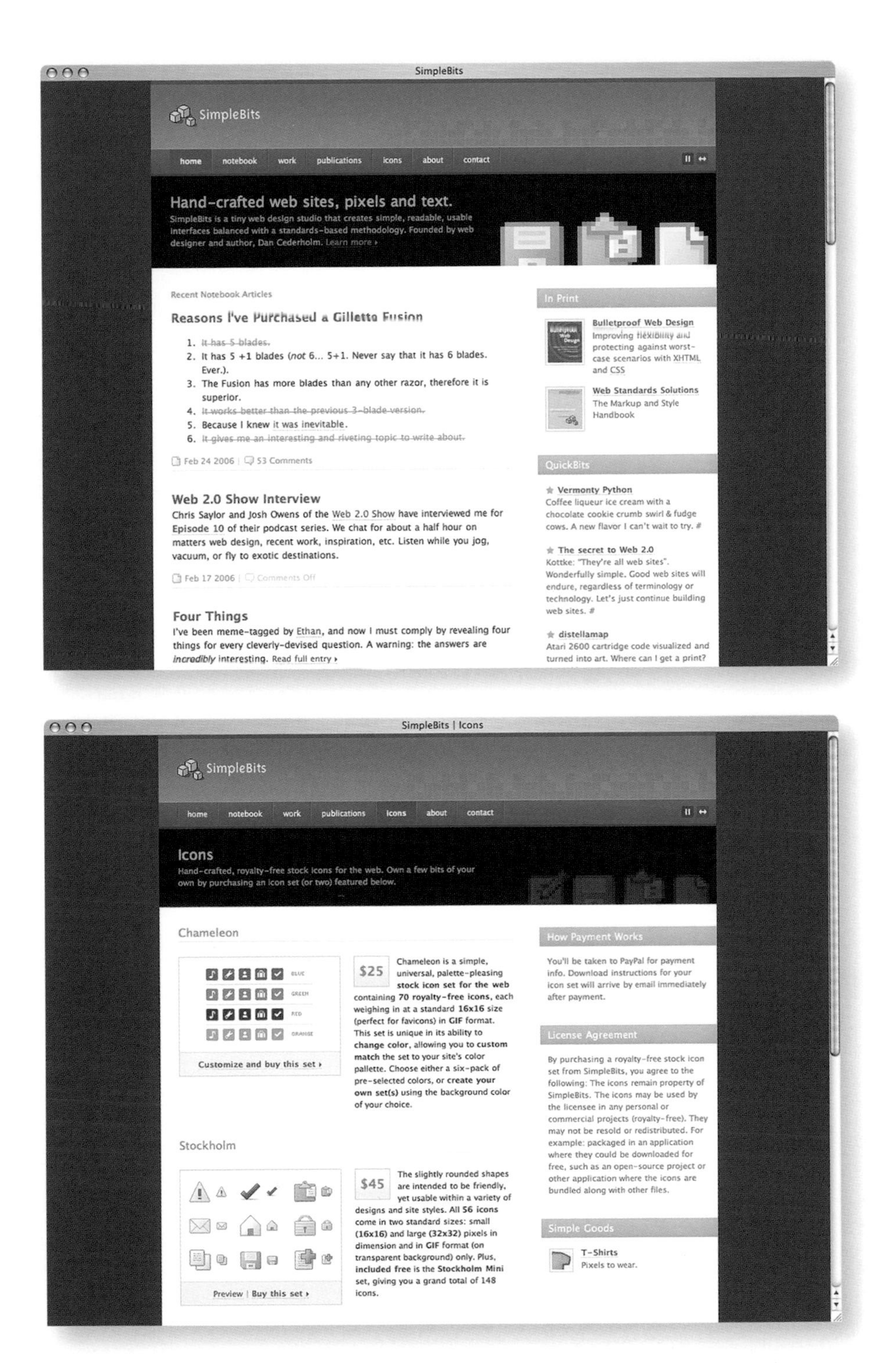

www.simplebits.com

D: dan cederholm

A: simplebits **M:** www.simplebits.com/contact

www.filipeduarte.com
D: filipe duarte
A: filipeduarte.com **M:** info@filipeduarte.com

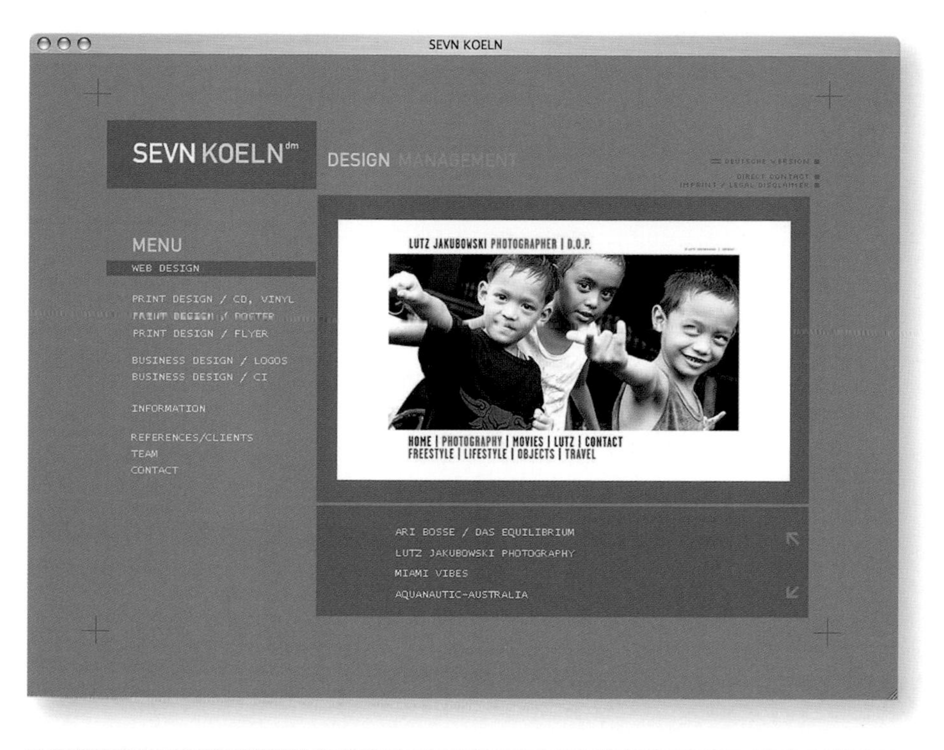

www.sevn.de

D: matthias klegraf **C:** christian spatz **P:** matthias klegraf

A: sevn koeln **M:** info@sevn.de

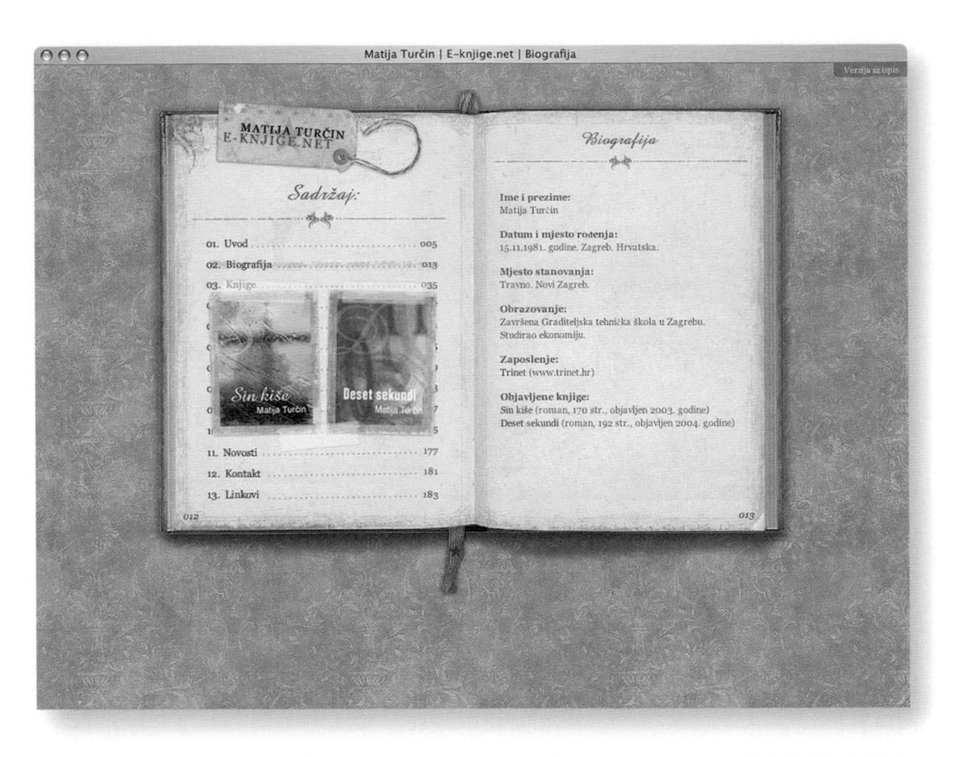

www.e-knjige.net

D: matija turcin

A: trinet **M:** info@trinet.hr

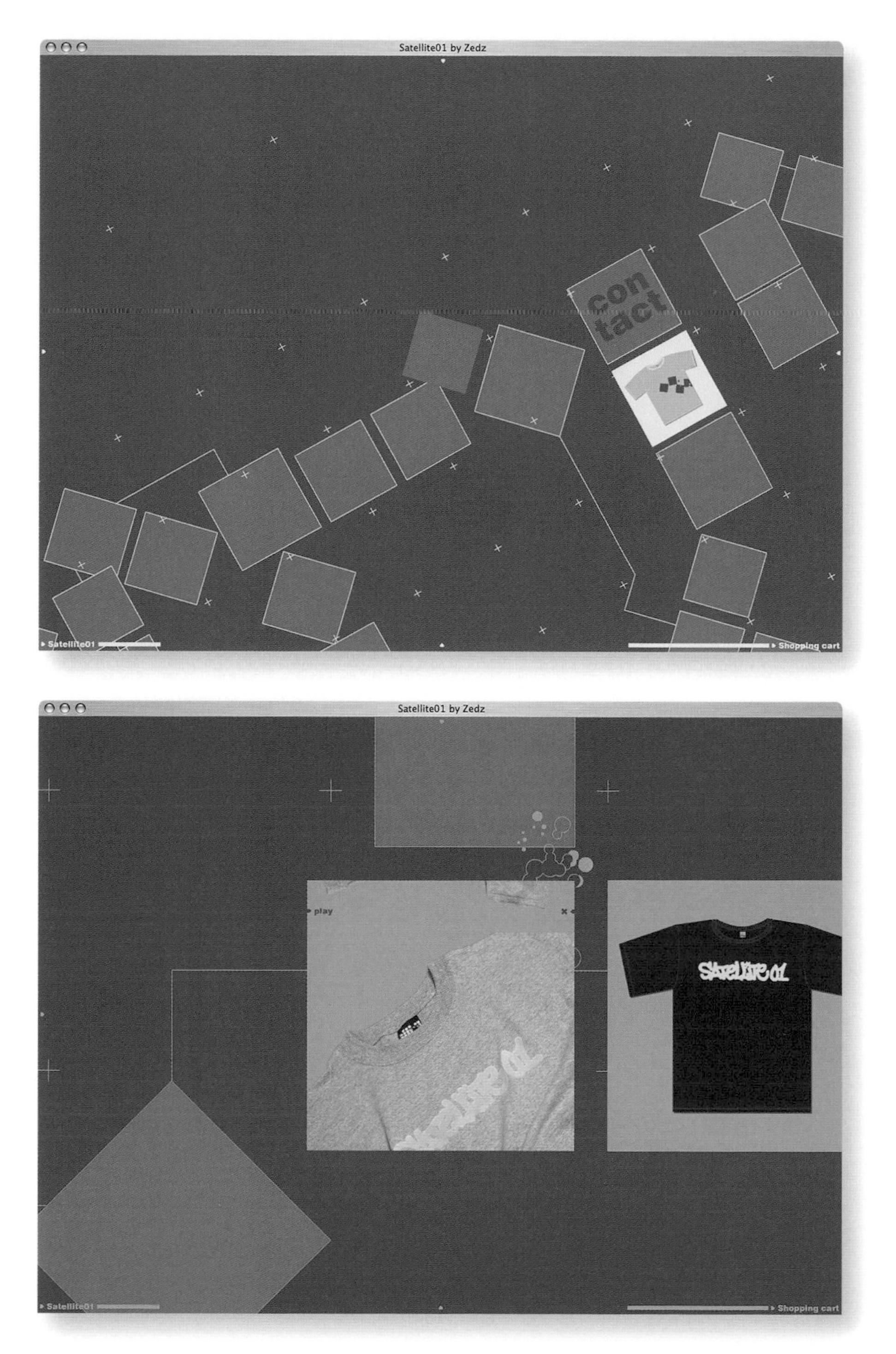

www.satellite01.com
D: ronald wisse
A: visualdata M: www.visualdata.org

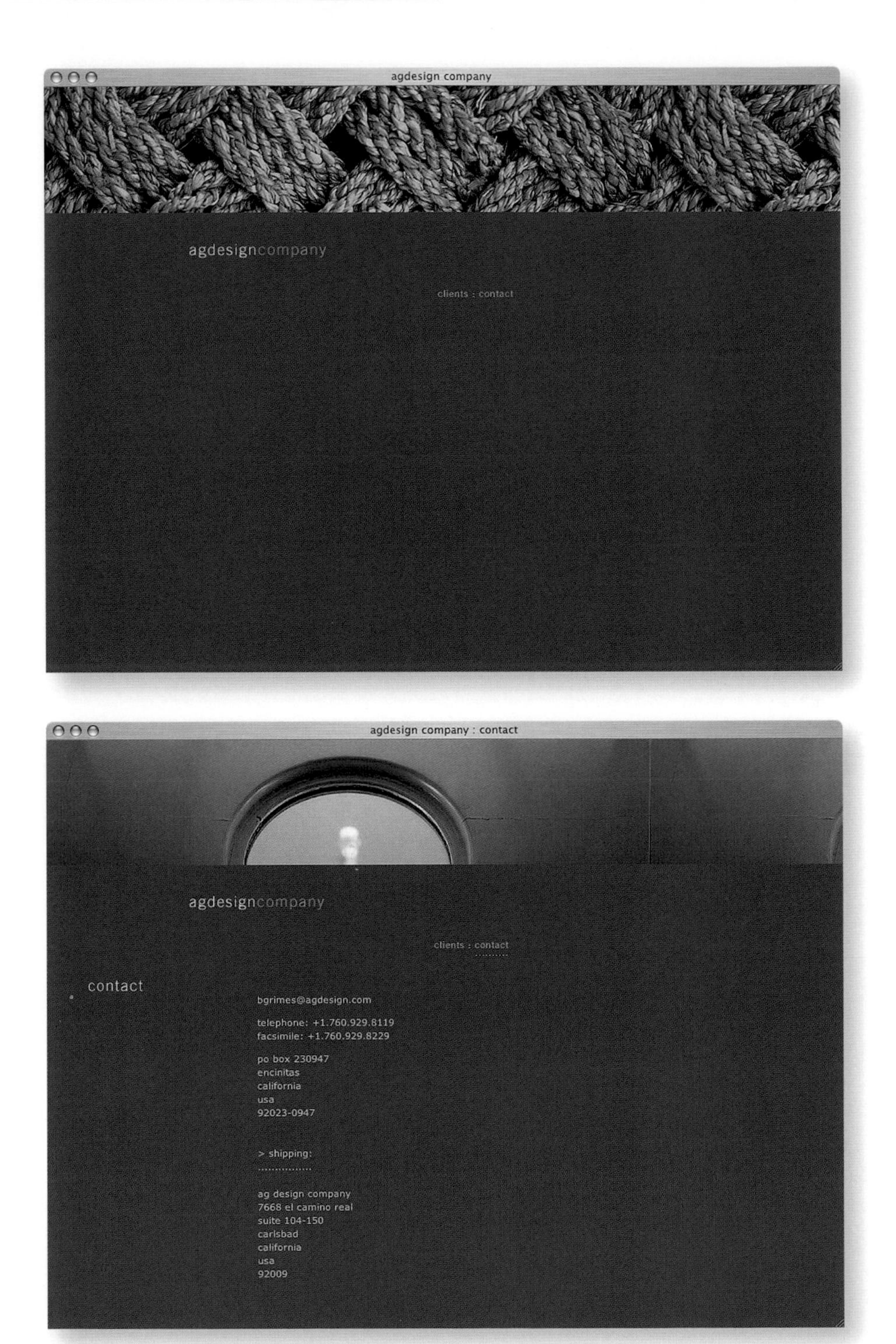

www.agdesign.com

D: barry grimes **C:** patrick dennis **P:** barry grimes

A: agdesign company **M:** barryg@agdesign.com

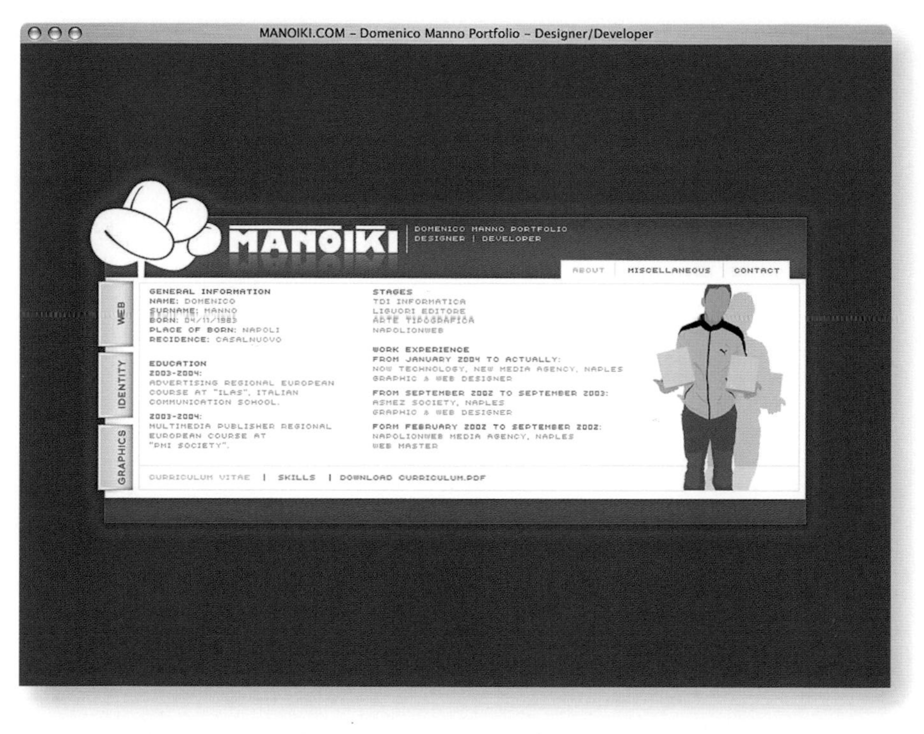

www.manoiki.com
D: domenico manno
M: domenico@manoiki.com

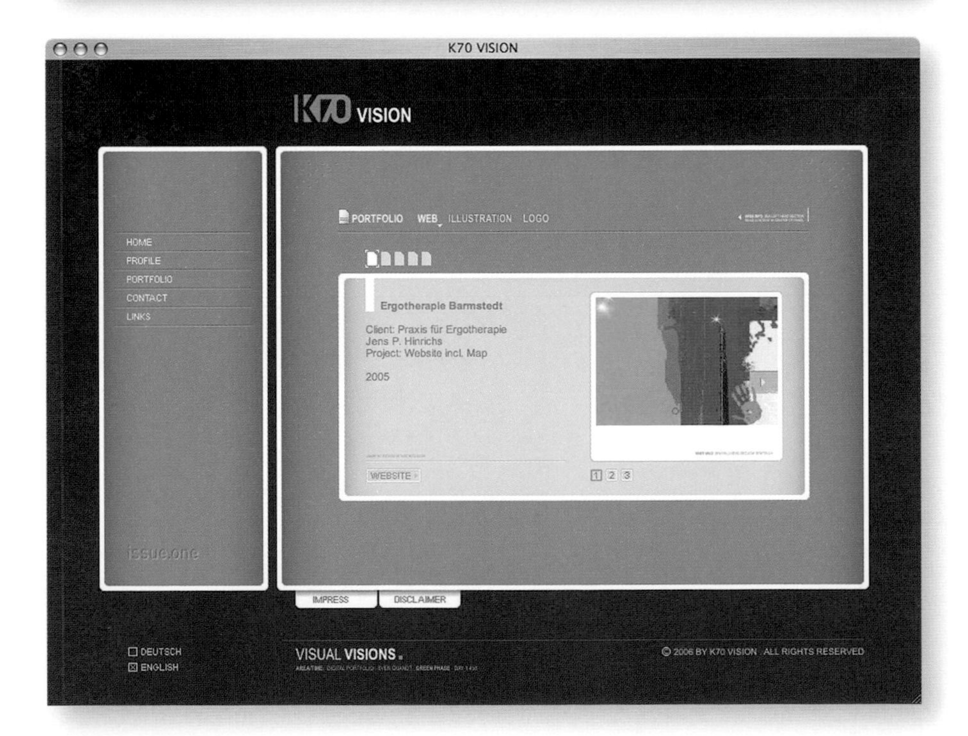

www.k70vision.com
D: sven quandt
M: info@k70vision.com

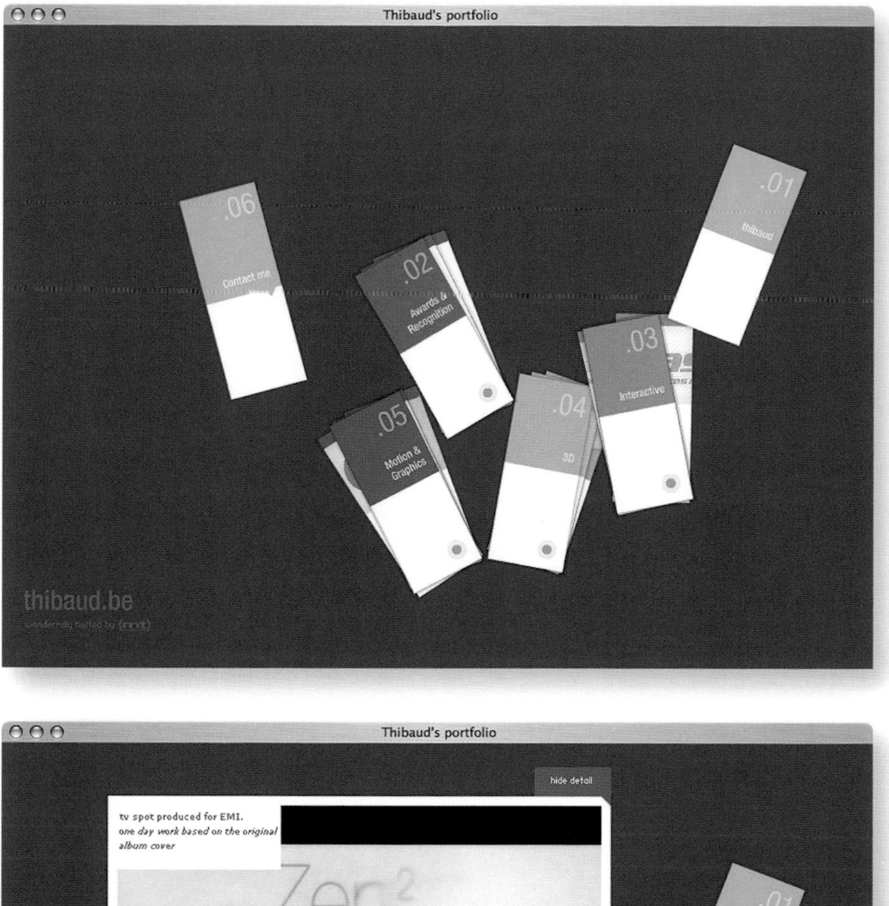

www.thibaud.be

D: thibaud van vreckem

A: apricus M: thibaud@apricus.be

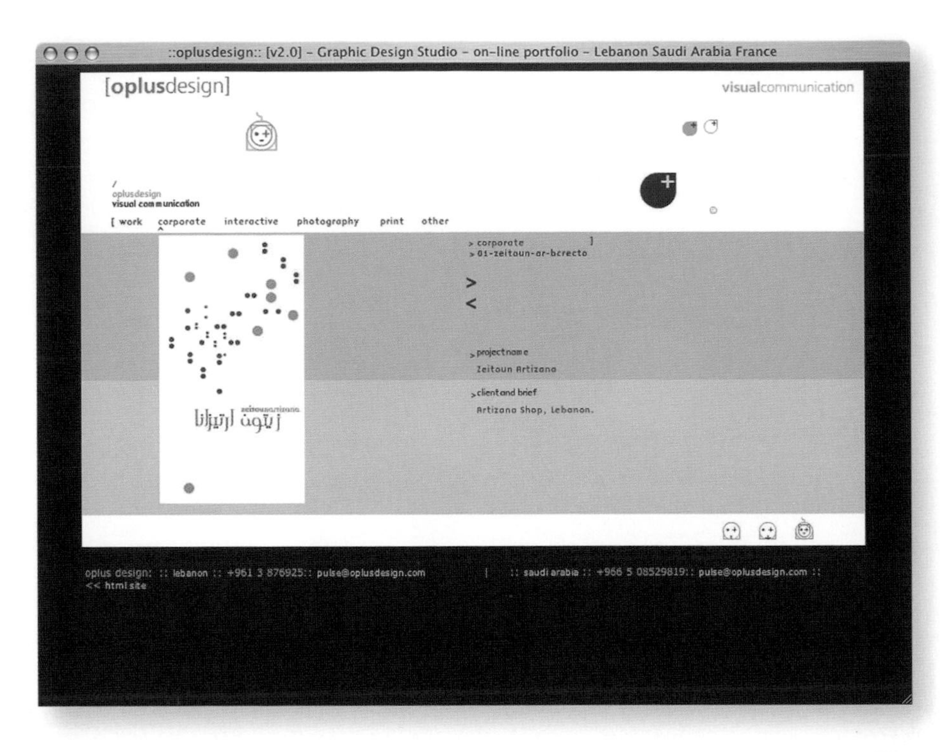

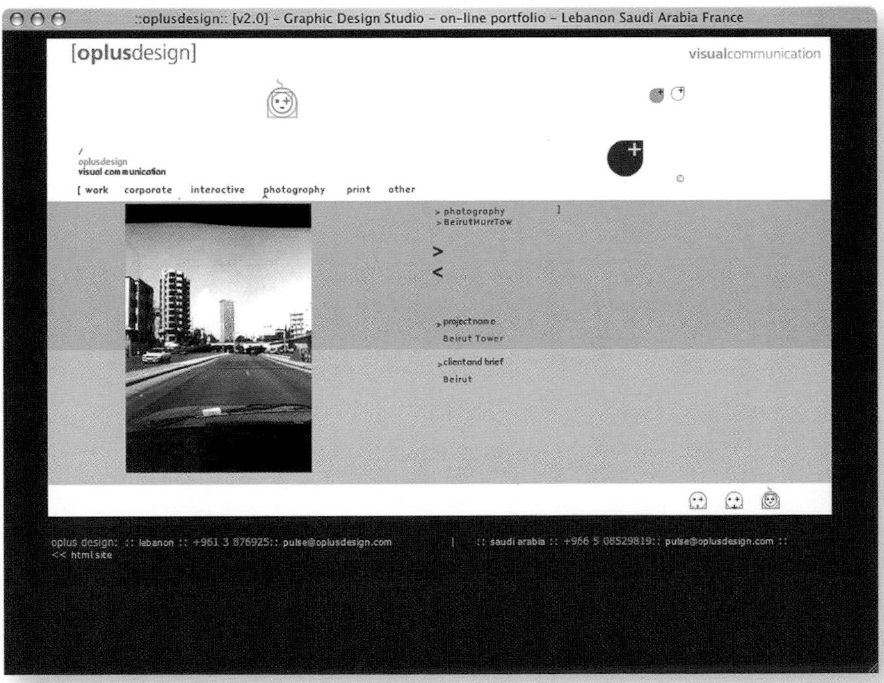

www.oplusdesign.com

D: samer lahoud, toufic tawil **C:** samer lahoud **P:** o plus design

A: oplus design **M:** pulse@oplusdesign.com

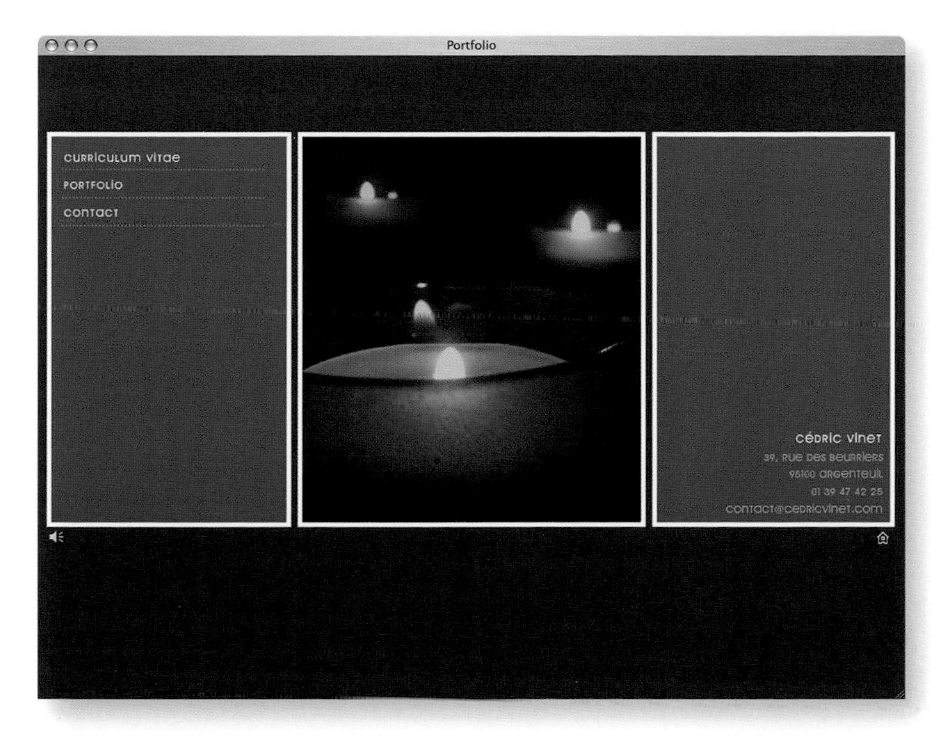

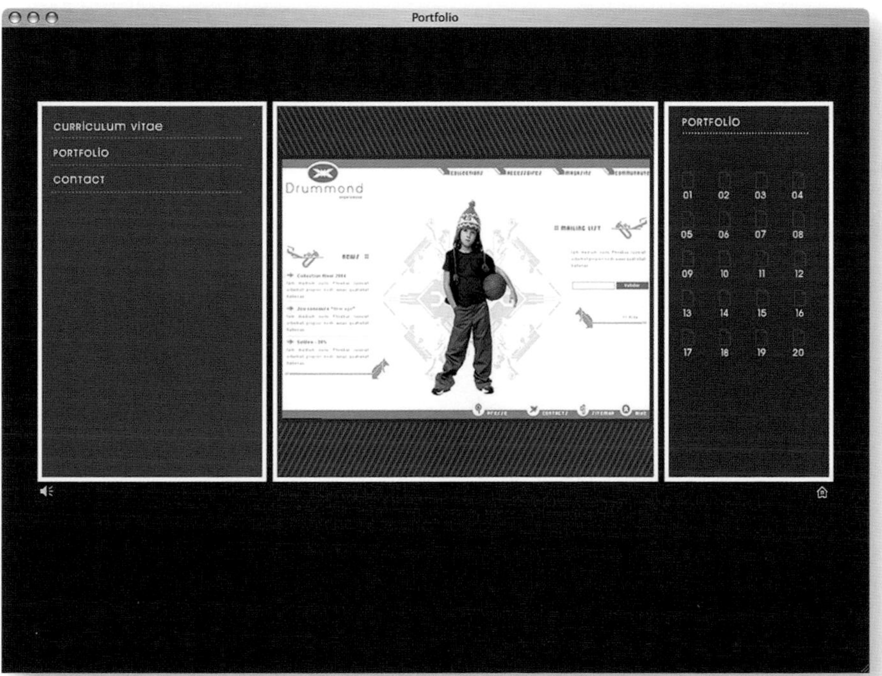

www.cedricvinet.com/site2/index.htm

D: cédric vinet

A: cédric vinet **M:** contact@cedricvinet.com

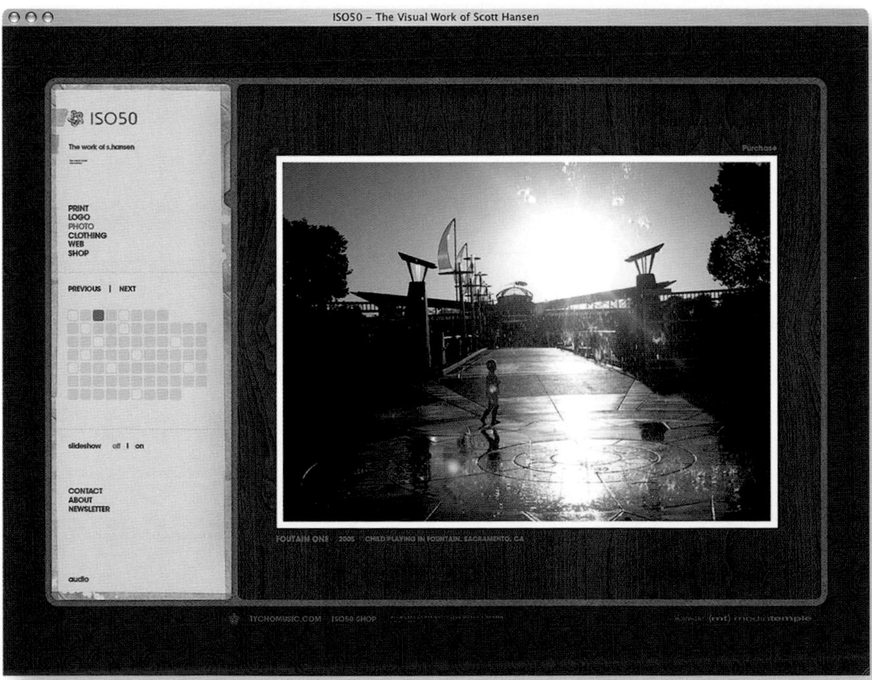

www.iso50.com

D: scott hansen **C:** dusty brown

A: iso50 **M:** scott@iso50.com

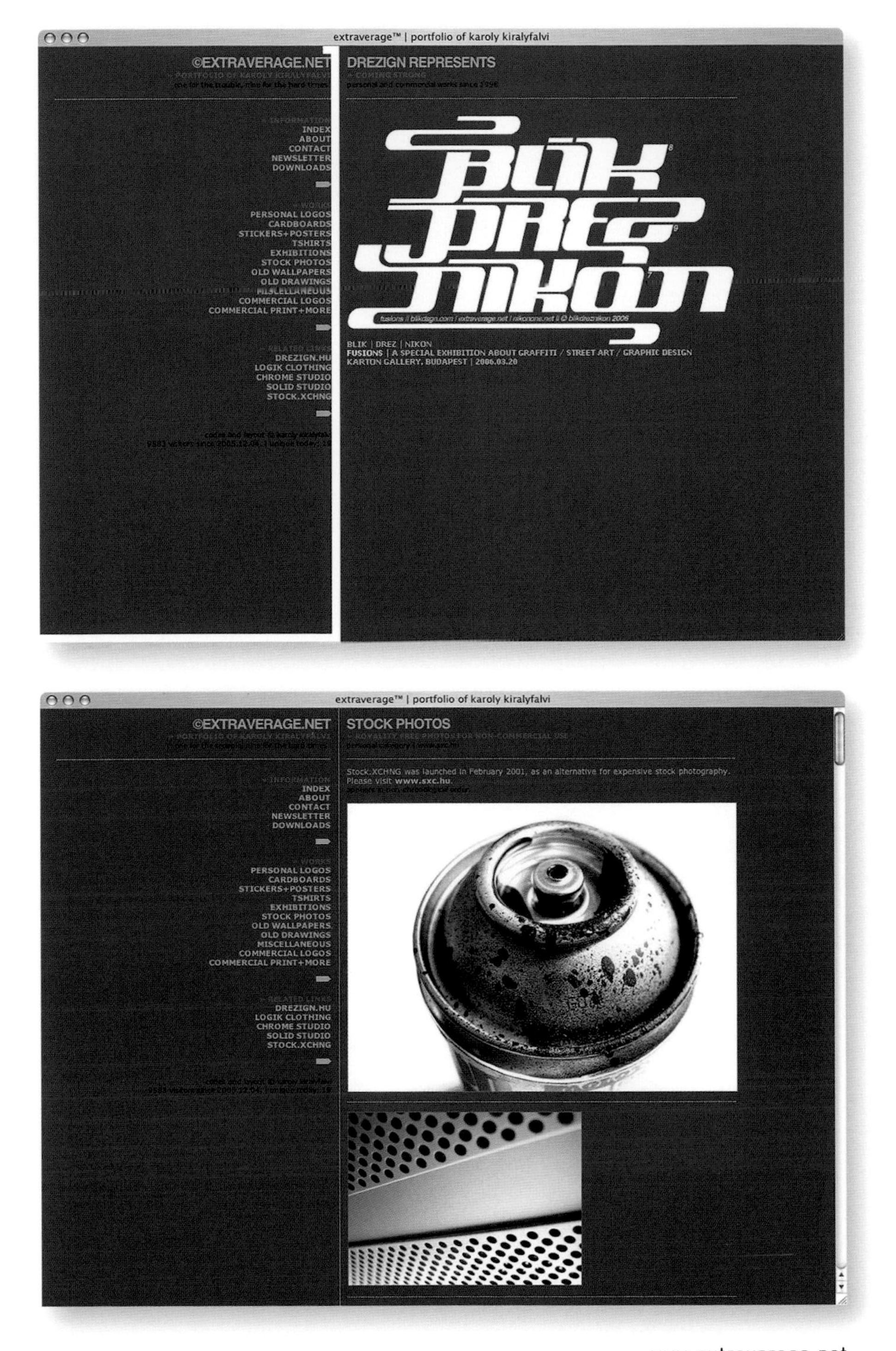

www.extraverage.net
D: karoly kiralyfalvi C: karoly kiralyfalvi P: drez
M: info@extraverage.net

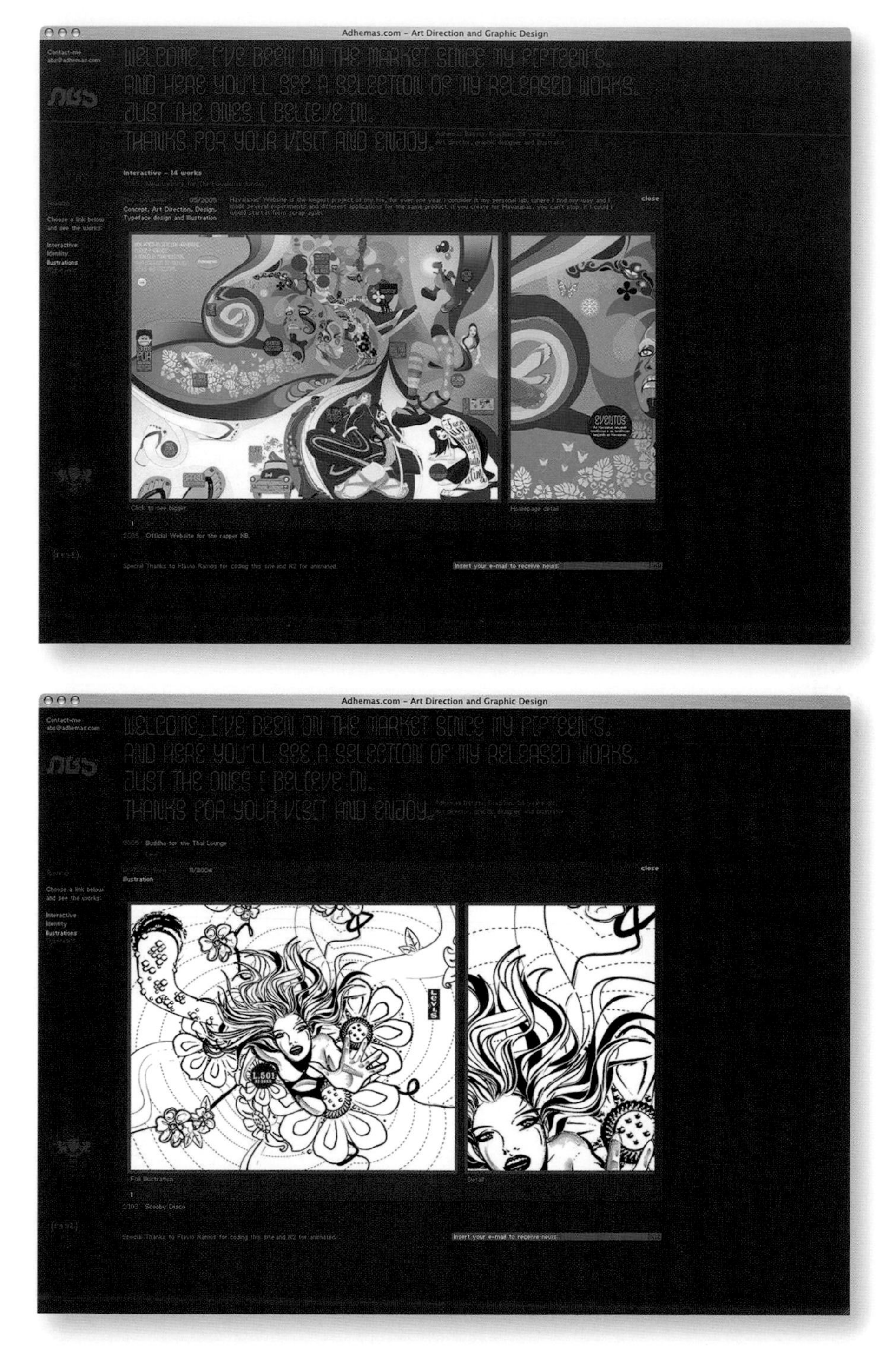

www.adhemas.com

D: adhemas batista **C:** flávio ramos **P:** adhemas batista

M: abs@adhemas.com

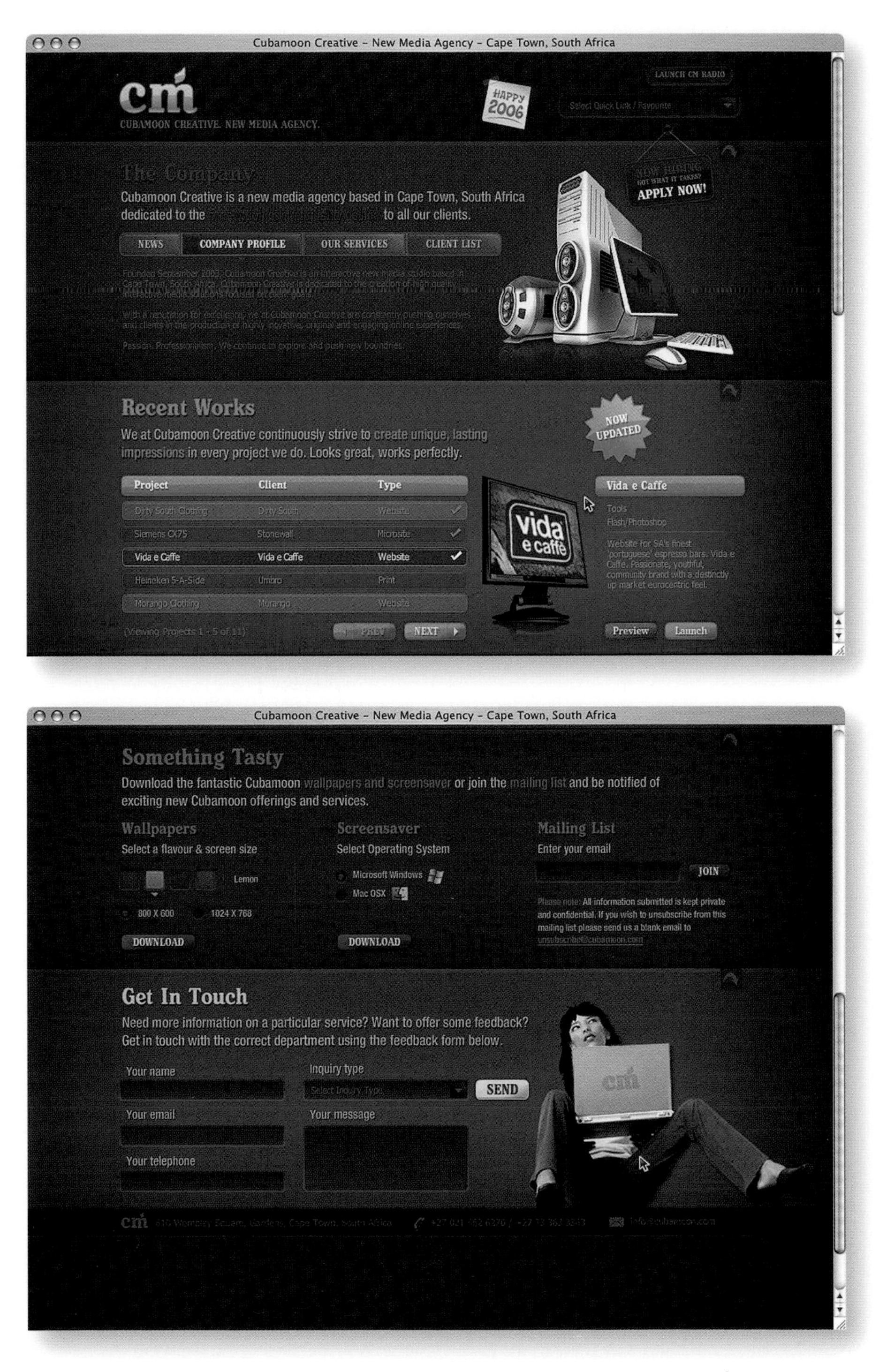

www.cubamoon.com

D: jimmy caravotas

A: cubamoon creative M: info@cubamoon.com

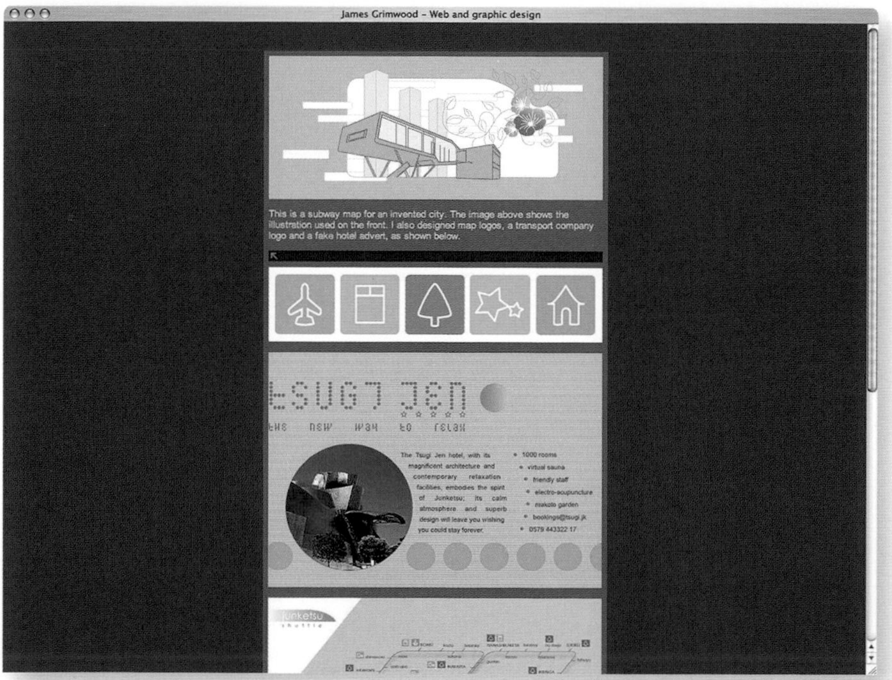

www.jamesgrimwood.co.uk

D: james grimwood

A: james grimwood **M:** james@jamesgrimwood.co.uk

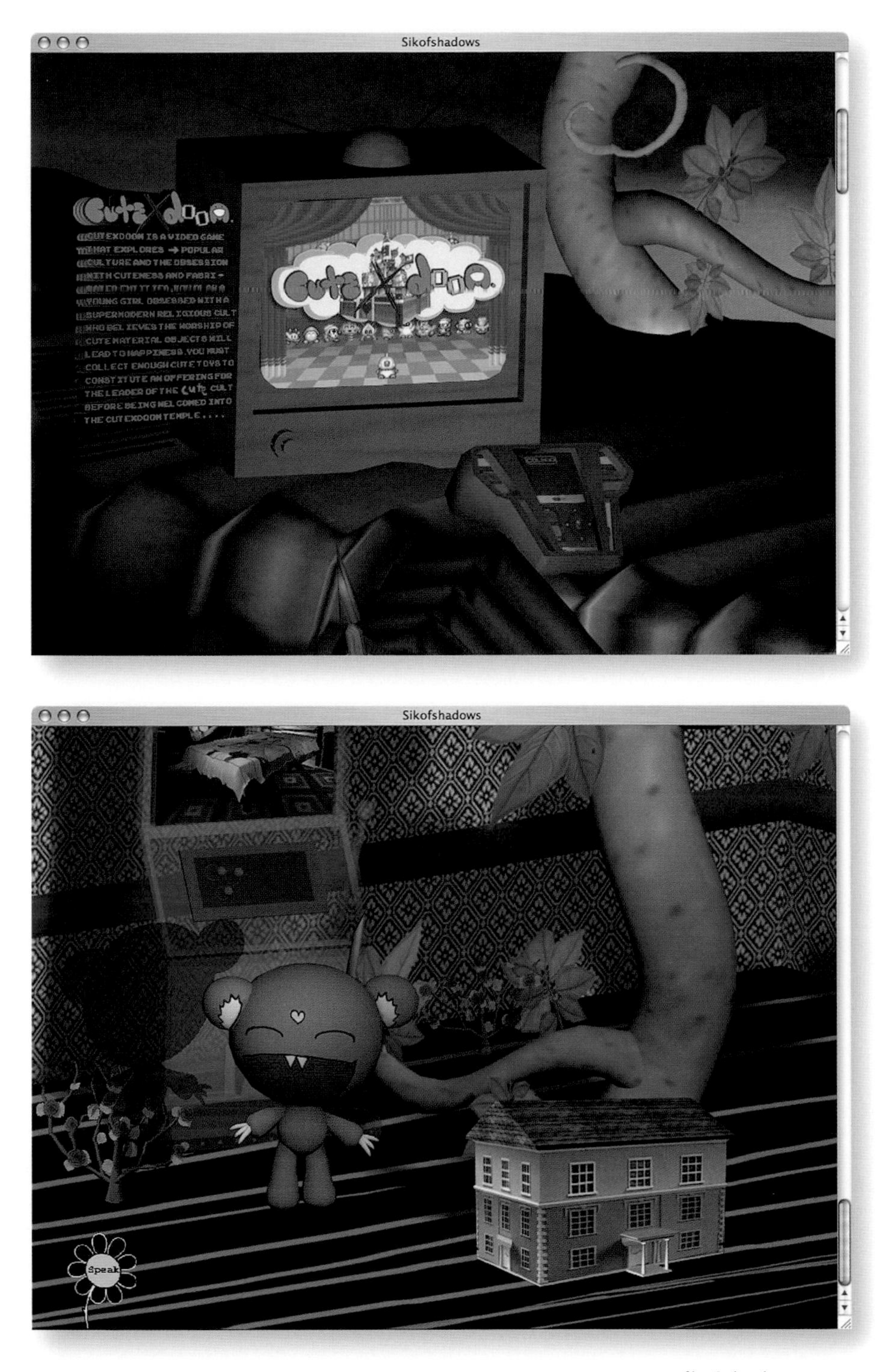

www.sikofshadows.com

D: anita fontaine

A: yumi-co **M:** ladybuggin@gmail.com

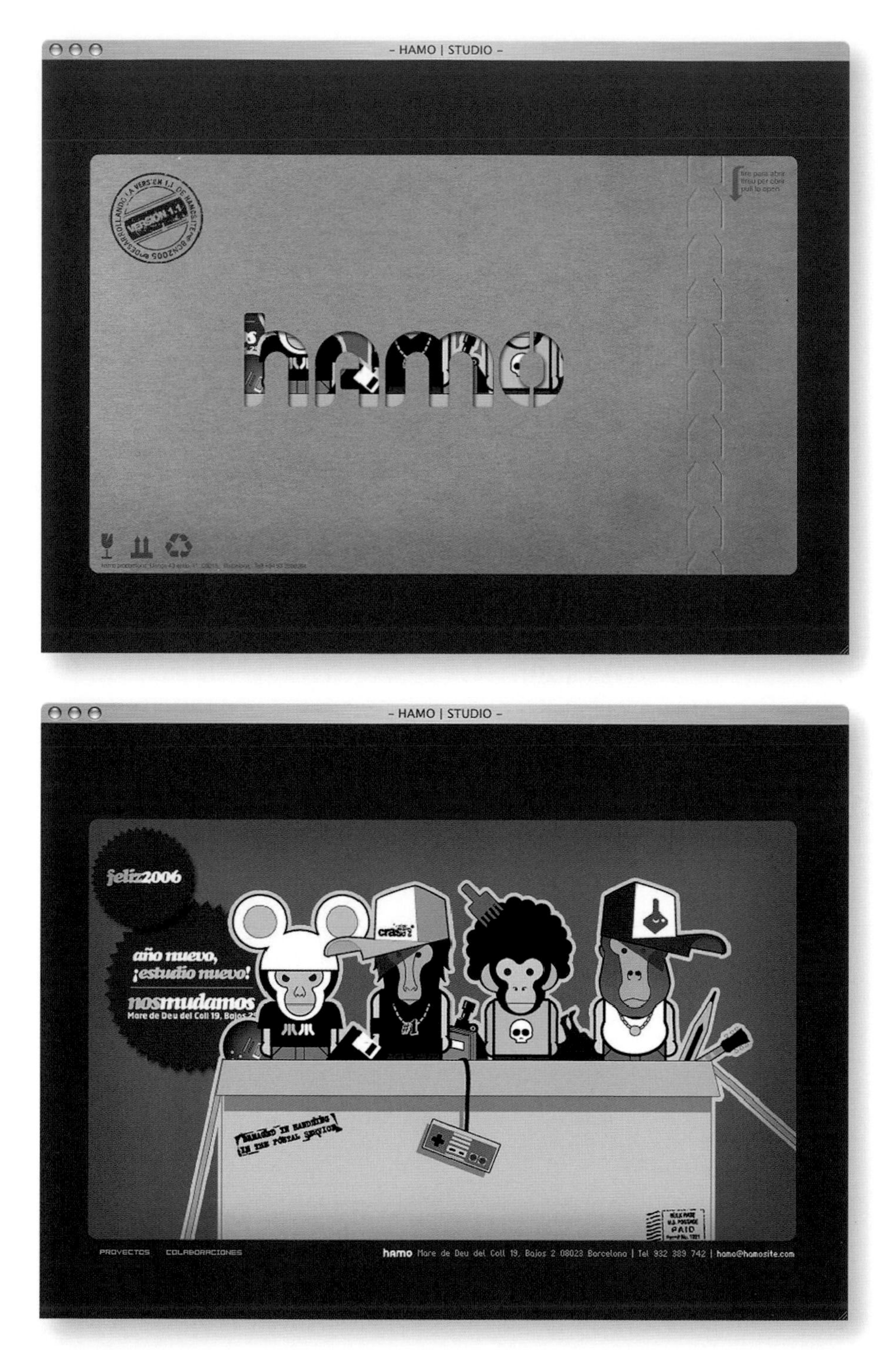

www.hamosite.com

D: pablo sánchez, lui villanueva **C:** ivan caño **P:** borja fusté

A: hamo studio **M:** hamo@hamosite.com

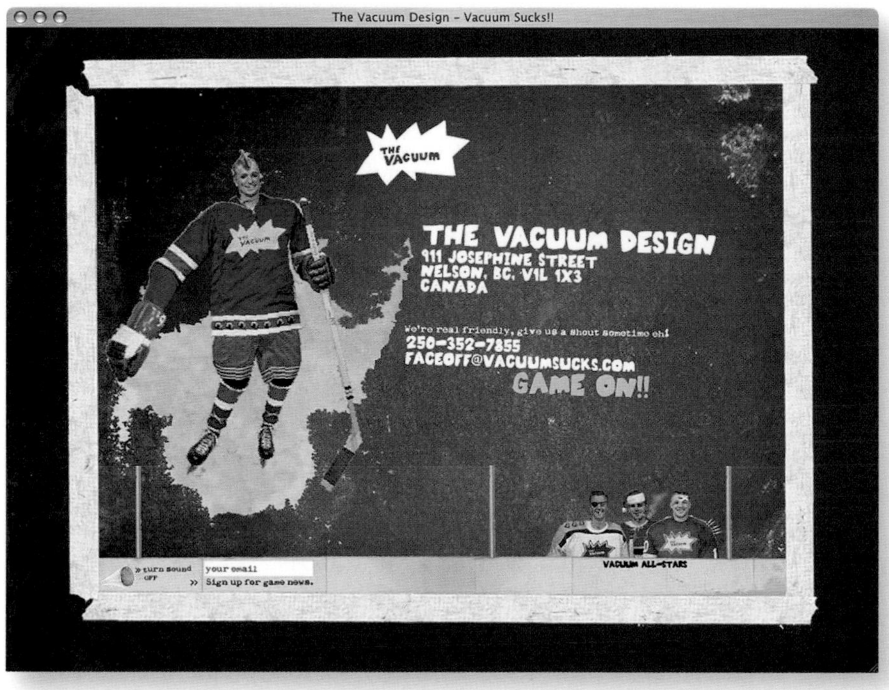

www.vacuumsucks.com

D: nate smith, tyler kealey **C:** kris mclaughlin **P:** team vacuum

A: the vacuum design **M:** faceoff@vacuumsucks.com

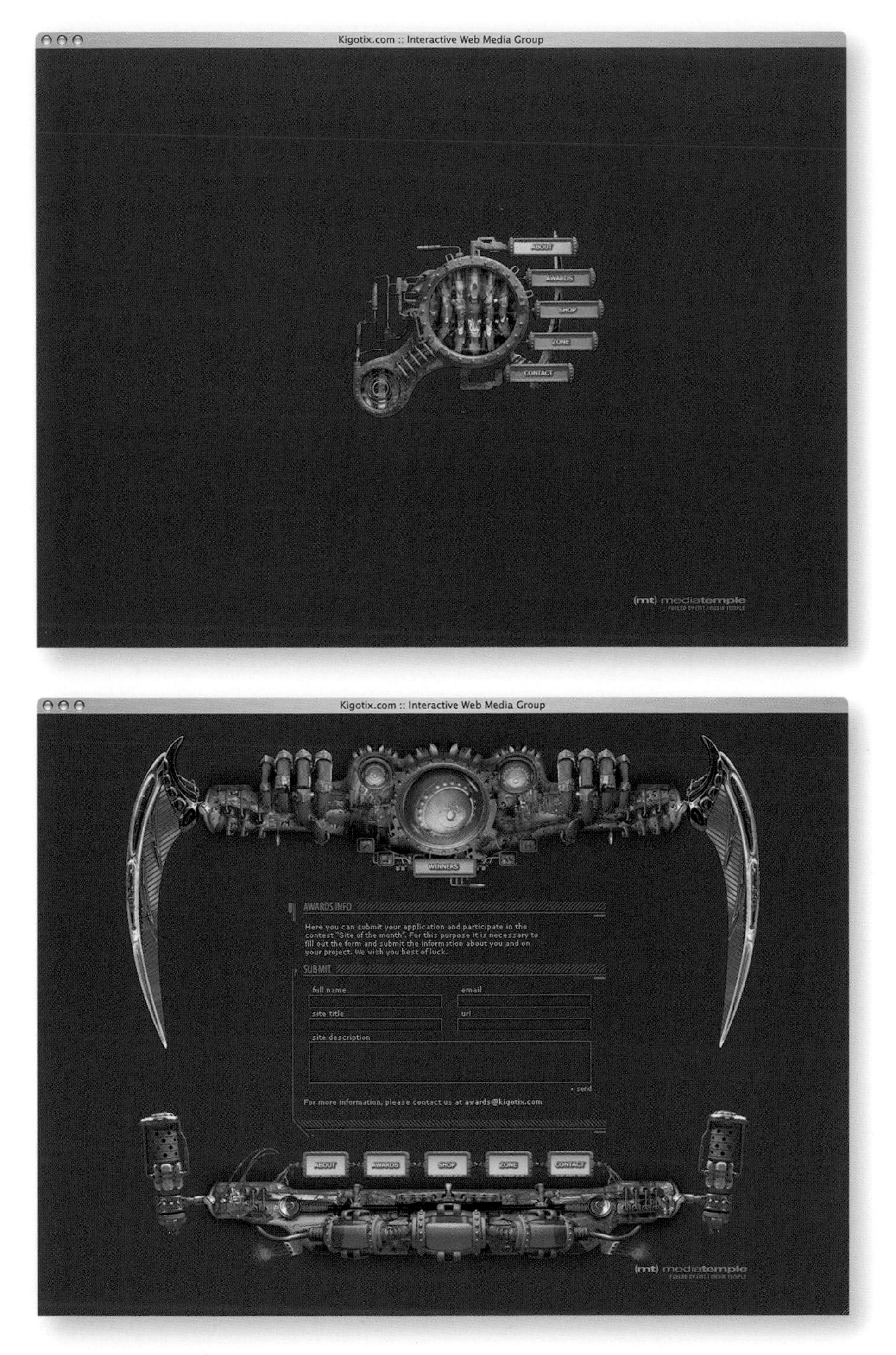

www.kigotix.com/kigotix

D: kuovoy roman **C:** jiganov artom **P:** kuovoy roman

A: kigotix **M:** info@kigotix.com

www.thehipperelement.com

D: joel marsh

A: the hipper element **M:** joel@thehipperelement.com

www.ilkilkilk.com

D: ilk

M: ilkone@gmail.com

www.fb.se

D: forsman, bodenfors **P:** thomson mediautveckling, north kingdom, astronaut

A: forsman & bodenfors **M:** info@fb.se

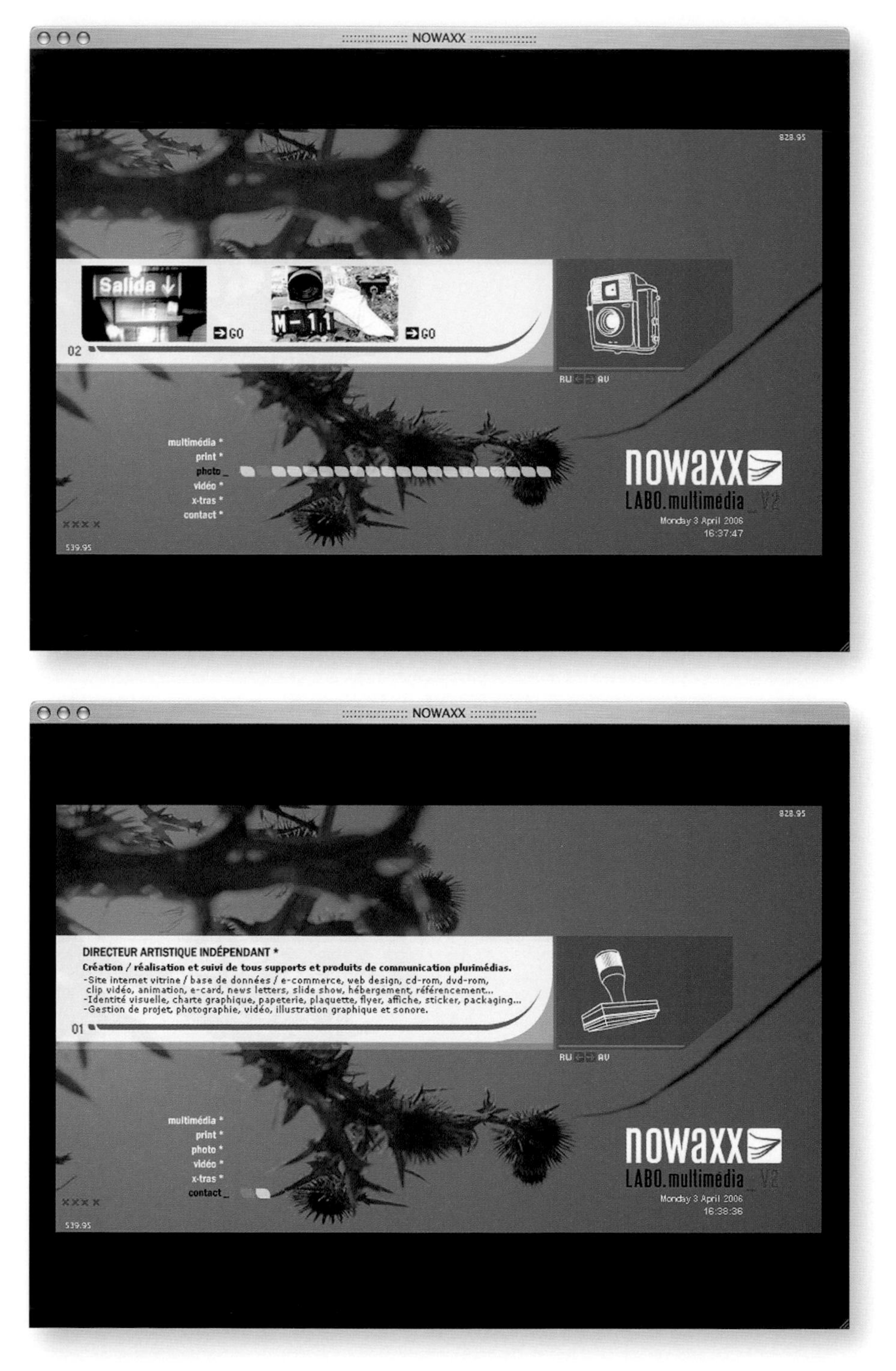

www.nowaxx.com

D: fabrice corneux

A: fabrice corneux **M:** fabrice@nowaxx.com

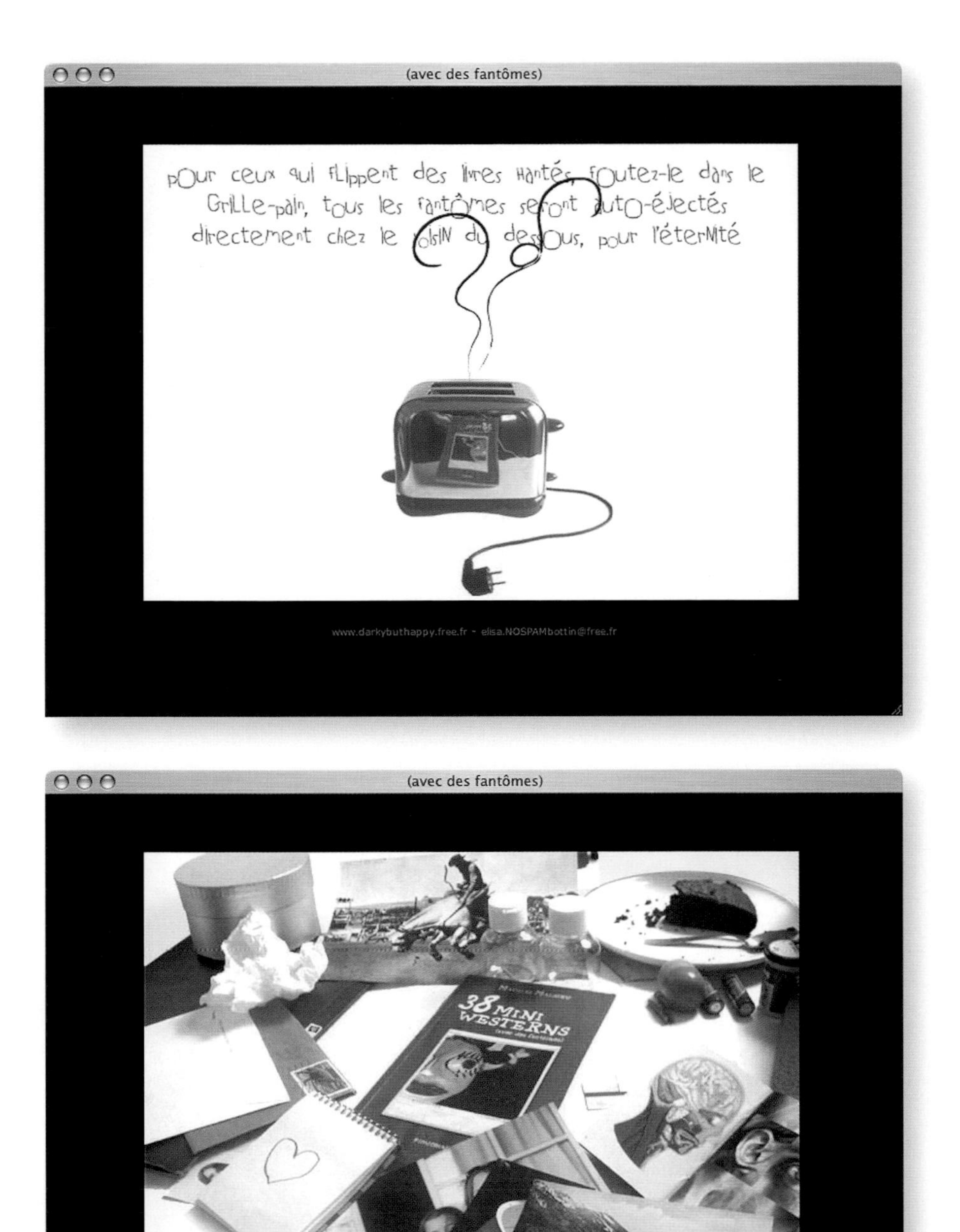

miniwesterns.free.fr

D: élisa bottin

M: elisa.bottin@free.fr

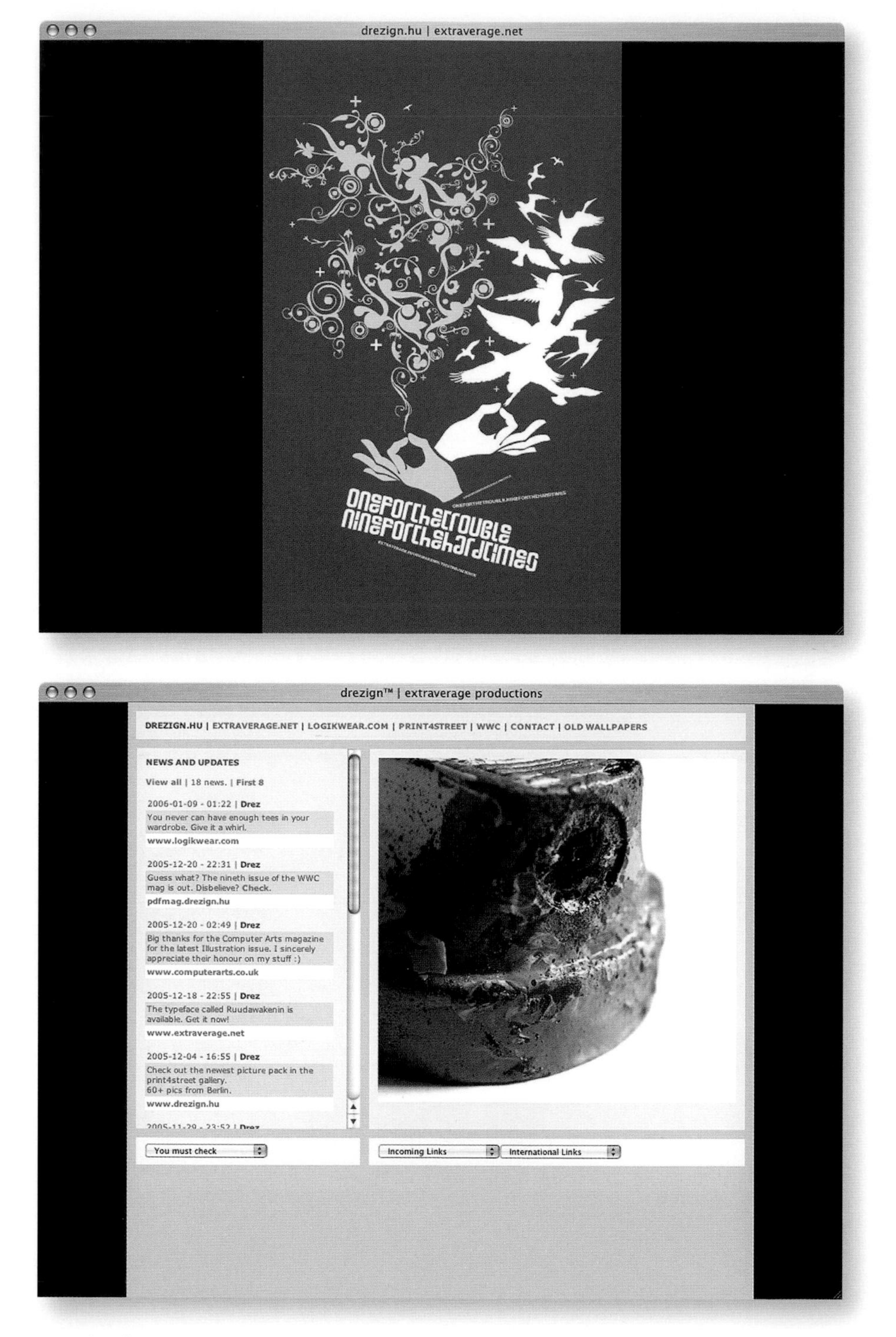

www.drezign.hu

D: karoly kiralyfalvi **C:** karoly kiralyfalvi **P:** drez

M: hello@drezign.hu

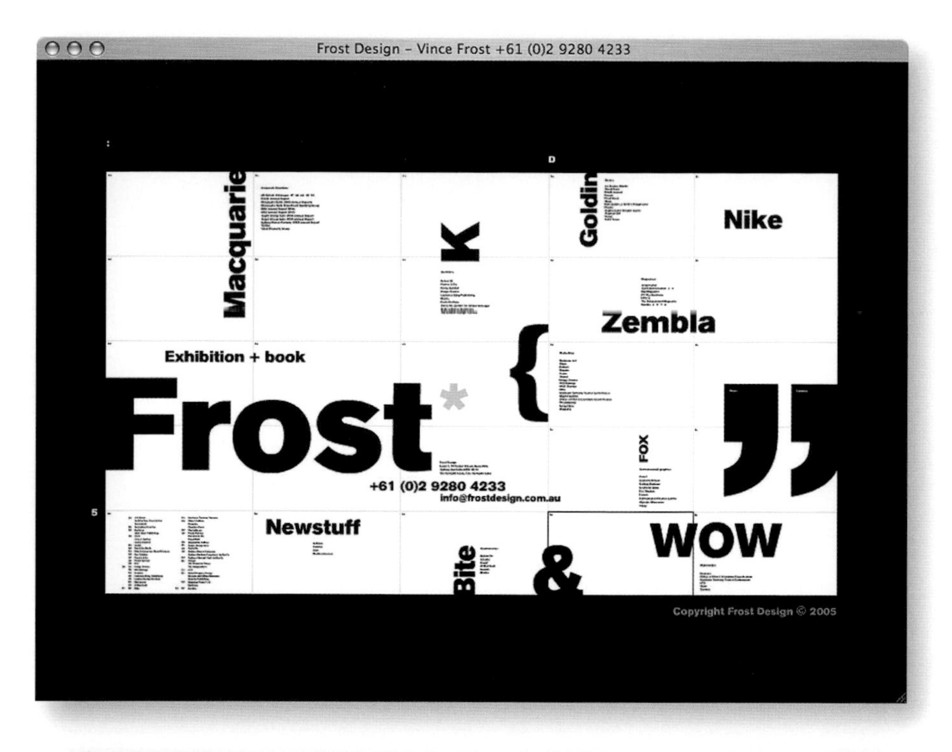

www.frostdesign.com.au
D: fred flade, vince frost
A: de-construct M: info@frostdesign.com.au

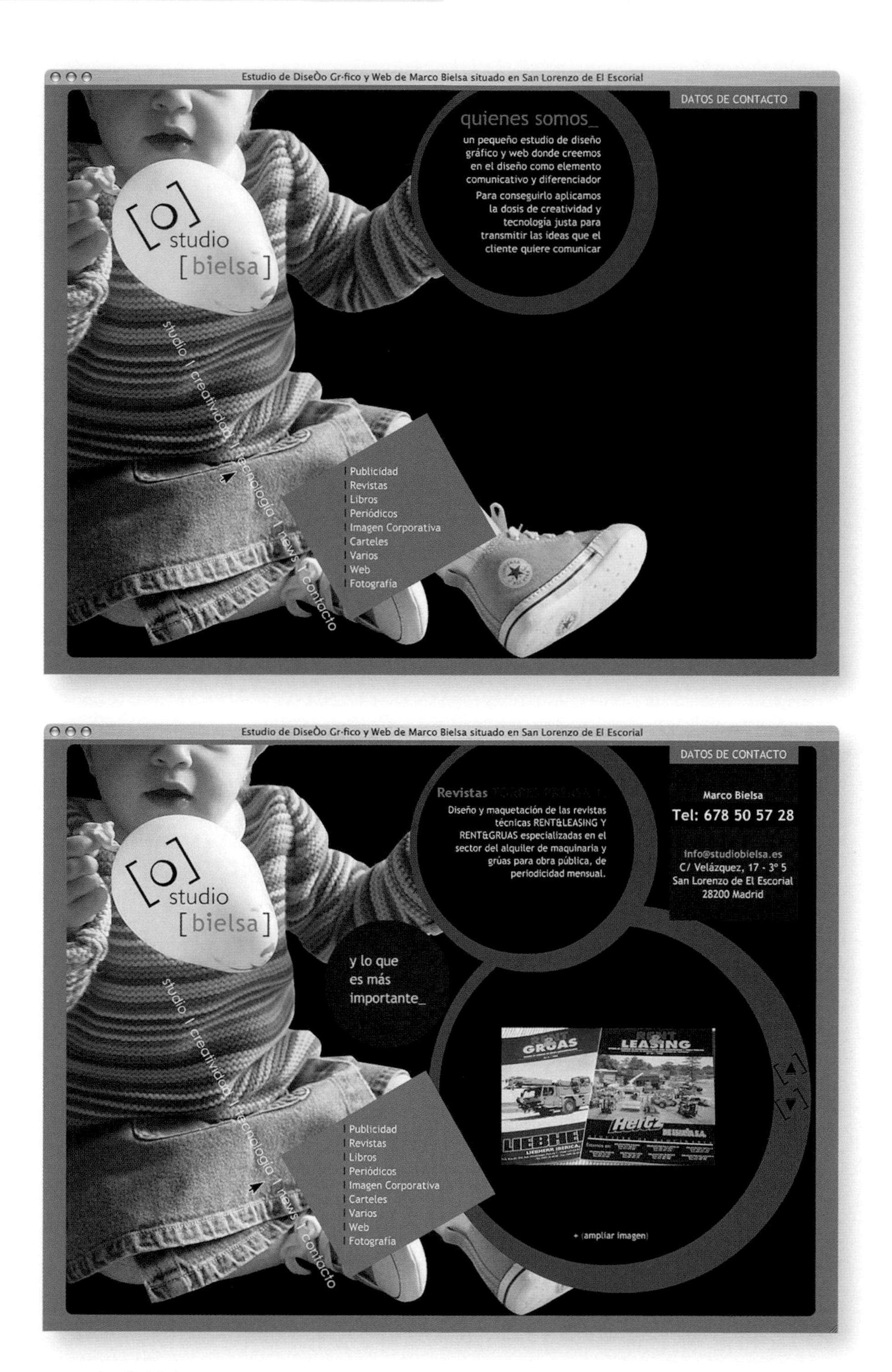

www.studiobielsa.es

D: marco bielsa

A: studiobielsa **M:** www.studiobielsa.es

spleener-creation.com
D: richard tran
M: spleener-creation.com

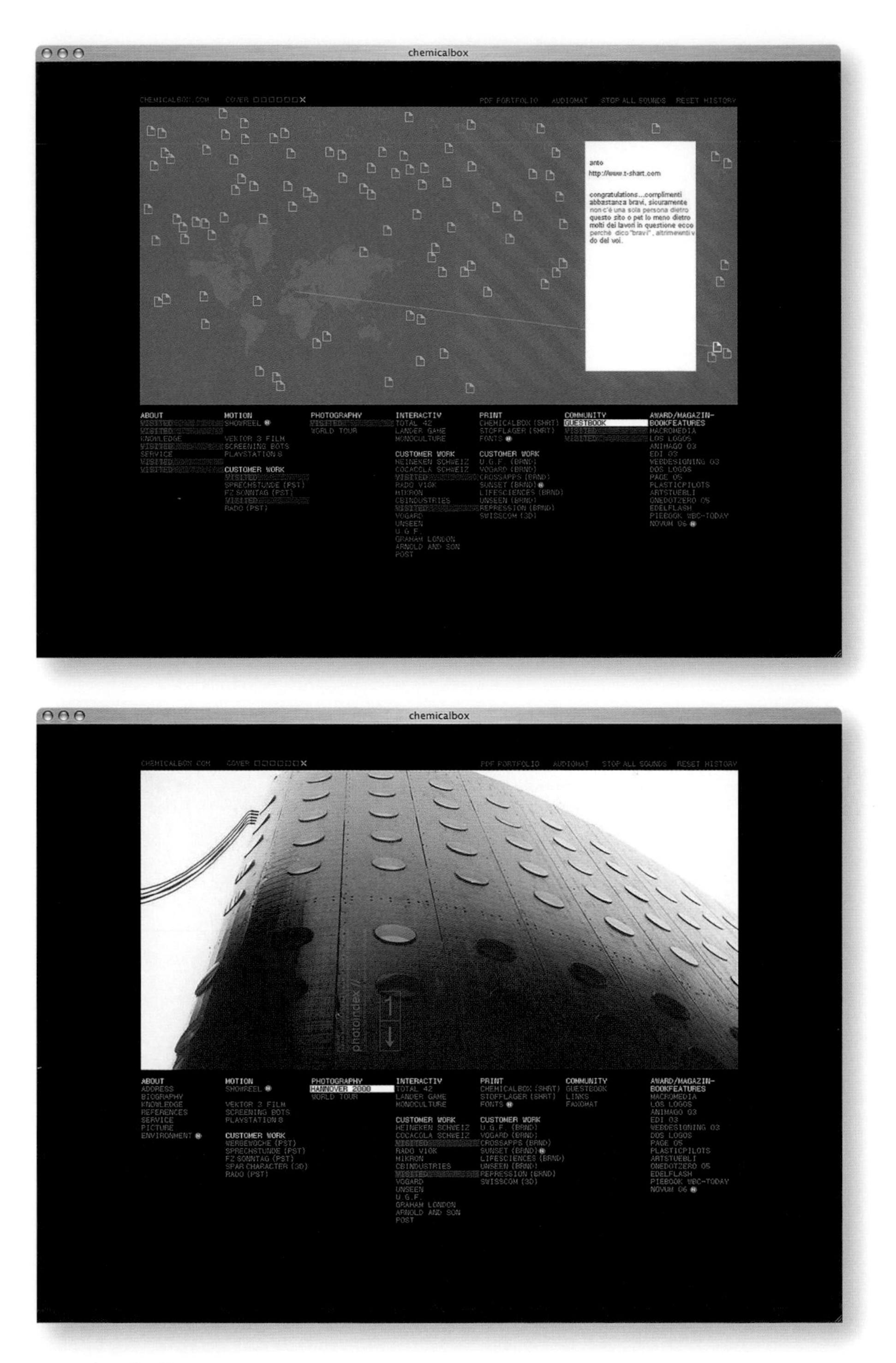

www.chemicalbox.com

D: mario buholzer

A: chemicalbox **M:** bureau@chemicalbox.com

www.oringe.com
D: benjamin wong
A: oringe M: www.oringe.com

www.fubon.co.uk

D: constantine yarosh, anna yarosh

A: fubon M: info@fubon.co.uk

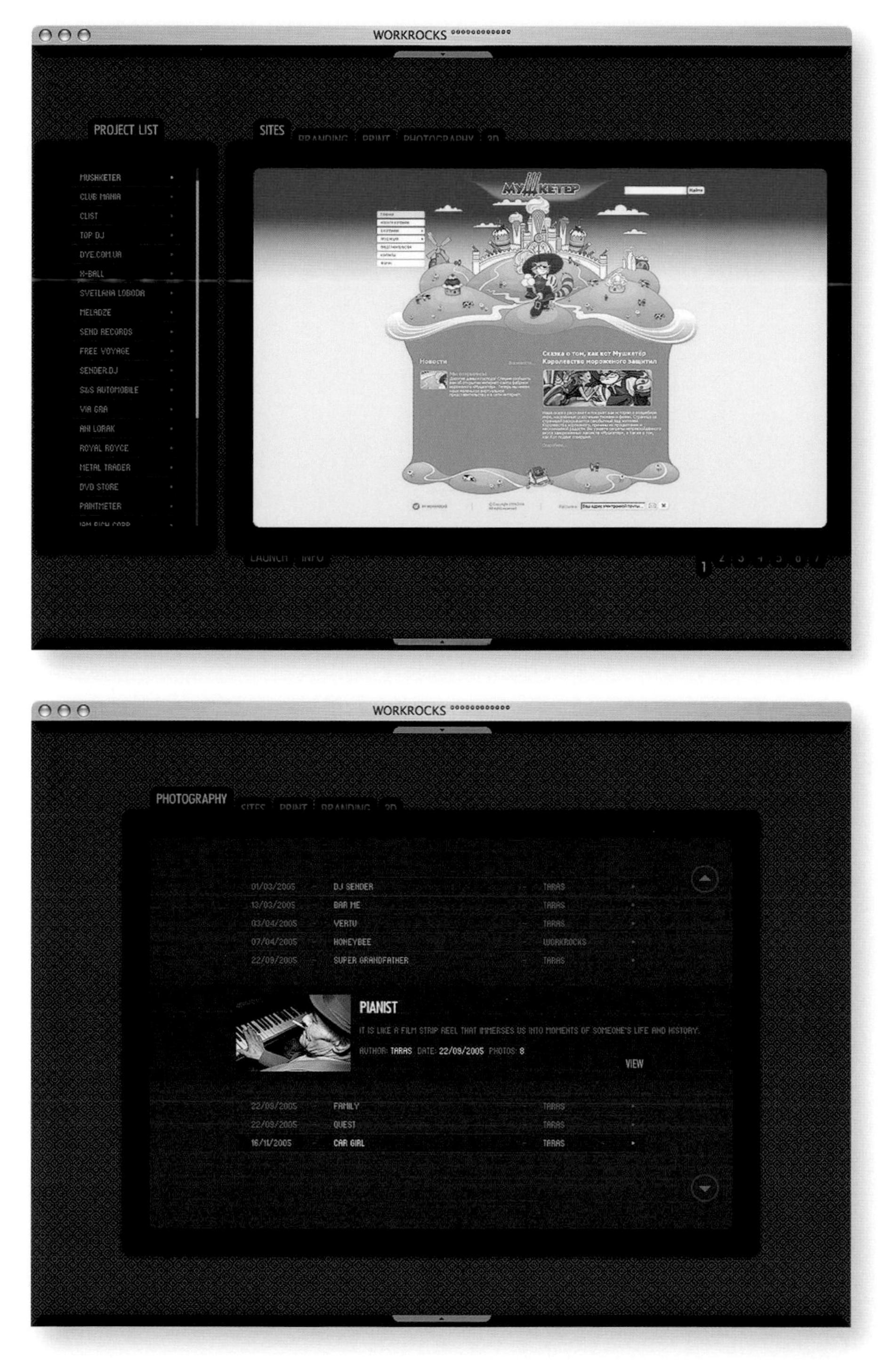

workrocks.com

D: workrocks

A: workrocks **M:** team@workrocks.com

www.lyo.com.br

D: leonardo rafael schneider

A: lyo design digital M: lyo@lyo.com.br

www.amberfly.com

D: peter barr **C:** douglas noble **P:** amberfly ltd

A: amberfly ltd **M:** enquiries@amberfly.com

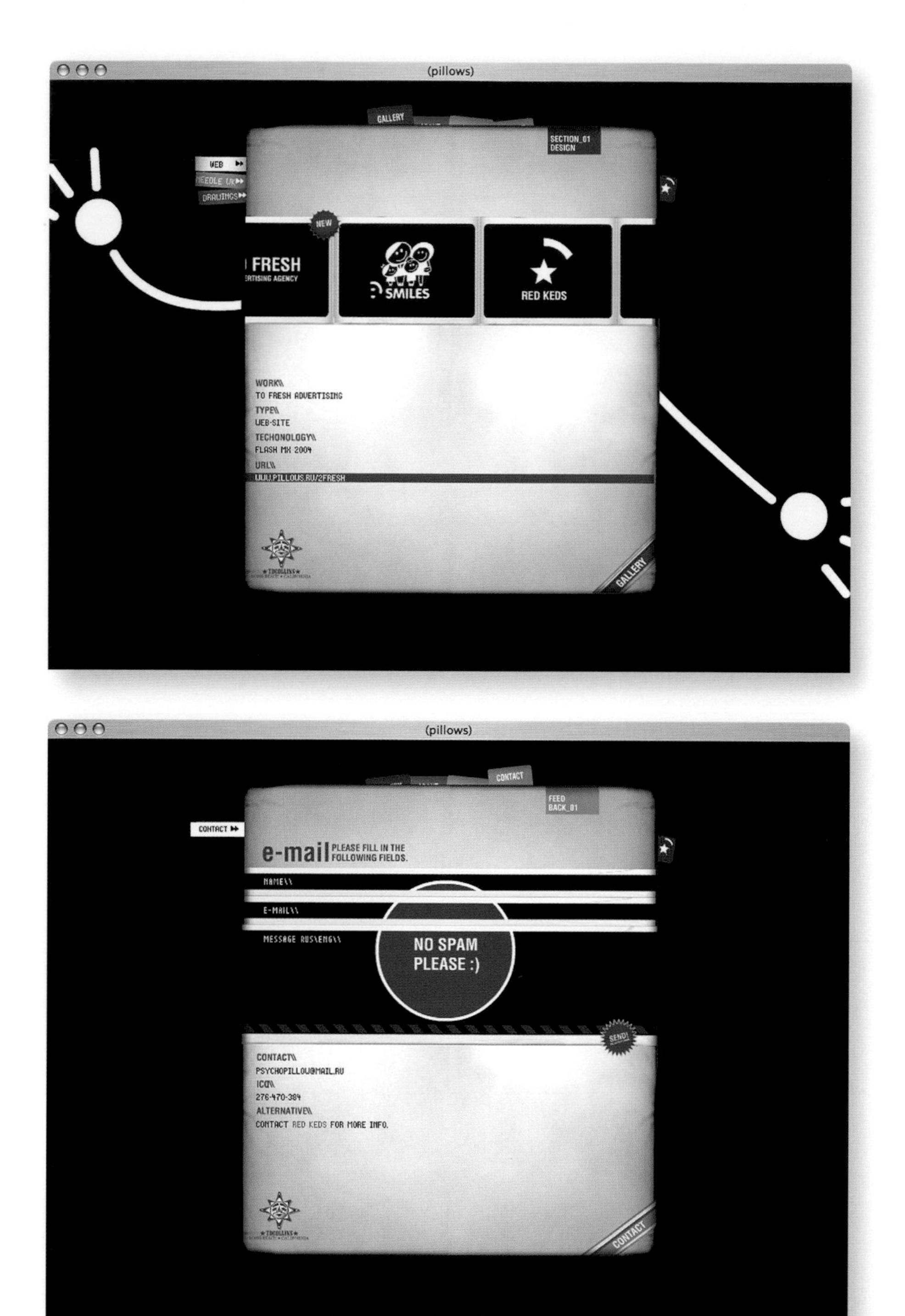

www.pillows.ru

D: sergey golnikov

A: pillows **M:** psychopillow@mail.ru

www.beatfly.com

D: patrizio C: macromedia studio P: macromedia

A: beat fly multimedia lab M: comunicazione@beatfly.com

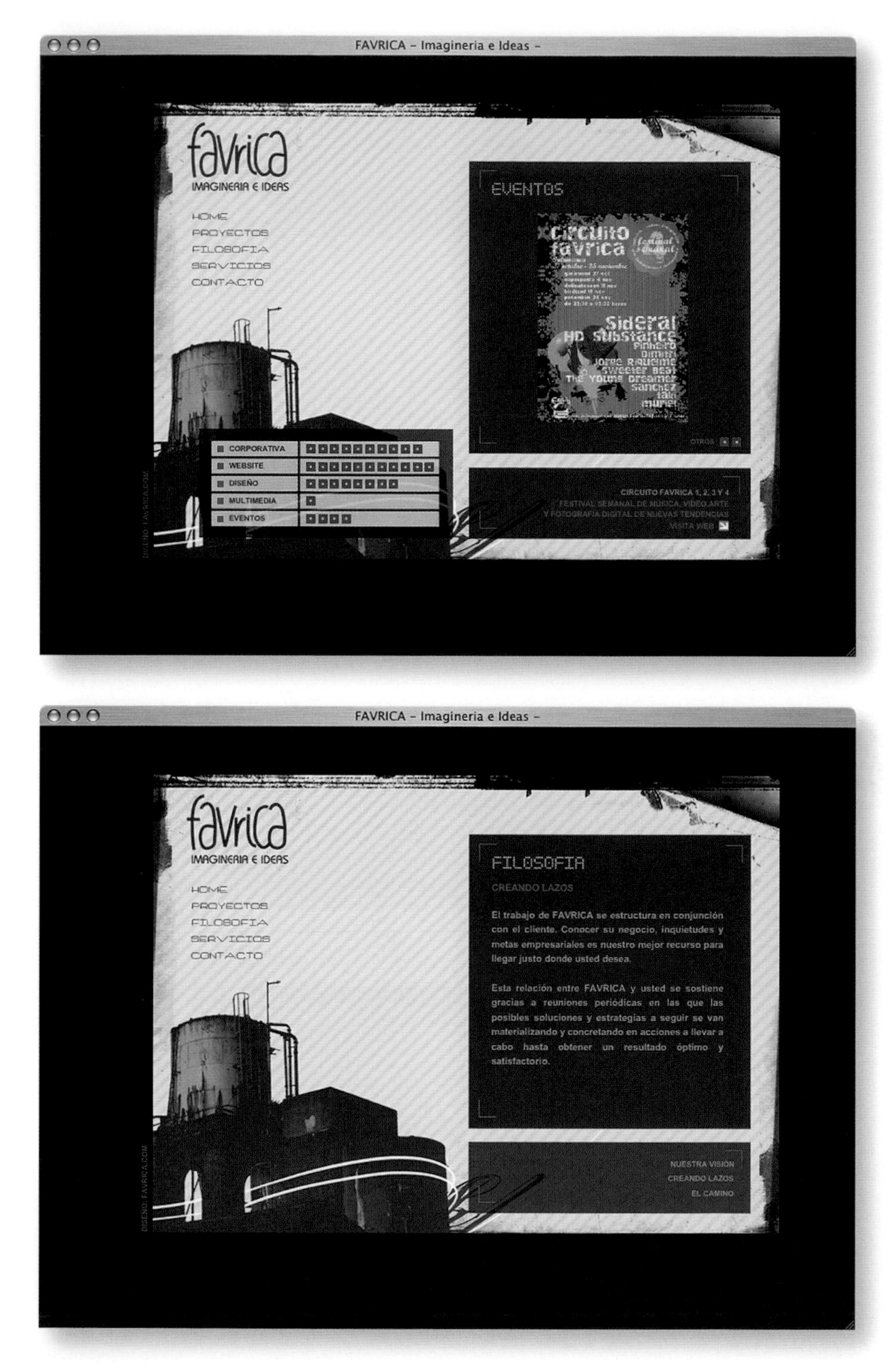

www.favrica.com

D: lydia gardón **C:** alex zuñiga **P:** fran martín

A: favrica imagineria e ideas **M:** info@favrica.com

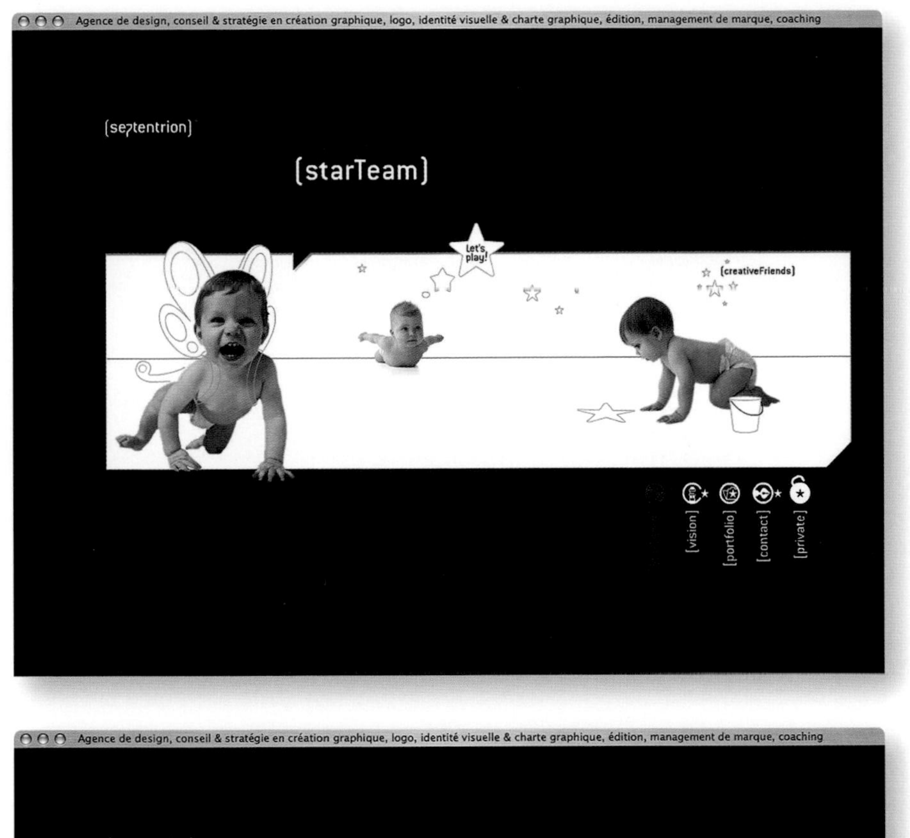

Agence de design, conseil & stratégie en création graphique, logo, identité visuelle & charte graphique, édition, management de marque, coaching

[se7tentrion]

[où sommes-nous?] *rue Blanche à Paris, entre Le Moulin Rouge et l'église de la Trinité, non loin des Grands Magasins.*

Septentrion
51, rue Blanche
F-75009 Paris
T +33 (0)1 49 95 95 15
F +33 (0)1 49 95 95 69

alpha@septentrion-design.com
Plan d'accés

www.septentrion-design.com

D: philippe delanghe **C:** guillaume garnier, arno roddier **P:** septentrion
A: macluhan's **M:** contact@macluhans.com

www.foreign.se
D: foreign
M: info@foreign.se

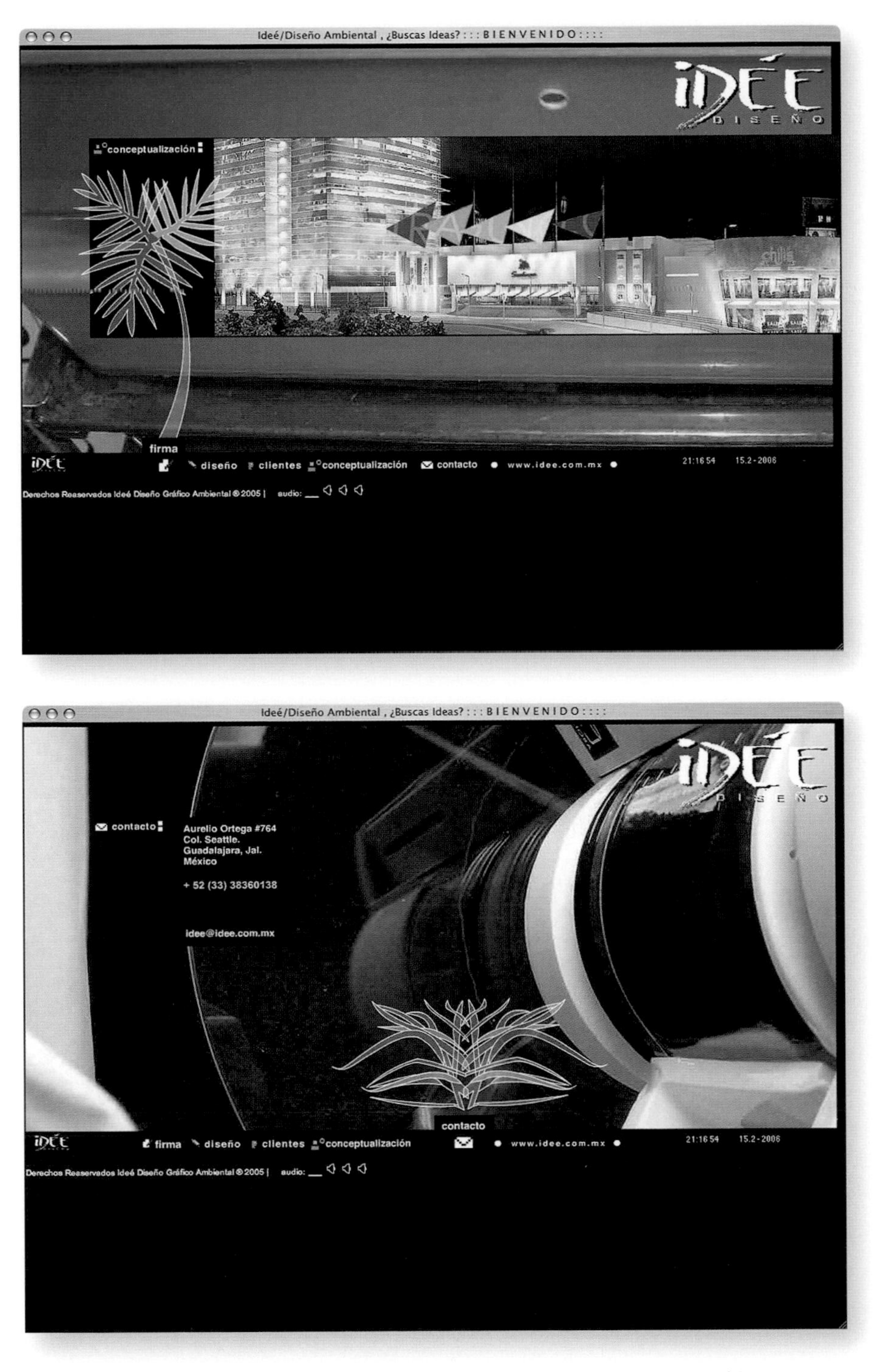

www.idee.com.mx
D: susana masso
A: susana masso M: smasso@idee.com.mx

www.pixel-delight.com

D: sharon erlich, sabo diab **C:** sharon erlich **P:** sabo diab

A: pixel delight **M:** info@pixel-delight.com

www.universaleverything.com

D: matt pyke **C:** kleber

A: universal everything **M:** www.universaleverything.com

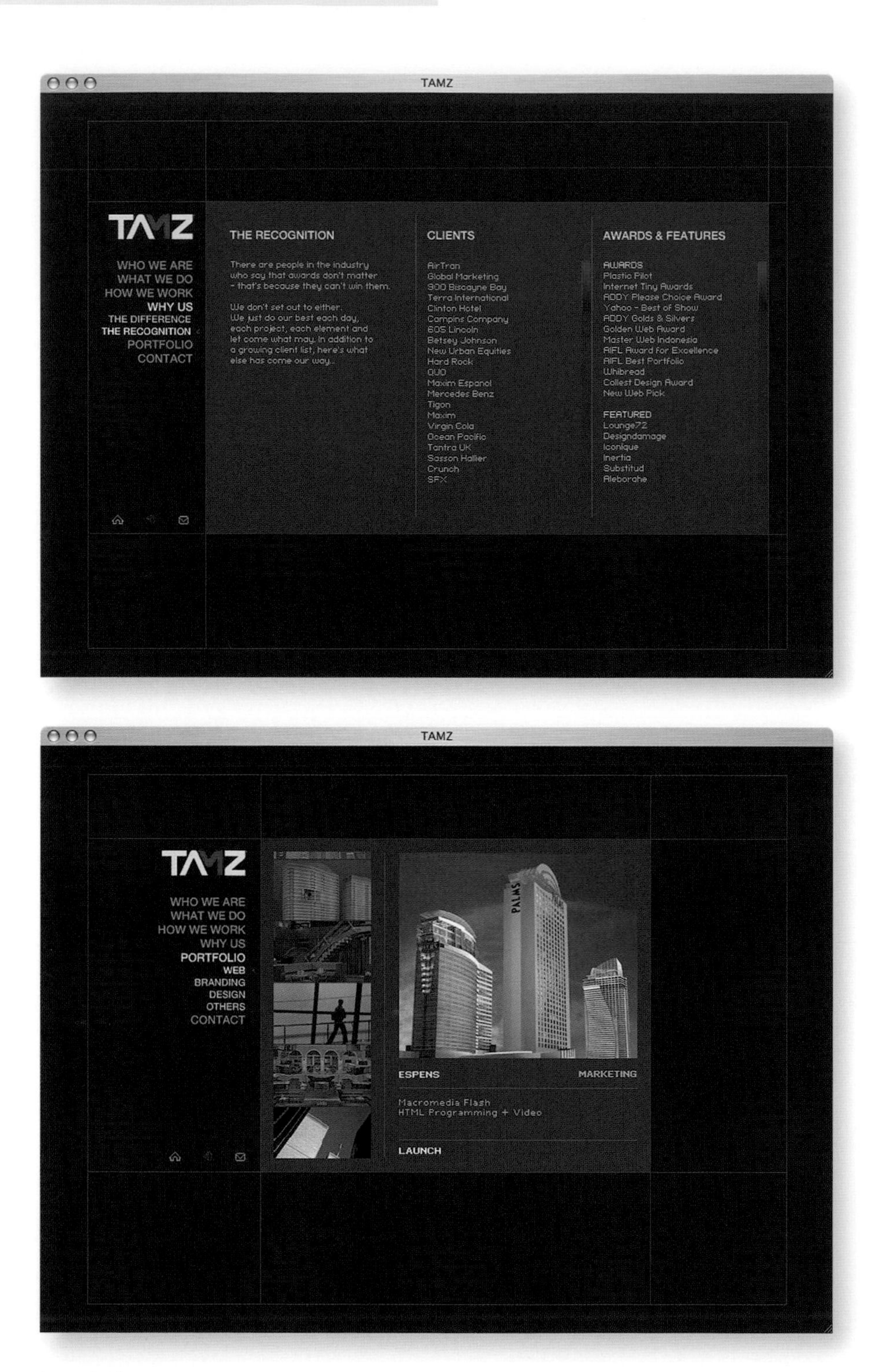

tamzdesigns.com

D: tamzdesigns

A: tamzil inc. **M:** mtamzil@tamzdesigns.com

www.crew11.net

D: crew11.net

A: hyper island **M:** rasmus.wangelin@hyperisland.se

www.nosurprises.it

D: kaneda

A: nosurprises **M:** kaneda@nosurprises.it

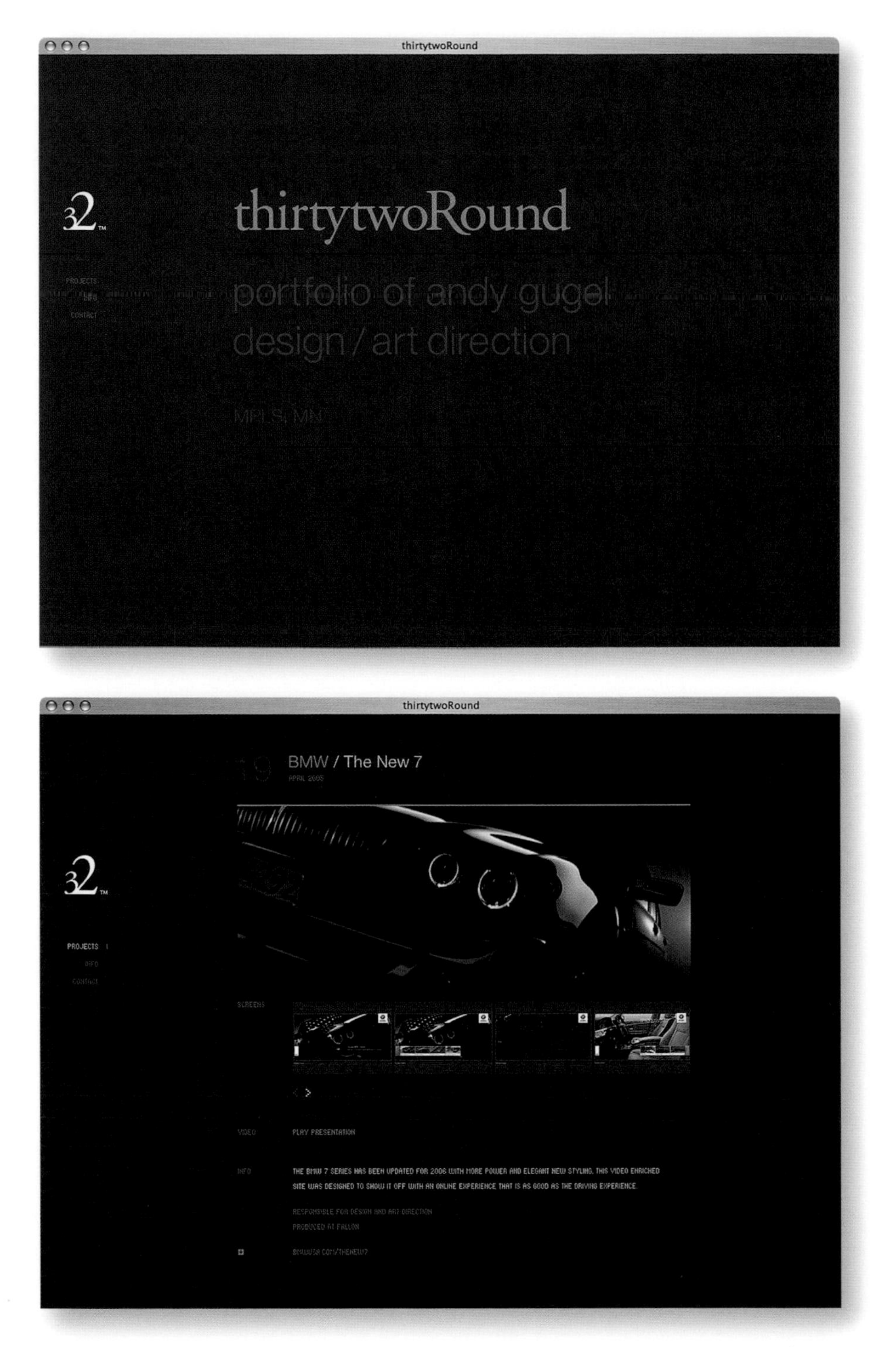

www.32round.com
D: andy gugel
A: thirtytworound **M:** info@32round.com

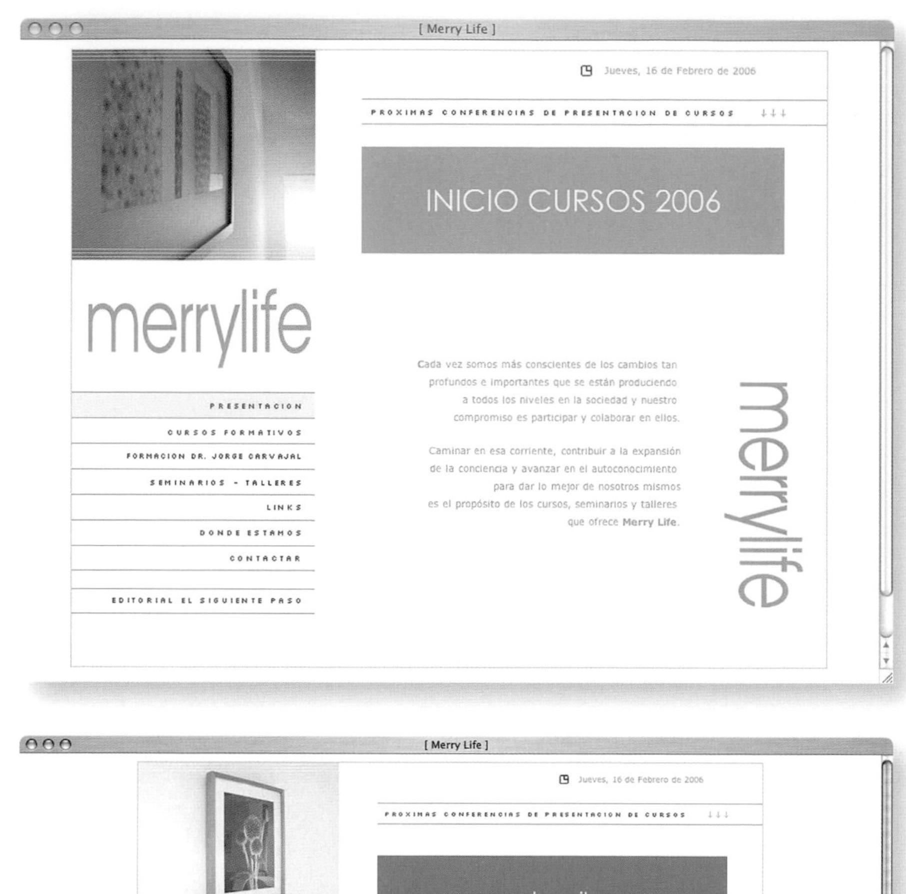

www.merrylife.org

D: sarah buyó jolibert

A: sarah buyó jolibert **M:** sbj@tinet.org

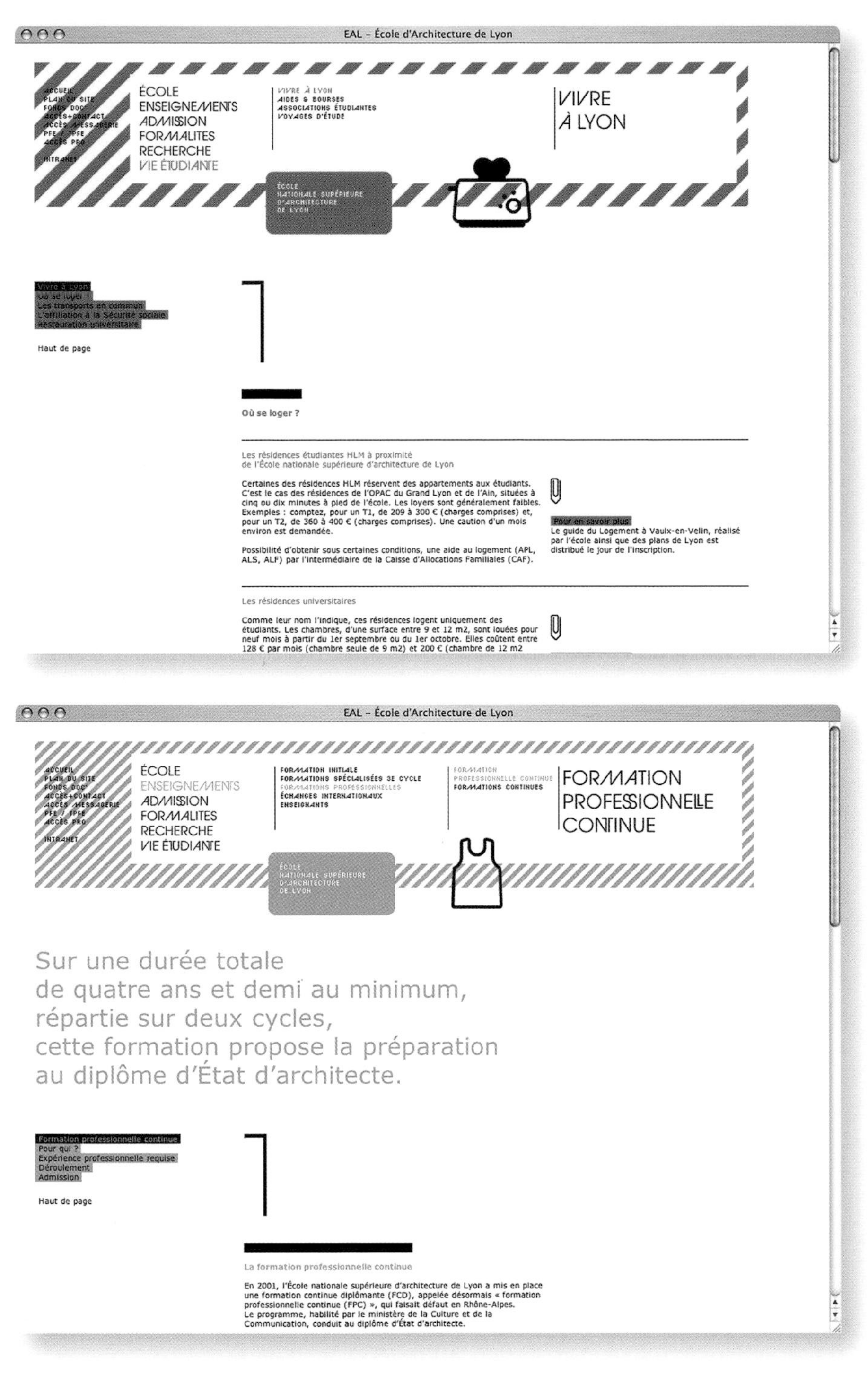

www.lyon.archi.fr
D: trafik
M: www.lavitrinedetrafik.com

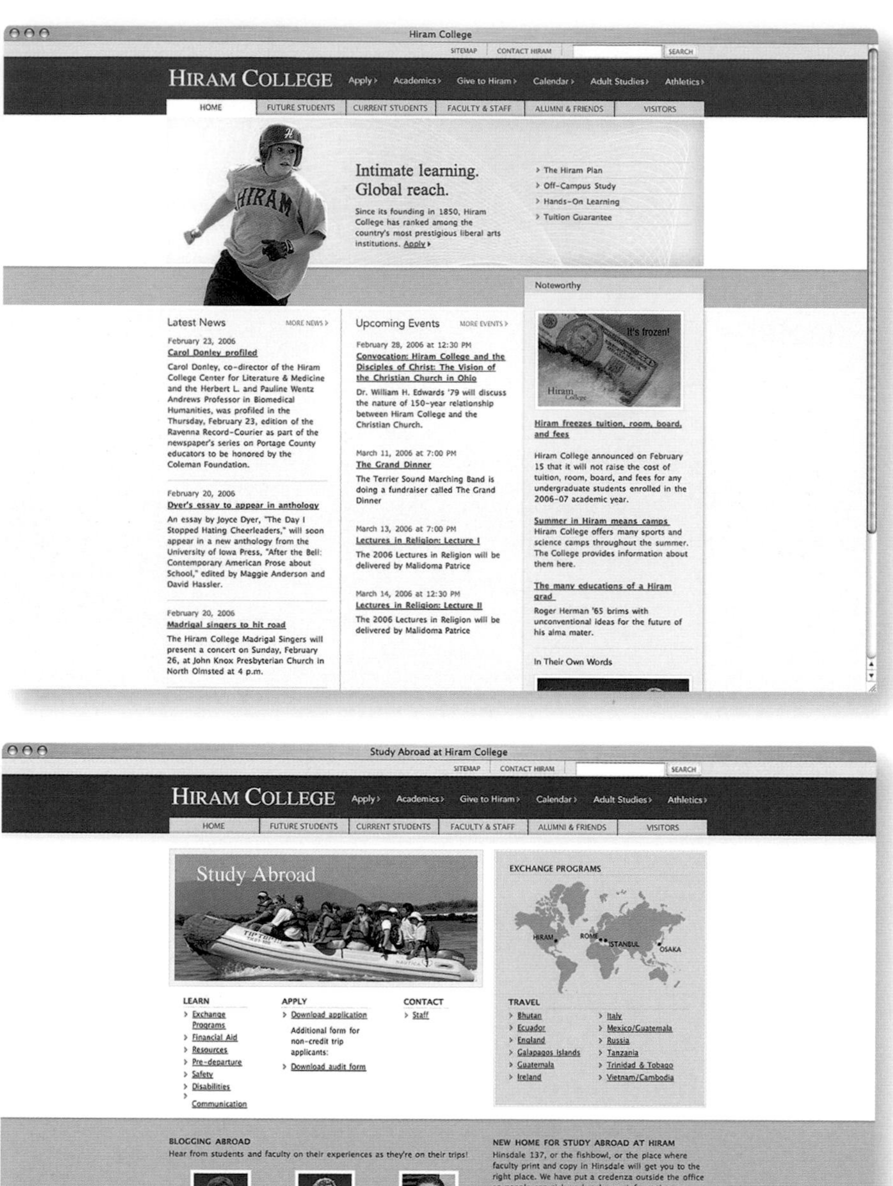

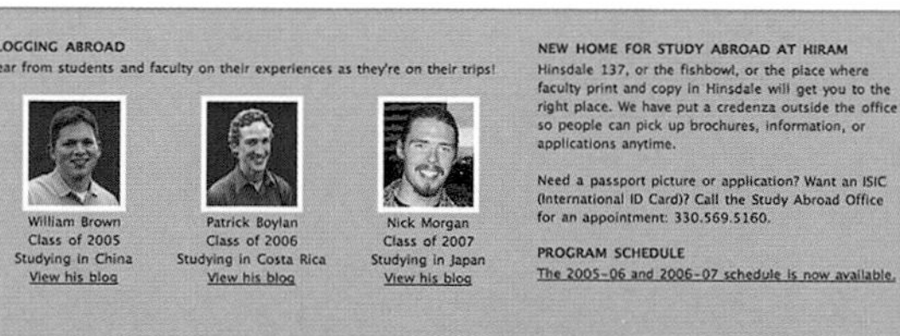

www.hiram.edu

D: cameron moll **C:** jonathan linczak

A: cameronmoll.com **M:** www.cameronmoll.com

ESPAÇO EVOE – o corpo das artes

ESPAÇO EVOÉ
O CORPO DAS ARTES

CURSO DE FORMAÇÃO DE ACTORES
[curso profissionalizante]

CURSOS
teatro
dança
consc. corporal

WORKSHOPS
programa sementes

WORKSHOPS
programaterra

ACTIVIDADES
aulas abertas
núcleo de investigação
dionisíacas
cabarés
evoé vai
conversas com Dionísio

EQUIPA

horários quero registar-me na maillinglist

EVOÉ é um grito de saudação a Dionísio, a Baco, a Évios, a Brómio, deus de muitos nomes, deus da dança, do teatro, do vinho, da fertilidade e das festividades corpóreas. É um grito de renascimento do deus nascido duas vezes. (...)

00 DESTAQUES
NOTÍCIAS

16-02-2006
21:36

Interpretação
Interdisciplinar
2ª, 4ª e 6ª
20h00 às 23h00

AGENDA EVOÉ

Workshop Pesquisa de Movimento/Aproximação à paisagem, com Ana Mira

Workshop de Clown, a comicidade do corpo, Ricardo Puccetti, de 1 a 5 de Abril

2º semestre - Inscrições abertas para o curso

CONTACTOS/MAPA HORÁRIOS
R. das Canastras, nº 40 | 1100-112 Lisboa | T. 218880838 evoe@evoe.pt

Webdesign: César Augusto [caugusto@portugalmail.pt]

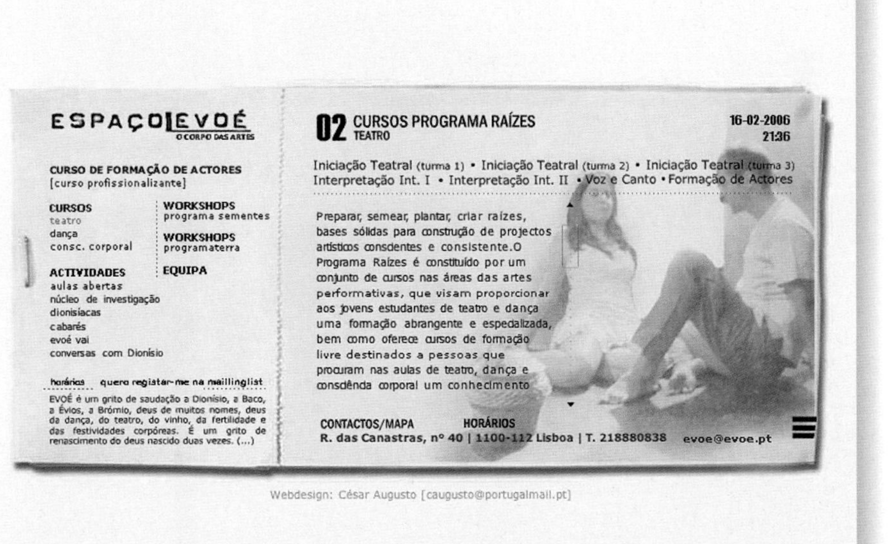

www.evoe.pt

D: césar augusto

M: caugusto@portugalmail.pt

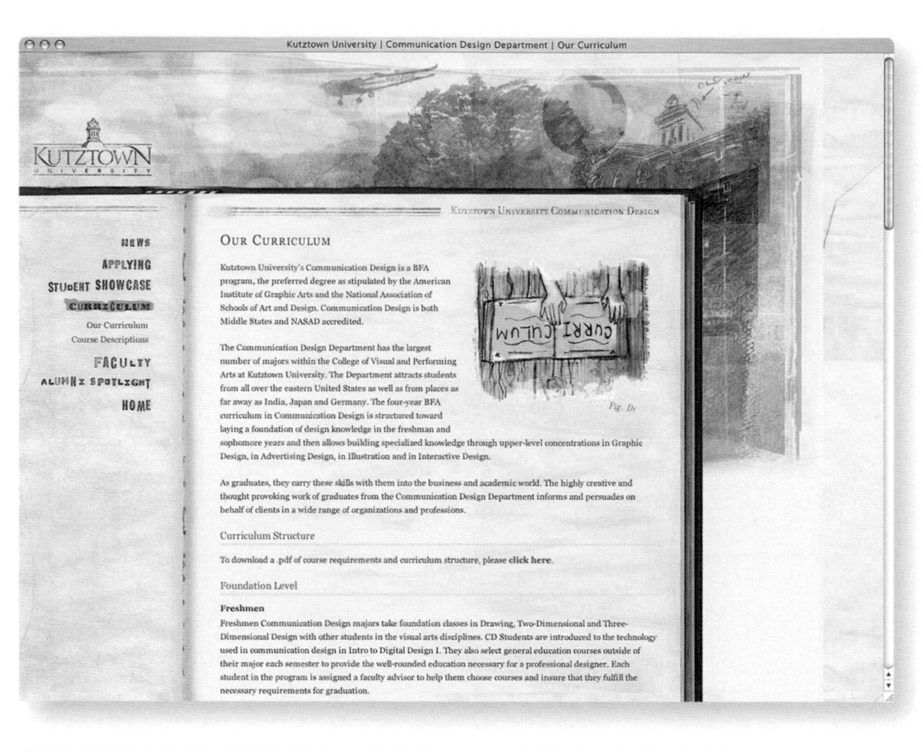

www.kutztown.edu/acad/commdes

D: scott reifsnyder **C:** michael mcaghon **P:** todd mcfeely

A: skybased, kutztown university communication design **M:** mcfeely@kutztown.edu

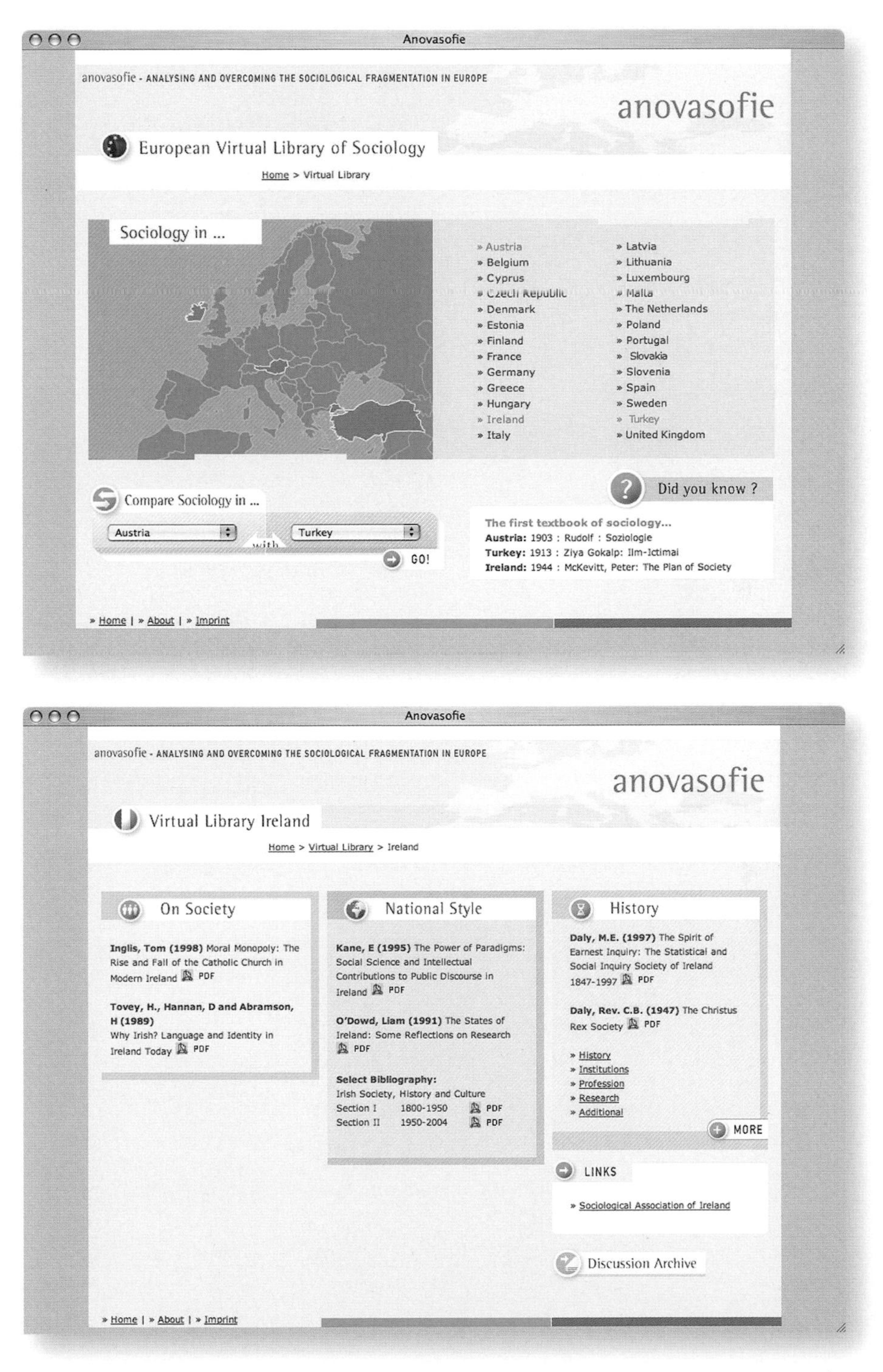

www.anovasofie.net/vl

D: chris poltensteiner **C:** philip wagner
A: wukonig.com **M:** joerg@wukonig.com

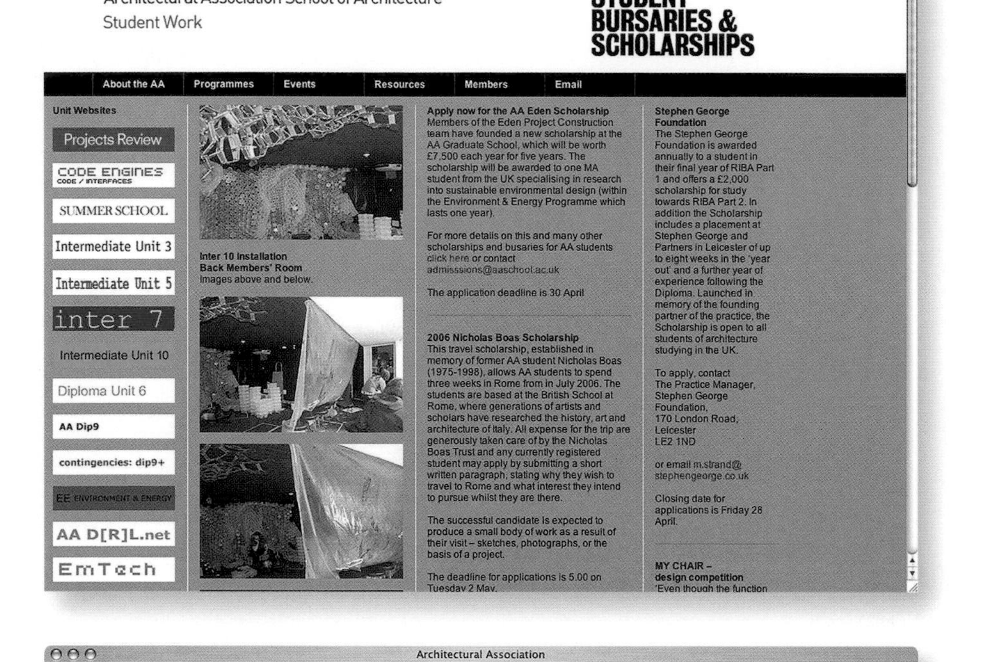

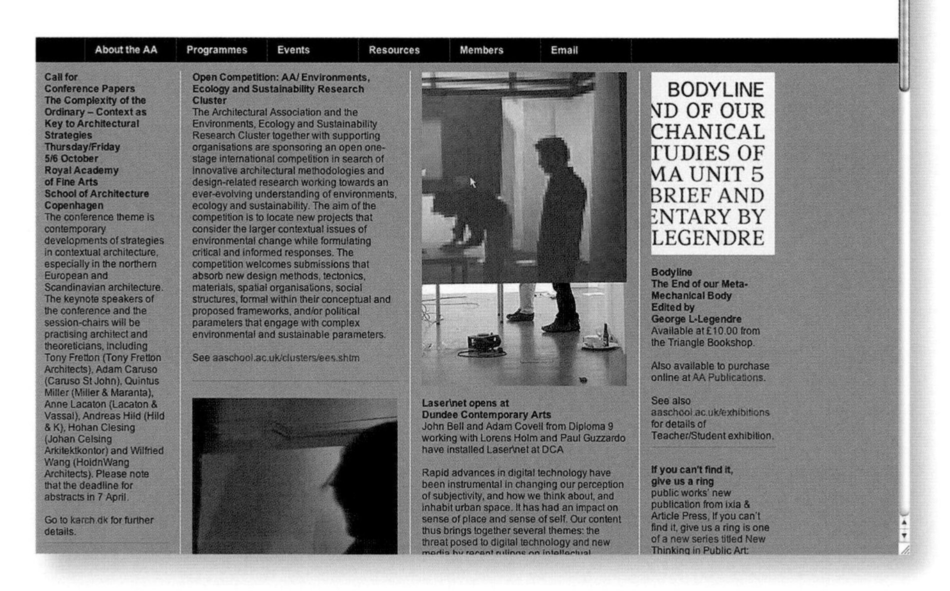

www.aaschool.ac.uk

D: chris fenn **C:** chris fenn **P:** rosa ainley

A: architectural association publications **M:** webmaster@aaschool.ac.uk

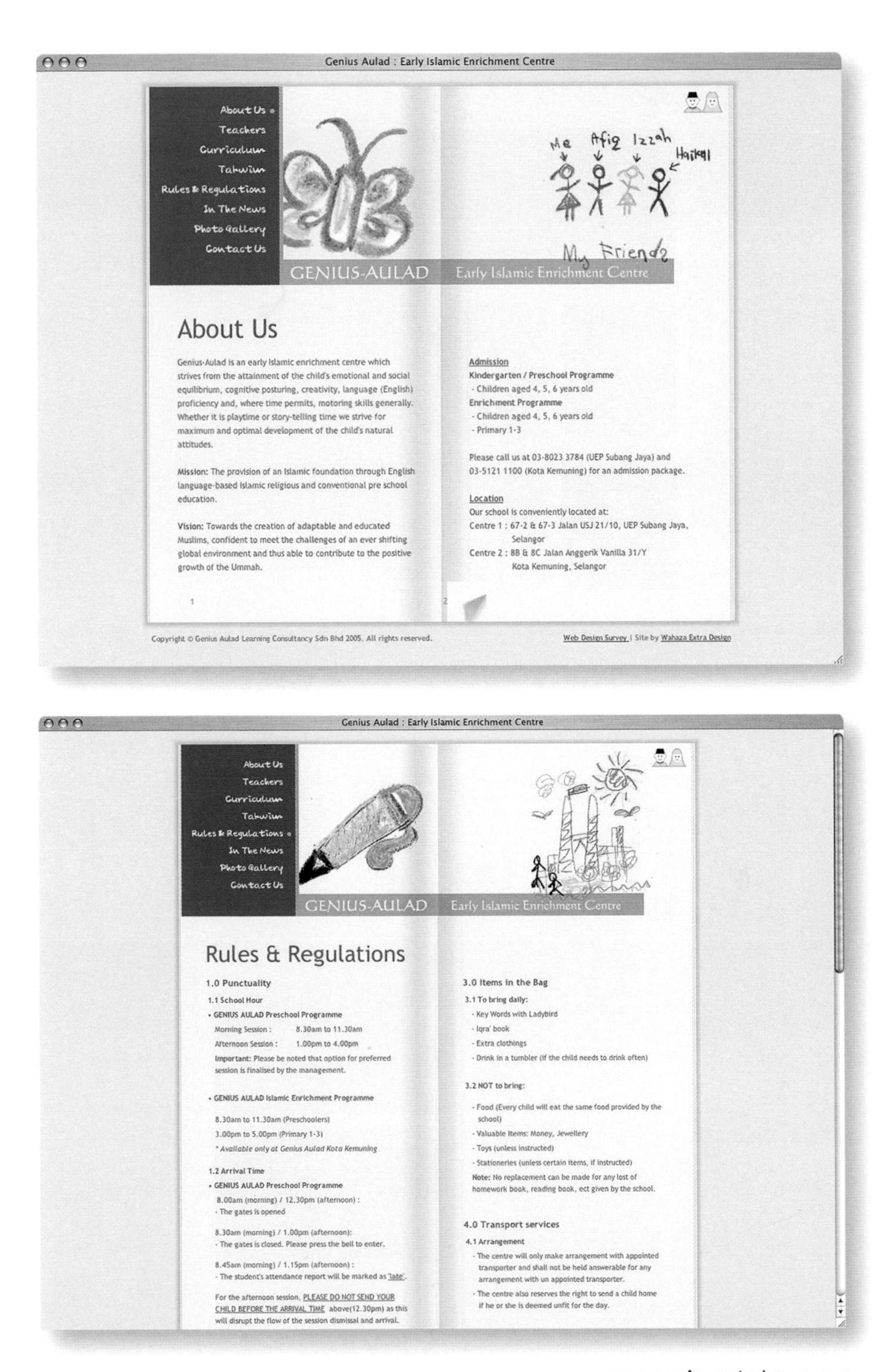

www.geniusaulad.com.my

D: mohd hisham saleh **C:** roby **P:** ian h. chris

A: wahaza extra design studio **M:** hisham@wahazaextra.com

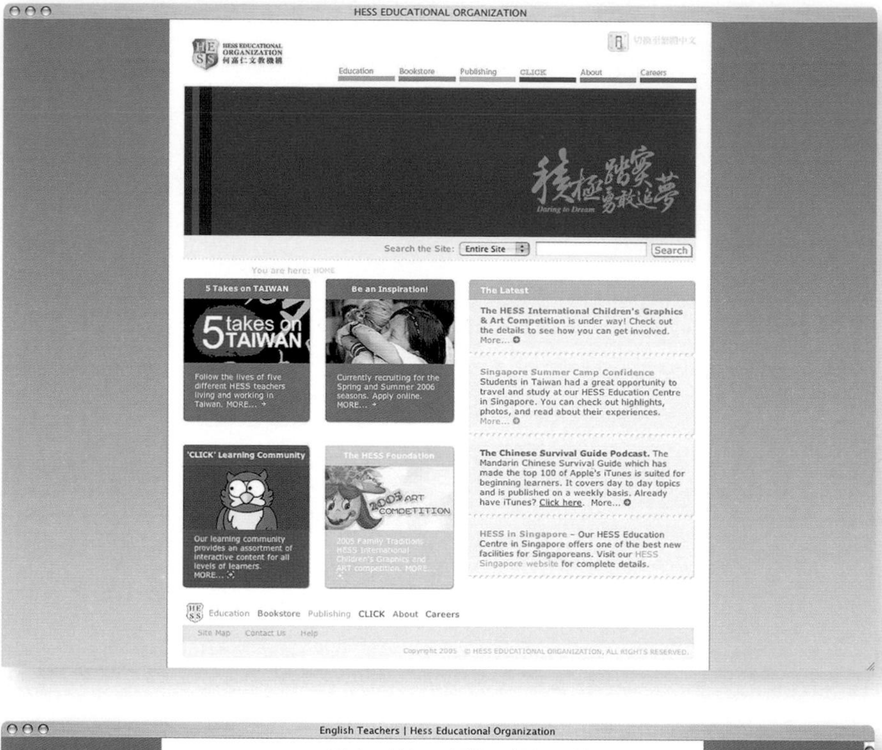

www.hess.com.tw

D: jason lee **C:** tony liu **P:** james li

A: hess educational organization **M:** jamesli@hess.com.tw

The Acting Room | Acting Classes in Hollywood, Los Angeles,...rnia by Acting Coach Kirsten Tretbar | Tel: +1.310.694.6621

About
Classes
Questions
Testimonials
Contact
Enroll Now!

The Acting Room

PROFESSIONAL ACTOR TRAINING PROGRAM

Join us in our Fall PROFESSIONAL ACTOR TRAINING CLASS! This is an ongoing, weekly three hour class on Monday nights at the Hollywood UMC, from 7 pm to 10:00 pm. These classes are for working actors only, age mature 16 to adult. We focus on each actor's individual levels and talents so feel free to join us if you're already a trained actor working in the industry or in the early stages of your career. Most of our students are full-time working actors, but we do permit a few beginners if talented.

We DO allow and recommend ONE FREE AUDIT. Students will be admitted by the instructor only after the initial audit. We want you to feel happy with your choice before you join us, and we'd like to get to know you better too.

These ongoing classes are small, and usually range from between 5 -15 students.

Page 1 of 3 Last Page Next Page

© Copyright 2004 Options

The Acting Room | Acting Classes in Hollywood, Los Angeles,...rnia by Acting Coach Kirsten Tretbar | Tel: +1.310.694.6621

About
Classes
Questions
Testimonials
Contact
Enroll Now!

The Acting Room

Thank you for your interest in joining The Acting Room. Please let us know who you are and which class you would like to take. Feel free to email us or call us and we will contact you shortly. We look forward to talking with you!

Your Last Name
Your Email Address
Your Address
Your City
Your State
Your Zip
Your Phone Number
Your Age

■ Weekly Professional Ongoing Acting Class (Monday Nights) - $200/month
☐ Spring Acting Program - TBA
☐ Summer Acting Program - TBA

Any Comments?

Submit

© Copyright 2004 Options

theactingroom.com

D: ozzy benn

A: toxic design **M:** ozzy@toxicdesign.com

www.ipincopallino.it

D: giacomo cavalleri **C:** micro-studio **P:** giacomo cavalleri

A: micro-studio **M:** g.cavalleri@micro-studio.it

sixxa.at

D: kathi macheiner **C:** mac krebernik **P:** lilo krebernik

A: d:vision visual communication gmbh **M:** studio@dvsn.at

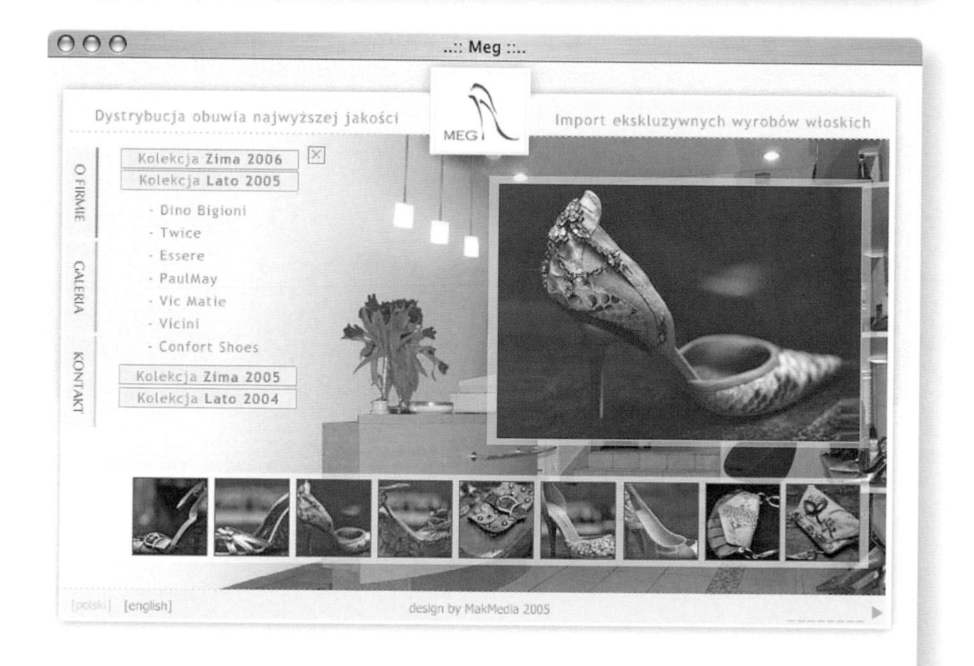

meg.pl

D: michal juszczyk

A: laflaf.net **M:** www.cwalineczka.prv.pl

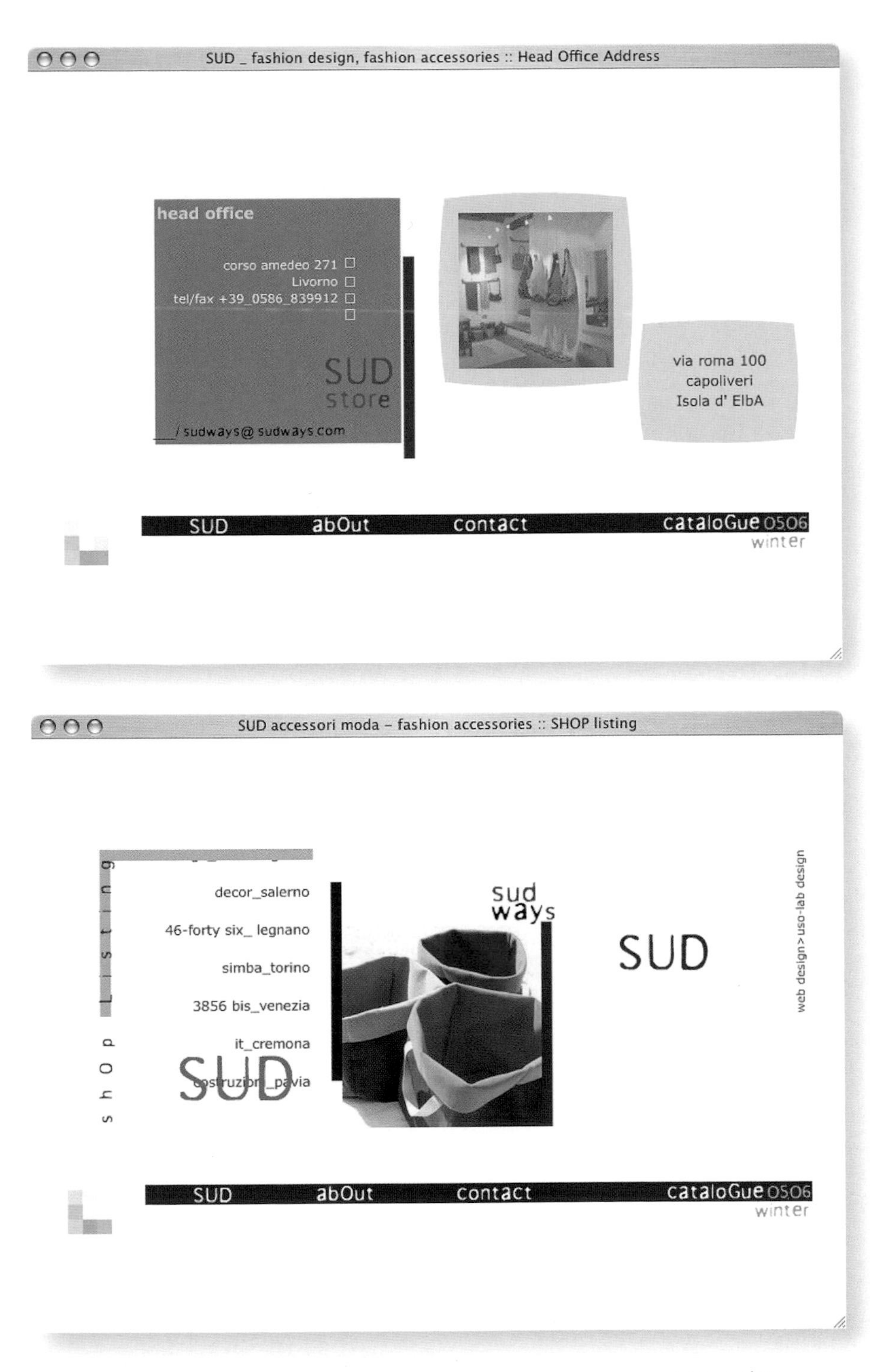

www.sudways.com

D: susanna ciacci

A: usolab design M: info@uso-lab.it

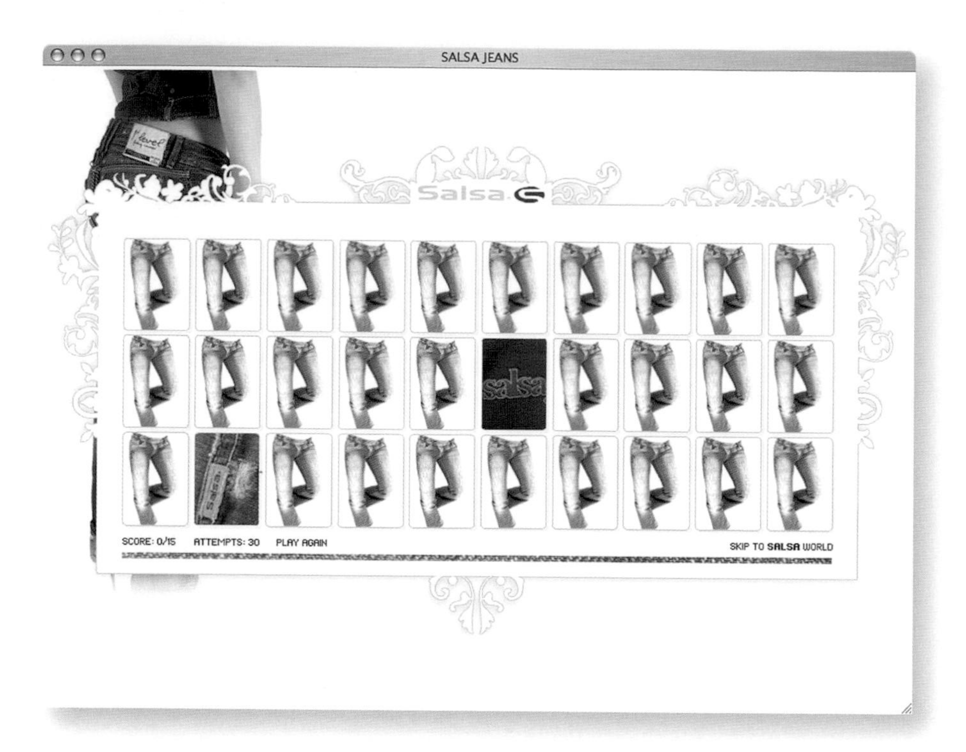

www.salsajeans.com

D: mourylise heymer **C:** simão vidinha **P:** joão ramos

A: redicom **M:** www.redicom.pt

www.comentrigo.com
D: dani martí
A: palmerita M: www.palmerita.com

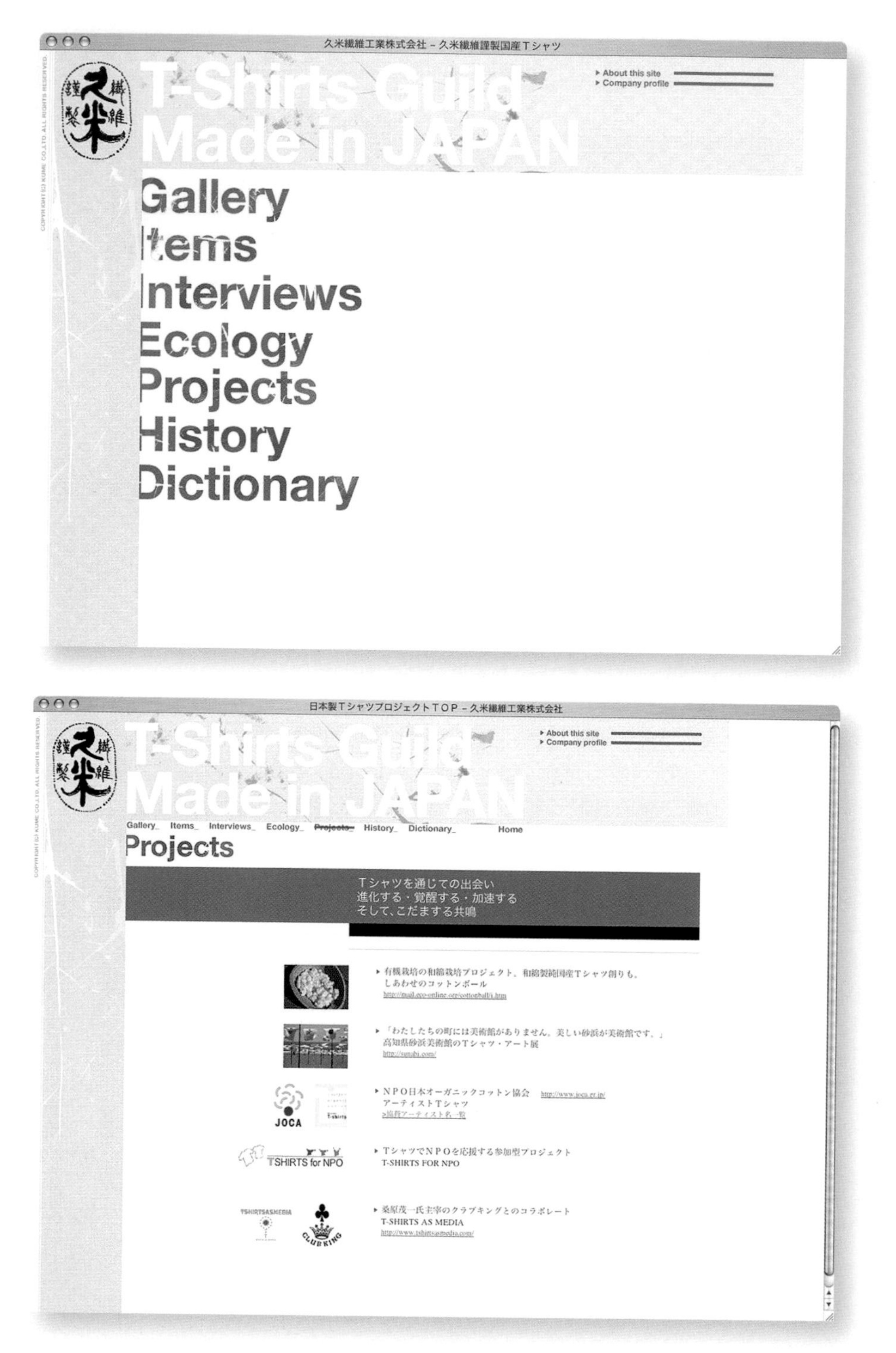

kume.jp

D: takayuki sugihara P: hiroyasu kume

A: roughark interaktiv M: www.roughark.com

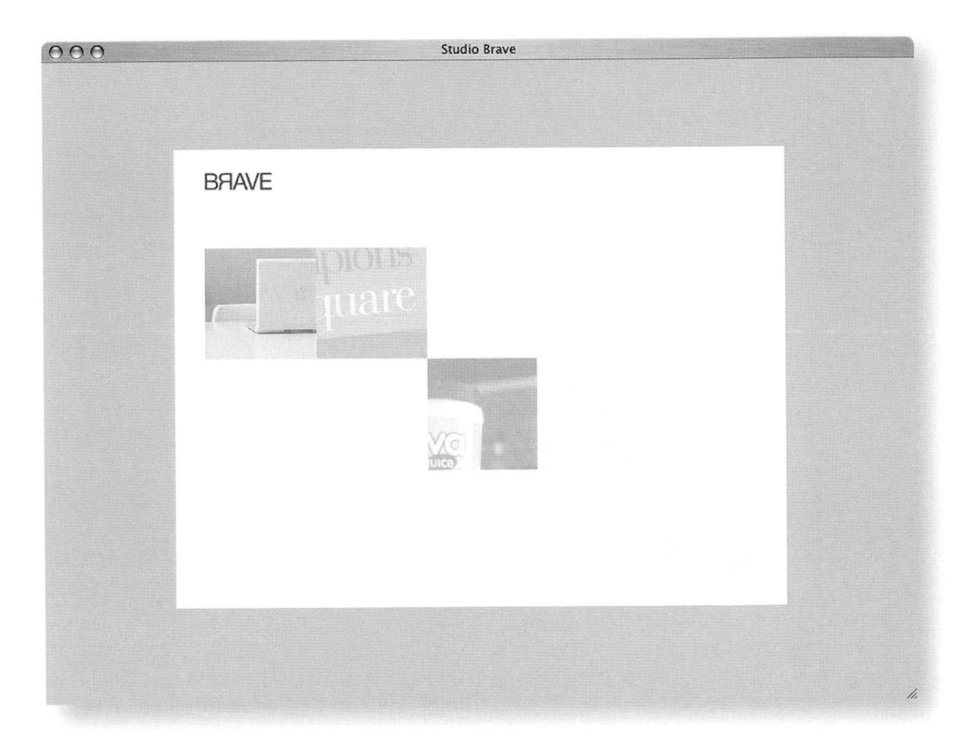

www.studiobrave.com.au
D: tim sutherland C: daniel fisher P: propagate
A: studio brave M: info@studiobrave.com.au

www.eleonoraboutique.com

D: claudio baldino

M: claudio.baldino@gmail.com

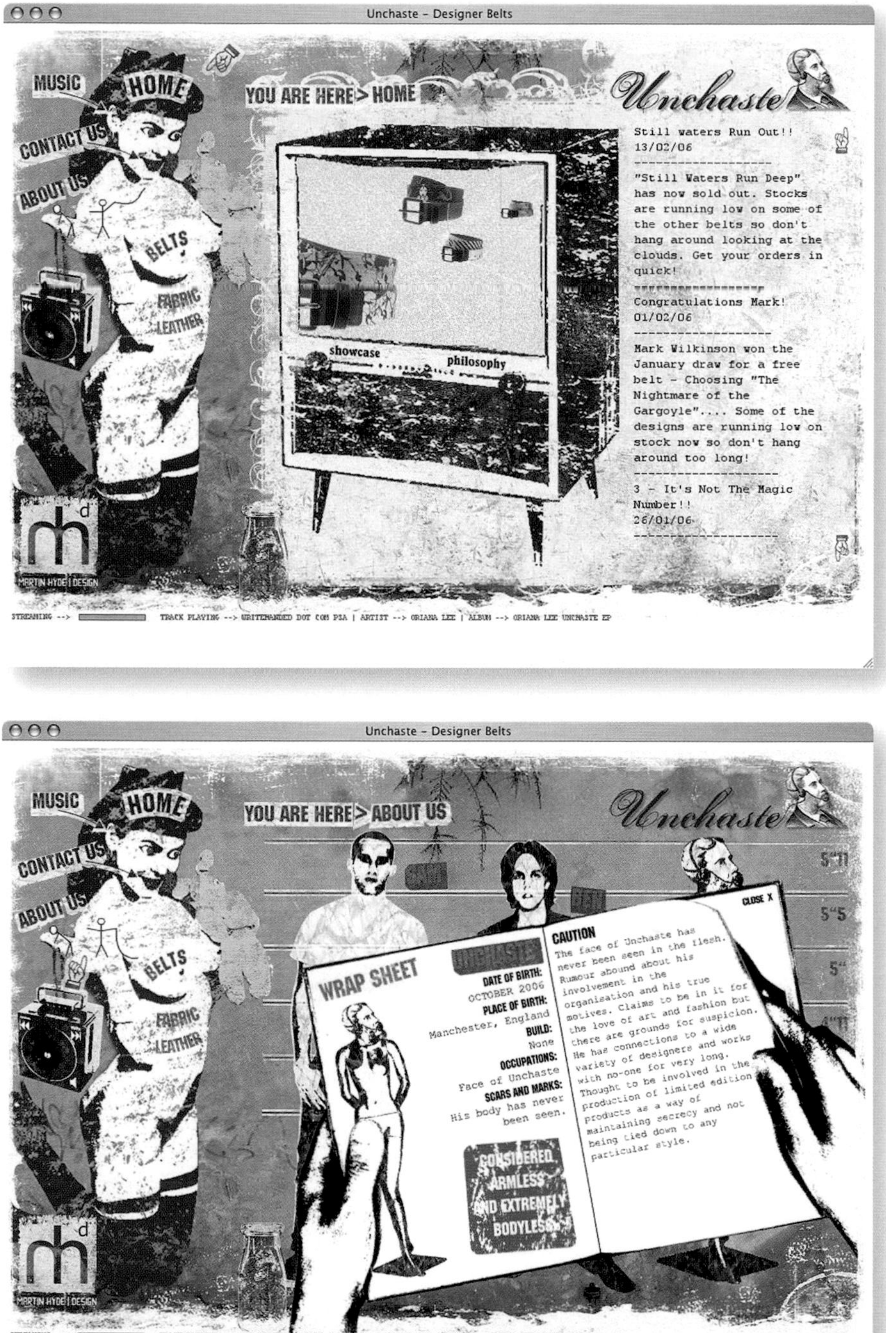

www.unchaste.co.uk
D: martin hyde
A: martin hyde | design **M:** www.martinhyde.co.uk

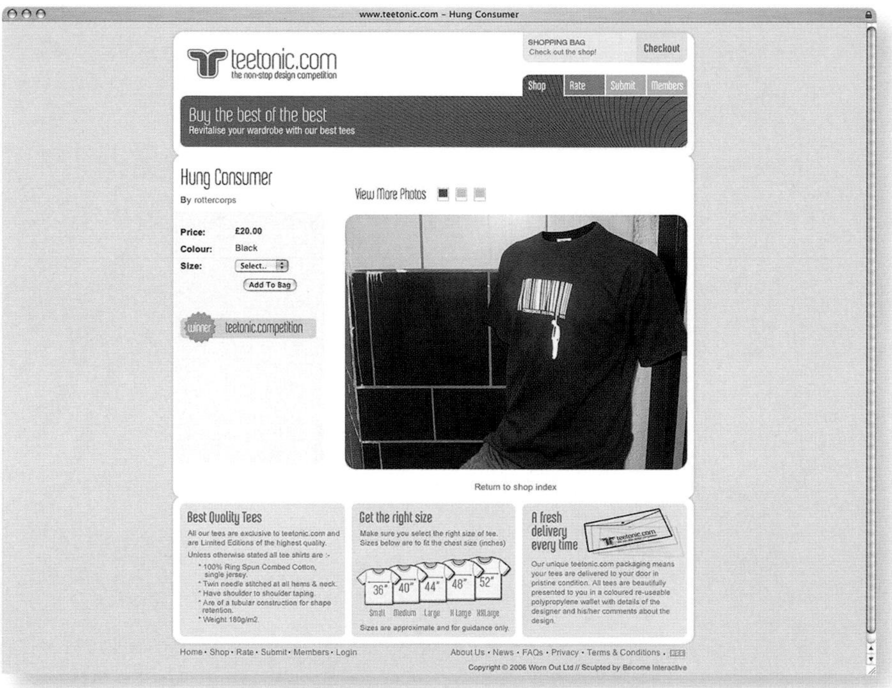

www.teetonic.com

D: paul derwin, tom beddard **C:** tom beddard, cameron yule **P:** paul derwin

A: become interactive **M:** paul@teetonic.com

TUTTO Frankfurt - Fashion, Mode, Accessoires, Lifestyle, Westend

TUTTO

BY MALENE BIRGER
CLOSED®
COCCINELLE
DEHA
DONDUP
GIRBAUD
MASON'S
SEVEN FOR ALL MANKIND
WEITERE LABELS...

Summer in the City.
We've got something to show.

Profil | News | Store | Labels | Kontakt | Location | Stichworte A-Z

Virtueller Rundgang
Spring 2006
Januar Highlights
Dezember Highlights

TUTTO SPOTLIGHTS

Donnerstag, 16. Februar 2006

News | Spring 2006 | Unsere Labels | Kontakt

Willkommen bei TUTTO
Seit mehr als 10 Jahren bieten wir Ihnen Fashion, Footwear und Accessoires internationaler Trend-Designer.

Unser symphatisches Team freut sich auf Sie! MEHR

TUTTO Kronberger Str. 42 60323 Frankfurt am Main Fon +49 (0) 69 - 17 35 65 Fax +49 (0) 69 - 72 21 21 E-Mail: info@tutto-frankfurt.de

www.tutto-frankfurt.de

D: dino pannozzo

A: schema f - new media solutions **M:** info@schema-f.de

www.soonline.net

D: ragde

A: ragde.com **M:** info@ragde.com

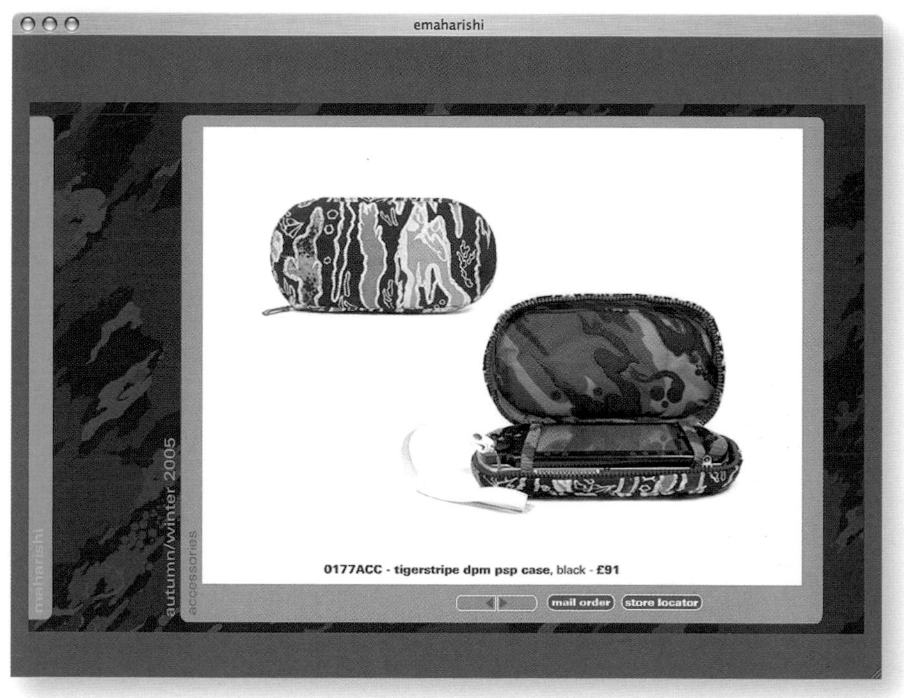

www.emaharishi.com

D: julia shapp **C:** julia shapp **P:** maharishi

A: maharishi **M:** info@emaharishi.com

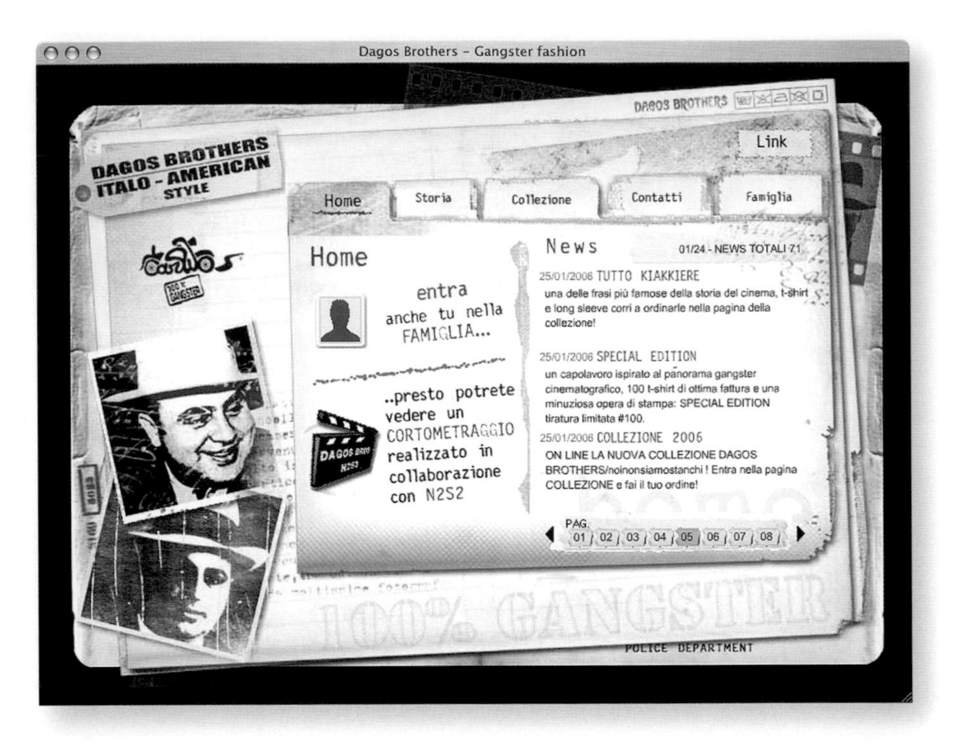

www.dagosbros.it

D: luca fadigati

A: effective studio **M:** www.effectivestudio.com

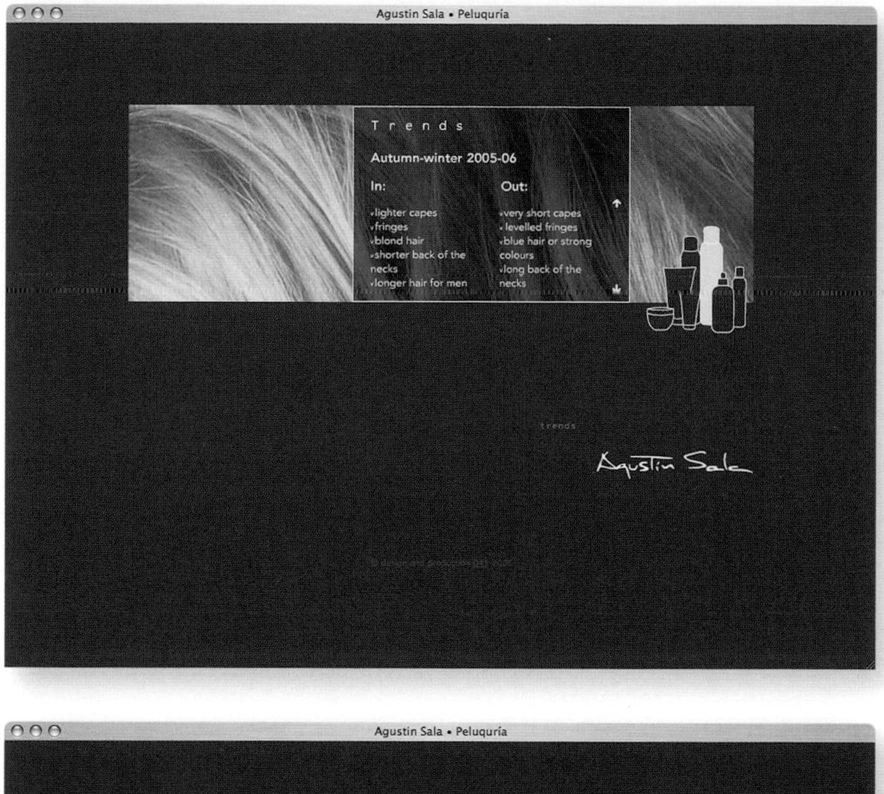

www.agustinsala.com

D: cristina guillén malluguiza, a. garcía saúco iglesias P: a. garcía saúco iglesias
A: crisipels M: antonio@enblanco.ws

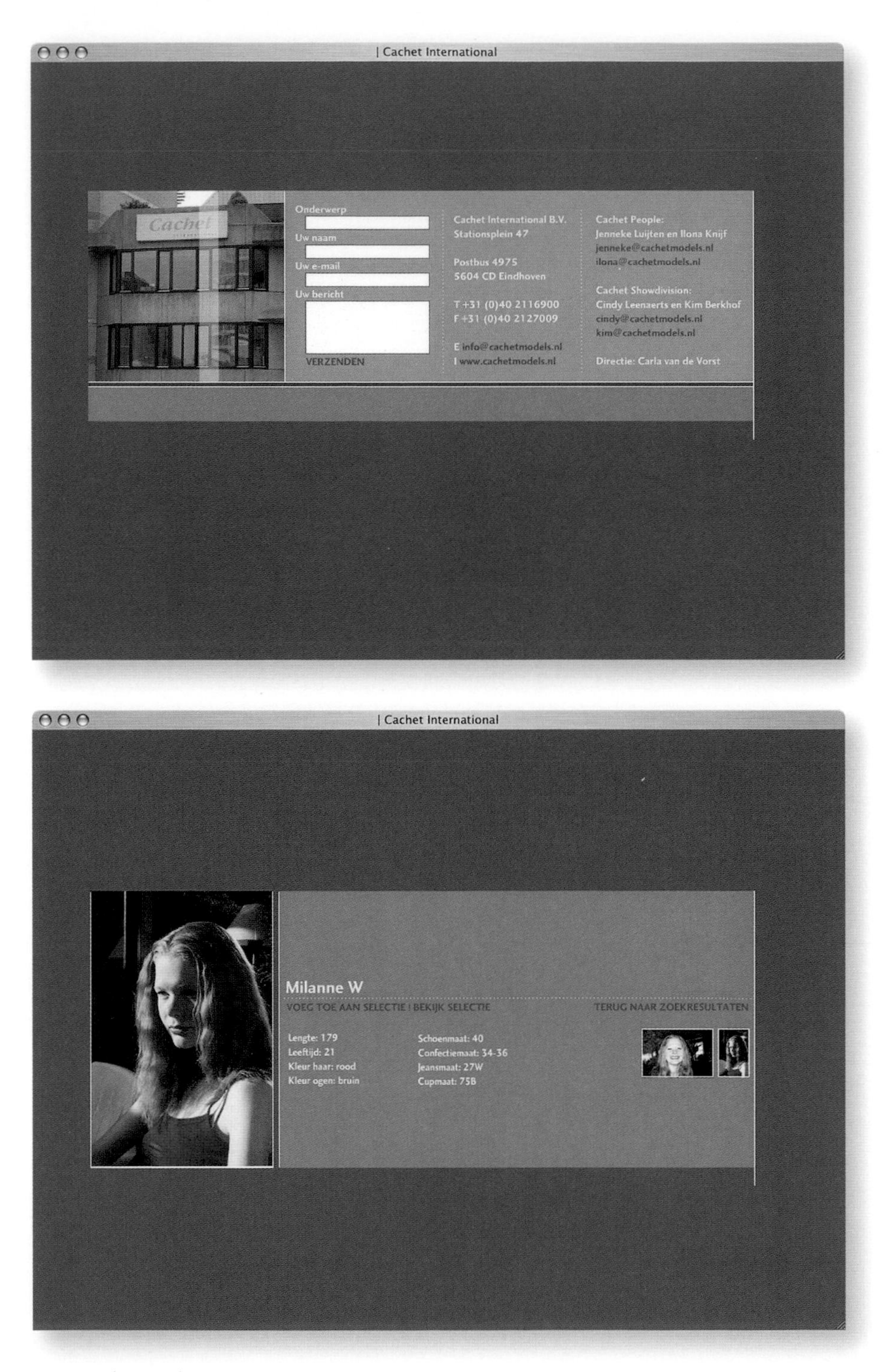

www.cachetmodels.nl

D: sander van der putten, rob hoekman **C:** jos van de laar **P:** carla van de vorst

A: parque creative **M:** info@parque.nl

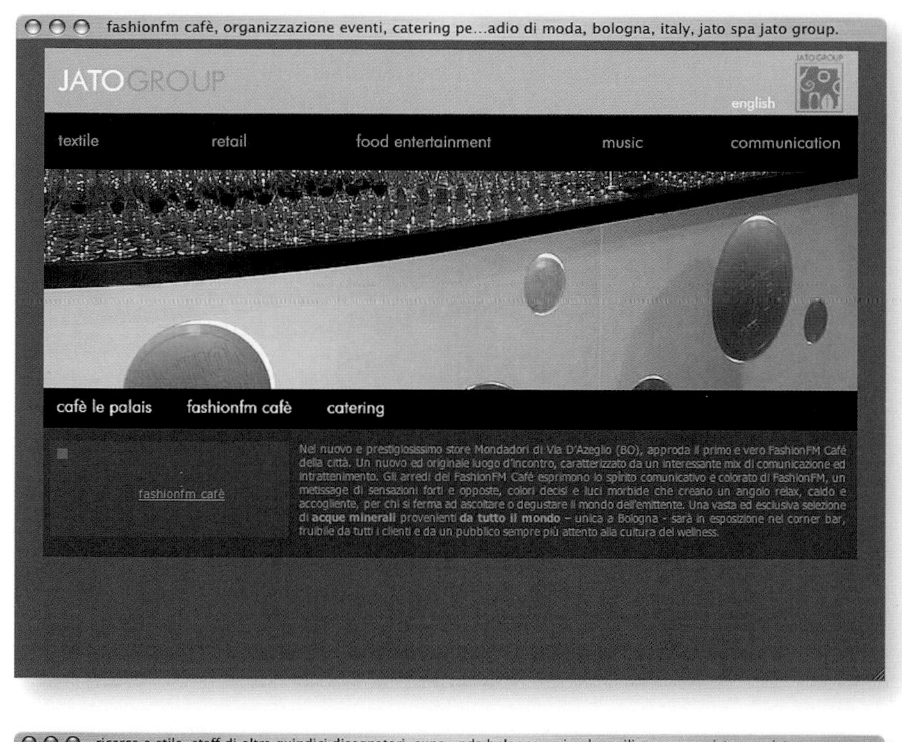

www.jato.it

D: antonello coghe

A: fashion communication **M:** antonello@fashionfm.it

Keller Company

keller
the school

Keller haircompany HAIR'N'MORE Keller the school TOP THEMA Jobs & Karriere Presse & Partner Impressum Schnellsuche...

ERFOLG KANN MAN LERNEN KELLER THE SCHOOL

Collectionen Modelle Vorteile Seminare Kalender Partnerkonzept AGB Kontakt

aktionen

WILLKOMMEN BEI KELLER THE SCHOOL

Wer hoch hinaus will, braucht eine solide Grundlage. Wir vermitteln jungen Menschen, die sich für eine Karriere in unserer Branche entschlossen haben, Fachwissen aus erster Hand. Erfahrene Friseure und Saloninhaber schätzen die vielfältigen Seminarkonzepte, loben die Inspiration und Motivation die sie daraus mitnehmen.

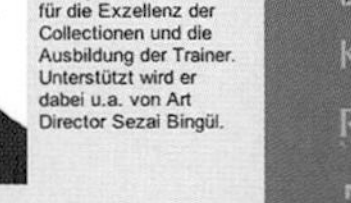

Bei Keller the school entstehen die zahlreichen vorbildlichen Collectionen unseres Creativ Teams, die immer wieder internationale Fachleute und unsere Kunden begeistern. Wir suchen die Herausforderung, die in den Extremen steckt und setzen uns ein hohes Ziel: mit innovativen Konzepten visionäres Hairstyling erlebbar machen.

Geschäftsführer Dieter Keller | Creativ Director Thomas Schug | Art Director Sezai Bingül

Creativ Director Thomas Schug ist verantwortlich für die Exzellenz der Collectionen und die Ausbildung der Trainer. Unterstützt wird er dabei u.a. von Art Director Sezai Bingül.

Erfolg macht Spaß und erfolgreich zu sein, kann man lernen! Fundiertes Grundwissen, handwerkliche Perfektion, ein Schuss Kreativität - das Ganze präsentiert von jungen Trainern, die mit Begeisterung bei der Sache sind.

Keller the school
Collectionspremiere 2006
Keller haircompany
Keller haircompany
NEWS ARCHIV

L'ORÉAL PROFESSIONNEL PARIS
KÉRASTASE PARIS
REDKEN
MCLEAN
PETER ZÖLLNER
FRÖHLICH & FRIENDS CONSULTING AG

www.keller-company.de

D: stefan behringer **C:** jürgen wunderle

A: d\sign creativeconcepts **M:** www.dsign.de

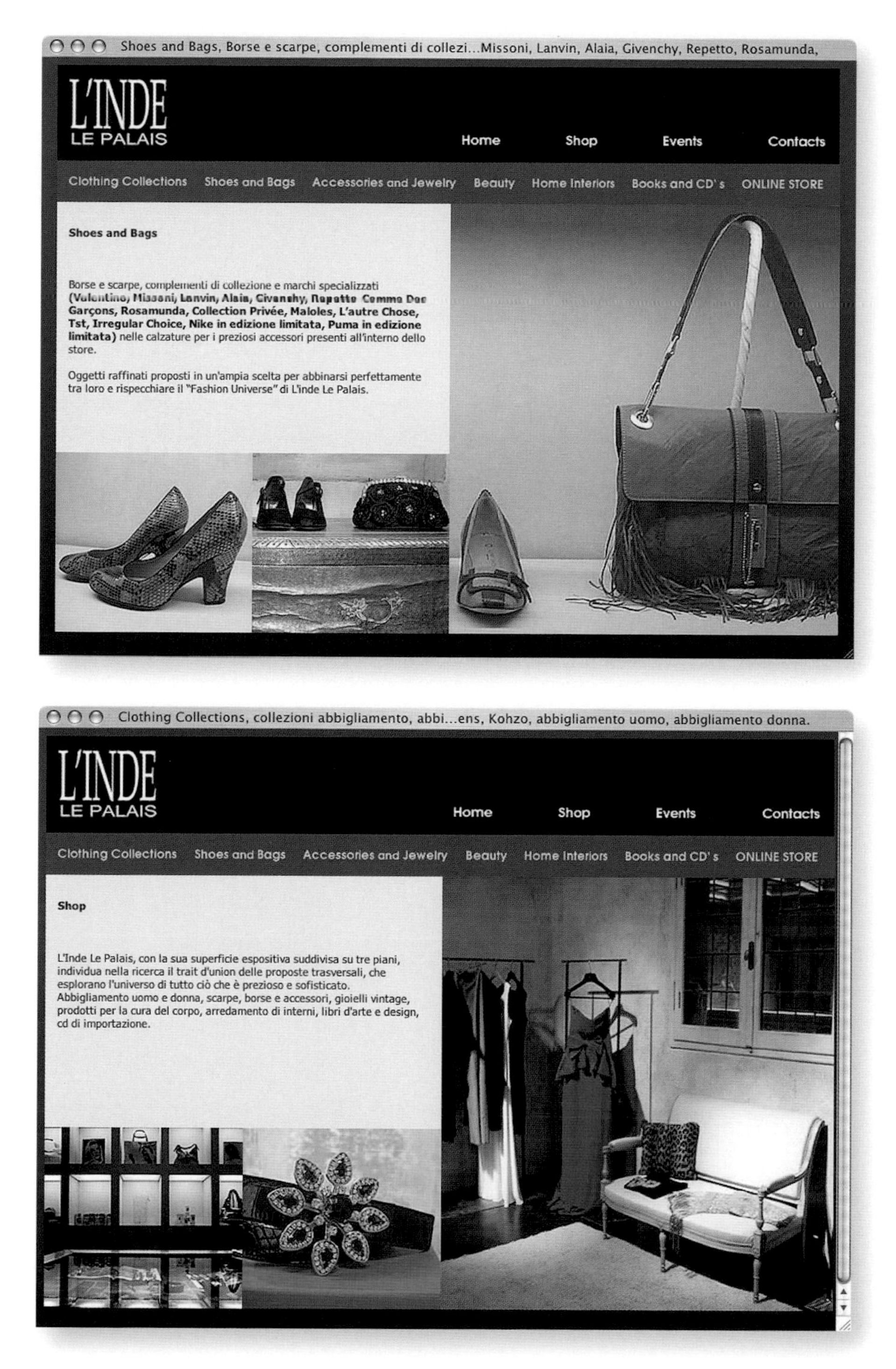

www.lindelepalais.com

D: antonello coghe

A: fashion communication **M:** antonello@fashionfm.it

www.anouskawink.nl

D: arnout schutte

A: id interactive **M:** arnoutschutte@gmail.com

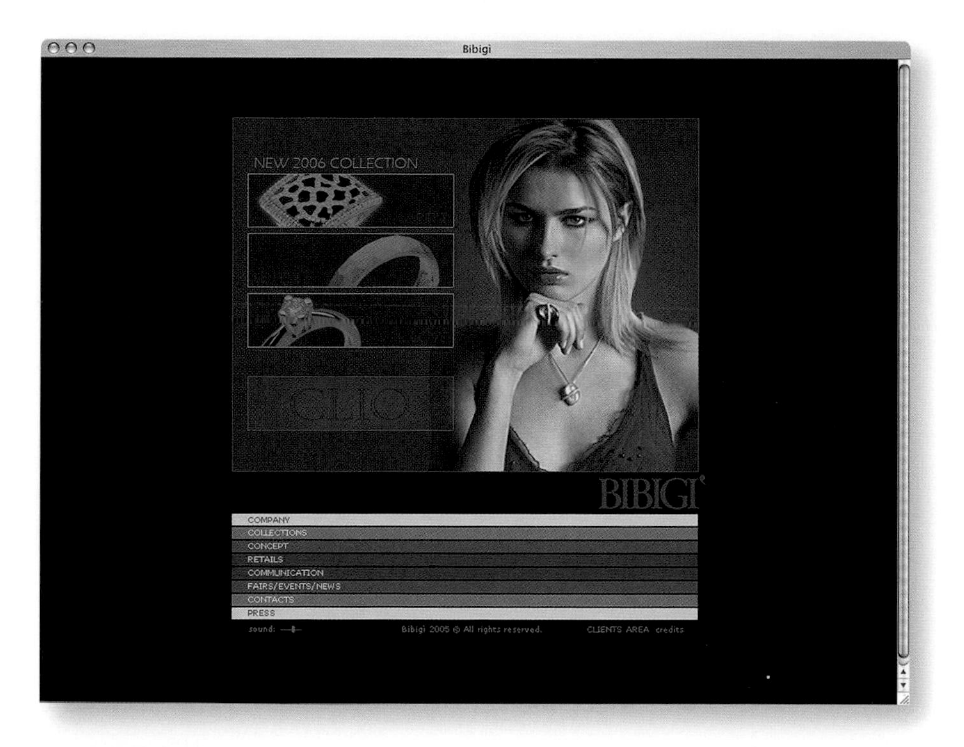

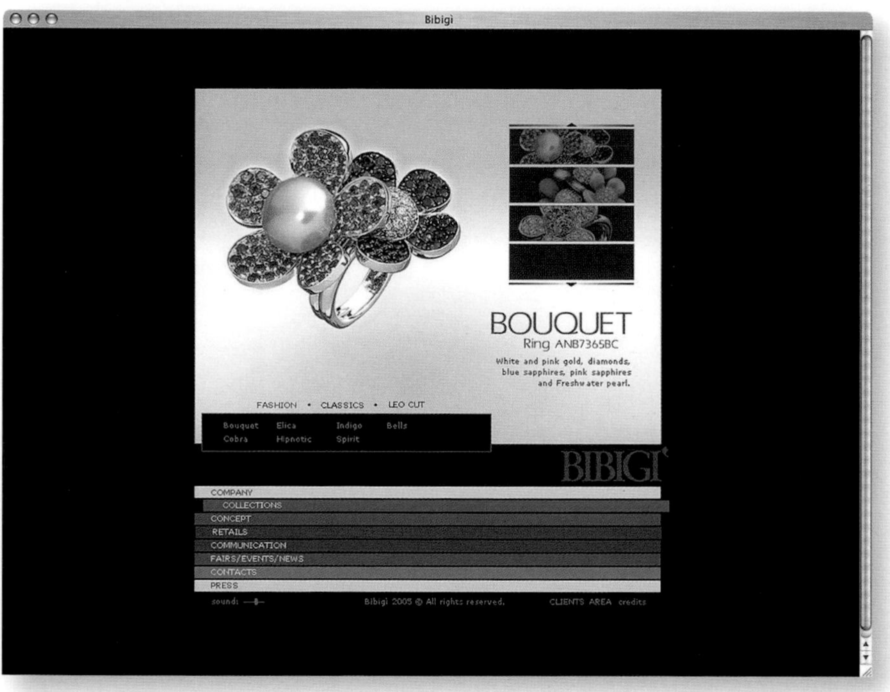

www.bibigi.com

D: federico guidi, luca guidi **C:** fabrizio fusi

A: equent **M:** info@equent.it

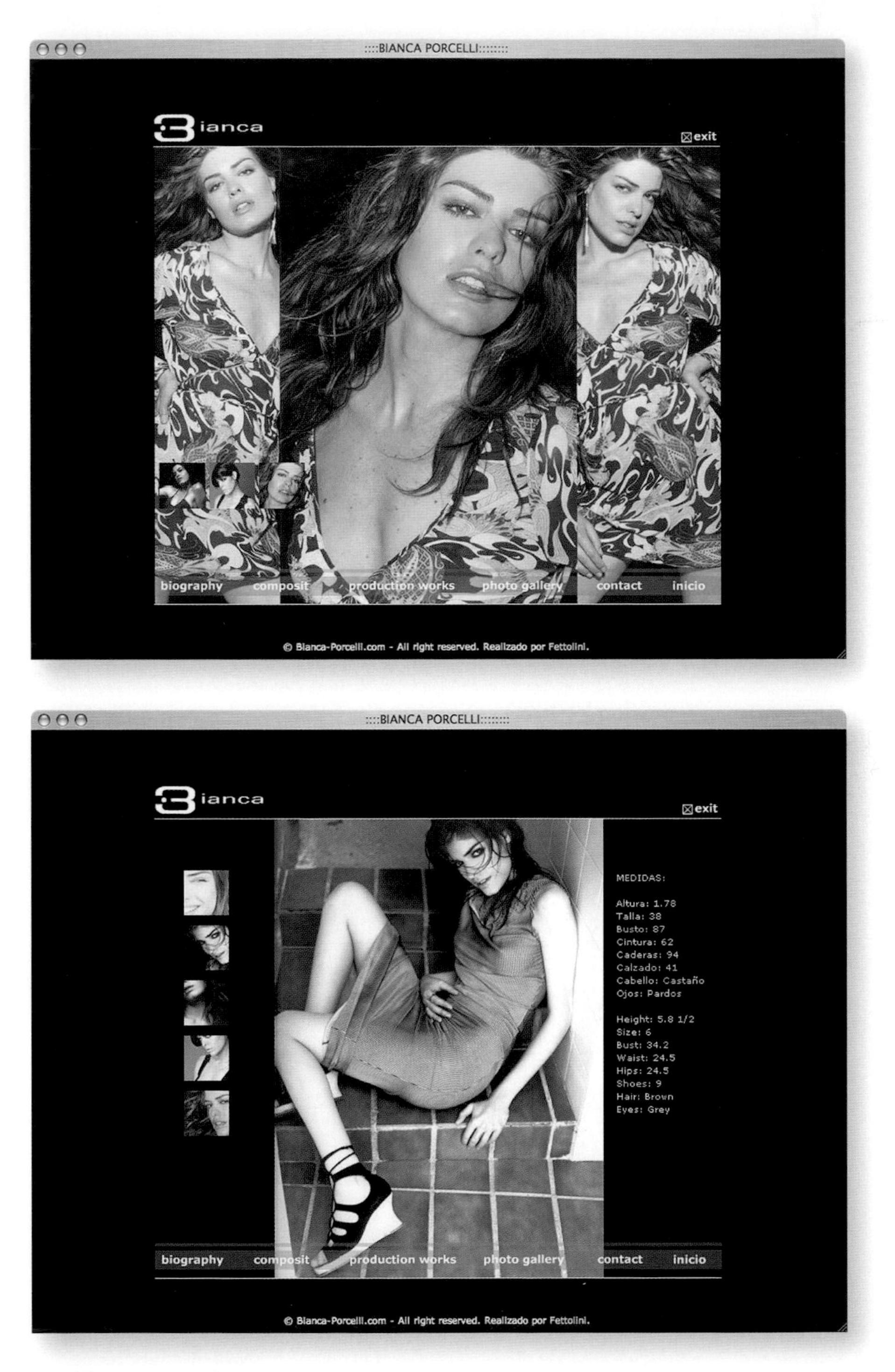

www.bianca-porcelli.com

D: fettolini design

A: fettolini design **M:** www.fettolini-design.net

www.enlaza.us

D: leonardo rafael schneider

A: lyo design digital **M:** www.lyo.com.br

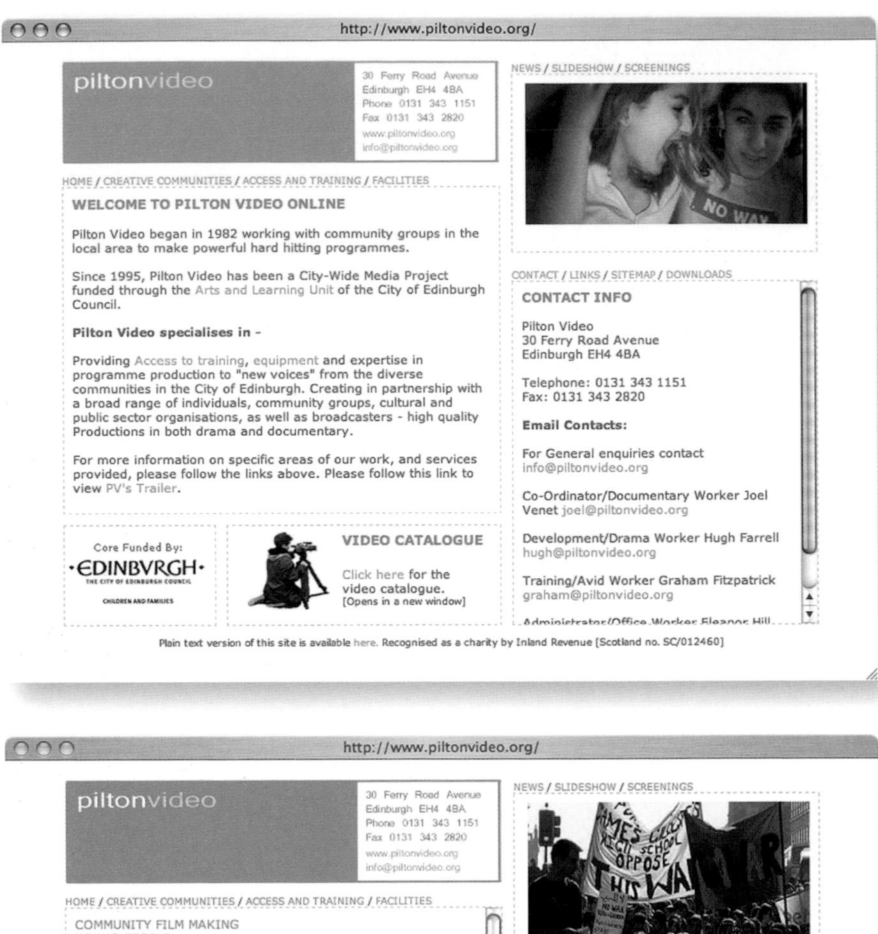

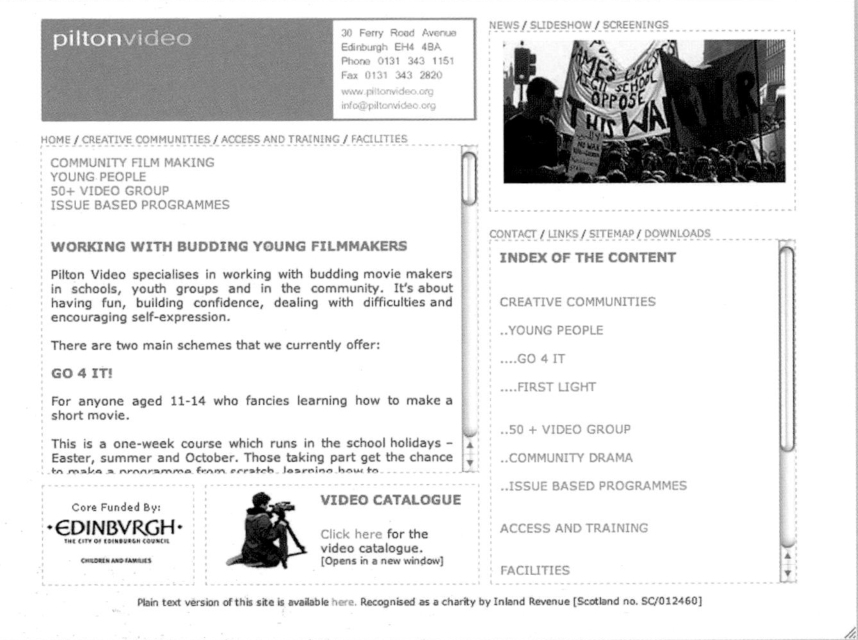

www.piltonvideo.org

D: minttu mantynen

A: my favourite tiger **M:** minttu@myfavouritetiger.co.uk

www.cedece-online.com

D: velcro

A: velcro **M:** www.velcrodesign.com

areatangent

PORTADA MENÚ

NOTÍCIES VEURE TOTES LES NOTÍCIES

09/03/2006
RODA DE PREMSA DIMECRES 15 a les 12:00h
El NAUMON invita AREAtangent RODA DE PREMSA DIMECRES 15 A LES 12:00h LLOC: Vaixell NAUMON, Moll de la Fusta, davant de l'IMAX El NAUMON, Centre Cultural del port de (...)

AGENDA ANAR A L'AGENDA COMPLETA

Dimarts 14 de març a les 21:00h
Càpsules a 1€ AUTORRETRATO
Experimental
Una proposta de Pau Palacios "Cuando retrato, autorretrato. Cuando me retrato, autorretrato. Si retrato un perro, (...)

Divendres 17 de març a les 22:30h
SUSANA SHEIMAN SEXTET
Jazz
SUSANA SHEIMAN SEXTET Divendres 17 de març 22:30h al NAUMON
Susana Sheiman és una de les joves veus del jazz actual. (...)

Dijous 16 de març a les 22'30h
IGNASI TERRAZA TRIO
Jazz
IGNASI TERRAZA El reconegut músic de jazz Ignasi Terraza, juntament amb el seu trio composat per Pierre Boussaguet i Jean (...)

AREATANGENT Espai de creació i visualització multidisciplinar · carrer Aurora 21 baixos. 08001 Barcelona

areatangent

AGENDA MENÚ

MARÇ 2006 MES

Dimarts 14 de març a les 21:00h
Càpsules a 1€ AUTORRETRATO
Experimental

Una proposta de Pau Palacios

"Cuando retrato, autorretrato.
Cuando me retrato, autorretrato.
Si retrato un perro, autorretrato.
Cuando la lluvia, autorretrato.
Si no retrato, autorretrato.

DATES

MARÇ 2006

		1	2	3	4	5
6	7	8	9	10	11	12
13	14	15	16	17	18	19
20	21	22	23	24	25	26
27	28	29	30	31		

Divendres 17 de març a les 22:30h
SUSANA SHEIMAN SEXTET
Jazz
SUSANA SHEIMAN SEXTET Divendres 17 de març 22:30h al NAUMON
Susana Sheiman és una de les joves veus del jazz actual. (...)

16 DIJOUS DIA

AREATANGENT Espai de creació i visualització multidisciplinar · carrer Aurora 21 baixos. 08001 Barcelona

www.areatangent.com

D: jorge ferrera **C:** raúl fernandez **P:** cristian cisa, josep mª marimon

A: tangent audiovisual **M:** info@tangent.es

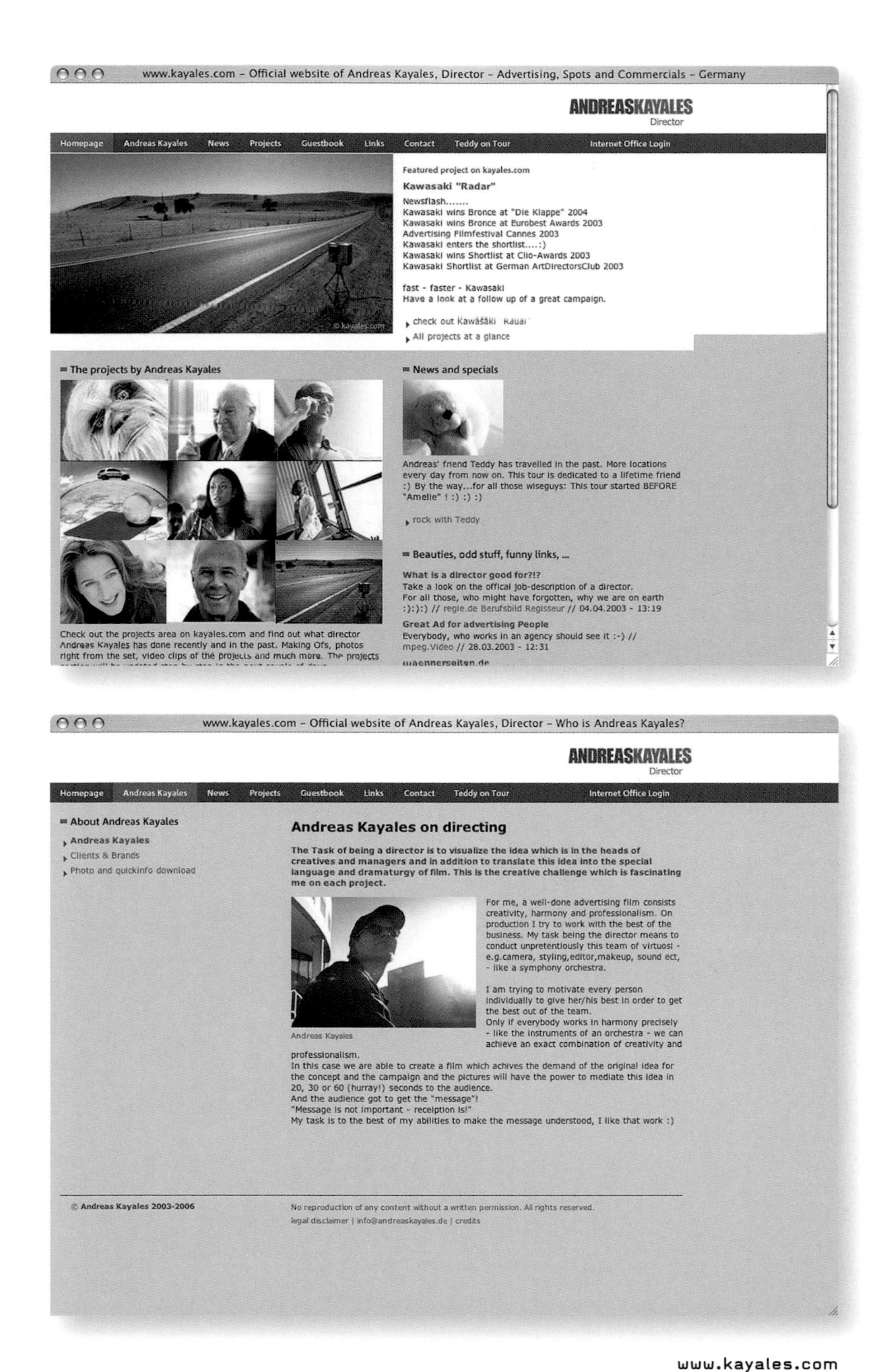

www.kayales.com

D: jan persiel **C:** jan persiel **P:** jan persiel, andreas kayales

A: schoengeist.de **M:** www.schoengeist.de

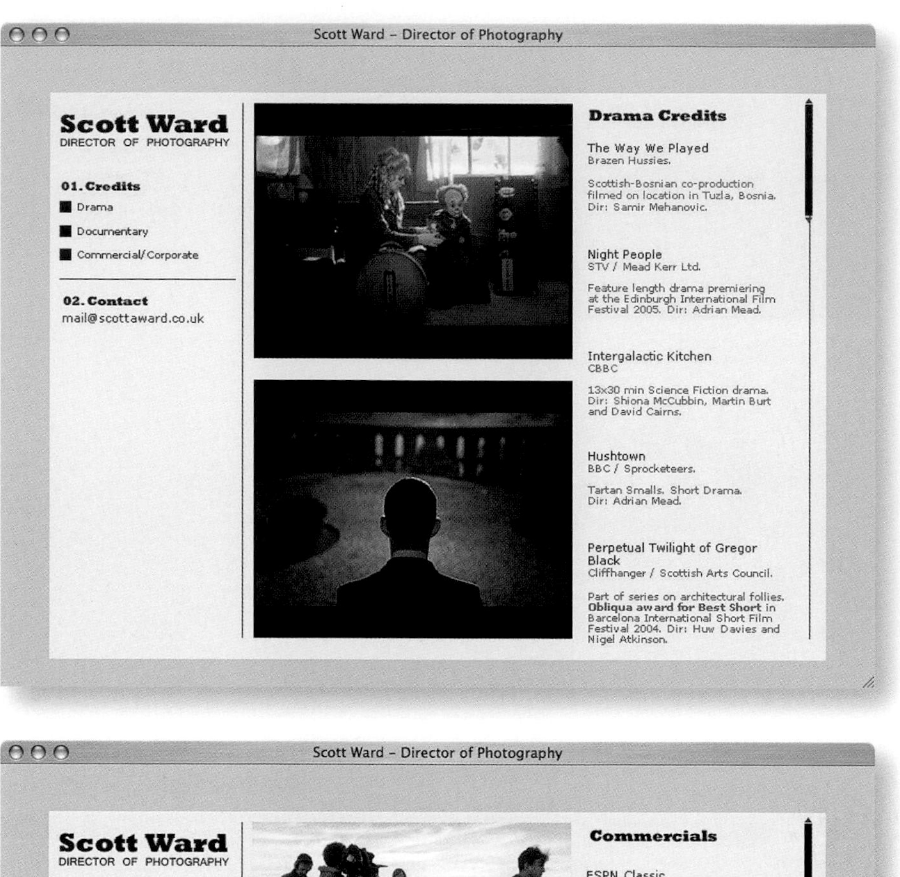

Scott Ward – Director of Photography

Scott Ward
DIRECTOR OF PHOTOGRAPHY

01. Credits
- Drama
- Documentary
- Commercial/Corporate

02. Contact
mail@scottaward.co.uk

Commercials

ESPN Classic
ESPN
Commercial shot in Rome for ESPN sports channel European launch.

Avante Channel Idents
UPC TV. NL.

Virgin Mobile
Spectre

Extreme Sports Channel Idents
UPC TV. NL.

Edinburgh International Film Festival
Cinema Commercial EIFF

ITV Digital
Homes Ondigital
As Director/Camera. Corporate video on analogue tv signal switch off.

Keep Edinburgh Clean
Skyline Productions
Two commercials for Keep Edinburgh Clean - campaign.

www.scottaward.co.uk

D: minttu mäntynen

A: my favourite tiger **M:** minttu@myfavouritetiger.co.uk

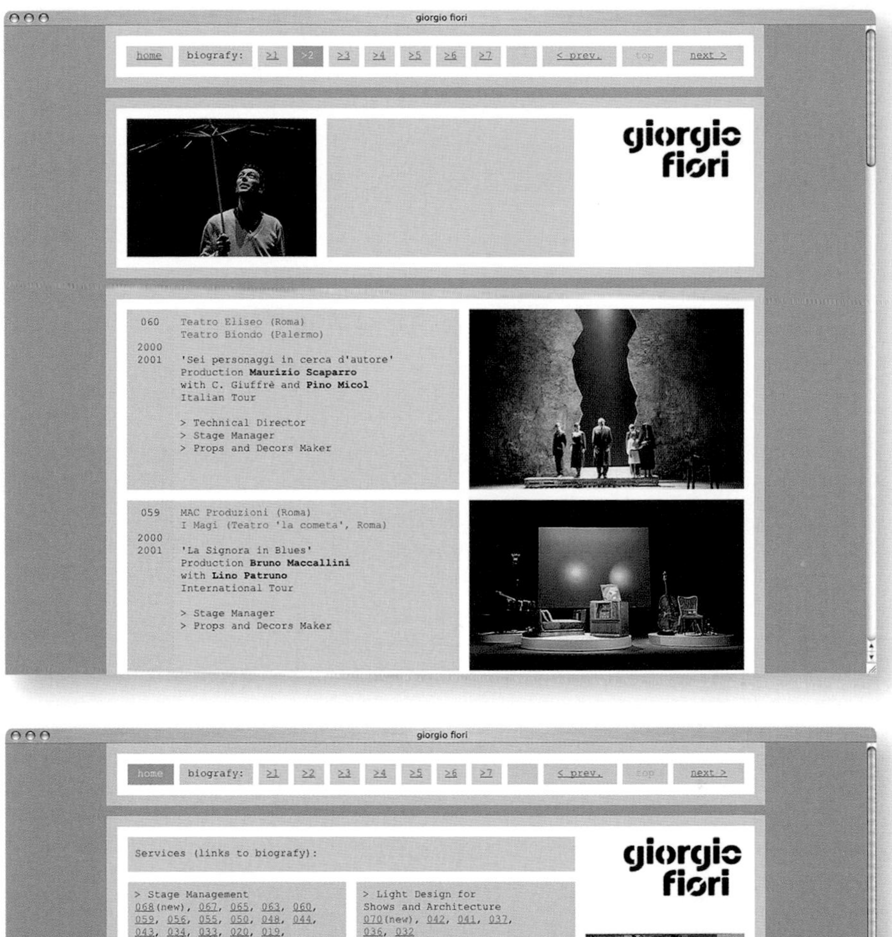

www.stagemanagement.info

D: marcel schneeberger

A: grafikpilot **M:** kerosin@grafikpilot.ch

www.daringplanet.com

D: paul corrigan

A: oddity studios, daring planet **M:** paul@daringplanet.com

www.leroythehand.com

D: 15 letters

M: www.15letters.com

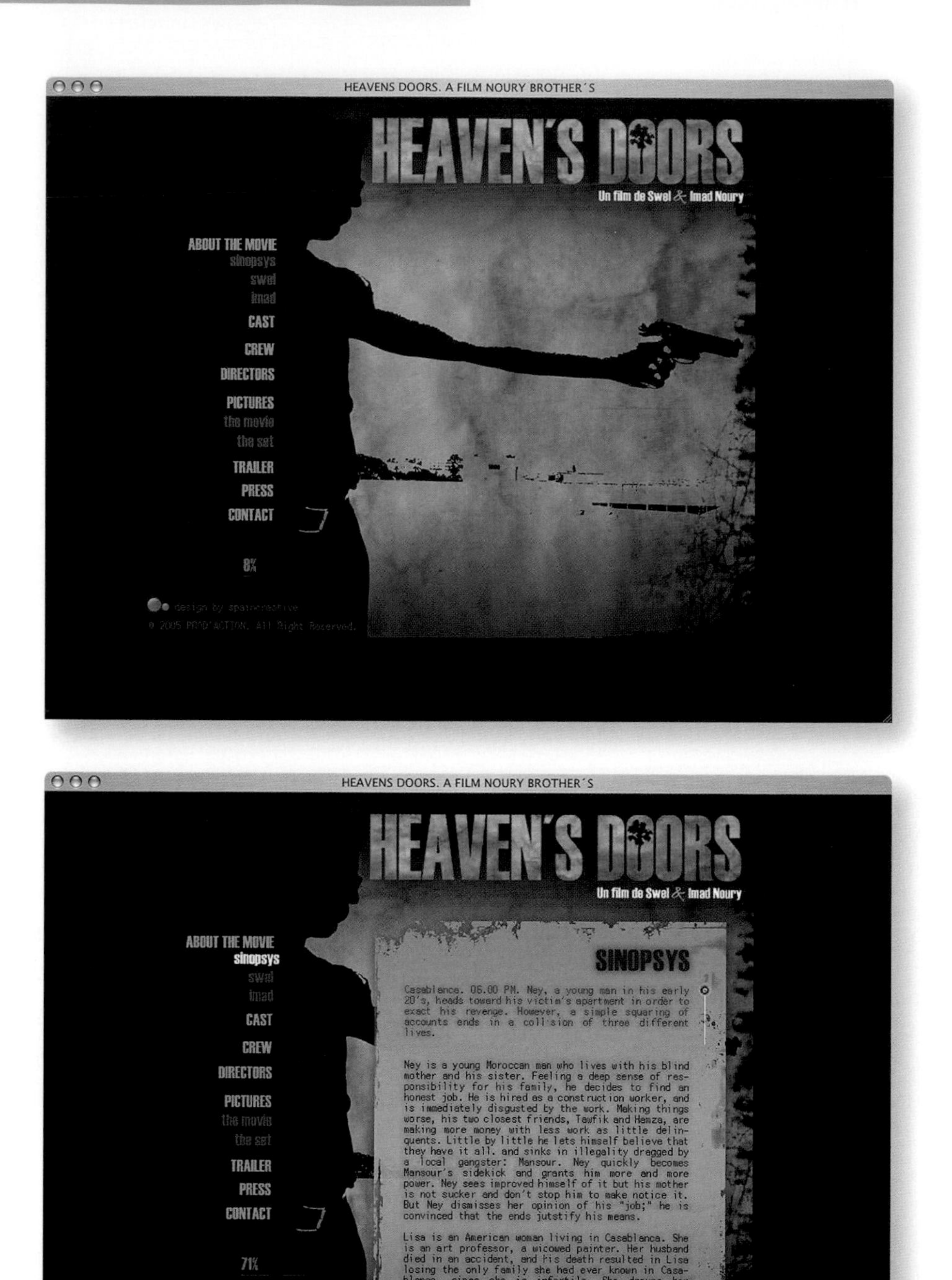

www.heavens-doors.com

D: lourdes molina

A: spaincreative **M:** info@antonioherraiz.com

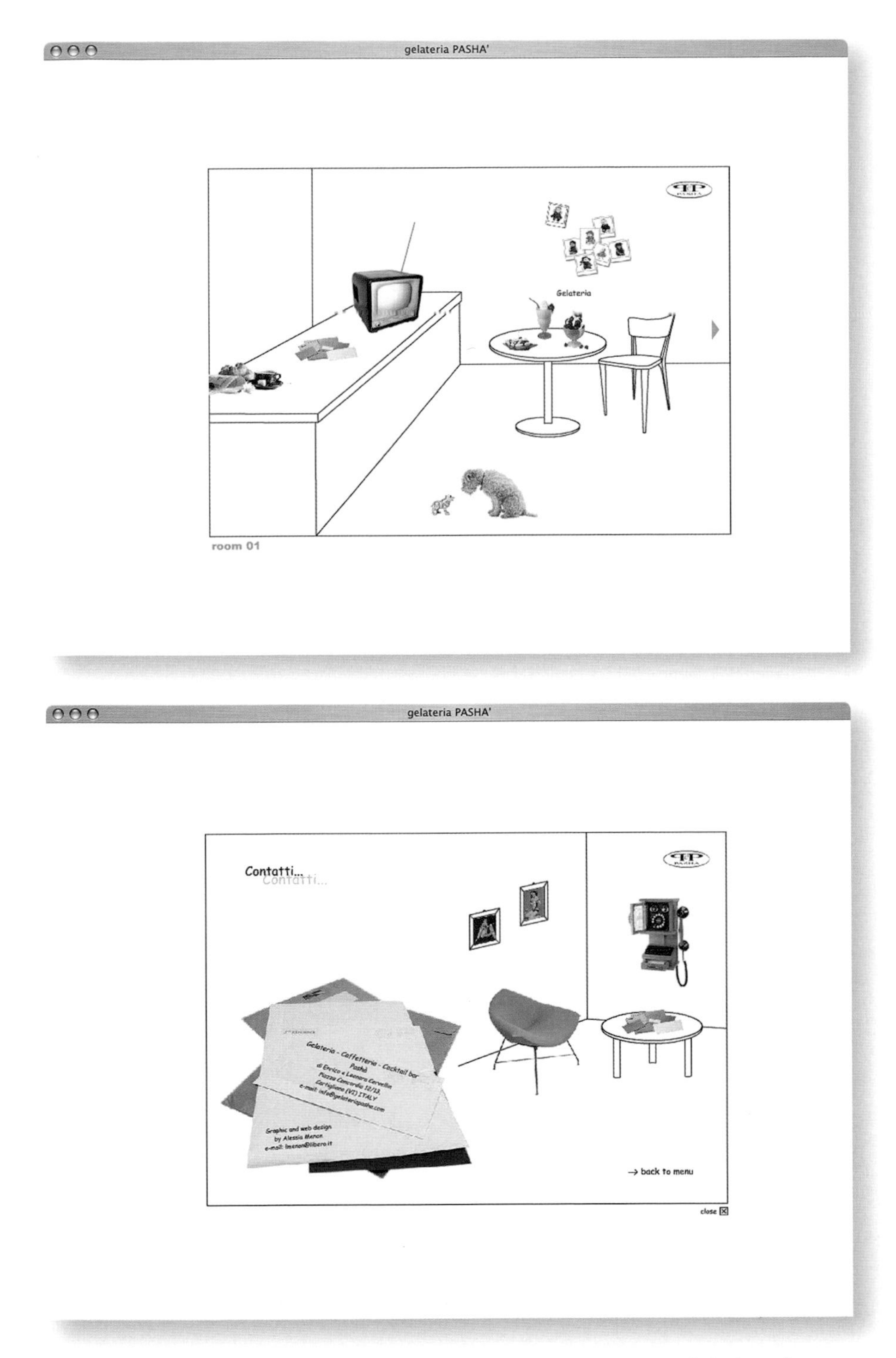

www.gelateriapasha.com
D: alessia menon
M: lmenon@libero.it

www.sumarroca.es

D: ignacio zorraquín

A: nomadesign **M:** www.nomadesign.info

www.genova.cl

D: nexprochile ltda.

A: nexprochile ltda. **M:** dcreativa@nexprochile.cl

www.bacardimojito.com

D: scott cook

A: driftlab **M:** www.driftlab.com

www.segugio.nl

D: natha **C:** natha **P:** adriano paolini

A: plush.nl **M:** natha@plush.nl

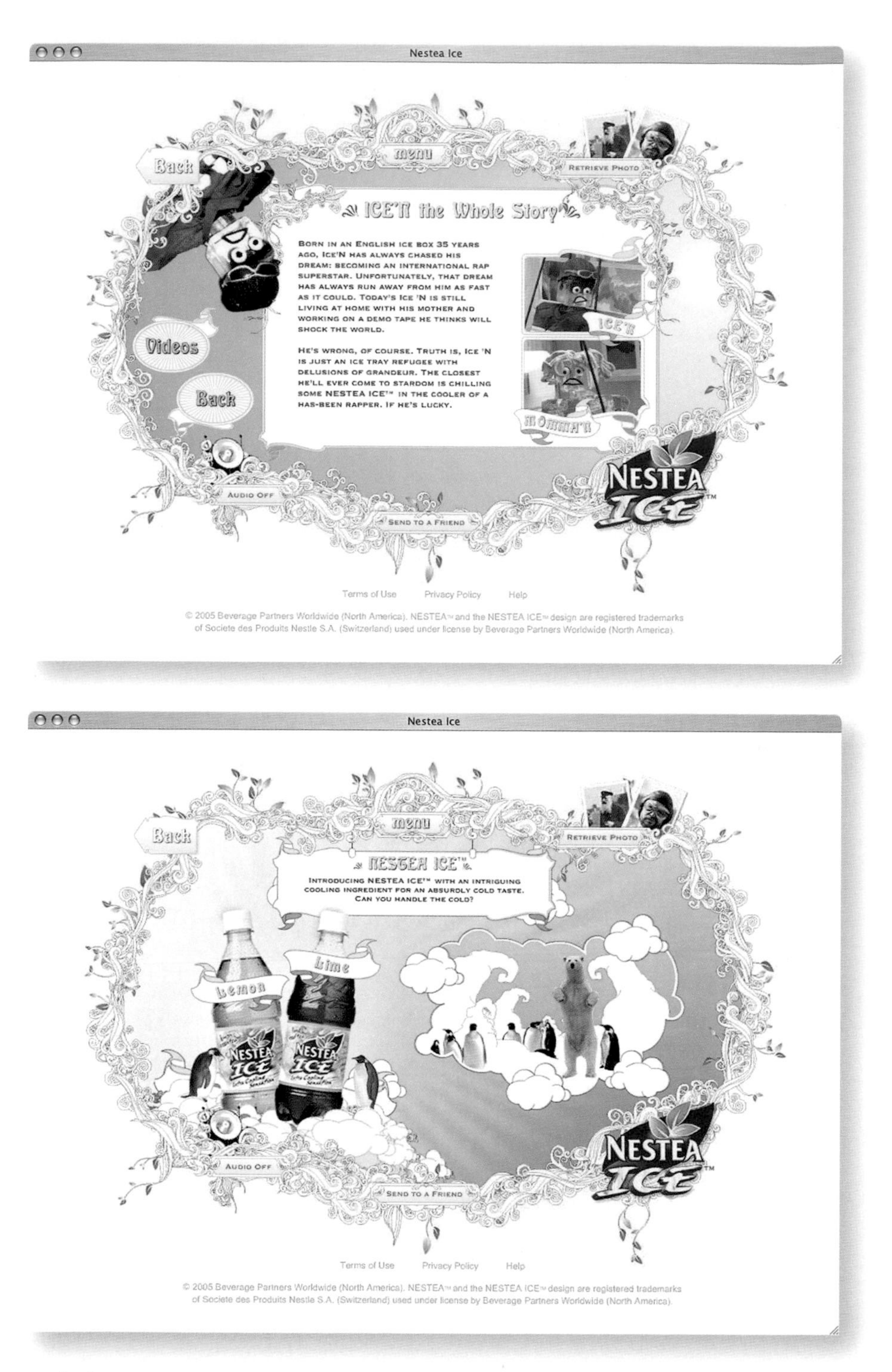

nesteaice.com

D: todd purgason, jorge calleja, ken macy, christian ayotte **P:** kristen myers

A: juxt interactive **M:** juxtinteractive.com

www.powwowcoffee.de

D: andreas reisewitz **C:** andreas reisewitz, yves vogl **P:** andreas reisewitz
A: compudrom creative services **M:** www.compudrom.de

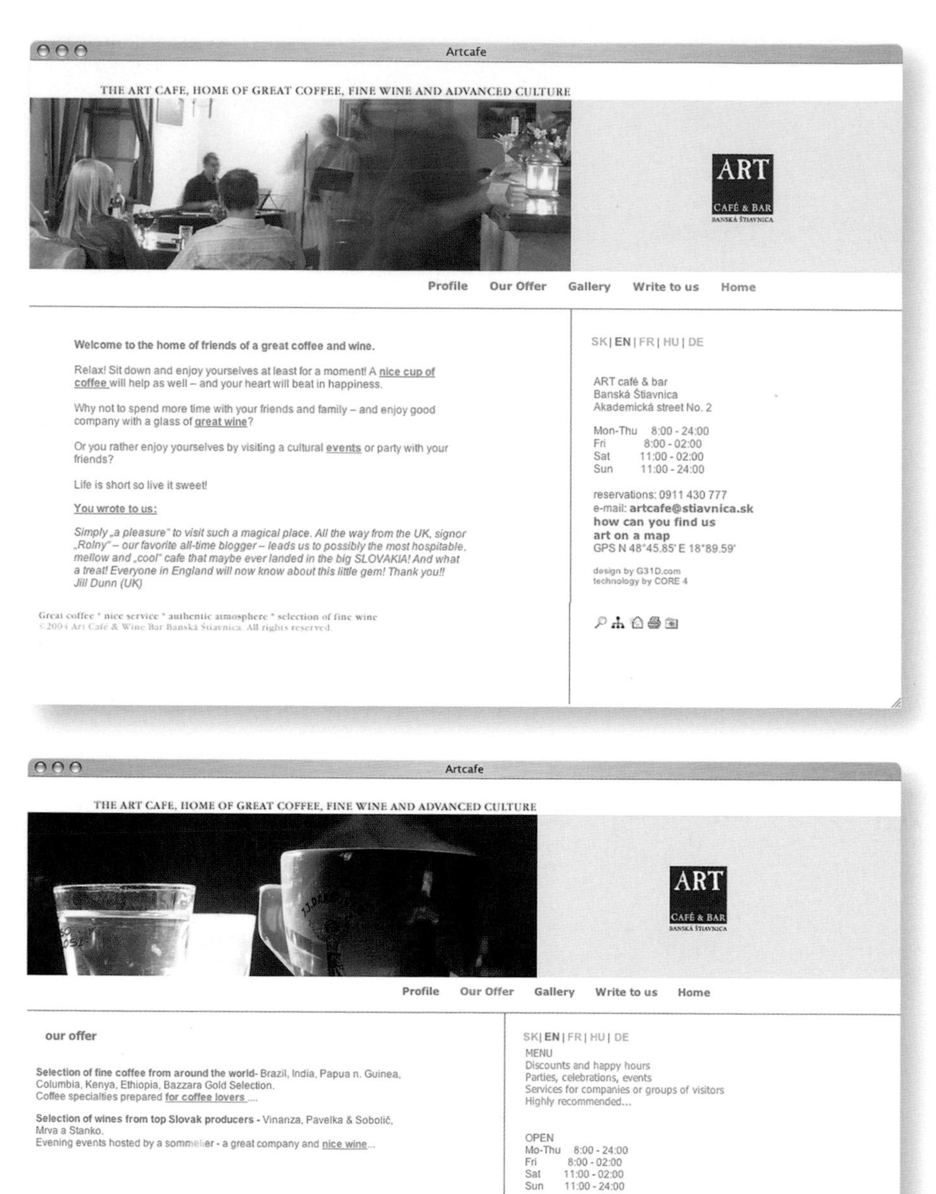

www.artcafe.sk

D: viktor kovac **C:** core 4

A: g31d.com creative agency **M:** info@g31d.com

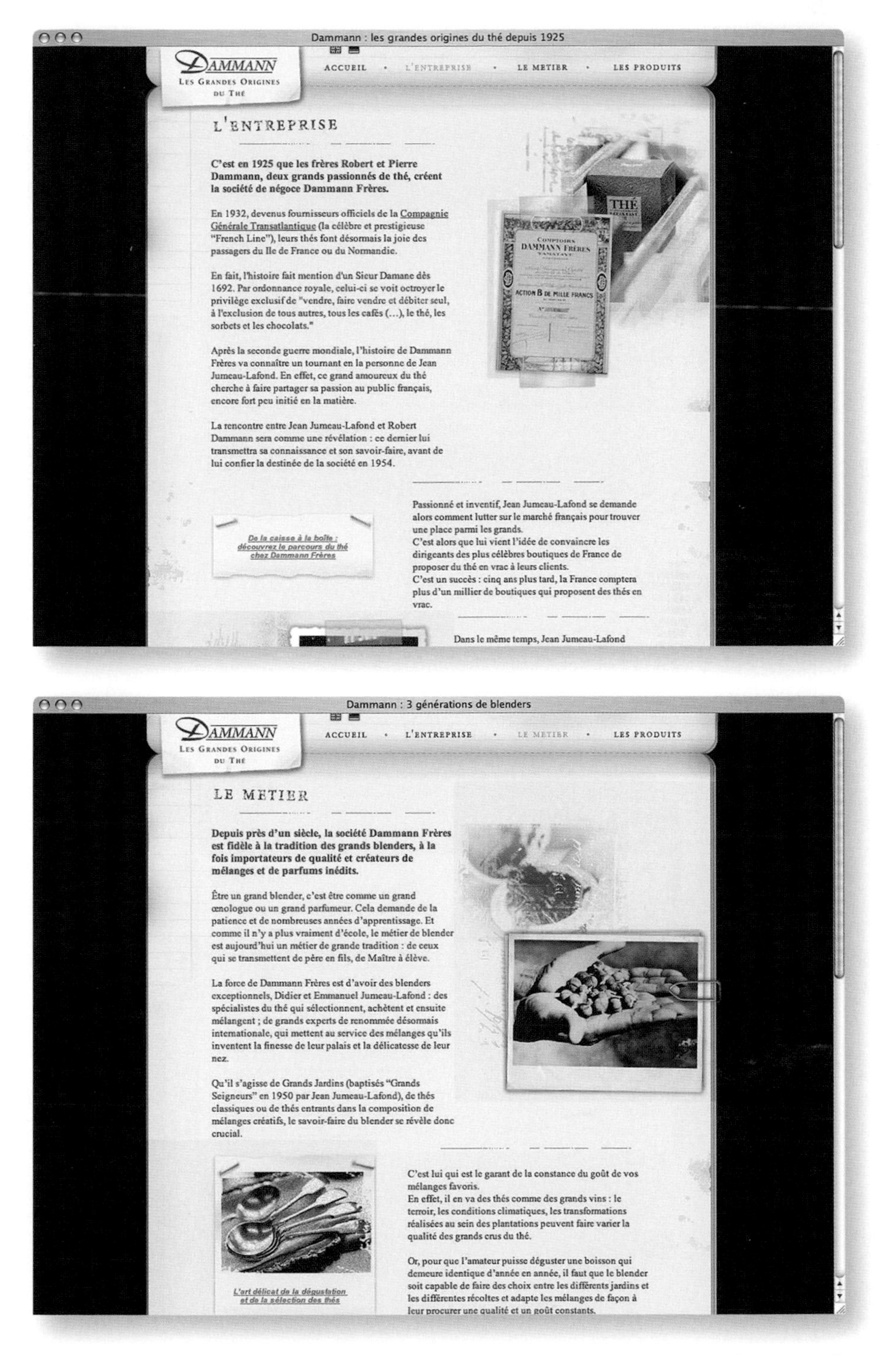

www.dammann.fr

D: laurent chomette pour sokovision **C:** sokovision **P:** dammann frères
A: sokovision **M:** eric.marillet@sokovision.com

___ Salotto 42 ___

Filosofia

salotto 42

Posto in fronte al Tempio di Adriano, uno dei monumenti più emblematici di Roma, nella Piazza di Pietra, area centralissima a pochi passi dal Parlamento e dal Pantheon, è nato il Salotto42.

Il "bookbar" Salotto42 è stato concepito come un vero e proprio salotto di una casa newyorkese: il penthouse. All'interno si respira una contaminazione di stili ed influenze diverse che variano dall'antichità al moderno. L'assemblamento non è casuale ma di rara ricchezza e di raffinata tendenza. Ed è così che nel nostro bookbar si è voluto unire divani anni 50 con lampadari Murano della prima metà dell'800, balaustre in marmo del '600, con broccati Art Nouveaux.

Non ci sono i quadri come in un vero salotto, ma ad attrarre l'occhio e a donare calore e fantasia allo spazio, ci sono i libri, di natura grafica e design, di moda e fotografia d'autore, di tendenza estrema ed erotismo raffinato.

Come si conviene in molti loft o penthouse di Manhattan, dove esiste preponderante, il camino, posto in corrispondenza delle sedute per amalgamare gli ospiti, il Salotto42, per ovviare alla mancanza del camino stesso, nelle giornate invernali e fredde, proietta in una cornice anni '30, un primo piano di fuoco

>>

chiudi

salotto 42

DSE by Alchimedia

www.salotto42.it

D: molinari **C:** andrea brauzzi **P:** salotto 42

A: alchimedia srl **M:** cmolinari@alchimedia.com

www.quintaeventos.com

D: bruno silva **C:** sidney veiga **P:** bruno silva

A: arta design **M:** bua@arta-design.com

www.champagne-rosesdejeanne.com

D: fabrice corneux

A: fabrice corneux **M:** fabrice@nowaxx.com

www.physiohk.com

D: michael clough **C:** teresa l. y. lee

A: compelite ltd **M:** www.compelite.net

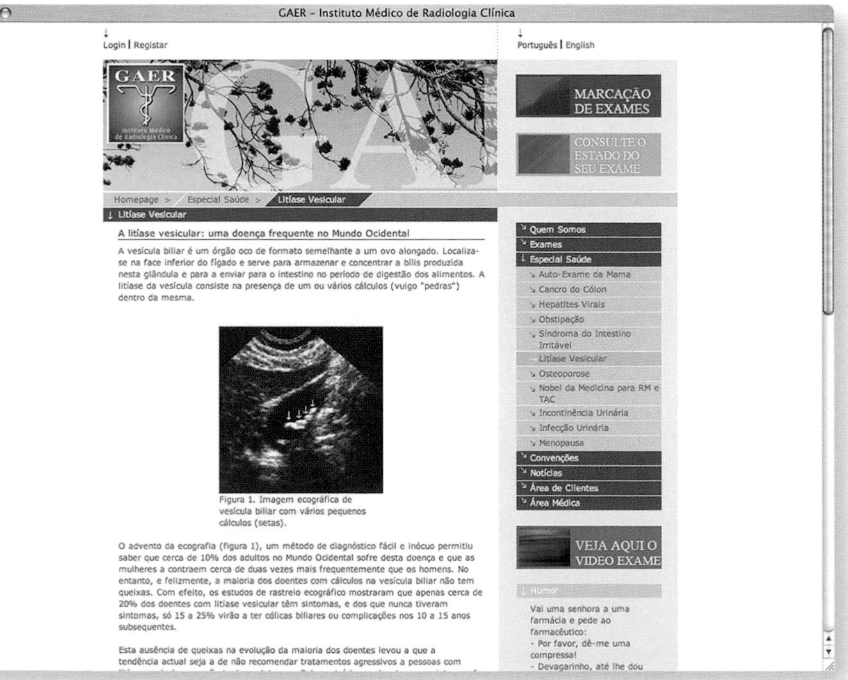

www.gaer.pt

D: nsolutions4u.com **C:** hélder ribeiro

A: gaer **M:** webmaster@gaer.pt

www.antibioticos.com.pt

D: sofia vitor **C:** wolfgang borgsmüller **P:** sofia vitor

A: aftamina **M:** www.aftamina.pl

www.meimon.nl

D: peter visser

A: illusoft M: p.visser@illusoft.com

www.orthovano.be

D: laurent lampaert

A: nookyalur **M:** info@nookyalur.com

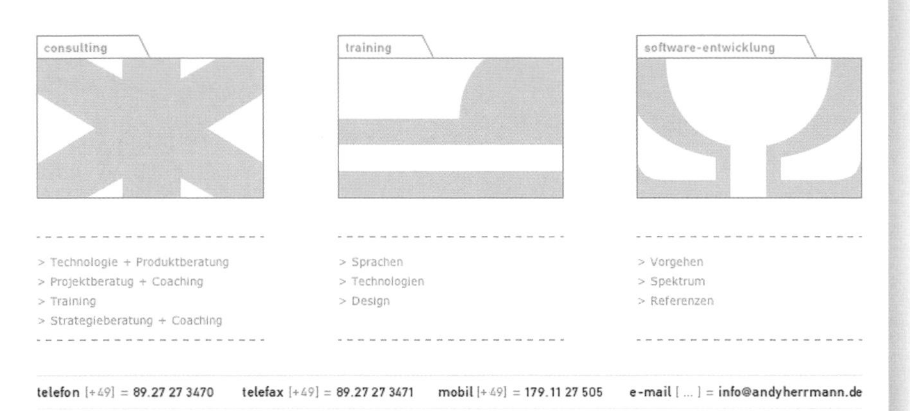

} andreas herrmann {

.do > (iT_design = } andreas herrmann {~ spec [Patterns]. y //: diplom-informatiker &
list [pro]. (> consulting) & (> training) = tec [++now] * (> software-entwicklung) !
{ > pdf-downloads }. req4_ { > support }~ref { > kontakt } .\ by { > impressum } + get (

Consulting

Kurzer Blick in die Kristallkugel gefällig?
Welche Technologie bestimmt unsere IT Welt von morgen? Welche Sprachen werden wir sprechen? Welche Software wird den Ton angeben? Wenn Sie etwas über die Welt der Zukunft und ihre Herausforderungen wissen wollen, können Sie einen Wahrsager konsultieren. Wir aber empfehlen Ihnen einen Besuch bei uns. Denn nur wer die Entwicklung der letzten Jahrzehnte kennt, hat den nötigen und vor allem kritischen Überblick über die Trends in der Software. Wir setzen nicht auf den kurzfristigen Hype, sondern - ganz die alte Schule - auf jahrelang bewährte Software ohne Kinderkrankheiten. Die läuft auch morgen noch fehlerlos. Das sagen wir Ihnen ganz frech, ohne einmal in die Kristallkugel zu gucken.

Eine Säule unseres Angebotes ist die Beratung rund um das Thema Software-Engineering. Je nach Kunde und Projektsituation kann diese Beratungstätigkeit unterschiedliche Schwerpunkte haben.

Auf den folgenden Seiten stellen wir einige typische Szenarien in Form von Fallbeispielen vor:
> Technologie-Entscheidungen
> Projekt-Coaching
> Training
> Strategieberatung

telefon [+49] = 89.27 27 3470 telefax [+49] = 89.27 27 3471 mobil [+49] = 179.11 27 505 e-mail [...] = info@andyherrmann.de

www.andyherrmann.de

D: sandra leister, alexander schäfer **C:** alexander schäfer

A: 372dpi - design print internet **M:** a.schaefer@372dpi.com

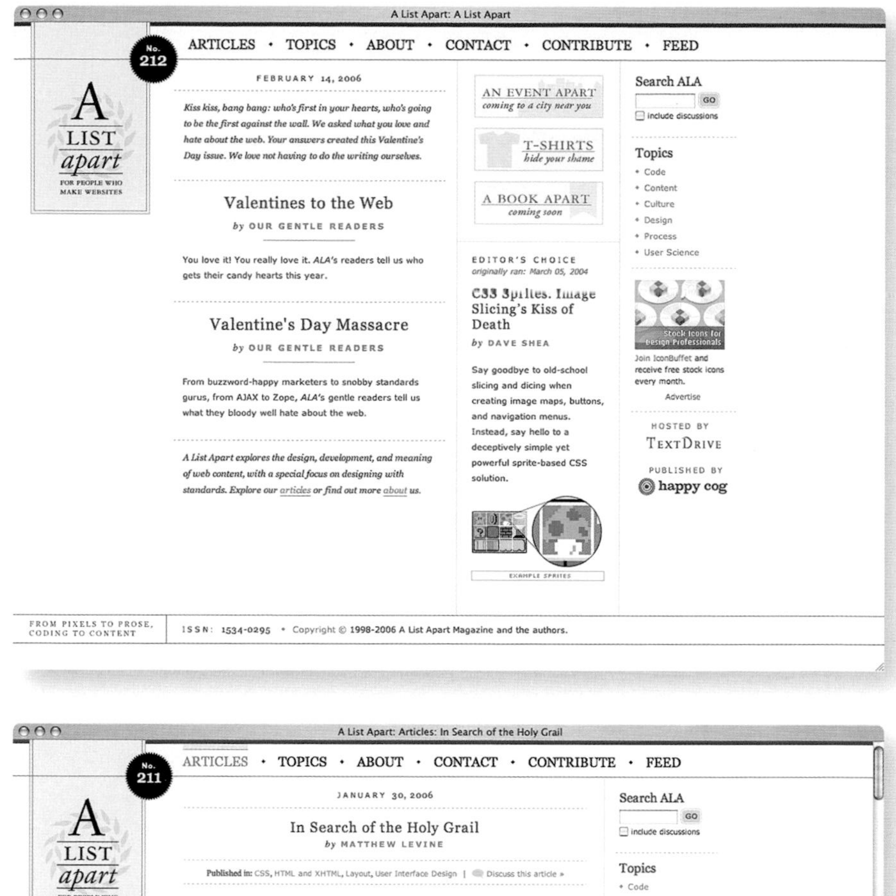

A List Apart: Articles: In Search of the Holy Grail

No. 211

ARTICLES • TOPICS • ABOUT • CONTACT • CONTRIBUTE • FEED

A LIST apart
FOR PEOPLE WHO MAKE WEBSITES

JANUARY 30, 2006

In Search of the Holy Grail
by MATTHEW LEVINE

Published in: CSS, HTML and XHTML, Layout, User Interface Design | Discuss this article »

I'm sorry. Really. I didn't name it. I don't mean to overstate its importance or trivialize the other and rather weightier Holy Grails.

But the name's out there, and we all know what it means.

Three columns. One fixed-width sidebar for your navigation, another for, say, your Google Ads or your Flickr photos—and, as in a fancy truffle, a liquid center for the real substance. Its wide applicability in this golden age of blogging, along with its considerable difficulty, is what has earned the layout the title of Holy Grail.

Many articles have been written about the grail, and several good templates exist. However, all the existing solutions involve sacrifices: proper source order, full-width footers, and lean markup are often compromised in the pursuit of this elusive layout.

A recent project has brought my personal grail quest to an end. The technique I'll describe will allow you to deploy the Holy Grail layout without compromising your code or your flexibility. It will:

1. have a fluid center with fixed width sidebars,
2. allow the center column to appear first in the source,
3. allow any column to be the tallest,
4. require only a single extra div of markup, and
5. require very simple CSS, with minimal ~~hacks~~ patches.

On the shoulders of giants

Search ALA
GO
include discussions

Topics
- Code
- Content
- Culture
- Design
- Process
- User Science

Snapshot
"Many articles have been written on the grail, and several good templates exist. However, all the existing solutions involve sacrifices: proper source order, full-width footers, and lean markup are the usual compromises made in pursuit of this elusive layout."

Free Stock Icons at IconBuffet
Join IconBuffet and receive free stock icons every month.
Advertise

HOSTED BY
TextDrive
PUBLISHED BY
happy cog

www.alistapart.com

D: jeffrey zeldman, j. santa maria C: e. meyer, d. benjamin P: e. kissane, j. zeldman
A: happy cog studios M: www.happycog.com

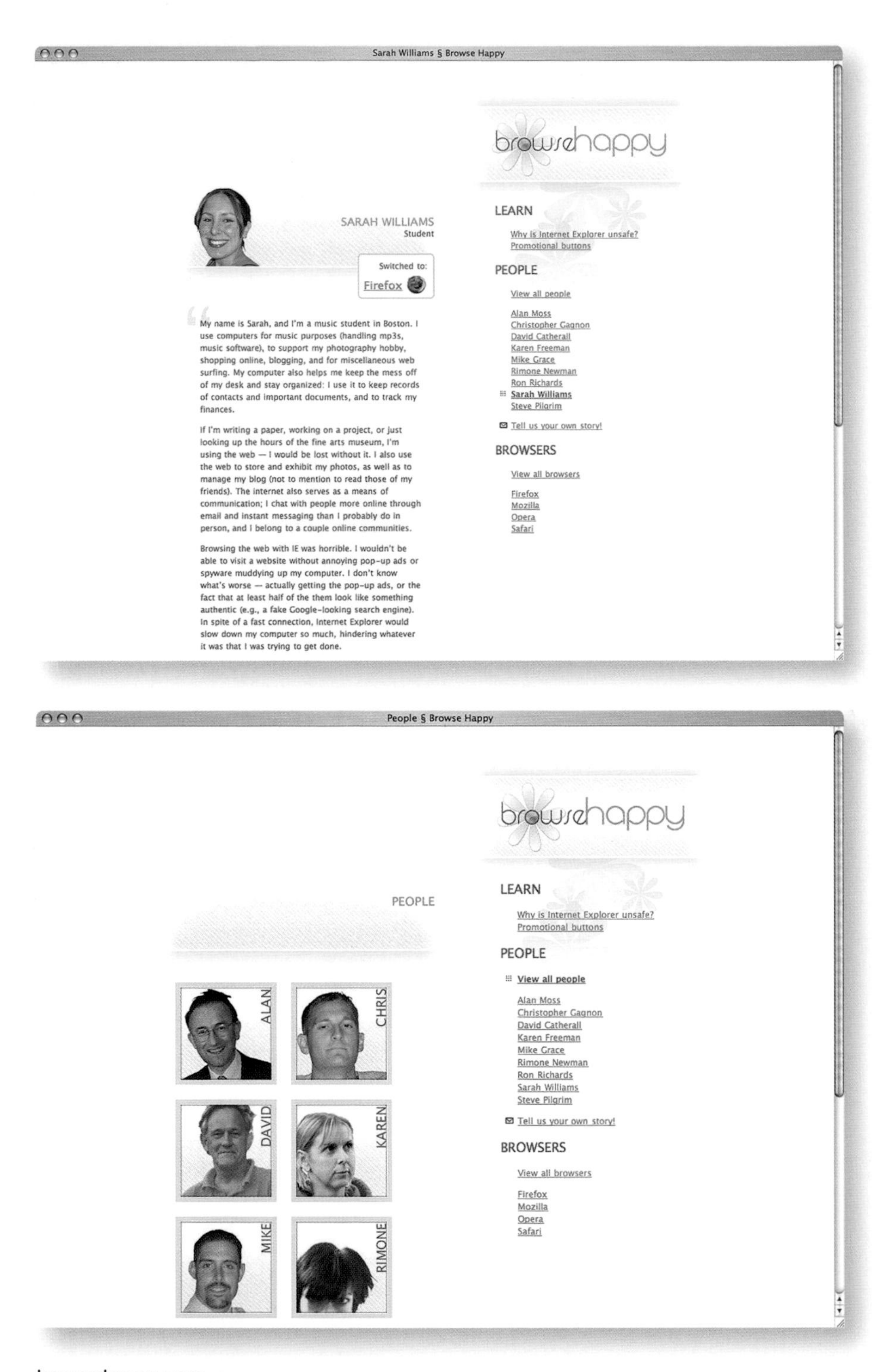

browsehappy.com

D: ethan marcotte **C:** ethan marcotte **P:** ethan marcotte, stephanie troeth

A: vertua studios **M:** vertua.com

www.brickhousemobile.com

D: david snyder, ian coyle **C:** ian coyle

A: fl2 **M:** www.fl-2.com

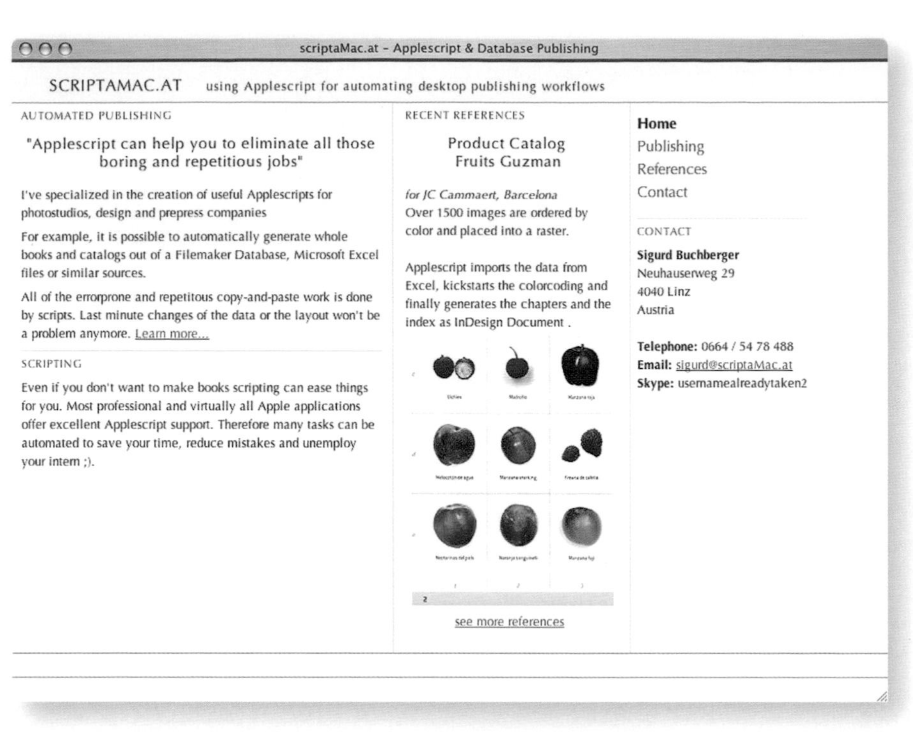

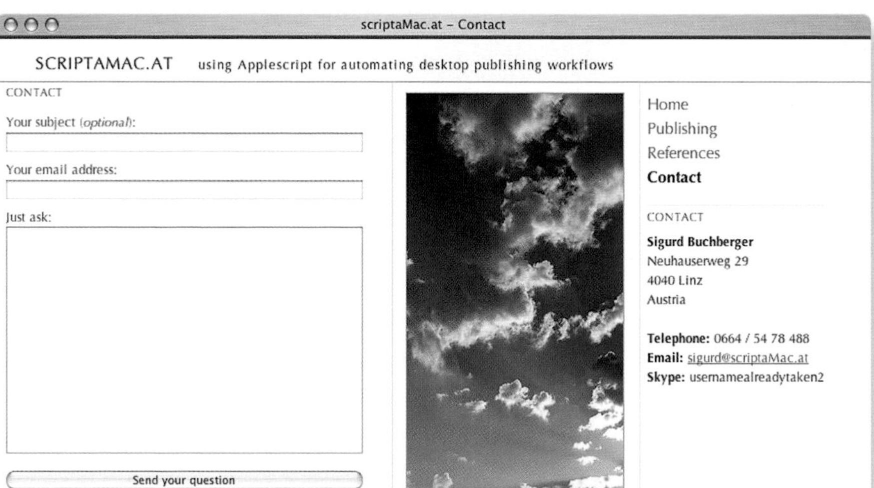

www.scriptamac.at

D: sigurd buchberger

M: sigurd@somemightsay.at

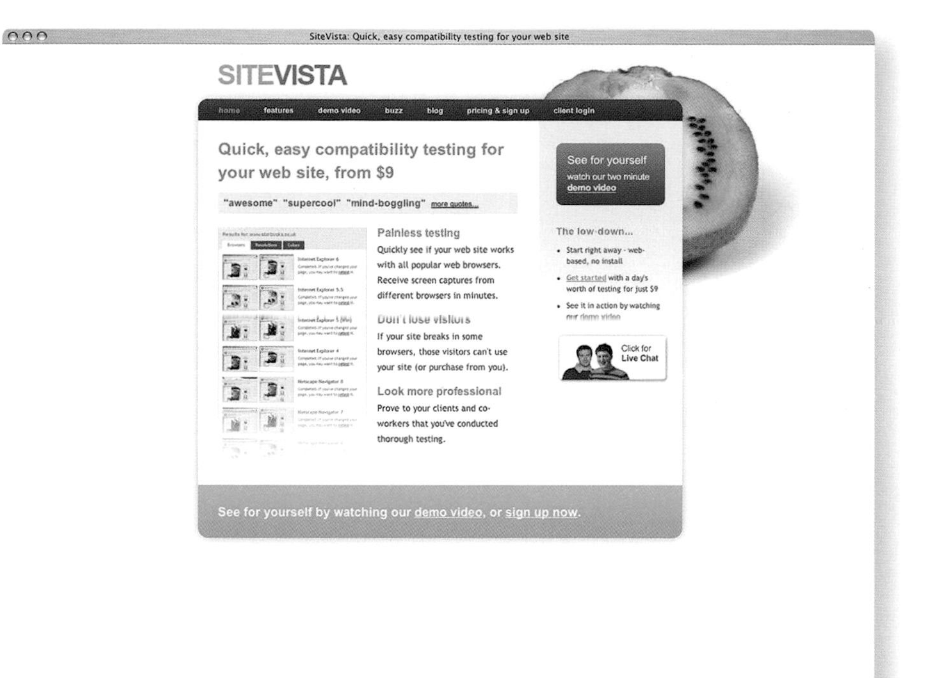

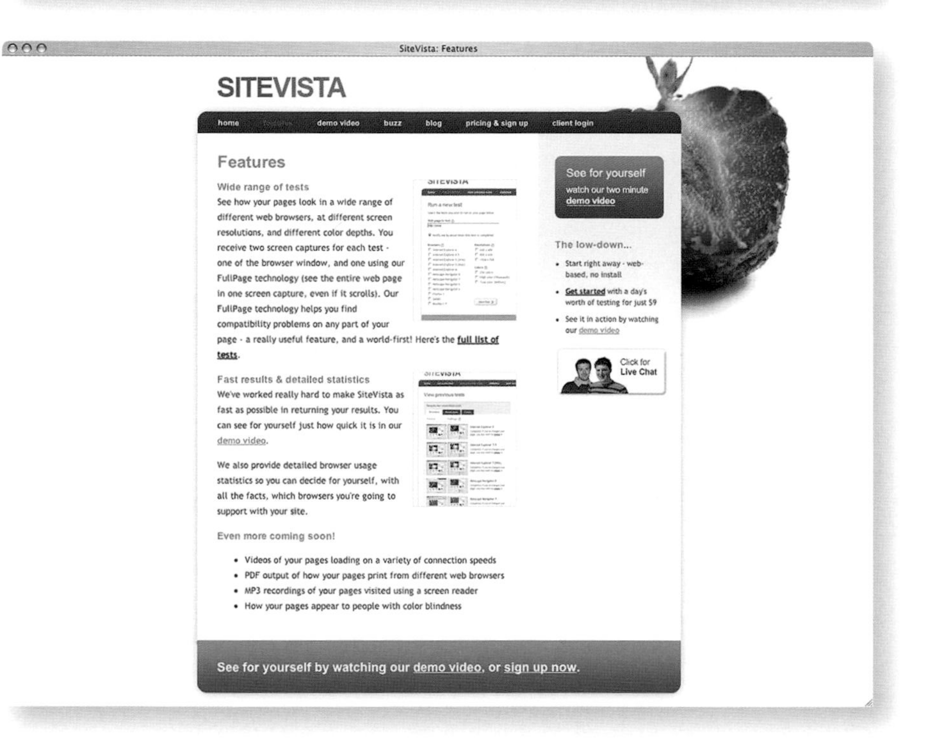

www.sitevista.com

D: paul farnell C: david smalley P: paul farnell

A: salted M: paul@salted.com

www.clearleft.com

D: andy budd **C:** jeremy keith **P:** richard rutter

A: clearleft ltd **M:** www.clearleft.com

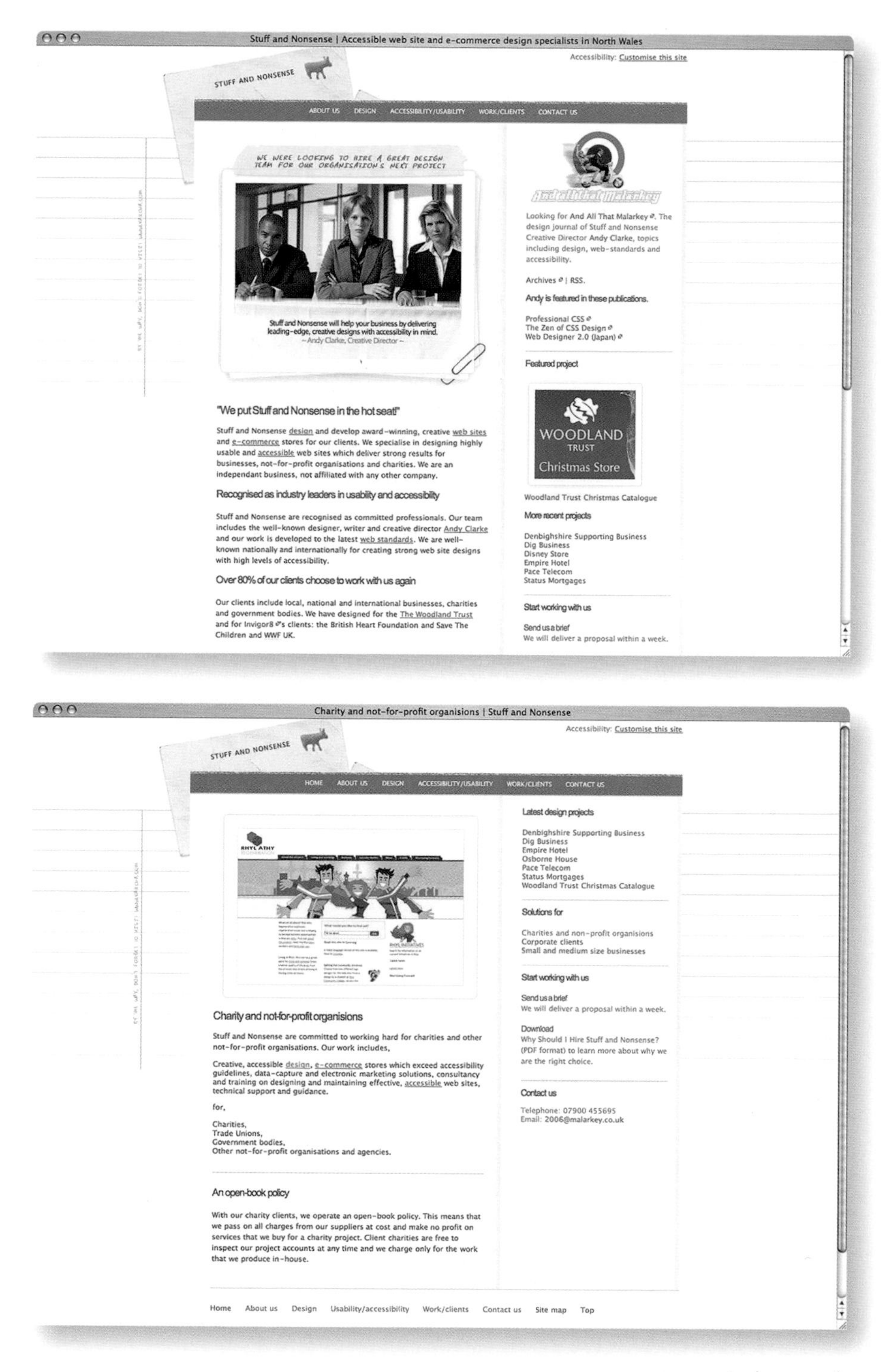

www.malarkey.co.uk

D: andy clarke

A: stuff and nonsense ltd. **M:** www.stuffandnonsense.co.uk

Zebra Productions

Prisbelønnet webdesign

zebra

Zebra Productions I Om web I Om stills I Om film I Om zebraen I Kontakt

Zebra Productions

Billedet har indtaget billedet

Stillbilledet er blevet tidens medie. Det fortæller historie, formidler budskaber, dokumenterer begivenheder, viderebringer stemninger og følelser. Overalt ser vi billeder, der appellerer til vores opmærksomhed. Stillbilledet spejler vores liv i alle dets afskygninger og er blevet et ikon på tilværelsen.

Hvis vi skal lægge mærke til et stillbillede, skal det være det rigtige billede i situationen. Det rigtige billede indeholder tilpas megen appeal og provokation til at bære budskabet igennem.

Vi indfanger og komponerer de helt rigtige billeder til de budskaber, vi arbejder med at formidle. Det væsentlige skal fremhæves og fremtræde troværdigt – måske med en fræk vinkel eller et lækkert lys.

Zebra Productions I Om web I Om stills I Om film I Om zebraen I Kontakt

zebra-pro.dk

D: zebra productions

A: zebra productions **M:** zebra@zebra-pro.dk

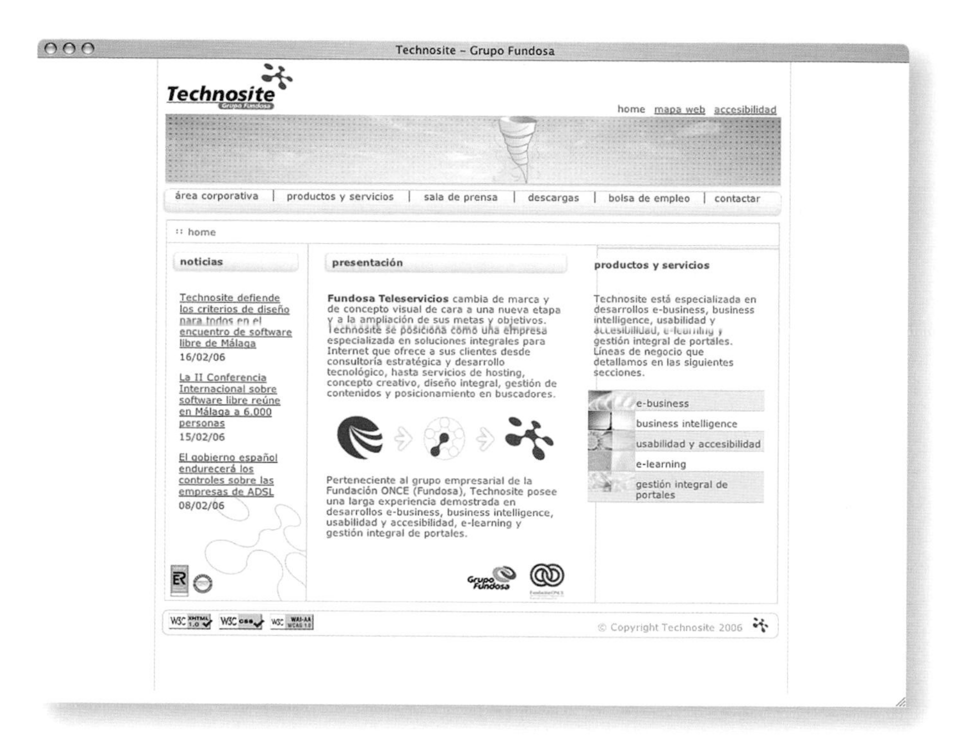

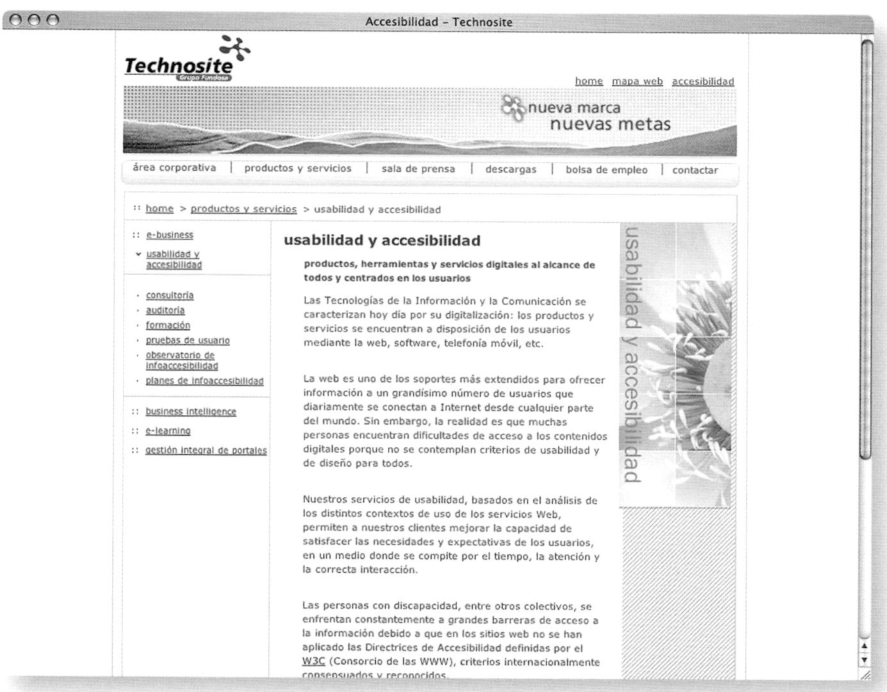

www.technosite.es
D: dept. diseño technosite
A: technosite **M:** tclosa@technosite.es

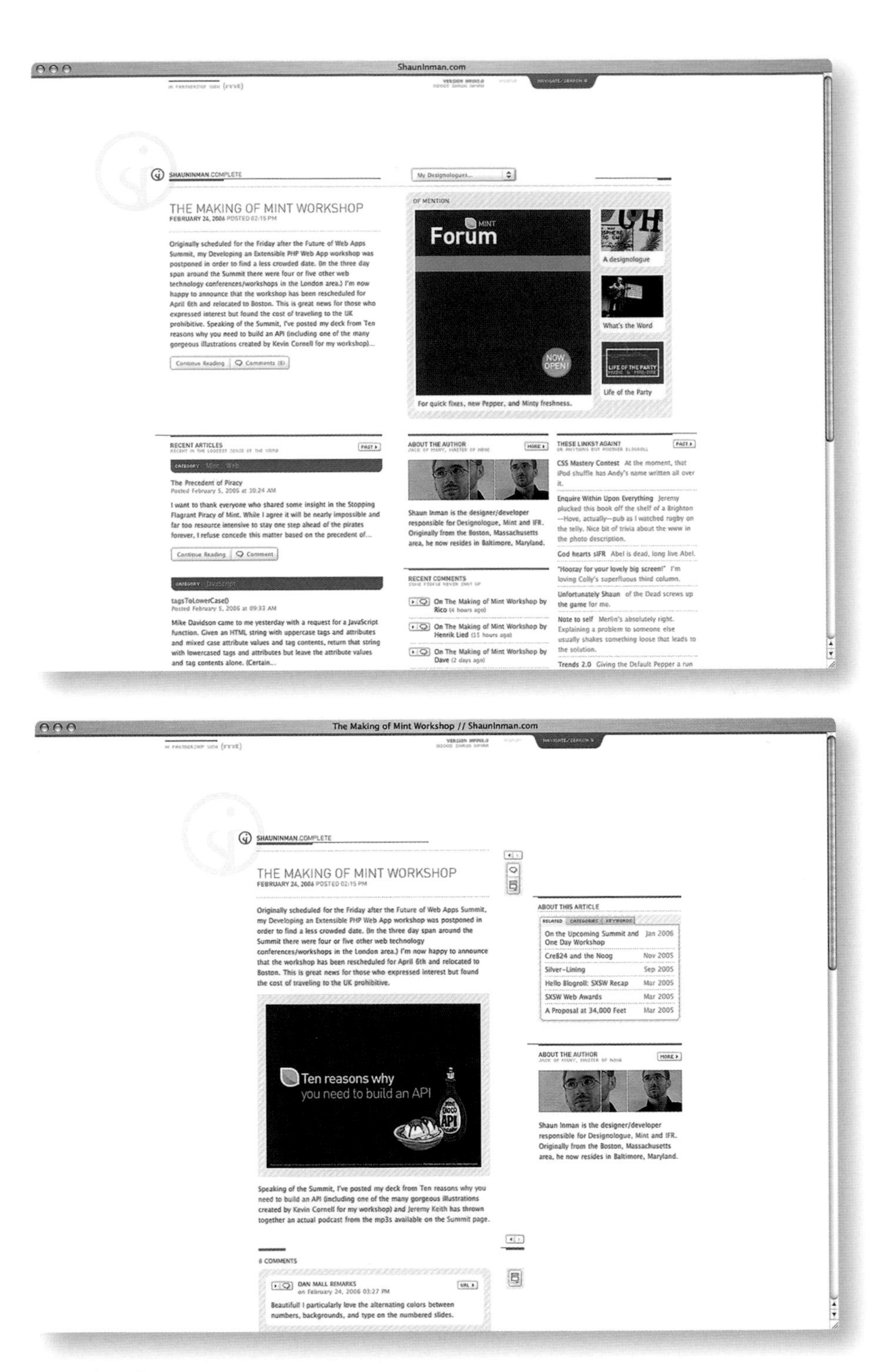

www.shauninman.com

D: shaun inman

A: shaun inman design & development **M:** www.shauninman.com/contact

www.binaryproductions.es

D: xavi royo **C:** xavi royo **P:** binary productions

A: xafdesign **M:** xavi@xafdesign.com

conceptlounge.nokia.nl

D: engin, beckers, van den broeck **C:** aallillou, verbruggen **P:** smith, michiels

A: these days **M:** www.thesedays.com

www.kanyoo.com

D: clement barlier

A: kanyoo **M:** clement@kanyoo.com

Ecommerce Web Page Development by A Professional Ecommerce Web Design Company

SWIFT MEDIA UK

SERVICES PORTFOLIO ABOUT US SUPPORT CONTROL PANEL WEBMAIL

Website Design Services
- Website Design
- Website Redesign
- Flash Web Design
- Ecommerce Design
- Intranet Design
- Website Maintenance
- Website Hosting
- Search Engine Optimisation
- Internet Marketing Service

Graphic Design Services
- Graphic Design
- Corporate Identity Design
- Logo Design

Articles
- Website Development
- Search Engine Optimisation
- Internet Marketing
- Website Hosting
- Computers
- Business

Tools & Information
- FAQs
- Downloads
- Link Exchange
- Add URL

Contact Us Now!

Custom Ecommerce Solution

An estimated 60% of all online transactions are abandoned because of poor functionality, less than intuitive navigational processes or concerns about security.

Swift Media UK has an edge when building e-commerce sites because we never lose sight of what the consumer wants and needs. Our approach is to make the process of purchasing online as familiar, easy and enjoyable for the user as possible.

Swift Media UK focus on **custom e-commerce development** that fit your business challenges. Whatever your business, we can help you market and sell your products and services more cost effectively.

The ingredients of a successful e-commerce website

Sites like Amazon.com lead the way in online sales, their success is proven and the process of buying is familiar to the online customer - so why reinvent the wheel?

Your new ecommerce solution will be familiar and engaging to customers, with the accent on clear navigation to products and easy to use interfaces. If the potential customer enjoys using your site and can easily find exactly what they want, then you are most of the way there to converting the sale.

Making it personal to maximise sales

Using a registration process allows you to personalise the shopping experience for your customers, making it easy and enjoyable to buy from you and enabling you to target them with specific products. On each visit you can greet them, Welcome Back Mr X, recommend specific products based on their preferences and previous purchases, and save them time by retrieving account and address information so they don't need to keep filling out forms.

www.swiftmediauk.co.uk

D: andy macdonald

M: www.swiftmediauk.co.uk

www.bee3.com

D: rasmus skjoldan **C:** christian jul jensen

A: bee3 **M:** rasmus@bee3.com

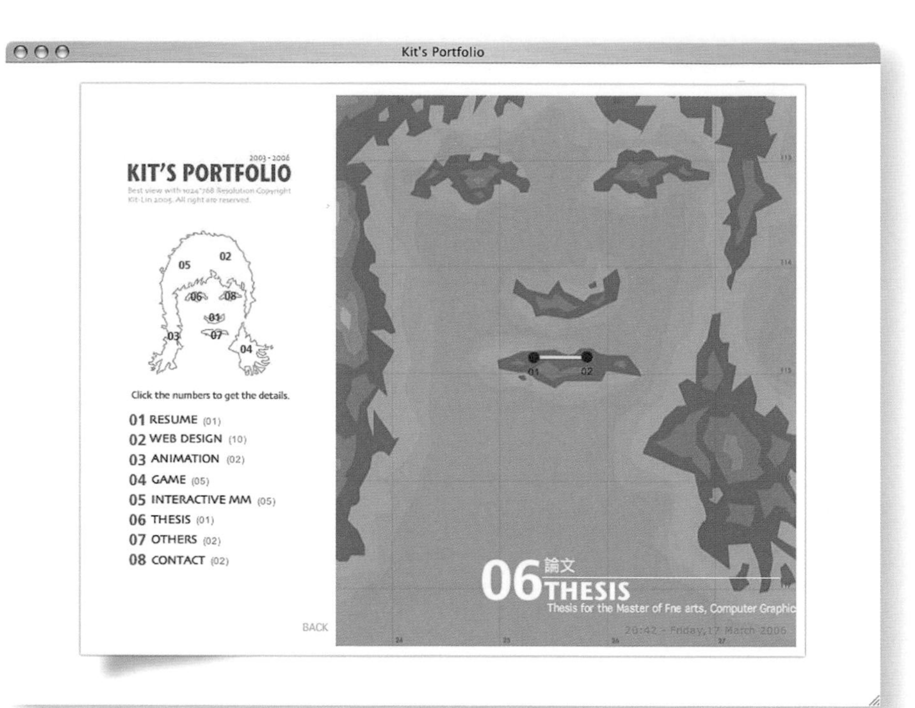

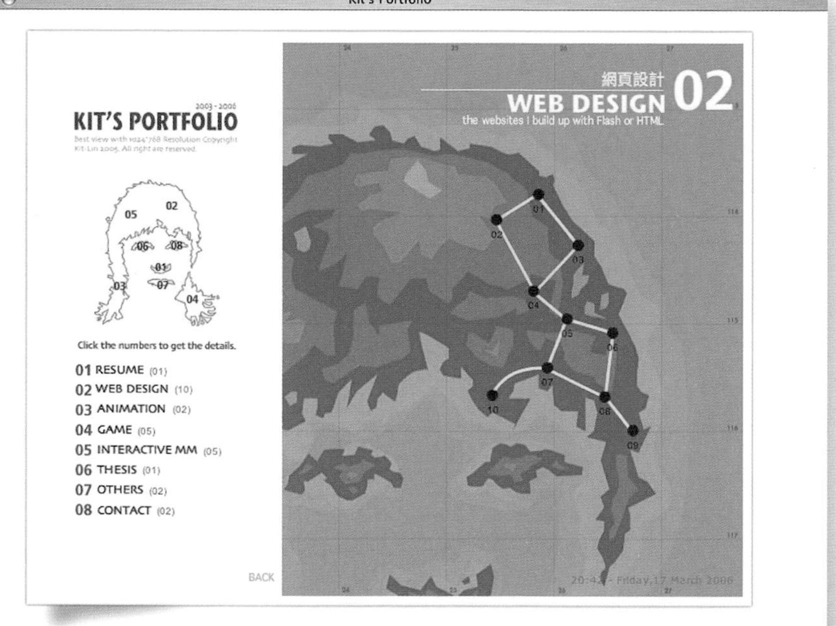

portfolio.kitlin.com

D: yi-chen lin

M: littleboww@yahoo.com.tw

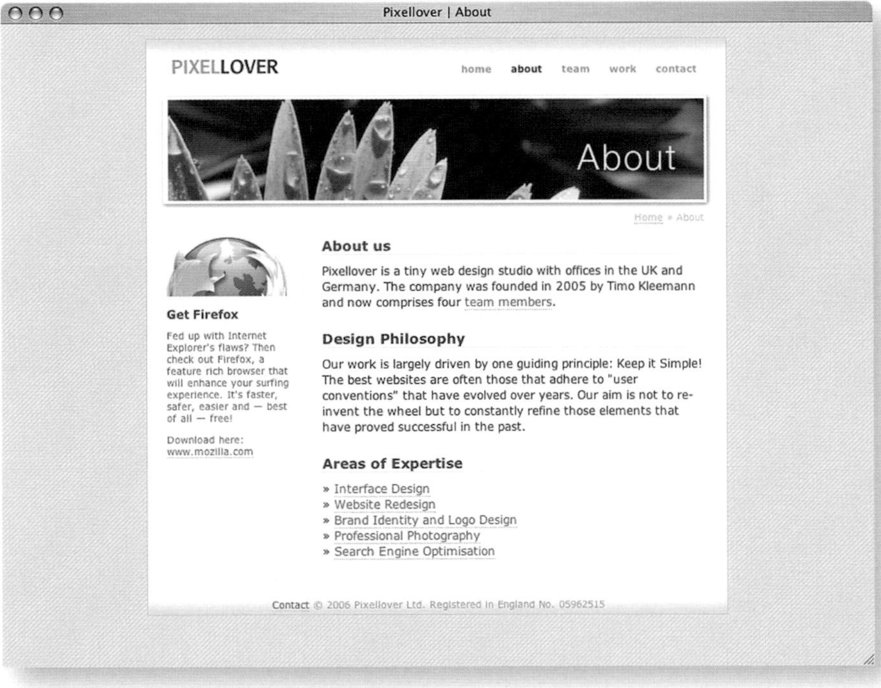

www.pixellover.net
D: timo kleemann
A: pixellover **M:** pizzadude81@gmail.com

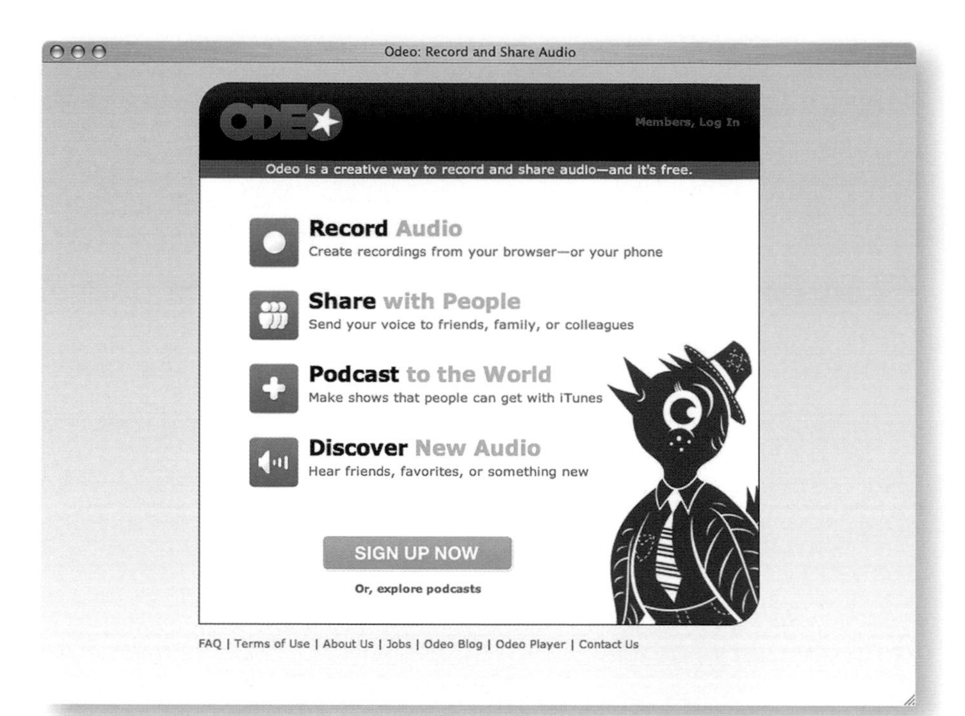

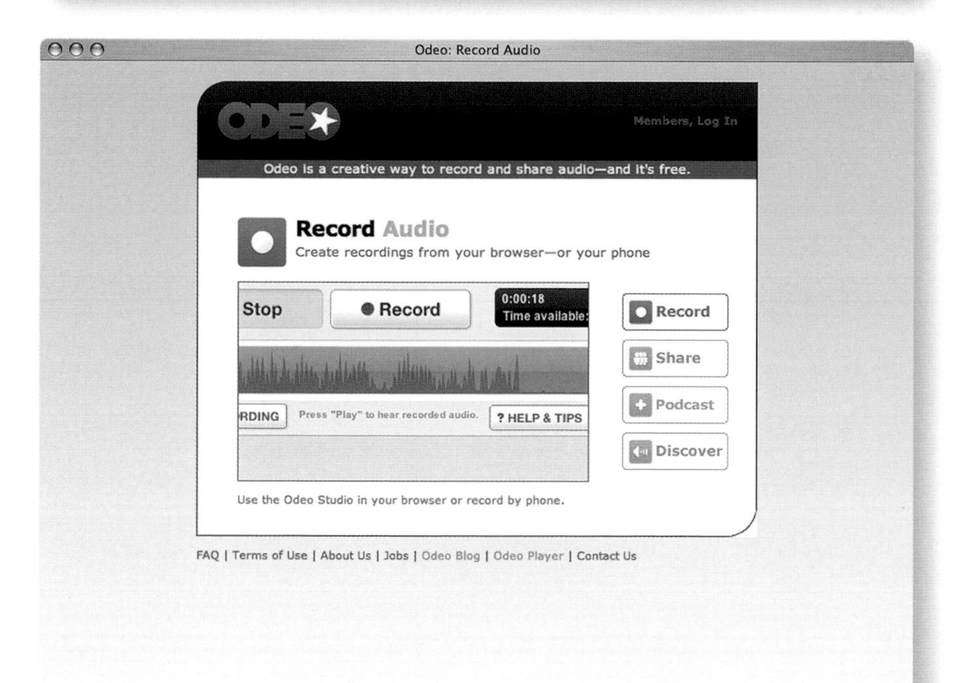

www.odeo.com

D: dan cederholm **C:** jack dorsey **P:** biz stone

A: simplebits **M:** biz@odeo.com

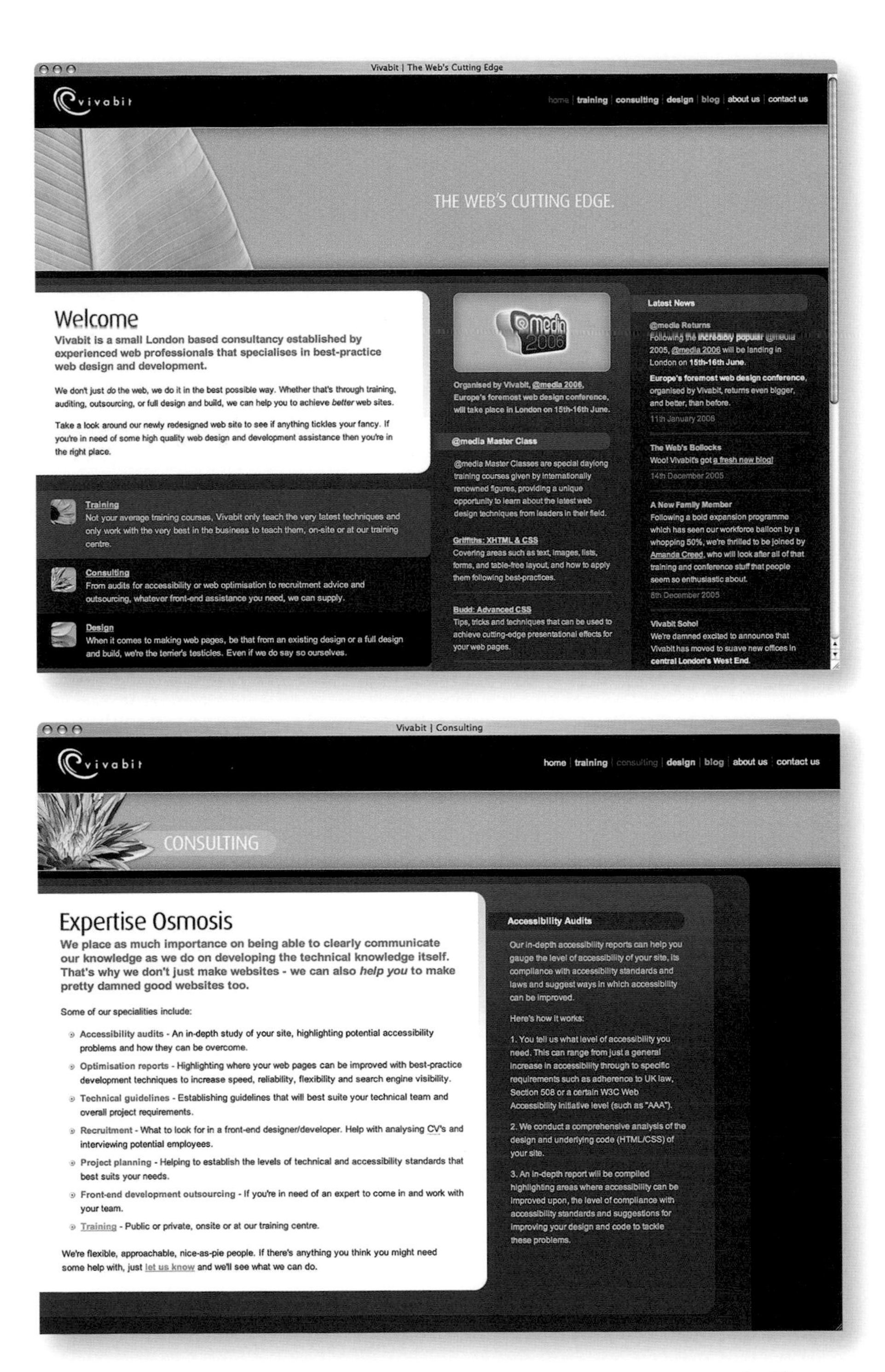

www.vivabit.com

D: cameron moll **C:** patrick griffiths

A: vivabit, cameronmoll.com **M:** www.vivabit.com

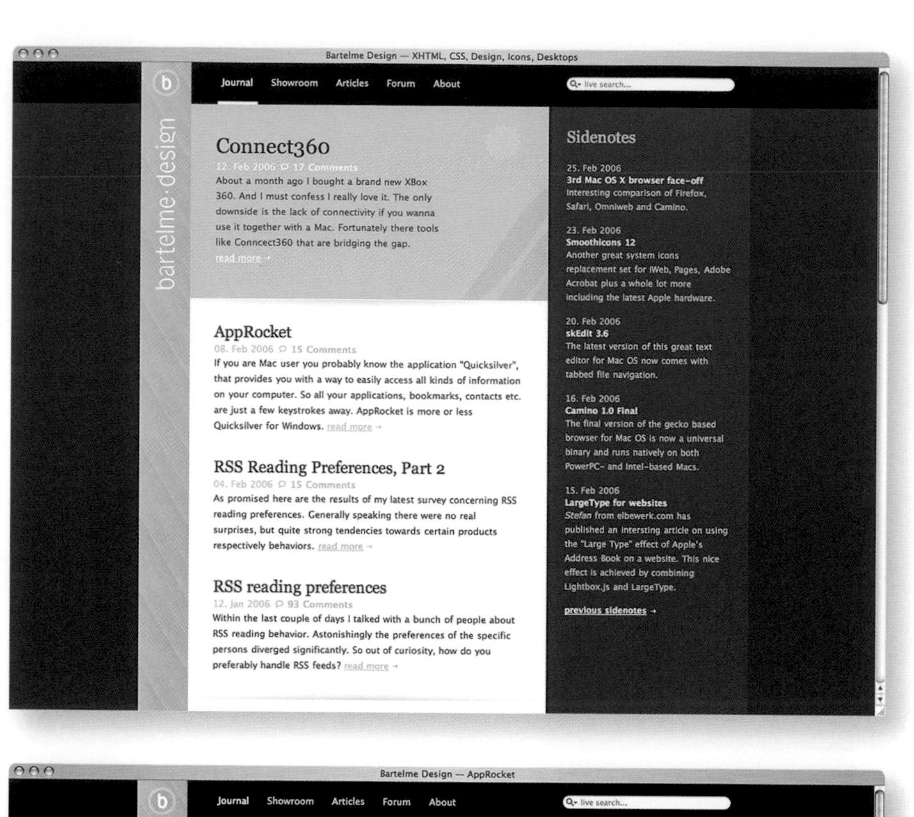

Bartelme Design — AppRocket

Journal Showroom Articles Forum About

live search...

bartelme·design

08. Feb 2006 15 Comments

If you are Mac user you probably know the application "Quicksilver", that provides you with a way to easily access all kinds of information on your computer. So all your applications, bookmarks, contacts etc. are just a few keystrokes away. AppRocket is more or less Quicksilver for Windows.

So what does AppRocket actually do? Well it's basically a small app that runs in the background and creates an index of all items on your computer. This includes applications, folders, files, bookmarks, playlists and so forth. Now for instance if you wanna launch Firefox, you just bring up the application by hitting "Alt+Space" and begin typing the first characters.

AppRocket now displays a list of potential results in small listing — with the most likely one at the very top. Now you just have to hit the return button in order to launch or view the respective item. That's it. Really simple, really fast, really convenient. Give it a try.

Mozilla Firefox
Mozilla Firefox-Schnellsuche benutzen
Mozilla Firefox Diskussionen
Mozilla Firefox Themes
Mozilla Firefox Erweiterungen
Mozilla Firefox (Safe Mode)
Mozilla Firefox • Quick Launch

Sidenotes

25. Feb 2006
3rd Mac OS X browser face-off
Interesting comparison of Firefox, Safari, Omniweb and Camino.

23. Feb 2006
SmoothIcons 12
Another great system icons replacement set for iWeb, Pages, Adobe Acrobat plus a whole lot more including the latest Apple hardware.

20. Feb 2006
skEdit 3.6
The latest version of this great text editor for Mac OS now comes with tabbed file navigation.

16. Feb 2006
Camino 1.0 Final
The final version of the gecko based browser for Mac OS is now a universal binary and runs natively on both PowerPC- and Intel-based Macs.

15. Feb 2006
LargeType for websites
Stefan from elbewerk.com has published an intersting article on using the "Large Type" effect of Apple's Address Book on a website. This nice effect is achieved by combining Lightbox.js and LargeType.

previous sidenotes →

bartelme.at

D: wolfgang bartelme
M: design@bartelme.at

www.duoh.com

D: veerle pieters **P:** geert leyseele

A: duoh! n.v. **M:** info@duoh.com

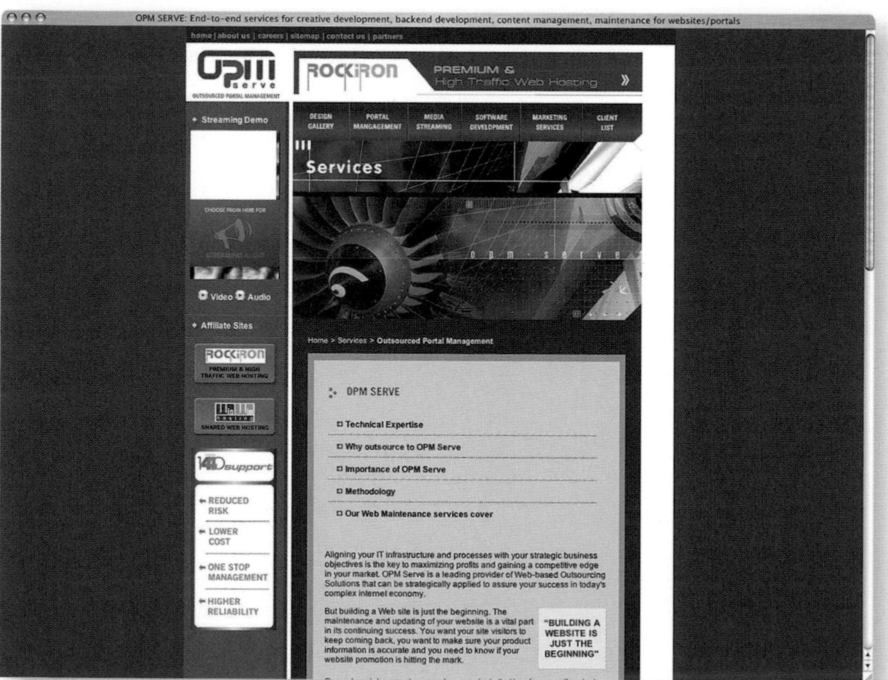

www.opmserve.com

D: kushal grover **P:** pugmarks

A: liquid designs india **M:** www.liquiddesignsindia.com

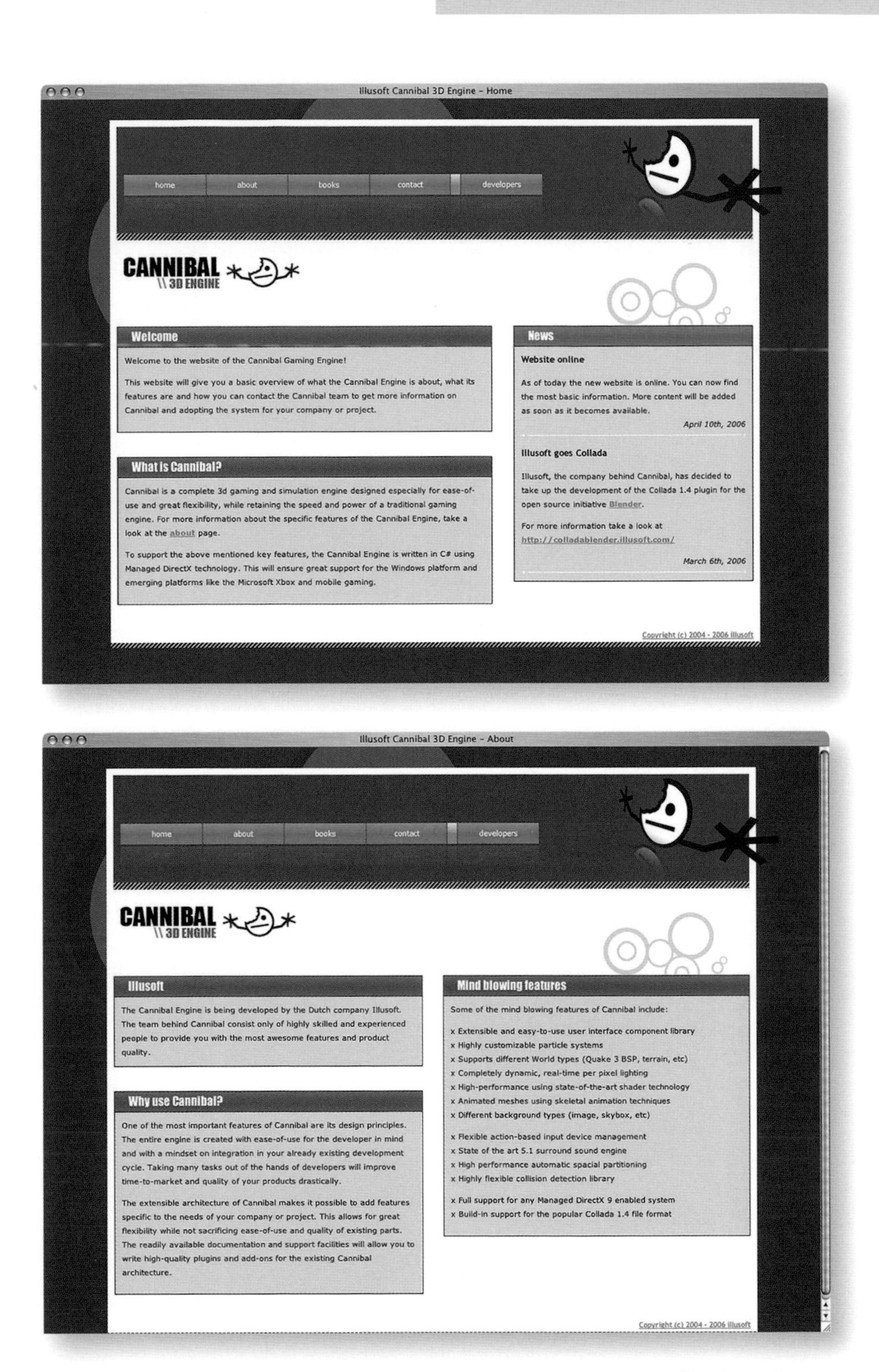

cannibal.illusoft.com
D: pieter visser
A: illusoft **M:** p.visser@illusoft.com

www.fantasy-interactive.com

D: david martin, krister karlsson **C:** hakim elhattab **P:** david martin

A: fantasy interactive **M:** interact@fantasy-interactive.com

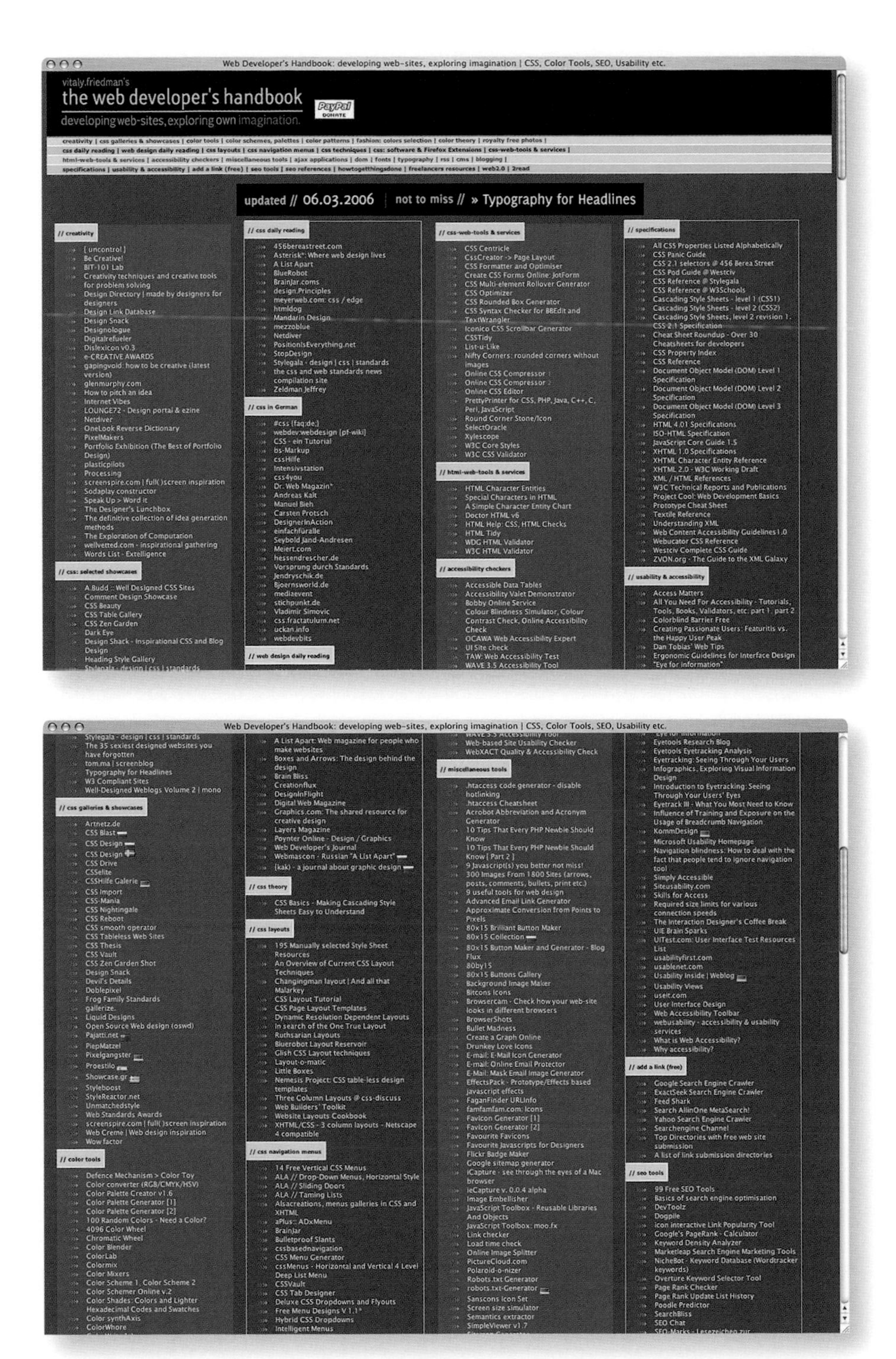

www.alvit.de/handbook

D: vitaly friedman

A: vitaly friedman **M:** web-dev@alvit.de

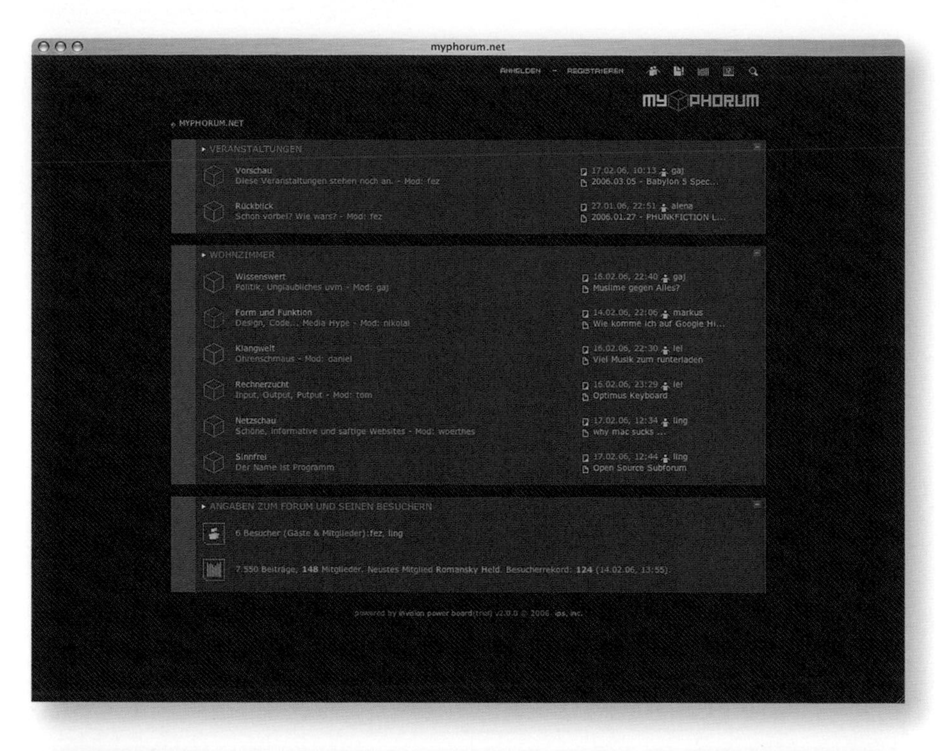

www.myphorum.net

D: gajendran somasundaram **C:** invision power services **P:** invision power services

A: www.somasundaram.net **M:** www.somasundaram.net

www.mug.pl

D: pawel rebisz, dariusz polarczyk **C:** dariusz polarczyk

A: interactive agency mug.pl **M:** office@mug.pl

kottke.org :: home of fine hypertext products

kottke.org home of fine hypertext products ARCHIVES + XML ABOUT CONTACT

I stumbled into an arcade this weekend for the first time in years, and it wasn't pretty: Lots of untranslated Japanese games, lots of Street Fighter clones (and lots of overlap between the two), only one game with a copyright date later than 2002, most much older than that. Might as well stay home. -- GK #

Like any good father, I'm trying to pass my values along to my children -- simple moral truths like: DC is better than Marvel. It turns out, that battle has already been fought. Spoiler results. It's a sick, sad world we live in. -- GK #

People are still getting AOL CDs. I got one recently, included in the box with a new printer, and A) it had Windows 3.1 installation instructions and B) the password was "GUSH-TEEN." Which pretty much sums up the reason for subscribing to AOL right there. -- GK #

As part of kottke.org's efforts towards the multi-David utopia of Way New Journalism (Note: ghost site), we proudly bring you the kind of original reporting that could only come from the blogosphere: We didn't find out what happened to TV shows that air at 2:00am during the time change because we fell asleep again. Windows (XP Home) Task scheduler skips tasks set for 2:30, though, while Linux's (Fedora Core 3) default cron executes them immediately after the adjustment, at the new 3:00. Take that, MSM! -- GK #

It's Daylight Saving Time time and early Sunday morning clocks should be moved forward, from 01:59:59 to 03:00:00. But what happens to all the television shows that start at 2:00? Or to computer tasks scheduled during the missing hour? Tomorrow: The Kottke Investigative Journalism Team reports. Blogs: Asking the questions those cowardly tratiors of the MSM consider far too stupid bother with. -- GK #

Jason Kottke and kottke.org, About | Contact me

Remaindered links
I read books and watch movies
Photography (@ Flickr, kottke tag)
Silkscreen font

RSS: Main weblog | Remaindered links

sites I've enjoyed recently

Airbag	990000
Anil Dash	Adam Greenfield
Blue Jake	Andre Torrez
Bluishorange	Andrea Harner
Boing Boing	Bitter Pill
Collision Detection	Black Belt Jones
Cynical-C	Caterina
Daring Fireball	Dooce
Design Observer	Google News
Flickr blog	Hchamp
Flickr friends	Ikeepadiary
Goldenfiddle	John Battelle
Gothamist	Justin Blanton
Greg.org	Lisa Whiteman
Gulfstream	Magnetbox
Hello, typepad	McSweeney's Lists
Lightningfield.com	Mighty Girl
Marginal Revolution	NYC Escorts Conf.
Matt's a.whole	Onfocus
Megnut	Paranoidfish
Morning News, The	ReBlog
Plasticbag	Scribbling.net
Slashdot	Signal vs. Noise
Slower	Sippey
The Superficial	Steven Johnson

About Jason and kottke.org (kottke.org)

kottke.org home of fine hypertext products ARCHIVES + XML ABOUT CONTACT

About Jason Kottke

Jason is currently dissatisfied with this page and writing about himself in the third person. Both will hopefully be remedied soonish. And something needs to be done about the outdated FAQ as well.

If you need to get in touch with me, here's what you need to know.

A reverse chronology of my life, intended to be less boring than the icky third-person "professional" bio above (updated 1.11.2005)

2006: Currently happening...

2005: In many ways, the opposite of sucked.

2004: Sucked, sucked.

2003: I'm having performance anxiety about this whole year summary thing...

2002: Crikey, now I'm in New York. Can't quite figure out how I got here. Not exactly a point A to point B kind of thing.

2001: Despite much interest, I'd never been to Europe before this year, when I went three times in the span of 6 months. Paris and Antwerp in May, London in July, and Berlin in October. I would like very much to live in Europe.

2000: Finally made the move to San Francisco after thinking about it for a couple years. Definitely a big change for a small town boy like myself.

1999: I think this was the year I really and truly discovered the joys of sour cream. I never used to like sour cream....and then I started eating

What kottke.org might be, a list:

- The personal site of Jason Kottke. But also his full-time gig.
- A weblog, which is a frequently updated, chronologically ordered collection of hypertext fragments. You'll find the most recent posted stuff on the front page and many ways to get at the older posts on the archive page.
- My wunderkammer. Wunderkammer is a German word meaning, roughly, "cabinet of wonders" or "cabinet of curiousities". Julian Dibbell wrote about weblogs as wunderkammers for the dearly-departed Feed.
- Updated almost daily since March 1998.
- Incomplete.
- Bigger than Jesus and the Beatles put together.

POWERED BY MOVABLETYPE

- An attempt to track and make sense of "material that connects the insights of science and culture, rather than using one to dismantle the other" (as Steven Johnson puts it).
- Sheer egoism, aesthetic enthusiasm, historical impulse, and even a bit of political purpose. (after George Orwell)
- Small pieces, loosely joined (after David Weinberger's book of the same name).
- Chock full of "wussy PoMo Sedaris-wannabe attitude" (source)
- Speed 3: The Weblog. If I stop writing, the bus will blow up. (source)
- A giant RFC document.
- Not all that it could be.
- Slashdot for the literati (comment via AIM).

www.kottke.org
D: jason kottke
M: jason@kottke.org

aroussi.com/weblog

D: ran aroussi

M: services@aroussi.com

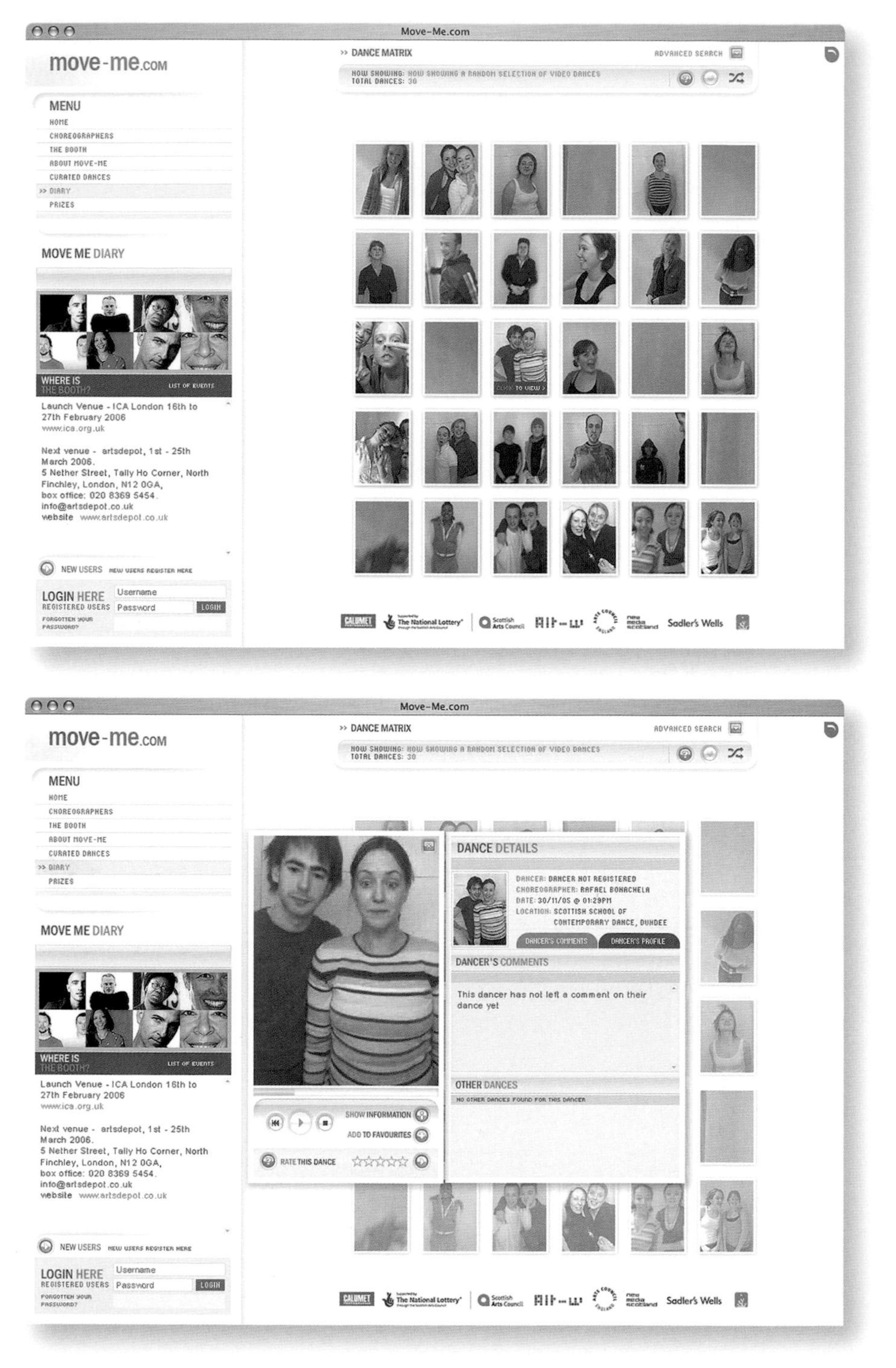

www.move-me.com

D: peter barr **C:** douglas noble **P:** ricochet dance productions, goat media ltd
A: amberfly ltd **M:** enquiries@amberfly.com

www.imnotabrand.com

D: kaneda **C:** pixelpost **P:** kaneda

A: nosurprises **M:** kaneda@nosurprises.it

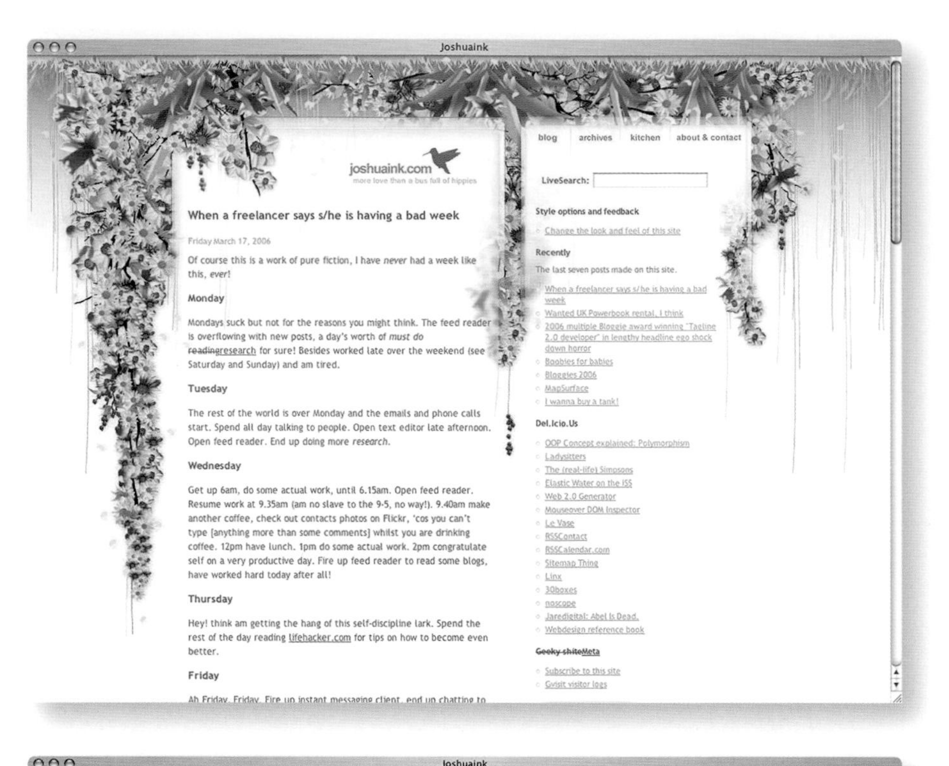

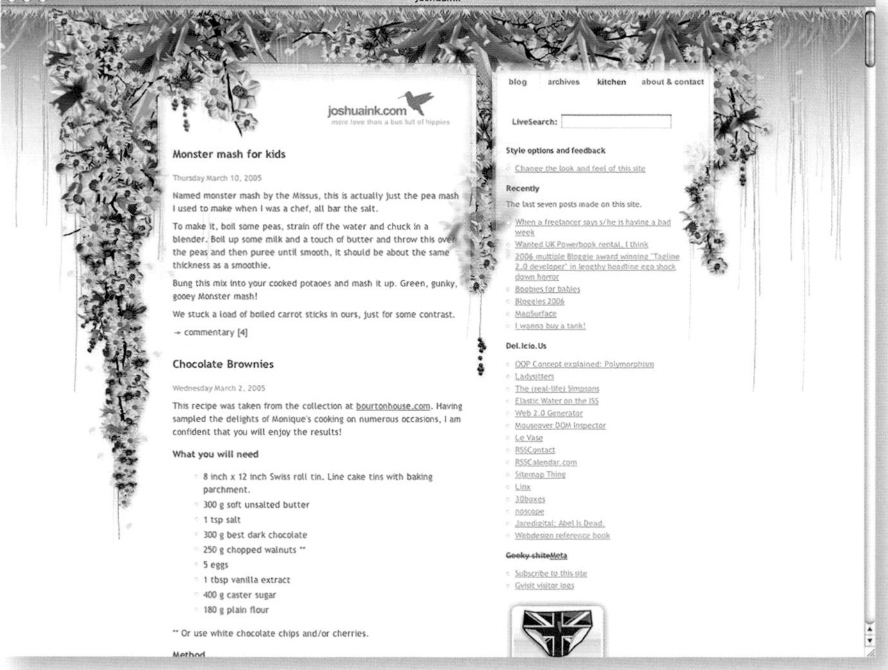

joshuaink.com

D: john oxton, denis radenkovic **P:** john oxton

M: mail@johnoxton.co.uk

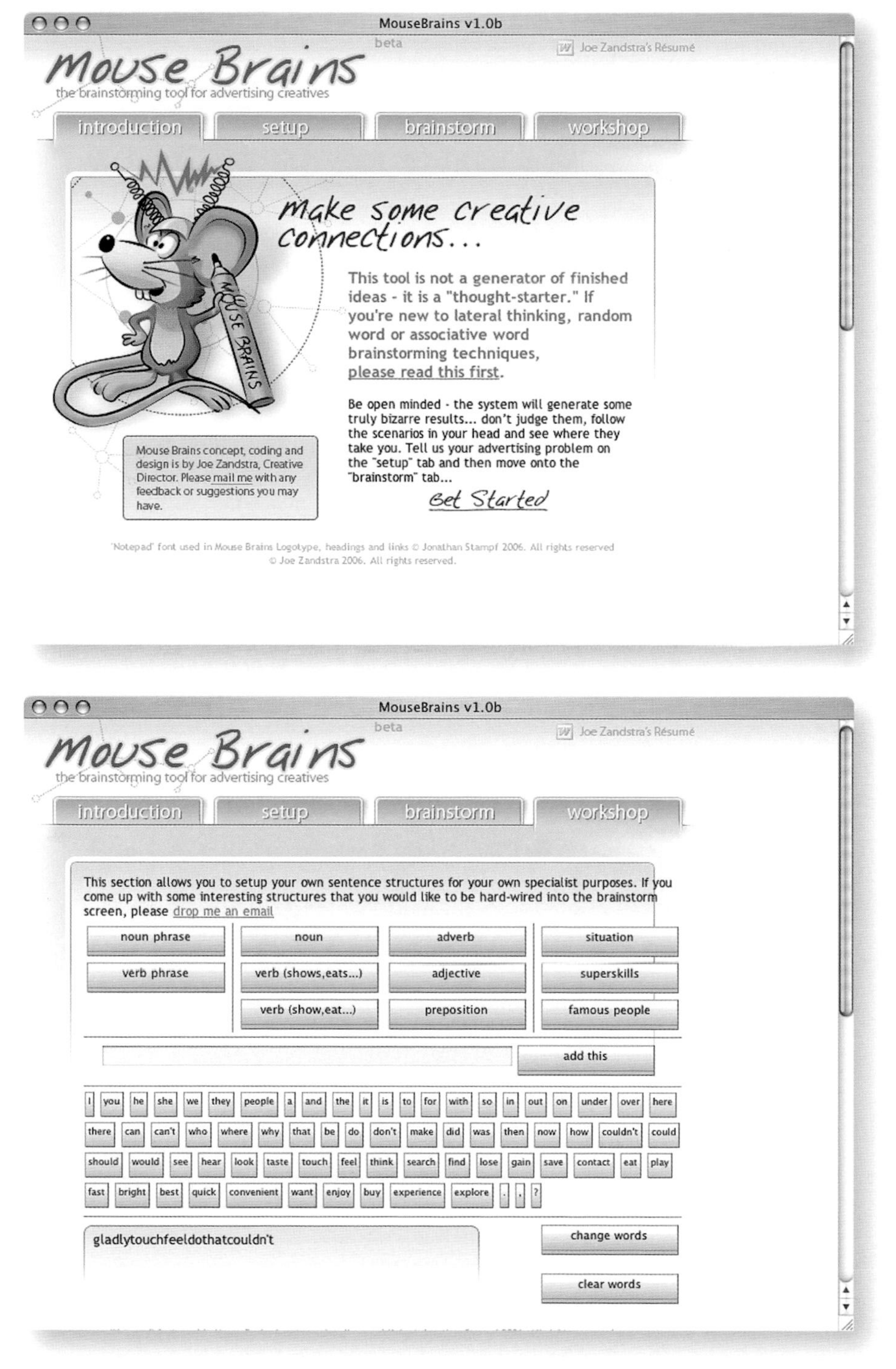

www.kennieting.com/mousebrains

D: joe zandstra

A: joe zandstra **M:** mousebrains@gmail.com

www.glsdesign.it/made

D: giuseppe la spada

A: gls design **M:** info@glsdesign.it

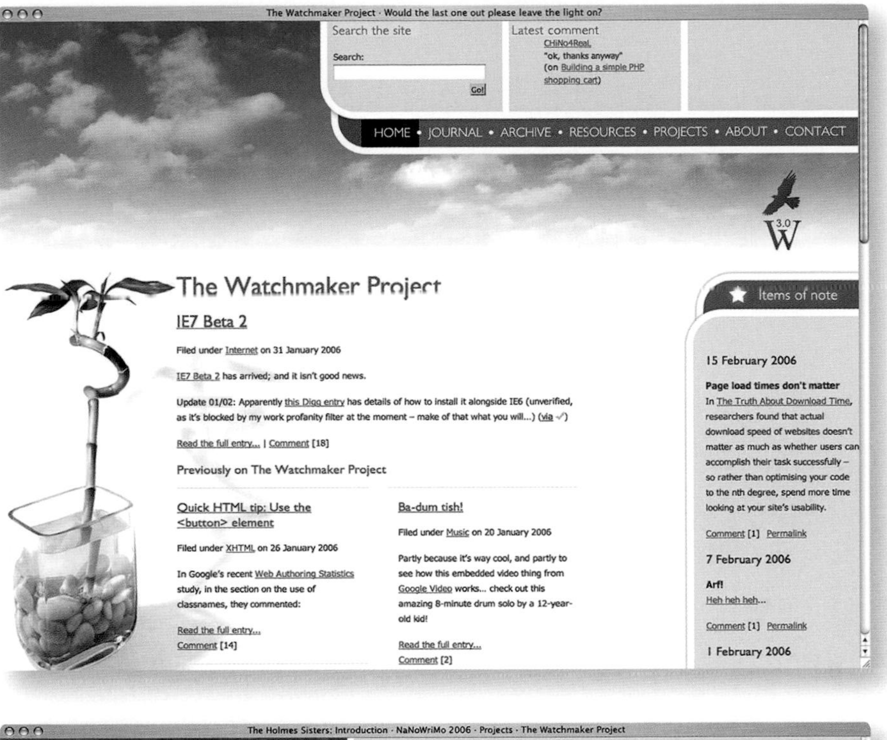

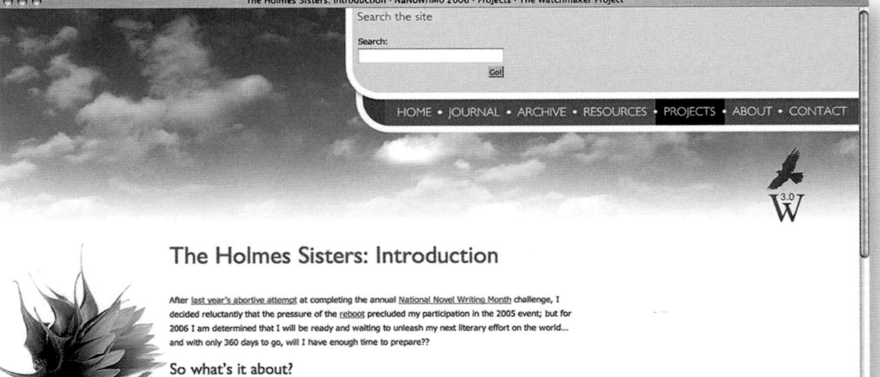

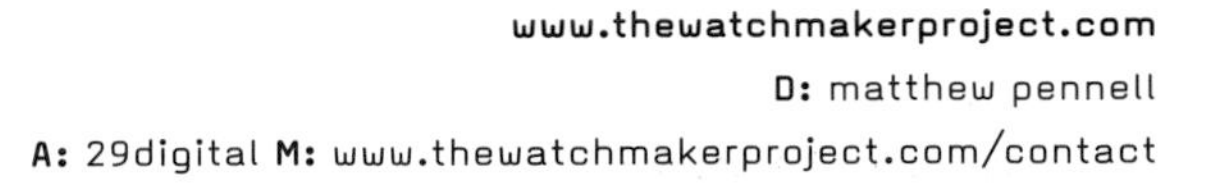
www.thewatchmakerproject.com

D: matthew pennell

A: 29digital M: www.thewatchmakerproject.com/contact

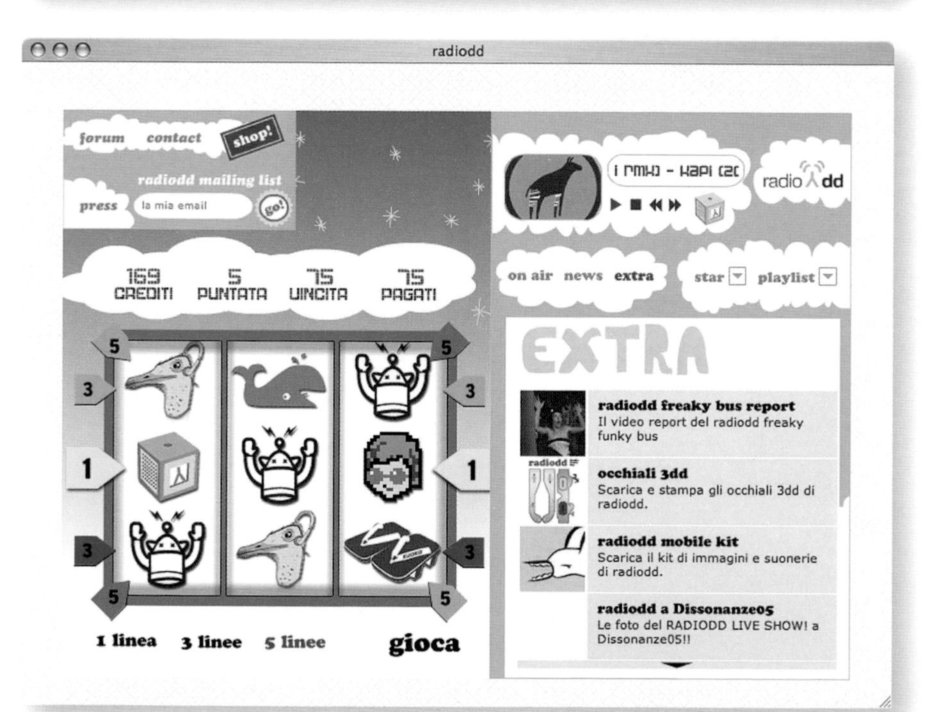

www.radiodd.com

D: digitaldelicatessen

M: contact@digitaldelicatessen.com

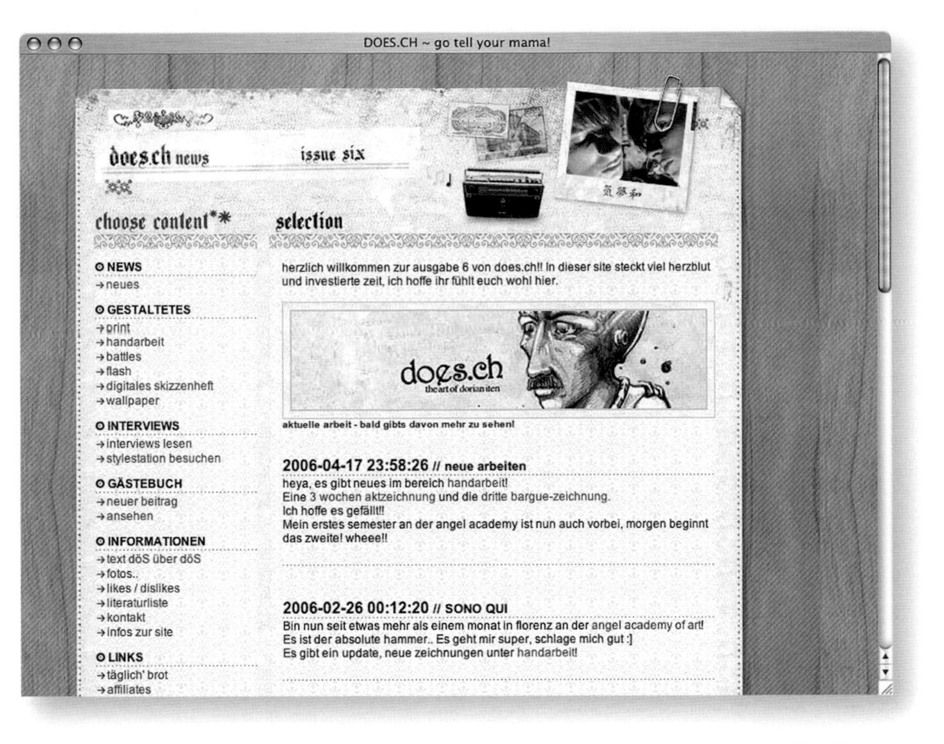

www.does.ch
D: dorian iten
M: dorian@does.ch

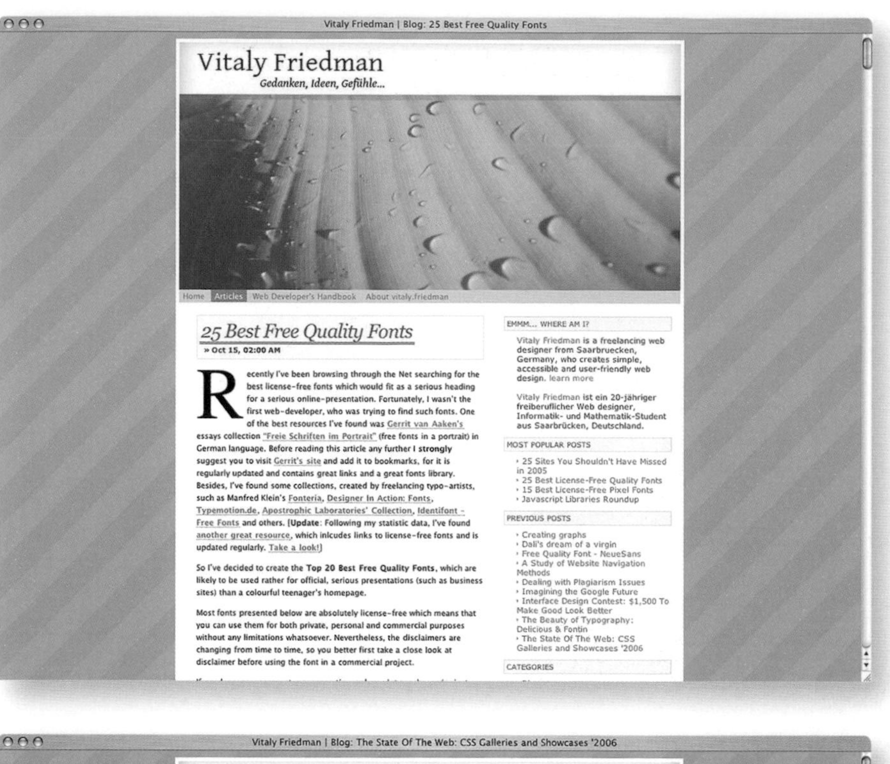

www.alvit.de/blog

D: vitaly friedman

A: vitaly friedman **M:** web-dev@alvit.de

www.jeroenwijering.com/whatsup

D: jeroen wijering

M: mail@jeroenwijering.com

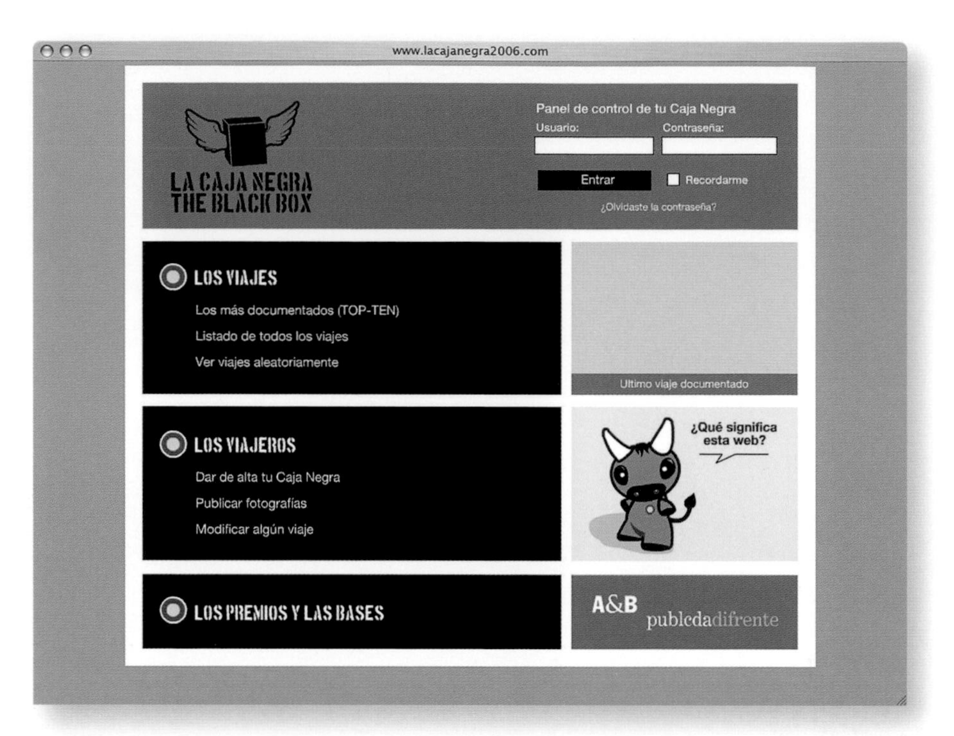

www.lacajanegra2006.com

D: javier gonzalez **C:** magalí piterman

A: arrontes y barrera, estudio de publicidad **M:** www.estudiodepublicidad.com

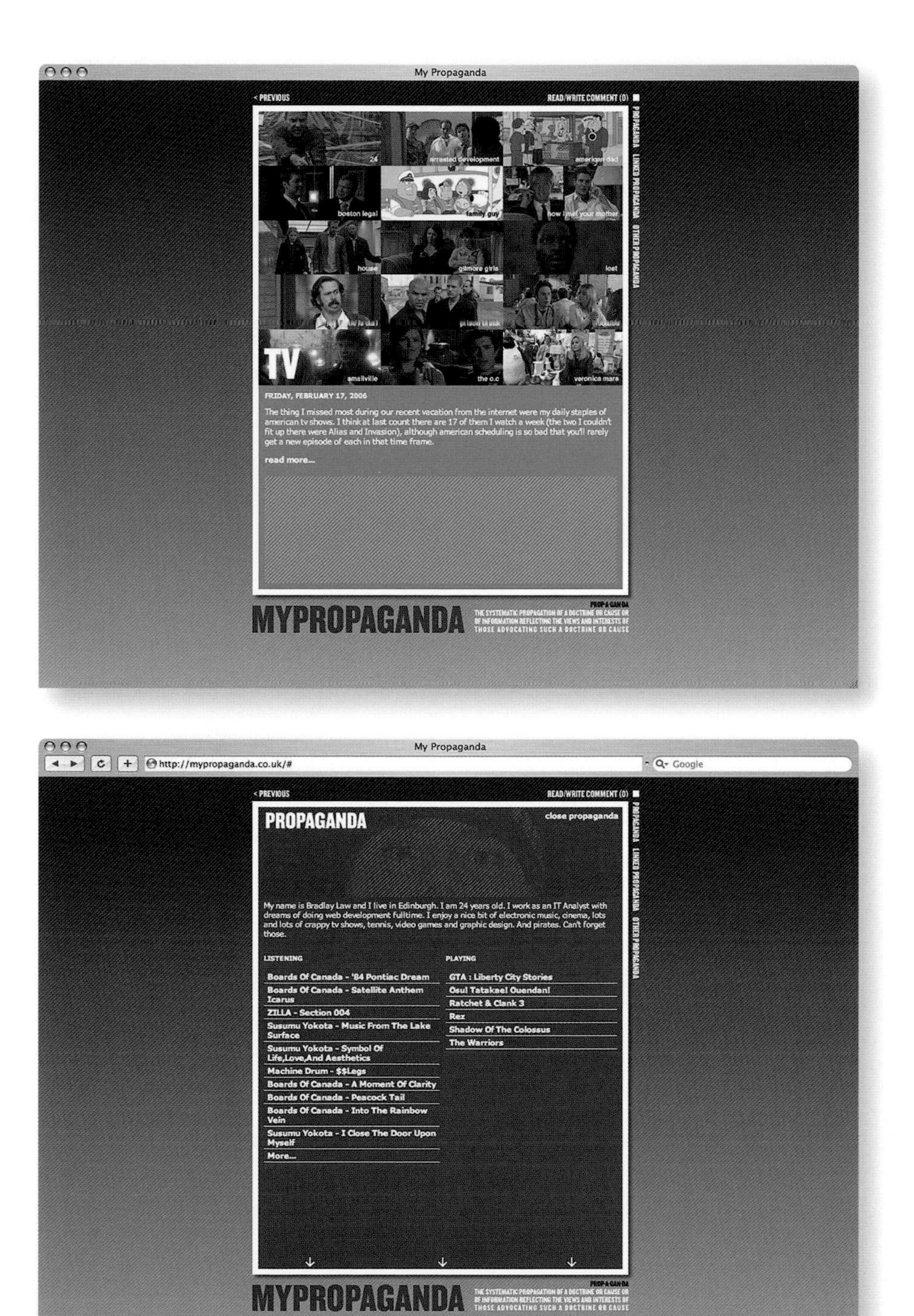

mypropaganda.co.uk

D: bradlay law

M: bradlaylaw@gmail.com

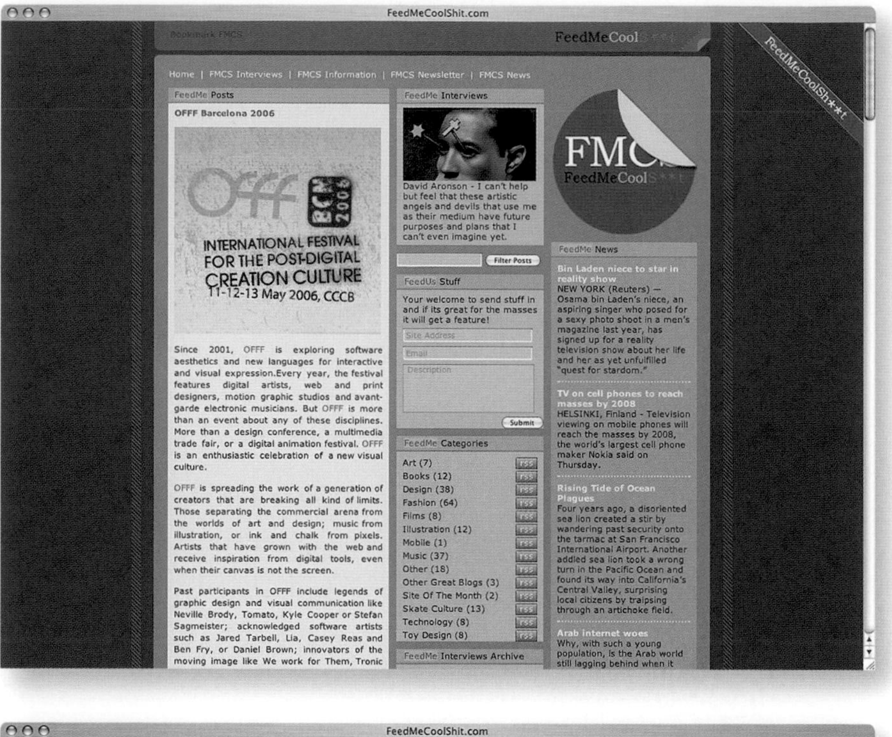

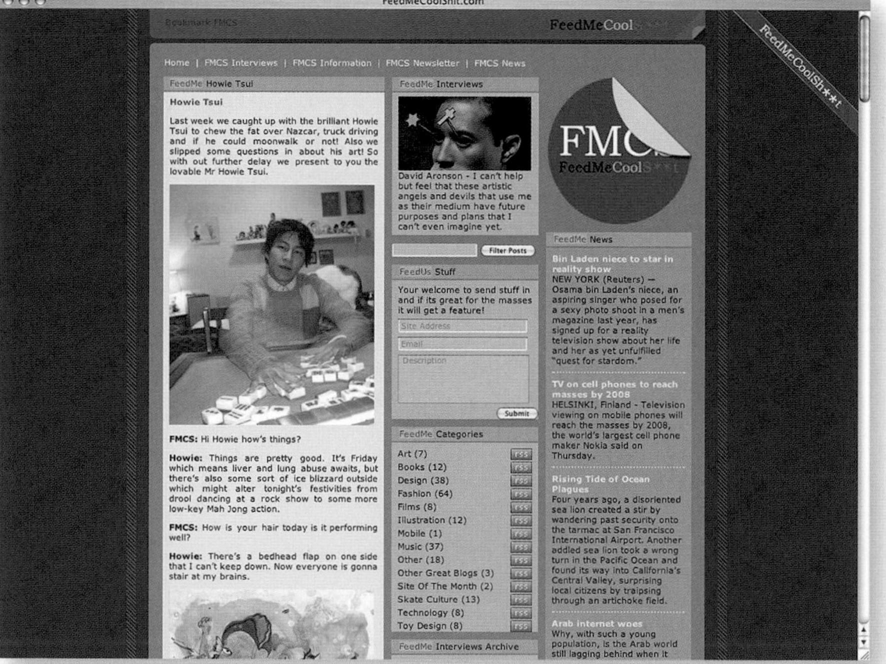

www.feedmecoolshit.com

D: johnny huntington **C:** z gavars

A: feedmenetwork **M:** johnny.huntington@gmail.com

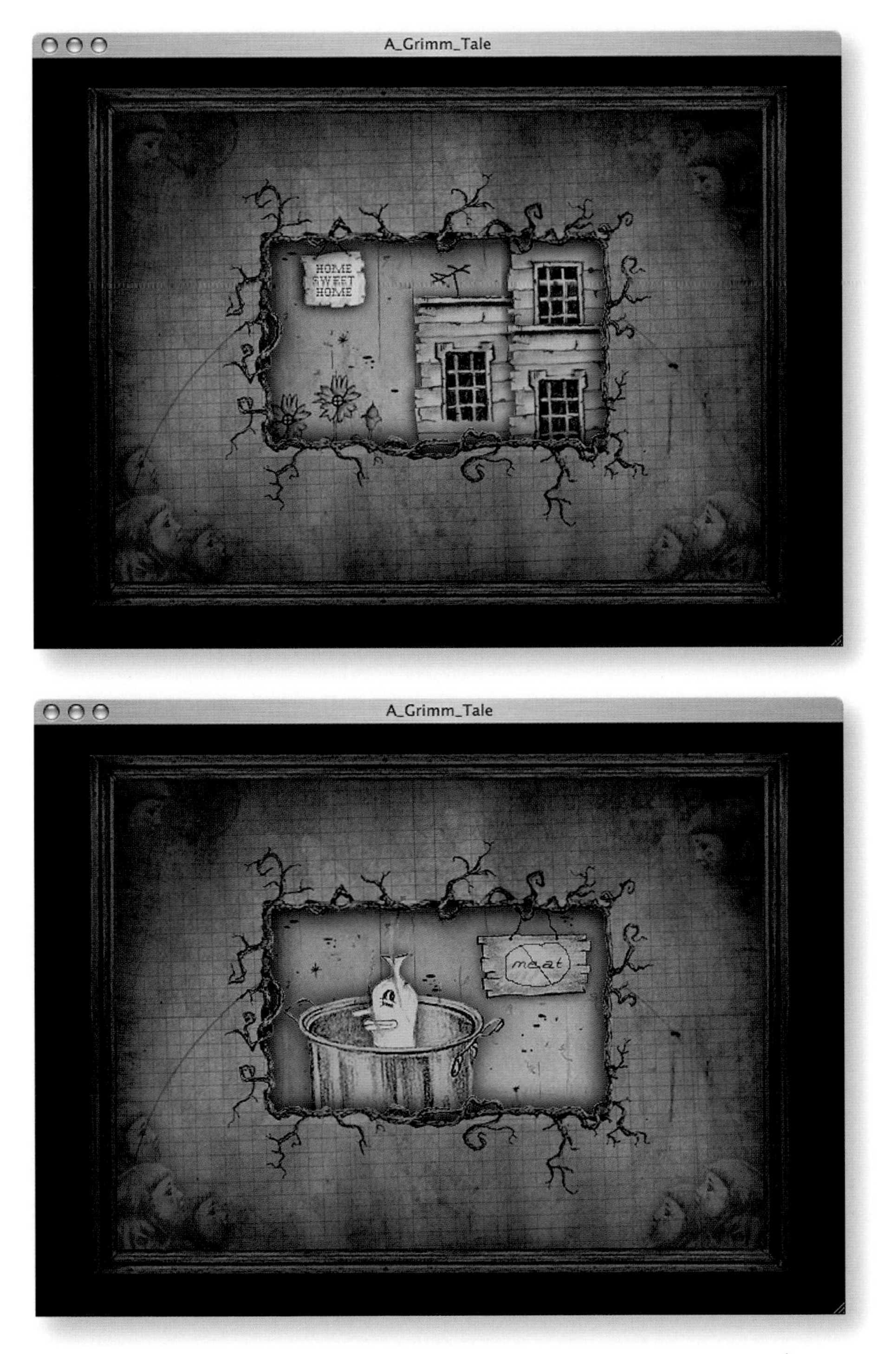

www.muttink.com/grimm

D: michael erazo-kase, jeremy holmes

A: mutt ink **M:** contactmutt@muttink.com

itch.in

D: arifuddin rahimi

A: nerdeeko labs **M:** mr.riff@itch.in

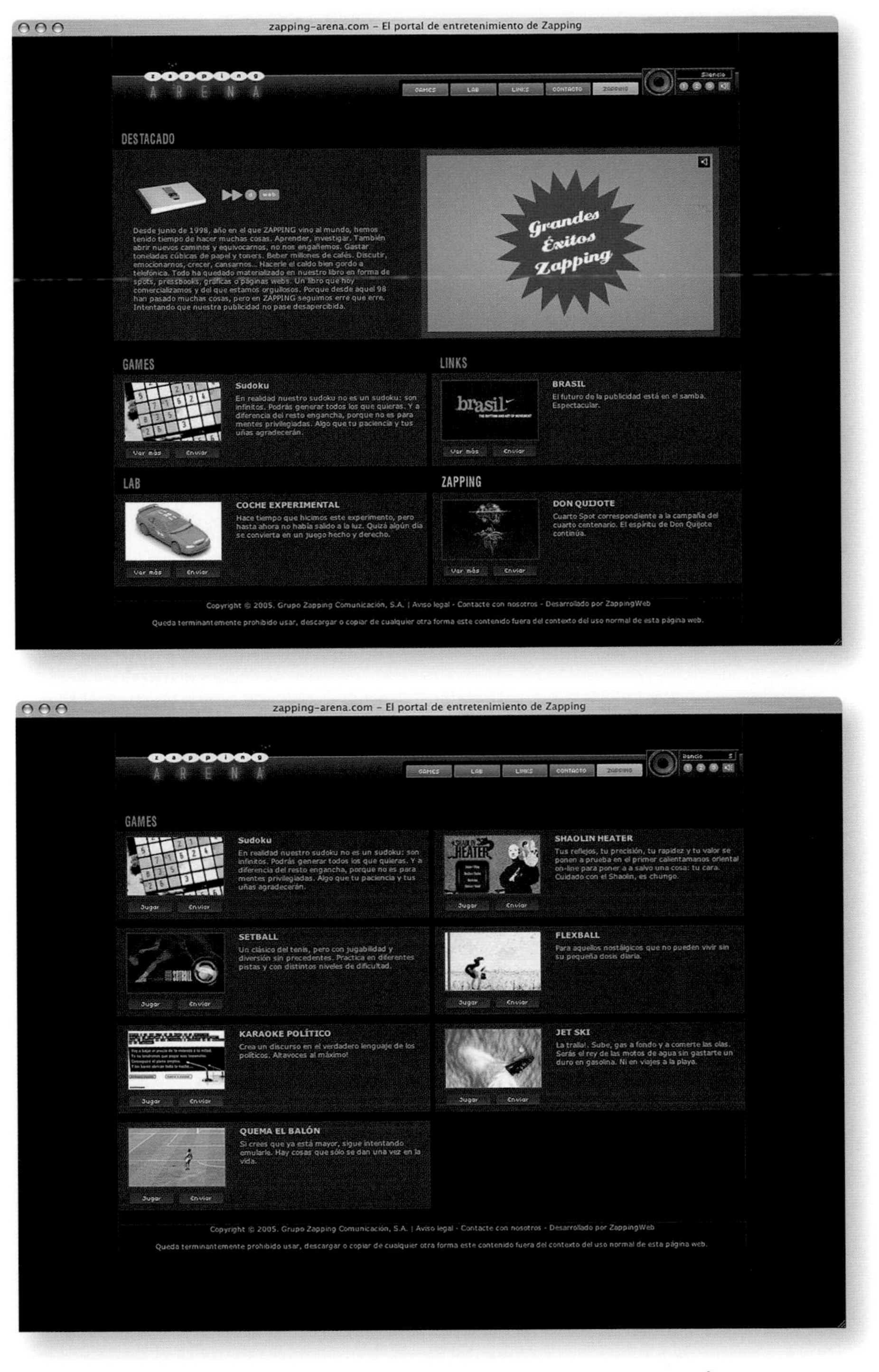

www.zapping-arena.com

D: zapping **C:** santiago rey **P:** juan searle

A: zapping **M:** jsearle@zaping.es

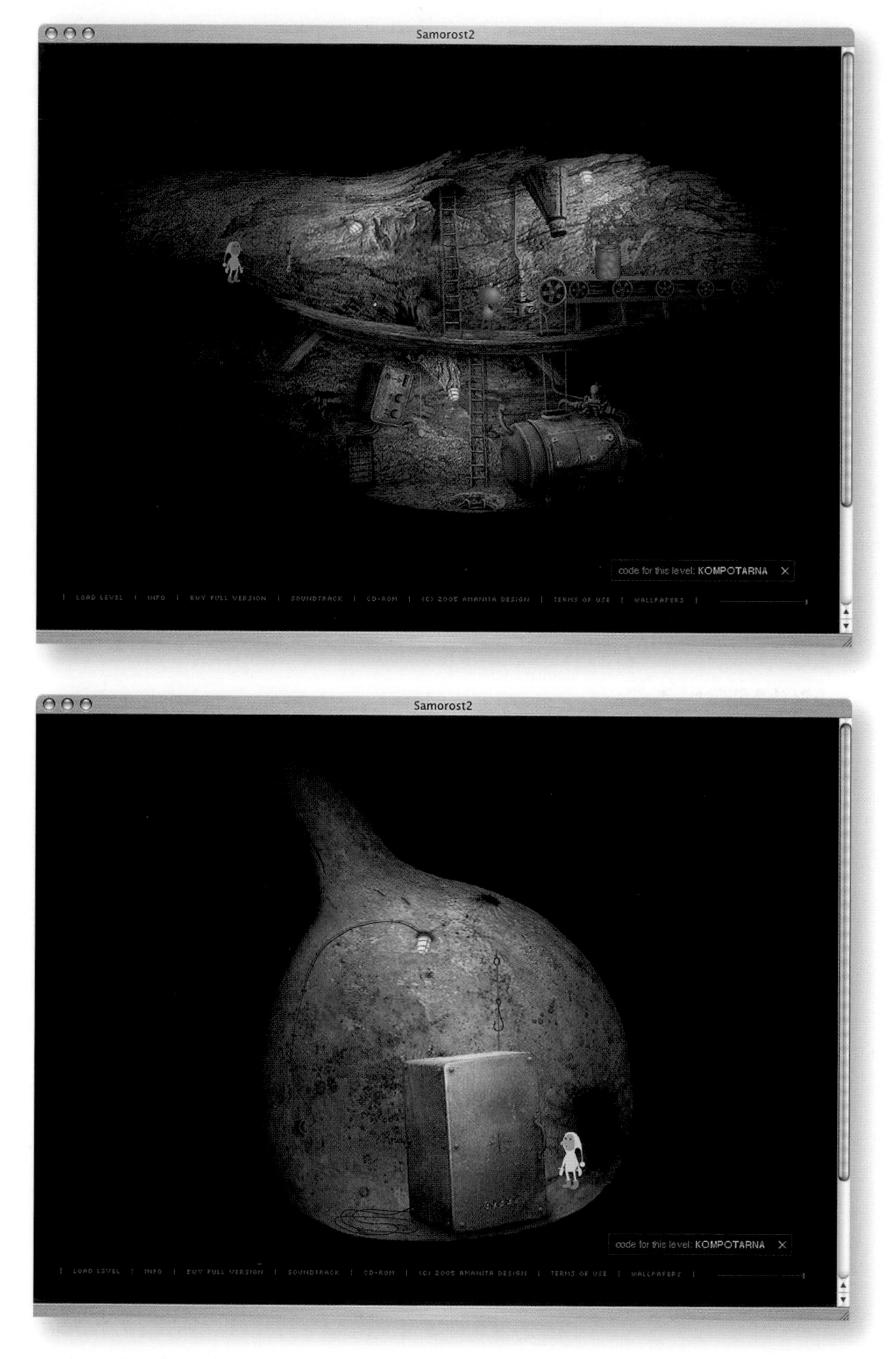

www.samorost2.net

D: amanita design

M: contact@amanitadesign.com

www.kikof.be

D: kevin van sande **C:** kevin van sande **P:** tim hovestadt

A: kikof **M:** kevin@kikof.be

2FRESH | Best Practices in Communication Design for the New Communication Age.

2FRESH

Corporate
Creative Process
Portfolio
Contact

Our process consists of four three major phases.

1. *First* is pre-design phase where we **listen**, **understand**, or **define** communication problems. The focus in this phase is on creating the ground which will function as the base of our design.

2. *Second* comes developing best fitting design solutions to defined problems in form of **creative idea** or **concept**. Then, client is given with appropriate **style** choices in accordance with concept(s).

3. *Third* phase, as concept and style are set, is **production**. First comes **visual design**, then **pre-implementation** (page layouts, animatics, etc.) and finally **implementation**. We also give room for an **adjustment** step where we play around with small things.

Actually there exists also a last and enduring phase where we keep **continuous communicaton** and **relation** with the client to **feed**, **develop** and **enhance** project we created over time.

2FRESH | Best Practices in Communication Design for the New Communication Age.

2FRESH

Corporate
Portfolio
Static
Contact

Project	Client	Format
Urbanism	-	Artwork
Abstractions	-	Artwork
Cities on Walls	-	Artwork
Dreams	-	Artwork
Economics Days	Galatasaray University	Logo
Economics Days	Galatasaray University	Invitation
Economics Days	Galatasaray University	Poster
RH+	Rotham Halas	Logo
RH+	Rotham Halas	Stationary
Love is in the Air	Sex Book Project	Artwork
The X	Sex Book Project	Artwork
Studying Abroad: Get Out!	DAAD	Poster
Record '03	Boğaziçi University	Book

www.2fresh.com

D: 2fresh

A: 2fresh M: contact@2fresh.com

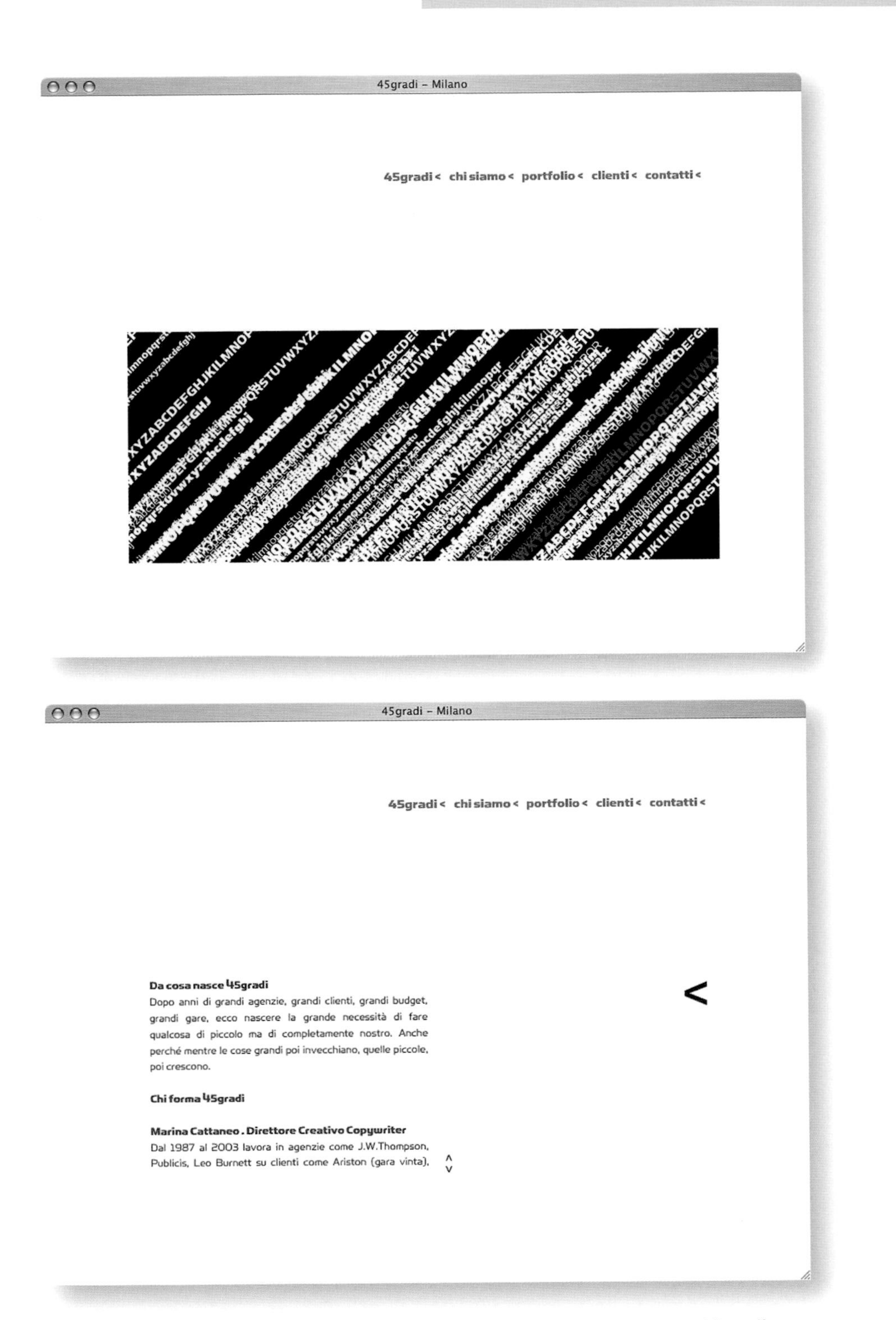

www.45gradi.com

D: silvia grazioli **C:** andrea rincon ray **P:** marina cattaneo

A: 45gradi **M:** marina.cattaneo@45gradi.com

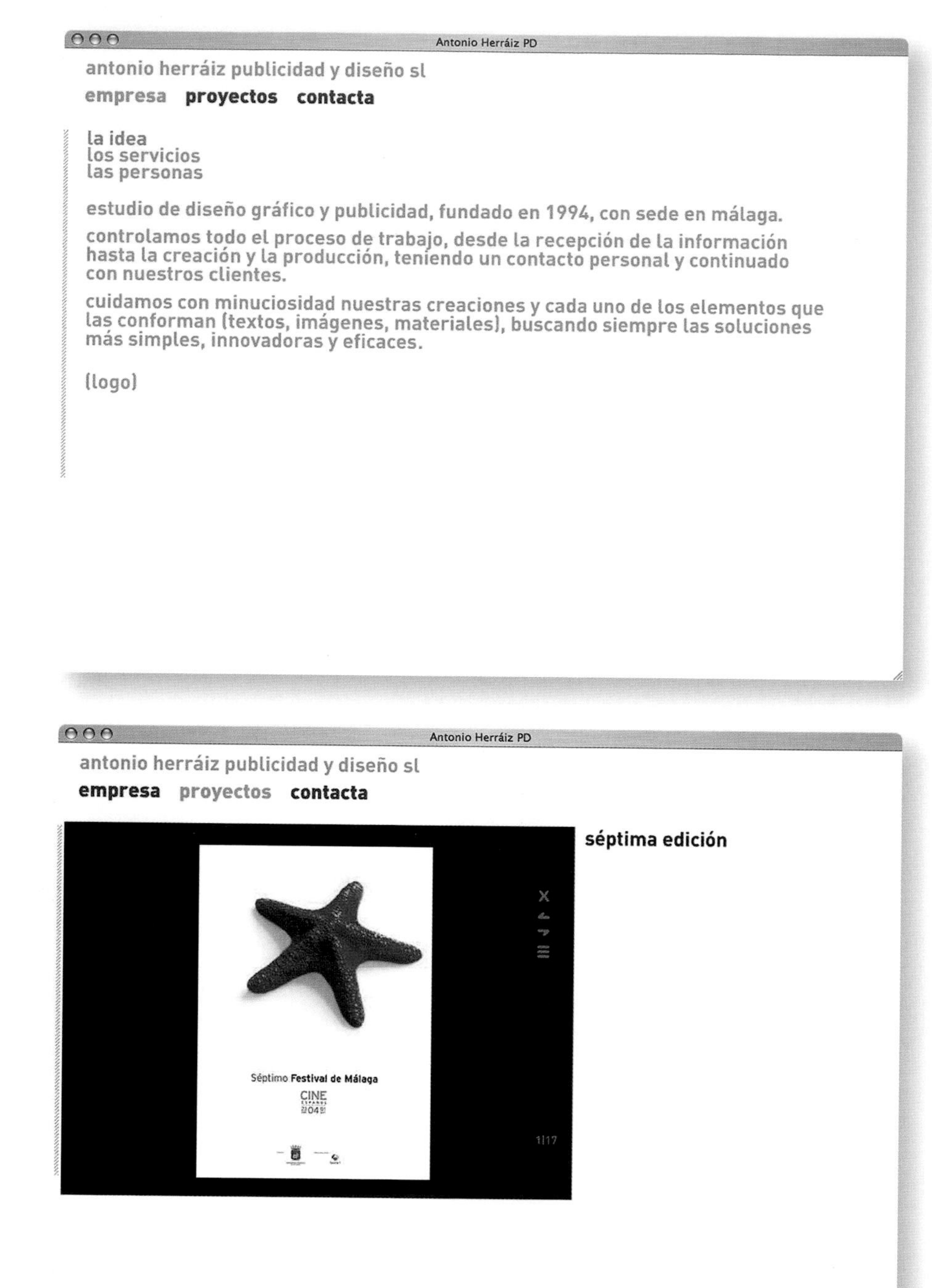

www.antonioherraiz.com

D: lourdes molina **C:** victor caballero **P:** antonio herráiz

A: antonio herráiz publicidad y diseño **M:** info@antonioherraiz.com

www.moses.nl

D: stephan de graaf **C:** stephan de graaf **P:** johan den heijer, moses
A: pixelfarm **M:** info@moses.nl

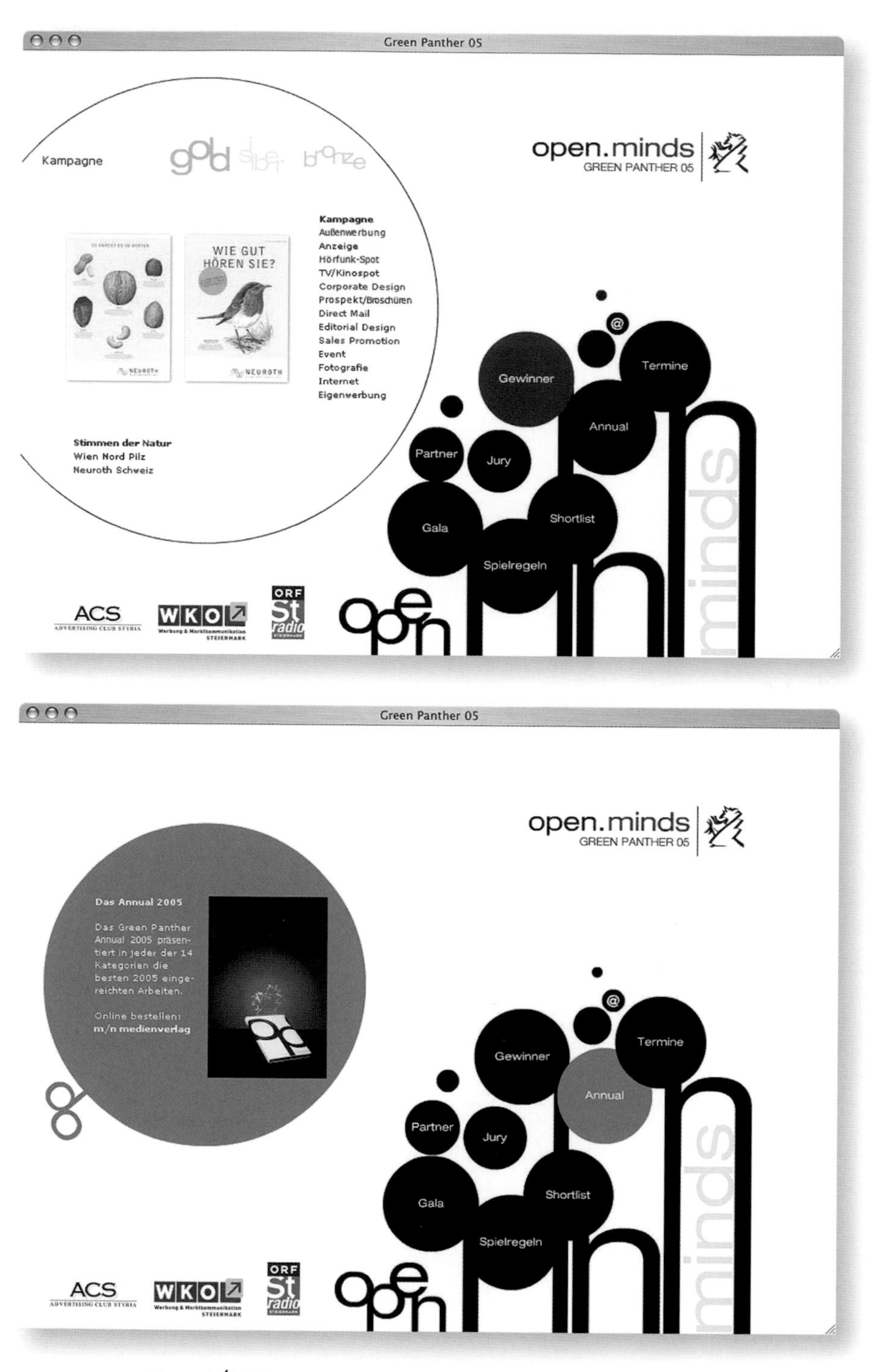

www.greenpanther.at/2005

D: nina markart, spreitzer & friends, c. poltensteiner **C:** p. wagner **P:** wukonig.com
A: wukonig.com **M:** joerg@wukonig.com

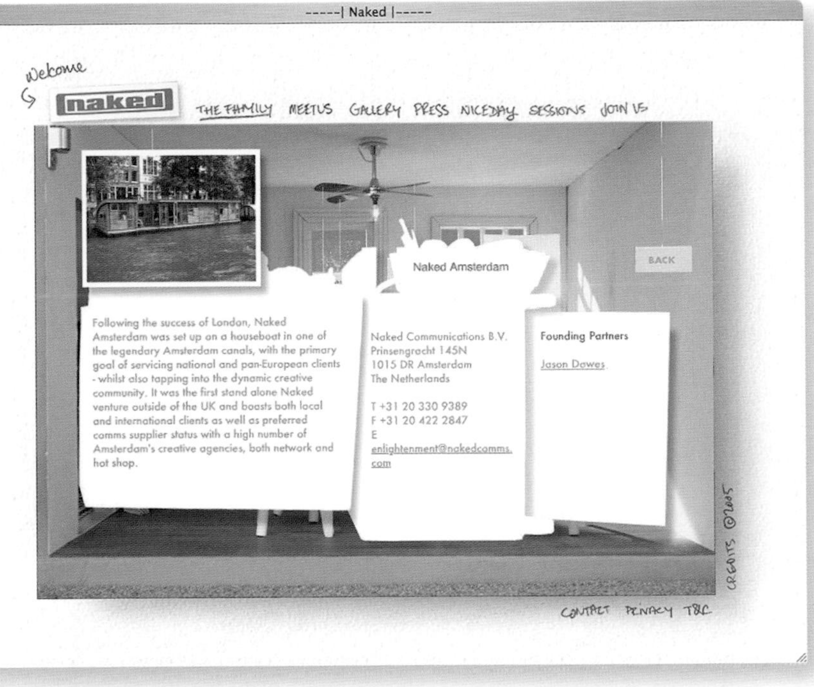

www.nakedcomms.com

D: carl burgess, marc kremers, brie wohler **C:** nils millahn **P:** nicky cameron

A: hi-res! **M:** www.hi-res.net

www.tgd.info

D: intercatius tgd

A: tgd comunicació **M:** sbuyo@tgd.es

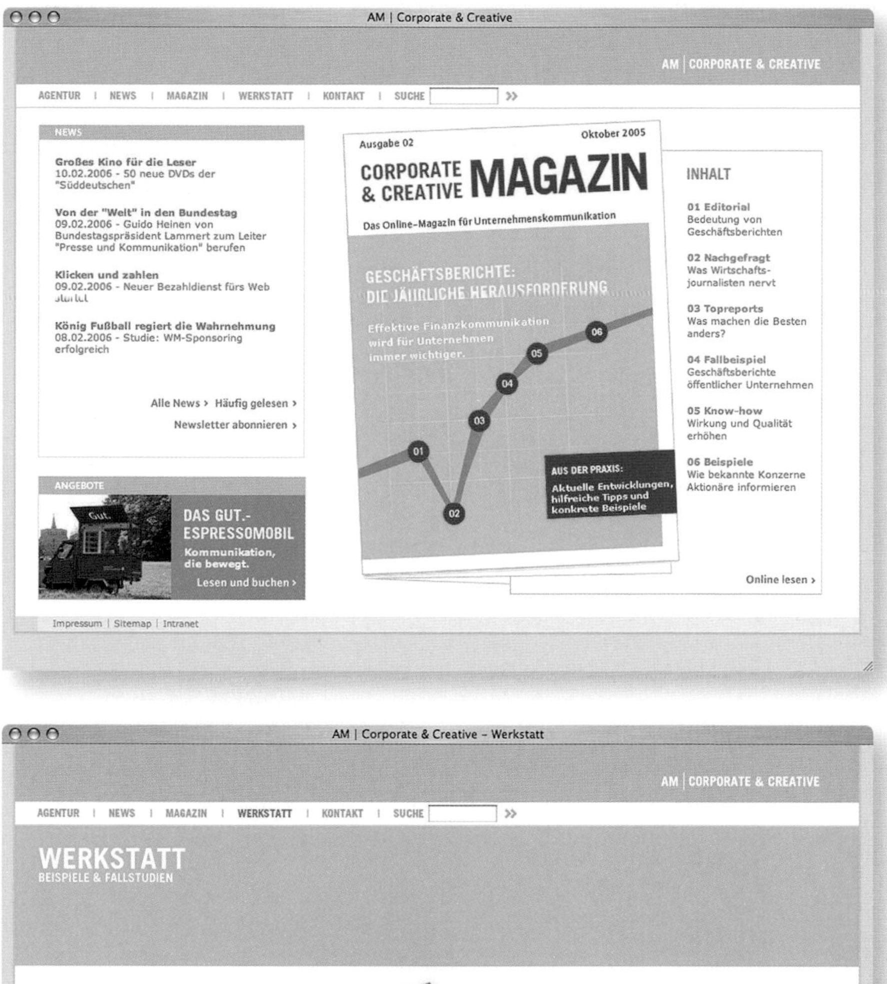

www.am-com.com

D: am | corporate & creative

A: am | corporate & creative **M:** koeln@am-com.com

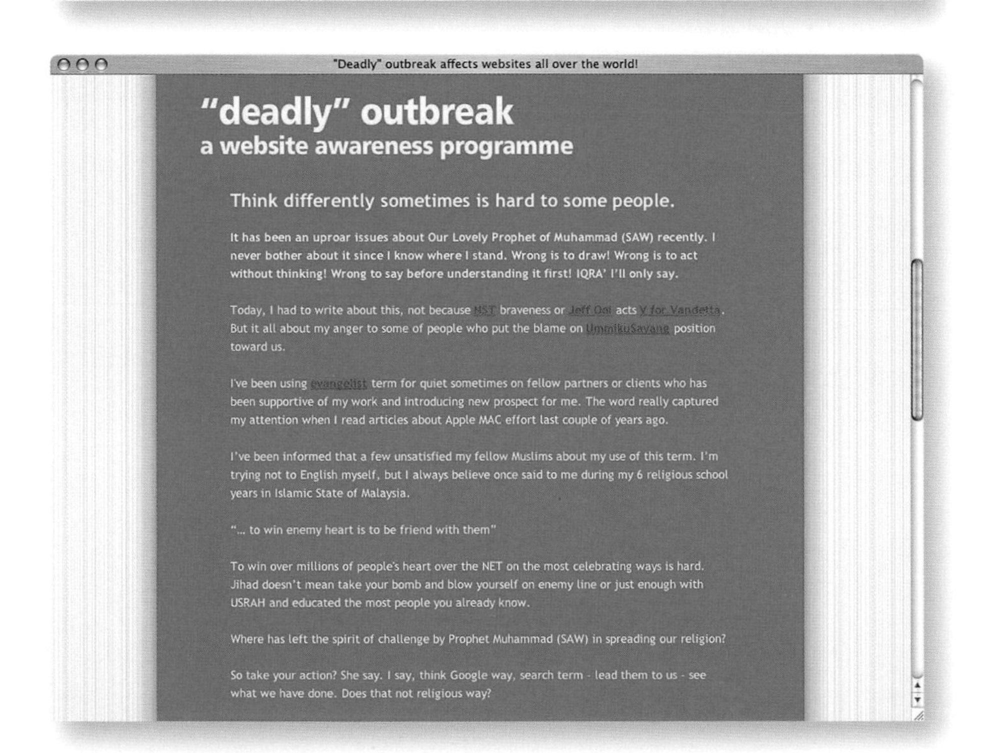

www.deadlyoutbreak.com

D: mohd hisham saleh **C:** roby **P:** ian h. chris

A: wahaza extra design studio **M:** www.wahazaextra.com

Agentur – achterdeck | Werbung | Corporate Design | Internet | Visualisierung

achterdeck

home
agentur
leistungen
projekte
kontakt

team kundenliste jobs

Die Mannschaft
macht das Schiff.

Wir betreuen den Marktauftritt unserer Kunden in allen relevanten Bearbeitungsphasen. Unsere Stärken sind die Innovationskraft und Geschwindigkeit, mit der wir gute Ideen umsetzen und auf Kundenwünsche eingehen sowie, ganz klar, unser höchst motiviertes, professionelles Team.

Wir verstehen unseren Beruf als Handwerk. Dieses hat viele Facetten und muss wie jedes andere gelernt werden, um hochwertige Lösungen für Internet und Druck garantieren zu können.

Kompetenz durch Erfahrung. Durch unsere bisherigen Arbeiten konnten wir die wichtigen, praktischen Erfahrungen sammeln, die man, wie auch in vielen anderen Bereichen, hier unbedingt benötigt.

Ende 2004 wurde beschlossen, die Fähigkeiten, die uns in den verschiedenen Bereichen auszeichnen, zu bündeln und von nun an offiziell als Team aufzutreten.

Impressum | © achterdeck

MAMBO AWARDS

Mamboaward: Winner for best content and best design with mambo open source is achterdeck.com

Werbung Uelzen – achterdeck | Werbung | Corporate Design | Internet | Visualisierung

achterdeck

home
agentur
leistungen
projekte
kontakt

Die Werbewerft.

Wir, die Werbeagentur achterdeck aus Uelzen, haben uns auf die Realisierung umfassender Projekte der visuellen Kommunikation spezialisiert. Diese beinhalten das Corporate Design (z.B. Logo, dynamische Websites, Geschäftsausstattung), aber auch klassische Werbung (z.B. Flyer, Plakate, Mailings, Broschüren).

Besuchen Sie unsere Projektbeispiele, um einen Eindruck zu erhalten, was wir für Sie tun können. Hier unser aktuelles Projekt:

Praxis für Therapie & Training

Impressum | © achterdeck

MAMBO AWARDS

Mamboaward: Winner for best content and best design with mambo open source is achterdeck.com

www.achterdeck.com
D: lars wendlandt **C:** stefan große
A: achterdeck **M:** www.achterdeck.com

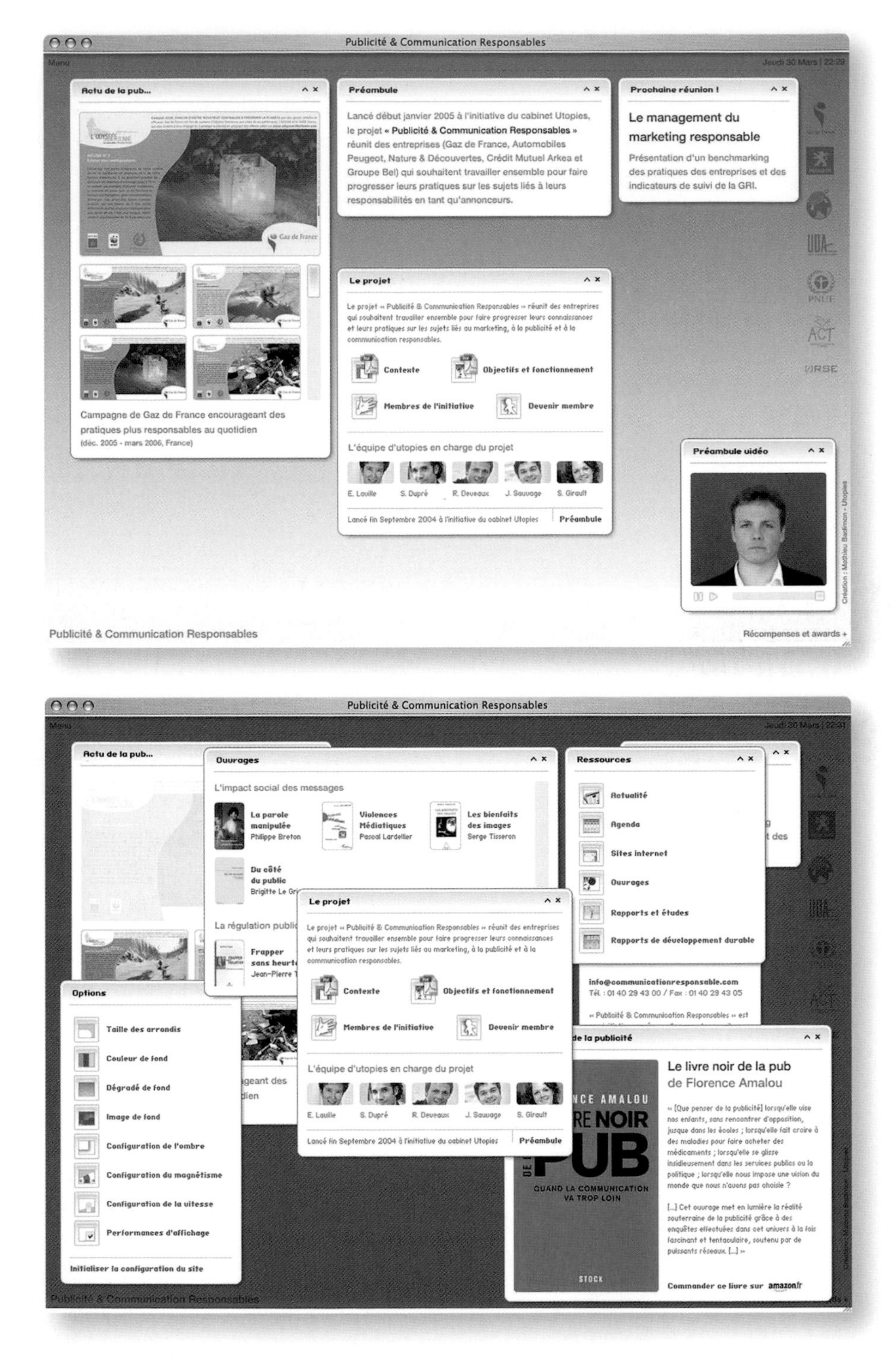

www.communicationresponsable.com

D: mathieu badimon

A: mathieu badimon **M:** contact@mathieu-badimon.com

www.unnpro.com

D: fabio berton **C:** christan giordano **P:** stefano stella
A: unnecessary production **M:** sstella@unnpro.com

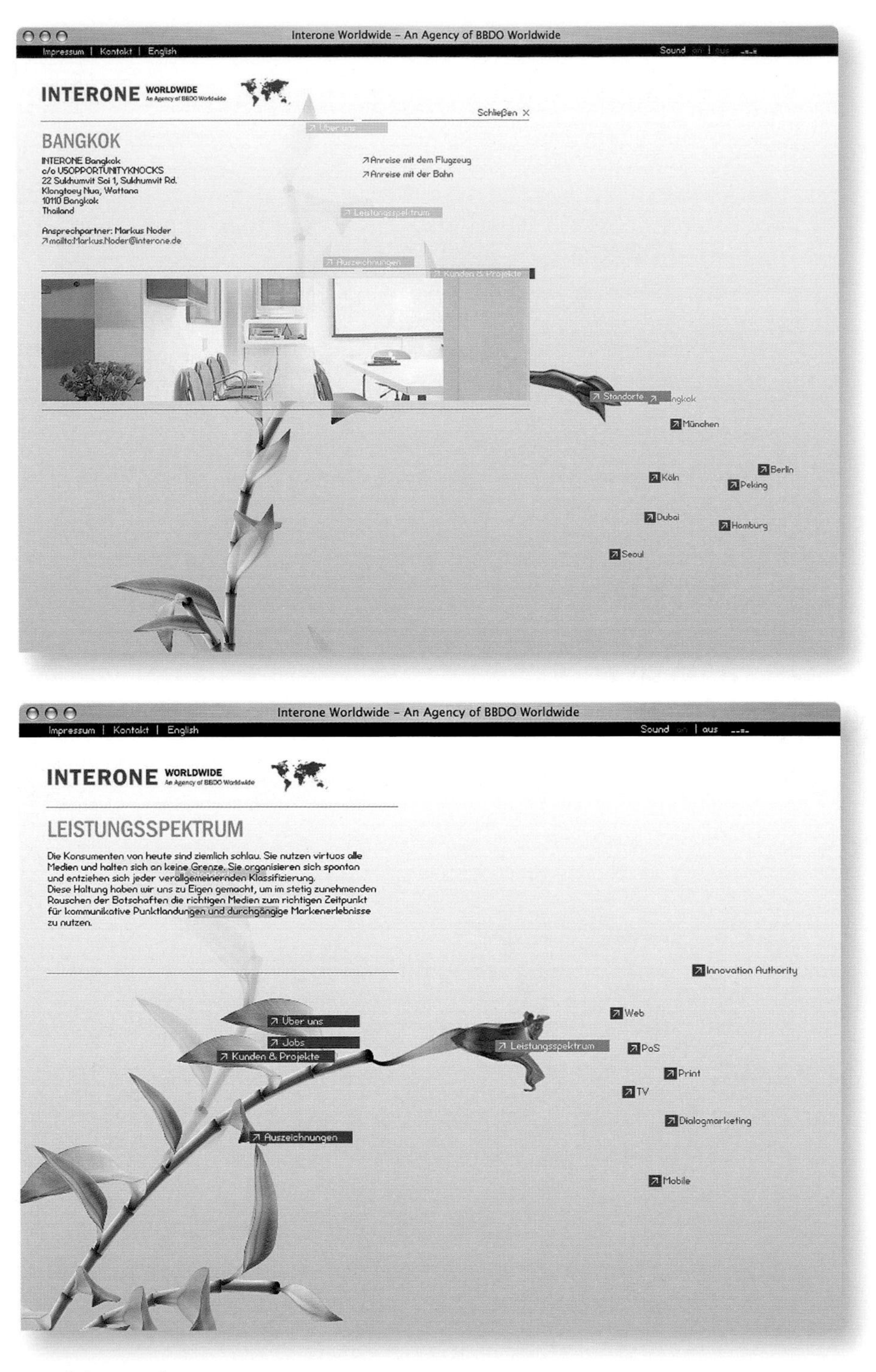

www.interone.de

D: mike john otto, thorben cording, f. genzmer **C:** l. gerckens **P:** c. bauer, m. j. otto

A: interone hamburg **M:** info@interone.de

www.bizart.lu

D: laurent daubach **C:** viktor dick **P:** raoul thill
A: atelier graphique bizart **M:** contact@bizart.lu

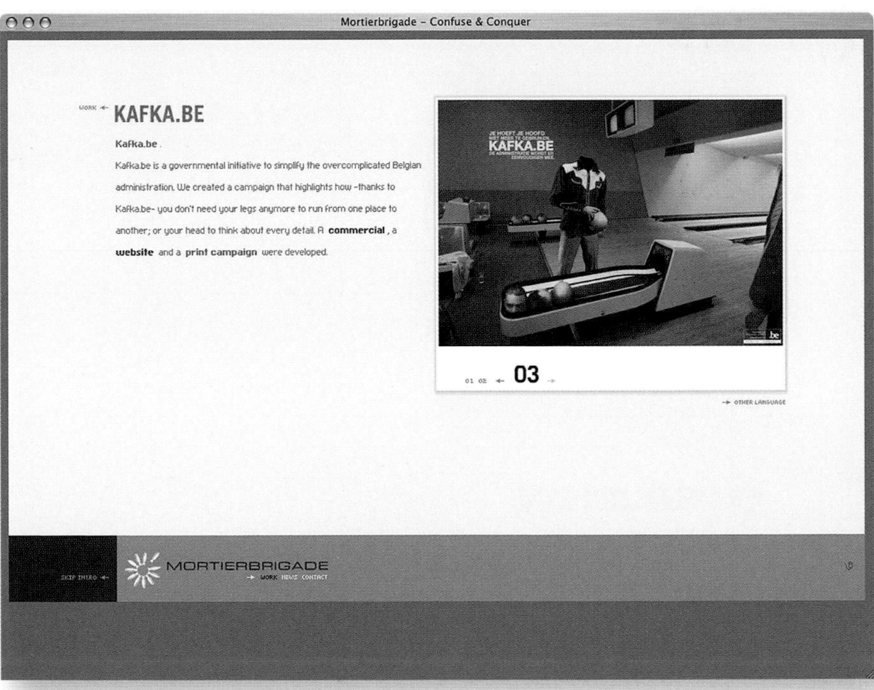

www.mortierbrigade.com

D: group94 **P:** mortierbrigade

M: info@group94.com

www.motherlondon.com

D: steve pearce, nico nuzzaci **C:** simon kallgard **P:** tom hostler

A: poke **M:** www.pokelondon.com

www.donaireydelaplaza.com

D: marc schmitt

A: donaire y de la plaza **M:** donaireydelaplaza.com

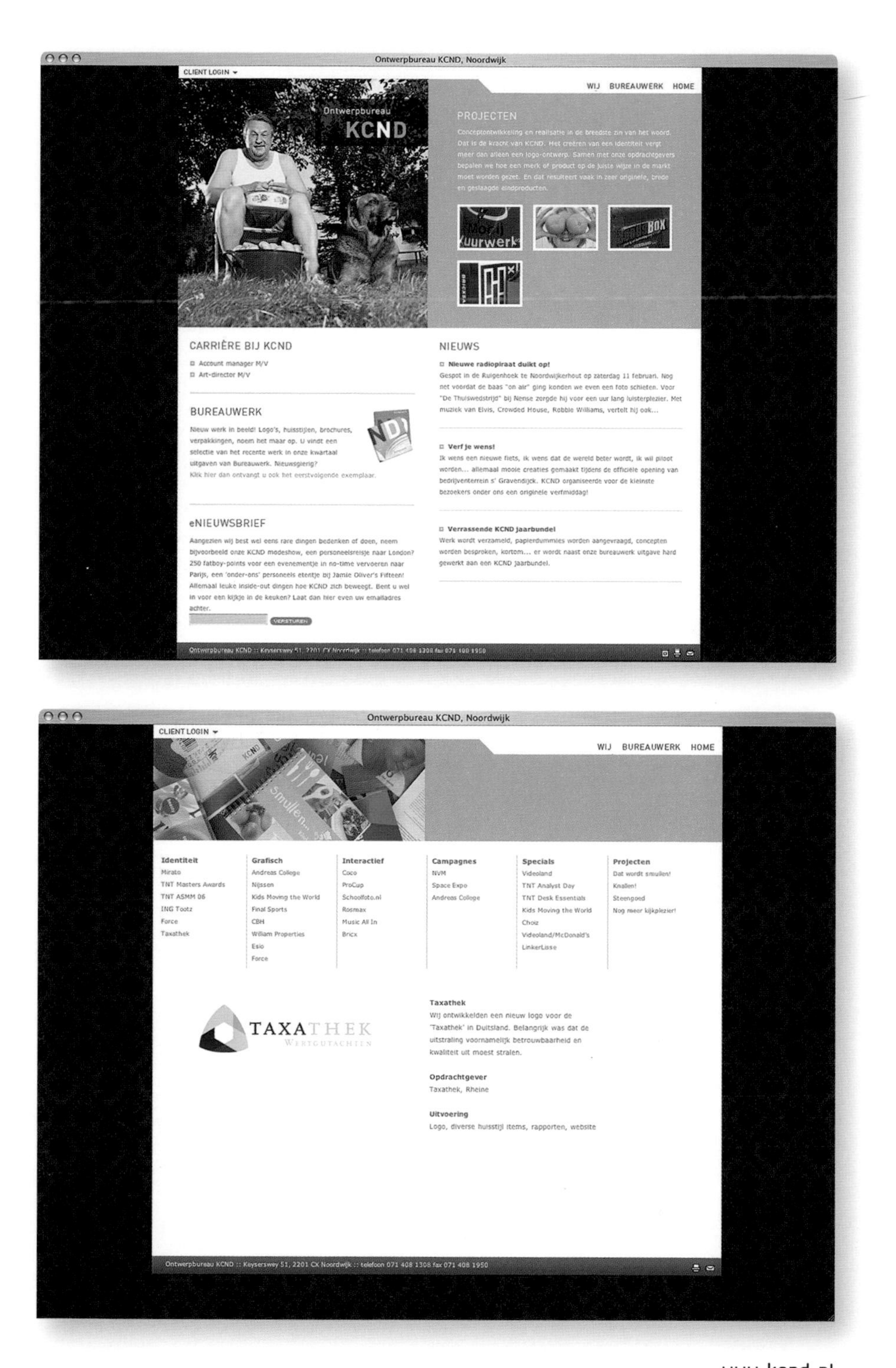

www.kcnd.nl

D: frank van den berg **C:** frank van den berg **P:** léon koelewijn
A: ontwerpbureau kcnd **M:** leon@kcnd.nl

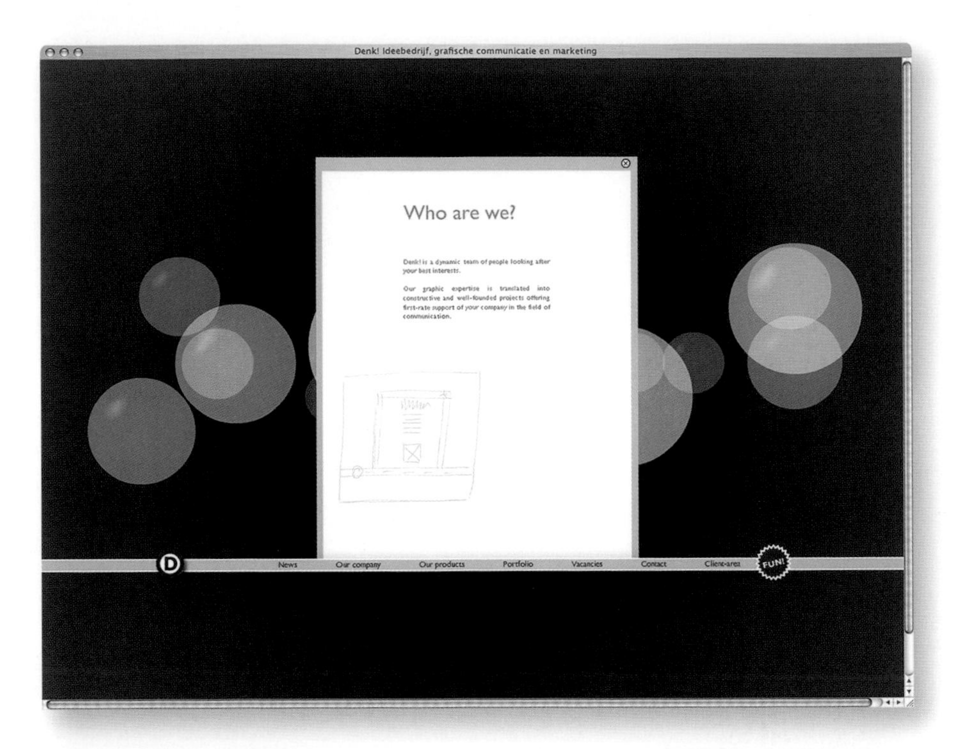

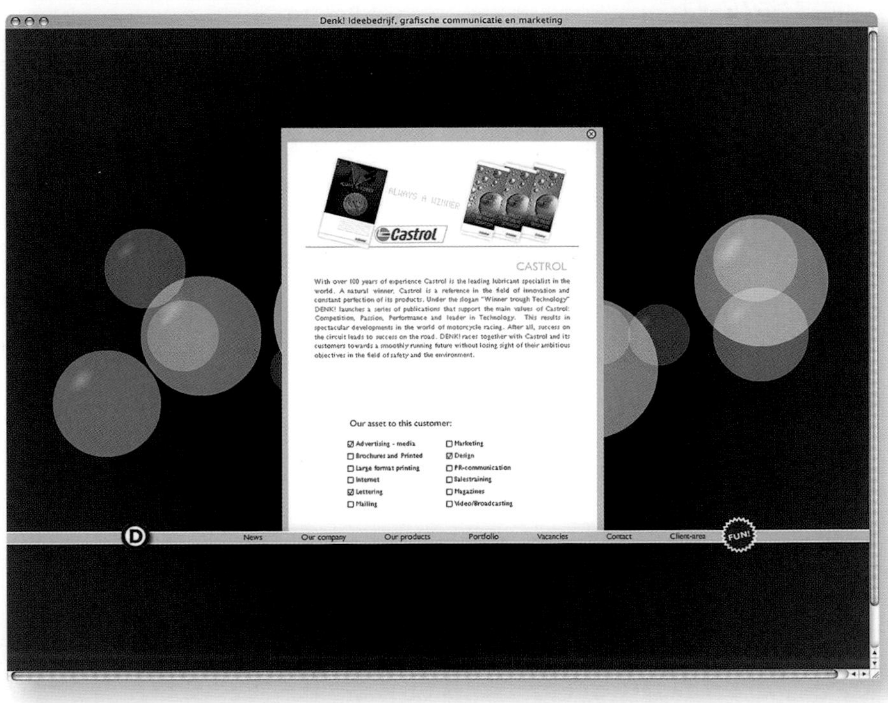

www.denk.be

D: kenny from denk! **C:** hans van de velde **P:** denk!

A: denk! **M:** hans@novio.be

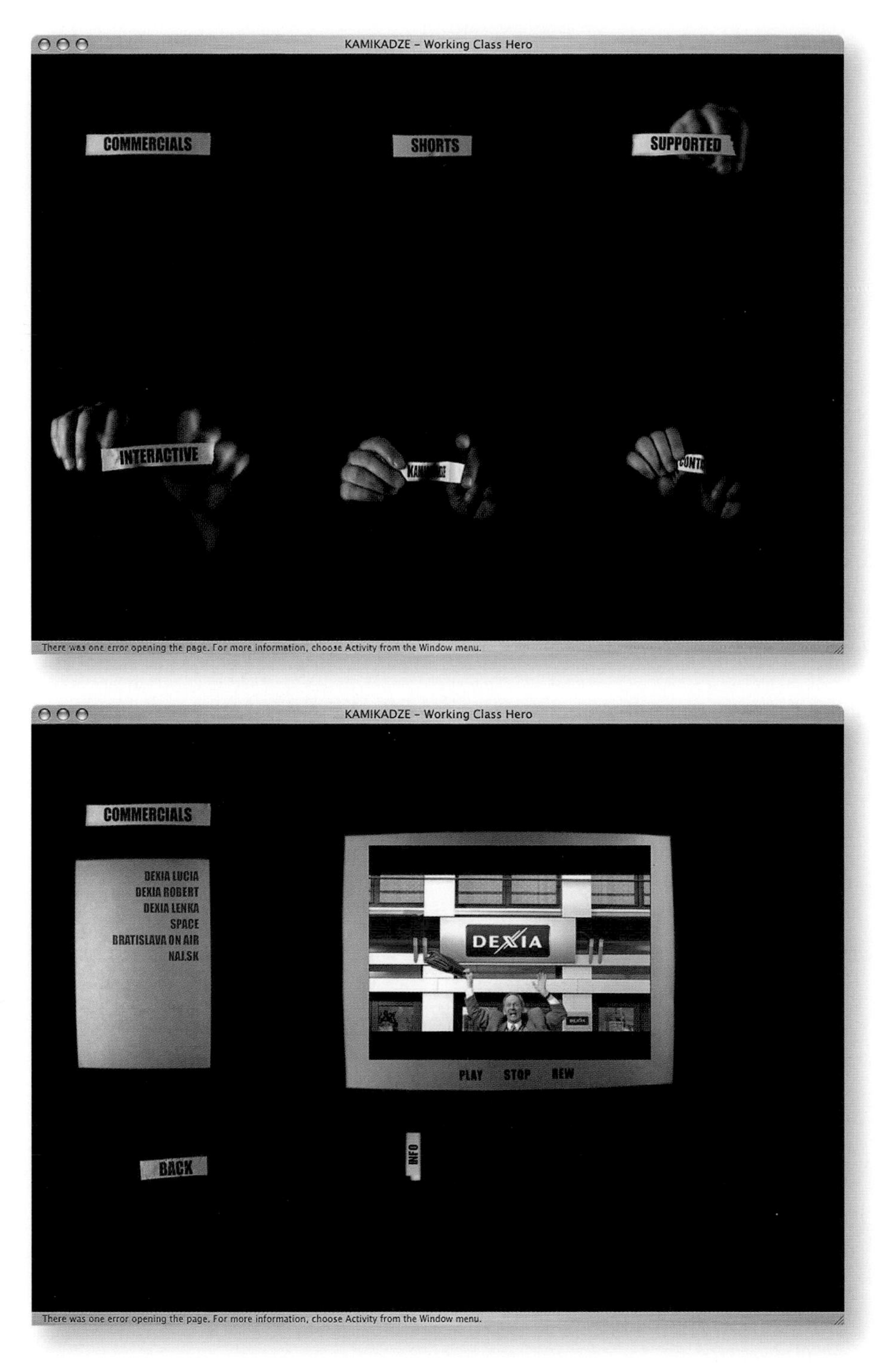

www.kamikadze.sk

D: brano pepel, vilo csino **C:** brano pepel

A: kamikadze **M:** info@kamikadze.sk

UnArt

WAS? WANN? WO? WIE? WER? WE LIKE:

NÄCHSTER EVENT: NEWSLETTER: FOTOGALERIE:

UnArt!

Schwullesbische* Landdisko im urbanen Stil.

* auch Hetero-, Bi-, Trans- und A-Sexuelle sind herzlich willkommen ;-)

Auf die Ohren gibts:
- ALTERNATIVE
- HIP HOP
- ELECTRONICA
und andere unartige Sounds von unseren Resident- und Guest-DJ's!

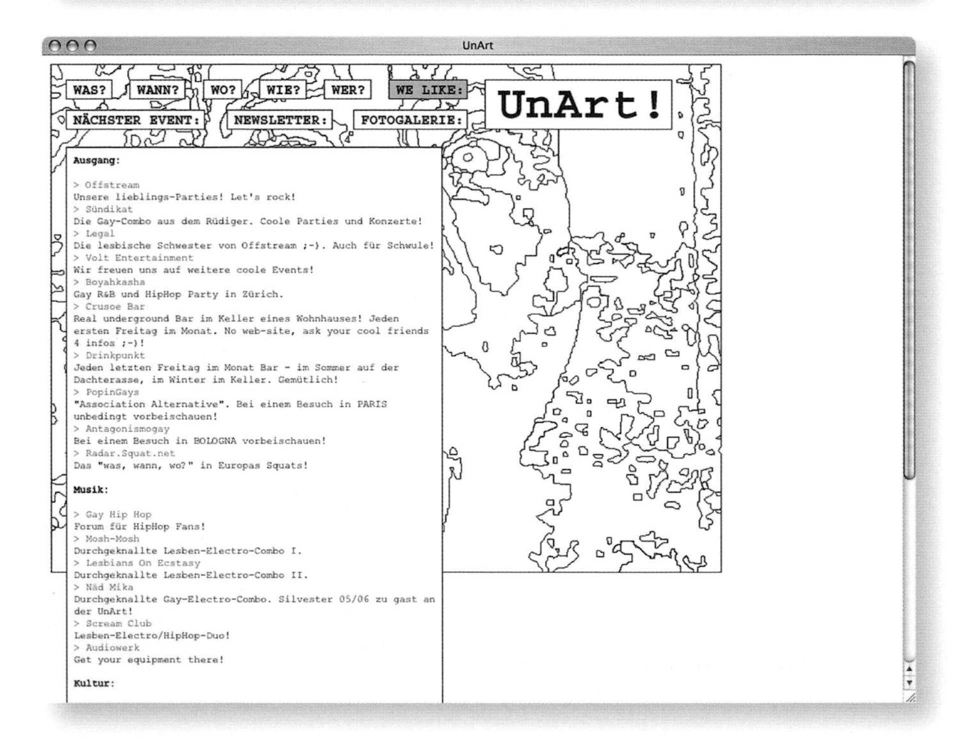

www.unart.ch.vu

D: dominik buser

A: 19m2 atelierkollektiv **M:** dominik@19m2.ch

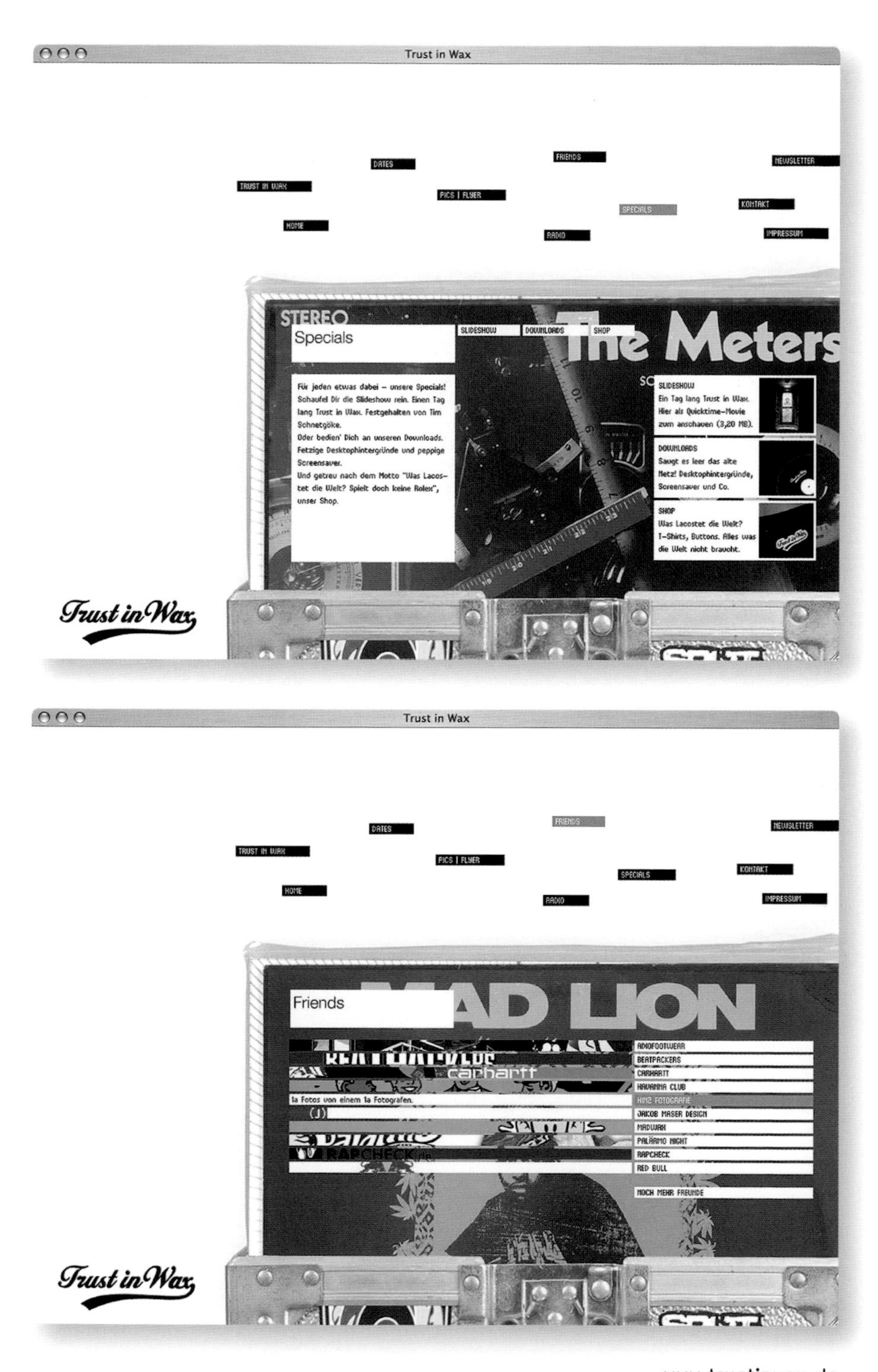

www.trustinwax.de

D: christian heidemann

A: christian heidemann - media design **M:** www.still-alive.de

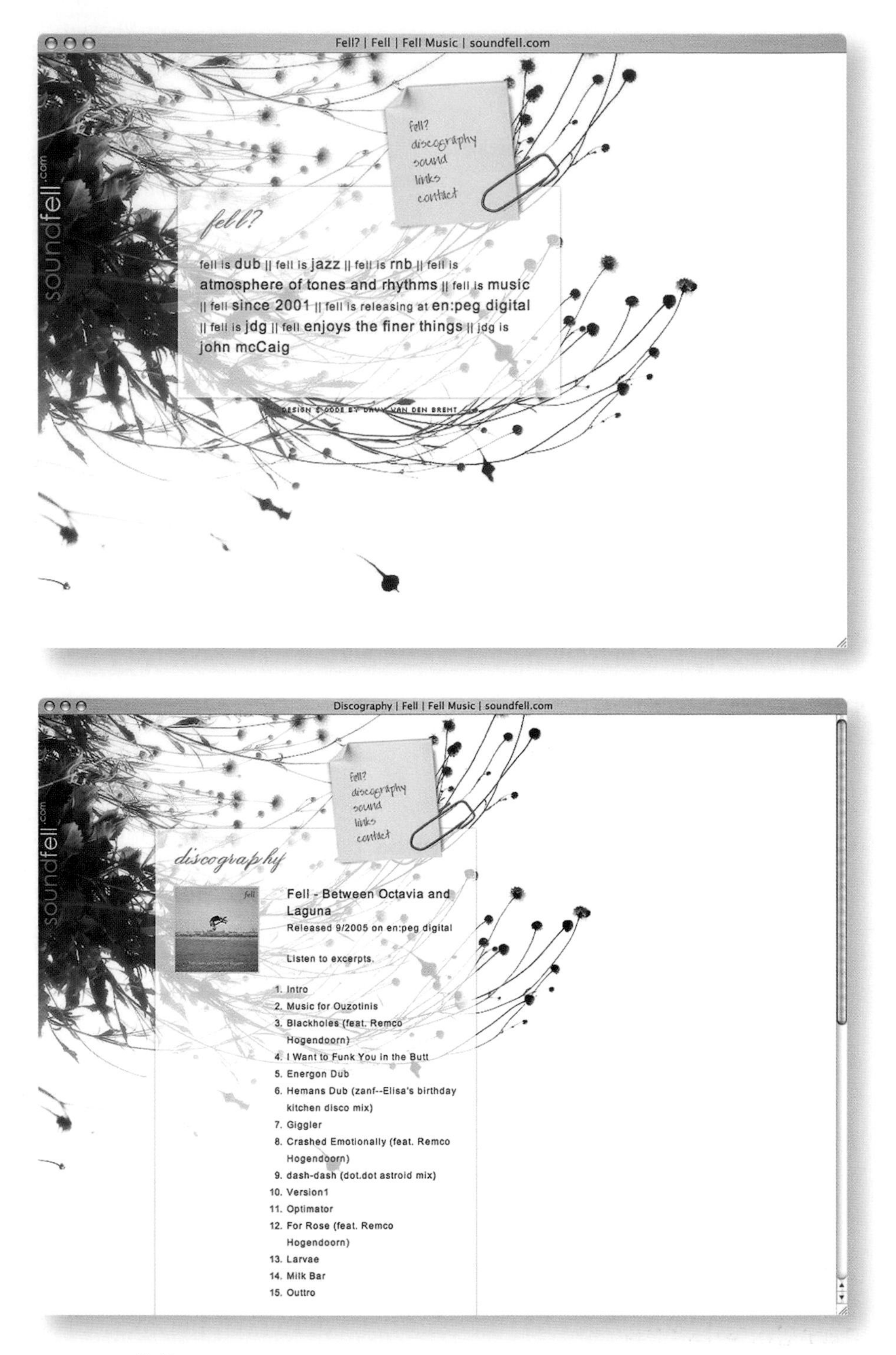

www.soundfell.com

D: davy van den bremt

A: davy van den bremt **M:** www.davyvandenbremt.be

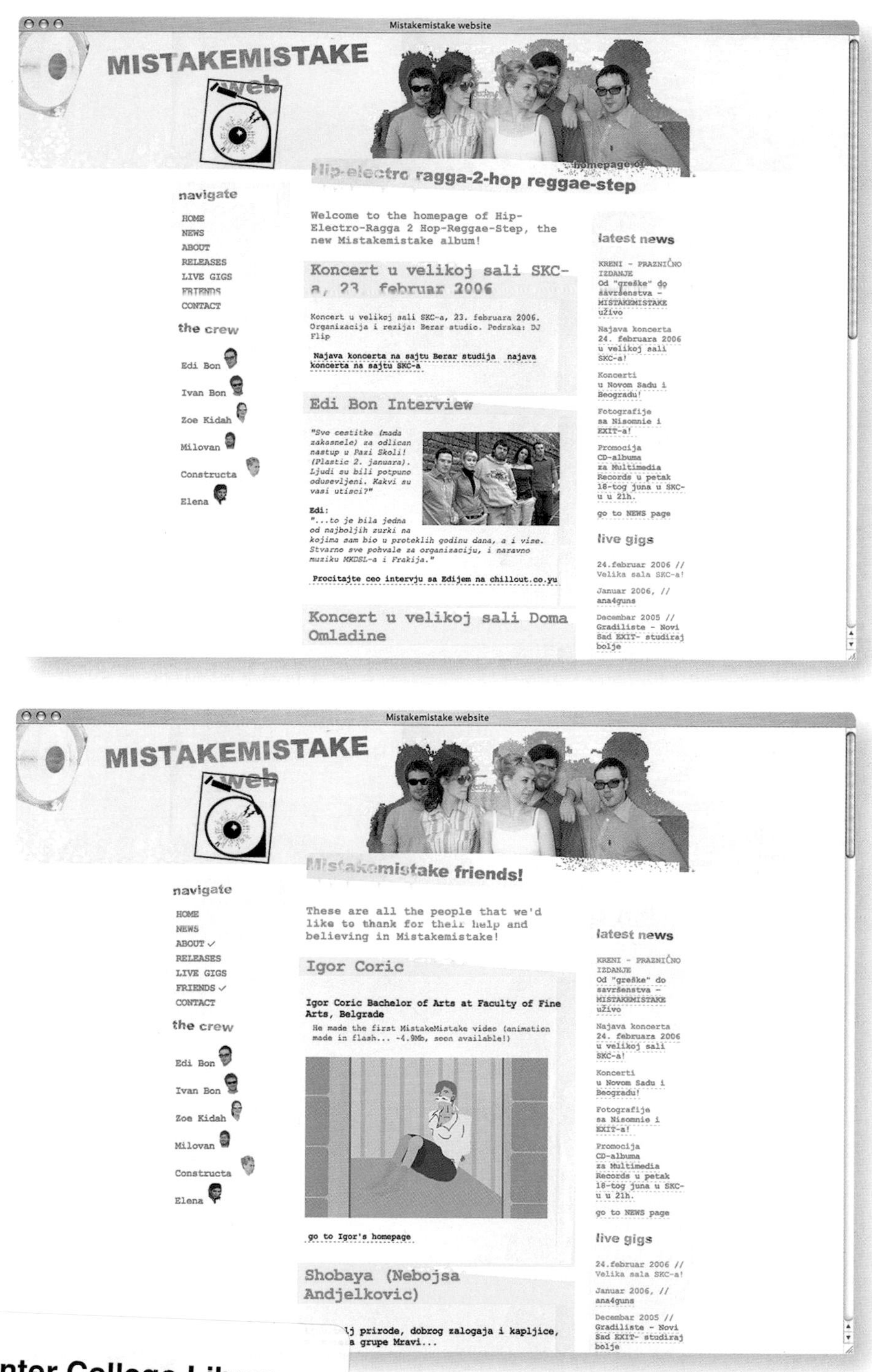

www.mistakemistake.com

D: denis radenkovic

A: 38one M: denis@38one.com

www.leogirardi.com

D: davide g. aquini

M: davide.aquini@libero.it

www.djbrunetto.com

D: pedro j. saavedra **C:** pedro j. saavedra **P:** irene novo

A: sit and die **M:** sitanddie@sitanddie.com

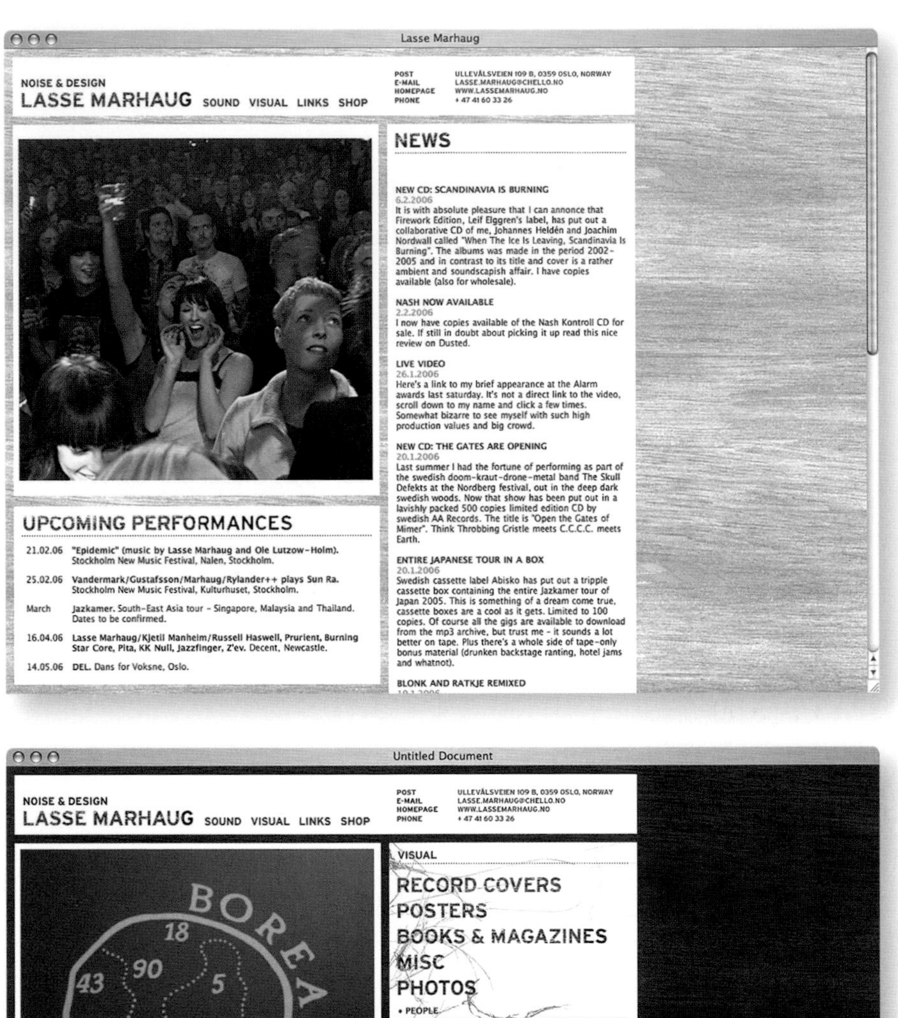

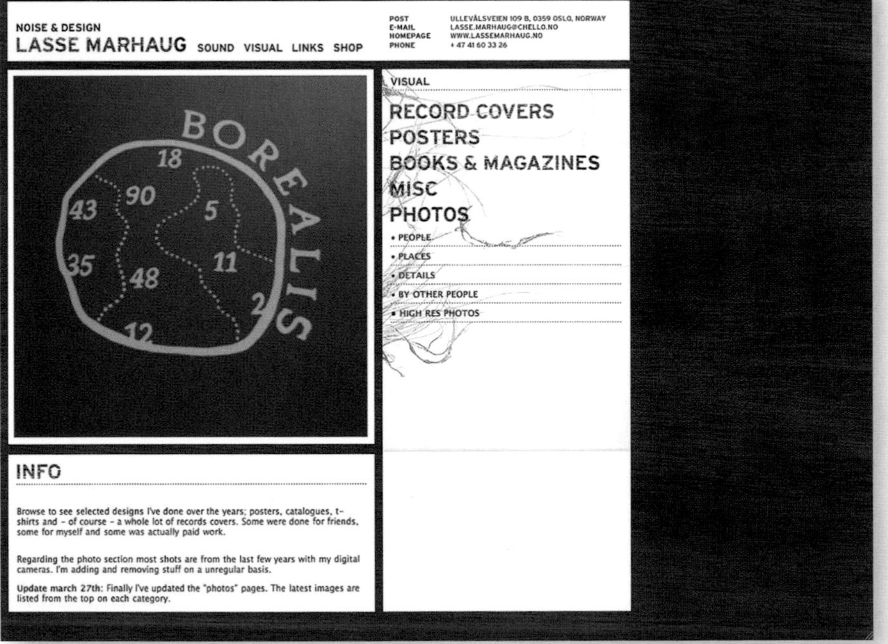

www.lassemarhaug.no

D: håvard gjelseth

A: this way design **M:** hgjelseth@thiswaydesign.com

www.nicelikethat.de
D: maika paetzold
A: mettage design M: www.mettage-design.de

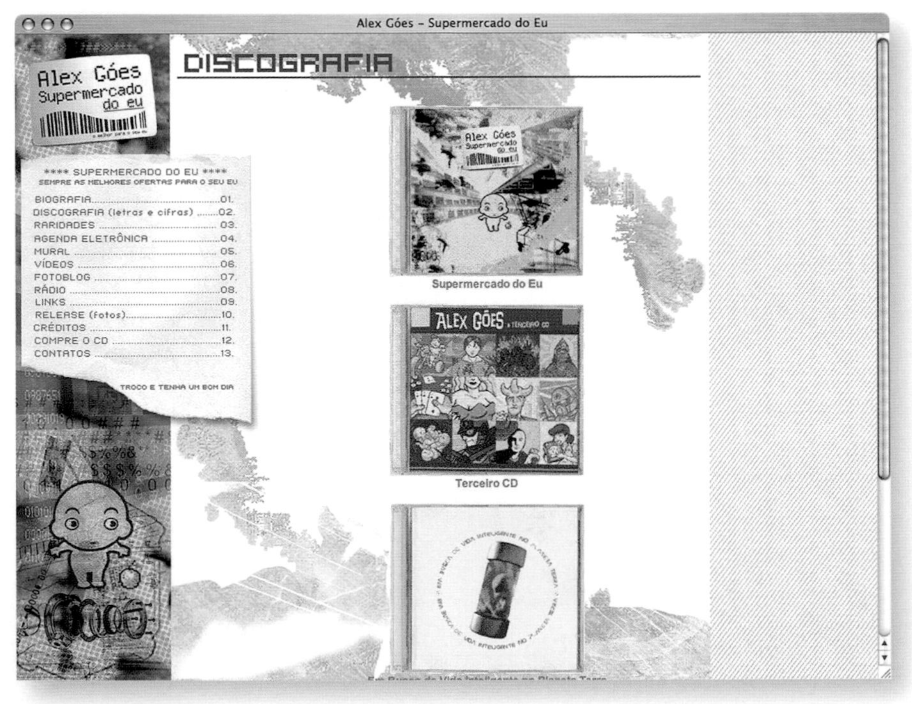

www.alexgoes.com.br

D: kaike **C:** max capellani **P:** kaike

A: elipse comunicação de marketing **M:** kaike@elipseweb.com.br

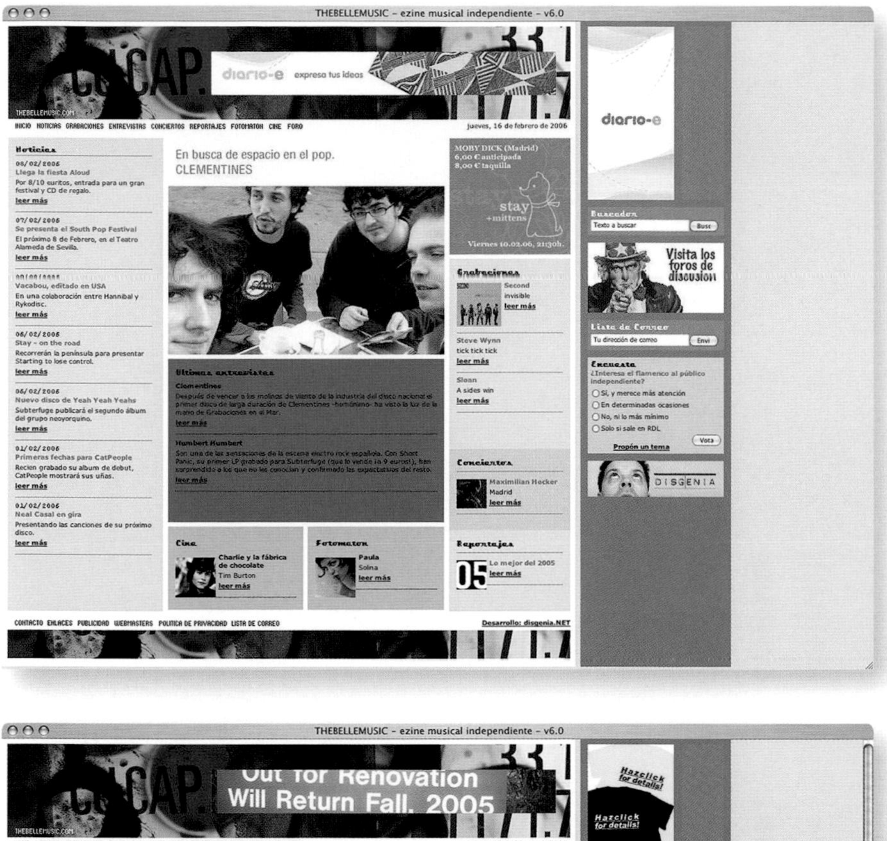

www.thebellemusic.com

D: alejandro ochoa alonso

M: contacto@thebellemusic.com

justforthefofit.com

D: todd purgason, brian miller **C:** casey corcoren **P:** sean gibson

A: juxt interactive **M:** juxtinteractive.com

www.petekronowitt.com
D: cristian strittmatter **C:** gabriel toledano **P:** sandra strittmatter
A: from scratch design studio **M:** contact@fromscratch.us

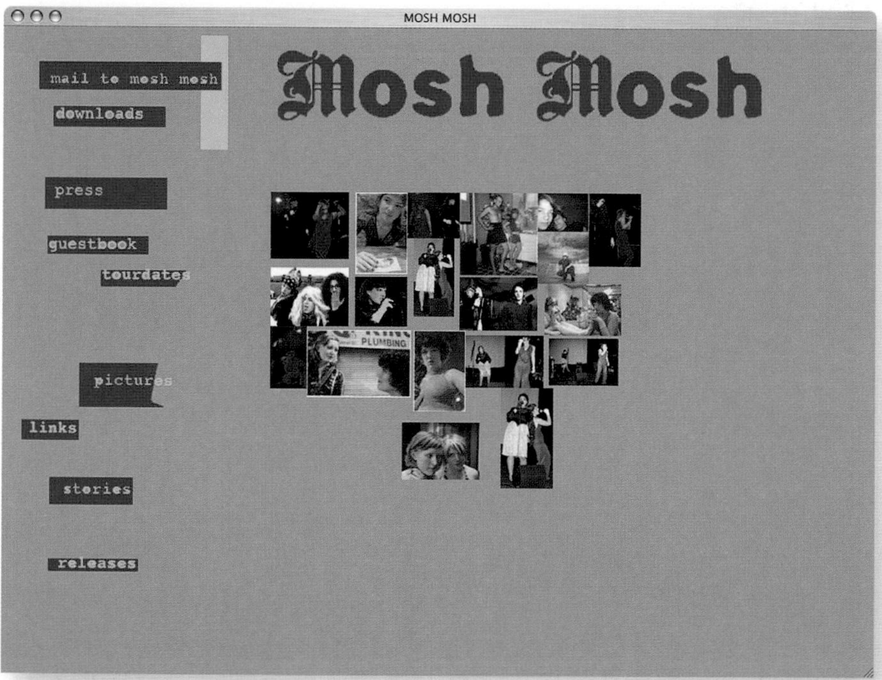

www.mosh-mosh.com

D: lady mosh

A: mosh art **M:** info@mosh-mosh.com

www.takeonemusic.com

D: ming-wen hsu

A: ming-wen hsu, design workshop M: dylan@mingwen.idv.tw

www.dj-fudido.com

D: mathieu saudel

A: mathieu saudel **M:** mathieu.saudel@wanadoo.fr

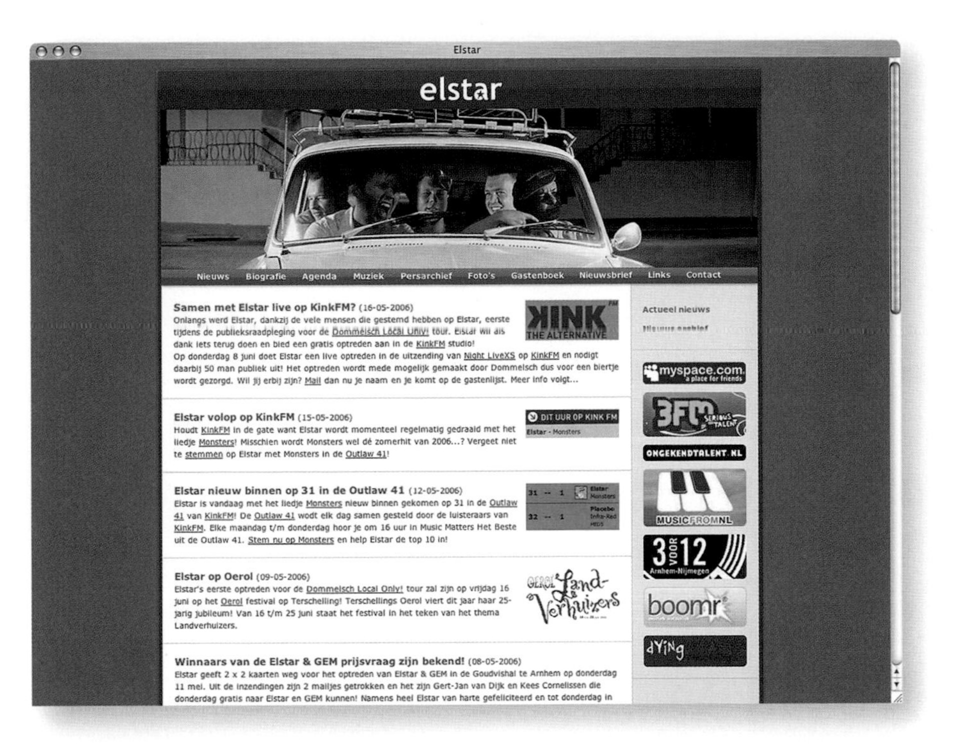

www.elstarmusic.com

D: bas boerman

A: adibas.nl M: info@adibas.nl

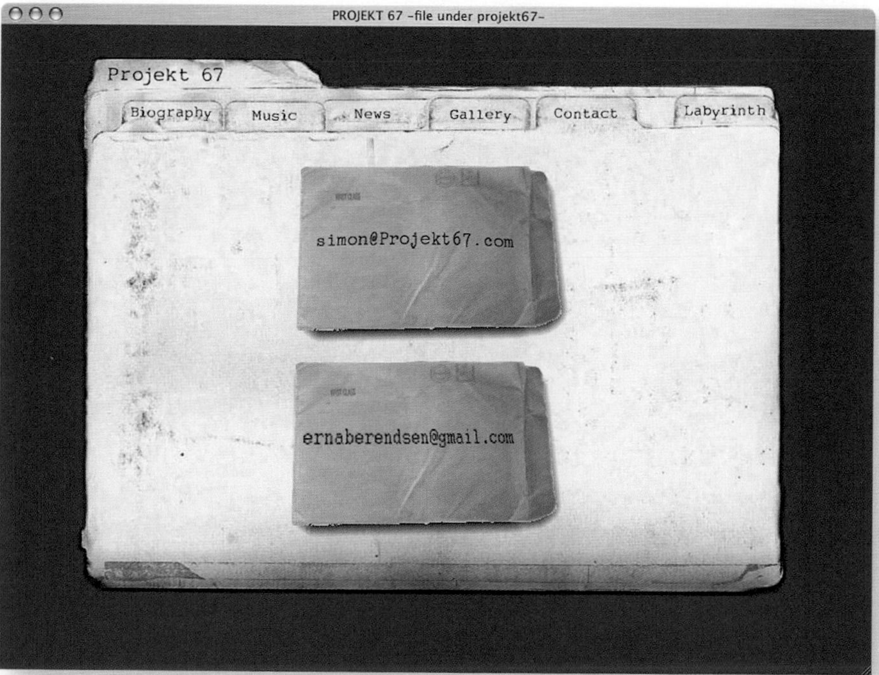

www.projekt67.com

D: simon van weelden

A: reddogproducts **M:** simon@projekt67.com

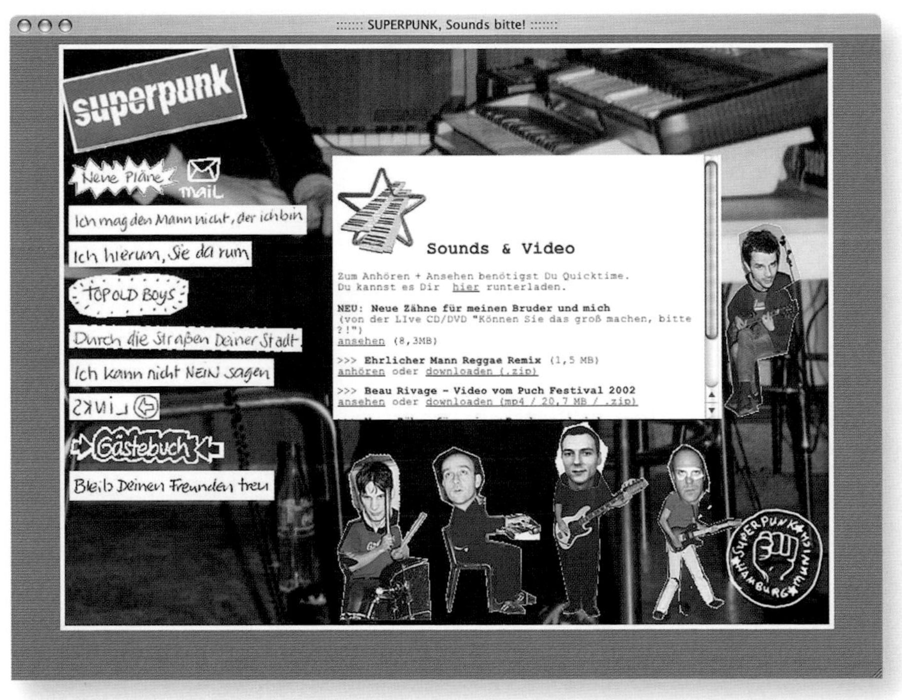

www.superpunk.de
D: kerstin holzwarth
A: kerstin holzwarth graphic design **M:** www.kokong.de

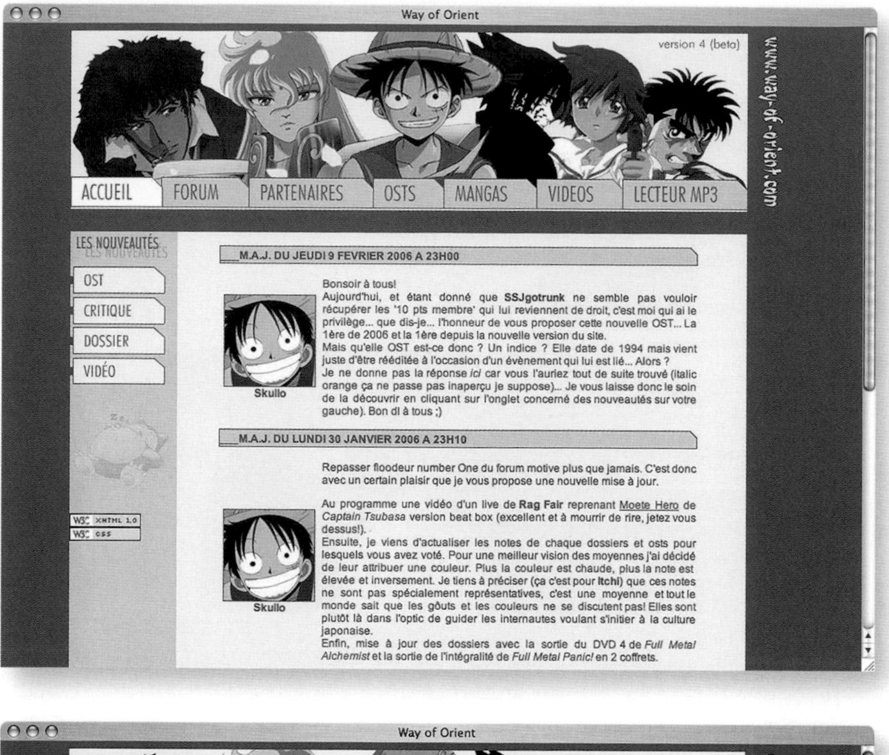

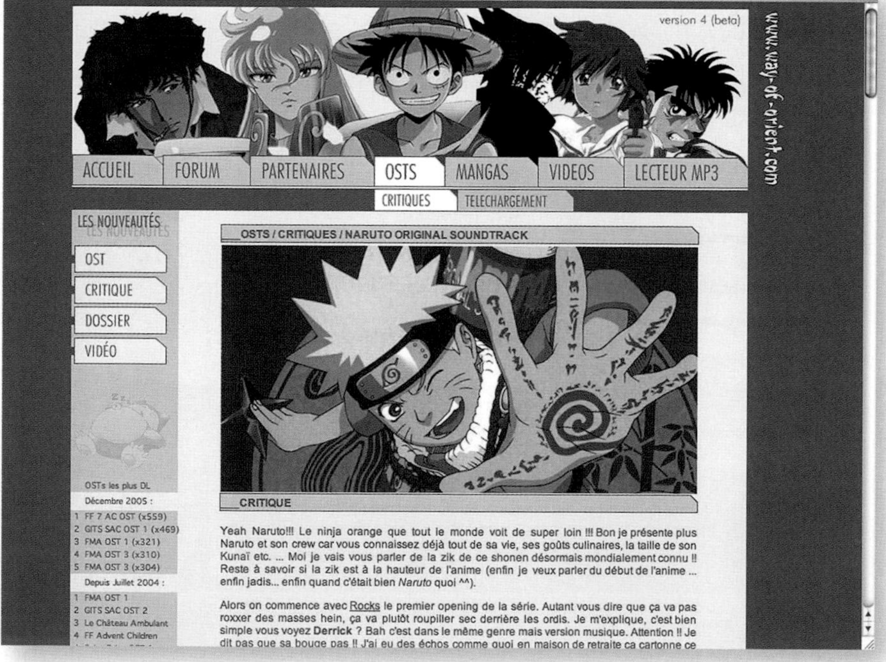

www.way-of-orient.com

D: rémy rey de barros

M: remy.reydebarros@caramailmax.com

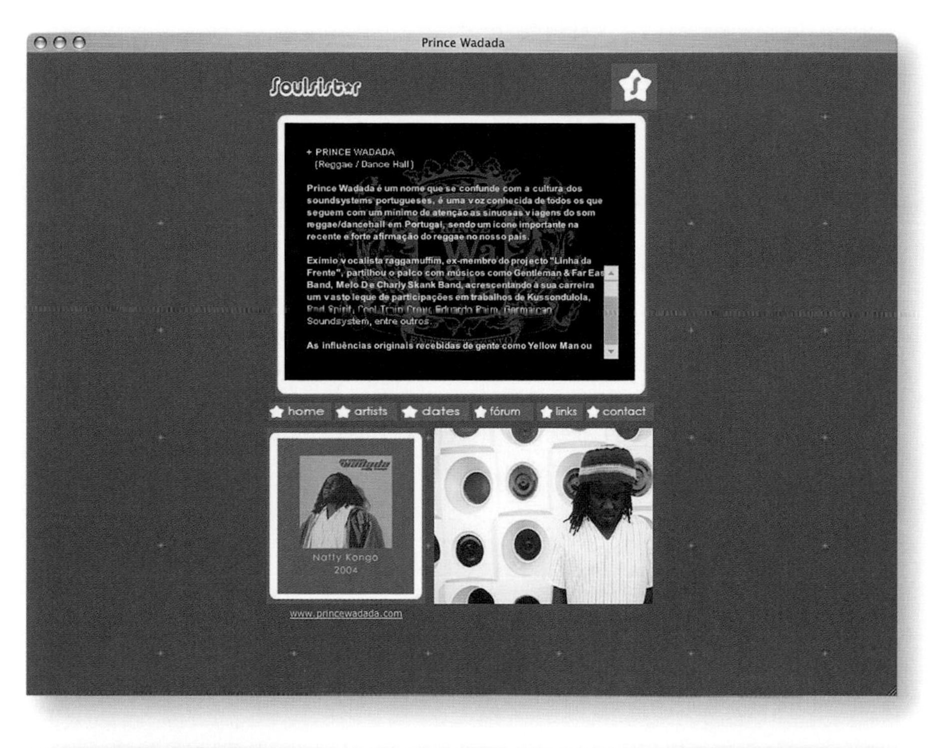

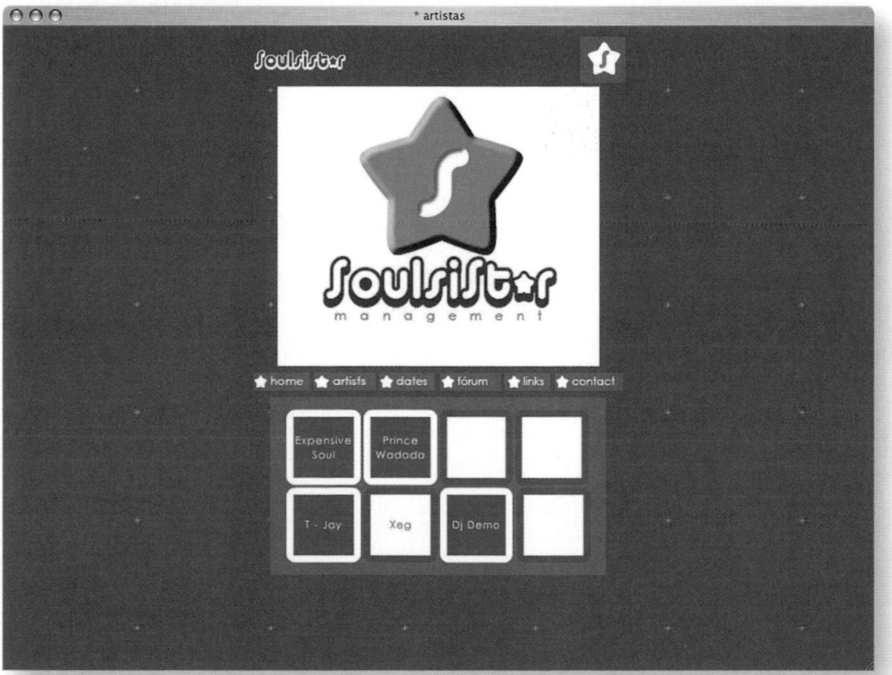

www.soulsistar.com

D: joana inês souza dias
M: joaninex@hotmail.com

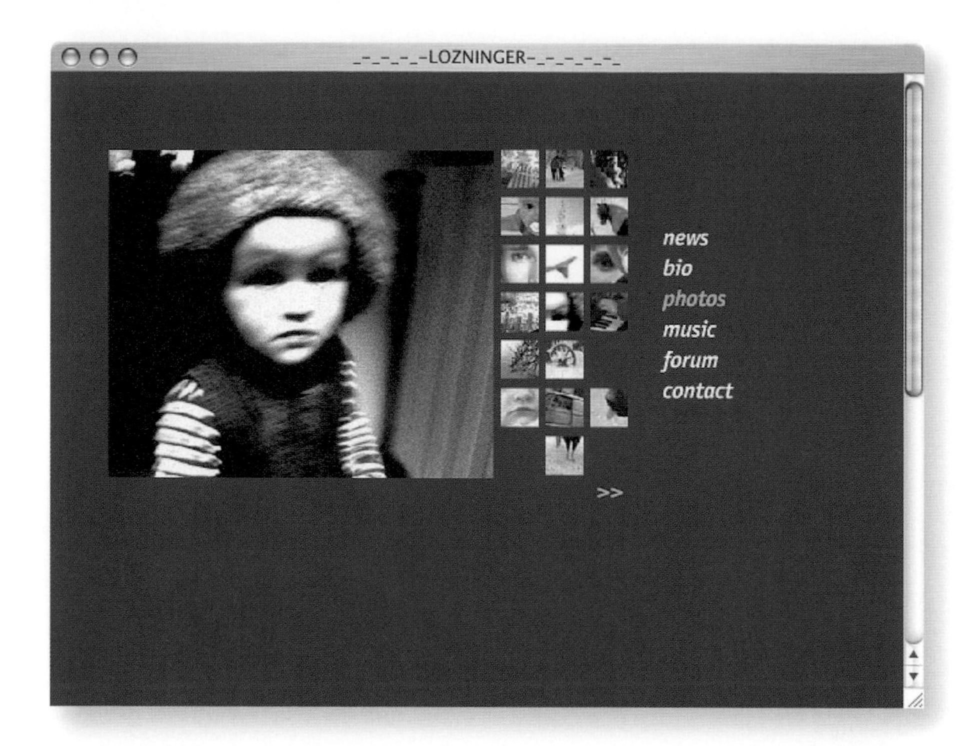

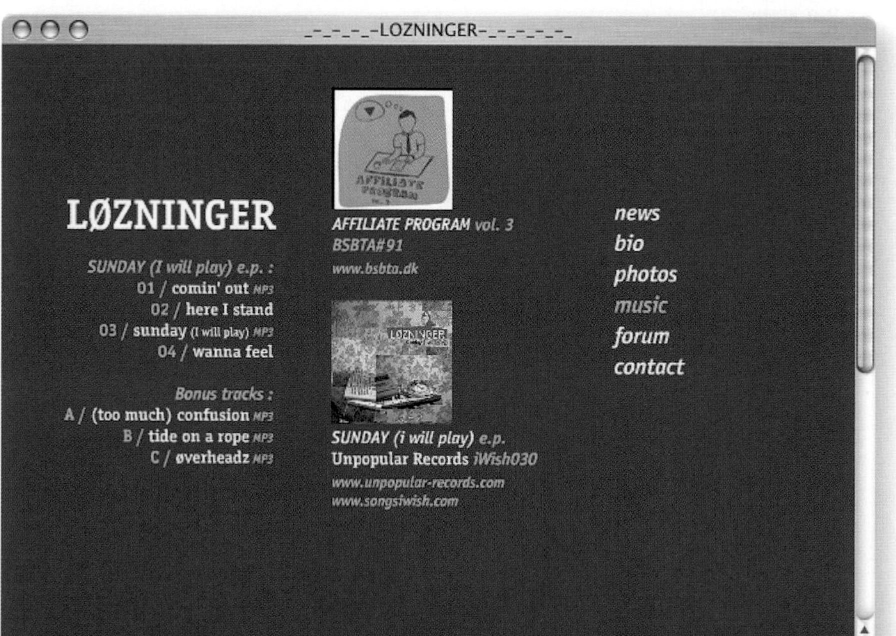

www.lozninger.com

D: + stasola design +

A: + stasola design + **M:** design@stasola.com

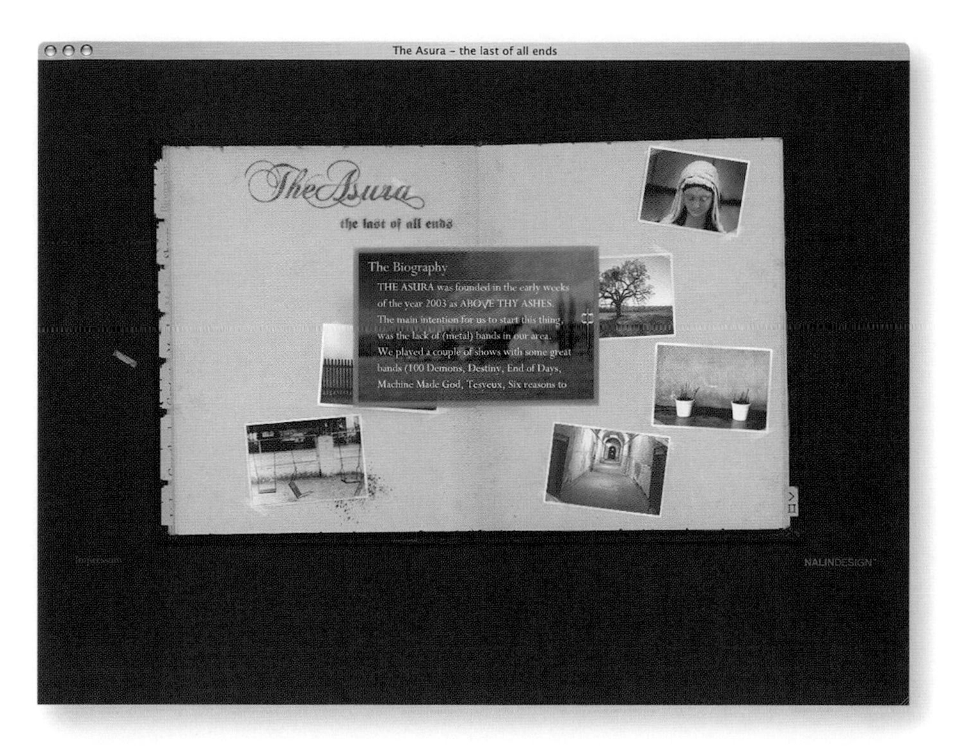

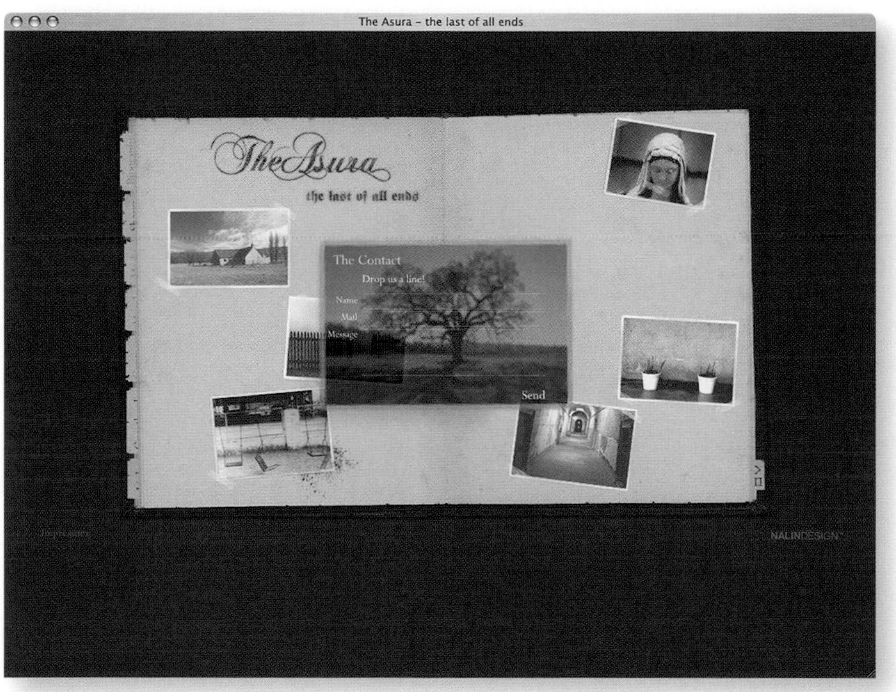

www.the-asura.com

D: andre weier

A: nalin-design **M:** www.nalin-design.com

www.mosesmusic.nl

D: stephan de graaf, johan den heijer **C:** s. de graaf **P:** j. den heijer, pauline schöder

A: pixelfarm, moses.music **M:** info@mosesmusic.nl

www.mangalavallis.it
D: max cavalli cocchi
M: max.cavallicocchi.it

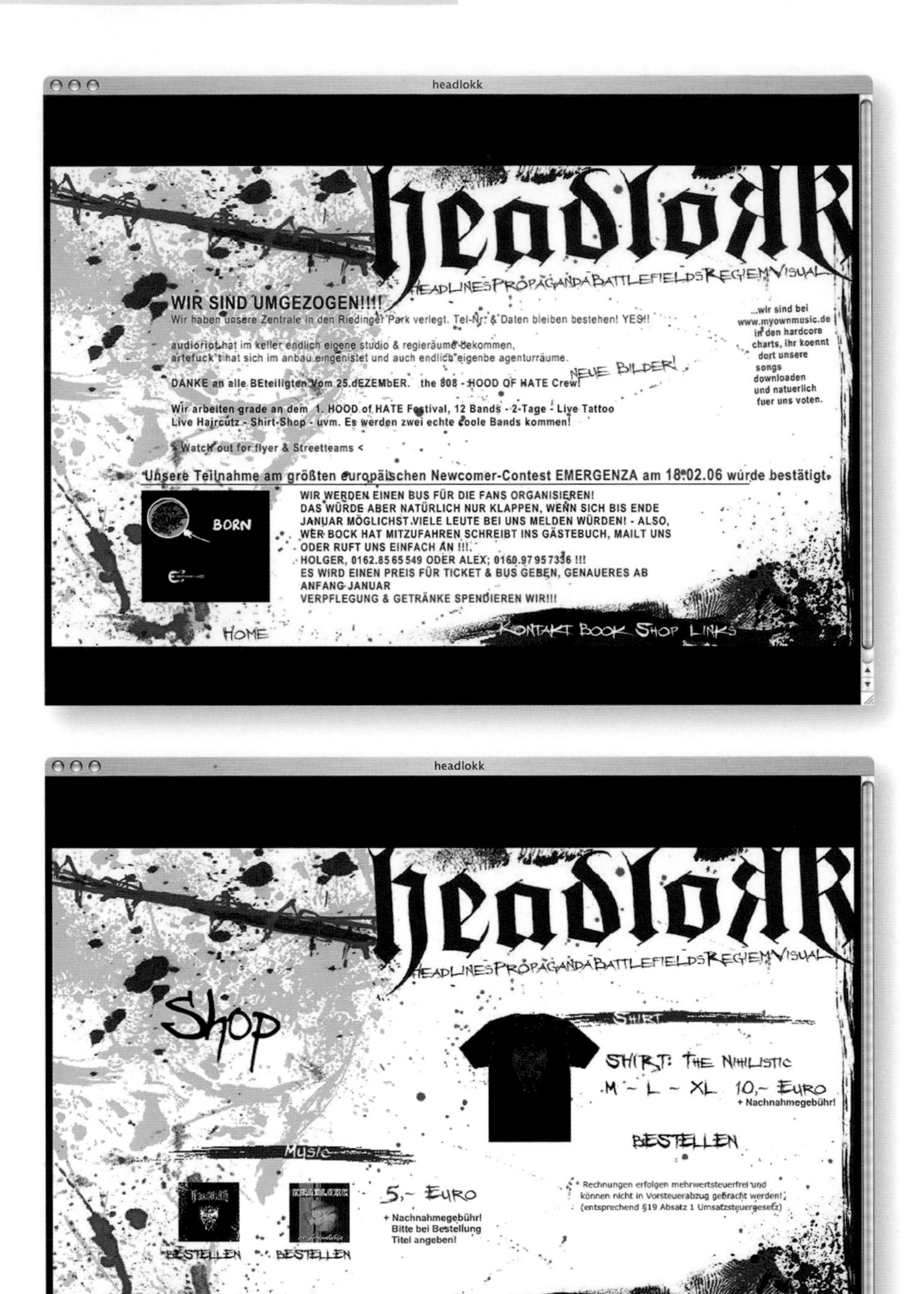

www.headlokk.com

D: alexander preböck

A: artefuck't **M:** headlokk@gmx.com

www.300yearslater.com

D: sam hayles **C:** joolz **P:** sam hayles

A: dose-productions **M:** www.dose-productions.com

www.wodb.ru

D: timoshenkov C: timoshenkov P: oding

A: artcifra M: www.artcifra.com

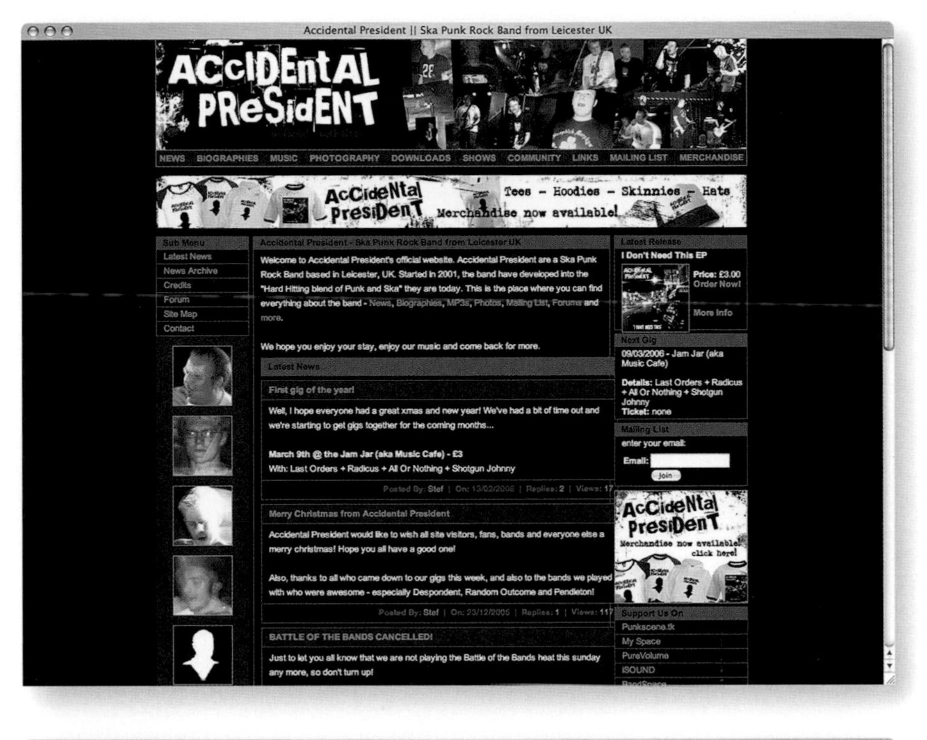

www.accidental-president.co.uk

D: stefan ashwell

M: band@accidental-president.co.uk

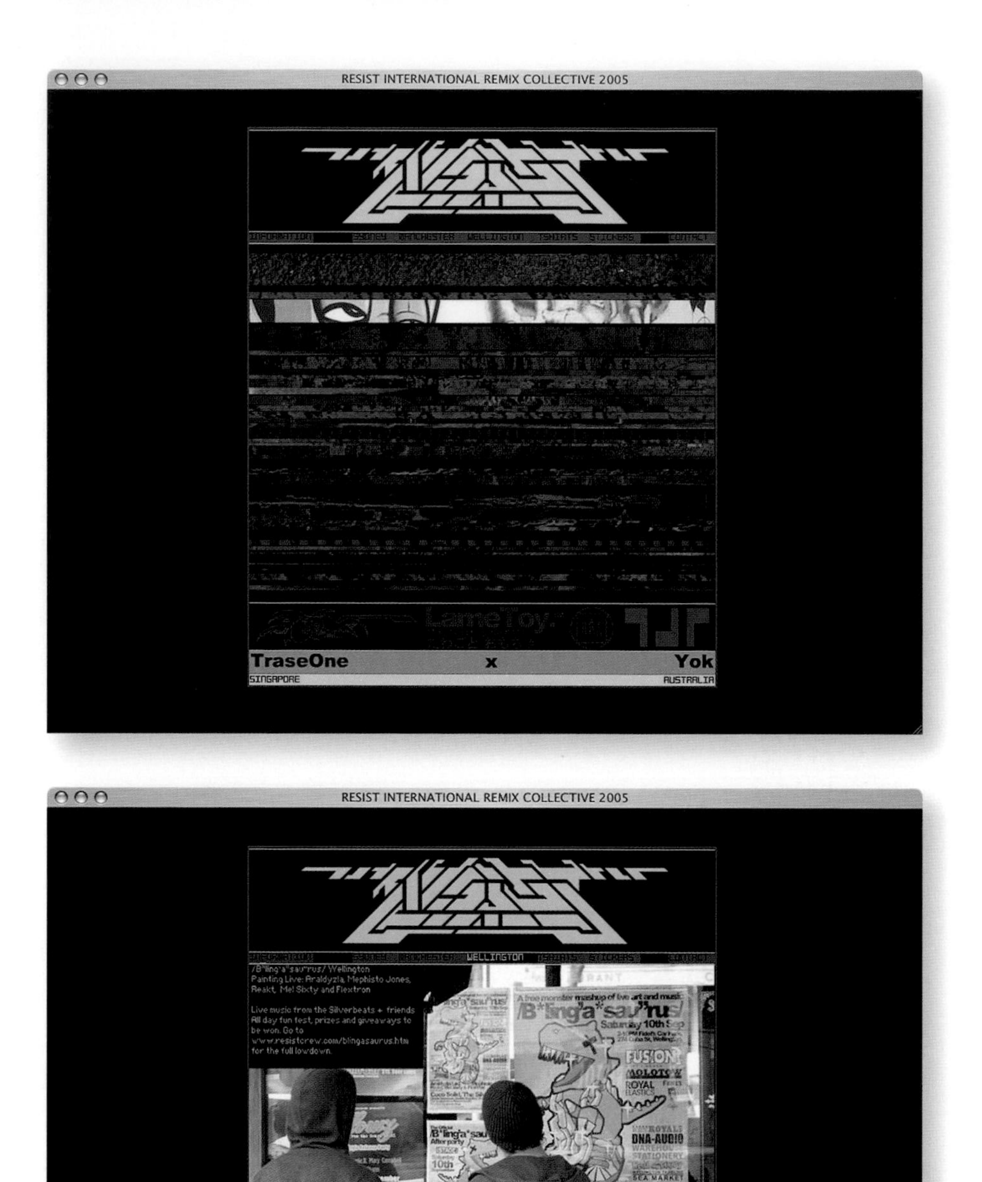

www.resistcrew.com
D: tom painter
A: tdpstudio **M:** info@tdpdesign.com

::: cleanoceanproject :::

There's no need to explain the irreversible impact pollution has on our environment. Unfortunately, it's very obvious. But there is definitely a need for action. And this change of attitude has to start at home, not only at the beach. The Cleanoceanproject lives this idea. And you're welcome to help. All it needs is a decision. <click para continuar>

www.CLEANOCEANPROJECT.org

<skip intro>

::: cleanoceanproject :::

04.12.2005 v
13.03.2005
27.11.2004
25.09.2004
05.09.2004
29.08.2004
06.06.2004
25.04.2004
30.11.2003
16.11.2003

beach clean up at the still virgen north shore of fuerteventura, aprox. 100 big 100 liter bags and 2 tons of big items!! many thanks to all people helping us out that day...

news
events
friends of cop
ocean care clothes
links
contact
press
newsletter

more pictures >

www.CLEANOCEANPROJECT.org

<home>

www.cleanoceanproject.org

D: rafaela stattmiller

A: www.oceano-digital.com **M:** info@oceano-digital.com

Van Abbemuseum

education

vanabbemuseum

exhibitions
collection

opening hours
how to find us

building
restaurant

education
activities
library

museum shop
publications

promotors
friends

newsletter
contact
links

- information in the museum
- infotexts
- novel
- El Lissitzky site
- [activities]

Education

The Education and Interpretation Department offers a wide range of activities to match the tastes of a diverse museum audience. The museum has special programmes for schools and its own courses for adults and children. These are all in Dutch.

Various types of guided tours are offered, including an architectural tour of the new building and a tour of masterpieces in the collection. For groups, guided tours are offered in Dutch, French, German and English. Click Guided Tours for more information.

The Getty Research Institute has produced an excellent website presenting the life and work of the artist El Lissitzky. Together with the Getty Research Institute, the Van Abbemuseum has made a Dutch translation of the website. This can be accessed through the Dutch-language section of the Van Abbemuseum's website.

More information

For questions on special programs and guided tours, please contact the Education and Interpretation Department, PO Box 235, 5600 AE Eindhoven, the Netherlands, e-mail: educatie@vanabbemuseum.nl

www.vanabbemuseum.nl

D: bic multimedia

A: bic multimedia **M:** www.bicmultimedia.nl

www.camaranavarra.com

D: david alegria **C:** spi **P:** camara navarra

A: ken **M:** www.ken.es

fame.ifdep.pt

D: filipe cavaco, adriano esteves, a. r. gomes **C:** alexandre r. gomes

A: bürocratik **M:** alex@burocratik.com

Seeing is believing.ca

seeingis**believing**

using new technologies to change the world

Joey's BLOG: A video activist's diary from the ground in the Philippines.

Teachers' E-ZINE: Study guides for understanding human rights and new technologies.

SEE the film: Check out when the film "Seeing is Believing" is playing in your town.

video

Double bill in our video screening room. Explore the film online and recap the history of the handicam revolution.

CONTRIBUTE to Nakamata's campaign to reclaim ancestral lands in the Philippines.

WRITE a letter: Join our campaign to demand justice in Nakamata territory.

BUY THE FILM: Get your own VHS copy of "Seeing is Believing".

NEW DVD IN RELEASE!:

support fund

Joey Lozano — star of *Seeing is Believing* film — died on September 16, 2005. Friends and colleagues have created the Lozano Support Fund for his family...

Participate: Join our FORUM and read the transcript of the WEB CHAT.

PRESS KIT: Background information about the film, high-res photos and more.

NEW FEATURE: New technologies in the hands of indigenous people.

technology

Discover how new technologies are causing revolutions around the globe.

Produced by Necessary Illusions in association with CBCnewsworld and SRC/RDI

with the participation of THE CANADIAN INDEPENDENT FILM & VIDEO FUND

Canadä

We acknowledge the financial support of the Government of Canada through the Human Rights Program, a program of the Department of Canadian Heritage.

Nous reconnaissons l'appui financier du gouvernement du Canada par le bias du Programme des droits de la personne, un programme de Patrimoine canadien.

Seeing is believing: Indigenous/new Tech

seeingis**believing** episode 1: autumn 2002

video | campaign | technology

indigenous/new tech

- GPS mapping: Risking lives
- The news source of Indian Country
- Tracking moose with GPS
- Red indgena wires Latin America
- Reznet fills journalistic void
- The battle over maps and names
- Native technology: A two-way street
- New tech: A matter of survival

When New Technologies are powered by Indigenous knowledge, the results can be amazing.

In this special collection of stories, we focus on how Indigenous Peoples around the world are picking up a multitude of new technologies to defend their rights, and protect their communities. From GPS mapping in dangerous conditions in the Philippines, to giving voice to young Aboriginal journalists in North America.

Select any of the eight stories in the left sidebar, and begin exploring the possiblities.

technology

cell phone **indigenous/new tech**

teachers' e-zine | forum | chat | credits | about the film | press room | resources and links

www.seeingisbelieving.ca

D: eric smith **C:** christopher murtagh **P:** katerina cizek, sandra dametto

M: kcizek@yahoo.com

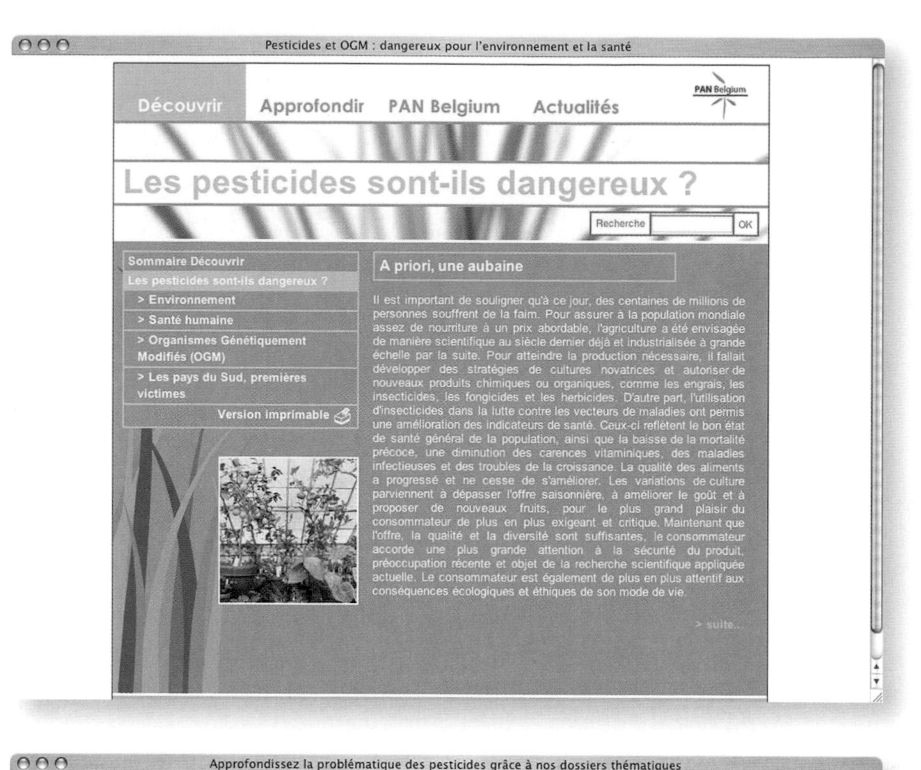

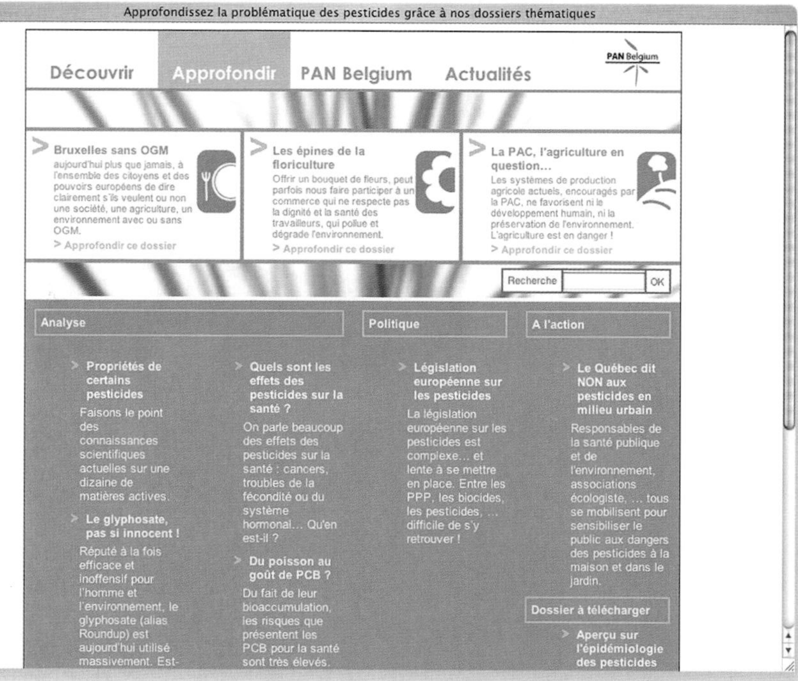

www.pan-belgium.be

D: vizzini romy **C:** serge de wever, j-f collier, d. küppers, r. vizzini **P:** pan belgium

M: info@romy-vizzini.be

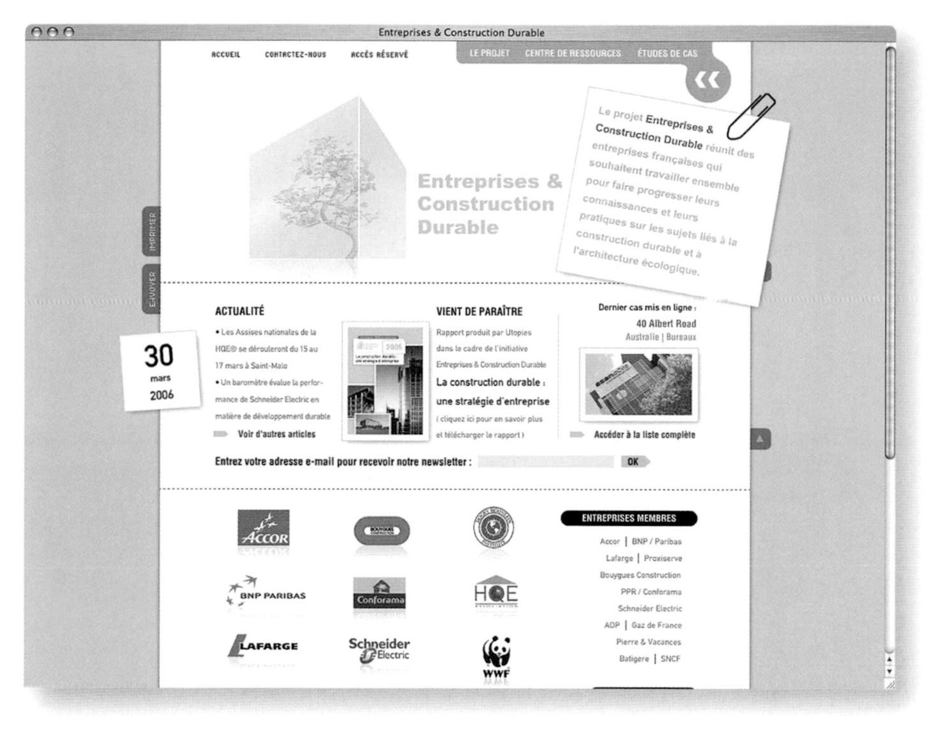

www.constructiondurable.com
D: mathieu badimon **P:** utopies
A: mathieu badimon **M:** contact@mathieu-badimon.com

www.helpeenroker.be

D: ilse pierard **C:** nascom **P:** carl de mey

A: snow **M:** www.snowbylgf.be

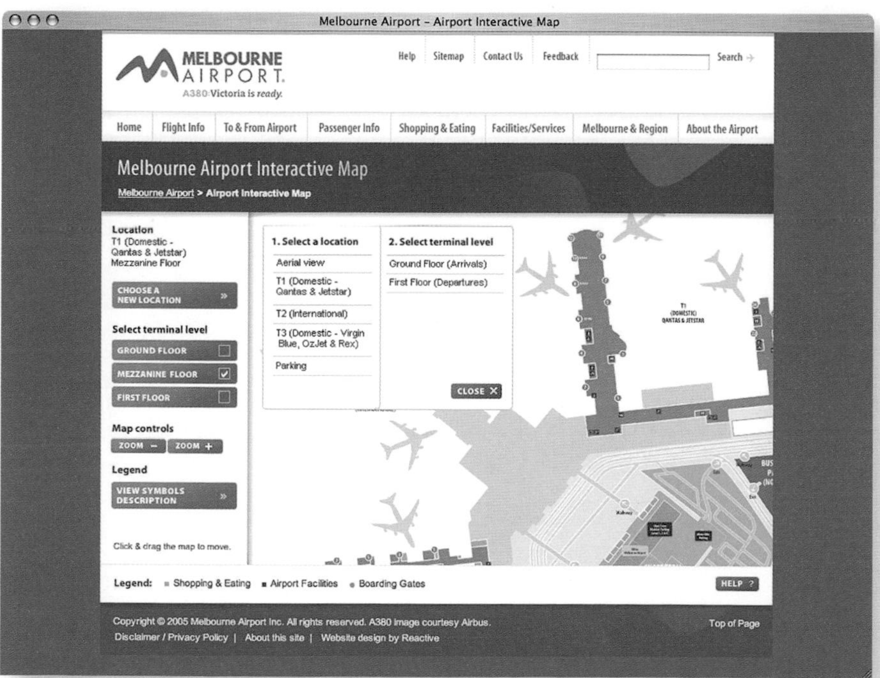

www.melbourne-airport.com.au

D: abby kelly **C:** ross richard, dan oxnam **P:** tim o'neill

A: reactive media **M:** chrisf@reactive.com

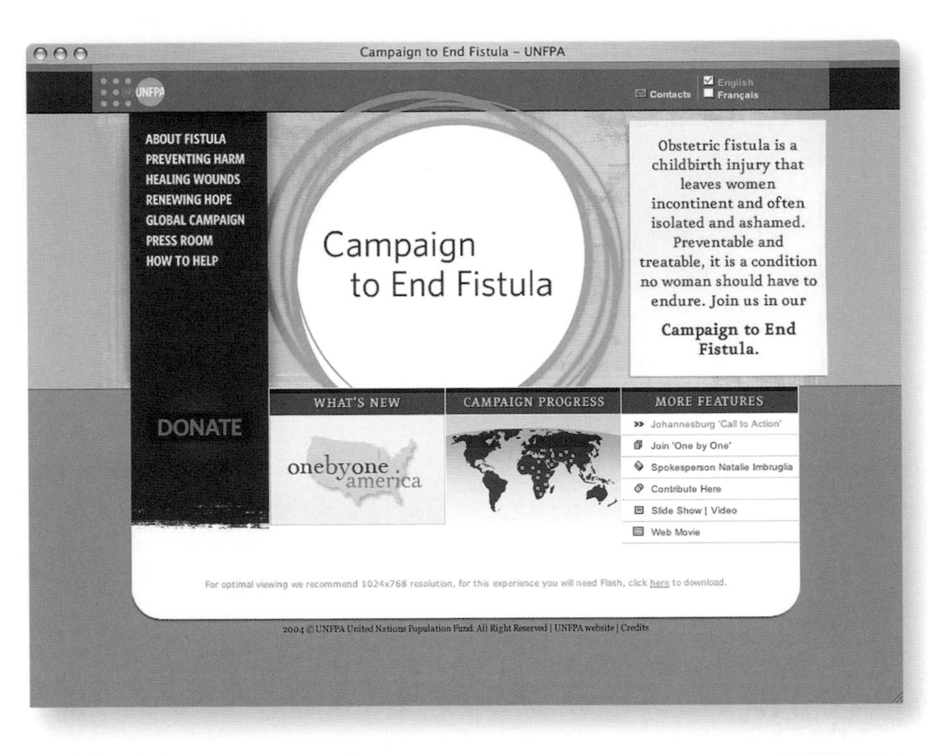

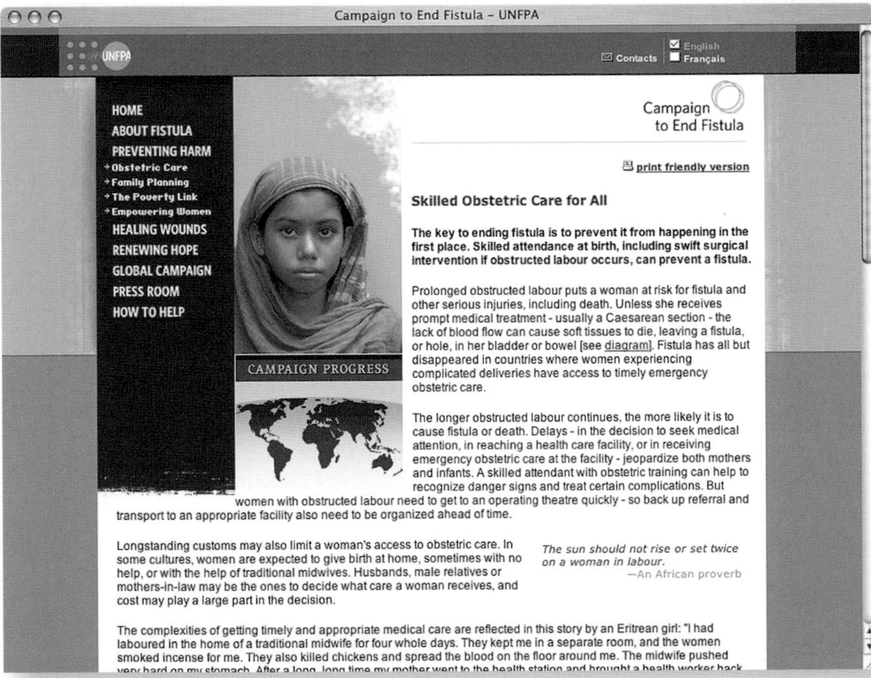

www.endfistula.org

D: allysson lucca **P:** micol zarb, saira stewart, alvaro serrano

A: unfpa **M:** www.unfpa.org

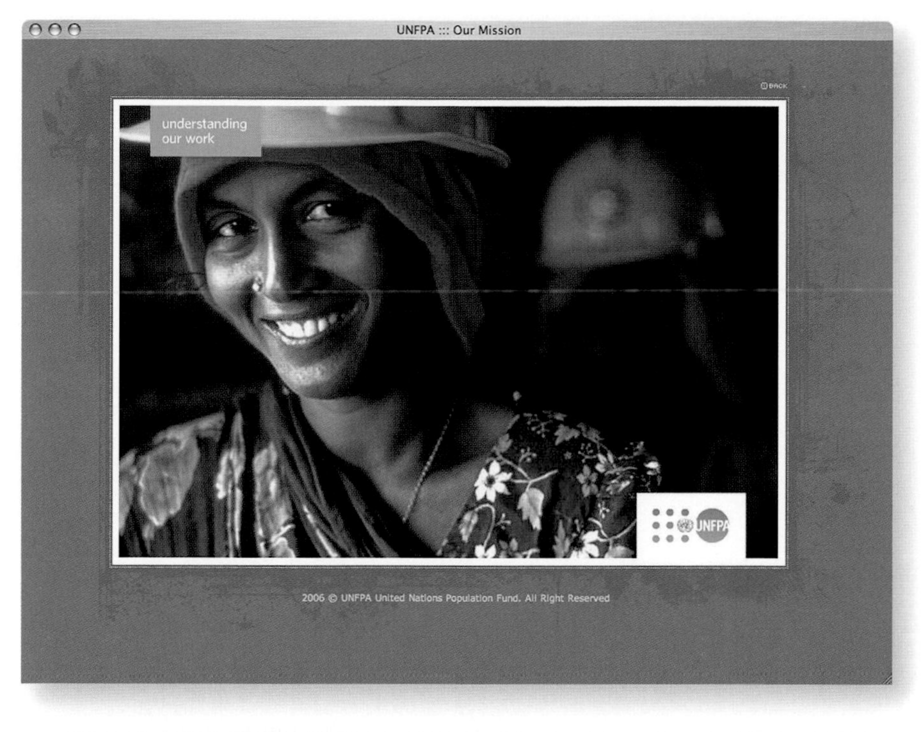

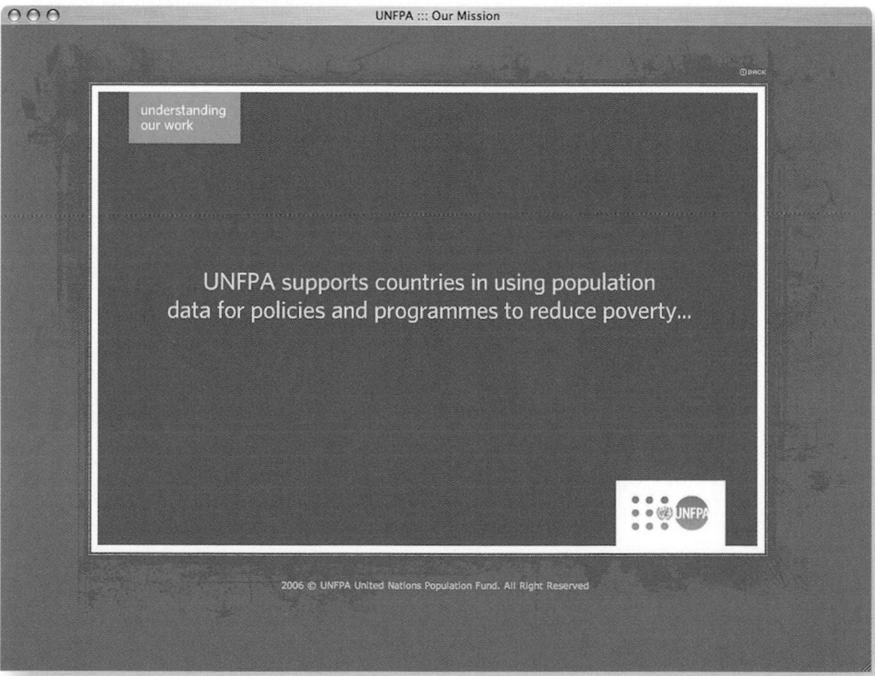

www.unfpa.org/ms

D: allysson lucca **P:** alvaro serrano

A: unfpa **M:** www.unfpa.org

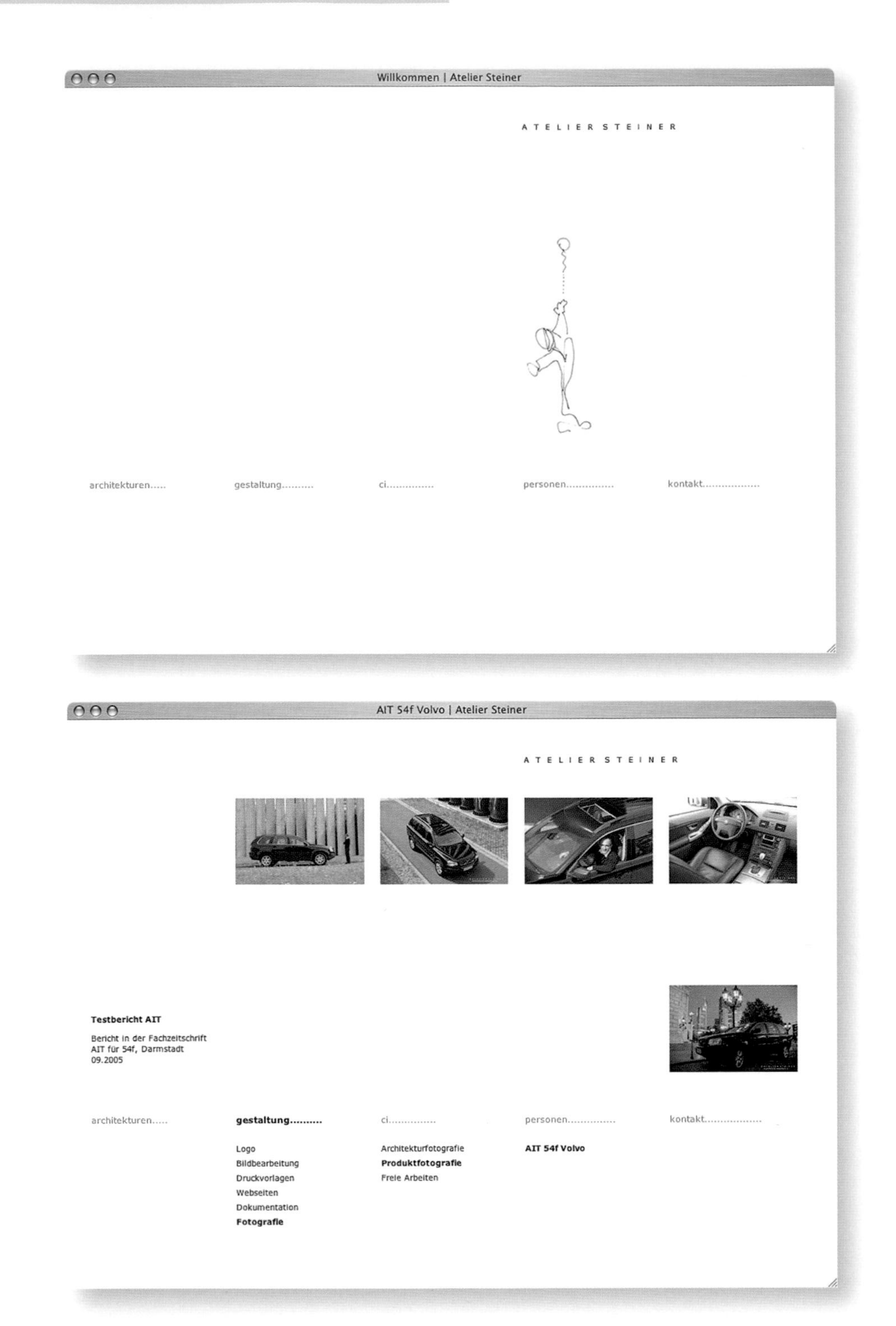

www.ateliersteiner.de

D: patrick steiner **C:** sebastian petters

A: 4wd media **M:** kontakt@4wdmedia.de

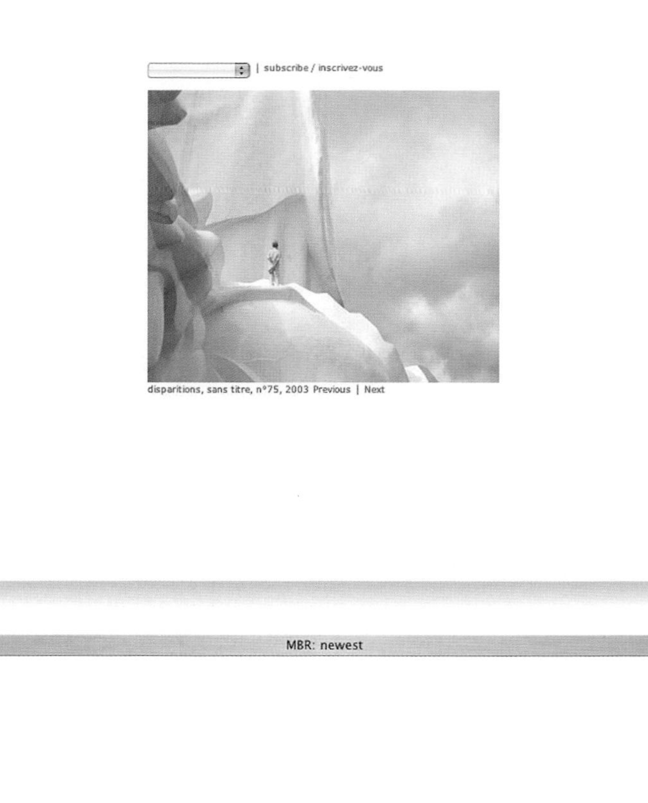

www.monsieurmathieu.com

D: mathieu bernard-reymond

M: info@monsieurmathieu.com

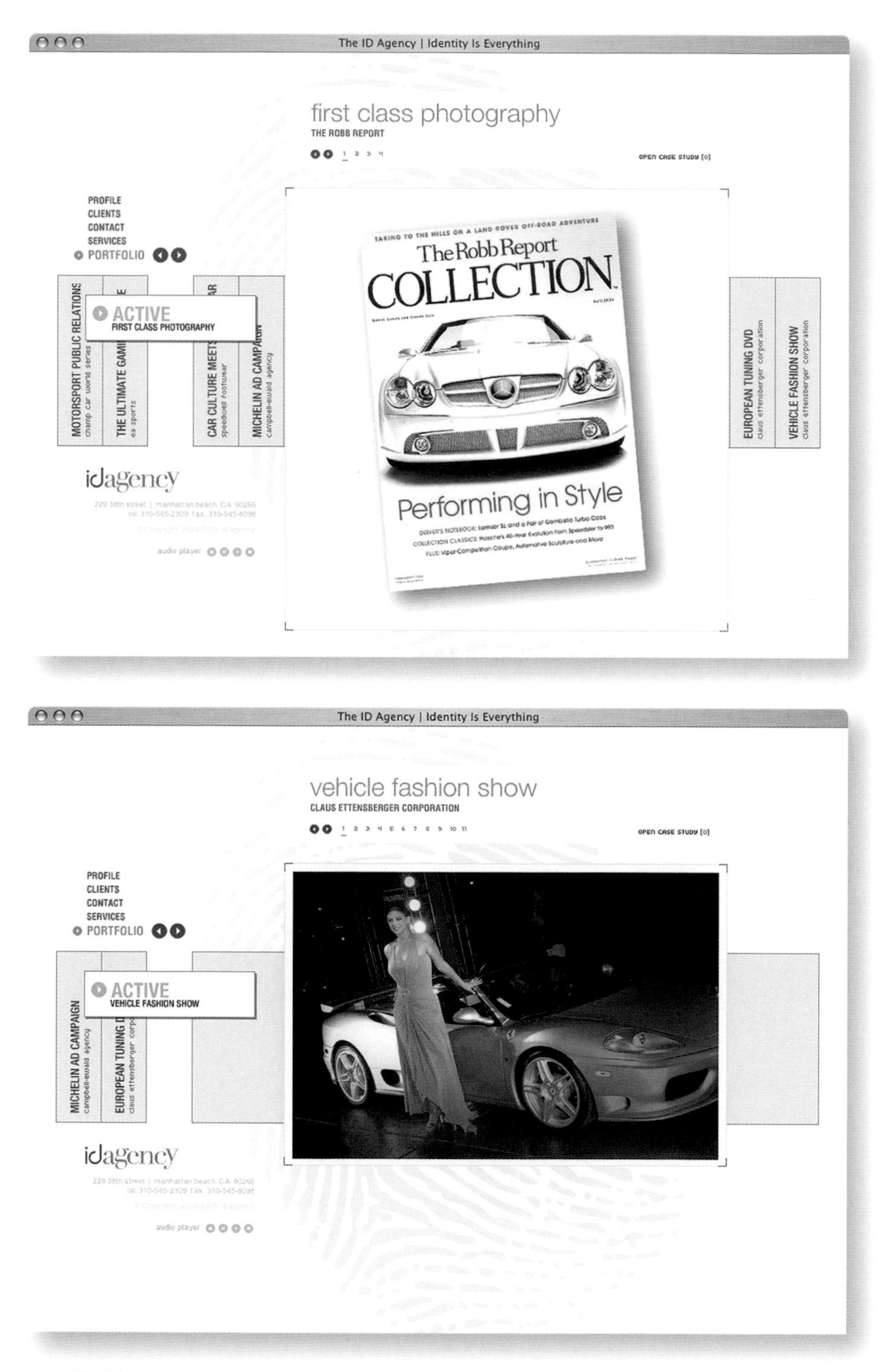

www.theidagency.com
D: greg huntoon **C:** jesse white-cinis **P:** greg huntoon
A: go farm **M:** www.gofarm.la

somemightsay.at

SIGURD BUCHBERGER
Neuhauserweg 29
4040 Linz
Austria

Wedekind
Wedekind Opiates Presentation
Chelsea, Vienna

somemightsay.at

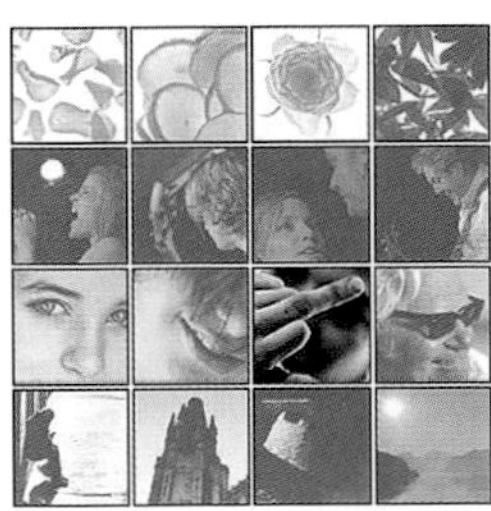

SIGURD BUCHBERGER
Neuhauserweg 29
4040 Linz
Austria

www.somemightsay.at

D: sigurd buchberger

A: webapplikationen.at M: sigurd@somemightsay.at

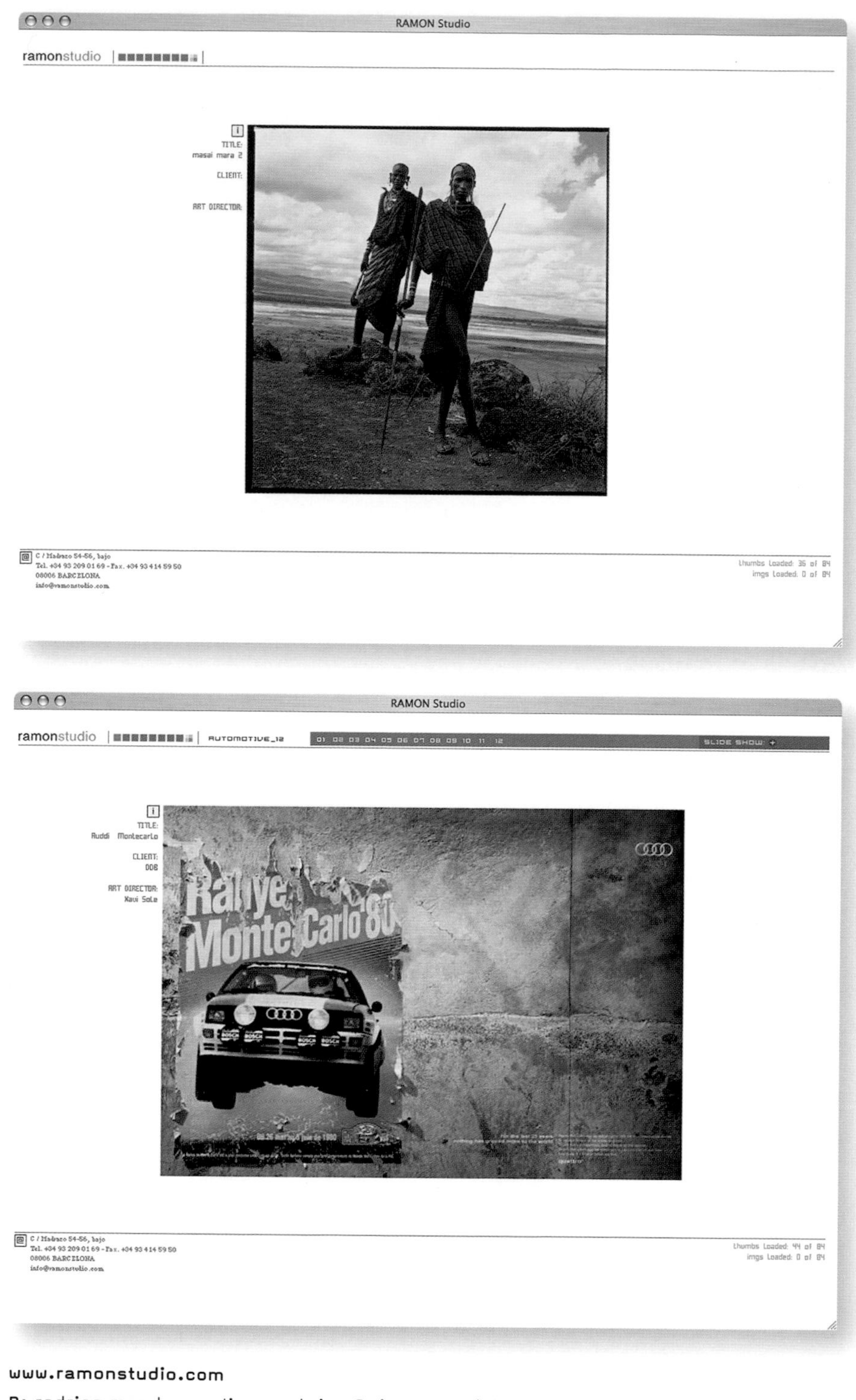

www.ramonstudio.com

D: rodrigo mendoza, eliana sobrino C: jorge agudelo P: s3design-studio

A: s3design-studio.com M: s3@s3design-studio.com

www.znyata.com
D: artur vakarov
M: sm@adliga.com

www.maaske.de

D: karolin maaske **C:** marc hämmerle **P:** karolin maaske, karsten maaske

A: ostkinder.de **M:** karo@ostkinder.de

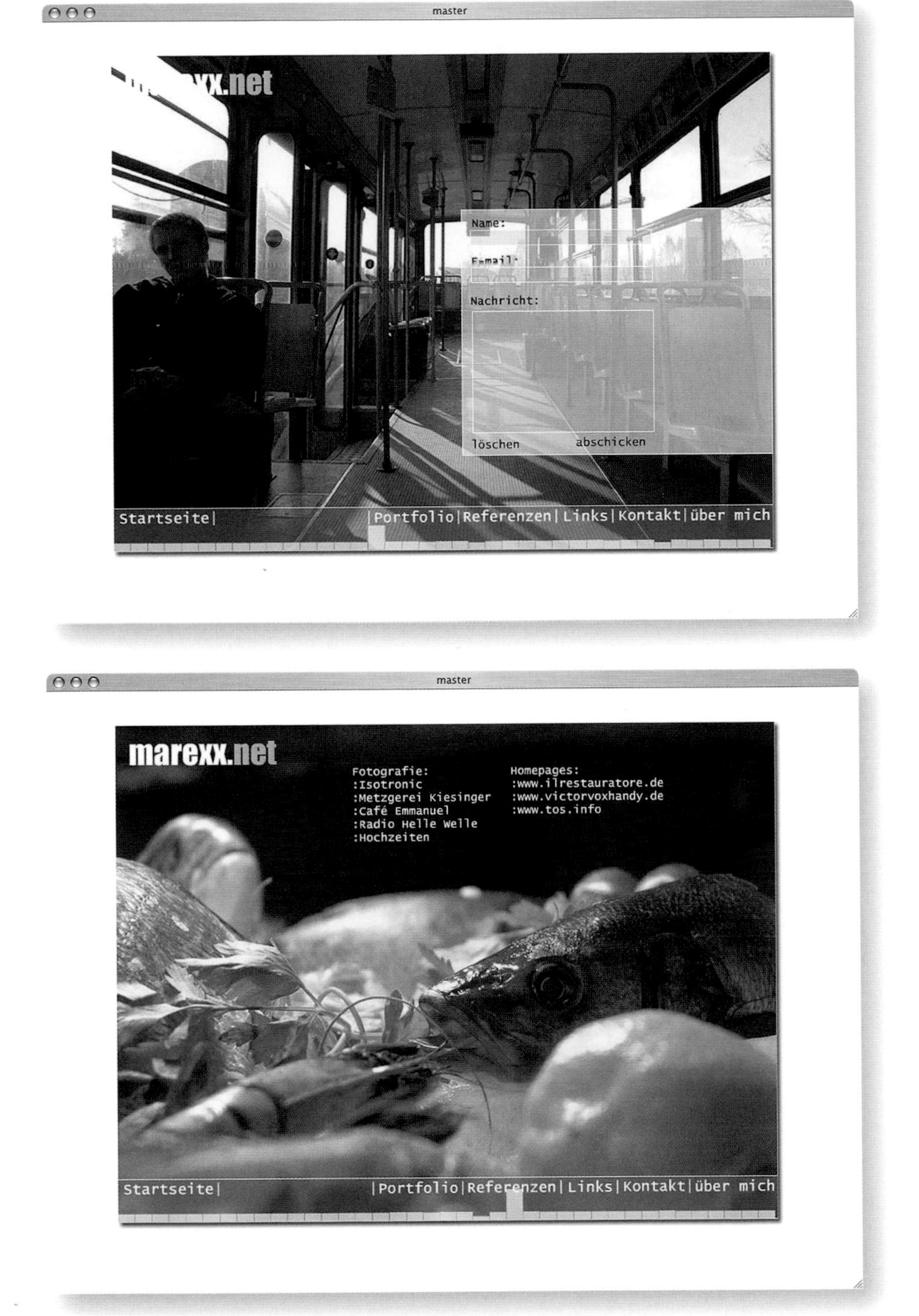

www.marexx.net

D: marek böttcher

A: marexx.net **M:** info@marexx.net

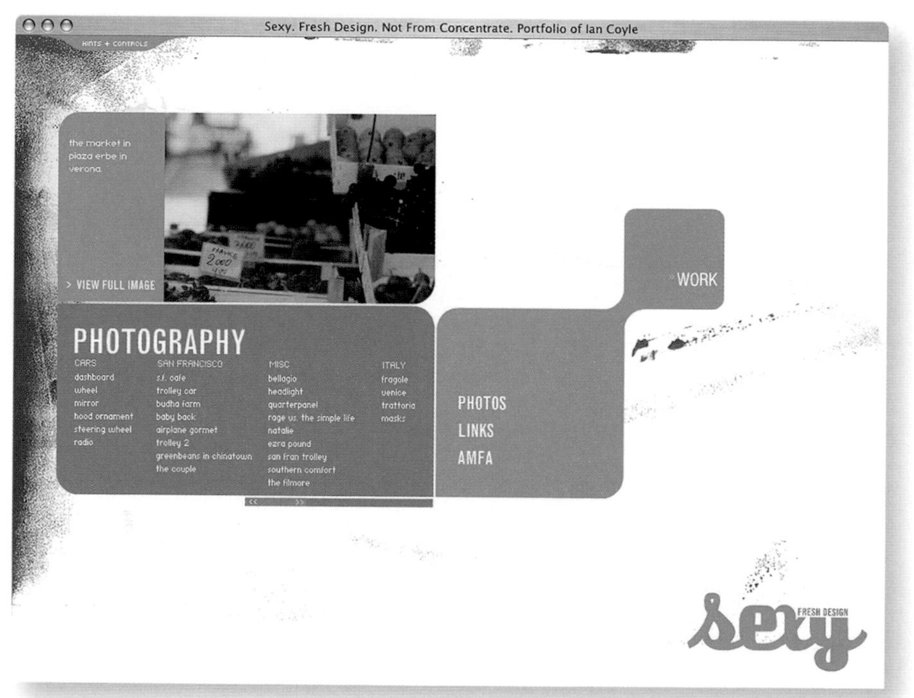

www.hello-sexy.com

D: ian coyle

A: sexy **M:** www.hello-sexy.com

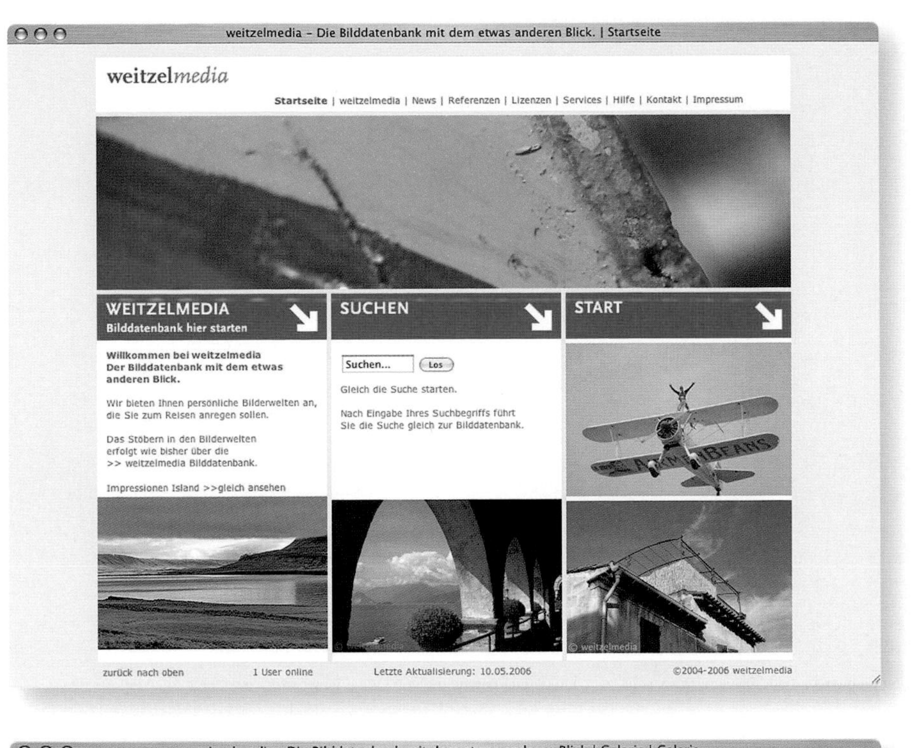

www.weitzelmedia.de

D: thomas weitzel

A: weitzeldesign **M:** info@weitzelmedia.de

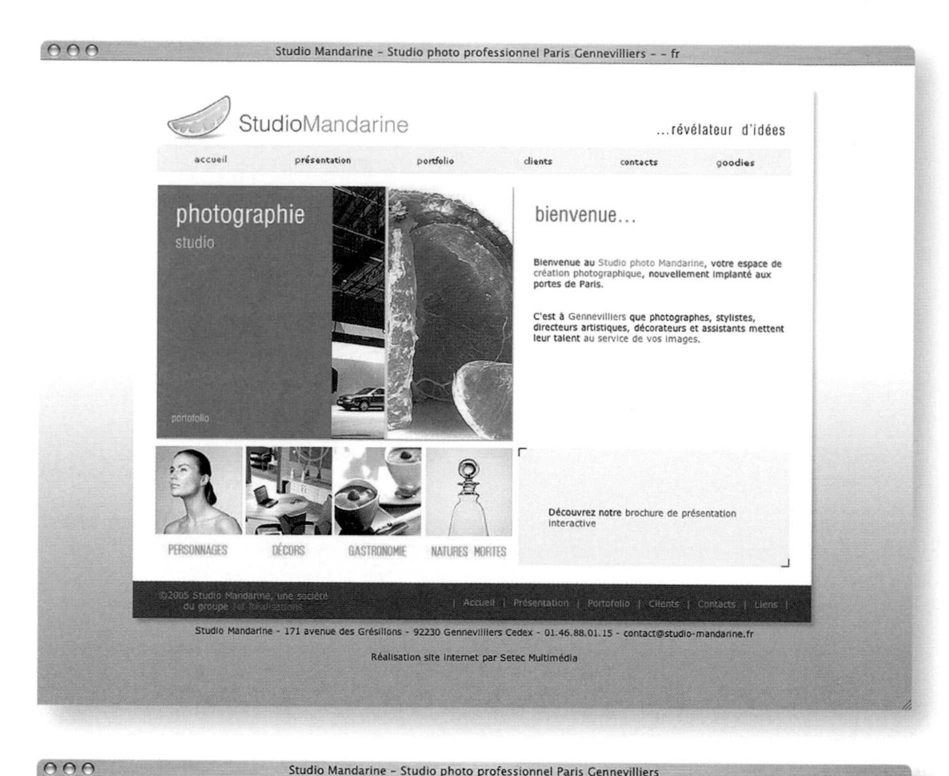

www.studio-mandarine.fr

D: aurélien durand **C:** benoît germond **P:** aurélien durand

A: setec multimédia **M:** aurelien@setec-multimedia.fr

Che Chapman | Photographer

Che Chapman | Photographer

CHE CHAPMAN PHOTOGRAPHER

Singles portfolio
AIDS Germany
River Boys
Saved from the Streets
AIDS Africa
Observing Sydney

Images | Contact

© 2006 | Julian Kommunikation

www.chechapman.com

D: karl hedner

A: julian kommunikation **M:** karl@julian.se

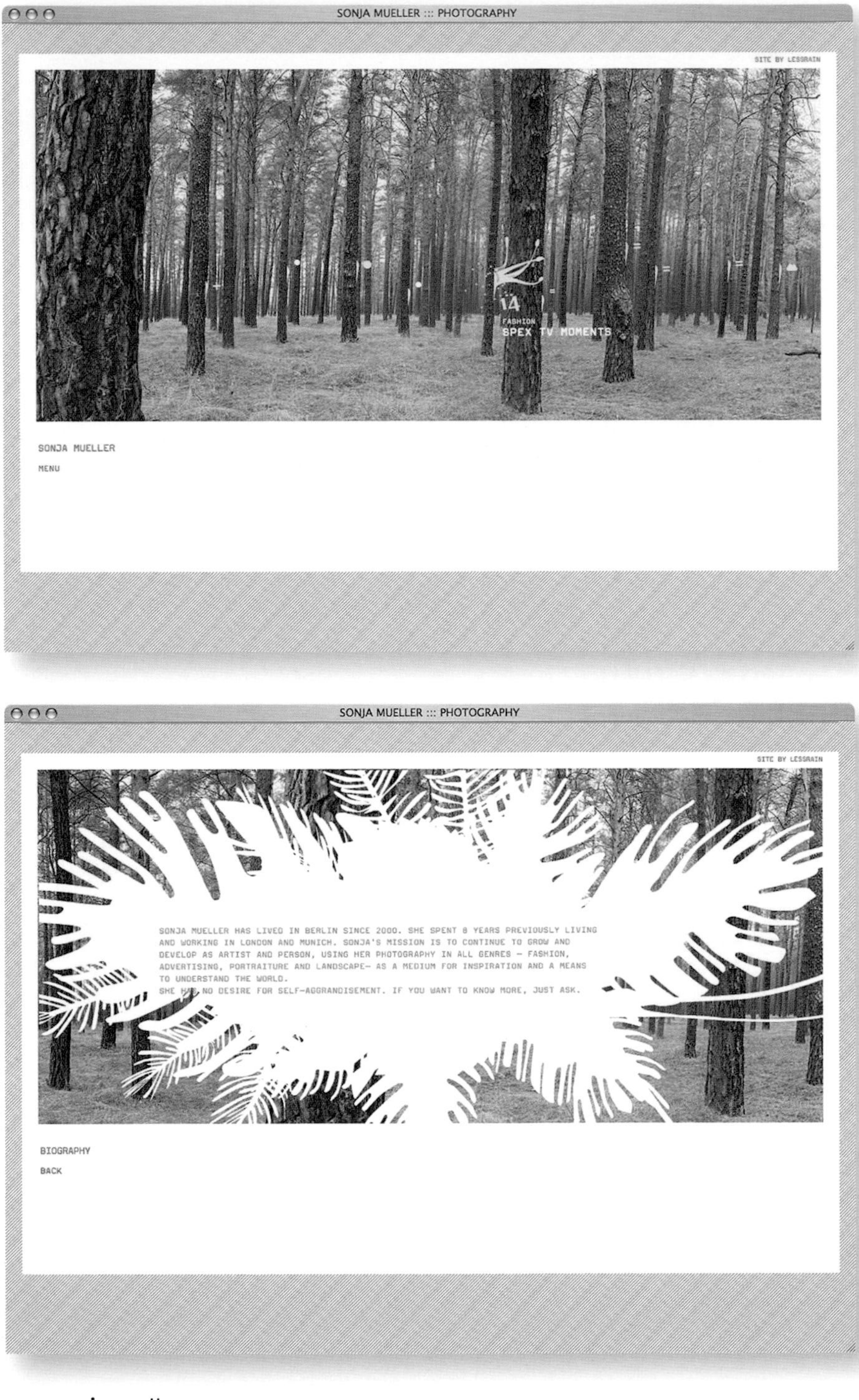

www.sonjamueller.org

D: matthias netzberger **C:** torsten haertel

A: less rain **M:** www.lessrain.com

www.kubikfoto.de

D: ole leifels, holger weber **C:** adrian runte

A: werberw **M:** info@kubikfoto.de

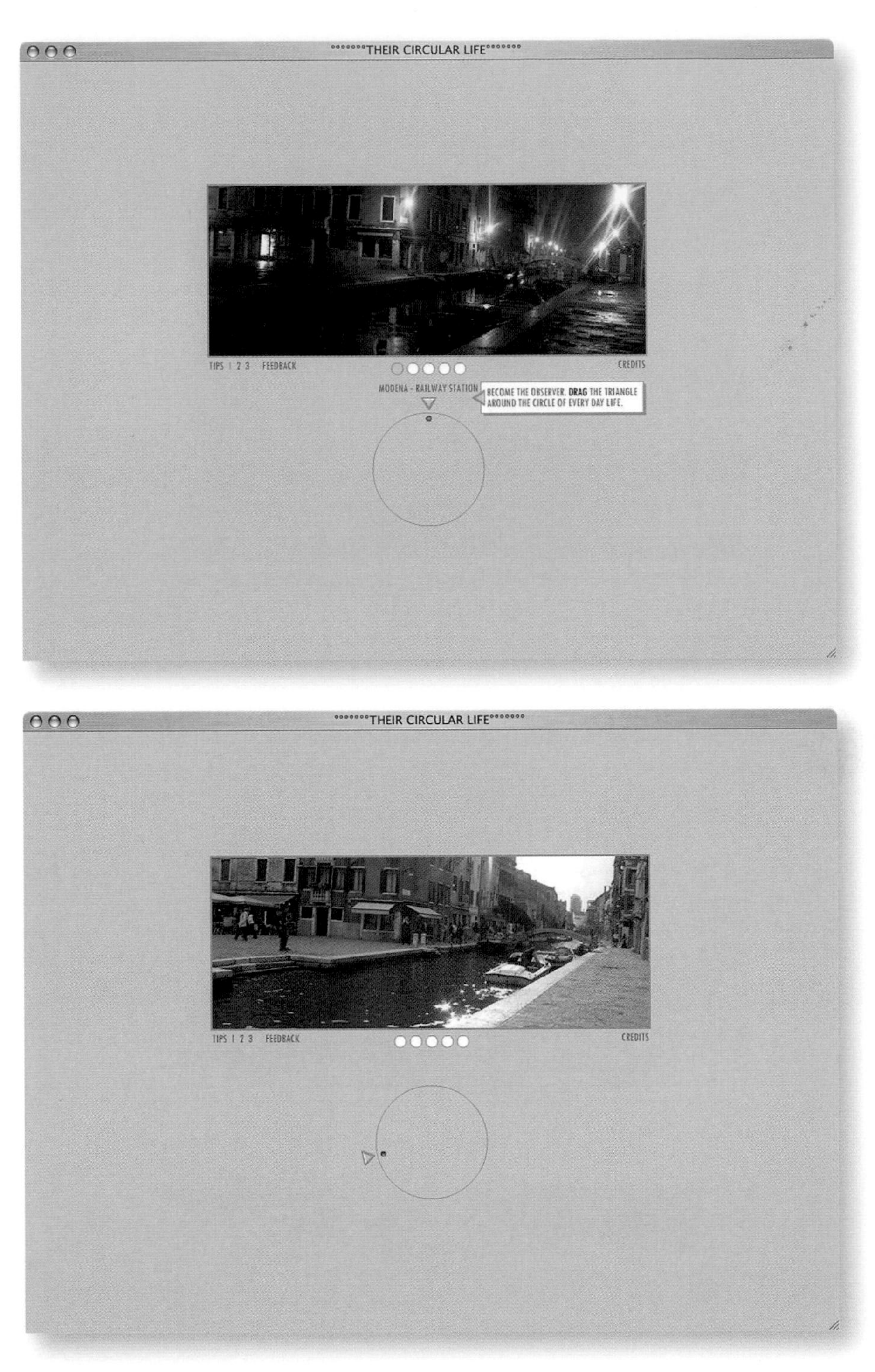

www.theircircularlife.it

D: lorenzo fonda **C:** davide terenzi

M: info@thericircularlife.it

www.jacquelinecallaghan.co.uk
D: alex atkinson P: rebecca keast
M: www.theconsult.com

www.virginieblachere.com

D: sandra leister, alexander schäfer **C:** dorothee bächle **P:** virginie blachère

A: 372dpi - design print internet **M:** www.372dpi.com

www.luisartus.com

D: eduardo de felipe

A: eduardo de felipe **M:** eduardo@elelec.com

www.levysheckler.com

D: matthew fordham **C:** matthew fordham **P:** marisa mckay

A: revolver creative **M:** www.revolvercreative.com

www.orange-project.com

D: jens franke

M: contact@jensfranke.com

www.electricgecko.de

D: malte müller

A: electricgecko* **M:** info@electricgecko.de

www.jesperludvigsen.dk

D: anders ojgaard

A: anders ojgaard kommunikation **M:** www.ojgaard.dk

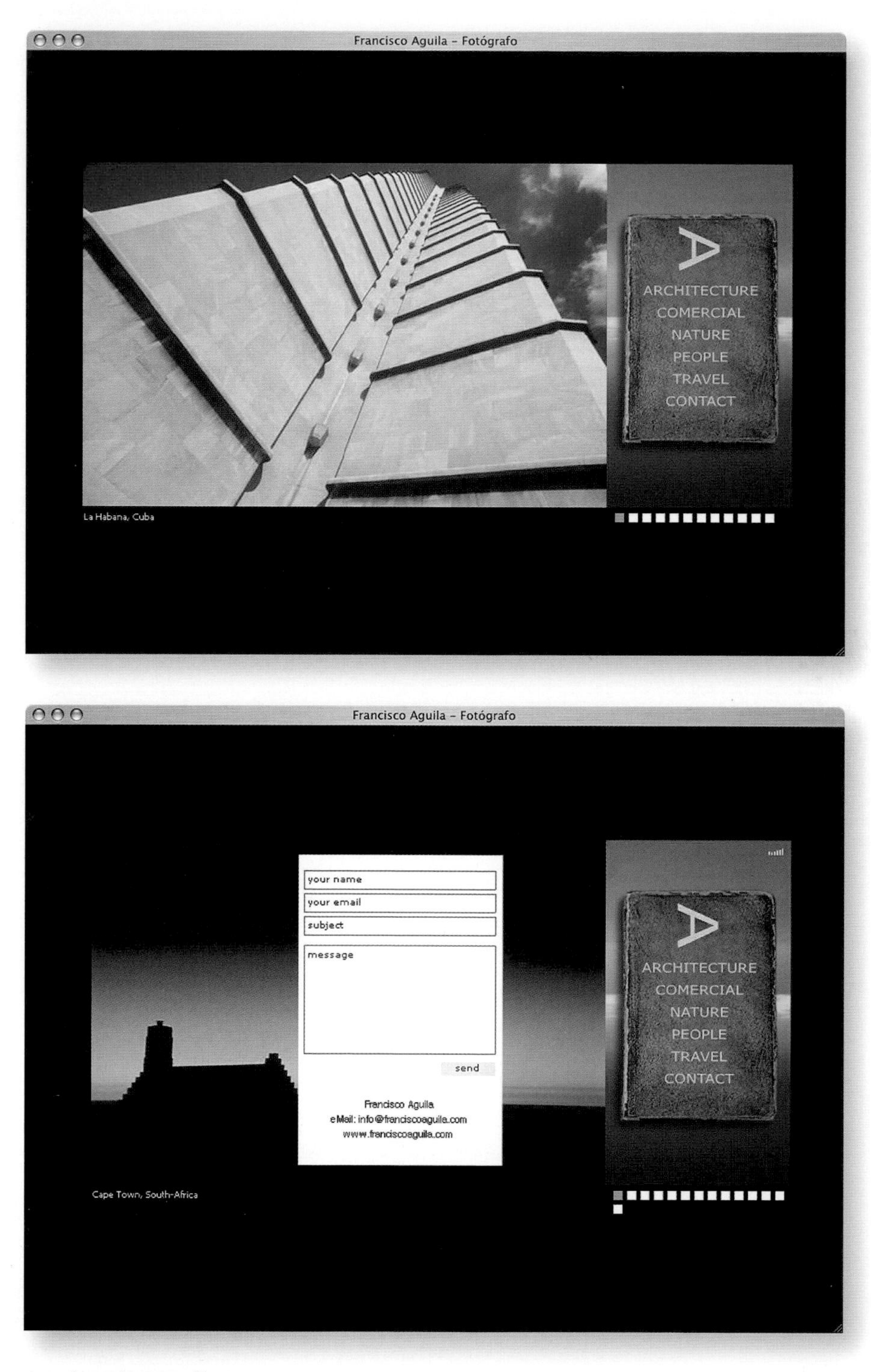

www.franciscoaguila.com

D: felipe alvarado

A: felipe alvarado **M:** felipealvarado@manquehue.net

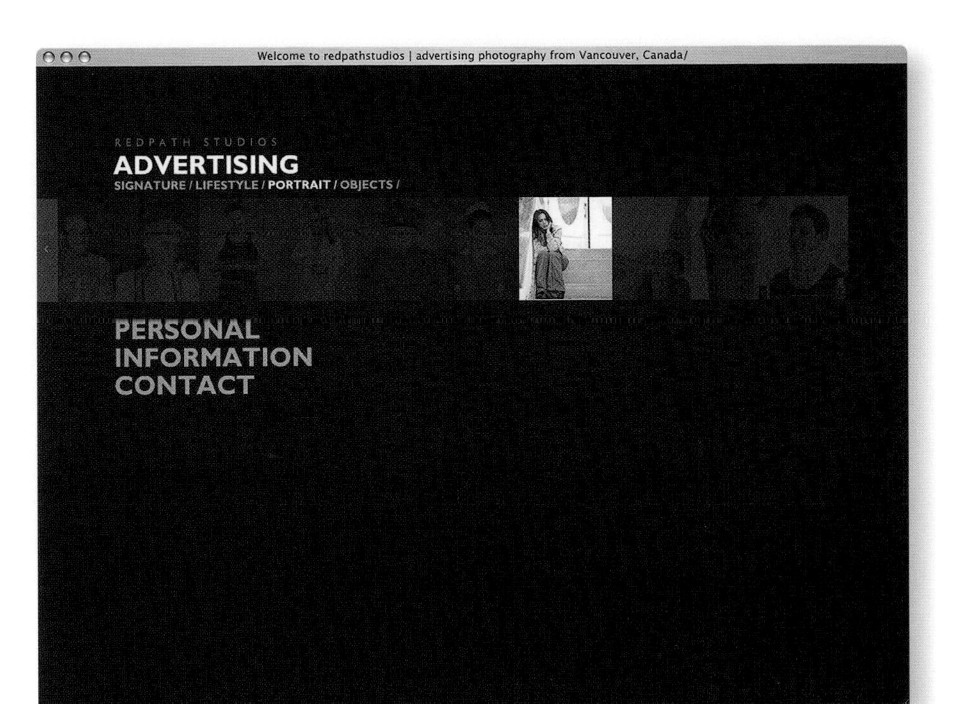

Welcome to redpathstudios | advertising photography from Vancouver, Canada/

INFORMATION

BIOGRAPHY / CLIENTS / AGENCIES

ANTHONY WEAVES A UNIQUE PERSONALITY DIRECTLY INTO HIS PHOTOGRAPHY. BORN AND RAISED IN BRITISH COLUMBIA, ANTHONY HAS SPENT HIS ENTIRE LIFE ENJOYING EVERYTHING THE WEST COAST HAS TO OFFER. BE IT SURFING THE AWESOME COASTLINE FROM MEXICO TO BRITISH COLUMBIA, OR SAVOURING THE TREASURES OF URBAN CULTURE IN BETWEEN, ANTHONY TRANSLATES HIS EXPERIENCES AND OBSERVATIONS INTO HIS PHOTOGRAPHY.

HE HAS BEEN HONING HIS VISION FOR TWENTY YEARS, WORKING PRIMARILY WITH ADVERTISING CLIENTELE, AS WELL AS SHOOTING PERSONAL PROJECTS. HIS WORK HAS WON MANY NATIONAL AND INTERNATIONAL AWARDS. HIS SURFING STYLE IS THE ENVY OF MANY.

CONTACT

www.redpathstudios.com
D: group94 **P:** redpath studios
M: info@group94.com

francisdreis.com
D: ozzy benn
A: toxic design **M:** toxicdesign.com

www.gingerstudiobcn.com

D: andrea llorca

A: macedònia studio! **M:** info@macedonia-studio.com

normajeanmarkus.com

D: curtis mcclain

A: sofierce.com **M:** curtis@sofierce.com

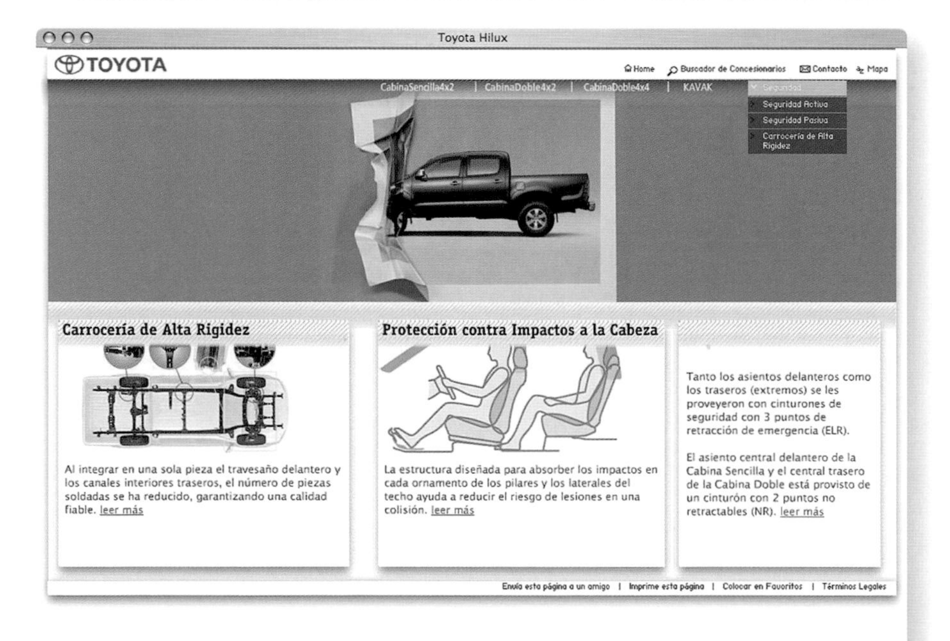

www.hilux.com.ve

D: ciro urdaneta **C:** luis giraldez, rodolfo sauce **P:** ciro urdaneta

A: image & web solution **M:** curdaneta@iws.com.ve

demo.fb.se/e/ikea/dreamkitchen/site/default.html

D: forsman & bodenfors

M: info@fb.se

www.tivoliaudiospain.com
D: frame girona
A: frame girona **M:** www.frame-works.net

www.helpjoe.be

D: stephane leborgne, kristof saelen **C:** sakri rosenstrom, patrik fagard

A: nascom **M:** www.nascom.be

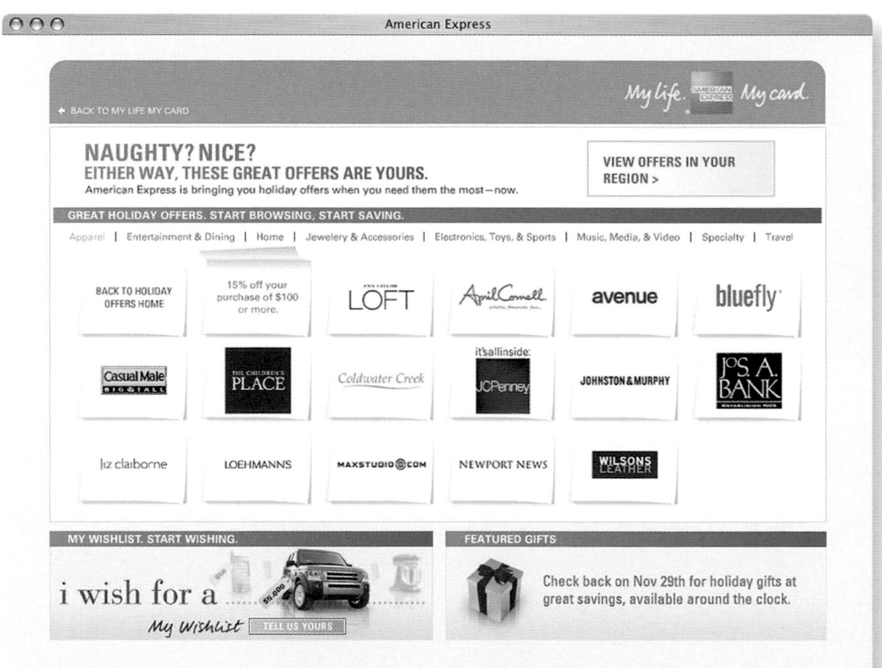

www.freedominteractivedesign.com/demos/digitas/index.htm

D: digitas **C:** shea gonyo, josh ott **P:** mark ferdman

A: digitas **M:** info@freedominteractivedesign.com

www.dnb-mag.com

D: stefan schröder **C:** marco matthäus

A: pixelsinmotion **M:** marco@pixelsinmotion.de

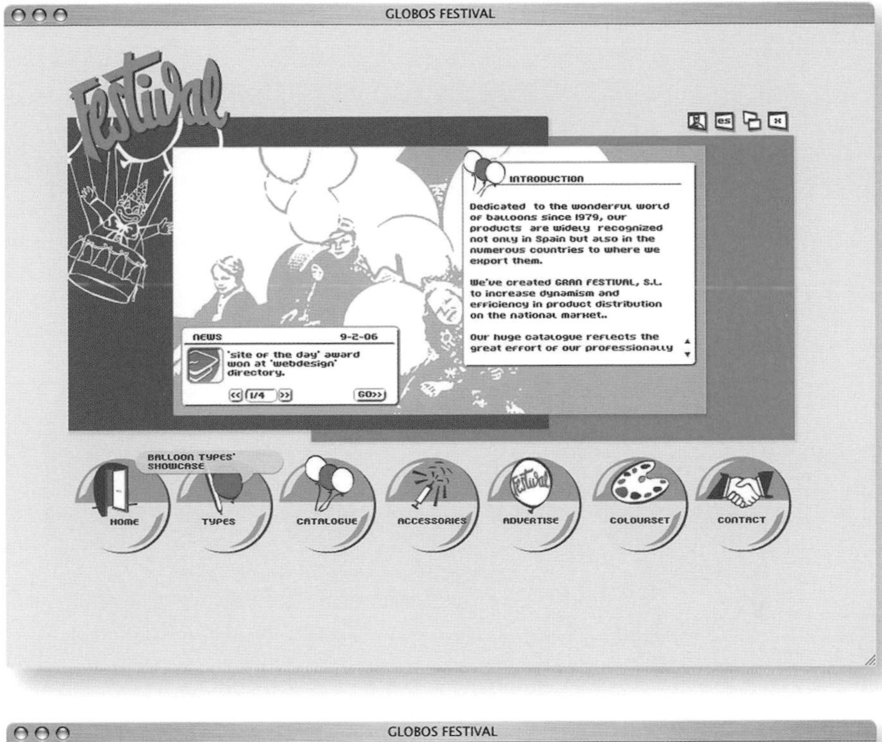

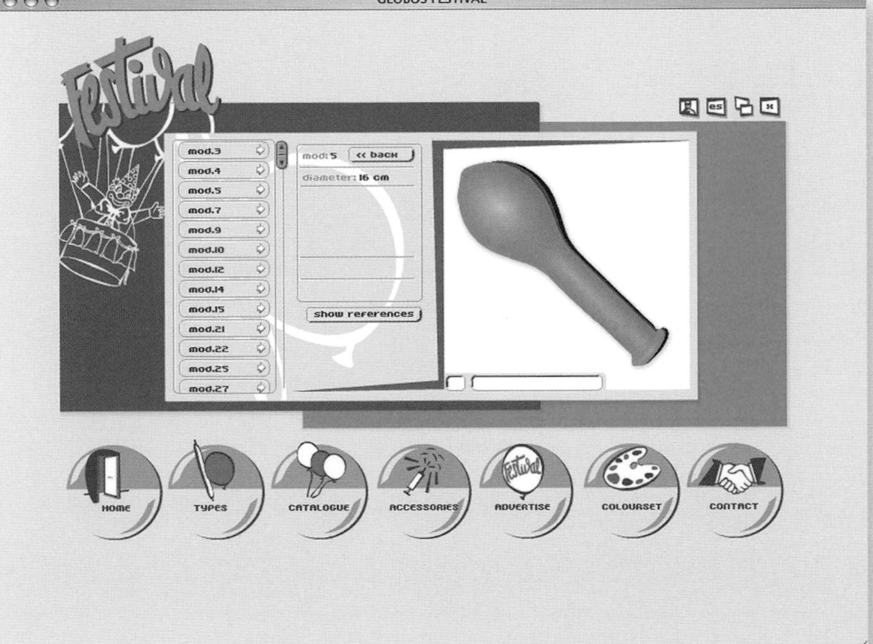

www.globosfestival.com

D: bibi gloaguen C: alberto álvarez

A: insane M: crash@insanelab.net

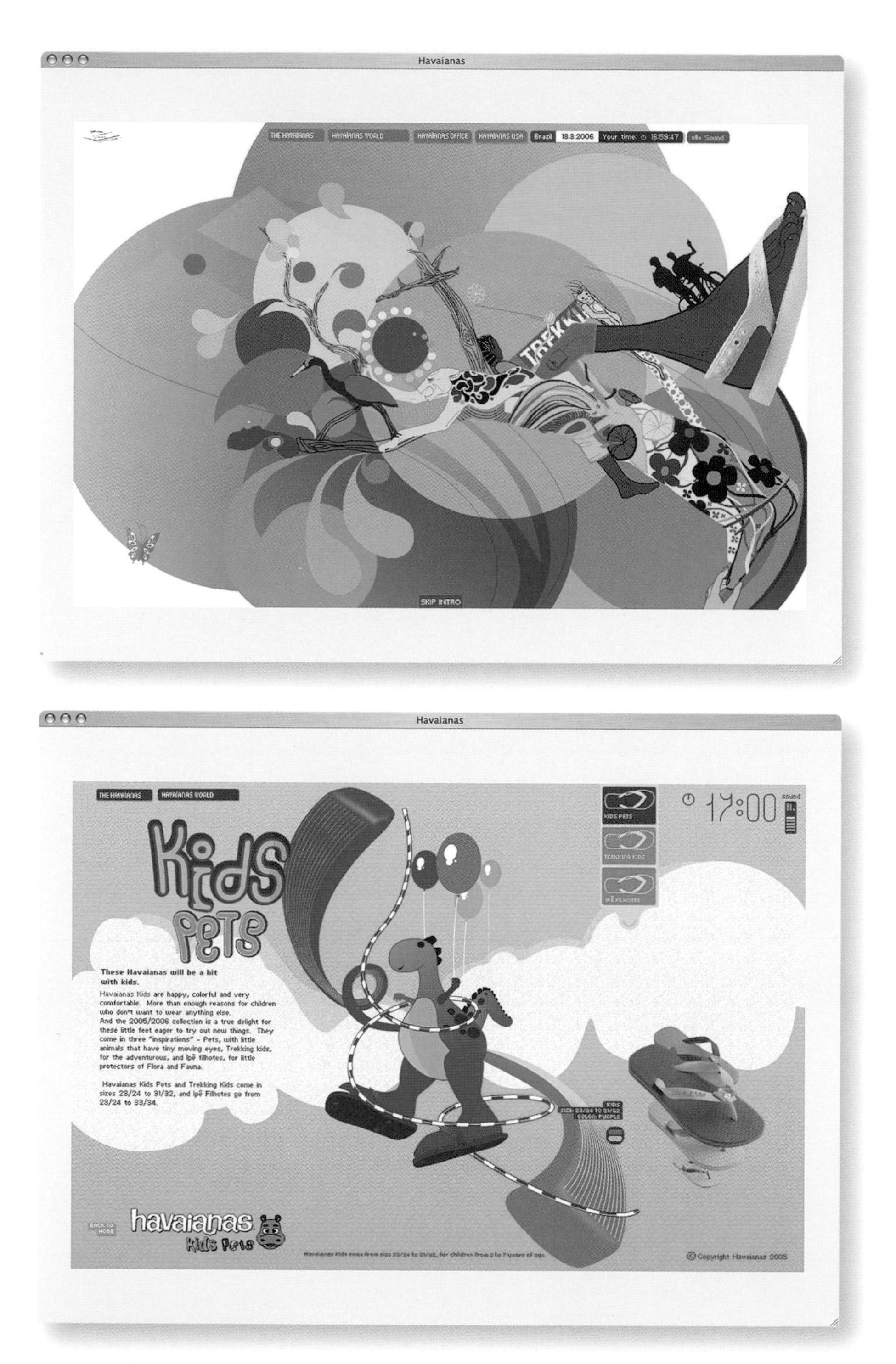

www.havaianas.com.br

D: adhemas batista **C:** flávio ramos **P:** ricardo almeida

A: almapbbdo **M:** www.almapbbdo.com.br

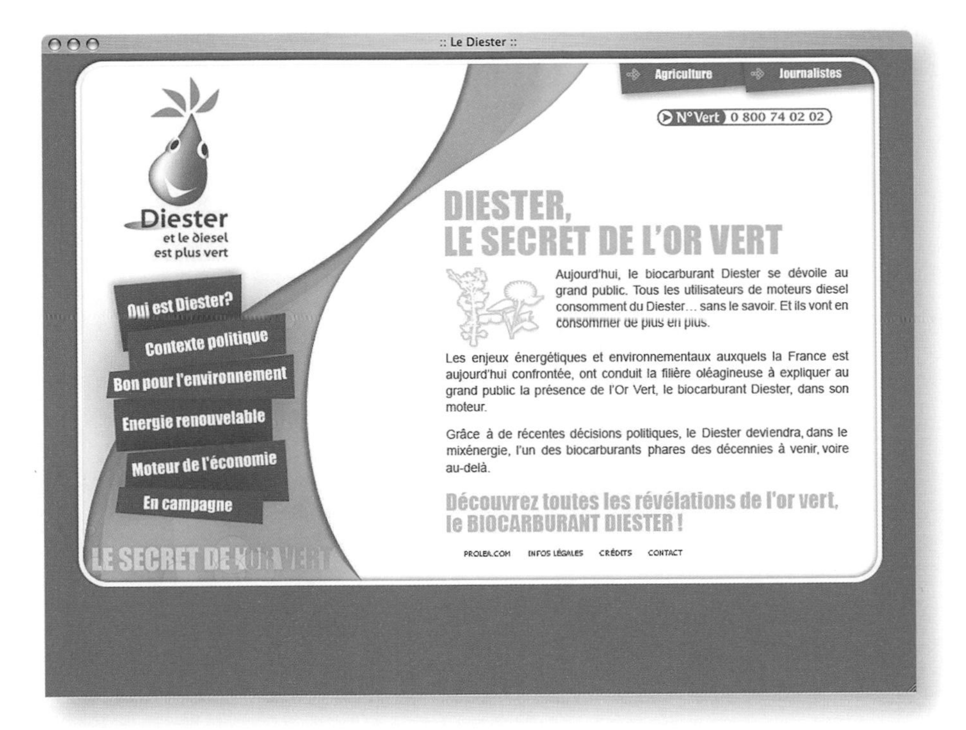

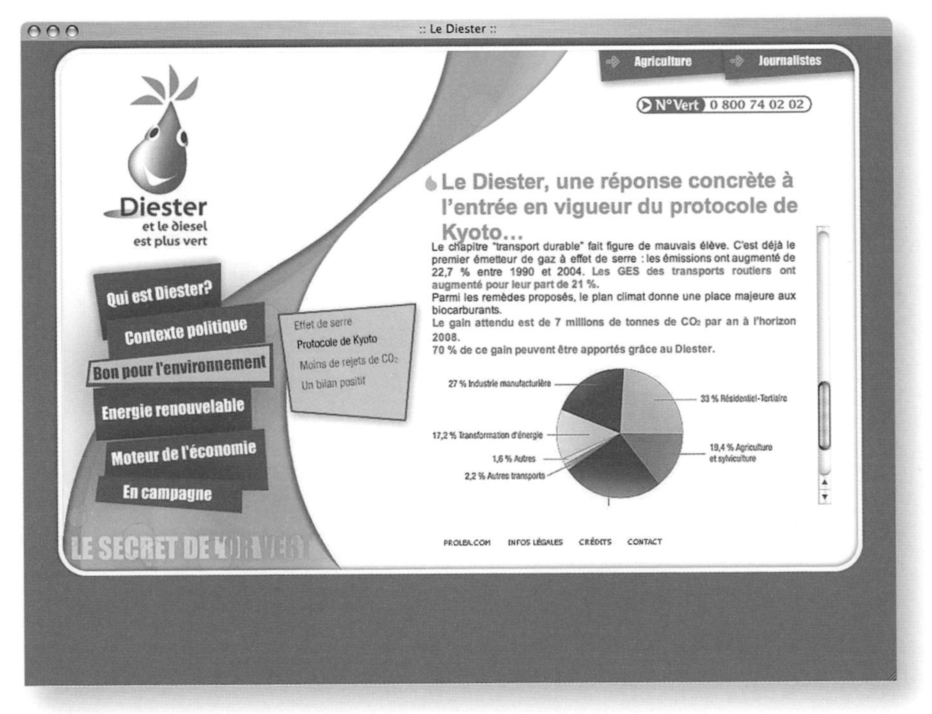

www.diester.fr

D: guillaume garnier

A: ligaris macluhan's M: contact@diester.fr

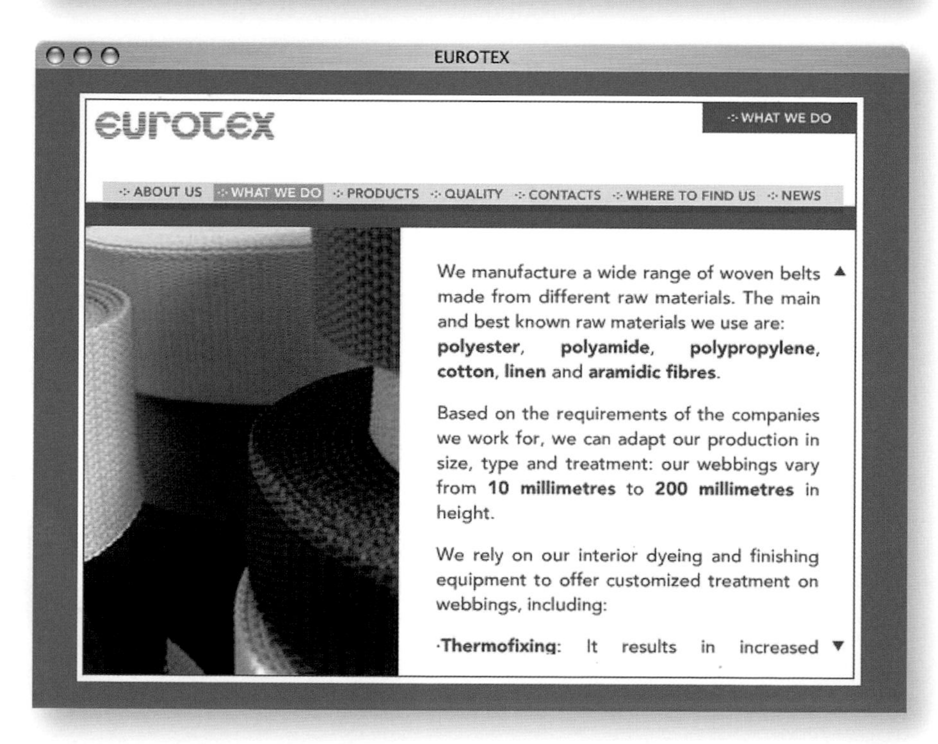

www.eurotexnastri.it

D: alessandro demicheli, nicola destefano

A: carsons&co advertising **M:** a.demicheli@carsons.it

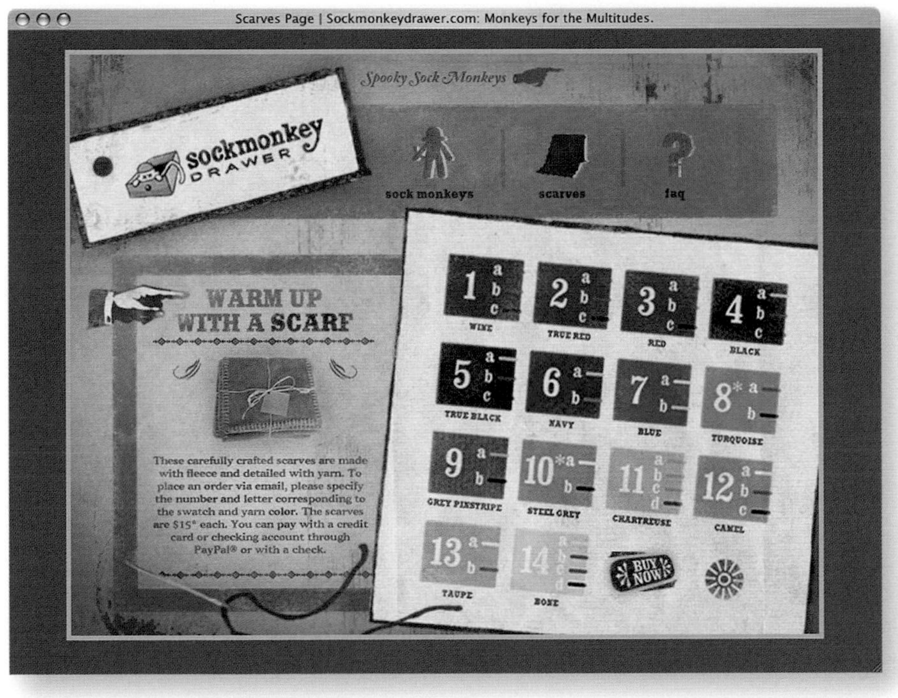

www.sockmonkeydrawer.com

D: kimlan cornell **C:** kimlan cornell, kevin cornell **P:** kimlan cornell

M: info@sockmonkeydrawer.com

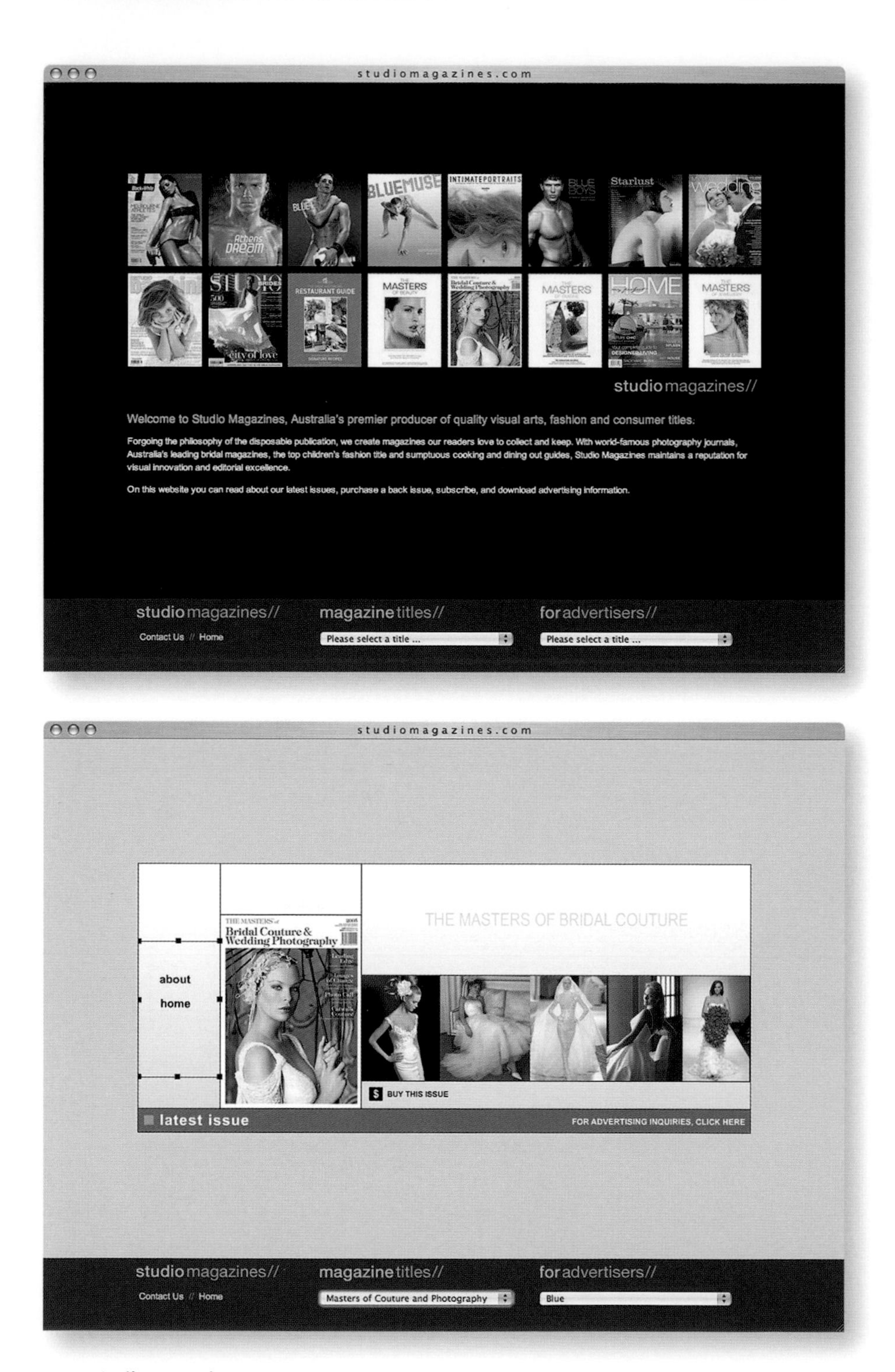

www.studiomagazines.com

D: daniel mcphee, marise watson **C:** daniel mcphee **P:** marise watson

A: soda creative **M:** marise@studio.com.au

www2.e-werk-stade.de

D: konstantin minster **C:** konstantin minster **P:** markus albrecht

A: city-map stade gmbh **M:** info@stade.city-map.de

www.vortrieb.com

D: andre berkmüller

A: berkmueller visuelle kommunikation **M:** www.berkmueller.de

www.freekmagazine.com

D: adolfo fernandez **C:** adolfo fernandez **P:** la mota ediciones s.l.

A: cerol diseño **M:** info@cerol.com

ANDREA JUNGWIRTH – Neue Medien

A N D R E A J U N G W I R T H
www.einfachgesagt.com

ZUR PERSON REFERENZEN KONTAKT IMPRESSUM | PREISÜBERSICHT

Neue Medien

Digitale Texte werden nicht gelesen sondern gescannt. Die LeserInnen überfliegen den Text, lesen zuerst Überschriften, Einleitung und Zwischenüberschriften und entscheiden dann, ob der Inhalt für sie relevant ist. Information muss zweckorientiert und leicht konsumierbar sein, der Text gut strukturiert.

Mein KnowHow
→ Struktur → Text → Bild → Style Guide

WEITEREMPFEHLEN
BY NIXDA + PARTNERS

Text
- Folder & Broschüren
- Neue Medien
- Vorträge & Workshops

Bild
lizenzfrei
- Individuelle Fotoserie
- Fotografie
- Foto-CDs (PopUp)
- Bildqualität

& mehr
- Ernährung
- Gesunde Küche

ANDREA JUNGWIRTH – Ernährung

A N D R E A J U N G W I R T H
www.einfachgesagt.com

ZUR PERSON REFERENZEN KONTAKT IMPRESSUM | PREISÜBERSICHT

Ernährung

"Frisch, bunt, abwechslungsreich und der Jahreszeit entsprechend, das ist gesunde Ernährung. Nehmen Sie sich Zeit zum Kochen und Genießen!"

Ökotrophologin Andrea Jungwirth

Mein KnowHow
→ Beratung und Vorträge
→ Hilfe zur Ernährungsumstellung
→ Personal nutrition guide

WEITEREMPFEHLEN
BY NIXDA + PARTNERS

Text
- Folder & Broschüren
- Neue Medien
- Vorträge & Workshops

Bild
lizenzfrei
- Individuelle Fotoserie
- Fotografie
- Foto-CDs (PopUp)
- Bildqualität

& mehr
- Ernährung
- Gesunde Küche

www.einfachgesagt.com
D: jürgen oberguggenberger
A: nixda + partners **M:** juergen@nixda.at

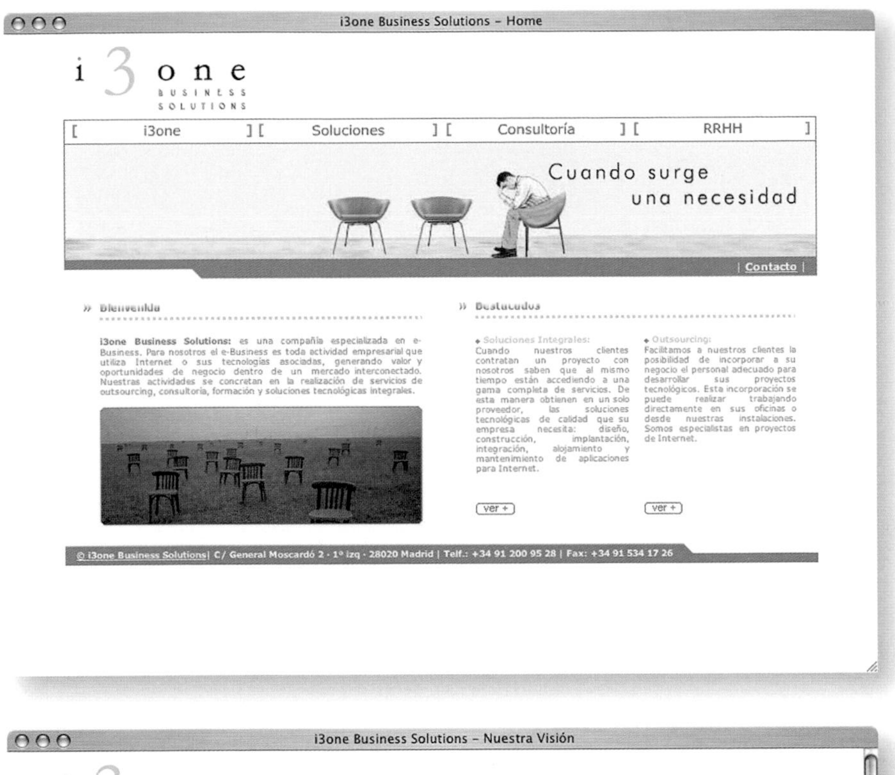

www.i3one.com

D: arturo sanz

A: i3one bussines solutions **M:** asanz@i3one.com

Cooking Crew | styling & food

Wanneer
Cooking Crew styling & food ?

* Bijvoorbeeld bij een huwelijk, een nieuw pand dat betrokken wordt, een bijzondere verjaardag, een afscheid, een zoveel-jarig bestaan, of welke gelegenheid maar denkbaar is. Met bijvoorbeeld familie, vrienden, in werkkring, met zakenrelaties, in een kleine of grotere groep. In eigen huis, in het nieuwe kantoor, op een speciale locatie, of waar dan ook (de Crew werkt voornamelijk binnen de provincie Utrecht, maar overleggen kan altijd).

* De Crew zorgt, met haar Crew-leden voor (een groot deel van) de voorbereiding en de uitvoering en de 'sores' achteraf. Geen gestress van tevoren en tijdens, en daarna het hele zaakje weer keurig op orde! Alles uit handen geven, het enige wat hoeft is aandacht geven aan de gasten.

site by frismedia.nl

Cooking Crew | styling & food

Boerenkool met kerst

Een gezond en niet-moeilijk gerecht, om lekker bij de televisie te eten, the day after....
(de hoeveelheden staan in het recept, maar het zijn allemaal ongeveer-hoeveelheden, vertrouw op je intuïtie en smaak):

Wat is er nodig voor het een:

Balsamicoazijn
Wijnazijn
Sherry
Suiker
Kaneelpoeder
Vier gedroogde vijgen

Doe 20 ml balsamicoazijn, 20 ml wijnazijn en 30 ml sherry in een pan en voeg 1 eetlepel suiker en een theelepel kaneelpoeder erbij.

lees verder 1 2 3 4 5

menu

&

Wanneer
Cooking Crew styling & food ?

* Bijvoorbeeld bij een huwelijk, een nieuw pand dat betrokken wordt, een bijzondere verjaardag, een afscheid, een zoveel-jarig bestaan, of welke gelegenheid maar denkbaar is. Met bijvoorbeeld familie, vrienden, in werkkring, met zakenrelaties, in een kleine of grotere groep. In eigen huis, in het nieuwe kantoor, op een speciale locatie, of waar dan ook (de Crew werkt voornamelijk binnen de provincie Utrecht, maar overleggen kan altijd).

* De Crew zorgt, met haar Crew-leden voor (een groot deel van) de voorbereiding en de uitvoering en de 'sores' achteraf. Geen gestress van tevoren en tijdens, en daarna het hele zaakje weer keurig op orde! Alles uit handen geven, het enige wat hoeft is aandacht geven aan de gasten.

site by frismedia.nl

www.cookingcrew.nl
D: donald harting **C:** nick bolink
A: frismedia.nl **M:** info@frismedia.nl

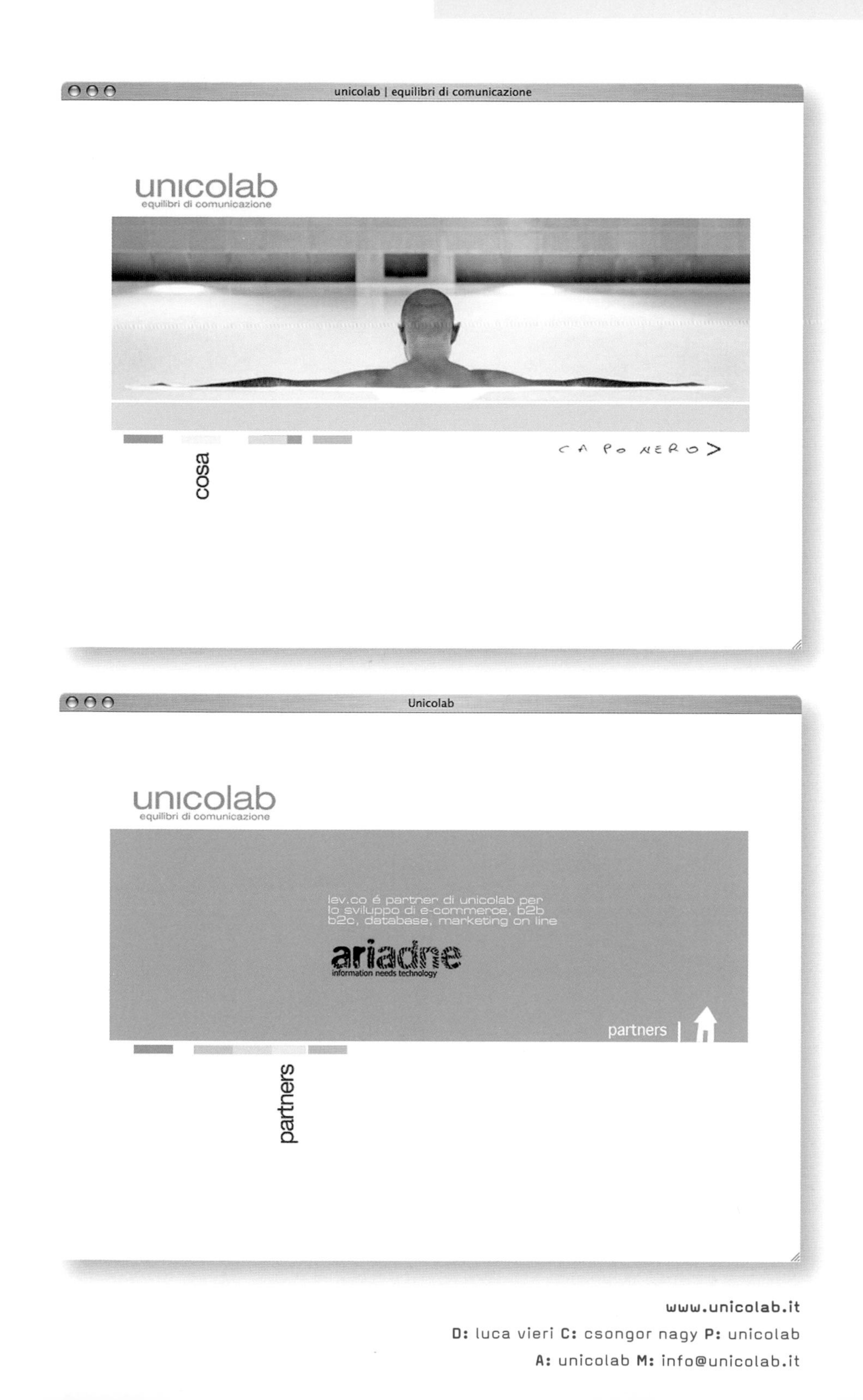

www.unicolab.it

D: luca vieri **C:** csongor nagy **P:** unicolab

A: unicolab **M:** info@unicolab.it

www.helge-haas.com

D: christopher schultz

A: liquid pixel **M:** info@liquid-pixel.de

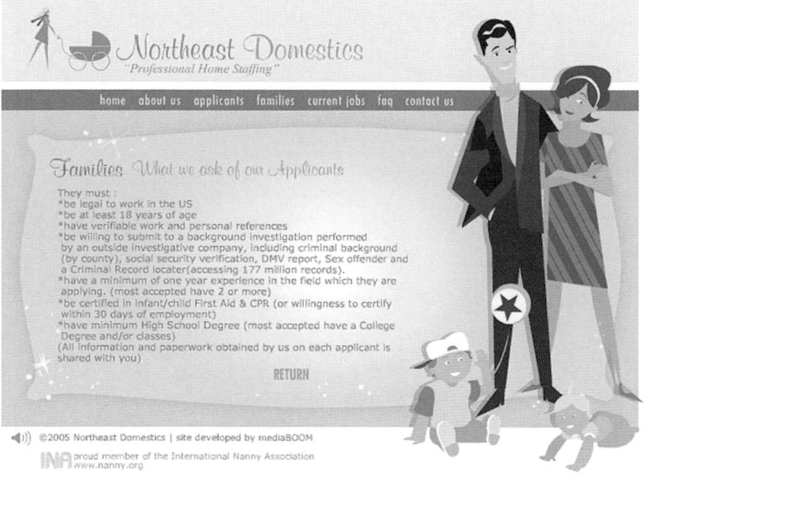

www.northeastdomestics.com

D: sean cooke **C:** sean cooke, frank depino **P:** frank depino

A: mediaboom **M:** www.mediaboom.com

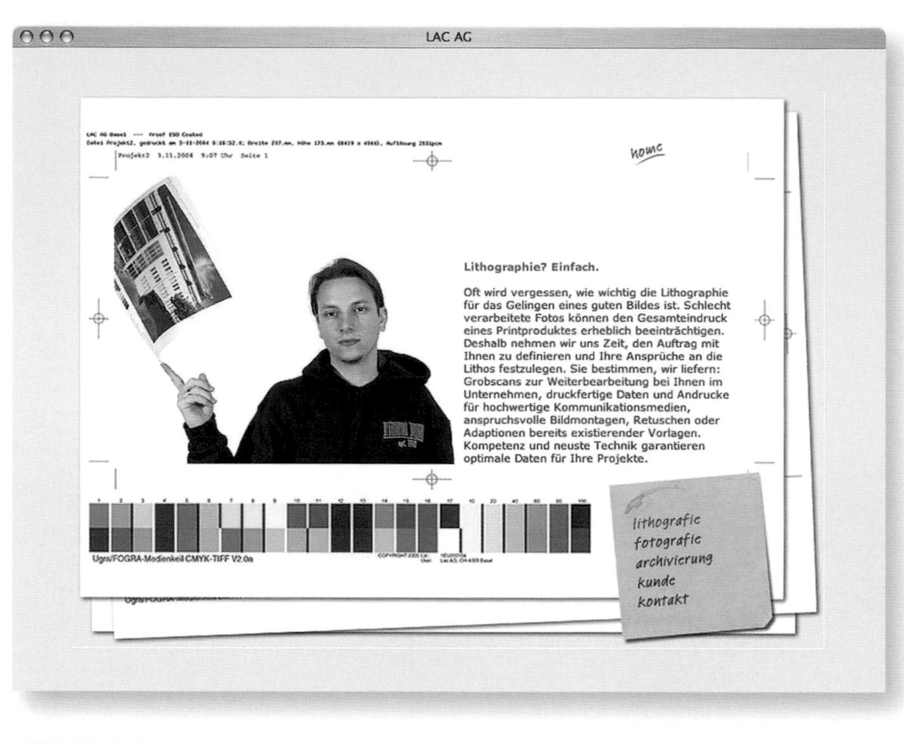

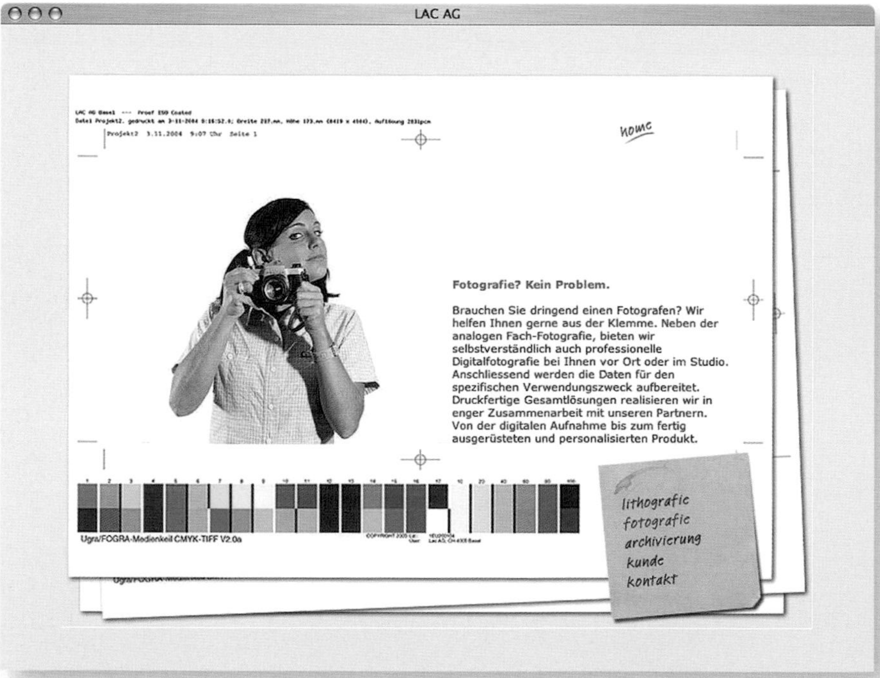

www.lac-basel.ch

D: michel seeliger

A: chameleon graphics gmbh **M:** www.chameleongraphics.ch

:: agenzia immobiliare Ballardini di Franco Rossi . mediatore . agente A.N.A.M.A :: Russi . RA .

agenzia immobiliare Ballardini di Franco Rossi

mediazione

agenzia · mediazione · contatti

affitti · appartamenti · case abbinate · case di campagna
capannoni & garage · terreni · attività com.ciali · ville

rif: 1/S/4
Località: PIANGIPANE(RA)
Tipologia: CASA AFFIANCATA

VENDESI IN PIANGIPANE CASA AFFIANCATA DEL 1980 (MAI ABITATA). CORTILE RETRO, GARAGE E PICCOLO SERVIZIO STACCATO CORPO CASA, INGRESSO, SCANTINATO, ALTRO GARAGE PER DUE AUTO, DUE STANZE, STANZA PREDISPOSTA PER BAGNO. PIANO RIALZATO: SALA, CUCINA PRANZO, DUE LETTO, BAGNO. IMPIANTI PUR MAI USATI NON SONO A NORMA. EURO 170.000 TRATTABILI. RIF. 1/S/4

agenzia immobiliare Ballardini . via Garibaldi 169 . 48026 Russi . Ra . tel / fax 0544 581950 . info@agenziaballardini.com

www.agenziaballardini.com

D: angelo pariano

A: angelo pariano **M:** info@artedopera.it

www.salonesbulevar.com

D: xavi royo **C:** xavi royo **P:** xafdesign

A: xafdesign **M:** xavi@xafdesign.com

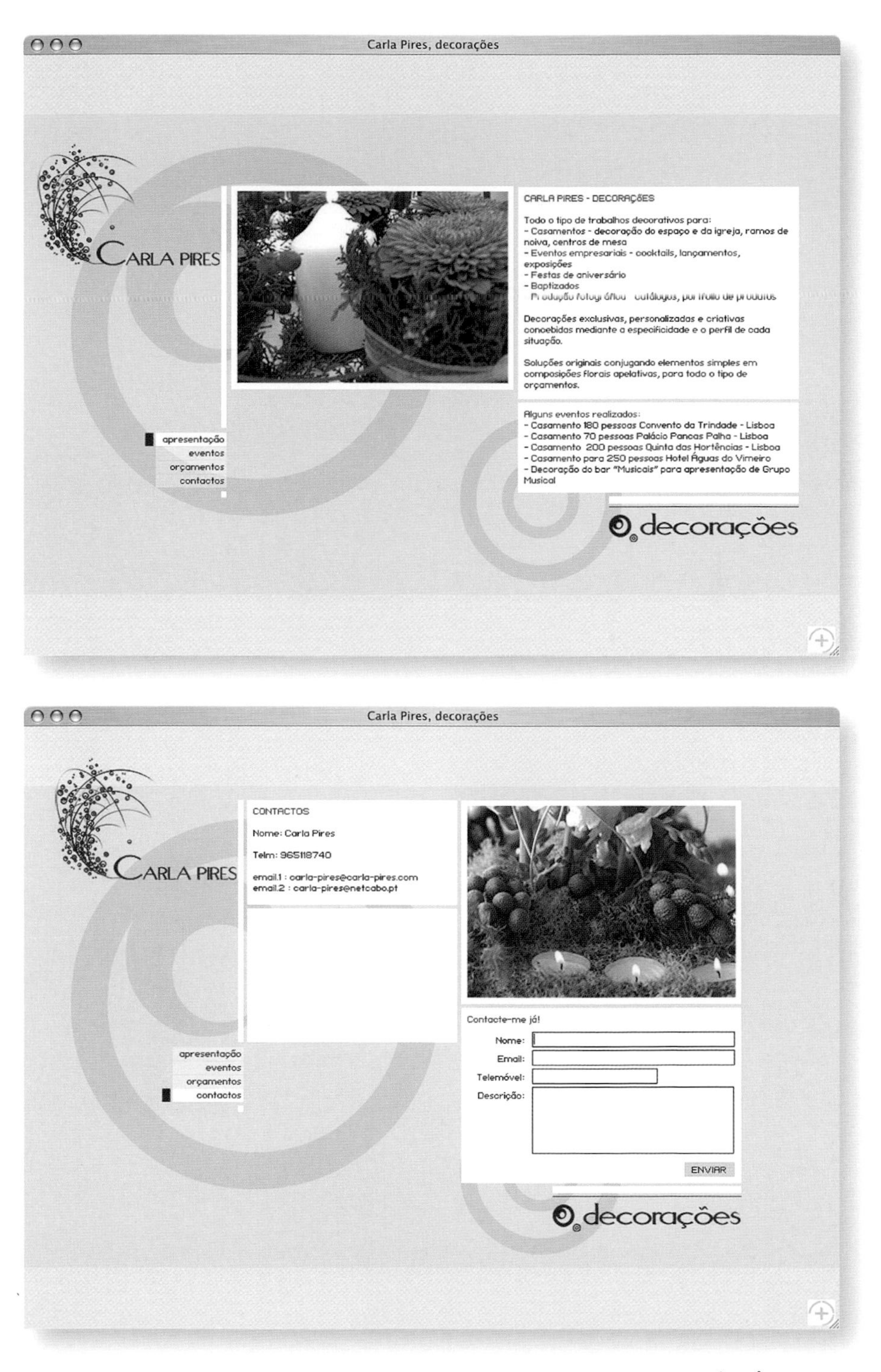

www.carla-pires.com

D: paulo afonso

A: semmais.com **M:** paulo.afonso@semmais.com

[ULTRA] SCHALL

[ultra]schall

LEISTUNGEN PROFIL SHOWREEL PROJEKTE REFERENZEN

Hier sehen Sie meine Leistungen im Überblick

FilmTon (Originalton - Aufnahmen)

- TV-Serie
- TV-Spielfilm
- Kinofilm
- Werbefilm

Sound Design

- SoundLogos
- Werbespots
- Live - Soundinstallationen
- Feuerwerke

Musik Komposition

- Film
- Werbung
- Internetauftritte
- CD -Produktionen

Equipment

- Protools 24Mix Plus System
- Logic Pro
- Audio Processing Software
- Röhren - Mikrofone und - Verstärker
- Mobiles Harddiscrecording
- Location Mischpulte
- Film Mikrofone
- Drahtlose Mikrofon &
- Komunikationanlagen
- Funk - TimecodeKlappe und
- TC Generatoren

Neuigkeiten

22.October 2005
Drehe Das Duo + + + Neues Musikprojekt
mehr

02. September 05
Habe gerade den TV-Film Die Blaumänner für NDR abgedreht
mehr

Die Top 5 aus unserem Showreel

001 002 003 004 005 mehr

Song 001 / Hold on

TIME 00:17 | VOLUME

BACK PLAY STOP NEXT

Kontakt

ultraschall
© 2005 Alle Rechte vorbehalten.

Impressum

www.uschall.de

D: ali rastagar **C:** cinthia c. mencia, hannes höß **P:** ali rastagar

A: 372.com network **M:** a.rastagar@3-72.com

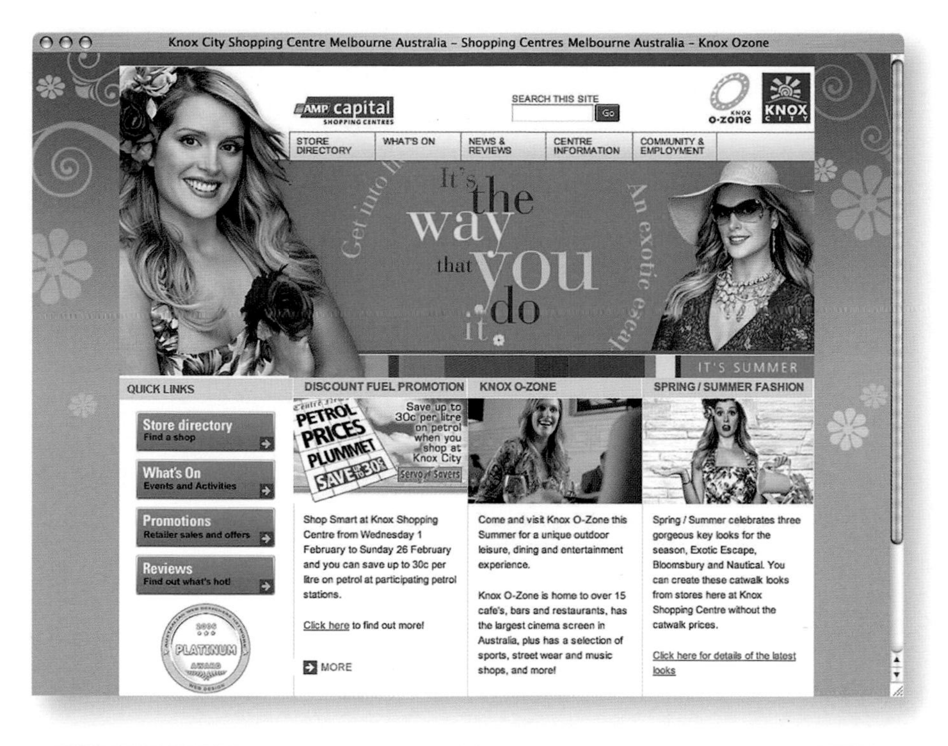

www.knoxcity.com.au

D: jonathan nicol **C:** skillsedit cms **P:** kristin mciver

A: skills media pty ltd **M:** www.skillsmedia.com

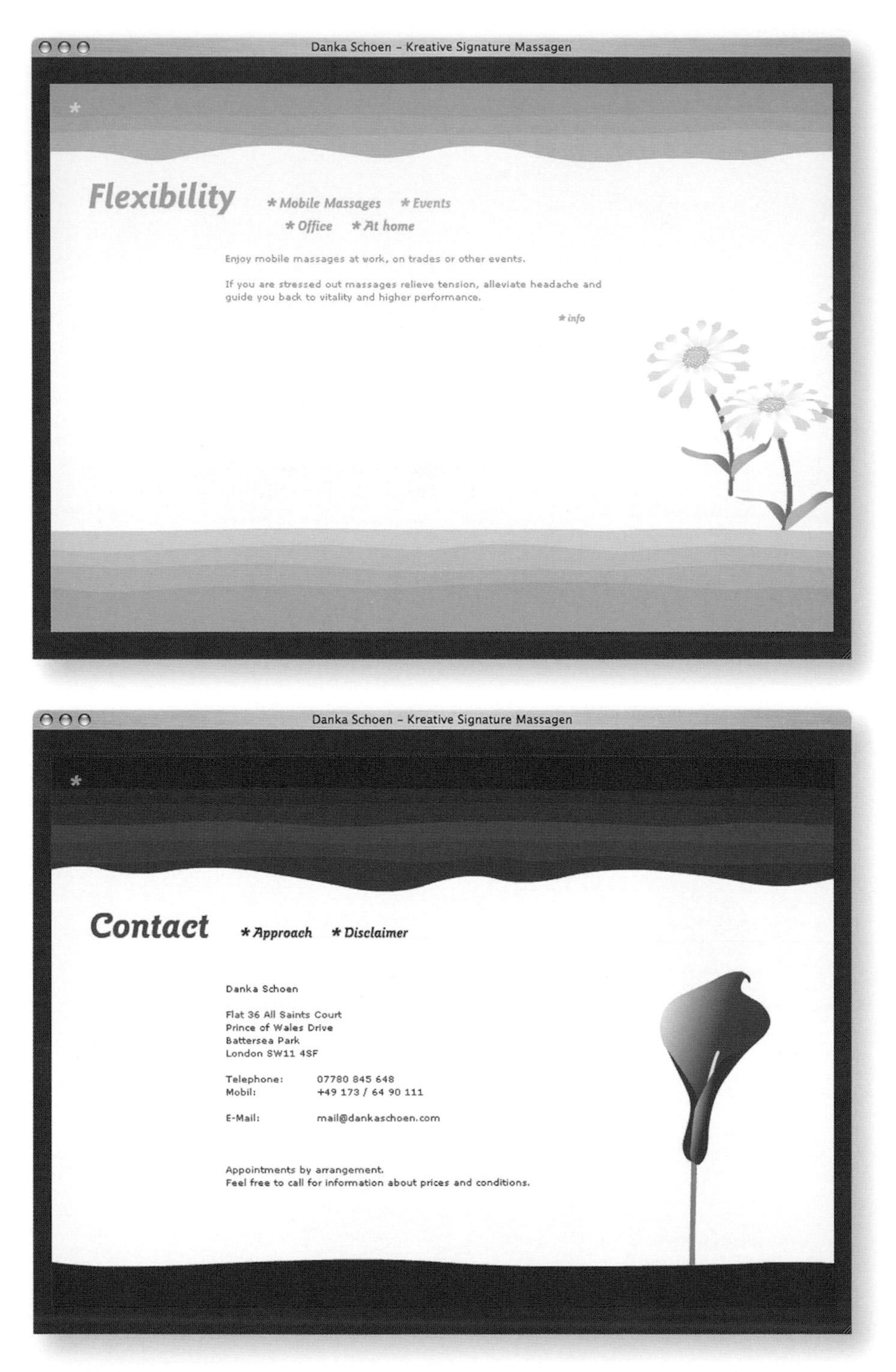

www.dankaschoen.de

D: daniel becker **C:** daniel becker **P:** short cuts | berlin

A: short cuts | berlin **M:** www.short-cuts.de

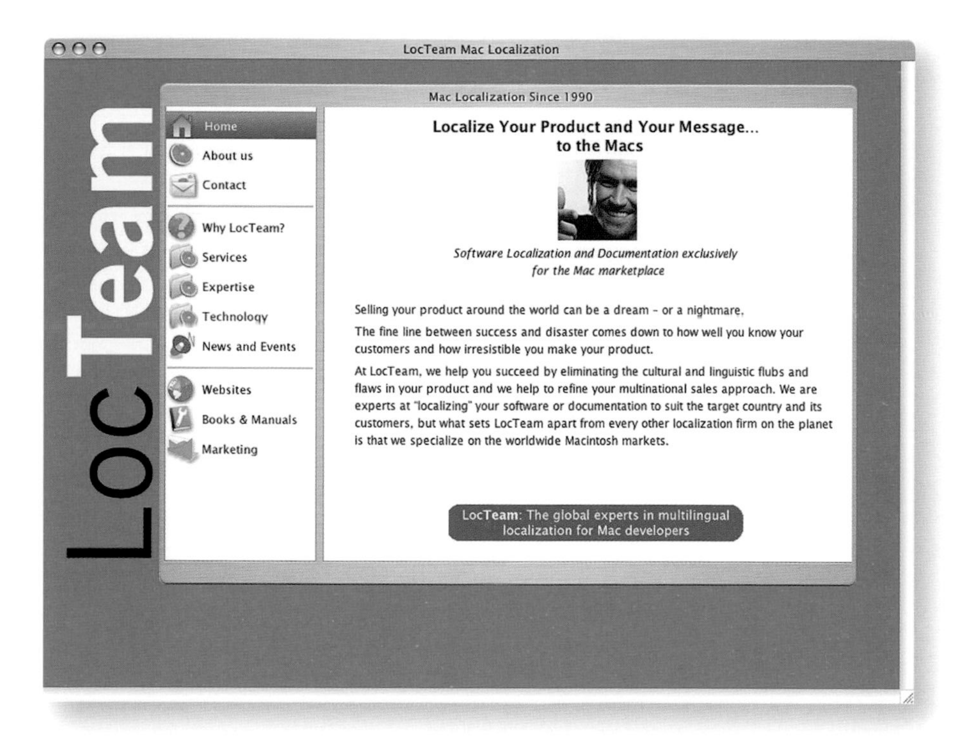

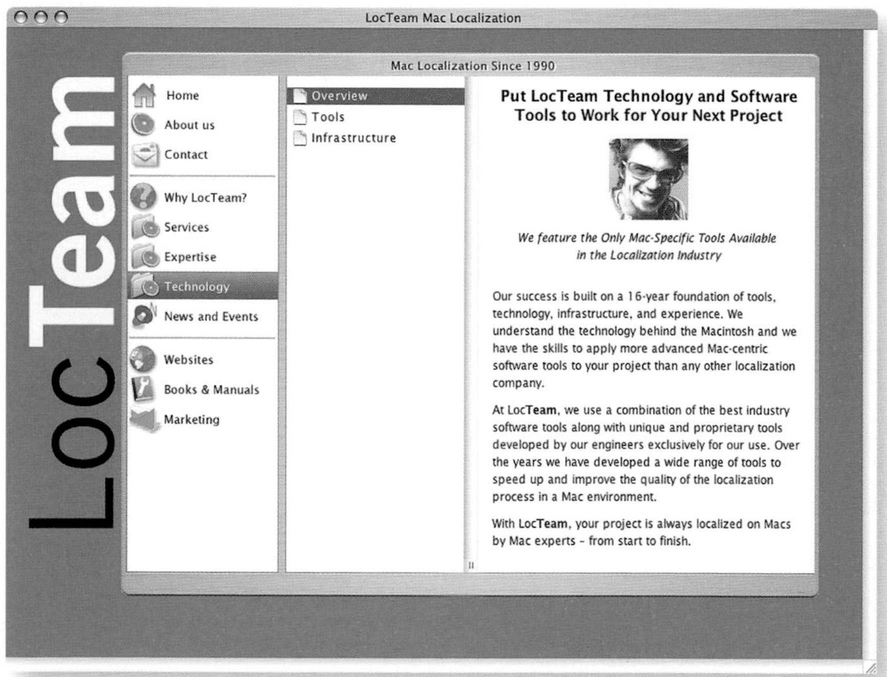

www.locteam.net

D: paco laluca **C:** rosa romeu **P:** magda garcia masana

A: locteam **M:** info@locteam.com

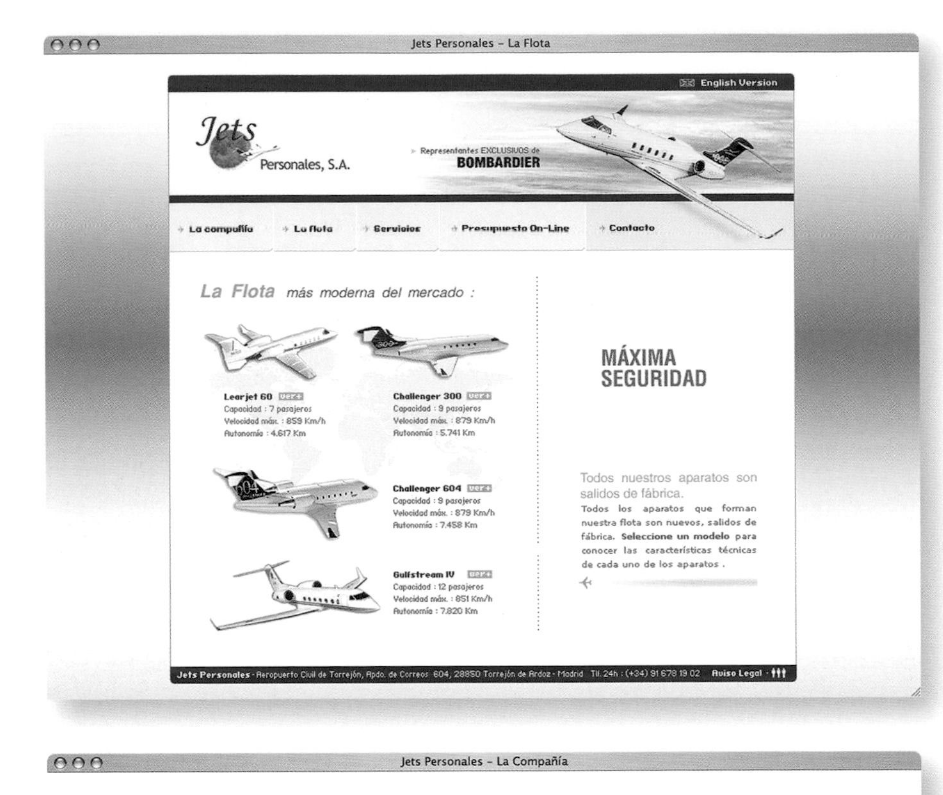

www.jetspersonales.com

D: miguel romanillos **C:** hamadi housami **P:** javier de miguel

A: dreamsite **M:** info@dreamsite.es

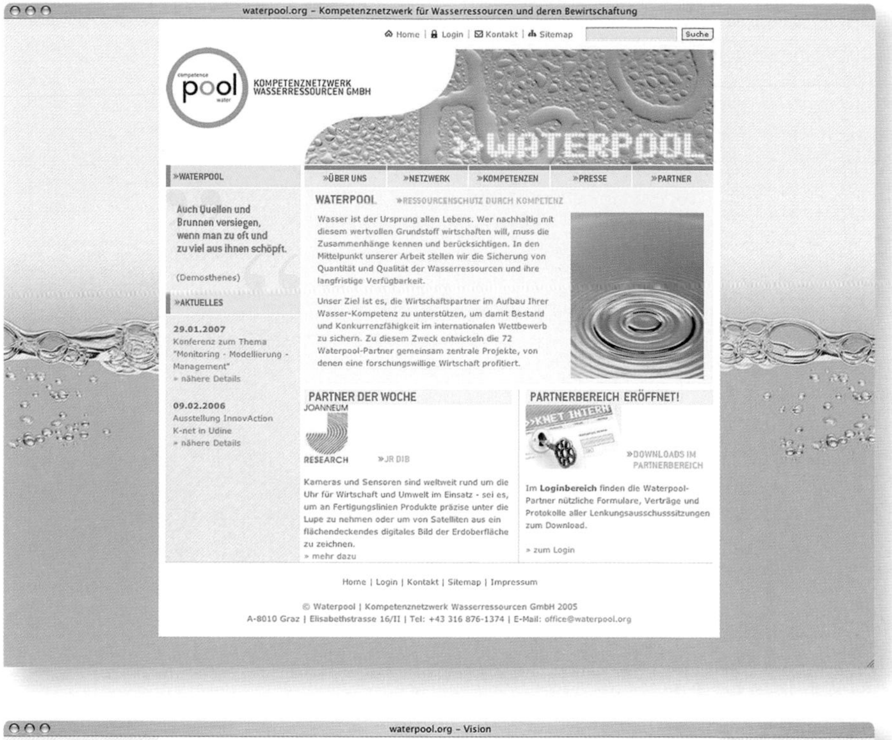

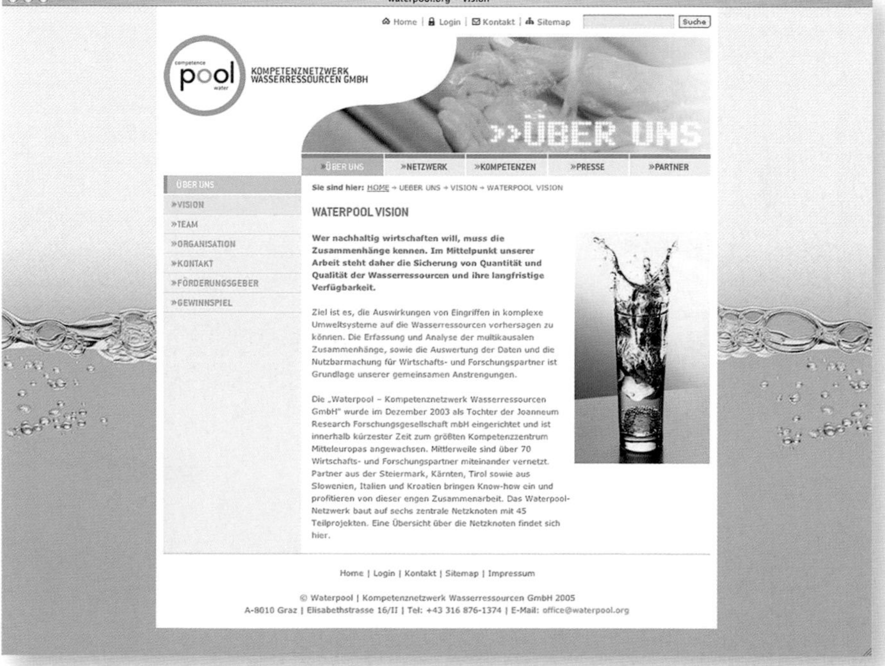

www.waterpool.org

D: daniela strassberger **C:** wukonig.com

A: der i-punkt. graz **M:** daniela.strassberger@ipu.at

www.mipatocuacua.com

D: daniel godoy

A: daniel godoy **M:** danielgodoym@gmail.com

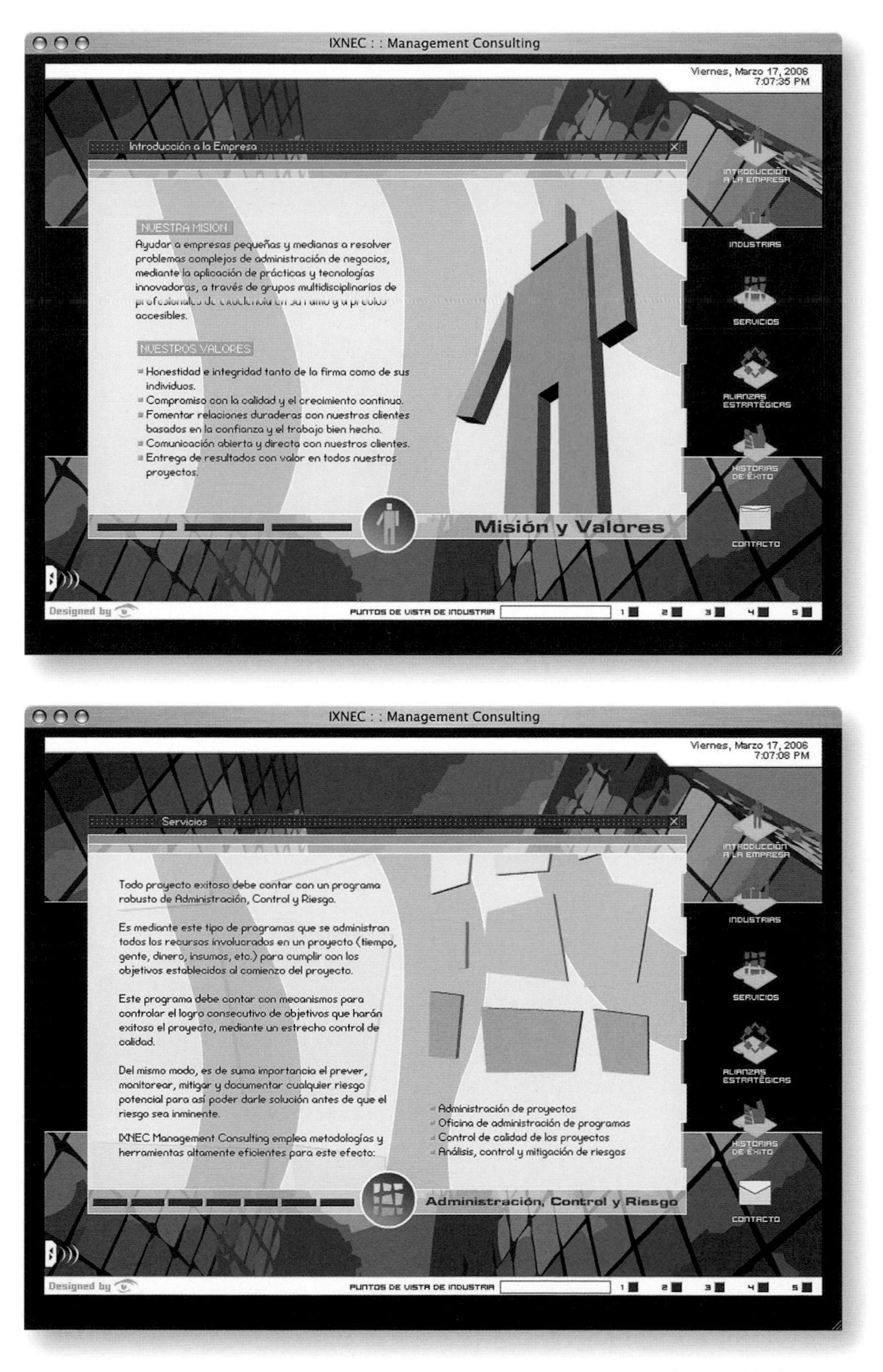

ixnec.at0mic.com
D: daniel serrano
A: at0mic **M:** darklight@at0mic.com

www.triple-m-gmbh.de

D: leif wasmuth

A: wasmuth.com **M:** www.wasmuth.com

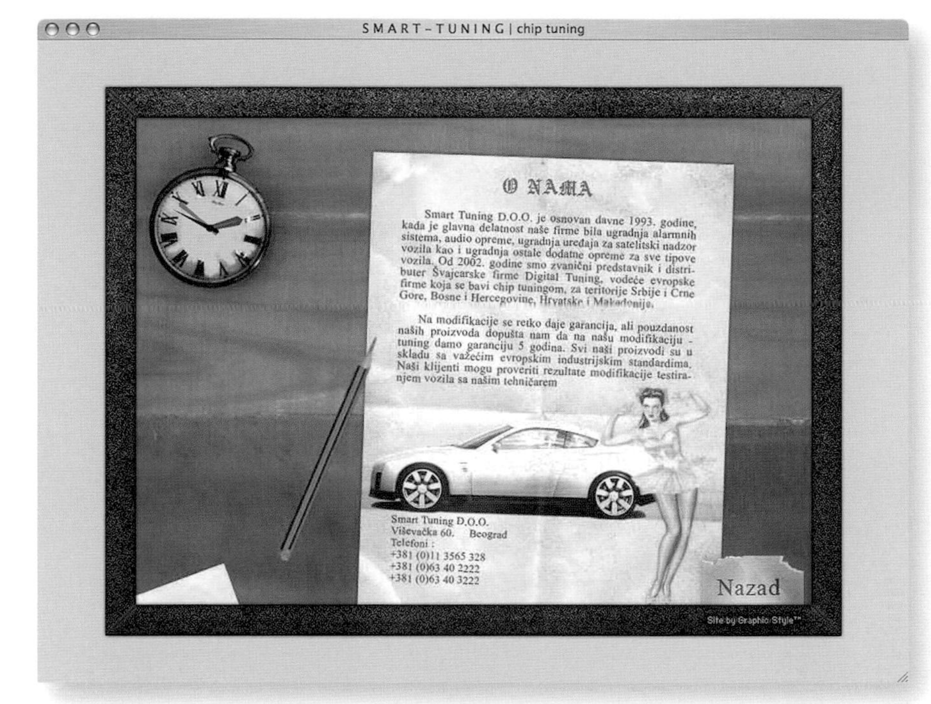

www.smarttuning.co.yu
D: nemanja nenadic
A: graphicstyle M: www.graphicstyle.net

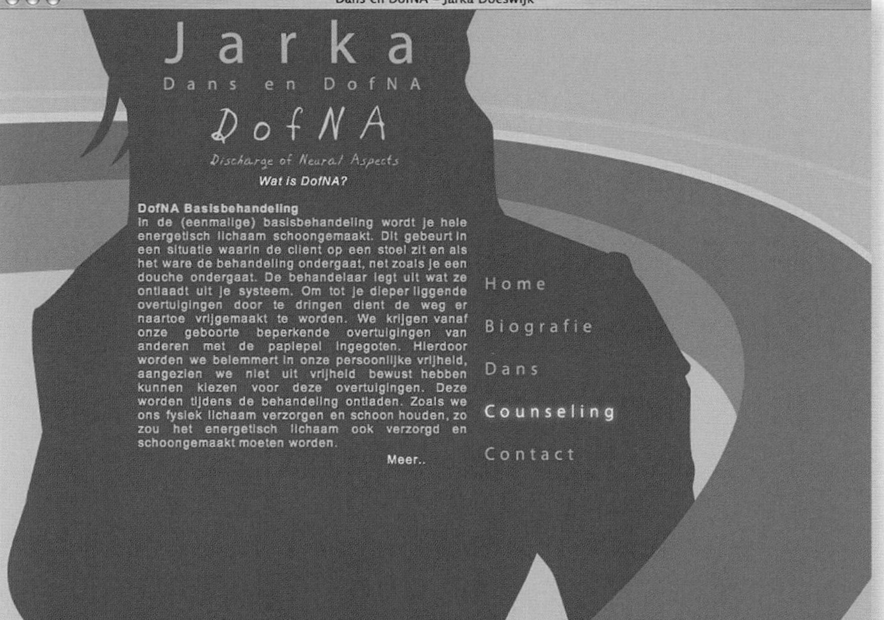

www.dans-dofna.nl

D: roy maassen

A: maassen creative studio **M:** www.maassencs.nl

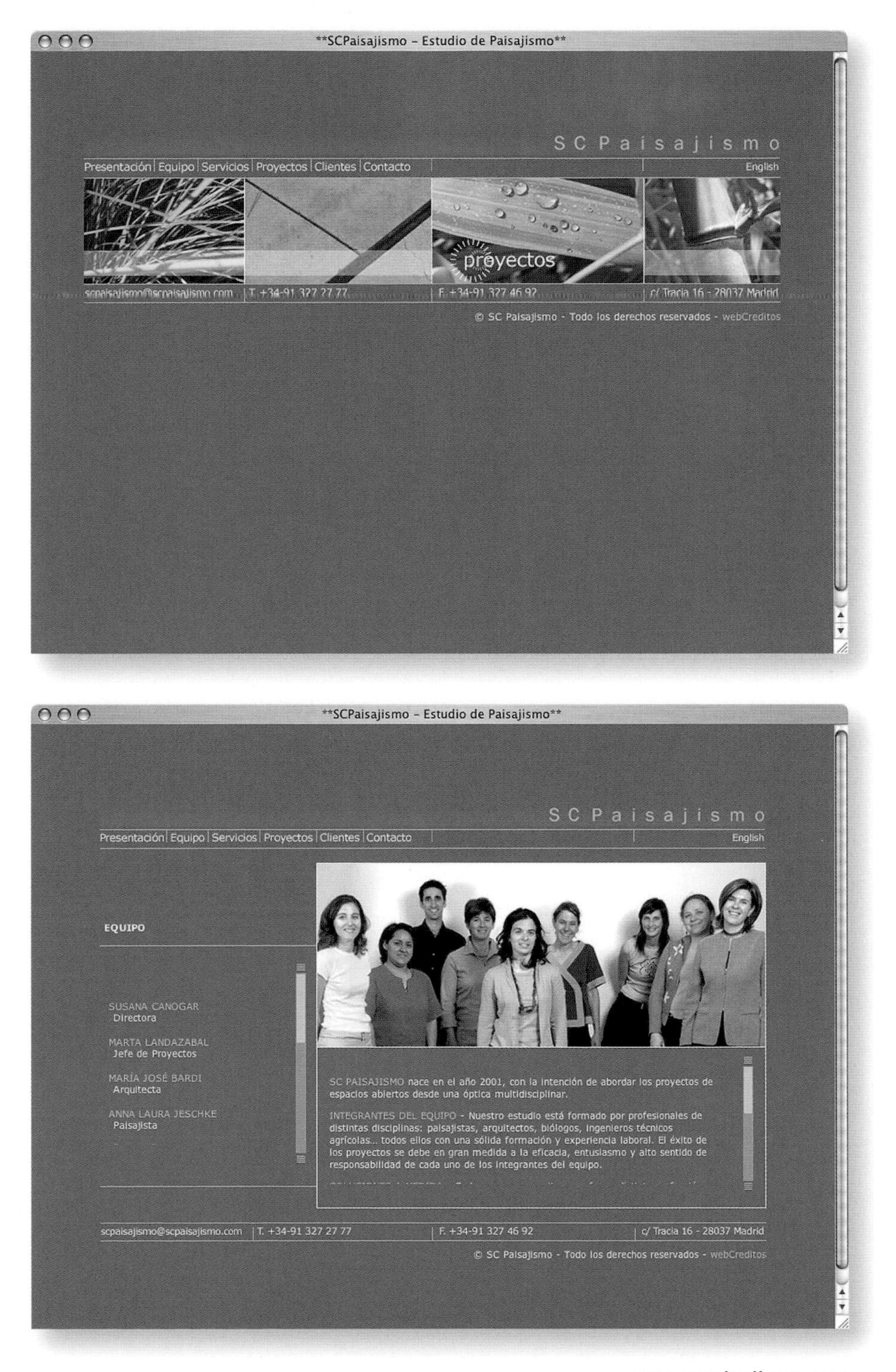

www.scpaisajismo.com

D: martin schneider

A: hierbabuena!communications **M:** www.hierbabuena-communications.com

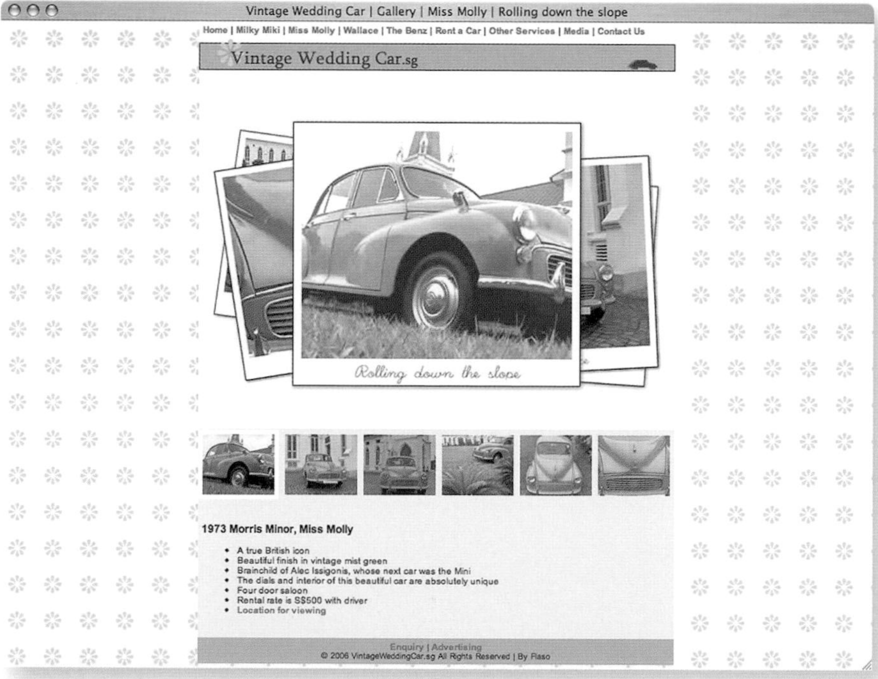

www.vintageweddingcar.sg

D: blithe koh

M: kaniza@pacific.net.sg

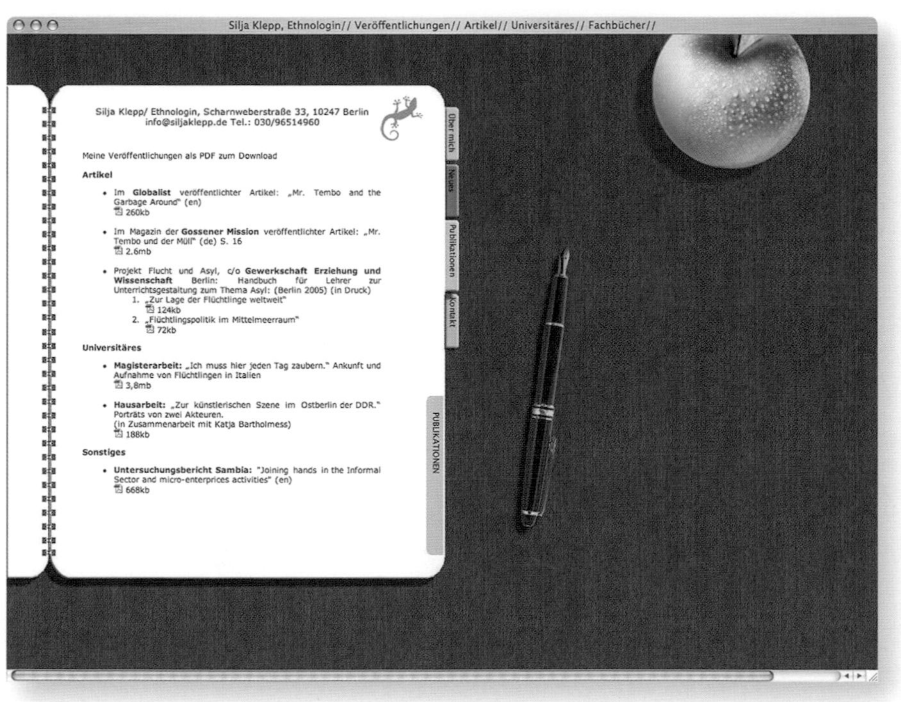

www.siljaklepp.de

D: matthias süßen

A: das hotel- kommunikationsstudio M: www.dashotel.net

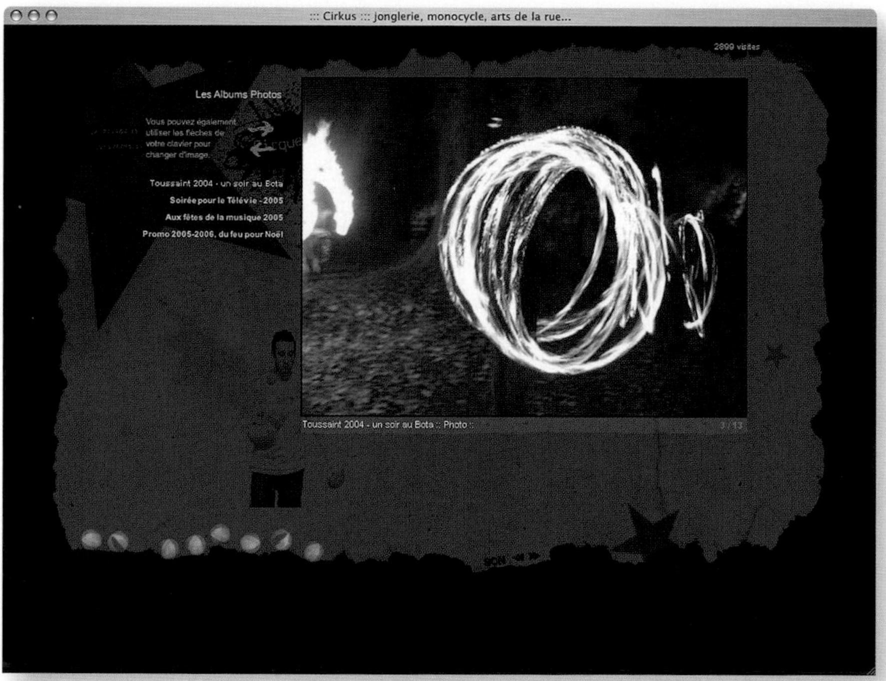

www.cirkus.be

D: joseph adam

A: visual shaker **M:** www.visual-shaker.be

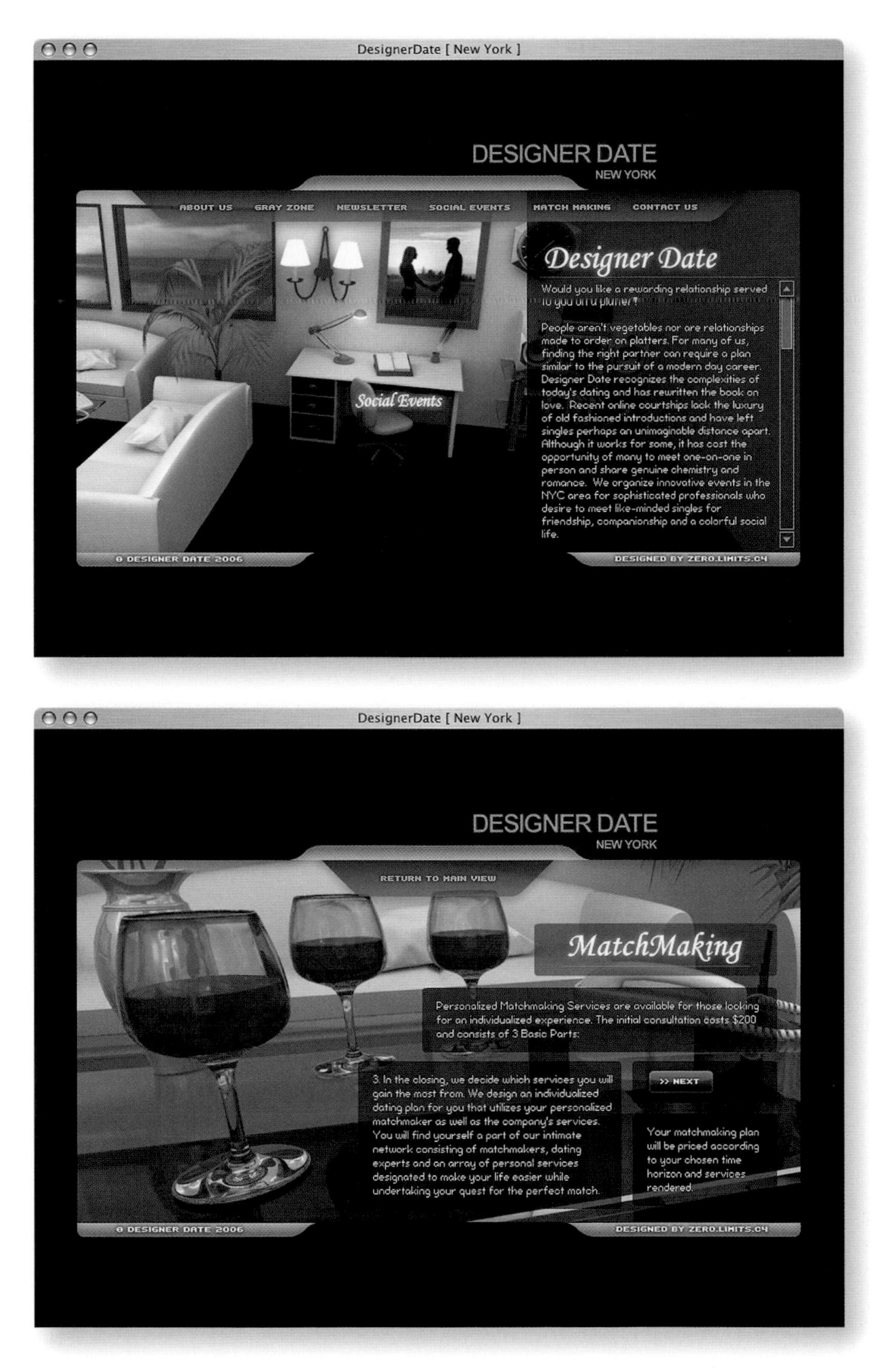

www.designerdate.com
D: yun tan
A: zero.limits.c4 **M:** www.zero-limits.net

www.peterranalloproductions.com

D: flug

M: iamflug@yahoo.ca

www.westcoastchoppers.com

D: greg huntoon **C:** brian kupetz **P:** greg huntoon

A: go farm **M:** www.gofarm.la

www.orangebag.nl

D: jorg van keulen, emiel van wanrooij **C:** colin raaijmakers, bas van hout

P: loek jurres **A:** the cre8ion.lab - schijndel **M:** www.cre8ion.com

www.videosell.it

D: chiara pontiggia **C:** massimiliano mureddu **P:** carlo molinari

A: alchimedia srl **M:** cmolinari@alchimedia.com

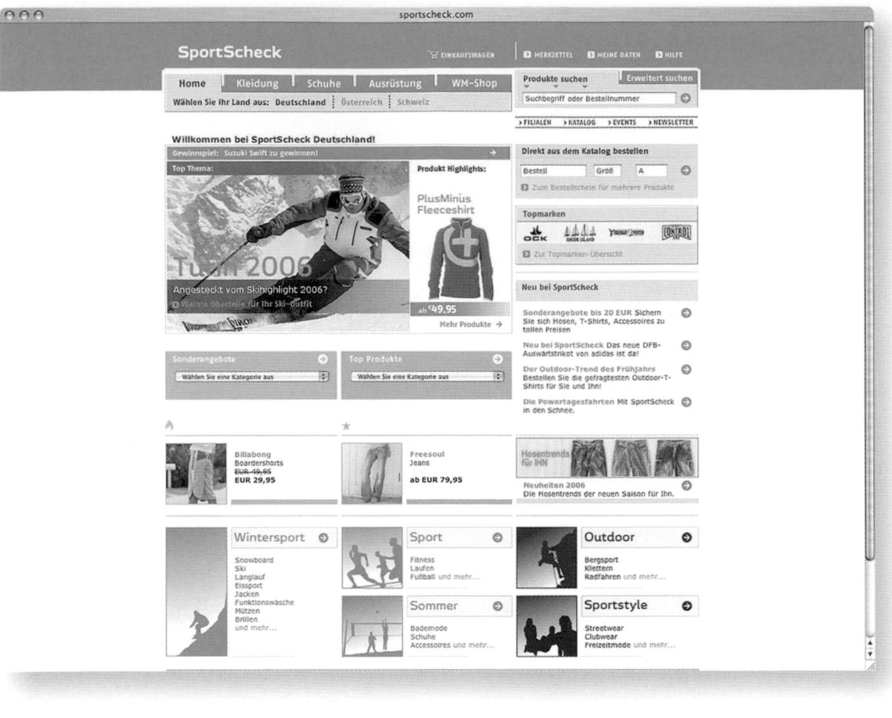

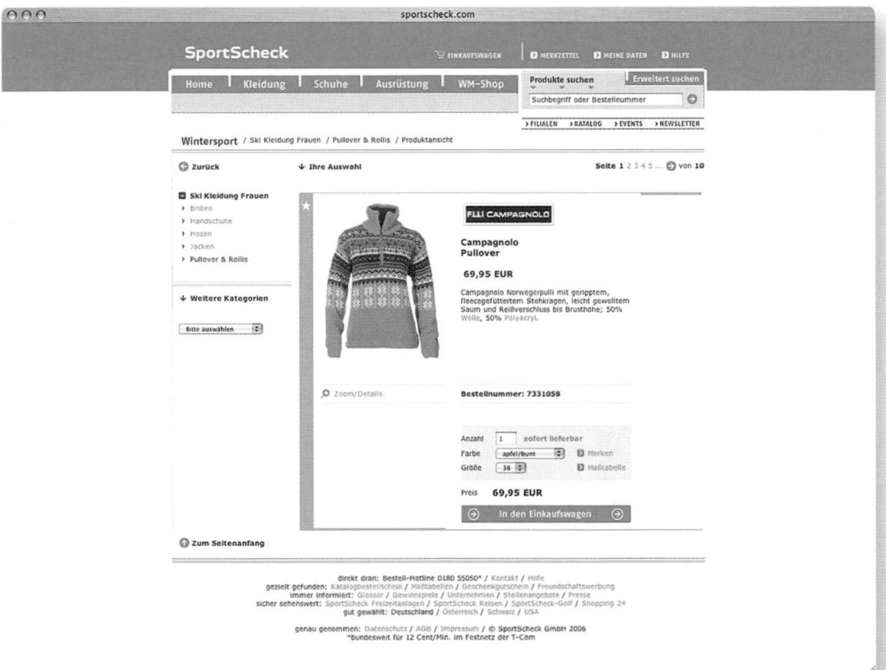

www.sportscheck.com

D: fork unstable media

A: fork unstable media **M:** bundesrepublik@fork.de

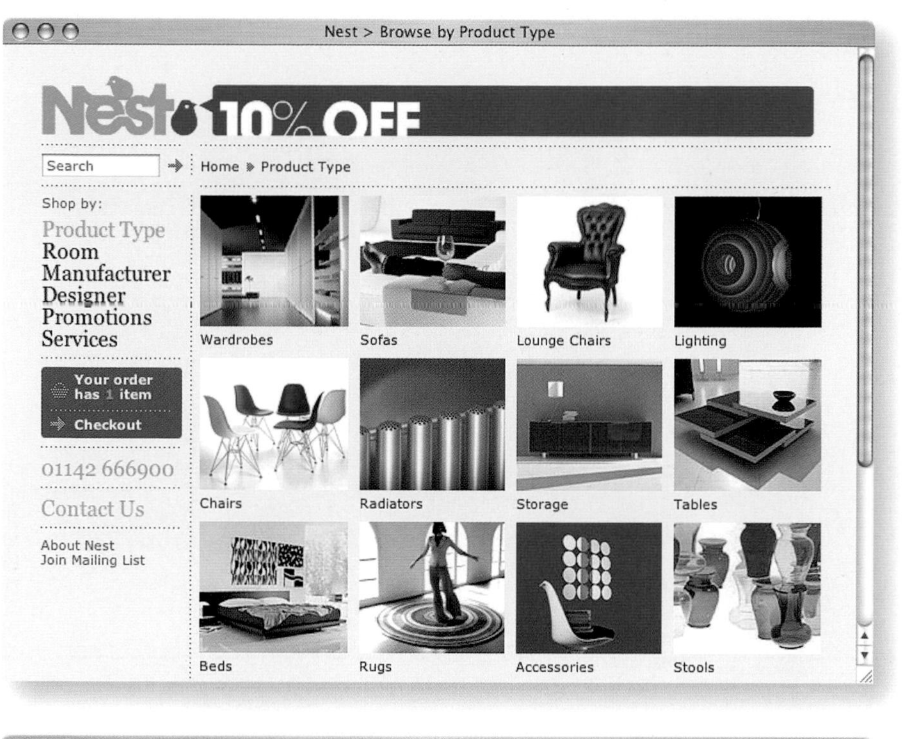

Nest > Your Order

Nest 10% OFF

Search

Home ▸ Room ▸ Bedroom ▸ PH Artichoke ▸ Your Order

Shop by:

Product Type
Room
Manufacturer
Designer
Promotions
Services

Your order has 1 item

Checkout

01142 666900

Contact Us

About Nest
Join Mailing List

Your Order

Your order contains the following items. You can change the quantities of items in your basket by changing the figure in the 'Quantity' box.

Product	Quantity	Price (£)
Louis Poulsen PH Artichoke Light PH Artichoke / Copper	1 Remove	3,350.00
Subtotal:		3,350.00
Shipping (UK):		FREE
Total:		£ 3,350.00

CONTINUE SHOPPING UPDATE CHECKOUT

Related Products

Other products to complement those in your order:

www.nest.co.uk

D: matt pyke **C:** kleber **P:** matt pyke

A: universal everything **M:** www.universaleverything.com

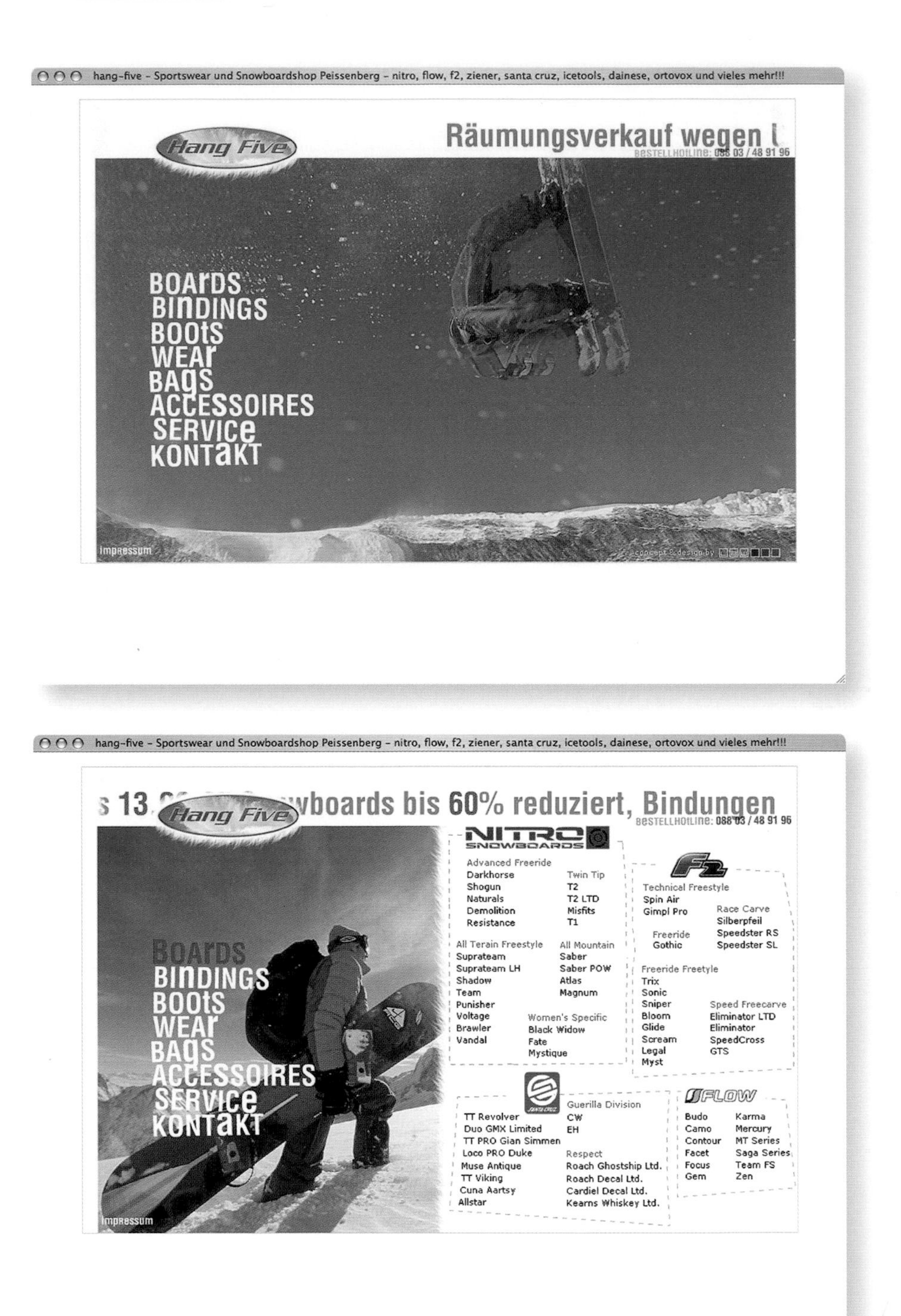

www.hang-five.de

D: leif wasmuth

A: wasmuth.com **M:** www.wasmuth.com

レディース / Ladies
▪ゴールデンベア
丸首カーディガン
ヘンリーネックセーター

www.kosugi.jp
D: parameter
A: nagi M: info@nagi.tv

www.tastedshapes.jp
D: takehiko ichimura
A: script **M:** info@tastedshapes.jp

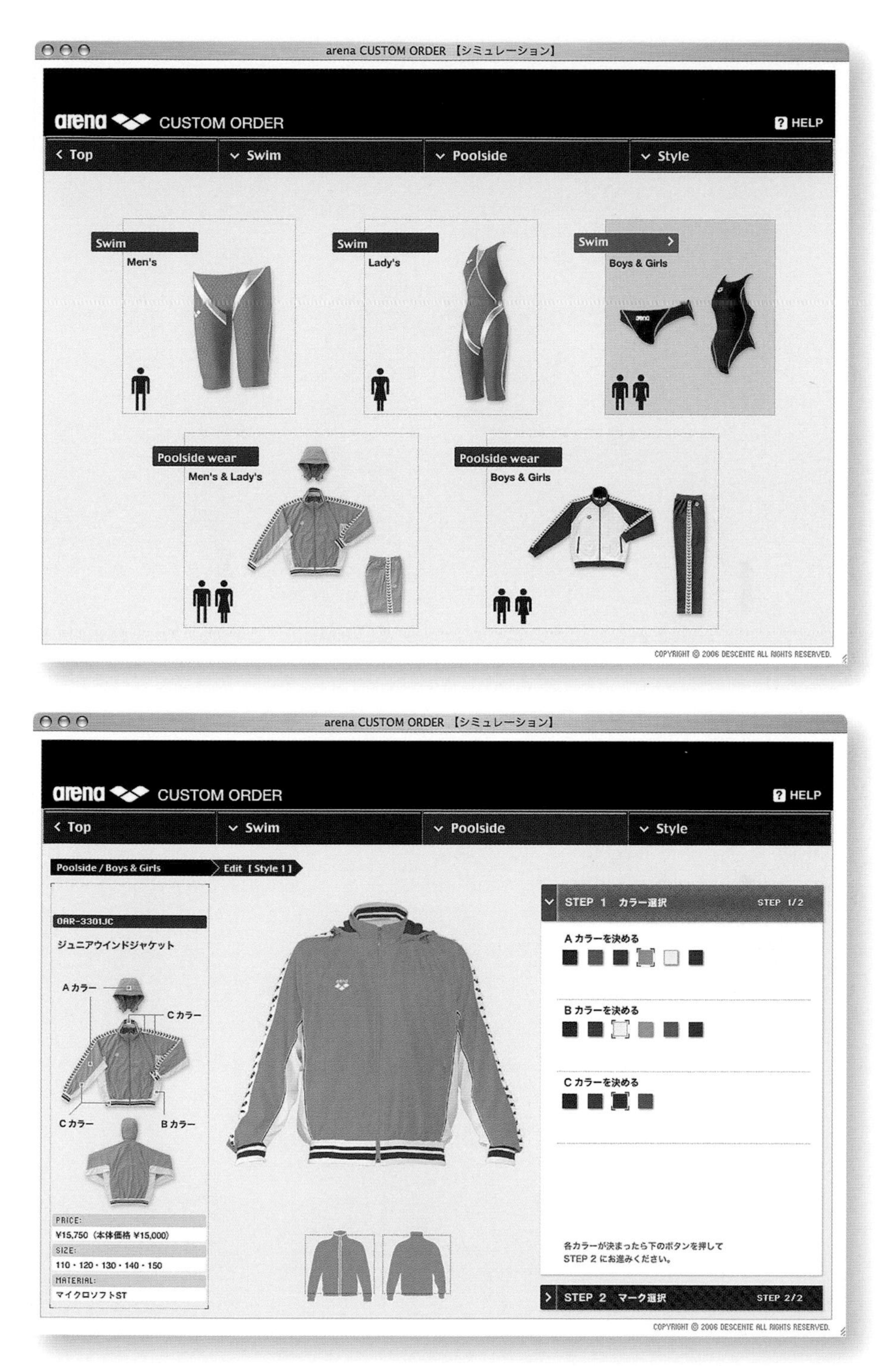

custom.arena-jp.com/simulation/index.html

D: roughark interaktiv

A: nagi M: info@nagi.tv

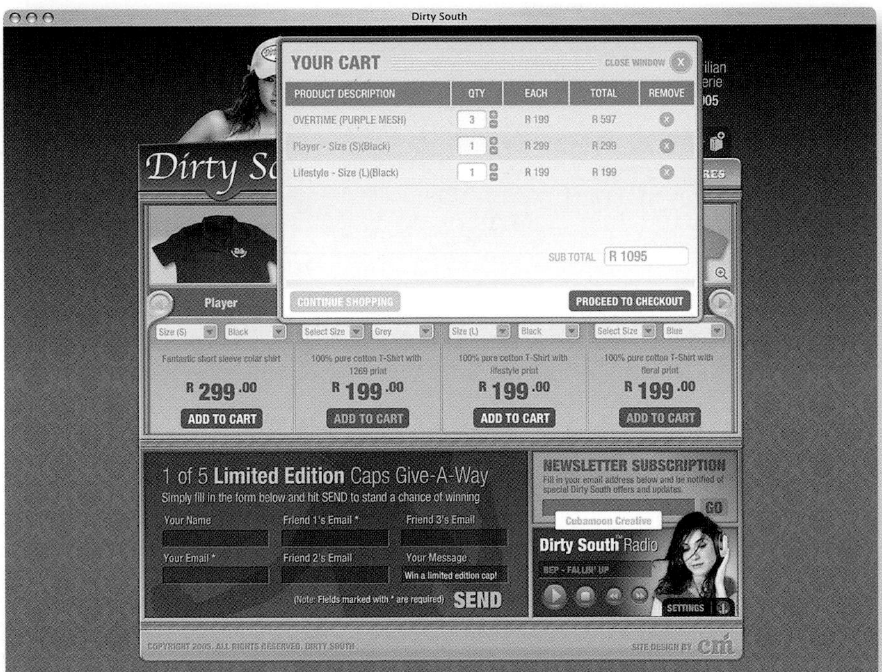

www.dirtysouth.co.za

D: jimmy caravotas

A: cubamoon creative **M:** info@cubamoon.com

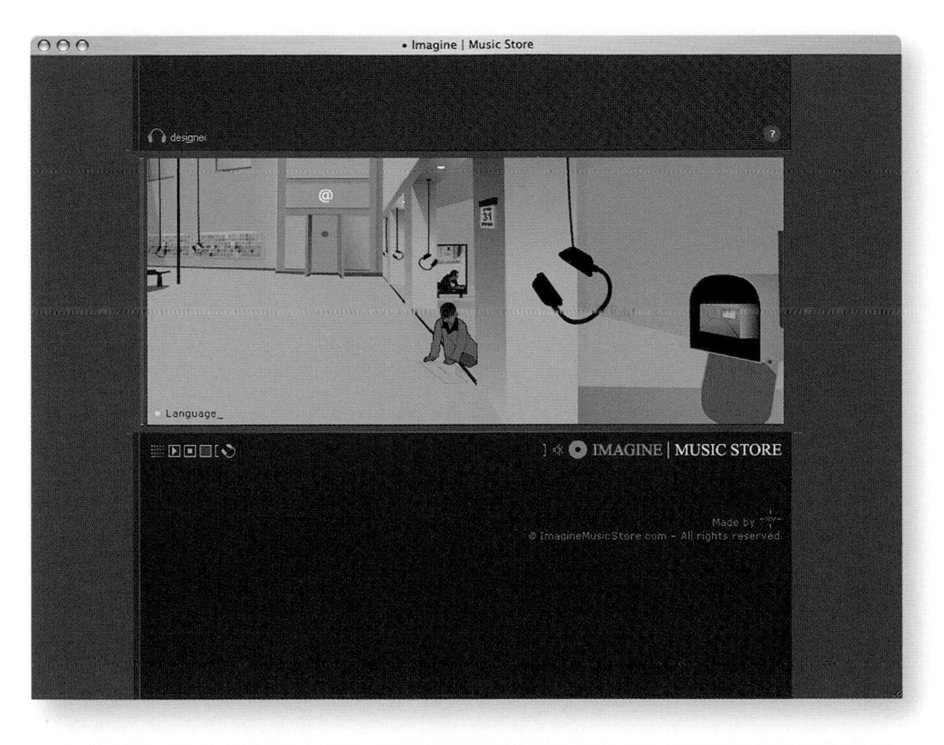

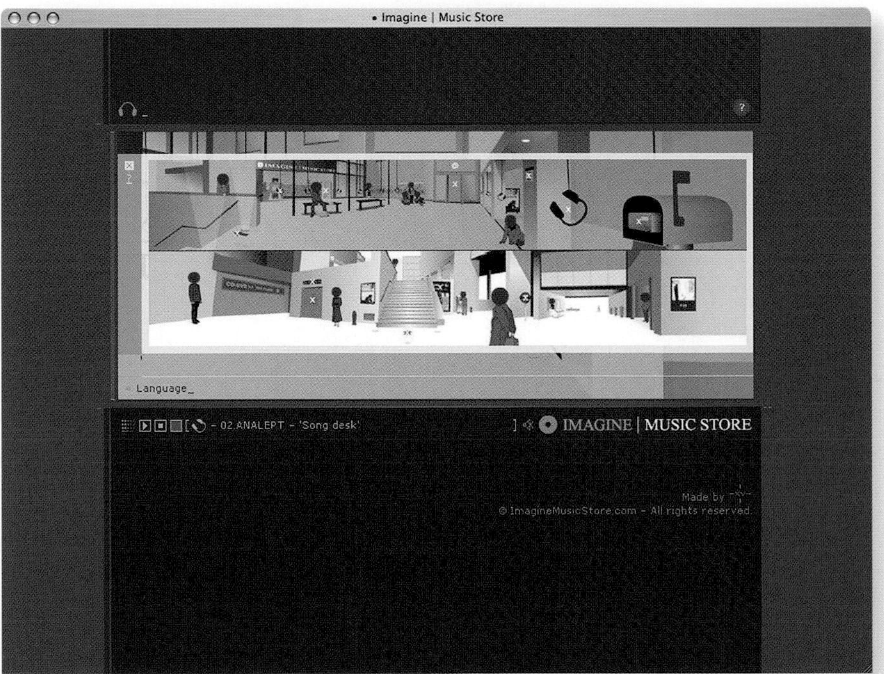

www.imaginemusicstore.com

D: fx. marciat, j. veronesi **C:** fx. marciat **P:** imagine music store

A: xy area **M:** xy@xyarea.com

www.billabongjrpro.com

D: billabong europe, septime creation **C:** septime creation

A: septime creation **M:** stephane.tenailleau@billabong.tm.fr

Fortschrittlicher Schweizer Fussball Verband

Alternative Liga Zürich

17 febraio 2006 FSFV seit 1977

Meisterschaft Copa Teams Forum Archiv Login Kontakt

MODERN WIBI STARTET SAISON 2006 MIT -4 PUNKTEN

07-12-2005

Wegen unentschuldigtem Nichterscheinen der drei Schiris am Finaltag (-3 Punkte gemäss FSFV-Reglement) und zu spätem Bezahlen der Cup-Teilnahmegebühr (-1 Punkt gemäss langjähriger ZK-Praxis) muss Modern WiBi mit total -4 Punkten in die Meisterschaft 2006 starten.

FSFV/ROTOR HALLENTURNIER

22-11-2005

Am 25./26. Februar findet das FSFV-Hallenturnier in Schlieren statt. Organisiert wird es erstmals von RotoR, anmelden kann man sich mit diesem Anmeldeformular. Anmeldeschluss ist der 10. Dezember.

DIE CUPSIEGER!

10-10-2005

Devils, Cuore e sangú und Traktor Emilie - das sind die Cupsieger der Saison 2005, die mit dem «letzten Kick» im Letzi endete. Finalberichte gibt's auf der Startseite, Bilder vom «letzten Kick» hier. Mit dem wunderbaren Abschluss von gestern entlassen wir euch in die Winterpause. Bis im Frühling!

Habemus Cupsieger!

Im Vorfeld der Cupfinals wurde erstmals «Der letzte Kick» ausgetragen, bei dem bunt gewürfelte Mannschaften in freundschaftlichen Rahmen und bei strahlendem Sonnenschein ein letztes Mal in diesem Jahr dem Ball nachjagen konnten. Der Anlass war so toll, dass wir bereits jetzt entschieden haben, das bald wieder durchzuführen.

In einer Super Atmosphäre mal andere Spielerinnen und Spieler kennen zu lernen, das müssen wir wiederholen!

Devils - unkontrolliert züri 2:1

Devils holen ersten Titel

Im Cupfinal der Frauen standen sich die finalerprobten Devils und die Neulinge von unkontrolliert züri gegenüber. Von Beginn an machten die Devils unter der Regie von Mary grossen Druck und erspielten sich Torchancen im Minutentakt, scheiterten aber entweder an der Torumrandung oder an Torfrau Evi, die sich in Hochform präsentierte. Völlig entgegen dem Spielverlauf ging dann unkontrolliert noch vor der Pause in Führung.
Doch die Devils steckten nicht auf und in der zweiten Halbzeit gelang ihnen der Ausgleich und kurz darauf das siegbringende 2:1.

Cuore e sangu - BSC Tram 5 3:1

Fortschrittlicher Schweizer Fussball Verband

Alternative Liga Zürich

17 febraio 2006 FSFV seit 1977

Meisterschaft Copa Teams Forum Archiv Login Kontakt

Dynamo Röntgen

Gegründet:	1991
Erfolge:	Meister 1993, 1996, 1997, 2002 Cupsieger 1996, 1997, 1998, 2000
Homepage:	www.dynamoroentgen.ch
Kontakt:	Manager: Mämä Sykora Albisriederstrasse 6 8003 Zürich Tel N: 079 703 25 21 fussballgott@dynamoroentgen.ch Trainer: Peti Heggli Spiserstrasse 16 8047 Zürich Tel P: 01 491 09 16

Dynamo Röntgen: der Name ist eine Referenz an Wacker Selnau, bei dem ein Mitbegründer 1990 als rechter Aussenverteidiger sein Debüt in der alternativen Liga gab - um ab 1991 im neu gegründeten Dynamo als Stürmer die gegnerischen Verteidigungen in Angst und Schrecken zu versetzen.

Obwohl der erfolgreichste Club der Liga: Harmonie war in der Dynamo-Historie so selten wie ein vollzähliges Training. Ideologische Differenzen um das ausgewogene Verhältnis zwischen fussballerischem Ehrgeiz und Teamgeist führten zu permanenten Debatten und prominenten Abgängen (Bruno Ziauddin, Chiarelotto-Brothers). Weitere Kaderveränderung erforderten ausgelaufene Bandscheiben (Michael Krobath) und zerfetzte Kniegelenke (Ruedi "Comeback" Bösiger), so dass heute von der Meistermannschaft 1993 gerademal noch 4 Spieler mit dabei sind, vom Siegerteam 1997 immerhin noch 10.

Doch trotz aller Krisen raufen sich die elf Dynamos auf dem Rasen immer wieder zusammen, um ihr gemeinsames Ziel zu verfolgen: ein Spiel ohne Schnörkel, aber mit viel Schmankerln in Form von Doppelpässen und Absatztricks garniert mit vollem Einsatz und Respekt vor dem Gegner. Kurz: den gepflegten Fussball. Das Ziel ist dann erreicht, wenn ein Schiedsrichter anerkennend in der Pause meint: "...das hat mich stark an Fussball

EUROPAMEISTERSCHAFTSSIEGER-BESIEGER

05-9-2005

Erfolg sättigt. Nach dem EM-Titel wurde RotoR von Dynamo gleich mit 6-2 vom Platz gefegt. Nach dem Fairplay-Titel streben wir nun das Double an.

EIN TITEL!

12-7-2005

Im Finale waren wir zwar nur Zuschauer (ausser unser Schiri-Trio - danke!), aber einen Titel haben wir 2005 nun doch noch gewonnen: den Fairplay-Preis! Wir danken unseren Gegnern für die faren Spiele und die Stimmen und versprechen, auch in Zukunft so zu spielen.

PEKKA BESIEGT SPUTNIK

17-6-2005

Mit einer wahrlich unmenschlichen Leistung hielt Dynamo-Keeper Pekka auch im vierten Spiel sein Tor rein und liess die Sputniks reihenweise verzweifeln. Zudem konnte er sich auf seine Torpfosten verlassen, die gleich viermal retteten. Sputnik hat wohl alles Pech für diese Saison aufgebraucht, Dynamo steht nach diesem 4:0 im Viertelfinale.

www.fsfv.ch

D: marc rinderknecht C: cyrill von planta P: marc rinderknecht

A: kobebeef M: mr@kobebeef.ch

avec Danone, Zizou et les A.G.I.T.E.S : FAUT QUE CA BOUGE !

Faut que ça Bouge!

Un programme DANONE soutenu par Zidane

Nutripark Faut que ça Bouge !

Un parcours fun et sportif qui va te faire bouger !

Viens te bouger avec nous !

Équipé comme une salle de sport mais fun comme un parc d'attraction, le chapiteau Nutripark « Faut que ça bouge ! » s'installe dans les plus grandes villes de France.

À l'intérieur, de nombreux ateliers autour des 3 thèmes principaux : courir, sauter et lancer.

C'est gratuit et c'est bon pour la forme !

Cap pas cap de relever les défis du Nutripark ?

Voilà le programme des activités :
- On commence par s'étirer et s'échauffer dans un univers très « danse »
- Ensuite, super rigolade avec une course où tu seras accroché(e) à un élastique en musique et lumière.
- puis saut en longueur : il faudra que tu franchisses la distance qui correspond à ta taille.
- Ensuite saut en hauteur un peu particulier : réussiras-tu à sauter très haut avec des poids accrochés à ta ceinture ?
- Concours d'adresse où tu devras réussir à lancer et à viser juste.
- puis tirs au but... Feras-tu mieux que Zinedine Zidane ?
- Et pour finir, parcours complet avec une course d'obstacles rigolos.

Que tu sois fille ou garçon, tu vas bouger et c'est le fun assuré !

Un super moment avec la bande des A.G.I.T.É.S.

Viens nous rendre visite sur le Nutripark « Faut que ça bouge ! ».
Et si tu participes aux épreuves du Nutripark, tu repartiras

Conseils des A.G.I.T.É.S.
Teste-toi
Réponses à tout
Agito'blog
Bouge ton corps
Rapid-o-top
Nutripark

Membre de la bande
Pour voir ton compte de points, dis-nous qui tu es :
e-mail
mot de passe
Mot de passe oublié
Pas encore membre ?
clique vite ici

Rejoins vite les A.G.I.T.É.S.
Tu peux gagner des supers cadeaux
Inscris-toi

Lequel des A.G.I.T.É.S. es-tu ?
Fais le test pour découvrir à qui tu ressembles le plus
Teste-toi

Relève les défis !
Participe au blog des A.G.I.T.É.S. et partage tes bonnes idées pour se bouger
Va voir le blog

www.fautquecabouge.com

D: laurent chomette **C:** eric marillet **P:** danone

A: sokovision **M:** info@sokovision.com

www.shorebreak.be

D: pieter deschutter **C:** rafaela stattmiller **P:** rafaela stattmiller

A: www.oceano-digital.com **M:** info@oceano-digital.com

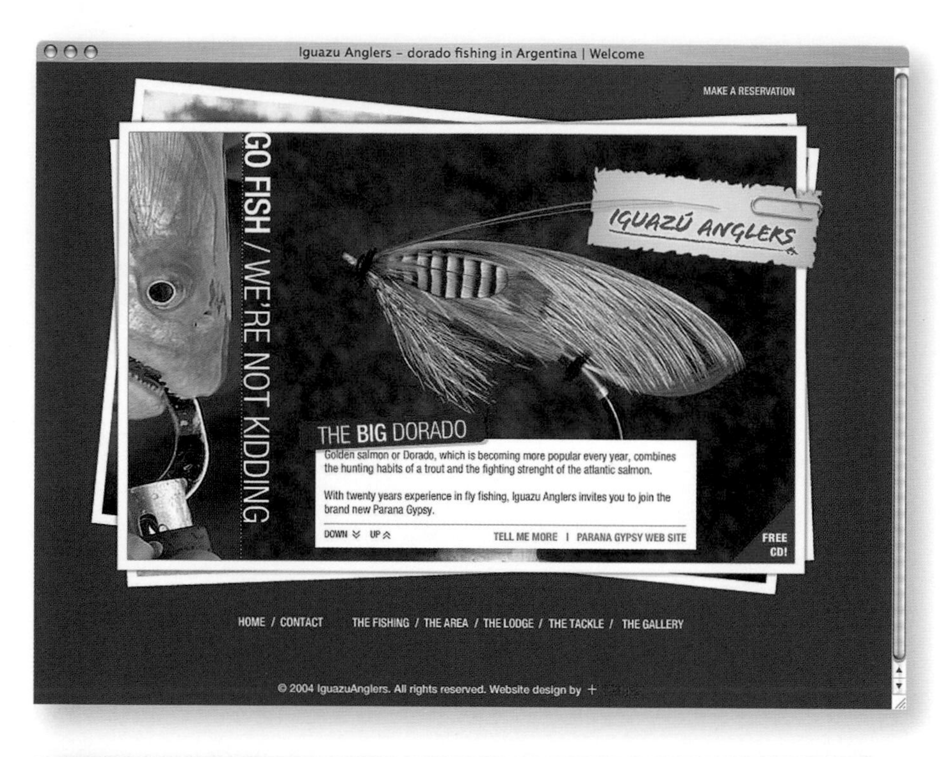

www.iguazuanglers.com

D: claudio lucero

A: 25diez **M:** www.25diez.com

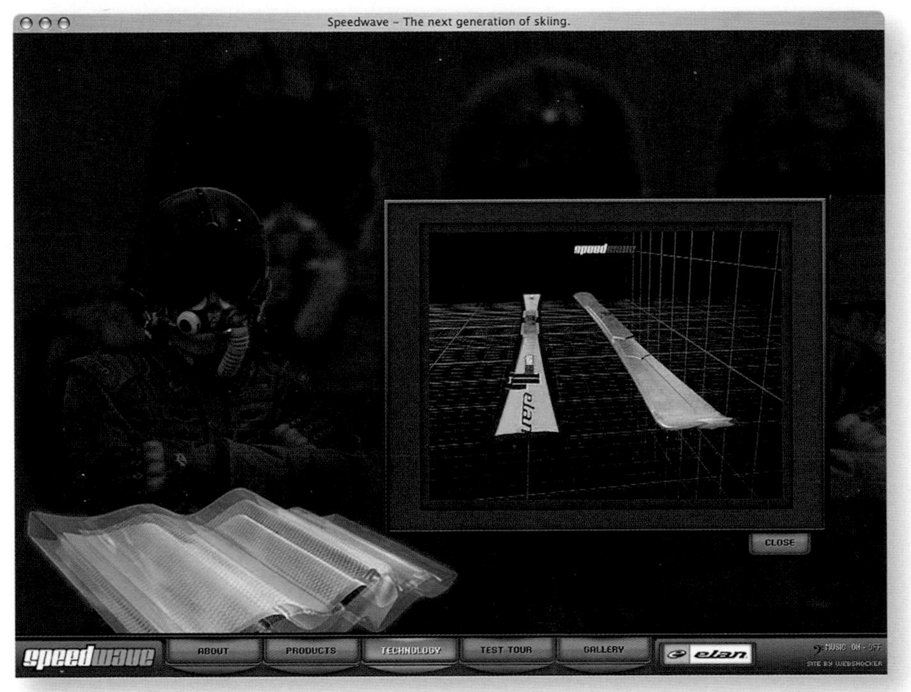

speedwave.elanskis.com

D: webshocker

M: www.webshocker.net

www.hotelsaodomingos.com

D: ronald de moraes **C:** josé de oliveira **P:** bernardo lúcio, ronald de moraes

A: elementos - publicidade e design **M:** www.elementos.com.pt

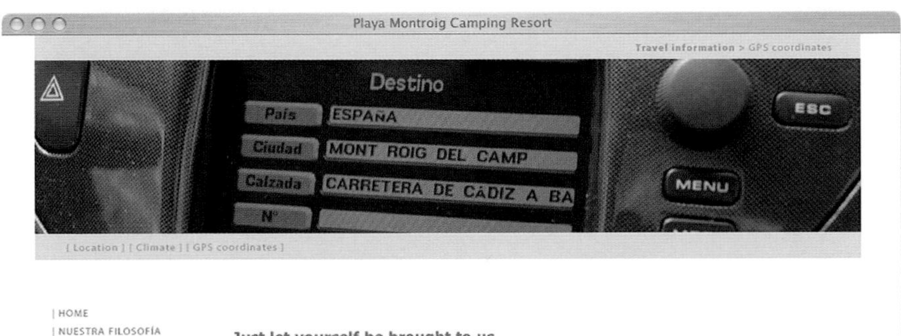

www.playamontroig.com

D: interactius tgd

A: tgd comunicació **M:** sbuyo@tgd.es

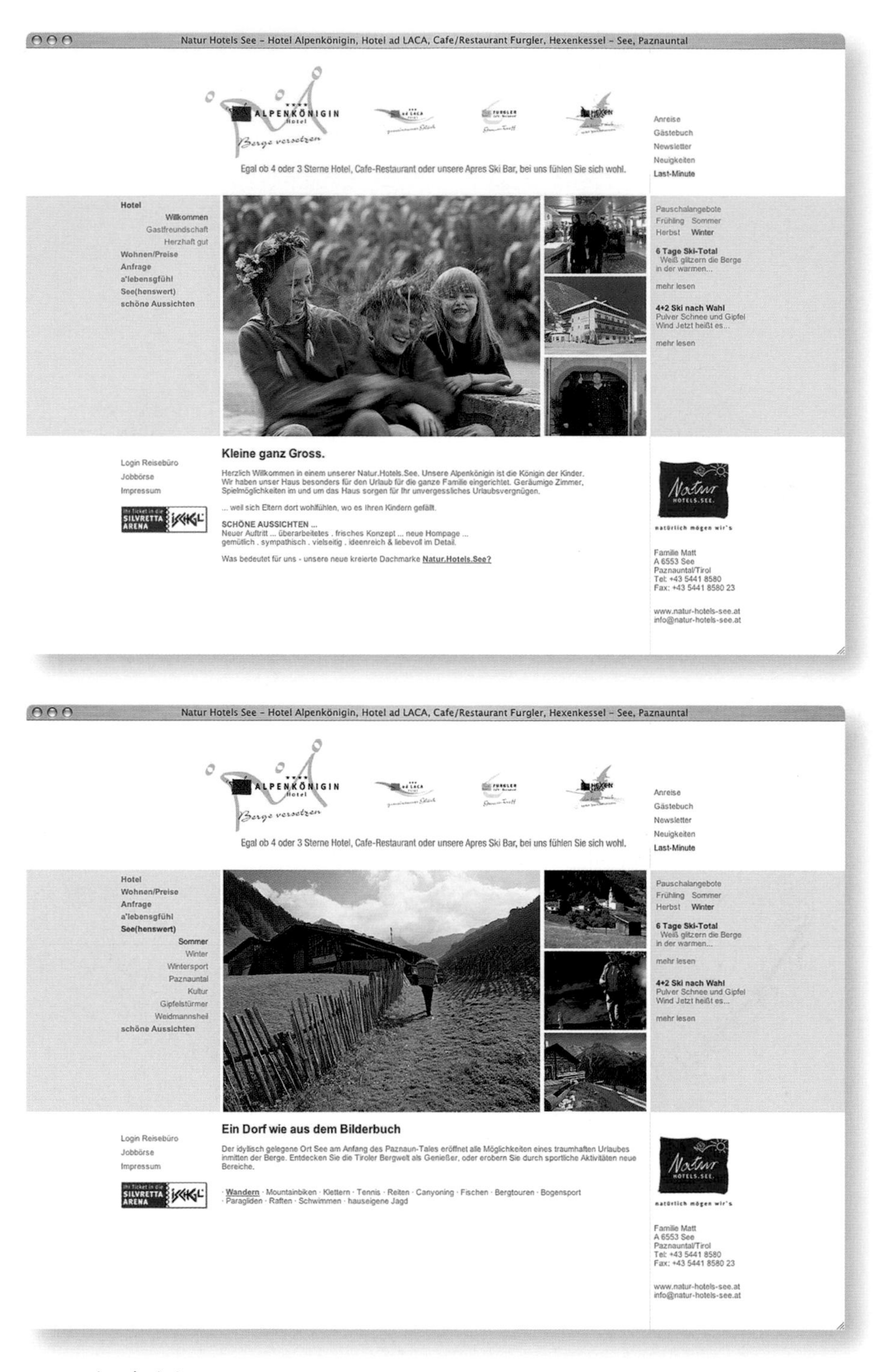

www.natur-hotels.com

D: christian baumann **C:** emanuel ulses **P:** natur hotels see

A: ccb baumann communication gmbh **M:** www.tiroldesign.at, www.ccb-baumann.at

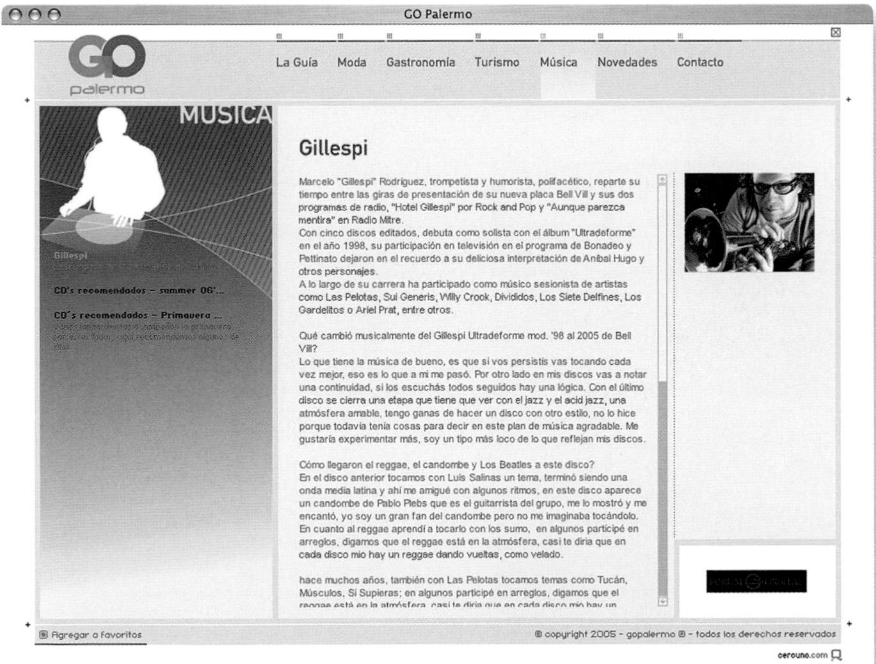

www.gopalermo.com.ar

D: bruno coppola, fabian garcía **C:** pablo gillari **P:** sergio ciaravino
A: cero uno **M:** info@cerouno.com

www.zollverein.de

D: karsten blaschke, theis müller **C:** lars wöhning, marcel dickhage

A: v2a.net **M:** md@v2a.net

Tablet Hotels: Unique Hotels for Global Nomads

TabletHotels
Unique Hotels for Global Nomads

Find a Hotel ▸ Great Deals ▸ Tablet 10 ▸ Weekends Around ▸ My Account ▸ Newsletter ▸ Corporate Plans ▸ Home ▸

Ten New Hotels : Europe 2006
A New Book From Tablet Hotels. Click Here to Peek Inside the Book ▸

Find A Hotel
▸ I Just Want To Get Away
(GIVE US AN IDEA AND WE'LL DO THE REST)
I Know The Hotel's Name ▸
I Know My Destination ▸
Great Deals On Great Hotels ▸

First, describe your perfect get away location:
(Click up to 3 items, and click on the item again to remove it from the list)

beach
city
island
countryside
jungle
mountains
coastal
desert
unusual

▸ beach
▸ unusual
▸ island

Now describe your agenda for this trip:
(Click up to 3 items, and click on the item again to remove it from the list)

romance
seduction
spa
great food
shopping
culture
pampering
escape
golf
water sports
ski
adventure
wine region
gambling
business
horseback riding
fishing

▸ escape

Show Me The Results

www.tablethotels.com

D: tablet inc.

M: info@tablethotels.com

www.taiwanstoryland.com

D: wu-chi-pei **C:** lin-bor-way **P:** denis t.l. lin

A: www.eyewasabi.com **M:** denis0516@gmail.com

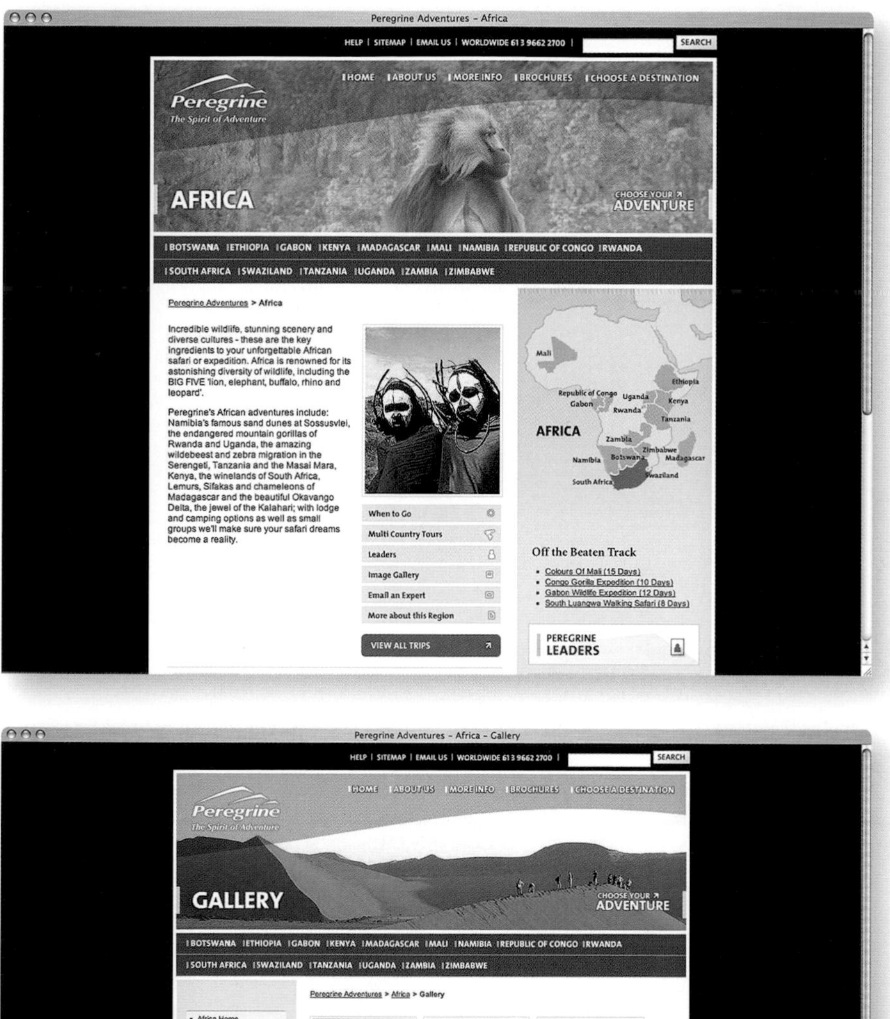

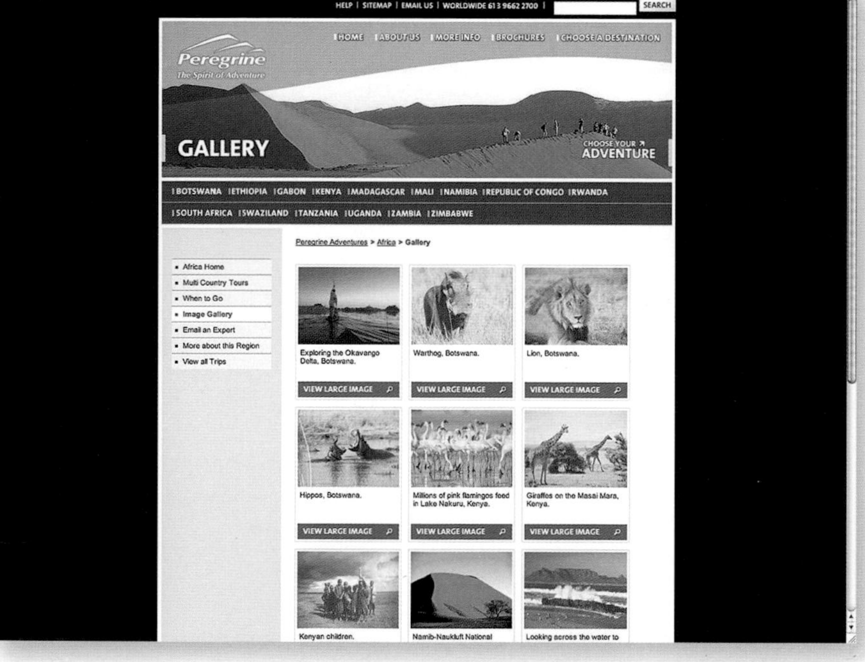

www.peregrineadventures.com

D: abby kelly **C:** alex williams, dan oxnam, kamil gottwald **P:** carl panczak

A: reactive media **M:** chrisf@reactive.com

www.centralparkhotel.com.hk

D: teresa l.y. lee **C:** yat-yu wu

A: compelite ltd **M:** garry@compelite.net

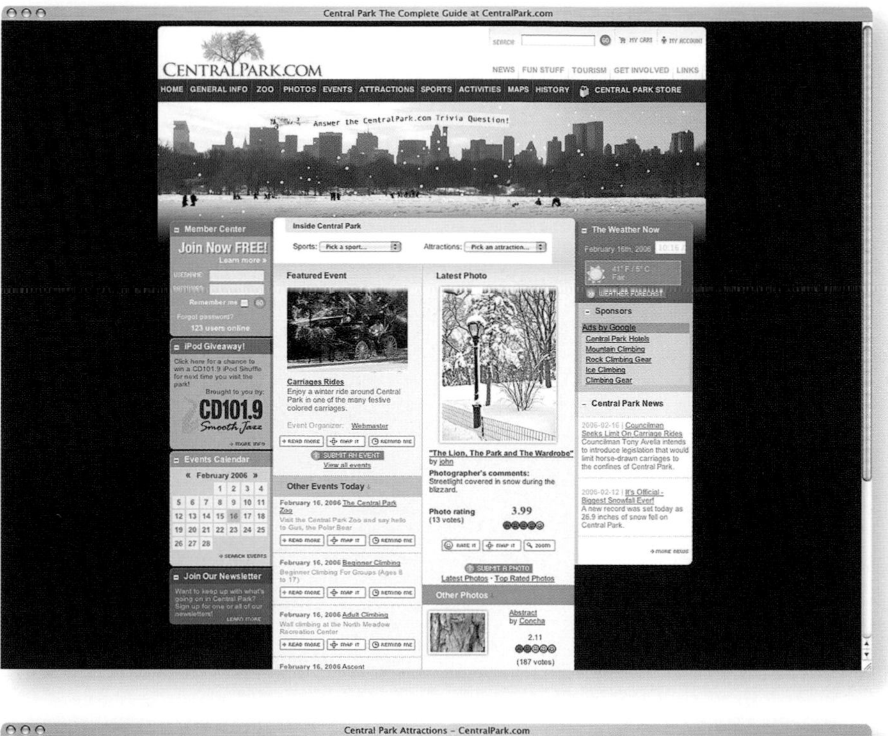

www.centralpark.com

D: aric boyles

A: centralpark.com **M:** erin@centralpark.com